OXFORD COMMENTARIES ON INTERNATIONAL LAW

The United Nations Convention on Jurisdictional Immunities of States and Their Property

The United Nations Convention on Jurisdictional Immunities of States and Their Property

A Commentary

Edited by

ROGER O'KEEFE
CHRISTIAN J. TAMS

Assistant Editor

ANTONIOS TZANAKOPOULOS

OXFORD
UNIVERSITY PRESS

OXFORD
UNIVERSITY PRESS

Great Clarendon Street, Oxford, OX2 6DP,
United Kingdom

Oxford University Press is a department of the University of Oxford.
It furthers the University's objective of excellence in research, scholarship,
and education by publishing worldwide. Oxford is a registered trade mark of
Oxford University Press in the UK and in certain other countries

First Edition published in 2013

British Library Cataloguing in Publication Data
Data available

ISBN 978–0–19–960183–7

Foreword

More than the law of jurisdiction (which favours concurrent jurisdiction), the international law of State immunity has always been of great importance as delineating the sovereign domain of each State vis-à-vis each other State. At a time when interactions between State domains were, perhaps, more limited than they now are and when, more importantly, the State and sovereignty were deemed indivisible, State immunity could afford to be unqualified. That is no longer the case and has not been so for at least 35 years, since the period of key decisions of the German, British, and US courts and the subsequent fashioning of legislation. But it took the international system a good number of those years to come to terms with these changes. Arguably, it has not fully done so yet. For example, the recent decision of the Hong Kong Court of Final Appeal in favour of immunity for a commercial transaction sounds a discordant note.[1] That case is probably to be explained on grounds of the subordination of Hong Kong to China in matters touching on foreign affairs; but it shows the continued attraction of absolute immunity to at least one major State.

As a field, State immunity is peculiar in at least three respects.

First, and least remarked on, it is the 'negative correlative' of a positive value, namely the autonomy of States within their own domain. Yet the point of that positive value does not appear to advantage in cases where, on the basis of the 'facts' alleged by the claimant, the respondent State has apparently misbehaved and is trying to avoid its accountability for doing so. Faced with an apparently deserving case, the temptation must often be to twist the rules or to expand the scope of exceptions to immunity.

Secondly, there is the point that international law in the matter of State immunity has been made almost exclusively by national courts, whose familiarity with international law may be less than complete and, even when it is not, whose perspective is always influenced by the constitutional arrangements and balance-of-power constraints of their own system. But two qualifications are in order here. One is that, by and large, national courts have treated State immunity seriously and sometimes with distinction—take the German Federal Constitutional Court and the then House of Lords in a series of cases. Another is that this situation of national domination is starting to change. The recent case-law of both the International Court of Justice and (even) the International Tribunal for the Law for the Sea includes important decisions concerning State immunity, each decided rather sweepingly in favour of the applicant State—that is, in favour of immunity.[2] So it seems that real international law has been formed despite the constitutional and other limitations of national courts.

[1] *Democratic Republic of the Congo v FG Hemisphere Associates LLC (No. 1)*, 147 ILR 376 (PRC (CFA HKSAR) 2011).

[2] *Jurisdictional Immunities of the State (Germany v Italy: Greece intervening), Judgment*, 3 February 2012 (International Court of Justice); *The 'ARA Libertad' Case (Argentina v Ghana), Request for the prescription of provisional measures, Order*, 15 December 2012 (International Tribunal for the Law of the Sea). The former decision is as remarkable for its articulation and careful reference to authority as the latter is for its lack of either, a contrast not fully justified by the distinction between merits and provisional measures.

This brings me to my third point, which is that international law, if it has been made during this period, has been made by a distinct minority of States. Although many courts have had occasion to consider issues of State immunity, the States whose courts have done so regularly can be counted on the fingers of two hands. The same is true of States (some of the same States) which have enacted comprehensive State immunity legislation. Yet international law is putatively universal, not made by a minority.

This is the importance of the 2004 United Nations Convention on Jurisdictional Immunities of States and Their Property, which has the potential, probably more than the occasional decisions of international courts and tribunals, to assist in the transition of a law of State immunity from the preferred positions of the world's preferred forums to a law generally accepted. Whether it will actually do so is a question, but that it has the potential to do so is undoubted. Texts of this kind can consolidate the law, at least in its general lines, and can form the basis of a consensus, even though they are often criticized for rigidity and for preventing desirable changes.

Just as it is too early to say that the 2004 UN Convention has consolidated anything, so it is too early to say that it has prevented anything. But many of the proposed developments—an exception to immunity in cases of universal civil jurisdiction over State 'crimes', for example—are themselves questionable, at least in the hands of national courts asserting extended jurisdiction over non-consenting foreign States. Indirectly, the law of State immunity also serves to limit the domain of national action and that of international jurisdiction, which limits some more recent proposals have seemed to ignore or transgress.

However all this may be, a detailed critical study of and commentary on the 2004 UN Convention has long been needed. The editors and other authors of this work are warmly to be congratulated for providing both these things.

James Crawford
Whewell Professor of International Law
Lauterpacht Centre for International Law
University of Cambridge
16 December 2012

Preface

State immunity is one of the canonical topics of international law. Until recently, however, there existed no comprehensive convention on the subject at the universal level. That situation changed with the adoption by the United Nations General Assembly in 2004—with a view, in the words of its Preamble, to 'enhanc[ing] the rule of law and legal certainty'—of the United Nations Convention on Jurisdictional Immunities of States and Their Property. Immediately praised as a major work of codification, the Convention has only gradually begun to attract States parties, and is unlikely to enter into force in the immediate future. Yet it has already become a standard point of reference on questions of State immunity for courts, both national and international, and legal scholars. Against this backdrop, we believe that a commentary on the Convention is anything but premature.

The Convention's often highly technical provisions call for careful analysis. The subsequent chapters—organized on an article-by-article basis, with additional cross-cutting contributions—seek to provide this. The commentary is intended to clarify, not problematize, although clarification may involve the unearthing of problems. The aim, in the words of Einstein, has been to make things as simple as possible but no simpler.

In preparing this book, we have been fortunate to count on the commitment of a dedicated team of talented authors willing to put up with tight deadlines and 'robust' editing. We owe each of them an enormous debt of gratitude.

At OUP, John Louth and Merel Alstein have supported the project from the start, while Briony Ryles and Mary Rose Flores have expertly seen it through the production process. To all of them we are very grateful.

Our particular thanks go to Dr Antonios Tzanakopoulos who, in addition to contributing as an author, has proved an untiring, efficient and cheerful assistant editor. Special mention is due also to James Russell, whose bibliographical and other assistance over summer 2012 was invaluable, and to Magdalene College, Cambridge, which funded this assistance.

Finally, it was not the editors' original intention that they should feature so heavily as authors. In this respect, the book is an example of the best-laid schemes o' mice an' men. To those readers who prefer more authorial variety in their edited volumes, apologies are owed and offered.

Cambridge and Glasgow, December 2012
RO'K/CJT

Contents

Table of Cases

Table of Treaties

List of Abbreviations

States

Arg	Argentina
Aus	Australia
Aut	Austria
Bel	Belgium
Bot	Botswana
BSSR	Byelorussian Soviet Socialist Republic
Can	Canada
Col	Colombia
Fin	Finland
Fra	France
FRG	Federal Republic of Germany
GDR	German Democratic Republic
Gre	Greece
Ire	Republic of Ireland
Isr	Israel
Ita	Italy
Jpn	Japan
Mal	Malaysia
Mex	Mexico
Nga	Nigeria
Nor	Norway
Nth	Netherlands
NZ	New Zealand
Pak	Pakistan
Pol	Poland
Por	Portugal
PRC	People's Republic of China
Qat	Qatar
Rus	Russian Federation
SA	Republic of South Africa
Sing	Singapore
Slo	Slovenia
Spa	Spain
Swi	Switzerland
UK	United Kingdom of Great Britain and Northern Ireland
US	United States of America
USSR	Union of Soviet Socialist Republics

Courts

1st Cir./2nd Cir./etc	US Court of Appeals for the First Circuit/Second Circuit/etc
CA	Court of Appeal
CC	Constitutional Court
CFA	Court of Final Appeal
CoC	Court of Cassation
CoJ	Court of Justice
CS	Council of State
DC	District Court
DC Cir.	Court of Appeals for the District of Columbia Circuit
DDC	District Court for the District of Columbia
EAT	Employment Appeal Tribunal
ECtHR	European Court of Human Rights
ECtHR (GC)	European Court of Human Rights (Grand Chamber)
EWCA	Court of Appeal of England and Wales
EWHC	High Court of England and Wales
Ex. Mag.	Examining Magistrate
FCC	Federal Constitutional Court
FLC	Federal Labour Court
FT	Federal Tribunal
HC	High Court
HL	House of Lords (Judicial Committee)
IC	Industrial Court
ICJ	International Court of Justice
IRC	Industrial Relations Court
IRComm	Industrial Relations Commission
LC	Labour Court
LT	Labour Tribunal
MC	Magistrates' Court
RLC	Regional Labour Court
SC	Supreme Court
SCJ	Supreme Court of Justice
SDC	Sub-District Court
SDNY	District Court for the Southern District of New York
SD Tex	District Court for the Southern District of Texas
SPC	Superior Provincial Court
TGI	Tribunal de Grande Instance

Other bodies

AALCC	Asian-African Legal Consultative Committee
AALCO	Asian-African Legal Consultative Organization
CAHDI	Committee of Legal Advisors on Public International Law (Council of Europe)
HKSAR	Hong Kong Special Administrative Region

ICSID	International Centre for Settlement of Investment Disputes
ILA	International Law Association
ILC	International Law Commission
IMF	International Monetary Fund
ITC	International Tin Council
OAS	Organization of American States
OSCE	Organization for Security and Cooperation in Europe
PCA	Permanent Court of Arbitration
UNCITRAL	United Nations Commission on International Trade Law
UNESCO	United Nations Educational, Scientific and Cultural Organization

Treaties

ECHR	Convention for the Protection of Human Rights and Fundamental Freedoms, Rome, 4 November 1950, CETS No. 005 ('European Convention on Human Rights')
ECSI	European Convention on State Immunity, Basel, 16 May 1972, 1495 UNTS 182
ICJ Statute	Statute of the International Court of Justice, San Francisco, 26 June 1945
UN Charter	Charter of the United Nations, San Francisco, 26 June 1945
UNCLOS	United Nations Convention on the Law of the Sea
UNCSI	United Nations Convention on Jurisdictional Immunities of States and Their Property, New York, 2 December 2004, UN doc. A/RES/59/38, Annex ('UN Convention on State Immunity')
VCLT	Vienna Convention on the Law of Treaties, Vienna, 23 May 1969, 1155 UNTS 331

Legislation

ACJJFS (Jpn)	Act on the Civil Jurisdiction of Japan with respect to a Foreign State, etc (Japan)
FSIA (US)	Foreign Sovereign Immunities Act (US)
FStIA (Aus)	Foreign States Immunities Act (Australia)
FStIA (SA)	Foreign States Immunities Act (South Africa)
FSIL (Isr)	Foreign States Immunity Law (Israel)
IFSJAC (Arg)	Immunity of Foreign States from the Jurisdiction of the Argentinean Courts (Argentina)
SIA (Can)	State Immunity Act (Canada)
SIA (Sing)	State Immunity Act (Singapore)
SIA (UK)	State Immunity Act (UK)
SIO (Pak)	State Immunity Ordinance (Pakistan)

Documents

Council of Europe

Expl. Rep. ECSI	Explanatory Report on the European Convention on State Immunity (Strasbourg: Council of Europe, 1972)

General Assembly

Draft UNCSI	Draft United Nations Convention on Jurisdictional Immunities of States and Their Property, *Report of the Ad Hoc Committee on Jurisdictional Immunities of States and Their Property, 1–5 March 2004,* GAOR, Fifty-ninth Session, Supplement No. 22, UN doc. A/59/22, Annex
1992 report Sixth Committee Working Group	Convention on Jurisdictional Immunities of States and Their Property: Report of the Working Group, GAOR, Forty-seventh session, Sixth Committee, Agenda item 130, UN doc. A/C.6/47/L.10 (3 November 1992)
1993 report Sixth Committee Working Group	Convention on Jurisdictional Immunities of States and Their Property: Report of the Working Group, GAOR, Forty-eighth session, Sixth Committee, Agenda item 147, UN doc. A/C.6/48/L.4 (11 November 1993)
Report Sixth Committee informal consultations	Convention on Jurisdictional Immunities of States and Their Property: Informal consultations held pursuant to General Assembly decision 48/413, GAOR, Forty-ninth session, Sixth Committee, Agenda item 143, UN doc. A/C.6/49/L.2 (4 October 1994)
1999 report Chairman Sixth Committee Working Group	Convention on Jurisdictional Immunities of States and Their Property: Report of the Chairman of the Working Group, Fifty-Fourth session, Sixth Committee, Agenda item 152, UN doc. A/C.6/54/L.12 (12 November 1999)
2000 report Chairman Sixth Committee Working Group	Convention on Jurisdictional Immunities of States and Their Property: Report of the Chairman of the Working Group, Fifty-fifth session, Sixth Committee, Agenda item 157, UN doc. A/C.6/55/L.12 (10 November 2000)
2002 report Ad Hoc Committee	Report of the Ad Hoc Committee on Jurisdictional Immunities of States and Their Property, GAOR, Fifty-seventh Session Supplement No. 22, UN doc. A/57/22 (4–15 February 2002)

2003 report Ad Hoc Committee	Report of the Ad Hoc Committee on Jurisdictional Immunities of States and Their Property, GAOR, Fifty-eighth Session Supplement No. 22, UN doc. A/58/22 (24–28 February 2003)
2004 report Ad Hoc Committee	Report of the Ad Hoc Committee on Jurisdictional Immunities of States and Their Property, GAOR, Fifty-ninth Session Supplement No. 22, UN doc. A/59/22 (1–5 March 2004)
2004 report Sixth Committee	Convention on jurisdictional immunities of States and their property: Report of the Sixth Committee, GAOR, Fifty-ninth Session, Agenda item 142, UN doc. A/59/508 (30 November 2004)
Suggestions of the Chairman	Suggestions of the Chairman, UN doc. A/AC.262/2004/DP.1 (27 February 2004)
Statement Chairman Ad Hoc Committee	Statement of the Chairman of the Ad Hoc Committee on Jurisdictional Immunities of States and Their Property introducing to the Sixth Committee the draft Convention on Jurisdictional Immunities of States and Their Property, GAOR, Fifty-ninth Session, Sixth Committee, 13th meeting, 25 October 2004, UN doc. A/C.6/59/SR.13 and Corr. 1

Institut de Droit International

Institut resolution	Institut de Droit International, Contemporary Problems Concerning the Immunity of States in Relation to Questions of Jurisdiction and Enforcement, Basel Session 1991, 64 *Annuaire de l'Institut de Droit International* (1992), vol. II, 389

International Law Association

ILA Draft Articles	International Law Association's Draft Articles for a Convention on State Immunity, adopted in Montreal, 29 August–4 September 1982, reproduced in International Law Association, Report of the Sixtieth Conference, 5–10; 22 ILM 287
ILA Revised Draft Articles	International Law Association's Revised Draft Articles for a Convention on State Immunity, adopted in Buenos Aires, 14–20 August 1994, reproduced in International Law Association, Report of the Sixty-sixth Conference, 21–27, 45–99

International Law Commission

Texts

Articles on Responsibility of States for Internationally Wrongful Acts	Articles on Responsibility of States for Internationally Wrongful Acts, UN doc. A/RES/56/83, Annex (28 January 2002)

Draft articles	Draft Articles on Jurisdictional Immunities of States and Their Property, reproduced in *Yearbook of the International Law Commission 1991*, vol. II(2), 13
ILC commentary	Commentary on Draft Articles on Jurisdictional Immunities of States and Their Property, reproduced in *Yearbook of the International Law Commission 1991*, vol. II(2), 13
ILC commentary DALT	Draft Articles on the Law of Treaties with commentaries, reproduced in *Yearbook of the International Law Commission 1966*, vol. II, 187

Sessional Reports of the Commission

Report ILC, tenth session	Report of the International Law Commission on the work of its tenth session, UN doc. A/3859 (28 April to 4 July 1958), reproduced in *Yearbook of the International Law Commission 1958*, vol. II, 78
Report ILC, thirtieth session	Report of the International Law Commission on the work of its thirtieth session, UN doc. A/33/10 (8 May to 28 July 1978), reproduced in *Yearbook of the International Law Commission 1978*, vol. II(2), 152
Report ILC, thirty-first session	Report of the International Law Commission on the work of its thirty-first session, UN doc. A/34/10 (14 May to 3 August 1979), reproduced in *Yearbook of the International Law Commission 1979*, vol. II(2), 166
Report ILC, thirty-second session	Report of the International Law Commission on the work of its thirty-second session, UN doc. A/35/10 (5 May to 25 July 1980), reproduced in *Yearbook of the International Law Commission 1980*, vol. II(2), 99
Report ILC, thirty-third session	Report of the International Law Commission on the work of its thirty-third session, UN doc. A/36/10 (4 May to 24 July 1981), reproduced in *Yearbook of the International Law Commission 1981*, vol. II(2), 200
Report ILC, thirty-fourth session	Report of the International Law Commission on the work of its thirty-fourth session, UN doc. A/37/10 (3 May to 23 July 1982), reproduced in *Yearbook of the International Law Commission 1982*, vol. II(2), 157
Report ILC, thirty-fifth session	Report of the International Law Commission on the work of its thirty-fifth session, UN doc. A/38/10 (3 May to 22 July 1983), reproduced in *Yearbook of the International Law Commission 1983*, vol. II(2), 17
Report ILC, thirty-sixth session	Report of the International Law Commission on the work of its thirty-sixth session, UN doc. A/39/10 (May to 22 July 1984), reproduced in *Yearbook of the International Law Commission 1984*, vol. II(2), 58

Report ILC, thirty-seventh session	Report of the International Law Commission on the work of its thirty-seventh session, UN doc. A/40/10 (6 May to 26 July 1985), reproduced in *Yearbook of the International Law Commission 1985*, vol. II (2), 51
Report ILC, thirty-eighth session	Report of the International Law Commission on the work of its thirty-eighth session, UN doc. A/41/10 (5 May to 11 July 1986), reproduced in *Yearbook of the International Law Commission 1986*, vol. II(2), 7
Report ILC, thirty-ninth session	Report of the International Law Commission on the work of its thirty-ninth session, UN doc. A/42/10 (4 May-17 July 1987), reproduced in *Yearbook of the International Law Commission 1987*, vol. II(2), 53
Report ILC, fortieth session	Report of the International Law Commission on the work of its fortieth session, UN doc. A/43/10, (9 May to 29 July 1988), reproduced in *Yearbook of the International Law Commission 1988* vol. II(2), 495
Report ILC, forty-first session	Report of the International Law Commission on the work of its forty-first session, UN doc. A/44/10 (2 May to 21 July 1989), reproduced in *Yearbook of the International Law Commission 1989*, vol. II(2), 97
Report ILC, forty-second session	Report of the International Law Commission on the work of its forty-second session, UN doc. A/45/10 (1 May to 20 July 1990), reproduced in *Yearbook of the International Law Commission 1990*, vol. II(2), 31
Report ILC, forty-third session	Report of the International Law Commission on the work of its forty-third session, UN doc. A/46/10 (29 April to 19 July 1991), reproduced in *Yearbook of the International Law Commission 1991*, vol. II(2), 12
Report ILC, fifty-first session	Report of the International Law Commission on the work of its fifty-first session, UN doc. A/54/10 (3 May to 23 July 1999), reproduced in *Yearbook of the International Law Commission 1999*, vol. II(2), 127
Report ILC, fifty-eighth session	Report of the International Law Commission on the work of its fifty-eighth session, UN doc. A/61/10 (1 May to 9 June and 3 July to 11 August 2006)
Report ILC, sixty-third session	Report of the International Law Commission on the work of its sixty-third session, UN doc. A/66/10 (26 April to 3 June and 4 July to 12 August 2011)

Reports of Special Rapporteurs

Preliminary report Sucharitkul	Preliminary report on the topic of jurisdictional immunities of States and their property, by Mr Sompong Sucharitkul, Special Rapporteur, UN doc. A/CN.4/323 (18 June 1979), reproduced

	in *Yearbook of the International Law Commission 1979*, vol. II (1), 227
Second report Sucharitkul	Second report on jurisdictional immunities of States and their property, by Mr Sompong Sucharitkul, Special Rapporteur, UN doc. A/CN.4/331 and Add.1 (11 April and 30 June 1980), reproduced in *Yearbook of the International Law Commission 1980*, vol. II(1), 199
Third report Sucharitkul	Third report on jurisdictional immunities of States and their property by Mr Sompong Sucharitkul, Special Rapporteur, UN doc. A/CN.4/340 & Corr.1 and Add.1 & Corr.1 (27 March and 18 May 1981), reproduced in *Yearbook of the International Law Commission 1981*, vol. II(1), 125
Fourth report Sucharitkul	Fourth report on jurisdictional immunities of States and their property, by Mr Sompong Sucharitkul, Special Rapporteur, UN doc. A/CN.4/357 and Corr.1 (31 March 1982), reproduced in *Yearbook of the International Law Commission 1982*, vol. II(1), 199
Fifth report Sucharitkul	Fifth report on jurisdictional immunities of States and their property, by Mr Sompong Sucharitkul, Special Rapporteur, UN doc. A/CN.4/363 & Corr.1 and Add.1 & Corr.1 (22 March and 11 April 1983), reproduced in *Yearbook of the International Law Commission 1983*, vol. II(1), 25
Sixth report Sucharitkul	Sixth report on jurisdictional immunities of States and their property, by Mr Sompong Sucharitkul, Special Rapporteur, UN doc. A/CN.4/376 and Add.1 and 2 (31 January and 18 April 1984), reproduced in *Yearbook of the International Law Commission 1984*, vol. II(1), 5
Seventh report Sucharitkul	Seventh report on jurisdictional immunities of States and their property, by Mr Sompong Sucharitkul, Special Rapporteur, UN doc. A/CN.4/388 and Corr.1 (E only) & Corr.2 (F only) (28 March 1985), reproduced in *Yearbook of the International Law Commission 1985*, vol. II(1), 21
Eighth report Surchartikul	Eighth report on jurisdictional immunities of States and their property, by Mr Sompong Sucharitkul, Special Rapporteur, UN doc. A/CN.4/396 and Corr.1 (3 March 1986), reproduced in *Yearbook of the International Law Commission 1986*, vol. II(1), 21
Preliminary report Ogiso	Preliminary report on jurisdictional immunities of States and their property, by Mr Motoo Ogiso, Special Rapporteur, UN doc. A/CN.4/415 and Corr.1 (20 May 1988), reproduced in *Yearbook of the International Law Commission 1988*, vol. II(1), 96
Second report Ogiso	Second report on jurisdictional immunities of States and their property, by Mr Motoo Ogiso, Special Rapporteur, UN doc. A/CN.4/422 & Corr.1 and Add.1 & Corr.1 (11 and 24 April

	1989), reproduced in *Yearbook of the International Law Commission 1989*, vol. II(1), 59
Third report Ogiso	Third report on jurisdictional immunities of States and their property, by Mr Motoo Ogiso, Special Rapporteur, UN doc. A/CN.4/431 and Corr.1 (11 April 1990), reproduced in *Yearbook of the International Law Commission 1990*, vol. II(1), 3

Reports of Working Groups

1999 report ILC Working Group	Report of the Working Group on Jurisdictional Immunities of States and Their Property, in Report of the International Law Commission on the work of its fifty-first session, UN doc. A/54/10 (3 May to 23 July 1999), reproduced in *Yearbook of the International Law Commission 1999*, vol. II(2), 1, Annex.

Other UN Bodies

Summary of Practice of the Secretary-General as Depositary	UN Office of Legal Affairs (Treaty Section), *Summary of Practice of the Secretary-General as Depositary of Multilateral Treaties*, UN doc. ST/LEG/7/Rev.1 (1999)
Treaty Handbook	UN Office of Legal Affairs (Treaty Section), *Treaty Handbook* (2006), UN Sales No. E.02.V.2
Final Clauses Handbook	UN Office of Legal Affairs (Treaty Section), *Final Clauses of Multilateral Treaties: Handbook* (2003), UN Sales No. E.04.V.3
United Nations Juridical Yearbook 1973	*United Nations Juridical Yearbook 1973*, UN Sales No. E.75.V.1
United Nations Juridical Yearbook 1974	*United Nations Juridical Yearbook 1974*, UN Sales No. E.76.V.1

Other Bodies

Inter-American Draft Convention	Inter-American Draft Convention on Jurisdictional Immunities of States, OEA/Ser.G-CP/doc. 1352/83, 30 March 1983

Journals

AJIL	American Journal of International Law
AJIL Supp	Supplement to the American Journal of International Law
ASIL Procs	Proceedings of the American Society of International Law
BYIL	British Year Book of International Law
Chinese JIL	Chinese Journal of International Law
EJIL	European Journal of International Law
ICLQ	International and Comparative Law Quarterly
IYIL	Italian Yearbook of International Law
JDI	Journal de Droit International

LQR	Law Quarterly Review
NYIL	Netherlands Yearbook of International Law
Polish YIL	Polish Yearbook of International Law
RBDI	Revue Belge de Droit International
RdC	Recueil des Cours de l'Académie de Droit International de La Haye
REDI	Revista española de derecho internacional / Revue espagnole de droit international
RIAA	Reports of International Arbitral Awards
YILC	Yearbook of the International Law Commission

List of Contributors

Silvia Borelli is Director of Research and Principal Lecturer in Public International Law in the School of Law at the University of Bedfordshire.

Chester Brown is Professor of International Law and International Arbitration at the Faculty of Law, University of Sydney, a Barrister at 7 Selborne Chambers, Sydney, and a door tenant at Essex Court Chambers, London, and Maxwell Chambers, Singapore.

Jean d'Aspremont is Professor of Public International Law, University of Manchester.

James G. Devaney is a PhD candidate at the European University Institute in Florence, and has worked as a research assistant at the University of Glasgow.

Andrew Dickinson divides his time between Australia, where he is Professor in Private International Law at Sydney Law School, University of Sydney, and the UK, where he is a practising solicitor, consultant to Clifford Chance LLP, and a Visiting Fellow at the British Institute of International and Comparative Law. He specializes in matters of private and public international law, including international immunities, and is one of the authors of *State Immunity: Selected Materials and Commentary* (Oxford: Oxford University Press, 2004).

Joanne Foakes is an Associate Fellow on the International Law Programme at Chatham House and a former Legal Counsellor of the Foreign and Commonwealth Office.

Tarcisio Gazzini is Associate professor of International Law at the Department of Transnational Legal Studies, VU University Amsterdam. He is a member of the editorial board of the Leiden Journal of International Law and of the ILA Committee on Non-State Actors.

Tom Grant is Senior Associate of the Lauterpacht Centre for International Law at the University of Cambridge and Senior Research Fellow of Wolfson College, Cambridge. He is also a practising lawyer.

Douglas Guilfoyle is Reader in Law at University College London. He is a member of the Contact Group on Piracy off the Coast of Somalia (Working Group 2 on legal issues) and has been a special adviser to the House of Commons Foreign Affairs Committee.

Gerhard Hafner is retired Professor of International Law at the University of Vienna and teaches at the Universities of Vienna and Bratislava (Slovakia). He was a member of the International Law Commission, is a member of the Institut de Droit International and he has worked as arbitrator and counsel on international cases. He was Chairman of the Ad hoc Committee of the UN General Assembly on jurisdictional immunities of States.

Roger O'Keefe is University Senior Lecturer in Law and Deputy Director of the Lauterpacht Centre for International Law at the University of Cambridge; Fellow of Magdalene College, Cambridge; and Visiting Professor at the Department of Legal Studies, Central European University, Budapest.

Simon Olleson is a member of the Bar of England and Wales. He is a tenant at 13 Old Square Chambers, Lincoln's Inn, London, where his practice specializes in public international law.

Kate Parlett is an Associate in public international law and international arbitration at Freshfields Bruckhaus Deringer LLP and is based in Paris. She was previously a Research Fellow at the Lauterpacht Centre for International Law at the University of Cambridge.

Christian J. Tams is Professor of International Law at the University of Glasgow. He is a member of the Royal Society of Edinburgh (Young Academy), of the ILA Committee on the Use of Force, and of the German Court of Arbitration for Sports.

Jörg Philipp Terhechte is Professor of German Public Law, European and International Law at Leuphana University, Lüneburg.

Tobias Thienel is a lawyer (*Rechtsanwalt*) with Weissleder Ewer in Kiel, Germany and a doctoral student at the Walther Schücking Institute of International Law at the University of Kiel.

Antonios Tzanakopoulos is University Lecturer in Public International Law at the University of Oxford and Fellow of St Anne's College, Oxford. He has worked on a number of cases involving international law before international and domestic courts.

Rosanne van Alebeek is Assistant Professor of international law at the Department of International and European Law and a research fellow of the Amsterdam Center of International Law at the University of Amsterdam.

Stephan Wittich is Associate Professor of International Law, University of Vienna.

Sir Michael Wood, KCMG, is a member of the International Law Commission, and a Senior Fellow of the Lauterpacht Centre for International Law at the University of Cambridge. He is a barrister at 20 Essex Street, London, where he practises in the field of public international law, including before international courts and tribunals. He was Legal Adviser to the UK's Foreign and Commonwealth Office between 1999 and 2006, having joined as an Assistant Legal Adviser in 1970.

General Introduction

Roger O'Keefe and Christian J. Tams

1. Introduction

State immunity—the idea that a State, including its individual organs, officials, and other emanations, may not be proceeded against in the courts of another State in certain instances—has long been and remains a source of international controversy. Although customary international law no longer recognizes the absolute immunity of States from foreign civil proceedings and has made inroads into what was the absolute immunity of State property from foreign judicial measures of constraint, the evolution of the contemporary notion of restrictive State immunity over the better part of a century has been an uncoordinated and contested process in which the legislatures and courts of individual States have, for want of a comprehensive, universal multilateral treaty on the subject, been compelled to run the risk inherent in unilaterally adopting a view on the parameters of the doctrine. Perhaps needless to say, these various national views have not always been consistent, leading to disputes between States.

With a view to reaching inter-State consensus on this fundamental question of international law, and 'bearing in mind its day-to-day practical importance', the International Law Commission (ILC) of the United Nations recommended in 1977 to the United Nations General Assembly the selection of the topic of the jurisdictional immunities of states and their property for codification and progressive development by the Commission.[1] In response, the General Assembly invited the Commission to commence work to this end.[2] The interim result was the Commission's final adoption on second reading in 1991 of a set of draft articles on jurisdictional immunities of States and their property.[3] Thirteen years, two Working Groups, and one Ad Hoc Committee later, the General Assembly adopted, by way of resolution 59/38 of 2 December 2004, the United Nations Convention on Jurisdictional Immunities of States and Their Property. The Convention currently has thirteen States parties and eighteen States signatories.[4] It will enter into force once thirty States are parties to it.

This book seeks to provide a systematic account of the Convention, also referred to herein as 'UNCSI', standing for 'United Nations Convention on State Immunity'. The latter is less of a mouthful, more precise,[5] and more accurate[6] than the Convention's

[1] Report ILC 29th session, *YILC 1977*, vol. II, Part 2, 130, para. 110.

[2] See UNGA res. 32/151, 19 December 1977, para. 7.

[3] See Report ILC 43rd session, *YILC 1991*, vol. II, Parts 2, 12, 13, para. 28. The draft articles are reproduced in the Appendix to this volume.

[4] For details, see the Appendix to this volume.

[5] Diplomatic, consular, and other cognate immunities are also—alongside the State immunity regulated by the Convention—jurisdictional immunities of States and their property. But, as Article 3(1) UNCSI makes clear, the Convention does not deal with, and is without prejudice to, these other immunities.

[6] As explained in the commentary to Article 1, any immunity from foreign measures of constraint from which State property may benefit is better conceived of in formal legal terms as the immunity of the State in respect of its property. That said, it is more convenient and by no means unacceptable to refer to 'the immunity

formal title, and is a nice counterpoint to the title of the only other comprehensive multilateral treaty on the same topic, namely the European Convention on State Immunity.

2. The Convention and Its Story, Status, and Significance

2.1 The drafting of the Convention

The drafting of the Convention, from the commencement in 1978 of the ILC's work on jurisdictional immunities of States and their property to the General Assembly's adoption of the Convention, was a protracted affair. Indeed, it is a minor miracle that the Convention was adopted at all. The ILC's work caught the tail-end of the ideological struggle between the West, with its instinctive and existing judicial and legislative preference for the restrictive doctrine of State immunity, and the Soviet bloc, with its staunch commitment to the absolute doctrine or to the salvage of as much of it as possible. The international legal dimensions of this divide, moreover, were replicated in the contemporaneous and continuing cleavage between developed and developing States, the source of much of the wrangling from the final adoption of the ILC's draft articles in 1991 to the adoption of the Convention in 2004. To make matters trickier still, superimposed on these geopolitical divisions were more abstract but no less passionately advanced national and personal differences over the doctrinal basis of State immunity and of the emergent restrictive approach thereto.

That agreement was eventually reached first on the draft articles and ultimately on the Convention is testament to the good will and good sense of the members of the ILC and its later Working Group, of the Sixth Committee and its Working Group, of the Ad Hoc Committee on Jurisdictional Immunities of States and Their Property, and of the General Assembly.[7] It also speaks to the technical expertise and diplomatic nous of the ILC's Drafting Committee; of the first Chairman of the Sixth Committee Working Group, Carlos Calero Rodrigues; of the Chairman of, respectively, the ILC Working Group, the reconvened Sixth Committee Working Group, and the Ad Hoc Committee, Gerhard Hafner; and of the coordinators of the Ad Hoc Committee's two informal consultative groups, Chusei Yamada and Michael Bliss. Most fundamentally, however, the adoption of the Convention reflects a tectonic shift in States' *opinio juris* from the early 1980s, accelerated by the waning and end of the Cold War and changes within the G77, in favour of the restrictive doctrine of State immunity in one form or another. In the final analysis, the Convention was capable of coming into being for the elementary reason that its essential principles were by 2004 broadly acceptable to States of all persuasions.

Nonetheless, the process of the Convention's elaboration was not ideal. The long hiatus between the final adoption of the ILC's draft articles and the eventual adoption of the Convention, during which time attention focused almost solely on five issues

of State property from measures of constraint'. Moreover, this formulation can usefully serve to highlight the distinction between this particular aspect of State immunity and the immunity of the State, in its various guises, from foreign proceedings (or, in the terminology adopted by the Convention, from 'jurisdiction').

[7] For details as to these various bodies, see especially G. Hafner, 'Historical Background to the Convention' in this volume.

identified as the most problematic, meant that most of the Convention's provisions were finalized or very nearly so thirteen years before the instrument was adopted. This lapse of time may have facilitated the adoption of the Convention: what seemed problematic in 1991 gradually became acceptable, and State practice and *opinio juris*, where not already generally consonant with the draft articles, coalesced and consolidated around them during the 1990s and early 2000s. But not all issues were given the attention they deserved, and the reluctance of the drafters between 1991 and 2004 to revisit previously settled matters affected the coherence of the final text.

2.2 The essence of the Convention

The Convention reflects a general acceptance among States that the restrictive doctrine of State immunity, if not yet universally subscribed to, is at least now the way forward. To the extent that this restrictive model of immunity levels the playing field as between private commercial interests and those of States, one could see the Convention as indicative of the post-Cold War hegemony of market capitalism. But private commercial actors do not have it all their own way under the Convention. The immunity of State property from foreign measures of constraint remains more expansive than the immunity of the State itself, in its various guises, from foreign proceedings. As a result, while, courtesy of the Convention, claimants may be able to proceed against States in foreign courts, any judgments they obtain may remain unenforced. In addition, State enterprises are treated perhaps marginally more favourably under the Convention than under the legislation and case-law of many developed states. To these extents and more, the Convention still reflects the striking of a bargain among different geopolitical constituencies.

2.3 The text of the Convention

The text of the Convention is easy to criticize. Infelicities, inconsistencies, and oversights are common. Key provisions, notably Articles 2, 10, and 19, are burdened by compromise clauses the proper application and, indeed, gist of which are not immediately apparent. The interplay between the operative provisions and the 'understandings' annexed and integral to the Convention, several of which are opaque in and of themselves, is not always straightforward.

Yet despite all this there is no reason why, with attentive reading, adherence to the general rules on the interpretation and application of treaties, and common sense, the Convention should not prove workable. Its textual flaws deserve to be of little consequence, the thrust of the relevant provisions being tolerably clear. Nor are the remaining issues by any means intractable.

That said, one surprising obstacle to a proper understanding of the Convention is the ILC's commentary to its Draft Articles on Jurisdictional Immunities of States and Their Property as finally adopted on second reading in 1991—or at least in undiscerning reliance on this commentary. Not only are the draft articles different in certain crucial respects from the eventual Convention, with the consequence that even the most reliable guide to the former would bear only imperfect relation to the latter. Even more to the point, the ILC commentary is not always a reliable guide to the former. Much of its content as finally adopted was simply carried over from the respective commentaries provisionally adopted on first reading, despite the fact that many draft articles underwent significant amendment in the interim. As a consequence, the commentary is unlikely to attain a status comparable to that of, for example, the Commission's commentaries to the 2001 Articles on Responsibility of States for Internationally Wrongful Acts and to the 1966 Draft Articles on the Law of Treaties. That said, a good deal of it remains useful, even if it is in no way formally authoritative, let alone conclusive, as to the correct interpretation and application of the Convention.

Nor is national case-law on State immunity necessarily a reliable indicator of how the Convention is to be interpreted and applied, based as it may be on legislative provisions or judicial understandings which differ in critical respects from the text of the Convention. This is not to suggest that case-law not based on the Convention is wholly irrelevant. Some of the treaty's terms were clearly intended to codify leading national decisions, while others borrow the language of extant national statutes of which there may exist judicial exegesis. But all such case-law should be approached with circumspection, with a view to sorting the wheat from the chaff.

2.4 The entry into force of the Convention and participation in it

Notwithstanding the effort preceding its adoption, to date the Convention has attracted only thirteen States parties out of the thirty necessary for its entry into force, although eighteen other States have signed it.

One possible explanation for the current situation is a 'Mexican standoff' whereby States, signatory or otherwise, are waiting for others to make the first move. Of course, thirteen States have already made such a move, and at least some of these represent not insignificant jurisdictions in terms of transnational commercial litigation. But it would nonetheless be understandable were other States to wish to see the Convention enter into force and perhaps a sizeable number of States, including certain key States, become parties to it before committing themselves. It would also stand to reason were States to wait and see whether other States enter reservations to particular provisions.

A second explanation, neither unrelated to nor mutually exclusive of the first, for the current low rate of participation in the Convention may be that States are waiting to gauge the content of contemporary customary international law on the contentious finer points of State immunity before tying themselves to the positions mandated by the Convention. Were this to be the case, one would expect a rise in the number of States parties if and when it became manifest through future State practice that customary international law and the bedevilling detail of the Convention were in substance indistinguishable.

There is a third, less optimistic, and again simultaneous possibility that at least some States would prefer as a matter of principle that their courts be guided by the customary international law of State immunity, rather than by any treaty obligation incumbent on the State, with the upshot that they have no intention of ever becoming parties to the Convention. The same attitude may explain in part the low rate of participation in the European Convention on State Immunity, which after almost forty years still has only eight contracting States out of the forty-seven members of the Council of Europe.

A fourth concurrent possibility, again pessimistic, is that some States, satisfied that the process of the Convention's drafting has identified or crystallized customary international rules on State immunity that accord sufficiently with the rules, legislative or otherwise, already applied by their courts, are content to proceed as presently, without the bother and risk of binding themselves to a treaty that may require legislative reform of municipal law with which commercial claimants in their courts are familiar and satisfied.

A final, qualitatively different but still concomitant possibility, is that some States believe the finer points of the Convention neither to correspond to current or foreseeable custom nor to reflect sound policy, and prefer instead their existing municipal law.

The current low rate of participation in the Convention is probably best explained by reference to all five reasons combined. Nor is there any obvious countervailing *cachet* to be had by a State by becoming a party to the Convention or any likely domestic pressure on it to do so, as might both be the case with a treaty in a field such as international human rights law, international humanitarian law, or international criminal law.

While its present status may be disappointing, the Convention is by no means the first important codifying treaty with a slow rate of uptake. No less an instrument than the Vienna Convention on the Law of Treaties[8] took eleven years to enter into force. The fact that today, although having as parties only a little over half the States of the world, it is seen as the definitive statement on the law of treaties suggests that the significance of a text need not be reflected in the number of States parties to it.

2.5 The significance of the Convention

The significance of the Convention as a treaty obviously depends on whether it enters into force and on how many and which States become parties to it. Should it attract widespread participation, its primary importance will lie simply in the fact that a substantial number of States will, for the first time since the onset of the decline of the absolute doctrine, be applying exactly the same rules—rather than substantially the same, or more or less similar, or diametrically opposed rules—of State immunity, at least in their mutual relations and in theory.[9] The result will be to 'enhance . . . legal certainty', in the words of the Convention's preamble, and to reduce the number of inter-State disputes over State immunity.

The Convention's significance, however, extends beyond the instrument's quality as a treaty. There can be little doubt that the process of the Convention's elaboration has, through the close involvement of States, revealed, and where not simply revealed then crystallized, the content of the contemporary customary international law of State immunity. This is not to say that each and every substantive provision in its entirety is necessarily consonant with custom. But far more than simply the essence of each is, and, as the following chapters show, both national and international courts have already looked to the Convention as persuasive evidence of today's customary rules on point. In *Jurisdictional Immunities of the State*, most notably, the International Court of Justice, outlining the material sources of the customary international law of State immunity, considered that 'State practice of particular significance is to be found in . . . the statements made by States, first in the course of the extensive study of the subject by the International Law Commission and then in the context of the adoption of the United Nations Convention'.[10]

[8] Vienna, 23 May 1969, 1155 UNTS 331 (VCLT). The VCLT currently has 112 States parties.

[9] In reality, much will depend on whether and what reservations are entered and on the vicissitudes of domestic judicial readings of the Convention's provisions.

[10] *Jurisdictional Immunities of the State (Germany v Italy: Greece intervening), Judgment*, 3 February 2012, para. 55.

Whether as treaty or evidence of custom, however, perhaps the Convention's most fundamental significance lies in its premise, namely that State immunity is not simply a matter of comity, and therefore discretionary, but is a rule of international law.[11] When the executive branches in States as diverse as China, a signatory to the Convention, and the United States of America continue to assert, at least in certain contexts, the power respectively to direct or 'suggest' that the judiciary decide a given way on a point of State immunity, this affirmation is welcome.

3. Conclusion

The United Nations Convention on Jurisdictional Immunities of States and Their Property is already a significant international instrument, less at present in its quality as a treaty than as a catalyst for the development of the modern customary international law of State immunity, of which it is largely declaratory. Quite how significant it becomes remains to be seen, but what is already self-evident is that a proper understanding of it is important. It is hoped that this book contributes to that understanding.

[11] See, in this light, *Jurisdictional Immunities of the State* (n. 10), para. 56: 'Although there has been much debate regarding the origins of State immunity and the identification of the principles underlying that immunity in the past, the International Law Commission concluded in 1980 that the rule of State immunity had been "adopted as a general rule of customary international law solidly rooted in the current practice of States" (*Yearbook of the International Law Commission*, 1980, Vol. II(2), p. 147, para. 26). That conclusion [. . .], in the opinion of the Court, is confirmed by [. . .] the comments of States on what became the United Nations Convention.'

Historical Background to the Convention

GERHARD HAFNER*

1. Introduction

The adoption of the United Nations Convention on Jurisdictional Immunities of States and Their Property marked the culmination of a long process of codification of the rules of State immunity.[1] The following contribution recalls the main stages of that process, focusing in particular on the work of the International Law Commission, of the Sixth Committee of the United Nations General Assembly, and of the General Assembly's Ad Hoc Committee on Jurisdictional Immunities of States and Their Property. Its aim is to sketch out a time-line, furnishing a concise summary of who did what and when, rather than to provide an in-depth conceptual account of the evolution of the restrictive doctrine of State immunity.[2]

2. Forerunners to the Convention

2.1 Non-governmental

It was the Institut de Droit international which pioneered the codification and, indeed, progressive development of the international rules on the jurisdictional immunities of States and their property, adopting at its Hamburg session in 1891 a resolution in which the earliest signs of the restrictive theory of State immunity are evident.[3] Subsequent resolutions adopted at the Institut's Aix-en-Provence session in 1954[4] and its Basel session in 1991[5] reflected the further evolution of international legal thinking away from an absolute notion of State immunity towards the restrictive doctrine. The Basel resolution, adopted the same year as the ILC's final adoption on second reading of its Draft Articles on Jurisdictional Immunities of States and Their Property, elaborated in

* This contribution was elaborated with the valuable assistance of Mr Gregor Novak.

[1] To be precise, the adoption of the Convention marked the culmination of the codification of State immunity in the context of non-criminal proceedings.

[2] For such an account, see H. Fox, *The Law of State Immunity* (2nd edn) (Oxford: Oxford University Press, 2008), chaps 8 and 9; Y. Xiaodong, *State Immunity in International Law* (Cambridge: Cambridge University Press, 2012), chap.1.

[3] See 'Projet de règlement international sur la compétence des tribunaux dans les procès contre les Etats, souverains ou chefs d'Etat étrangers' (Hamburg session, 11 September 1891), reproduced in Institut de Droit international, *Tableau général des résolutions (1873–1956)* (Basel: Karger, 1957), 14. The resolution proposed subjecting a foreign State's immunity from proceedings to a small number of exceptions relating to specific non-sovereign acts undertaken within the forum State's territory. It also proposed an exception to the immunity of the former State's property from judicial seizure where that State had set aside the property for the satisfaction of a debt.

[4] See 'L'immunité de juridiction et d'exécution forcées des Etats étrangers' (Aix-en-Provence session, 30 April 1954), reproduced in Institut de Droit international (n. 3), 17.

[5] See 'Contemporary Problems Concerning the Immunity of States in Relation to Questions of Jurisdiction and Enforcement' (Basel session, 2 September 1991), in 64 *Annuaire de l'Institut de Droit international* (1992), vol. II, 388.

concrete terms on the abstract *jure imperii/jure gestionis* distinction posited in respect of a foreign State's immunity from proceedings in the Aix-en-Provence resolution and reflected in the interim in widespread State practice, providing detailed criteria indicative of the competence of the forum State's courts (or quasi-judicial organs[6]) to determine the substance of a claim against a foreign State.[7] As for the immunity of the foreign State's property from 'measures of constraint', by which was meant 'any process or order of the courts or other organs of the forum State for the satisfaction or enforcement of a judgment or order, or for the purpose of prejudgment measures in preparation for execution', the resolution proposed that this remain unqualified in relation to certain categories of State property but be unavailable in relation to others if the latter had been 'allocated or earmarked by the State for the satisfaction of the claim in question' or, failing the sufficiency of this, if the property was within the territory of the forum State and was 'in use or intended for use for commercial purposes'.[8] The Institut's Basel resolution would prove influential in discussions in 1999 within the ILC's Working Group on Jurisdictional Immunities of States and Their Property.[9]

The Institut, however, was not alone among private groups in seeking to codify the international rules on State immunity.

In 1932, the Harvard Research in International Law project, responsible for a range of codification initiatives across several fields of international law, put forward a draft convention entitled 'Competence of Courts in Regard to Foreign States'.[10] The instrument anticipated the subsequent structure of both international and national instruments embodying restrictive State immunity by positing a general immunity from proceedings qualified in succeeding provisions by an exhaustive enumeration of exceptions[11]—exceptions the substance of which would also in time become familiar.

The International Law Association, for its part, came relatively late to the codification of State immunity, adopting resolutions on the topic only in 1982, in Montreal,[12] and again in 1994, in Buenos Aires.[13] The former resolution approved a set of 'Draft Articles for a Convention on State Immunity', the latter—which postdate the ILC's draft articles—a revised version of the same. Debates preceding the adoption of the Buenos Aires text centred on the criteria for distinguishing *acta jure imperii* from *acta jure gestionis* and on questions of execution.

2.2 Intergovernmental

Although for much of the twentieth century no comprehensive codification of State immunity was formally agreed among States, certain specific questions pertaining to such

[6] See Institut resolution (n. 5), art. 1.

[7] See Institut resolution (n. 5), art. 2(2). For the most part, these criteria corresponded in substance to the exceptions to a foreign State's immunity from proceedings recognized simultaneously in the ILC's draft articles.

[8] See Institut resolution (n. 5), art. 4. In accordance with art. 5 of the resolution, both immunity from proceedings and immunity from measures of constraint were to be unavailable where they had been expressly waived, although waiver of the former was not to imply waiver of the latter.

[9] See section 3.4.

[10] 'Competence of Courts in Regard to Foreign States' (1932) 26 *AJIL Supp* 451.

[11] See 'Competence of Courts in Regard to Foreign States' (n. 10), art. 7.

[12] See 'State Immunity', in International Law Association, *Report of the Sixtieth Conference, held at Montreal, August 29th, 1982, to September 4th, 1982* (1983), 5.

[13] See 'State Immunity', in International Law Association, *Report of the Sixty-Sixth Conference, held at Buenos Aires, Argentina, 14 to 20 August 1994* (1994), 21.

immunity came from the interwar period onwards to be regulated by treaty.[14] The most important of these treaties is the International Convention for the Unification of Certain Rules relating to the Immunity of State-owned Vessels 1926 (1926 Brussels Convention),[15] as elaborated on by its 1934 Additional Protocol,[16] which reflects the restrictive theory of State immunity. The 1926 Brussels Convention provides that '[s]ea-going ships owned or operated by States, cargoes owned by them, and cargoes and passengers carried on State-owned ships, as well as the States which own or operate such ships and own such cargoes'[17] are not to enjoy immunity from foreign proceedings in respect of the operation of such ships or in respect of the carriage of such cargoes or from measures of judicial constraint in connection with them.[18]

As for more general regulation of the topic, brief and impressionistic provisions on State immunity, conforming to an extent to the restrictive doctrine, were agreed at the regional level in the form of Articles 333 to 339 Convention on Private International Law 1928 (Bustamante Code),[19] concluded by the Sixth International Conference of American States. When it came to the stipulated immunity of a contracting State from proceedings in the courts of another,[20] Article 335 Bustamante Code provided an exception in respect of real (as distinct from personal) and mixed actions arising out of acts performed by the first State 'as a individual or private person'.[21]

In terms of efforts towards more comprehensive intergovernmental codification, the Committee of Experts for the Progressive Codification of International Law established by the Council of the League of Nations in 1924 reported to the Council four years later that the topic of the 'Competence of Courts in regard to Foreign States' was apt for codification. But the Council decided to reserve the question to a later date,[22] which never came; and after the Second World War, it was in the regional and interregional context that initially States more actively pursued the comprehensive codification of the international law of State immunity.

The Asian-African Legal Consultative Committee[23] led the way with its work on State immunity in the late 1950s. The AALCC's final report on the topic, adopted at its third session in Colombo in 1960, proceeded from the premise that a State which entered into a transaction of a commercial or otherwise private character ought not to

[14] In addition, in the wake of the First World War, the defeated Powers were deprived by treaty of the 'rights, privileges and immunities of sovereignty' in respect of their future engagement in international trade. See Art. 281 Treaty of Peace between the Allied and Associated Powers and Germany, Versailles, 28 June 1919, 225 CTS 188; Art. 283 Treaty of Peace between the Allied and Associated Powers and Austria, St Germain-en-Laye, 10 September 1919, 226 CTS 8; Art. 161 Treaty of Peace between the Allied and Associated Powers and Bulgaria, Neuilly, 27 November 1919, 226 CTS 332; Art. 216 Treaty of Peace between the Allied and Associated Powers and Hungary, Trianon, 4 June 1920, 6 LNTS 187. See also Art. 268 Treaty of Peace between the Allied and Associated Powers and Turkey, Sèvres, 10 August 1920 (unratified).

[15] Brussels, 10 April 1926, 176 LNTS 199. The 1926 Brussels Convention currently has only 24 States parties.

[16] Brussels, 24 May 1934, 176 LNTS 214.

[17] Art. 1 1926 Brussels Convention (n. 15/16).

[18] See Art. 2 1926 Brussels Convention (n. 15/16).

[19] Bustamante Code, Havana, 20 February 1928, 86 LNTS 111.

[20] See Art. 333 Bustamante Code (n. 19).

[21] Under no circumstances, however, was a court competent to take coercive measures against an embassy or consulate without the consent of its diplomatic agents or consular officers. See Art. 339 Bustamante Code (n. 19).

[22] See LNOJ Supp. No. 64 (1928), 143.

[23] Since 2001, the AALCC has been known as the Asian-African Legal Consultative Organization.

enjoy immunity from proceedings in another State's courts in respect of that transaction.[24] But the Committee equally considered that a judgment obtained against a foreign State could not be executed against its public property, the latter being defined to exclude property of a 'state trading organisation which has a separate juristic entity' [*sic*] under the municipal law of the State of incorporation.[25]

The first legally binding comprehensive codification of State immunity was agreed under the auspices of the Council of Europe[26] in the form of the European Convention on State Immunity 1972.[27] The ECSI, which served as one of the material bases for the ILC's subsequent work, embodies the restrictive approach to a foreign State's immunity from proceedings; and it does so, following the model of the Harvard Research draft convention, by positing a general rule of immunity qualified by an exhaustive range of detailed exceptions, most of them relating to conduct of a commercial or otherwise private character having some link to the forum State, usually to its territory. On the other hand, despite cleaving to a more-or-less common view of the appropriate relationship between the state and the economy, the western European States which elaborated the ECSI were still not prepared to admit of coercive measures by foreign courts against their property,[28] providing instead for a complicated regime for the execution of foreign judgments by the courts of the judgment-debtor State.[29]

A third regional effort at complete codification of the law of State immunity came in 1983, when the Inter-American Juridical Committee of the Organization of American States, which is to the OAS what the ILC is to the UN, approved an Inter-American draft Convention on Jurisdictional Immunities of States.[30] The Inter-American draft Convention emulates the structure and mirrors, albeit in more condensed form, the substance of the ECSI, but it remains a draft, never having been submitted to the General Assembly of the OAS.

3. The Evolution of the Convention

3.1 Preparatory Work

Attempts on the universal plane to codify the international rules on State immunity were pursued after the Second World War within the framework of the United Nations. In its

[24] See Asian-African Legal Consultative Committee, *Final Report of the Committee on Immunity of States in respect of Commercial and other Transactions of a Private Character, as revised in the third session of the AALCC* (New Delhi: 1960), 68, partly reprinted in M.M. Whiteman (ed.), *Digest of International Law* (Washington, DC: USGPO, 1968), vol. 6, 553, 573.

[25] See AALCC report (n. 24), 573.

[26] The Council of Europe returned to the question of State immunity in 2001, with the initiation of a 'Pilot Project on State Practice regarding State Immunities', in the framework of which 27 member States submitted information on their judicial, executive, and legislative practice in the field. See CAHDI (Committee of Legal Advisors on International Law) Working Documents, CAHDI (2004) 5 Part II (A) rev & rev 2 and CAHDI (2004) 5 Part II (B) & (B) rev. See also G. Hafner et al. (eds), *State Practice Regarding State Immunities* (Leiden: Martinus Nijhoff/Council of Europe, 2006).

[27] As per Art. 33, nothing in the ECSI 'shall affect existing or future international agreements in special fields which relate to matters deal with in the [ECSI]'. In addition, Art. 30 specifically carves out from the scope of the ECSI the sorts of proceedings covered by the 1926 Brussels Convention.

[28] See Art. 23 ECSI.

[29] See Arts 21–22 ECSI.

[30] 22 ILM (1983) 292.

Survey of International Law in relation to the Work of Codification of the International Law Commission, produced in 1949 to facilitate the efforts of the nascent ILC, the UN Secretariat indicated a need, on account of divergence and uncertainty among States as to certain aspects of the question, to codify the jurisdictional immunities of foreign States, and it suggested that such codification was feasible.[31] That same year the Commission included 'Jurisdictional immunities of States and their property' among its provisional list of topics for codification,[32] although the matter was not accorded priority.[33]

3.2 The ILC's Draft Articles on Jurisdictional Immunities of States and Their Property, 1978–1991

In 1971, in view of the ILC's decision to review its long-term programme of work, the UN Secretariat produced a further *Survey of International Law*, in which, noting a trend towards a restrictive concept of State immunity as reflected in the report of the AALCC,[34] it observed:

> Differences of view exist [as to the jurisdictional immunities of foreign States] . . . But it may be suggested that the differences are not in all cases large, although they can nevertheless cause friction and uncertainty; that, as was said in the 1948 Survey, it is doubtful whether considerations of any national interest of decisive importance stand in the way of a codified statement of the law on this topic, commanding general acceptance; and that its day-to-day importance makes it suitable for codification and progressive development.[35]

It was against this backdrop that, in 1977, the General Assembly invited the ILC to commence work on the topic of jurisdictional immunities of States and their property 'at an appropriate time and in the light of progress made on . . . topics in its [then] current programme of work'.[36]

The following year, on receipt of the report of a working group established during its thirtieth session to examine the issue, the ILC included the topic of 'Jurisdictional immunities of State and their property' in its programme of work, appointing Sompong Sucharitkul as Special Rapporteur.[37] On the Commission's request, the UN Secretary-General invited member States to submit to him relevant materials on the topic, including national legislation, decisions of national courts, and diplomatic and other official correspondence.[38]

Special Rapporteur Sucharitkul presented eight reports to the ILC, on the basis of which the latter adopted on first reading, in 1986, a complete set of draft articles,[39] which the Secretary-General transmitted to governments for comments and observations. The

[31] See *Survey of International Law in relation to the Work of Codification of the International Law Commission*, UN doc. A/C.4/1/Rev.1 (10 February 1949), 31, para. 52.

[32] See *YILC 1949*, 281, para. 16. See also *YILC 1949*, 281, 40–1, paras 37–39.

[33] See *YILC 1949*, 281, paras 19–20.

[34] See *Survey of international law. Working paper prepared by the Secretary-General*, reproduced in *YILC 1971*, vol. II(2), 1, 19, para. 70.

[35] *Survey of international law* (n. 35), 20, para. 75.

[36] GA res. 32/151, 19 December 1977, para. 7.

[37] See Report ILC, thirtieth session, 153, paras 188–190.

[38] For the resultant materials, see UN doc. A/CN.4/343 and Adds 1–4, reproduced in United Nations Legislative Series, *Materials on Jurisdictional Immunities of States and their Property* (UN Sales No. E/F 81. V.10).

[39] See Report ILC, thirty-eighth session, 8–12.

following year the Commission appointed Motoo Ogiso as its new Special Rapporteur on jurisdictional immunities of States and their property. In the light of the input received from governments,[40] Special Rapporteur Ogiso proposed various amendments to the draft articles over the course of his three reports. The Commission, refraining from discussing doctrinal views in favour of a focus on concrete situations, proceeded in 1991 to the final adoption on second reading of twenty-two Draft Articles on Jurisdictional Immunities of States and Their Property, with commentaries.[41] In addition, it recommended to the General Assembly that the latter 'should convene an international conference of plenipotentiaries to examine the draft articles . . . and to conclude a convention on the subject'.[42]

3.3 The Sixth Committee's Working Group and informal consultations, 1992–1994

The fundamental changes wrought, however, by the collapse of communism on the political and economic systems of the States of the former eastern bloc meant that the time was not ripe for a conference. Instead, the General Assembly established an open-ended Working Group of the Sixth Committee to examine, in the light of States' written comments and observations on the draft articles[43] and of the views expressed during the Assembly's forty-sixth session, both '[i]ssues of substance arising out of the draft articles, in order to facilitate a successful conclusion of a convention through the promotion of general agreement', and the question of the convening of a conference.[44] The Sixth Committee's Working Group, under the chairmanship of ILC member Carlos Calero-Rodrigues (Brazil), held ten meetings throughout 1992,[45] in which discussion focused on (*i*) the definition of the term 'State', in particular on the question of federal subdivisions; (*ii*) the definition of the term 'commercial transaction' for the purposes of the exception in respect of such transactions to a foreign State's immunity from proceedings; (*iii*) the exception in respect of contracts of employment to a foreign State's immunity from proceedings; (*iv*) issues pertaining to State enterprises in the context of commercial transactions; and (*v*) the immunity of State property from measures of constraint. No general agreement was reached, and 'the prevailing view was that consideration of issues of substance arising out of the draft articles should continue in order to facilitate a successful conclusion of a convention through the promotion of general agreement'.[46] In response, the General Assembly decided to re-establish the Working Group,[47] which held a further thirteen meetings in 1993,[48] focusing on the same core issues, with essentially the same outcome.

The General Assembly decided this time that informal consultations on the topic, still within the framework of the Sixth Committee and under the chairmanship of Carlos

[40] See *YILC 1988*, vol. II(1), 45–91.

[41] See Report ILC, forty-third session, 13–62.

[42] Report ILC, forty-third session, 13, para. 25.

[43] The General Assembly invited such written comments and observations in GA res. 46/55, 9 December 1991, para. 2.

[44] GA res. 46/55, para. 4.

[45] See 1992 report Sixth Committee Working Group.

[46] 1992 report Sixth Committee Working Group, 8, para. 38.

[47] See GA decision 47/414, 25 November 1992.

[48] See 1993 report Sixth Committee Working Group.

Calero-Rodrigues, should take place the following year,[49] which they did.[50] But agreement on the five key issues proved elusive once more. As a consequence, the Assembly, although agreeing ultimately with the ILC's recommendation to convene an international conference with a view to concluding a convention on jurisdictional immunities of States and their property, deferred further consideration of the topic until 1997, inviting States to submit to the Secretary-General in the interim comments on the Sixth Committee's work to date.[51]

3.4 The ILC's Working Group on Jurisdictional Immunities of States and Their Property and the Sixth Committee's Working Group, 1999–2000

The General Assembly resumed consideration of a convention on jurisdictional immunities of States and their property in 1997, envisaging the establishment once more, in two sessions' time, of a working group.[52] The following year the Assembly duly decided to establish at its next session an open-ended Working Group of the Sixth Committee 'to consider outstanding substantive issues related to the draft articles on jurisdictional immunities of States and their property adopted by the International Law Commission . . . and to consider whether there [were] any issues identified by the working group upon which it would be useful to seek further comments and recommendations of the Commission'.[53] It also invited the ILC to present to it by 31 August 1999 any preliminary comments the latter had on these outstanding substantive issues.[54]

Since the ILC lacked explicit authority under its Statute to conduct a third reading of its Draft Articles on Jurisdictional Immunities of States and Their Property,[55] it chose instead to establish a Working Group on Jurisdictional Immunities of States and Their Property, with Gerhard Hafner (Austria) as Chairman and Chusei Yamada (Japan) as Rapporteur, the remit of which was confined to a consideration of the five key substantive issues. The Working Group's report[56] summarized the evolution of the contested questions and any recent case-law relevant to them, and suggested possible solutions, which 'often contain[ed] various possible technical alternatives, a final selection among which require[d] a decision by the General Assembly'.[57] In addition, in an appendix to its report, the Working Group considered the availability or otherwise of jurisdictional immunity in actions arising out of, among other things, violations of *jus cogens* norms, a question it merely brought to the attention of the Commission.[58] In the event, the Commission took note of the Working Group's report and adopted its suggestions,[59] while for its part the General Assembly twice took note of the report 'with appreciation'.[60]

49 See GA decision 48/413, 9 December 1993.
50 See Report Sixth Committee informal consultations.
51 See GA res. 49/61, 9 December 1994.
52 See GA res. 52/151, 15 December 1997.
53 GA res. 53/98, 8 December 1998, para. 1.
54 GA res. 53/98, para. 2.
55 See Art. 16 ILC Statute.
56 See 1999 report ILC Working Group.
57 1999 report ILC Working Group, 155, para. 8.
58 1999 report ILC Working Group, 155, para. 9.
59 Report ILC, fifty-first session, 128, para. 484.
60 GA res. 54/101, 9 December 1999, para. 1; GA res. 55/150, 12 December 2000, para. 1.

The open-ended Working Group of the Sixth Committee established the previous year met later in 1999 and again in 2000,[61] under the chairmanship of Gerhard Hafner, seeking to achieve compromise on the various bones of contention. It also turned its collective mind to the form the outcome of its work might take. In this latter regard, a number of delegations supported a convention on grounds of legal certainty, consistency, and clarity. They emphasized that the rules of State immunity were to be applied by domestic courts and that only a binding instrument could ensure uniform State practice in this respect. Other delegations ventured instead the idea of a model law on State immunity, which, they argued, stood a better chance of broad acceptance on account of its non-binding character.[62] In response, the General Assembly decided to establish an Ad Hoc Committee on Jurisdictional Immunities of States and Their Property, which was to meet for two weeks in 2002 'to further the work done, consolidate areas of agreement and resolve outstanding issues with a view to elaborating a generally acceptable instrument based on the draft articles on jurisdictional immunities of States and their property . . . and also on the discussions of the open-ended working group of the Sixth Committee and their results'.[63]

3.5 The Ad Hoc Committee on Jurisdictional Immunities of States and Their Property, 2002–2004

The Ad Hoc Committee on Jurisdictional Immunities of States and Their Property met in three annual sessions from 2002 to 2004, again under the chairmanship of Gerhard Hafner.

A. 2002 session

At its 2002 session, the Ad Hoc Committee decided to proceed in a Working Group of the Whole, which first discussed the five outstanding substantive issues identified by the open-ended Working Group of the Sixth Committee, 'namely: (a) concept of a State for purposes of immunity; (b) criteria for determining the commercial character of a contract or transaction; (c) concept of a State enterprise or other entity in relation to commercial transactions; (d) contracts of employment; and (e) measures of constraint against State property'.[64] Substantial progress was made, in particular on the definition of 'State' and on measures of constraint against State property, the treatment of the latter in the now-amended draft articles being divided between provisions on pre-judgment and post-judgment measures respectively. The Working Group of the Whole then considered the remainder of the ILC's draft articles 'with a view to identifying and resolving any further issues arising from the text'.[65]

The General Assembly—'[n]oting that only a few issues remain[ed] outstanding' and '[s]tressing the importance of uniformity and clarity in the law applicable to

[61] See 1999 report Chairman Sixth Committee Working Group and 2000 report Chairman Sixth Committee Working Group.

[62] Reference was made in this connection to the UNCITRAL Model Law on International Commercial Arbitration, UN doc. A/40/17, annex I.

[63] GA res. 55/150, 12 December 2000, para. 3 (quote) and para. 4. See also GA res. 56/78, 12 December 2001.

[64] 2002 report Ad Hoc Committee, 1, para. 9.

[65] 2002 report Ad Hoc Committee, 2, para. 9.

jurisdictional immunities of States and their property'—took note of the Ad Hoc Committee's report, and decided to reconvene the Committee the following year.[66]

B. 2003 session

In order to facilitate negotiations at its 2003 session, the Ad Hoc Committee, proceeding again in a Working Group of the Whole, divided the key outstanding issues among two informal consultative groups, chaired by Chusei Yamada and Michael Bliss (Australia) respectively. The first group dealt with the criteria for determining the commercial character of a contract or transaction, the second with the concept of a State enterprise or other entity in the context of commercial transactions, with contracts of employment, with the inapplicability of the draft articles to criminal proceedings, and with the relationship between the draft articles and other international agreements on the same subject-matter. The remaining matters of substance and the question of the eventual form of the outcome of the Committee's work were examined by the Working Group of the Whole.[67]

Progress was greatly facilitated by agreement on a set of 'understandings' with respect to specific draft articles, each of them giving effect to a compromise in relation to the provision in question. Agreement on these understandings also led to growing support for an eventual convention. But the precise relationship between the understandings and the draft articles remained a matter of debate.

The question of the availability or otherwise to a State of immunity from actions alleging, *inter alia*, violations of *jus cogens* resurfaced in the course of the session. The general view, however, was that the denial of immunity in such situations had not attained, and was unlikely to attain, the status of a rule of customary international law. As the inclusion of an exception to immunity from jurisdiction in such cases was seen to jeopardize general acceptance of the prospective convention in its entirety, the issue was dropped.

As to the relationship between the future convention and existing treaties dealing with State immunity, among them the ECSI, agreement was reached that the convention would not affect rights and obligations under any such treaties. As to reservations, although some States favoured their explicit exclusion, it was by and large thought that the regime laid down in Articles 19(*c*) to 23 VCLT would enable States to participate in any eventual convention despite their difficulties with one or other of its provisions. The upshot was that no provision on reservations was included in what was to become the Convention.

In the event, the Working Group of the Whole was able to resolve all outstanding issues. As a consequence, the Ad Hoc Committee was in a position to submit to the General Assembly a completed text of the revised draft articles, together with the understandings.

The General Assembly—'[n]oting the adoption of the draft articles and the understandings by the Ad Hoc Committee' and '[n]oting also the broad support for the conclusion of a convention on jurisdictional immunities of States and their property'—took note 'with appreciation' of the Ad Hoc Committee's report, and decided to reconvene the Committee the following year 'with the mandate to formulate a preamble

[66] GA res. 57/16, 19 November 2002.

[67] See 2003 report Ad Hoc Committee, 2, para. 9.

and final clauses, with a view to completing a convention on jurisdictional immunities of States and their property'.[68]

C. 2004 session

At its third and final session, held in March 2004, the Ad Hoc Committee, proceeding once more in a Working Group of the Whole, formulated a preamble to and the final clauses of what it styled the draft United Nations Convention on Jurisdictional Immunities of States and Their Property. The Working Group of the Whole also settled the question of the relationship between the Convention and the understandings, which were eventually annexed to the Convention. Finally, the Working Group 'reiterated the general understanding, which was initially contained in the annex to the [Ad Hoc Committee's] draft articles on jurisdictional immunities of States and their property, that the draft Convention did not cover criminal proceedings', although it 'was of the view that a more appropriate placement for that issue was in a General Assembly resolution'.[69]

At its eighth plenary meeting, the Ad Hoc Committee adopted its report, which contained the finalized text of the draft Convention.

3.6 The Chairman of the Ad Hoc Committee's statement to the Sixth Committee

Gerhard Hafner, Chairman of the Ad Hoc Committee on Jurisdictional Immunities of States and Their Property, introduced the draft Convention to the Sixth Committee on 25 October 2004, noting that the finalization[70] of the text 'had been possible only because several States belonging to different legal systems and regions had made considerable concessions and shown great flexibility'.[71] He drew the Sixth Committee's attention to the recommendation by the Ad Hoc Committee that the General Assembly adopt the draft Convention.[72]

The Chairman of the Ad Hoc Committee prefaced his remarks on specific issues with a more systemic observation:

> Generally, it must be borne in mind that the Convention would have to be read in conjunction with the commentary prepared by the International Law Commission, at least insofar as the text submitted by the Commission had remained unchanged. The Commission's commentary, the reports of the Ad Hoc Committee and the General Assembly resolution adopting the Convention would form an important part of the *travaux préparatoires* of the Convention.[73]

'That common reading of the text of the Convention and the commentary', the Chairman continued, 'would certainly clarify the text if certain questions of interpretation remained'.[74]

[68] GA res. 58/74, 9 December 2003.

[69] 2004 report Ad Hoc Committee, 3, para. 11.

[70] Strictly speaking, the text was not quite finalized. The Chairman of the Ad Hoc Committee noted a handful of minor textual corrections that were required before the adoption of the draft Convention. See Statement Chairman Ad Hoc Committee, 6, paras 33–34.

[71] Statement Chairman Ad Hoc Committee, 5, para. 30. See also Statement Chairman Ad Hoc Committee, 6, para. 38.

[72] See Statement Chairman Ad Hoc Committee, 6, para. 32.

[73] Statement Chairman Ad Hoc Committee, 6, para. 35.

[74] Statement Chairman Ad Hoc Committee, 6, para. 35.

The Chairman of the Ad Hoc Committee then touched on three particular issues in connection with the draft Convention. First, he emphasized the Ad Hoc Committee's recommendation that the General Assembly 'include in its resolution adopting the draft Convention the general understanding that it did not cover criminal proceedings'.[75] Secondly, he declared that a 'general understanding had always prevailed' to the effect that military activities were not covered by the Convention.[76] 'In any case', he added in this regard,

> reference should be made to the [International Law] Commission's commentary on article 12, stating that 'neither did the article affect the question of diplomatic immunities, as provided in article 3, nor did it apply to situations involving armed conflicts'. It had to be borne in mind [as well] that the preamble stated that the rules of customary international law continued to govern matters not regulated by the provisions of the Convention.[77]

Thirdly, he explained that the exclusion of military activities was but one example of 'the general approach of the Convention' whereby 'it did not apply where there was a special immunity regime, including immunities *ratione personae* (*lex specialis*)'.[78] He noted that '[s]ometimes [this] was expressly stated in the text, sometimes not'.[79] By way of example, the Chairman specified that 'the express mention of heads of State in article 3 should not be read as suggesting that the immunity *ratione personae* of other state officials was affected by the Convention'.[80]

3.7 The adoption of the Convention via General Assembly resolution 59/38

The Convention was adopted by the General Assembly without a vote on 2 December 2004 by way of resolution 59/38, to which the text of the Convention, including the understandings, was annexed.

A proposal that reference be made in the operative part of General Assembly resolution 59/38 to the statement to the Sixth Committee by the Chairman of the Ad Hoc Committee met with strong resistance. Last-minute negotiations alighted on a compromise whereby the statement was referred to instead in the resolution's preamble. As a consequence, in the ninth recital of the preamble to resolution 59/38, the General Assembly is described as '[t]aking into account the statement of the Chairman of the Ad Hoc Committee introducing the report of the Ad Hoc Committee'.[81]

In operative paragraph 2 of resolution 59/38, the General Assembly '[a]grees with the general understanding reached in the Ad Hoc Committee that the United Nations Convention on Jurisdictional Immunities of States and Their Property does not cover criminal proceedings'.

[75] Statement Chairman Ad Hoc Committee, 6, para. 32.
[76] Statement Chairman Ad Hoc Committee, 6, para. 36, citation omitted.
[77] Statement Chairman Ad Hoc Committee, 6, para. 36.
[78] Statement Chairman Ad Hoc Committee, 6, para. 37.
[79] Statement Chairman Ad Hoc Committee, 6, para. 37.
[80] Statement Chairman Ad Hoc Committee, 6, para. 37.
[81] The recital is followed by a footnote reference to GAOR, Fifty-ninth session, Sixth Committee, 13th meeting (A/C.6/59/SR.13) and corrigendum.

4. Concluding Remarks

'Given the strong interest elicited by [this] increasingly important and ever-developing area of the law, it should be seen as a significant accomplishment to have reached agreement on an instrument which . . . promise[s] to harmonize the practice of States and facilitate commercial relations between States and private actors.'[82] So spoke the present author when, as Chairman of the Ad Hoc Committee on Jurisdictional Immunities of States and Their Property, he presented the draft text of the Convention to the Sixth Committee. Now, as then, it is appropriate to pay tribute in this connection to 'the flexibility and creativity demonstrated by delegations during the negotiations'. It is also imperative to recognize the work over many years of the ILC and especially of its Special Rapporteurs.

The evolution of the Convention, albeit not of its text, will recommence in due course through the instrument's interpretation and application by domestic and international courts. In this regard, questions have been raised as to the use that may permissibly be made both of the Chairman of the Ad Hoc Committee's statement to the Sixth Committee, as taken note of by the General Assembly in the preamble to resolution 59/38 when adopting the Convention, and of operative paragraph 2 of resolution 59/38, in which the General Assembly agrees with 'the general understanding reached in the Ad Hoc Committee' that the Convention does not apply to criminal proceedings. The answer in each case is that General Assembly resolution 59/38 is best considered '[an] instrument which was made by one or more parties in connection with the conclusion of the treaty and accepted by the other parties as an instrument related to the treaty', within the meaning of Article 31(2)(*b*) VCLT, making it part of the context in which, in accordance with Article 31(1) VCLT, any relevant term of the Convention must be read.[83] Alternatively, and at the very least, both the Chairman's statement and paragraph 2 of resolution 59/38 can be considered elements of the Convention's *travaux préparatoires* for the purposes of Article 32 VCLT. Neither possibility means that the Chairman's statement, of which the General Assembly is said in the preamble to resolution 59/38 merely to take note, and the General Assembly's express agreement in paragraph 2 of the resolution with the 'general understanding' that the Convention does not apply to criminal proceedings must be accorded equal weight. But it does mean that both have a role to play in the Convention's future interpretation.

[82] Statement Chairman Ad Hoc Committee, 6, para. 38.

[83] In *Jurisdictional Immunities of the State (Germany v Italy: Greece intervening), Judgment*, International Court of Justice, 3 February 2012, para. 69, the International Court of Justice placed considerable evidentiary weight, when assessing the alleged customary status of the exception to immunity from proceedings embodied in Art. 12 UNCSI, on the fact that '[n]o State questioned the interpretation' advanced by the Chairman of the Ad Hoc Committee.

Immunity from Jurisdiction and Immunity from Measures of Constraint

Sir Michael Wood

1. Introduction

In its judgment of 3 February 2012 in *Jurisdictional Immunities of the State*, the International Court of Justice observed:

[T]he immunity from enforcement enjoyed by States in regard to their property situated on foreign territory goes further than the jurisdictional immunity enjoyed by those same States before foreign courts. Even if a judgment has been lawfully rendered against a foreign State, in circumstances such that the latter could not claim immunity from jurisdiction, it does not follow *ipso facto* that the State against which judgment has been given can be the subject of measures of constraint on the territory of the forum State or on that of a third State, with a view to enforcing the judgment in question. Similarly, any waiver by a State of its jurisdictional immunity before a foreign court does not in itself mean that that State has waived its immunity from enforcement as regards property belonging to it situated in foreign territory.

The rules of customary international law governing immunity from enforcement and those governing jurisdictional immunity (understood *stricto sensu* as the right of a State not to be the subject of judicial proceedings in the courts of another State) are distinct, and must be applied separately.[1]

Later in the judgment, the Court applied this distinction in the context of Germany's claim that the Italian judgments declaring Greek decisions enforceable in Italy violated Germany's jurisdictional immunity. The Court noted:

[T]he claim in Germany's third submission is entirely separate and distinct from that set out in the preceding one... The Court is no longer concerned to determine here whether a measure of constraint—such as the legal charge on the Villa Vigoni—violated Germany's immunity from enforcement, but to decide whether the Italian judgments declaring enforceable the pecuniary awards pronounced in Greece did themselves—independently of any subsequent measures of enforcement—constitute a violation of the Applicant's immunity from jurisdiction.[2]

In these passages, the Court confirmed the general opinion that immunity from suit and immunity from execution are two separate matters.[3] As Ian Sinclair wrote in 1979,

[1] *Jurisdictional Immunities of the State (Germany v Italy: Greece intervening), Judgment*, 3 February 2012, International Court of Justice, para. 113.

[2] *Jurisdictional Immunities of the State* (n. 1), para. 124.

[3] Among the writings on State immunity, including immunity from execution, see J. Crawford, 'Execution of Judgments and Foreign Sovereign Immunity' (1981) 75 *AJIL* 820; R. Jennings and A. Watts (eds), *Oppenheim's International Law. Volume I: Peace* (9th edn) (London: Longmans, 1992), 341–65; N. Turck, 'French and US Courts Define Limits of Sovereign Immunity in Execution and Enforcement of Arbitral Awards' (2001) 17 *Arbitration International* 327; A. Dickinson, R. Lindsay, and J. Loonam, *State Immunity: Selected Materials and Commentary* (Oxford: Oxford University Press, 2004); G. Hafner and U. Köhler, 'The United Nations Convention on Jurisdictional Immunities of States and Their Property' (2004) 35 *NYIL* 3; D. Stewart, 'The UN Convention on Jurisdictional Immunities of States and Their Property' (2005) 99 *AJIL* 194; A. Reinisch, 'European Court State Practice Concerning State Immunity from Enforcement Measures'

whatever may be the theoretical relationship between jurisdictional immunity and immunity from execution, the sensitivities of foreign States are likely to be aroused if, following upon the denial of a claim to jurisdictional immunity, the courts of the State of the forum authorize the levying of forced execution against the property of the defendant State.[4]

It follows from this separateness that one should not view restrictions on immunity from execution as flowing automatically from restrictions on immunity from suit. The Swiss courts are sometimes cited for a different view, but if one looks beyond the rhetoric it is clear that in fact they admit the distinction,[5] which is also reflected in various codification projects[6] and national laws.[7]

The Convention embodies this important conceptual and practical distinction, differentiating between 'immunity from jurisdiction', as regulated by Parts II and III and the accompanying 'understandings' annexed to the Convention, and 'immunity from measures of constraint', as dealt with in Part IV and in the understanding with respect to Article 19.

2. Background

In the International Law Commission's oft-cited words, immunity from execution may be viewed as 'the last bastion of immunity'.[8] This is meant in the sense that, procedurally, immunity from execution may be a long-stop protection for the State even when immunity from suit has been removed. Such protection is of particular importance where the defendant State does not accept, in principle, the restriction on immunity applied by the courts of the forum or does not accept that the restriction has been properly applied.

As a practical matter, once the restrictive doctrine of immunity became established in the last century, immunity from measures of constraint became one of the most important issues within the law of State immunity. The ability, should it prove necessary, to enforce a judgment is obviously vital for a claimant, since there is, for most litigants, little point in securing a favourable judgment if the defendant State can simply refuse to pay the judgment debt and get away with it.[9] However satisfactory the rules on immunity

(2006) 17 *EJIL* 803; E. Wiesinger, 'State Immunity from Enforcement Measures' (2006) http://intlaw.univie.ac.at/fileadmin/user_upload/int_beziehungen/Internetpubl/wiesinger.pdf; H. Fox, *The Law of State Immunity* (2nd edn) (Oxford: Oxford University Press, 2008), chap. 18; M. Shaw, *International Law* (6th edn) (Cambridge: Cambridge University Press, 2008), 697–750; G. Hafner, 'United Nations Convention on Jurisdictional Immunities of States and Their Property', in R. Wolfrum (ed.), *Max Planck Encyclopedia of Public International Law* (Oxford: Oxford University Press, 2012), vol. X, 319; S. Murphy, *Principles of International Law* (2nd edn) (St Paul, MN: West Law, 2012), 302–23; J. Crawford (ed.), *Brownlie's Principles of International Law* (8th edn) (Oxford: Oxford University Press, 2012), 502–5; X. Yang, *State Immunity in International Law* (Cambridge: Cambridge University Press, 2012), chap. 9.

[4] I. Sinclair, 'Law of Sovereign Immunity: Recent Developments' (1979) 167 *RdC* 113, 219–20. Hazel Fox likewise refers (n. 3), 605, to 'the separate regime of immunity from execution'.

[5] See Fox (n. 3), 604.

[6] See eg the Institut de Droit international's 1991 resolution 'Contemporary Problems Concerning the Immunity of States in Relation to Questions of Jurisdiction and Enforcement' (Basel session, 2 September 1991), in 64 *Annuaire de l'Institut de Droit international* (1992), vol. II, 388. See also the ILA Revised Draft Articles.

[7] See the laws discussed with respect to Part IV UNCSI.

[8] ILC commentary, draft art. 18, para. 2.

[9] An exception would be those cases, increasingly frequent, where legal proceedings are instituted against a State as part of a campaign against the government's policies, for example the various Falun Gong cases against the People's Republic of China. In such cases, principle rather than money is what matters to the claimant.

from jurisdiction may be, if a judgment cannot be executed against a recalcitrant State, it may prove to be worth little or nothing. But execution is also a very sensitive matter in inter-State relations. Execution against State property located in the territory of another State can be a source of intense friction.

It is not, therefore, surprising that immunity from execution has been one of the most contested aspects of State immunity, indeed an 'intractable aspect'.[10] As Gerhard Hafner has put it, 'enforcement measures are considered to be more likely to intrude into the sovereign rights of a State so that States apply a more cautious approach'.[11] Even after the acceptance of restrictions on immunity from suit, immunity from execution was often regarded as absolute, absent treaty exceptions. There were in fact a number of early treaty exceptions. Article 281 of the Treaty of Versailles provided that, '[i]f the German Government engages in international trade, it shall not in respect thereof have or be deemed to have any rights, privileges or immunities of sovereignty'.[12] Under the International Convention for the Unification of Certain Rules concerning the Immunity of State-owned Ships (1926 Brussels Convention),[13] State-owned ships, except warships etc, may be arrested and detained in the same way as privately owned merchant vessels. But these are specific treaty provisions addressing particular circumstances or classes of property, and it is difficult to discern in them any move towards the development of customary exceptions to immunity from execution.

The reluctance on the part of States, even within Europe, to acknowledge exceptions to immunity from execution is reflected in the European Convention on State Immunity, adopted under the auspices of the Council of Europe in 1972.[14] The ECSI was based on a unique (and complex) approach, which took as a starting point that States are immune from measures of execution. The Convention provided that '[n]o measures of execution or preventive measures against the property of a Contracting State may be taken in the territory of another Contracting State except where and to the extent that the State has expressly consented thereto in writing in any particular case'.[15] At the same time, the Contracting States undertook, in most circumstances, to give effect to any judgment given against them in application of the Convention's exceptions to immunity for jurisdiction.[16] In addition, there were optional provisions under which, if accepted, Contracting States accepted enforcement in limited circumstances.[17] As of 2012 the ECSI had secured eight Contracting States, of which six had accepted the optional provisions.[18]

The insistence on retaining immunity from execution may be thought to raise doubts about the reality of States' acceptance of the restrictive doctrine of immunity. Can it

[10] Fox (n. 3), 8.

[11] Hafner (n. 3), para. 37.

[12] The same language appeared in the treaties of peace with Austria, Bulgaria, Hungary, and Turkey.

[13] Brussels, 10 April 1926, 176 LNTS 199. See also its Additional Protocol, Brussels, 24 May 1934, 176 LNTS 215.

[14] Basel, 16 May 1972, 1495 UNTS 182. See Expl. Rep. ECSI, paras 76–95 and 104–106; R. O'Keefe, 'European Convention on State Immunity (1972)', in R. Wolfrum (ed.), *Max Planck Encyclopedia of Public International Law* (Oxford: Oxford University Press, 2012), vol. III, 889.

[15] Art. 23 ECSI.

[16] See Art. 20 ECSI.

[17] Art. 26 ECSI.

[18] The relationship between the ECSI and the UNCSI has been discussed within the Council of Europe. See O'Keefe (n. 14). It seems to be generally accepted that the UNCSI will supersede the ECSI as and when the latter enters into force for the parties to the former. For details see the commentary to Art. 26.

really be said that the restrictive doctrine is gaining headway if judgments cannot be enforced against the State? The better view is that the prevalence of the restrictive doctrine in the context of immunity from jurisdiction is nonetheless significant, since most States most of the time give effect to judgments, sometimes even if they do not themselves accept the restrictive doctrine.

3. The Convention

The United Nations Convention on Jurisdictional Immunities of States and Their Property embodies two important distinctions: first, between immunity from jurisdiction (or immunity from suit) and immunity from measures of constraint (or immunity from execution),[19] which are dealt with in separate Parts; and, second, between measures of constraint that are taken before judgment on the merits and those that are taken to enforce a judgment on the merits, as elaborated in Part IV.[20]

The first distinction, the origins of which lie deep in the history of State immunity, was always fundamental to work on the Convention. The distinction between immunity from jurisdiction and immunity from measures of constraint is reasonably easy to draw, although in *Jurisdictional Immunities of the State* the Court was compelled to explain in some detail that a court decision declaring a foreign judgment enforceable constituted a violation of immunity from jurisdiction, rather than immunity from execution.[21]

The second distinction is novel,[22] and only came to the fore in the 1999 Working Group of the ILC. It had not been present in the Commission's 1991 draft articles. The Working Group 'concluded that a distinction between prejudgement and post-judgement measures of constraint may help to sort out the difficulties inherent in this issue'.[23]

The provisions on measures of constraint are among the most important and innovative of the Convention. They were the subject of difficult negotiations, especially in the period after the ILC adopted its final draft articles in 1991.[24] They were discussed at length by States in the context of the ILC Working Group, the Working Group of the Sixth Committee, the Sixth Committee itself, and the Ad Hoc Committee on Jurisdictional Immunities of States and Their Property. The provisions of Part IV of the

[19] The term 'measures of constraint' was viewed in the ILC as broader or less technical than 'execution'. See ILC commentary, draft Part IV, para. 2. The terminology of the Convention, including 'measures of constraint', seems to have been adopted by the ICJ in *Jurisdictional Immunities of the State*, an example of the contribution of the Commission's output to the harmonization of the use of terms in international law. See the commentary to Part IV.

[20] See Art. 18 (pre-judgment measures) and Arts 19 and 21 (post-judgment measures) UNCSI. See also the commentaries to Part IV and Arts 18, 19, and 21 UNCSI.

[21] See *Jurisdictional Immunities of the State* (n. 1), paras 121–133. The Court said, para. 128, that '[w]hen a court is seised, as in the present case, of an application for *exequatur* of a foreign judgment against a third State, it is itself being called upon to exercise its jurisdiction in respect of the third State in question'.

[22] The only national legislation to embody the distinction is the FSIA (US), which recognizes a broader immunity from pre-judgment than from post-judgment measures. See s. 1610(*a*) and (*b*) versus 1610(*d*) FSIA (US), although see also s. 1610(*e*), on the immunity of State vessels. As for the ECSI, the immunity accorded by Art. 23 ECSI is the same as between 'measures of execution' and 'preventive measures'. At the same time, Art. 26, an optional provision, seeks to restrict immunity from execution only.

[23] 1999 report ILC Working Group, 171, para. 126.

[24] See the commentaries to Arts 18, 19, and 21.

Convention as ultimately adopted reflect a workable compromise between those States that were opposed to any form of execution against State property and those that wanted execution to be widely available. The outcome represents a fair balance. It largely protects the State against pre-judgment measures of constraint while permitting, in certain circumstances, execution of an eventual judgment against property 'specifically in use or intended for use by the State for other than government non-commercial purposes'.

Achieving a reasonable compromise on immunity from measures of constraint was probably the most important step on the long march towards the adoption of the Convention by the UN General Assembly in December 2004. Adoption was without a vote—that is to say, without a single State objecting. The solution found in Article 19 (including the 'understanding' in the annex) has been described as 'a major achievement of the Convention'.[25] It was also a major achievement by two members of the ILC who were also active in the Sixth Committee, namely Ambassador Carlos Calero-Rodrigues of Brazil and Professor Gerhard Hafner of Austria. It was largely due to their knowledge, skill, and persistence that the complex negotiations were eventually brought to a successful conclusion.[26]

How far do the provisions of Part IV of the Convention reflect customary international law? This is part of the wider question concerning the Convention as a whole, and retains all its importance, since there are very few relevant treaties, or treaty provisions, in force. The Convention itself is not (yet) in force, and it may well be a very long time, if ever, before it is binding, as a treaty, for most States. Nevertheless, the signs are there that many of its provisions are already viewed by international and domestic courts, by governments, and by writers as reflecting customary international law.[27] This is likely to become even more the case with the passage of time. But it remains important to assess the Convention's provisions individually to see how far this is justified.[28] The provisions on measures of constraint, when negotiated, probably involved a degree of progressive development as well as codification. But the reception of these provisions by States over time, including their adoption by the General Assembly without a vote, means that courts and tribunals called on to apply customary international law in this field may well regard the content of this Part as largely reflecting custom. At the very least they will treat its provisions as an important element in the identification of the rules of customary international law in this field.

[25] Hafner (n. 3), para. 40.

[26] For tributes to Carlos Calero-Rodrigues, including his work on the topic of jurisdictional immunities of States and their property, see summary record 3129th ILC meeting, UN doc. A/CN.4/SR.3129.

[27] See eg P.-T. Stoll, 'State Immunity', in R. Wolfrum (ed.), *Max Planck Encyclopedia of Public International Law* (2012), vol. IX, 498, para. 4, stating that the Convention 'is already widely acknowledged as an accurate, extensive, learned, and systematic reflection of this field of the law, and is widely used as a basis for legal practice and scholarly reflection'. See also para. 83.

[28] One might, for example, question the European Court of Human Rights' statement in *Cudak v Lithuania*, application no. 15869/02, Judgment (Merits and Just Satisfaction), ECtHR (GC), 23 March 2010, para. 67, that 'it is possible to affirm that Article 11 of the International Law Commission's 1991 Draft Articles, on which the 2004 Convention was based, applies to the respondent State under customary international law'. Art. 11, on contracts of employment, is a very specific provision, and sets out in a detailed manner a particular negotiated compromise. This is perhaps why the Court focused on the 1991 draft, which was quite unusual when the General Assembly had already adopted a Convention with a quite different provision. See the commentary to Art. 11 UNCSI for details.

4. Conclusion

In *Jurisdictional Immunities of the State*, the Court noted that 'both Parties agree that immunity is governed by international law and is not a mere matter of comity', and emphasized 'that the rule of State immunity occupies an important place in international law and international relations'.[29] The Preamble to the United Nations Convention on Jurisdictional Immunities of States and Their Property expresses the belief that

> an international convention on the jurisdictional immunities of States and their property would enhance the rule of law and legal certainty, particularly in dealings of States with natural or juridical persons, and would contribute to the codification and development of international law and the harmonization of practice in this area.

One matter of particular importance for the future acceptance of common rules of law of State immunity is a proper appreciation of the distinction between the rules relating to immunity from jurisdiction and those relating to immunity from measures of constraint, as set out in the Convention and as they are to be found in customary international law.

[29] *Jurisdictional Immunities of the State* (n. 1), paras 53 and 57.

The 'General Understandings'

Roger O'Keefe

1. Introduction

The '[u]nderstandings with respect to certain provisions of the Convention' contained in the annex, which forms an integral part of the Convention,[1] are not the only 'understandings' subject to which the Convention must be read. There exists in addition what is referred to as a 'general understanding', applicable not just in respect of a specific provision or provisions but in respect of the Convention as a whole, that the Convention does not apply to criminal proceedings. There is alleged also to be a 'general understanding' that the Convention does not apply to military activities. The first of these across-the-board understandings is verifiable, and, as it is, merely articulates what even a superficial analysis of the text itself reveals to be the Convention's inapplicability in the criminal context. The second is more contentious, and it remains to be seen whether the States parties truly understand the Convention not to apply to military activities.

2. Outline and Analysis

2.1 Criminal proceedings

No provision of the Convention expressly excludes criminal proceedings from the treaty's scope. At the same time, the ILC's commentary to its draft articles states that it 'should be understood that [the draft articles] do not cover criminal proceedings'.[2] Moreover, and of more significance, the Chairman of the Ad Hoc Committee, when introducing the draft Convention to the Sixth Committee on 25 October 2004, emphasized the Ad Hoc Committee's recommendation that the General Assembly 'include in its resolution adopting the draft Convention the general understanding that it did not cover criminal proceedings'.[3] Most importantly, the General Assembly took up this recommendation. In operative paragraph 2 of resolution 59/38,[4] the resolution by which the Convention was adopted, the General Assembly '[a]grees with the general understanding reached in the Ad Hoc Committee that the United Nations Convention on Jurisdictional Immunities of States and Their Property does not cover criminal proceedings'.

Writing in his personal capacity with Ulrike Köhler, Gerhard Hafner, who served as Chairman of the Ad Hoc Committee, has argued that resolution 59/38 as a whole

[1] See Art. 25 UNCSI. [2] ILC commentary, draft art. 2, para. 2.

[3] Statement Chairman Ad Hoc Committee, 6, para. 32. This 'general understanding' had originally been included by the Ad Hoc Committee in the understandings annexed to the draft articles. See 2003 report Ad Hoc Committee, annex II. It was removed seemingly on account of its incongruity, in that it represented a 'general' understanding, in the sense of being applicable to the draft articles in their entirety, whereas the other understandings were, as the annex's title put it at the time, '[u]nderstandings with respect to certain provisions of the draft articles' or, as the title to the annex to the eventual Convention now calls them, '[u]nderstandings with respect to certain provisions of the Convention'.

[4] GA res. 59/38, 2 December 2004.

'must... be considered as part of the context for the purposes of interpretation according to Article 31(2)(*b*) VCLT as it could be ranked among the instruments "made by one of the parties in connection with the conclusion of the treaty and accepted by the other parties as an instrument related to the treaty"'.[5] Equally, there is no obvious reason—except, conceivably, the eventual participation in the Convention of States which did not exist on 2 December 2004 and were therefore not parties to the adoption of the resolution by the General Assembly—why the agreement with the 'general understanding' as to criminal proceedings manifest on the part of all the members of the General Assembly in operative paragraph 2 of resolution 59/38 could not constitute an 'agreement relating to the treaty which was made between all the parties in connection with the conclusion of the treaty' within the meaning of Article 31(2)(*a*) VCLT, which again would make it an element of the context in which the provisions of the Convention must be read. Alternatively, Hafner and Köhler suggest that 'the resolution must in any case be considered as belonging to the *travaux préparatoires* according to Article 32 VCLT'.[6] Either way, albeit in different ways, the General Assembly's endorsement of the 'general understanding' that the Convention does not apply to criminal proceedings can permissibly be brought to bear on the term 'proceedings' as found in the relevant provisions of the Convention.

But recourse to paragraph 2 of General Assembly resolution 59/38 is not actually necessary in order to establish conclusively that the Convention does not apply to criminal proceedings. Even the most perfunctory perusal of the text makes this abundantly clear. First and foremost, the term 'State' is defined in such a way in Article 2(1)(*b*) as to include, in addition to natural persons,[7] a range of legal (or 'juridical' or 'moral') persons—'the State and its various organs of government',[8] 'constituent units of a federal State or political subdivisions of the State',[9] and 'agencies or instrumentalities of the State or other entities'[10]—and the overwhelming majority of national justice systems, to 'proceedings' in which the Convention is designed to apply, do not recognize the criminal responsibility of legal persons. Secondly, with the sole exception of the exception in respect of personal injury and damage to property recognized in Article 12, it would be nonsensical (or, in the language of Article 32(*b*) VCLT, 'manifestly absurd') to attempt to apply to criminal proceedings the exceptions to immunity from jurisdiction enumerated in Part III of the Convention. That is, the 'proceedings in which State immunity cannot be invoked' listed in Part III cannot, if Part III as a whole is to be operable, refer to both civil and criminal proceedings. Finally, were the Convention to apply additionally to criminal proceedings, it is curious that Parts IV or V should refer only to 'judgment', and not to 'conviction' or more generally to a 'verdict'; why Part IV should make no reference to the immunity of State property from seizure and forfeiture; and why there should be reference to neither a warrant of arrest or summons to appear in Article 22 ('Service of process') nor to trial *in absentia* in Article 23 ('Default judgment'). In short, virtually every provision of the Convention bespeaks the latter's application to civil proceedings alone.

[5] G. Hafner and U. Köhler, 'The United Nations Convention on Jurisdictional Immunities of States and their Property' (2004) 35 *NYIL* 3, 46.

[6] Hafner and Köhler (n. 5), 46.

[7] See Art. 2(1)(*b*)(iv) UNCSI, referring to 'representatives of the State acting in that capacity'.

[8] Art. 2(1)(*b*)(i) UNCSI.

[9] Art. 2(1)(*b*)(ii) UNCSI.

[10] Art. 2(1)(*b*)(iii) UNCSI.

That the Convention does not apply to criminal proceedings has been affirmed, in word and deed, in the context of the International Law Commission's current work on the immunity of State officials from foreign criminal jurisdiction. In its syllabus on the topic, prepared with a view to the Commission's inclusion of the latter in its programme of work, the ILC's Working Group on the Long-term Programme of Work drew attention to the General Assembly's stated agreement in paragraph 2 of resolution 59/38 with the 'general understanding' reached in the Ad Hoc Committee regarding criminal proceedings.[11] In its subsequent memorandum of 2008, prepared at the request of the ILC to assist the latter with its work on the topic, the UN Secretariat stated categorically that 'the Convention does not deal with immunity in respect of criminal jurisdiction', citing in this regard paragraph 2 of resolution 59/38[12] and reiterating the point later as follows:

> The term 'proceedings' is not defined by the Convention. However, it was clearly indicated that it should be understood that it does not cover criminal proceedings in any organ of a State empowered to exercise judicial functions regardless of the level or the nomenclature used. This has been confirmed in the relevant General Assembly resolution 59/38, to which the Convention is annexed . . . [13]

It has never been suggested since within the ILC, let alone by any State when the Commission's work on the topic has been considered in the Sixth Committee, that the Convention applies to criminal proceedings.

To date, one State, Switzerland, has entered a general interpretative declaration on becoming party to the Convention in which, '[i]n accordance with General Assembly resolution 59/38, adopted on 2 December 2004', it 'understands that the Convention does not cover criminal proceedings'.[14]

In sum, it cannot seriously be doubted that the Convention is inapplicable to criminal proceedings.

2.2 Activities of armed forces

Far more challenging than the straightforward question of criminal proceedings is whether the Convention applies to proceedings[15] against[16] or otherwise in respect

[11] See Report ILC, fifty-eighth session, 439–40, para. 11.

[12] UN Secretariat, *Immunity of State officials from foreign criminal jurisdiction. Memorandum by the Secretariat*, UN doc. A/CN.4/596 (31 March 2008), 30, para. 45.

[13] UN Secretariat (n. 12), 32, para. 47.

[14] C.N.223.2010.TREATIES-2 (Switzerland: Ratification), 20 April 2010.

[15] When it comes, on the other hand, to post-judgment measures of constraint, see Art. 21(1)(*b*) UNCSI (cross-referable to Art. 19(*c*) UNCSI), which provides in effect that, in the absence of express consent to the taking of such measures or of the allocation or earmarking of such property for the satisfaction of the claim, no such measures are to be taken against 'property of a military character or used or intended for use in the performance of military functions'. The same is more straightforwardly the case in relation to pre-judgment measures of constraint in accordance with Art. 18 UNCSI. As for the specific and longstanding immunity of warships from both proceedings and measures of constraint in connection with them, aspects of this are recognized in Arts 32 and 96 United Nations Convention on the Law of the Sea, Montego Bay, 10 December 1982, 1833 UNTS 3 (UNCLOS), as applicable among States parties to both UNCSI and UNCLOS by virtue of Art. 26 UNCSI; and Art. 16(2) and (4) UNCSI disapply in relation to warships the exceptions to a State's immunity from proceedings provided for in Art. 16(1) and (3) (proceedings relating to the operation of a State-owned or -operated ship).

[16] Note that members of the armed forces of a State acting in that capacity qualify as the State for the purposes of the immunity from proceedings, and the exceptions thereto, recognized in the Convention, in accordance with Art. 2(1)(*b*)(iv) UNCSI.

of[17] the activities of a foreign State's armed forces, particularly when such activities are carried out in the territory of the forum State. Neither Article 3 nor any other provision of the Convention expressly excludes such proceedings *ipso facto* from the Convention's scope. This is in contrast to Article 31 ECSI[18] and to several national State immunity provisions.[19]

Although Special Rapporteur Sucharitkul took the view at the outset that the ILC's draft articles did not apply to the '[i]mmunities extended to foreign visiting forces',[20] as 'generally' regulated by status of forces agreements,[21] he proposed no provision to this effect. Not dissimilarly, when the UK suggested 'the addition [to draft article 3] of a new paragraph which would provide that the [draft] articles are without prejudice to the question of the privileges and immunities enjoyed by the armed forces of one State while present in another State with the latter's consent',[22] Special Rapporteur Ogiso, opposing the suggestion but seemingly not its spirit, replied that

> the privileges and immunities of the armed forces of a State while present in another State are determined by agreement between the States concerned rather than by customary international law, and it may not be relevant to refer to such privileges and immunities in [draft article 3].[23]

For its part, however, the ILC commentary, while saying nothing to the effect in relation to draft article 3, asserted—with no recorded basis in the Commission's discussions for doing so[24]—that draft article 12 (which became Article 12 of the Convention) did not

[17] It may be that a claimant is permitted by the law of the forum State to sue the foreign State as such, or its government or ministry of defence, in respect of the activities of that foreign State's armed forces.

[18] Art. 31 ECSI provides: 'Nothing in this Convention shall affect any immunities or privileges enjoyed by a Contracting State in respect of anything done or omitted to be done by, or in relation to, its armed forces when on the territory of another Contracting State.' The rationale for Art. 31 provided in Expl. Rep. ECSI, para. 116, is that '[t]hese problems are generally dealt with by special agreements'. As acknowledged, however, in the accompanying cross-reference to Art. 33 ECSI ('Nothing in the present Convention shall affect existing or future international agreements in special fields which relate to matters dealt with in the present Convention'), such agreements are the subject of their own savings clause in the ECSI.

[19] S. 16(2) of the SIA (UK), enacted to give effect to Art. 31 ECSI, provides that Part I of the Act, which deals with immunity from proceedings, does not apply to 'proceedings relating to anything done by or in relation to the armed forces of a State while present in the United Kingdom'. See also, in similar terms, s. 6 FStIA (Aus); s. 17(2)(*a*) SIO (Pak); s. 19(2)(*a*) SIA (Sing). See too, more precisely, s. 22 FSIL (Isr), which reads: 'Notwithstanding the provisions of this statute, legal actions based on any act or omission committed by foreign military forces whose rights and status in Israel were determined by agreement between the State of Israel and the state to which the foreign military forces belong shall be governed by that agreement.'

[20] Second report Sucharitkul, 212, para. 52.

[21] Second report Sucharitkul, 212, para. 52, fn. 55.

[22] Preliminary report Ogiso, 103, para. 47. See also Report ILC, forty-first session, 103, para. 446. Earlier, during the discussion of what became draft article 12 and eventually Art. 12 of the Convention, Sir Ian Sinclair had stated: 'It was customary for status-of-forces agreements to regulate comprehensively the making of claims by local residents against the authorities of foreign armed forces present, by agreement, in the territory of the host State, and he presumed that the Special Rapporteur intended to formulate a corresponding exclusion in the draft articles.' See summary record 1767th ILC meeting, *YILC 1983*, vol. I, 74, 78, para. 30.

[23] Preliminary report Ogiso, 103, para. 49. See also Report ILC, forty-first session, 103, para. 446.

[24] The apparent source of the assertion is Fifth report Sucharitkul, 40, para. 74, where, in discussing 'the basis for . . . non-immunity' in accordance with what became the exception to immunity embodied in draft art. 12 (and, eventually, Art. 12 of the Convention), the Special Rapporteur elaborates: 'While, in general, it is possible to conceive of day-to-day activities of States which could be covered by an insurance policy in case of fire or accident or other natural disaster or calamity attributable to an agency or instrumentality of a State, the possibility that State immunity is still needed should not be precluded, particularly in cases where the State has performed an act exclusively in the domain of the laws of war, such as in military operations or military exercises or manoeuvres, or indeed in operations to quell riots, disturbances, civil war or civil strife, which are not generally covered by

apply 'to situations involving armed conflicts'.[25] Subsequently, the Working Group of the Sixth Committee, reporting in 1993 the seemingly shared view that the 'jurisdictional immunity of foreign armed forces should be dealt with bilaterally between the sending State and the host State', thought that 'the issue of jurisdictional immunity of armed forces of a State stationed in another State should be uniformly excluded from the scope of the . . . draft articles'.[26]

No such uniform exclusion found its way into the text of the eventual Convention, whether in Article 3, Article 12, or otherwise. When presenting the draft Convention to the Sixth Committee, however, the Chairman of the Ad Hoc Committee stated:

> One of the issues that had been raised was whether military activities were covered by the Convention. The general understanding had always prevailed that they were not. In any case, reference should be made to the Commission's commentary on article 12, stating that 'neither did the article affect the question of diplomatic immunities, as provided in article 3, nor did it apply to situations involving armed conflicts'. It had to be borne in mind that the preamble stated that the rules of customary international law continued to govern matters not regulated by the provisions of the Convention.[27]

The Chairman went on to explain that the exclusion of military activities was but one example of 'the general approach of the Convention' whereby 'it did not apply where there was a special immunity regime . . . (*lex specialis*)'.[28] But a proposal to refer to the Chairman's statement in the operative provisions of General Assembly resolution 59/38 met with firm opposition.[29] In the event, whereas in paragraph 2 of resolution 59/38 the General Assembly explicitly agrees with the general understanding reached in the Ad Hoc Committee that the Convention does not apply to criminal proceedings, any indication of the exclusion from the Convention's scope of 'military activities' (to quote the Chairman) must be implied from the recognition in the ninth recital of the resolution's preamble that the General Assembly, in adopting the Convention, '[took] into account the statement of the Chairman of the Ad Hoc Committee introducing the report of the Ad Hoc Committee'.

Hafner and Köhler argue persuasively that the mention in the preamble to General Assembly resolution 59/38 of the Chairman of the Ad Hoc Committee's statement to the Sixth Committee 'allows for . . . reference to [this] introductory statement in the interpretation of the convention'.[30] The real question, however, is not whether the Chairman's statement can be used for interpretative purposes[31] but whether what it

peacetime insurance.' The remark—which makes no mention of the exclusion of the activities alluded to from the scope of application of the draft articles, as distinct from the State's retention of immunity from proceedings in respect of them—was seemingly not the subject of discussion in the Commission.

[25] ILC commentary, draft art. 12, para. 10.

[26] 1993 report Sixth Committee Working Group, para. 91. See also, subsequently, GAOR, forty-eighth session, Sixth Committee, summary record 29th meeting (Monday, 15 November 1993), UN doc. A/C.6/48/SR.29 (22 December 1993), 16, paras 75–78 (Japan).

[27] Statement Chairman Ad Hoc Committee, 6, para. 36.

[28] Statement Chairman Ad Hoc Committee, 6, para. 37.

[29] See Hafner and Köhler (n. 5), 9. See also section 3.7 of Hafner, 'Historical Background to the Convention' in this volume.

[30] Hafner and Köhler (n. 5), 10.

[31] It would nonetheless remain to be shown to which specific provision or provisions of the Convention any relevant act of interpretation might relate—something not obvious in the case of the purported exclusion of 'military activities' referred to by the Chairman in his statement.

says about 'military activities' is of any probative value. The same goes for the ILC commentary to draft article 12 quoted by the Chairman of the Ad Hoc Committee—which, as it is, refers to 'situations of armed conflicts', a phrase not coterminous with the 'military activities' referred to by the Chairman himself.[32]

The fact is that nothing on the record prior to the Chairman of the Ad Hoc Committee's statement points to a 'general understanding' that proceedings in respect of either 'military activities' (as per the Chairman) or 'situations of armed conflicts' (as per the ILC commentary to draft article 12) are *ipso facto* excluded from the Convention's scope. Rather, the words of both Special Rapporteurs and of the Working Group of the Sixth Committee, as recounted above, suggest a prevailing assumption that what is left undisturbed by the Convention are no more than such rights and obligations in relation to a State's jurisdictional immunities as may variously accrue to and bind a sending-defendant State and a receiving-forum State under any status of forces agreement (SOFA) or status of mission agreement (SOMA) in force between them. Indeed, SOFAs and SOMAs constitute the only 'special immunity regime... (*lex specialis*)'[33] (as per the Chairman of the Ad Hoc Committee)—or, more accurately, the only special immunity regimes, each agreement needing to be approached on its own terms—in relation to 'military activities'. No special immunity regime, whether of a customary or conventional character, pertains to military activities as such. Even less does a special immunity regime pertain to 'situations of armed conflicts'.

The fact that what was understood to be left undisturbed by the Convention was rights and obligations under SOFAs and SOMAs, along with the fact that it was never thought necessary to follow the advice of the Sixth Committee's Working Group by inserting into the Convention what became a specific safeguard clause in relation to the 'jurisdictional immunity of armed forces of a State stationed in another State',[34] suggest in turn that the Convention's generally assumed lack of effect on what are referred to over-inclusively as 'military activities' was viewed as no more than a function of Article 26,[35] in relation to existing SOFAs or SOMAs, and, alternatively or additionally, of the opening words of Article 12,[36] as specifically regards proceedings for pecuniary compensation for death or personal injury or for damage to or loss of tangible property allegedly caused by visiting forces in the forum State's territory. Had the supposed 'general understanding' as to the exclusion of 'military activities' from the Convention's scope been something other than this, it is unfathomable why explicit provision for it was not inserted into the text.

[32] See also A. Dickinson, 'Status of Forces under the UN Convention on State Immunity' (2006) 55 *ICLQ* 427, 431.

[33] Statement Chairman Ad Hoc Committee, 6, para. 37.

[34] 1993 report Sixth Committee Working Group, 17, para. 91.

[35] Art. 26 ('Other international agreements') UNCSI provides: 'Nothing in the present Convention shall affect the rights and obligations of States Parties under existing international agreements which relate to matters dealt with in the present Convention as between the parties to those agreements.' See commentary to Art. 26. See also summary record 1868th ILC meeting, *YILC 1984*, vol. I, 320, 324, para. 29. See too *Moore v United Kingdom*, 384 F.3d 1079 (US (9th Cir.) 2004) for the application of a similar provision in the FSIA to the Agreement between the Parties to the North Atlantic Treaty regarding the Status of their Forces, London, 19 June 1951, 199 UNTS 67.

[36] The opening words of Art. 12 ('Personal injuries and damage to property') UNCSI read: 'Unless otherwise agreed between the States concerned...'. ILC commentary, draft art. 12, para. 8, fn. 152 refers explicitly to SOFAs in this regard. See also summary record 1768th ILC meeting, *YILC 1983*, vol. I, 81, 83, para. 11 (Motoo Ogiso); summary record 2120th ILC meeting, *YILC 1989*, vol. I, 176, 178, para. 12 (Emmanuel Roucounas).

In short, 'in the absence of an express exclusion or understanding such as that in relation to criminal proceedings', the more persuasive conclusion to be drawn is that 'the Convention regulates the immunity of a State in all civil proceedings, including those relating to military activities',[37] even if it may be trumped by a SOFA or SOMA by virtue of Article 26. It is perhaps telling in this regard that the ILC Secretariat's 2008 memorandum to the ILC on the immunity of State officials, while forthright in endorsing the Chairman of the Ad Hoc Committee's statement insofar as it relates to criminal proceedings and immunities *ratione personae*,[38] concludes in contrast that 'there are divergent views as to the extent to which jurisdictional immunities of armed forces of a State are covered by the Convention'.[39]

None of this should be taken to mean that a State, including its armed forces, would not, in accordance with the Convention, enjoy immunity from foreign proceedings in respect of any activities of those armed forces not covered by a SOFA or SOMA in force between that State and the forum State. What it means is simply that the availability of any such immunity would be a consequence of the application of the Convention in the usual way—that is, it would proceed from the general immunity from foreign proceedings recognized in Article 5 and from the absence of any relevant exception to it. Nor does the fact that a SOFA or SOMA may govern proceedings against the sending State in the courts of the receiving State in relation to the activities of the former's armed forces in the latter's territory mean that a State will necessarily enjoy immunity from such proceedings. It will depend on the terms of the applicable SOFA or SOMA.

All this said, in the declarations attached to their respective instruments of ratification of the Convention, both Norway and Sweden have expressed their understanding that the Convention 'does not apply to military activities, including the activities of armed forces during an armed conflict, as those terms are understood in international humanitarian law, and activities undertaken by military forces of a State in exercise of their official duties'.[40] Subsequently, moreover, in *Jurisdictional Immunities of the State*, the ICJ—while stopping short of conclusively endorsing the proposition that the Convention as such does not apply to military activities[41]—placed decisive evidentiary weight, when assessing the alleged customary status of the exception to immunity from proceedings embodied in Article 12, not only on the declarations by Norway and Sweden but also on the fact that '[n]o State questioned the interpretation' advanced by the Chairman

[37] Dickinson (n. 32), 430. See, similarly, C.K. Hall, 'UN Convention on State Immunity: The Need for a Human Rights Protocol' (2006) 55 *ICLQ* 411, 422. But see, *contra*, D.P. Stewart, 'The UN Convention on Jurisdictional Immunities of States and their Property' (2005) 99 *AJIL* 194, 197; H. Fox, *The Law of State Immunity* (2nd edn) (Oxford: Oxford University Press, 2008), 384 and H. Fox, 'In Defence of State Immunity: Why the UN Convention on State Immunity Is Important' (2006) 55 *ICLQ* 399, 402.

[38] UN Secretariat (n. 12), 30, para. 45.

[39] UN Secretariat (n. 12), 30–1, para. 45.

[40] See UNCSI depositary notifications C.N.280.2006.TREATIES–2 (Norway: Ratification), 6 April 2006; C.N.912.2009.TREATIES–1 (Sweden: Ratification), 24 December 2009.

[41] The Court relied on the statements of the Chairman of the Ad Hoc Committee, Sweden and Norway to reach the distinct conclusion that 'the inclusion in the Convention of Article 12 cannot be taken as affording any support to the contention that customary international law denies State immunity in tort proceedings relating to acts occasioning death, personal injury or damage to property committed in the territory of the forum State by the armed forces and associated organs of another State in the context of an armed conflict'. See *Jurisdictional Immunities of the State (Germany v Italy: Greece intervening), Judgment*, International Court of Justice, 3 February 2012, para. 69.

of the Ad Hoc Committee.[42] Although it is perfectly possible and perhaps more likely that the States present in the Sixth Committee and later in the General Assembly in plenary understood the Chairman's loose mention of 'military activities' to refer more precisely to what in fact seems to have been the subject of the general understanding in question, namely (in the words of the Sixth Committee's Working Group) 'the issue of jurisdictional immunity of armed forces of a State stationed in another State',[43] it remains to be seen if more States, in the light of what the Court has said, follow the lead of Norway and Sweden. Should declarations to the same effect as theirs become sufficiently widespread and representative, they may eventually establish beyond doubt a general understanding on the part of the States parties as to the Convention's non-application to military activities per se. That said, it may pay to recall that Norway and Sweden are only two of what are presently thirteen States parties to the Convention. It is also worth mentioning, as the ICJ did not, that the sole State party to have enacted legislation so far to implement the Convention, namely Japan, has excluded neither military activities nor situations involving armed conflicts from the scope of application of either its statute as a whole or of the 'territorial tort' exception embodied in it.[44]

An understanding to the effect that the Convention does not apply to military activities per se would differ qualitatively from the safeguarding of a special regime of immunity as effected by Article 3's various 'without prejudice' clauses[45] and by Article 31 ECSI.[46] It would constitute not a means of resolving a conflict of norms but a 'carve-out' of a given subject-matter from the ambit of the Convention regardless of the former's normative content.

The formal legal basis on which any such understanding could be brought to bear on the Convention is far from clear. It is not self-evident, *pace* the ICJ, that the issue would be one of interpretation, as would bring into play Article 31(3)(*b*) VCLT. One can interpret, strictly speaking, only what is in the text. Nor could one deploy the logic relied on to safeguard from the effect of the Convention the immunities *ratione personae* not mentioned in Article 3, for the reason that one is dealing here not with what would otherwise be the tacit abrogation *inter partes*, without convincing indication of the intention to do so, of 'an important principle of customary international law'.[47] All this said, it would seem a doctrinaire denial of reality to suppose that a compellingly evidenced extraneous understanding on the part of a convincing majority of the States parties could not somehow be permissibly brought to bear on the Convention.[48]

It is also uncertain what the precise scope of any exclusion in relation to 'military activities'—insofar as this exclusion is not limited to activities in respect of which claims for compensation are regulated by a SOFA or SOMA—might be, even if such activities were stated to include 'the activities of armed forces during an armed conflict, as those terms are understood in international humanitarian law, and activities undertaken by

[42] *Jurisdictional Immunities of the State* (n. 41), para. 69.

[43] 1993 report Sixth Committee Working Group, 17, para. 91.

[44] See ACJJFS (Jpn), especially Art. 10.

[45] The gist of Art. 3 is encapsulated in its title, *viz* 'Privileges and immunities not affected by the present Convention'.

[46] Recall n. 18.

[47] See the commentary to Art. 3 UNCSI, quoting *Elettronica Sicula S.p.A. (ELSI) (United States of America v Italy), Judgment*, ICJ Rep 1989, 15, 42, para. 50.

[48] See W. Shakespeare, *Hamlet*, Act I, scene 5, lines 66–67.

military forces of a State in exercise of their official duties'.[49] For example, would such 'activities' include the procurement by a quartermaster-general, in time of armed conflict or otherwise, of food, clothing, or sanitary or building supplies—the sort of transaction that would otherwise fall within the exception to a State's immunity from proceedings provided for in Article 10 of the Convention? Or would the exclusion be restricted to activities causing death or injury to the person or damage to or loss of tangible property?

It is worth emphasizing that the consequence of the Convention's non-application to military activities would not necessarily be the immunity of the State (including members of its armed forces acting in that capacity) from all foreign proceedings in relation to such activities. All it would mean is that the question of the State's immunity would fall to be answered by reference to such other rules of international law as may apply.

3. Conclusion

Whether it is true that '[t]he severest criticism of the Convention lies in the failure to state clearly in its provisions the matters covered and those which are excluded'[50] is a matter of opinion. The criticism certainly has a wealth of worthy competitors. It is nonetheless doubtless true that the necessity of recourse to extraneous and not always verifiable 'general understandings' for a full picture of its scope of application is one of the 'peculiarities'[51] of the Convention, and is in principle an unsatisfactory way of going about things, even if in the Convention's case it may have been an imaginative expedient.

[49] See n. 40.

[50] H. Fox, 'The Merits and Defects of the 2004 UN Convention on State Immunity: Gerhard Hafner's Contribution to its Adoption by the United Nations', in I. Buffard et al. (eds), *International Law between Universalism and Fragmentation: Festschrift in Honour of Gerhard Hafner* (Leiden: Martinus Nijhoff, 2008), 413, 419.

[51] See T. Treves, 'Some Peculiarities of the UN Convention on Jurisdictional Immunities of States and Their Property: a Footnote on the Codification Technique', in I. Buffard et al. (eds) (n. 50), 503.

Preamble

Christian J. Tams

The States Parties to the present Convention,

Considering that the jurisdictional immunities of States and their property are generally accepted as a principle of customary international law,

Having in mind the principles of international law embodied in the Charter of the United Nations,

Believing that an international convention on the jurisdictional immunities of States and their property would enhance the rule of law and legal certainty, particularly in dealings of States with natural or juridical persons, and would contribute to the codification and development of international law and the harmonization of practice in this area,

Taking into account developments in State practice with regard to the jurisdictional immunities of States and their property,

Affirming that the rules of customary international law continue to govern matters not regulated by the provisions of the present Convention,

Have agreed as follows:

1. Introduction

Like nearly all multilateral agreements, the Convention begins with a preamble introducing the main body of the treaty. Preambles typically set out the motives for the conclusion of the treaty; they often help identify its object and purpose and they try to clarify the relationship between the treaty and other rules of international law.[1] The Convention's Preamble does all that. Like most other preambles, it is 'binding in character . . . , [but] does not contain . . . directly operative provisions'.[2] Its chief legal relevance is that, as part of the treaty context, and by identifying its object and purpose, the Preamble can aid the interpretation of the treaty.[3]

The Convention's Preamble follows the standard 'preambular style' for treaties elaborated within the United Nations ('*The States Parties to the present Convention, . . .*

[1] For details see eg M.M. Mbengue, 'Preamble', in R. Wolfrum (ed.), *Max Planck Encyclopedia of Public International Law* (Oxford: Oxford University Press, 2012), vol. VIII, 397; A. Aust, *Modern Treaty Law and Practice* (2nd edn) (Cambridge: Cambridge University Press, 2007), 424–7.

[2] G.G. Fitzmaurice, 'The Law and Procedure of the International Court of Justice 1951–54' (1957) 33 *BYIL* 203, 229.

[3] See Art. 31 VCLT: '1. A treaty shall be interpreted in good faith in accordance with the ordinary meaning to be given to the terms of the treaty in their context and *in the light of its object and purpose.*
2. The context for the purpose of the interpretation of a treaty shall comprise, in addition to the text, *including its preamble* and annexes . . . ' (emphases added).

Have agreed as follows . . .').[4] With five preambular recitals, and at 138 words, it is fairly concise by UN standards.[5]

2. Drafting History

In line with general practice, the Convention's drafters deferred discussion of a preambular text until a decision on the final outcome of the text was taken. In its 2003 Report, the Ad Hoc Committee noted that '[i]f and when the General Assembly decided to adopt the draft articles as a convention, the draft articles would need a preamble . . . '.[6] By 2004, the if and when having been decided, the Committee discussed, and agreed on, a text.[7] It did so on the basis of a draft suggested by its Chairman,[8] which in most respects was identical to the eventual wording, but mentioned specific principles of international law in the second recital, while not referring to 'codification and development' in the third. The Chairman's draft also contained a sixth recital, placed in square brackets, which '*[r]ecogniz[ed]* the general understanding that the provisions of the present Convention do not cover criminal proceedings', which was not adopted but would appear in paragraph 2 of General Assembly resolution 59/38.[9] The Chairman's draft was closely modelled on a draft text suggested by the EU Presidency in early 2004.[10] The Ad Hoc Committee's Report provides no information on how the Chairman's draft was received or why it was modified.

3. Key Points

3.1 Recognition and evolution of the principle of State immunity

The first, third, and fourth recitals describe the background against which the Convention was elaborated, and do so in a deliberately ambiguous way. On the one hand, jurisdictional immunities of States and their property are considered to be 'generally accepted as a principle of customary international law'; on the other, the Convention is said to take account of 'developments in State practice'. The background thus evoked is one of tradition and contemporaneity, or continuity and change: firmly based on a legal principle that precedes its elaboration, the Convention translates this principle[11] into

[4] See Aust (n. 1), 424 and 427.

[5] By contrast the Preamble to the United Nations Convention on the Law of the Sea, Montego Bay, 10 December 1982, 1833 UNTS 3, comprises 410 words; that to the VCLT 266; and that to the Convention on the Prohibition of the Use, Stockpiling, Production and Transfer of Anti-Personnel Mines and on their Destruction, Oslo, 18 September 1997, 2056 UNTS 211 (Ottawa Convention), 502. As for treaties elaborated outside the UN framework, the Preamble to the Convention on Access to Information, Public Participation in Decision-Making and Access to Justice in Environmental Matters, Aarhus, 25 June 1998, 2161 UNTS 447 (Aarhus Convention), at 722 words, is worth mentioning.

[6] 2003 report Ad Hoc Committee, para. 12.

[7] See 2004 report Ad Hoc Committee, paras 9–10.

[8] See Suggestions of the Chairman, 3, preamble.

[9] See O'Keefe, 'The "General Understandings"' in this volume.

[10] EU Presidency Statement—Convention on Jurisdictional Immunities of States and their Property, doc. PRES04-018EN, 1 March 2004, http://www.eu-un.europa.eu/articles/en/article_3276_en.htm. Note that this text, in the second recital, had referred to jurisdictional immunities of States and their property as 'rules'—as opposed to 'principles'—of customary international law.

[11] Recall the EU proposal (n. 10) which had spoken of '*rules* of immunity' (emphasis added), section 2.

treaty provisions in the light of developments in State practice. The third recital's reference to 'codification' and 'development' of international law (to which the Convention is believed to contribute) takes up the same idea. As is usual, and no doubt wisely, it does not indicate which aspects of the Convention codify rules of international law (ie aim at 'the more precise formulation and systematization in fields where there already has been extensive State practice, precedent and doctrine'[12]) and which amount to the development of international law in areas in which 'the law has not yet been sufficiently developed in the practice of States'.[13]

To emphasize continuity is a common device in preambles that intends to allay concerns among potential States parties. It indicates that the Convention does not intend to break with tradition, or re-write the law of State immunity. Conversely, the reference to 'developments' suggests that while generally (and traditionally) accepted, the principle of State immunity is not static, but has undergone changes of which the Convention takes account. While the Preamble does not spell out the character of these 'developments' expressly, it seems most likely that the reference was meant to highlight the gradual recognition of restrictions to immunity. As the process has been described elsewhere in considerable detail,[14] suffice it to mention the growing recognition of immunity exceptions (at least with respect to immunity from jurisdiction) in international instruments,[15] domestic legislation,[16] and domestic case-law.[17] Towards the end of the Convention's drafting, this trend—which the Preamble, again seeking to accommodate potential concerns, expressly characterizes as a trend *in practice*, as opposed to lofty ideas, possibly even voiced by academics—had become so consolidated that, notwithstanding discussions about points of detail, it was clear that the Convention would qualify the principle of State immunity by adding a number of important exceptions.

In mentioning continuity/tradition alongside change/contemporaneity, the Preamble captures the spirit of the Convention as an instrument of codification and development. At the same time, the balanced nature of the characterization reduces the Preamble's potential impact on the interpretation of specific treaty provisions. Whereas, read on its own, the first recital might support a construction in the light of traditional customary

[12] To take up the 'definition' of codification used in Art. 15 ILC Statute.

[13] *Cf* Art. 15 ILC Statute (referring to 'progressive development').

[14] See eg H. Fox, *The Law of State Immunity* (2nd edn) (Oxford: Oxford University Press, 2008), 204–36; G.M. Badr, *State Immunity: An Analytical and Prognostic View* (The Hague: Martinus Nijhoff, 1984), 21–34 and 41–62; and the collection of decisions in *Materials on Jurisdictional Immunities of States and Their Property* (New York: United Nations, 1982), UN Legislative Series, vol. 20, Sales No. E/F.81.V.10. For a succinct account see also G. Hafner, 'Historical Background to the Convention' in this volume.

[15] Notably the ECSI; the Inter-American draft Convention on Jurisdictional Immunities of States (1983) 22 ILM 292; the Basel Resolution adopted by the Institut de Droit international on 'Contemporary Problems Concerning the Immunity of States in Relation to Questions of Jurisdiction and Enforcement', in 64 *Annuaire de l'Institut de Droit international* (1992), vol. II, 388; and the ILA Draft Articles and ILA Revised Draft Articles.

[16] Notwithstanding differences in detail, influential pieces of domestic legislation all adopted versions of the restrictive approach: see FSIA (USA), SIA (UK); SIA (Can), SIA (Sing), SIO (Pak), FSIL (Isr), FStIA (SA), FStIA (Aus), IPA (Mal), IFSJAC (Arg).

[17] Jurisprudence is abundant and is referred to in the analysis of specific exceptions recognized in Part III of the Convention. When focusing on countries that have not adopted domestic legislation, the following decisions seem to have proved particularly influential: *Dralle v Republic of Czechoslovakia*, 17 ILR 155 (Aut (SC) 1950); *Administration des Chemins de Fer du Gouvernement Iranien v Société Levant Express Transport*, 52 ILR 315 (Fra (CoC) 1969); *Claim against the Empire of Iran Case*, 45 ILR 57 (FRG (FCC) 1963).

international law, the reference to 'developments' in the fourth recital emphasizes recent trends, even where these modify the content of the principle. As a result, it seems difficult to rely on the Preamble to support a particularly static or particularly dynamic construction of the Convention's provision.

3.2 Enhancing legal certainty and the rule of law

The third and longest recital describes the main motive that led to the elaboration of the Convention. Building on the generally accepted principle of State immunity and taking into account developments in State practice, the Convention is believed to 'enhance the rule of law and legal certainty, particularly in dealings of States with natural or juridical persons' and to 'contribute to . . . the harmonization of practice'.[18] The third recital emphasizes what is a key aim of multilateral treaty-making generally. In the Convention's context, the emphasis on (domestic) practice is of particular relevance as the international rules on jurisdictional immunities have traditionally been shaped by domestic laws, executive decisions, and court decisions. While the language employed is modest ('[b]elieving', 'enhance', 'contribute'), underlining that 'legal certainty' and 'the rule of law' can only be realized progressively and hardly ever completely, the cautious optimism informing the third recital would seem justified. As the subsequent analysis of specific provisions makes clear, in many respects the Convention clarifies the state of international law and (to adapt a phrase used in relation to another long-term codification project) seems to 'encod[e] the way in which we think about [State immunity]'[19] even at a time its fate as a treaty is uncertain.

Whether the third recital will affect the interpretation of specific provisions is difficult to predict. At some level, the express mentioning of 'legal certainty', 'rule of law', and 'the harmonization of practice' could support a strict construction of the Convention, eg supporting the uniform interpretation of terms that have been interpreted differently in domestic legal systems. Yet the cautious language used, and qualifications added, means that this will only be a very general interpretative guideline.

3.3 Principles of international law embodied in the UN Charter

According to the second recital, the States parties 'hav[e] in mind the principles of international law embodied in the Charter of the United Nations'. The reference, common in UN treaty practice, is to the main principles of international law, spelled out in Articles 1 and 2 of the UN Charter and elaborated in subsequent UN practice,[20]

[18] The Preamble to the ECSI puts this much more clearly: 'Desiring to establish in their mutual relations common rules relating to the scope of the immunity of one State from the jurisdiction of the courts of another State.'

[19] *Cf* James Crawford's remarks on the impact of the ILC's 2001 Articles on Responsibility of States for Internationally Wrongful Acts: J. Crawford, 'The International Court of Justice and the Law of State Responsibility', in J. Sloan and C.J. Tams (eds), *The Development of International Law by the International Court of Justice* (Oxford: Oxford University Press, forthcoming 2013), 14 (manuscript).

[20] See notably GA res. 2625 (XXV) (the 'Declaration on Principles of International Law Concerning Friendly Relations and Cooperation Among States in Accordance with the Charter of the United Nations', or 'Friendly Relations Declaration'); GA res. 55/2 (2000) (the 'United Nations Millennium Declaration') and GA res. 60/1 (the 'World Summit Outcome Document').

such as the prohibition against the use of force and the principles of sovereign equality and non-intervention, good faith, peaceful dispute resolution, and individual rights and self-determination.

The recital intends to ensure that the Convention is construed in line with the (Charter) principles of international law, which is unsurprising given that it was elaborated within the UN framework. It affirms the general rule of treaty interpretation pursuant to which a provision is to be interpreted in the light of other 'relevant rules of international law applicable between the parties';[21] and it singles out 'Charter principles' as particularly relevant rules. However, the impact of this statement is affected by the generality of the reference: not one principle specifically, but 'Charter principles' *en bloc* are referred to. Given their breadth, and their interconnectedness, it is thus rather difficult to derive specific guidance from them, which could influence the interpretation of specific provisions of the Convention in a decisive way.

3.4 The role of customary international law

Pursuant to fifth recital, 'matters not regulated by the provisions of the . . . Convention' remain governed by customary international law. This is at once an obvious statement and a useful clarification. It is obvious because it would be difficult for a treaty to disapply customary law on matters which it itself does not address; hence the Preamble merely 'affirms' (in a declaratory manner) the continued application of customary rules. What is more, it does not specify (nor could it be expected to) what matters *are* regulated by the Convention; this is to be determined by interpreting the treaty and its provisions. Yet to affirm that where the treaty does not apply customary law continues to apply is important as it implies that the Convention's substantive scope is limited.[22] The Convention regulates aspects of the law of jurisdictional immunities, but is by no means exhaustive. This important point is taken up in subsequent provisions of the Convention, notably in the 'without prejudice' clause of Article 3 and in Article 1's description of the scope of the Convention. In conjunction with these provisions, the fifth recital can be read as a safeguard against expansive treaty interpretation. While it does not predetermine the results of the interpretative process, it emphasizes the finite scope of the Convention.

The fifth paragraph affirms the continued application of customary international law, ie of one particular source of general international law. This is in line with the first recital, pursuant to which immunity, unless regulated by treaty, is recognized as a principle of customary international law. However, it should not be read to exclude other sources of general international law. While the matter is not specifically affirmed, questions not regulated by the Convention could also be governed by, for example, general principles of law in the sense of Article 38(1)(*c*) ICJ Statute; just as a State could accept specific obligations in relation to immunity unilaterally.

[21] *Cf* Art. 31(3)(*c*) VCLT (now often referred to as 'systemic integration').

[22] The same point can be made with respect to the other 'dimensions' of the Convention's scope, namely its temporal scope (addressed in Art. 4 UNCSI) and its territorial scope (governed by Art. 29 VCLT and the general rules of treaty law).

4. Evaluation

While its balanced nature may reduce its impact on treaty interpretation, the Preamble seems to capture the essence of the Convention. Fittingly, given the Convention's subject-matter, it avoids the flowery rhetoric characterizing preambles of other treaties. Adapting words used to describe the Preamble to the Vienna Convention on the Law of Treaties, one might perhaps say that it is 'an eminently practical preamble for a Convention whose content [is] eminently practical'.[23]

[23] *Cf* UN doc. A/CONF.39, OR 1969 (Plenary), 171, para. 33: 'an eminently legal preamble for a Convention whose content was eminently legal'.

PART I: INTRODUCTION

Article 1

Roger O'Keefe and Christian J. Tams

Article 1

Scope of the present Convention

The present Convention applies to the immunity of a State and its property from the jurisdiction of the courts of another State.

1. Introduction

It is not unusual for the opening operative provision of a multilateral standard-setting treaty to comprise a general statement delineating the treaty's scope.[1] This is the form and ostensible function of Article 1 of the Convention. But like numerous provisions of its sort,[2] it says little more than what might otherwise be gleaned from the succeeding provisions of the treaty. Rather than meaningfully circumscribing the application of the Convention, it serves by way of mere overture to the action that follows. In doing so, however, it sounds some discordant notes.

2. Drafting History

In his second report, submitted to the ILC in 1980, Special Rapporteur Sucharitkul proposed a wordy introductory provision according to which the draft articles applied to 'questions relating to jurisdictional immunities accorded or extended by territorial States to foreign States and their property'.[3] The Commission expressed misgivings as to this formulation. Reference to a 'foreign' State was to be avoided in a treaty;[4] the mention of the 'territorial' State seemed misleadingly to presuppose a territorial basis of jurisdiction;[5] the alternative verbs 'extended' and 'accorded' appeared to imply a discretion on

[1] See eg Art. 1 VCLT; Art. 1 Vienna Convention on the Law of Treaties between States and International Organizations or between International Organizations, 25 ILM 543 (1986); Art. 1 Vienna Convention on Succession of States in respect of Treaties, 1946 UNTS 3; Art. 1 Vienna Convention on Succession of States in respect of State Property, Archives and Debts, 22 ILM 306 (1983); Art. 1 Convention on the Law of the Non-Navigational Uses of International Watercourses, 36 ILM 700 (1997). See also draft art. 1 Draft Articles on Responsibility of International Organizations, UN doc. A/64/10 (2009), 13.

[2] See eg Art. 1 VCLT; Art. 1 Vienna Convention on the Law of Treaties between States and International Organizations or between International Organizations; Art. 1 Vienna Convention on Succession of States in respect of Treaties; Art. 1 Vienna Convention on Succession of States in respect of State Property, Archives and Debts; draft art. 1 Draft Articles on Responsibility of International Organizations.

[3] Second report Sucharitkul, 203, para. 14.

[4] See eg summary record 1623rd ILC meeting, *YILC 1980*, vol. I, 199, 201, para. 17 (Sir Francis Vallat); summary record 1625th ILC meeting, *YILC 1980*, vol. I, 214, 215, para. 5 (Stephen Schwebel), 215, para. 7 (Laurel B. Francis).

[5] See summary record 1623rd ILC meeting (n. 4), 201, para. 17 (Sir Francis Vallat); summary record 1625th ILC meeting (n. 4) 215, para. 5 (Stephen Schwebel).

the part of the forum State whether or not to give effect to State immunity;[6] and the expression 'jurisdictional immunities', 'not the happiest combination of words', was considered too complex,[7] despite featuring in the title of the topic before the ILC. A leaner version of the provision[8] was provisionally adopted by the Drafting Committee in 1983 on the understanding that 'it was not possible at th[at] stage to cast the draft article in more specific terms';[9] and, after the deletion of the phrase 'questions relating to', draft article 1 was adopted in this form on first reading in 1986.[10] On second reading, 'one State' was changed to 'a State',[11] before the final adoption of draft article 1 in 1991. When the decision to adopt the text as a binding agreement had been taken, the phrase 'the present draft articles' was changed to 'the present Convention', and Article 1 was adopted along with the rest of the Convention in December 2004.

3. Key Points

3.1 'the immunity of a State and its property'

Article 1 announces the application of the Convention to 'the immunity of a State and its property'. The formulation, which echoes the Convention's title, is not without its difficulties. As a matter of international law, it is in the State alone, and not in its property, that any entitlement to immunity from the jurisdiction of the courts of another State vests. This international legal truism is reflected in the wording of Article 5 of the Convention—the cornerstone of Parts II and III of the Convention, dealing with immunity from proceedings—which provides that a State 'enjoys immunity, in respect of itself and its property, from the jurisdiction of the courts of another State'. It is further manifest in Part IV of the Convention, on immunity from measures of constraint, which contains no general provision akin to Article 5 whereby State property is said to 'enjoy' immunity and in which Articles 18 and 19, the key provisions, are formulated as bare prohibitions on measures by the forum State against another State's property. In short, under the Convention as under general international law, the property of a State is not the bearer of any entitlement to immunity, either from proceedings *in rem* or from measures of constraint in connection with proceedings against the State or that property. Only the State is, where relevant in respect of its property.

The gist, however, of the relevant words of Article 1 and, indeed, of the Convention's title is that, although any entitlement to immunity vests as a matter of international law—and, indeed, perhaps municipal law—in the State alone, any immunity actually accorded by the courts of another State serves to bar proceedings and measures of

[6] See eg summary record 1623rd ILC meeting (n. 4), 201, para. 17 (Sir Francis Vallat), 202, para. 3 (Juan José Calle y Calle); summary record 1625th ILC meeting (n. 4), 218, para. 25 (Christopher Walter Pinto [Chairman]).

[7] Summary record 1625th ILC meeting (n. 4), 218, para. 25 (Christopher Walter Pinto [Chairman]). See also summary record 1623rd ILC meeting (n. 4), 201, para. 16 (Sir Francis Vallat), 202, para. 4 (Juan José Calle y Calle).

[8] This was proposed by Sir Francis Vallat, summary record 1623rd ILC meeting (n. 4), 201, para. 17.

[9] Summary record 1634th ILC meeting, *YILC 1980*, vol. I, 260, 265, para. 47 (Stephan Verosta [Chairman of the Drafting Committee]).

[10] See Report ILC, thirty-eighth session, 8.

[11] See Report ILC, forty-third session, 13.

constraint as much against the foreign State's property as against the foreign State itself. In other words, the reference in Article 1 to the immunity of State property is no more than functional. A State's property itself may well enjoy no international legal entitlements under the Convention, but this does not alter the fact that the forum State is not permitted, for example, to take judicial measures of constraint against that property. In this light, it is not incorrect, at least in this purely practical sense, to refer, as Article 1 does, to 'the immunity of a State and its property from the jurisdiction of the courts of another State'.

Whether this formulation was advisable, let alone necessary, is another matter, and there is force in the criticism that the Convention as a whole betrays a confused approach in this regard. It by no means fosters conceptual clarity that the relevant provisions of Part IV of the Convention, on State immunity from measures of constraint in connection with proceedings ('No ... measures of constraint ... against property of a State may be taken'), are formulated so differently from those of Part III, on State immunity from proceedings ('a State cannot invoke immunity') or that no provision does for Part IV what Article 5 does for Parts II and III by declaring, as an introductory article to Part IV could have done, that a State 'enjoys immunity, in respect of itself and its property, from measures of constraint in connection with a proceeding before a court of another State'. It would certainly have been preferable had the Convention conceived and spoken at all times of the immunity of the State, in respect of itself and its property, rather than of the immunity of the State and its property.

3.2 'immunity ... from the jurisdiction of the courts of another State'

A. 'of another State'

As Article 1 makes clear, it is from the jurisdiction of the courts solely of another State that the Convention deals with the immunity of a State and its property. Whether the government of a State, the ministries and departments of that government, individual State officials, and so on enjoy immunity from the jurisdiction of the courts of their own State is a matter not for the Convention, or indeed for the international law of jurisdictional immunities more generally, but for the municipal law of that State alone.

B. 'the jurisdiction of the courts'

The word 'jurisdiction' is a protean one, being semantically capable of embracing all enjoyment and exercise of State power. Article 1 suggests that the term is limited for the purposes of the Convention to the exercise of authority by a State's courts. But the suggestion is not in fact accurate.

While it is evident that the Convention does not apply to the assertion of State authority via the legislature,[12] Part IV, dealing with State immunity from measures of constraint, regulates the exercise of authority by a State party as much via its executive organs as via its courts. Articles 18 and 19 provide in general terms that '[n]o ... measures of constraint ... may be taken in connection with a proceeding before a court of another State'; and the word 'taken', while capable of applying to the mere order by a court of measures of constraint, is clearly also capable of embracing the execution of any such

[12] That said, it may obviously be the case that a State party is compelled, either practically or as a matter of its municipal law, to enact legislation to implement the Convention.

judicial order by the bailiffs or the equivalent—that is, by whatever coercive authorities are vested by the law of the forum State with the authority physically to compel compliance with an order by a civil court. The ILC commentary to draft article 1 (which elsewhere explains, oxymoronically and self-contradictorily, that 'the phrase "of the courts" is designed to confirm the understanding that the scope of the current topic is confined primarily to immunity from the jurisdiction "of the courts" of States'[13]) says as much. It explains that the draft articles apply 'not only in relation . . . to exemption from the exercise of the power to adjudicate, normally assumed by the judiciary or magistrate within a legal system of the territorial State, but also in relation to the non-exercise of all other administrative and executive powers, by whatever measures or procedures and by whatever authorities of the territorial State, in relation to a judicial proceeding'.[14]

Insofar as Part IV prohibits the taking of measures of constraint against State property 'in connection with a proceeding before a court', one might be forgiven for using 'the jurisdiction of the courts' by way of shorthand. That said, convenience would not appear to have been the rationale for the wording of Article 1, which owes more to the ILC's overwhelming focus—perhaps understandable at the time, given the state of development in 1980, 1983, 1986, and even 1991 of the rules on State immunity from measures of constraint—on immunity from proceedings. Indeed, it may well have been that, as originally conceived,[15] the formulation of what would become Article 1 took no account whatsoever of measures of constraint, in which light the reference to the jurisdiction 'of the courts' would have made perfect sense.

C. *'immunity . . . from . . . jurisdiction'*

More problematic than Article 1's exclusive reference to the courts is the way the provision uses the constructive phrase 'immunity . . . from . . . jurisdiction', as embedded in the expression 'immunity from the jurisdiction of the courts of another State'. Given that the Convention regulates State immunity both from proceedings and from measures of constraint taken in connection with proceedings, Article 1 must be taken to employ the term 'immunity . . . from . . . jurisdiction' to refer to both immunity from proceedings and immunity from measures of constraint. This usage, however, is starkly inconsistent with the later use of the term 'immunity . . . from . . . jurisdiction' in the selfsame expression 'immunity . . . from the jurisdiction of the courts of another State' as found in Article 5 of the Convention, as well as with the use of 'immunity from . . . jurisdiction' and 'immunity from jurisdiction' in Articles 7 to 17 of the Convention. As employed in Parts II[16] and III (Articles 5 to 17) of the Convention, 'immunity from jurisdiction' relates solely to immunity from proceedings. It does not extend to immunity from measures of constraint, the subject of Part IV of the Convention.

[13] ILC commentary, draft art. 1, para. 3. In terms of oxymoron, a scope cannot be 'confined primarily' to something. It is confined to something or not.

[14] ILC commentary, draft art. 1, para. 2.

[15] It will be recalled from section 2 that the expression 'immunity . . . from the jurisdiction of the courts of another State' did not feature in Special Rapporteur Sucharitkul's original draft, having been proposed later by Sir Francis Vallat.

[16] Note that Part II of the Convention, despite being entitled 'General principles', pertains solely to immunity from proceedings—that is, in the language of both Part II and Part III of the Convention, immunity from 'jurisdiction'—and not also to immunity from measures of constraint. See the commentary to Part II UNCSI.

The explanation for the disjuncture would again appear to lie in the distinctly subordinate position occupied by immunity from measures of constraint in the ILC's outlook on the topic. Indeed, as originally conceived, it may have been that, as with its reference solely to the courts, Article 1's use of the term 'immunity . . . from . . . jurisdiction' took no account of immunity from measures of constraint, in which light this usage would have been on all fours with the use of the same term in Parts II and III of the Convention and in the title to and provisions of Chapter I ECSI.

As used in Article 1, but in contrast to its use in Parts II and III of the Convention, the term 'immunity . . . from . . . jurisdiction' is synonymous with the term 'jurisdictional immunities' found in the title of the ILC's work, in draft article 1 as originally proposed by Special Rapporteur Sucharitkul, and in the title of and Preamble to the eventual Convention. The expression 'jurisdictional immunities of States and their property' more obviously encompasses both the 'immunity from jurisdiction' regulated by Parts II and III and the 'immunity from measures of constraint' regulated by Part IV;[17] and it is telling in this regard that the ILC commentary to draft article 1 elaborates on the phrase 'jurisdictional immunities', rather than on the words 'immunity . . . from . . . jurisdiction' as actually found in the provision.[18]

4. Evaluation

Overtures are best composed when it has become clear what they are supposed to introduce. The essence of Article 1 was agreed very early on. Indeed, leaving aside subsequent inconsequential changes, the provision was among the first to be formulated. For an overture, this was too early. As a result, its terminology is surprisingly at odds with the remainder of the Convention.

[17] See eg ILC commentary, draft art. 1, para. 2.
[18] See ILC commentary, draft art. 1, para. 2.

Article 2(1)(*a*) and (*b*)

Tom Grant

Article 2(1)

Use of terms

1. For the purposes of the present Convention:
   (*a*) 'court' means any organ of a State, however named, entitled to exercise judicial functions;
   (*b*) 'State' means:
      (i) the State and its various organs of government;
      (ii) constituent units of a federal State or political subdivisions of the State, which are entitled to perform acts in the exercise of sovereign authority, and are acting in that capacity;
      (iii) agencies or instrumentalities of the State or other entities, to the extent that they are entitled to perform and are actually performing acts in the exercise of sovereign authority of the State;
      (iv) representatives of the State acting in that capacity[.]

1. Introduction

Article 2, entitled 'Use of terms', sets out the definitions of three terms for the purposes of the Convention. Subparagraphs (*a*) and (*b*) of Article 2(1) define 'court' and 'State' respectively. Given that the Convention applies, in the words of Article 1, to 'the immunity of a State and its property from the jurisdiction of the courts of another State', the content of the terms 'court' and 'State' is obviously crucial.

In the context of immunity from jurisdiction, as dealt with in Parts II and III, the basic rule, laid down in Article 5, is that a 'State' enjoys immunity from proceedings in the courts of another State subject to Articles 7 to 17 of the Convention. In terms of immunity from measures of constraint, the basic rule, posited in Article 18 and 19, is that no measures of constraint may be taken against property of a 'State' unless the exceptions to the rule specified in those provisions are made out. In this light, satisfying Article 2(1)(*b*)'s definition of 'State' is a necessary, albeit not sufficient, criterion for the availability of State immunity in both contexts. Given this, it is perhaps not surprising that the drafting of at least certain aspects of this definition gave rise to considerable controversy.

The term 'court', as defined in Article 2(1)(*a*), is fundamental as well, but was easier for the drafters to agree on.

2. Drafting History

Paul Reuter, as ILC chairman, observed that '[i]t was not unusual that the early articles of a draft could only be evaluated in relation to the subsequent articles and that the latter sometimes obliged the Commission to revise the former'.[1] The section on use of terms in particular, he noted, required repeated consideration. The Commission's draft articles on jurisdictional immunities of States and their property proved no exception.

It was in his Second Report that Special Rapporteur Sucharitkul first proposed a draft article 2, on the use of terms,[2] of which he assumed it would be necessary to define a relatively large number. He began with a list of seven, but this was 'clearly not exhaustive', constituting instead merely 'an initial minimum'.[3] The list comprised 'immunity', 'jurisdictional immunities', 'territorial State', 'foreign State', 'State property', 'trading or commercial activity', and 'jurisdiction'.[4] In addition, the Special Rapporteur proposed a separate draft article containing interpretative provisions referring to 'at least two or three' of these terms.[5] Over the course of the drafting, however, although the word 'court' was added and the term 'trading or commercial activity' substituted by 'commercial transaction', the list was shortened overall to leave, eventually, only the two fundamental terms, 'court' and 'State', and, under Article 2(1)(*c*), 'commercial transaction'.

2.1 Article 2(1)(*a*)

The drafting of Article 2(1)(*a*), defining the term 'court', was considerably less difficult than that of Article 2(1)(*b*). Although Special Rapporteur Sucharitkul's initial list of terms did not include 'court', the Special Rapporteur suggested that 'courts', for the purposes of the draft articles, should be taken to include 'the judicial as well as . . . the administrative authorities of the territorial State'.[6] The Drafting Committee, however, defined 'court' to mean 'any organ of a State, however named, entitled to exercise judicial functions'.[7] The Commission endorsed this,[8] preferring, as the Drafting Committee had as well, 'judicial functions' to 'adjudicatory functions', which some civil law systems might have interpreted too narrowly.[9] The text adopted on first reading remained unchanged on second reading, and passed from there into the Convention.

2.2 Article 2(1)(*b*)

A. General

The 'highly disputed'[10] definition of a 'State', or at least parts of it, proved one of the most contentious issues over the course of the Convention's drafting.[11]

Special Rapporteur Sucharitkul's initial scheme contained a draft article on the use of terms which set out short definitions of key concepts (including, at the time, 'foreign

[1] Summary record 1749th ILC meeting, *YILC 1982*, vol. I, 317, 322, para. 41.

[2] See Second report Sucharitkul, 206–9, paras 34–42.

[3] Second report Sucharitkul, 203, para. 15.

[4] Second report Sucharitkul, 203, para. 15.

[5] Second report Sucharitkul, 206, para. 34.

[6] Second report Sucharitkul, 204, para. 22.

[7] Summary record ILC 1749th meeting (n. 1), 320, para. 23 (Sompong Sucharitkul). See also Eighth report Sucharitkul, 24, para. 6.

[8] See summary record ILC 1750th meeting, *YILC 1982*, vol. I, 324, 330, paras 60 and 75.

[9] See summary record ILC 1750th meeting (n. 8), 321–2, para. 34 (Zhengyu Ni), referring to the fact that some legal systems had officers, such as procurators, who exercised judicial functions but did not adjudicate.

[10] G. Hafner and U. Köhler, 'The United Nations Convention on Jurisdictional Immunities of States and Their Property' (2005) 35 *NYIL* 3, 13.

[11] See 1999 report Chairman Sixth Committee Working Group, 2, para. 5.

State' and 'territorial State'), with the term 'foreign State' being elaborated on in a further article containing '[i]nterpretative provisions'.[12] Even after the Commission's decision not to distinguish between 'territorial' and 'foreign' States, the division between draft article 2, on the use of terms, and the 'interpretative provisions' of draft article 3 was retained; and in the text adopted on first reading in 1986, it was the latter that set out the Commission's understanding of 'State'.[13] It was only on second reading and in the light of comments by governments[14] that the two provisions were merged and the substance of what was to become Article 2(1)(*b*) was moved into the provision on the use of terms.[15]

While specific issues remained contested right up to the adoption of the Convention, the broad contours of what would become Article 2(1)(*b*) were sketched on first reading and not revisited. Draft article 3 as proposed in Special Rapporteur Sucharitkul's second report included four categories of legal or natural person within the definition of 'foreign State'.[16] One of these categories, namely 'the sovereign head of State', was dropped before adoption on first reading, while a new category of 'representatives of the State' was added.[17]

The debate on second reading and beyond went to drafting details.

B. *The four categories of legal and natural persons*

(i) 'the State and its various organs of government'

What would become Article 2(1)(*b*)(i) attracted little comment throughout the drafting. A version of the provision appeared in Special Rapporteur Sucharitkul's second report,[18] from where it carried over into draft article 3 on first reading and draft article 2 on second reading.

(ii) 'constituent units of a federal State or political subdivisions of the State'

In contrast, the eventual Article 2(1)(*b*)(ii), on 'constituent units of a federal State or political subdivisions of the State', gave rise to protracted debate, both as regards the entities covered and the conditions under which they would be treated as a 'State'.

Early versions of the text had referred only to a State's 'political subdivisions',[19] which were considered a 'State' when they exercised 'sovereign authority'. In 1986, however, the Drafting Committee inserted the further requirement that such subdivisions be 'entitled to perform acts in the exercise of the sovereign authority of the State', retaining the term 'sovereign authority' as 'the nearest equivalent to the French expression "*prérogatives de la puissance publique*"', even if others preferred the term 'governmental authority'.[20]

It was on second reading that debate began in earnest. In their comments and observations, a number of States suggested including federal constituent units as distinct

[12] Second report Sucharitkul, 206, para. 33 and 211, para. 48.

[13] See Report ILC thirty-eighth session, 8–9.

[14] See Preliminary report Ogiso, 101–2, paras 23, 35 (Australia, Byelorussia, the GDR, and Venezuela).

[15] See Preliminary report Ogiso, 101, para. 29.

[16] See Second report Sucharitkul, 211, para. 48.

[17] See summary record ILC 1968th meeting, *YILC 1986*, vol. I, 165, 166, para. 15.

[18] See Second report Sucharitkul, 211, para. 48 ('the central government and its various organs or departments').

[19] Second report Sucharitkul, 211, para. 48; *YILC 1986*, vol. II(2), 9, para. 22.

[20] Report ILC, thirty-eighth session, 14 (commentary to draft art. 3).

from other 'political subdivisions',[21] especially as these were said, under certain federal systems, not to participate in the exercise of the sovereign authority of the State as such but to exercise powers of their own.[22] In response, Special Rapporteur Ogiso proposed in his Third Report a separate draft article covering 'constituent States of a federal State' conditioned on the State's declaration that its constituent States could invoke those draft articles applicable to a State and accepted the corresponding obligations.[23] The Drafting Committee, and eventually the Commission, agreed to include federal constituent entities, but simplified the provision to read 'constituent units of a federal State'.[24] The Commission also again considered replacing 'sovereign authority' with 'governmental authority', which would have brought the text into line with the terminology adopted in the ILC's work on State responsibility and clarified that the question was one of municipal law; but again some members felt that 'sovereign authority' better expressed the attribute of the State by virtue of which it enjoyed immunity. In the absence of consensus, the existing term was retained.[25]

After the final adoption of the draft articles on second reading in 1991, the controversy over federal constituent units continued in the Sixth Committee Working Group and the ILC Working Group. A number of governments believed that the diversity of federal and other administrative arrangements in States made it impractical to incorporate a provision on constituent units of a federal State.[26] France in particular rejected the idea that 'territorial subdivisions of a foreign State' enjoyed immunity from jurisdiction.[27] Partly in response to these criticisms, the ILC Working Group proposed in 1999 to restrict the clause to those constituent units of a federal State 'which are entitled to perform acts in the exercise of the governmental authority of the State, [provided that it was established that such entities were acting in that capacity]'.[28] It also suggested the merger of what were still separate provisions on political subdivisions and federal units, since 'the difference in treatment [was] confusing';[29] and, reversing the ILC's previous decision, it suggested the substitution of the term 'sovereign authority' with 'governmental authority', so as to bring the text of the draft article into line with the ILC's draft articles on State responsibility.[30]

[21] See 'Comments and observations received from Governments', *YILC 1988*, vol. II(1), 45, 70, para. 2 (FRG); Preliminary report Ogiso, 101, para. 33. Austria thought it self-evident that the expression 'the State and its various organs of government' would be 'wide enough to cover any political subdivision of a State'. See 'Comments and observations' (n. 21), 56, para. 4 (Aut).

[22] See summary record ILC 2191st meeting, *YILC 1990*, vol. I, 306, 309, para. 29 (Ahmed Mahiou, Chairman of the Drafting Committee). See also ILC Report, forty-first session, 100–1, para. 426.

[23] Third report Ogiso, 7 (draft art. 2(1)(*b*)(*i bis*)). See also summary record ILC 2158th meeting, *YILC 1990*, vol. I, 61, 65, para. 4 (Motoo Ogiso). The proposal drew on Art. 28 ECSI. It was taken up again later. See 1992 report Sixth Committee Working Group, 2, paras 9–10.

[24] See summary record ILC 2191st meeting (n. 22), 309, para. 29; summary record ILC 2218th meeting, *YILC 1991*, vol. I, 66, 69, para. 24. See also ILC commentary, draft art. 2, para. 11.

[25] Summary record ILC 2191st meeting (n. 22), 309, para. 30.

[26] See eg Comments of Belgium, 12 August 1993, UN doc. A/48/313, 2.

[27] Reply received from France, 15 October 1992, UN doc. A/47/326/Add.5, 2 (section B). See also Comments of Belgium, 12 August 1993, UN doc. A/48/313, 2; Reply received from Chile, 8 May 2000, UN doc. A/55/298, 4, para. 22.

[28] 1999 report ILC Working Group, 158, para. 30.

[29] Summary record ILC 2601st meeting, *YILC 1999*, vol. I, 246, 257, para. 75 (Gerhard Hafner, Chairman of Working Group).

[30] Summary record ILC 2601st meeting (n. 29), para. 74. See also 1999 report Chairman Sixth Committee Working Group, 3, para. 13.

When the report of the ILC Working Group was considered in the Commission, members from federal States felt that the Working Group, in its reformulation of the provision on federal States, had gone 'too far in giving satisfaction to States organized along unitary and centralized lines', especially since the proposed text 'gave the impression that the constituent units of federal States could enjoy jurisdictional immunity only when they exercised the governmental authority of the central State'.[31] Gerhard Hafner, Chairman of the Working Group, agreed that 'of the State' could be deleted,[32] and it was.[33] Drawing on the ILC's debates and on comments by governments, the Working Group of the Sixth Committee subsequently endorsed the qualification, bracketed up to that point, that constituent units or political subdivisions were to enjoy immunity 'where at the time of the dispute it was clearly established' that they had acted in the exercise of their authority.

Final changes to the provision were made in the Ad Hoc Committee on Jurisdictional Immunities of States and Their Property. The requirement that constituent units or political subdivisions actually exercise authority was simplified. More significantly, the Ad Hoc Committee reverted to the term 'sovereign authority', rather than 'governmental authority', and inserted the definite article before it. As amended, the provision appeared in the Ad Hoc Committee's reports of 2003 and 2004,[34] and was introduced to the Sixth Committee.[35] Yet there was to be a final twist. The Chairman of the Ad Hoc Committee indicated to the Sixth Committee that, among the final corrections entrusted to the Secretariat, 'the word "the" should be deleted before the words "sovereign authority"',[36] a change that 'would not in any case change the substance of the draft text'.[37]

(iii) 'agencies or instrumentalities of the State or other entities'

Special Rapporteur Sucharitkul's proposed draft article 3 had referred to 'agencies or instrumentalities acting as organs of a foreign State in the exercise of its sovereign authority, whether or not endowed with a separate legal personality and whether or not forming part of the operational machinery of the central government'. The formulation was significantly simplified after debate in the Commission and Drafting Committee. The requirement that agencies or instrumentalities be 'acting as organs' was dispensed with, as were the references to separate legal personality and 'the operational machinery of government'. Draft article 3(1)(*c*) as adopted on first reading in 1986, which spoke of 'agencies or instrumentalities of the State, to the extent that they are entitled to perform acts in the exercise of the sovereign authority of the State',[38] was left largely unchanged on second reading. The Commission did, however, add the phrase 'and other entities', which was meant to 'cover nongovernmental entities . . . vested with governmental authority in exceptional cases', for example commercial banks authorized by the State to deal with import and export licensing.[39]

[31] See summary record ILC 2602nd meeting, *YILC 1999*, vol. I, 255, 255–6, para. 1 (Bruno Simma).

[32] See summary record ILC 2602nd meeting (n. 31), 259, para. 36 (Gerhard Hafner, Chairman of the Working Group).

[33] See summary record ILC 2602nd meeting (n. 31), 260, para. 47.

[34] See 2003 report Ad Hoc Committee (Annex 1); 2004 report Ad Hoc Committee (Annex 1).

[35] See Statement Chairman Ad Hoc Committee.

[36] Statement Chairman Ad Hoc Committee, 6, para. 34.

[37] Statement Chairman Ad Hoc Committee, 6, para. 33.

[38] Report ILC, thirty-eighth session, 9.

[39] Summary record ILC 2218th meeting (n. 24), 69, para. 26 (chairman of the Drafting Committee).

The main challenge to the eventual Article 2(1)(*b*)(iii) came in the Sixth Committee Working Group, where a number of States advocated the deletion of the provision.[40] The UK in particular sought to exclude separate legal entities, with the exception of central banks and other monetary authorities, from the definition of 'State', but to have them accorded immunity in proceedings relating to acts performed in the exercise of sovereign authority.[41] This was ultimately not pursued.

Debate between 1999 and 2004 was more narrowly focused. Two changes were agreed. First, the text was tightened up to refer to agencies and instrumentalities 'to the extent that they are entitled to perform and are actually performing acts in the exercise of sovereign authority of the State'.[42] Secondly, the conjunctive link between 'agencies or instrumentalities of the State' and 'other entities' was made disjunctive.[43]

The provision was adopted in this form in 2004.

(iv) 'representatives of the State'

The eventual Article 2(1)(*b*)(iv), dealing with 'representatives of the State acting in that capacity', attracted relatively little debate. The Drafting Committee inserted the provision in 1986 into what was then draft article 3, the interpretative provision, and the Commission adopted it on first reading. Governments made no comment on it, and it was included unchanged in draft article 2(1)(*b*)(v) as finally adopted on second reading in 1991. From there it passed renumbered but otherwise unchanged into the Convention.

3. Key Points

The purpose of the drafters in specifying the meaning of the terms 'court' and 'State' was to assist in the application of the substantive provisions of the Convention, given that the State is the entity whose immunities the Convention concerns, while the organs against which such immunities may be invoked are the courts of other States. The definitions in subparagraphs (*a*) and (*b*) of Article 2(1) are to be applied to all provisions of the Convention. Conversely, their interpretation is properly referable to the Convention as a whole.[44]

3.1 Article 2(1)(*a*)

According to Article 2(1)(*a*), the term 'court' as used in the Convention means 'any organ of a State, however named, entitled to exercise judicial functions'. The term 'judicial functions' is not itself defined in the Convention. The omission was deliberate, given that 'such functions vary under different constitutional and legal systems'.[45] The ILC commentary to draft article 2 nonetheless states:

> [J]udicial functions may include adjudication of litigation or dispute settlement, determination of questions of law and of fact, order of interim and enforcement measures at all stages of legal

[40] See also Reply received from Austria, 9 July 1992, UN doc. A/47/326, 11, para. 6; 1993 report Sixth Committee Working Group, 23 (US, Proposal N).

[41] 1993 report Sixth Committee Working Group, 22 (Proposal K).

[42] 1999 report Chairman Sixth Committee Working Group, 24, para. 88.

[43] See 1999 report Chairman Sixth Committee Working Group, 4, para. 16.

[44] Art. 31(1) and (2) VCLT.

[45] ILC commentary, draft art. 2, para. 3.

proceedings and such other administrative and executive functions as are normally exercised by, or under, the judicial authorities of a State in connection with, in the course of, or pursuant to, a legal proceeding. Although judicial functions are determined by the internal organizational structure of each State, the term does not, for the purposes of the present articles, cover the administration of justice in all its aspects which, at least under certain legal systems, might include other functions related to the appointment of judges.[46]

The commentary adds that 'this definition may, under different constitutional and legal systems, cover the exercise of the power to order or adopt enforcement measures (sometimes called "quasi-judicial functions") by specific administrative organs of the State'.[47]

The term 'court' is unlikely in practice to cause great difficulties.

3.2 Article 2(1)(*b*)

Article 2(1)(*b*) defines the term 'State' by reference to four categories of legal or natural person, the first three of which are themselves compounds of two or more categories. The definition given is essentially circular, insofar as it relies repeatedly on the word 'State' to define the term 'State'.[48] The four basic categories comprise: the State as such, along with its various organs of government, as treated under Article 2(1)(*b*)(i); the constituent units of a federal State and other political subdivisions of a State, as treated under Article 2(1)(*b*)(ii); agencies or instrumentalities of a State and other analogous entities, as treated under Article 2(1)(*b*)(iii); and individual representatives of a State, as treated under Article 2(1)(*b*)(iv). Of the various legal and natural persons comprising the four categories, those under Article 2(1)(*b*)(ii), (iii), and (iv) are considered a 'State' for the purposes of the Convention only if they satisfy further conditions as to, variously, their entitlement to perform acts in the exercise of the sovereign authority of the State, the capacity in which they were acting at the relevant time, and the character of the conduct performed by them that forms the subject of the relevant proceedings.

Under Article 2(1)(*b*)(ii) and (iii), a determination as to whether the legal entity in question is to be treated as a 'State' for the purposes of the Convention will entail a prior determination as to whether the entity is 'entitled to perform acts in the exercise of sovereign authority'. Whether the entity is so entitled will be a question of the municipal law of the State (as the term is used in international law) whose immunities are in issue. In order to ascertain whether the entity is so entitled, the court—which will necessarily be a court of another State—may find it useful to have recourse to expert evidence or to invite submissions by the government of the State invoking immunity.[49] As for the subsequent question under Article 2(1)(*b*)(ii) and (iii) as to whether the entity was actually performing acts in the exercise of sovereign authority at the time of the impugned conduct, this, in contrast, is largely a factual question.[50]

It merits emphasis that the provisions of Article 2(1)(*b*) are not rules of attribution for the purposes of either international or municipal law. Whether, for example, the

[46] ILC commentary, draft art. 2, para. 3.
[47] ILC commentary, draft art. 2, para. 4.
[48] See eg summary record ILC 2218th meeting (n. 24), 69–70, para. 27 (Pemmaraju Sreenivasa Rao).
[49] See eg Preliminary report Sucharitkul, 235, para. 37.
[50] See eg Report of the Working Group, 6, para. 31.

acts or omissions of an agency, instrumentality, or other entity within the meaning of Article 2(1)(*b*)(iii) are attributable to the State for the purposes of the international law of State responsibility is a question of the rules on attribution of conduct provided for by the international law of State responsibility,[51] not of Article 2(1)(*b*) of the Convention.[52] Whether, by way of similar example, the State as such or the government of that State or the relevant ministry of that State can be held liable under the municipal law applied by the court for the acts and omissions of an agency, instrumentality, or other entity within the meaning of Article 2(1)(*b*)(iii) is a substantive question of the applicable municipal law—whether it be the rules on vicarious liability or agency or the rules of company law or of the law of unincorporated associations or, indeed, the rules of customary international law on attribution of conduct to a State as given direct effect by the applicable municipal law.

The specifically municipal legal aspects of the foregoing point call for reiteration. The sole question regulated by Article 2(1)(*b*) is whether a given respondent is to be treated as a 'State' for the purposes of the rules of State immunity from both jurisdiction and measures of constraint laid down in the Convention. Article 2(1)(*b*) does not regulate whether the emanation of the State named as respondent to the claim may be held legally answerable under the applicable municipal law for the acts or omissions of another emanation of the State. So, for example, if the claimant elects to sue the State as such for the acts of a separate municipal legal person like a State enterprise, Article 2(1)(*b*)(i) will determine only whether the State as such is to be considered a 'State' so as to benefit procedurally from the *prima facie* availability to a 'State' of immunity from jurisdiction, as posited in Article 5 of the Convention. Whether the claimant can 'pierce the corporate veil' and hold the State itself liable for the acts or omissions of a State enterprise is, in contrast, a question of substantive municipal law to be determined by reference to whatever body of rules is applicable under that law.

A. The State as such and its various organs of government

In accordance with Article 2(1)(*b*)(i), the term 'State' encompasses 'the State and its various organs of government'. The ILC commentary elaborates on this straightforward category as follows:

> The first category includes the State itself, acting in its own name and through its various organs of government, however designated, such as . . . the central government, various ministries and departments of government, ministerial or sub-ministerial departments, offices or bureaux, as well as subordinate organs and missions representing the State, including diplomatic missions and consular posts, permanent missions and delegations. The use of the expression 'various organs of government' is intended to include all branches of government and is not limited to the executive branch only.[53]

The form of government of the State is immaterial.[54]

[51] See, in this regard, Arts 4–11 Articles on Responsibility of States for Internationally Wrongful Acts, UN doc. A/RES/56/83, Annex (28 January 2002).

[52] For apparent confusion in this regard, see 'Convention on Jurisdictional Immunities of States and Their Property: Report of the Secretary-General', UN doc. A/47/326/Add.1 (25 August 1992), 2–3, para. 3 (China).

[53] ILC commentary, draft art. 2, para. 6.

[54] See n. 55, para. 7.

The suggestion in the ILC commentary that Article 2(1)(*b*)(i) encompasses the head of State in his or her public capacity is incorrect.[55] Article 3(2) excludes from the Convention's scope the question of the jurisdictional immunity of heads of State in both their private and public capacities.

B. Constituent units of a federal State and other political subdivisions

Article 2(1)(*b*)(ii) brings within the meaning of 'State' for the purposes of the Convention 'constituent units of a federal State or political subdivisions of the State, which are entitled to perform acts in the exercise of sovereign authority, and are acting in that capacity'.[56] The phrase 'political subdivisions of the State'—which perhaps would have been clearer as 'other political subdivisions of the State', given that a constituent unit of a federal State, at least in the ordinary sense of the term, is itself a political subdivision of the State—would appear to mean tiers of government other than the central government or constituent federal units, such as provinces (where these do not constitute federal units), cantons, counties, municipalities, and so on.

In bringing constituent units of a federal State within its definition of 'State', the Convention differs from the ECSI, under Article 28(1) of which the constituent units of a federal State do not, as a general rule,[57] enjoy immunity from jurisdiction, although they may be granted immunity in accordance with the rule in Article 27(2) applicable to separate entities if the proceedings relate to 'acts performed by [them] in the exercise of sovereign authority (*acta jure imperii*)'. The Convention also contrasts to this extent with the legislation of various States, which is either to the same effect as the ECSI[58] or rules out the immunity of constituent federal units altogether.[59] At the same time, several other, federal States do treat constituent units of other federal States as a foreign 'State' for the purposes of State immunity.[60] In the final analysis, the difference between the position under the Convention and that under the ECSI and some national State immunity legislation would appear to be more of form than substance, given the twin requirements of Article 2(1)(*b*)(ii) that the constituent federal unit or other political subdivision be entitled to perform, and at the relevant time actually be performing, acts in the exercise of sovereign authority—requirements almost identical to those applicable to separate entities (or, in the terminology of the Convention, 'agencies or instrumentalities or other entities')

[55] See ILC commentary, draft art. 2, paras 6 and 8. The mistaken assertion is the obverse of the incorrect statement in ILC commentary, draft art. 3, para. 6, that a foreign head of State benefits from immunity *ratione personae* only in respect of acts performed in a private capacity. For a full discussion of the issue, see section 3.2 (B) of the commentary to Art. 3.

[56] It might be noted that, as is prevalent throughout the text of the Convention, the comma before 'which' is extraneous, turning what is clearly intended as a qualifying phrase into what, at least at first sight, is an otiose descriptor. Applying the canon of construction that militates against textual redundancy (and dispensing also with the extraneous comma before 'and'), Art. 2(1)(*b*)(ii) should read 'constituent units of a federal State or political subdivisions of the State which are entitled to perform acts in the exercise of sovereign authority and are acting in that capacity'.

[57] But see Art. 28(2) ECSI, pursuant to which a federal State may declare that its federal constituent units may invoke the provisions of the ECSI. Austria, Belgium, and Germany have made declarations under Art. 28(2).

[58] See eg s. 14(1) and (6) SIA (UK), although s. 14(5) makes provision for the application of Part I of the Act to constituent territories on a territory-by-territory basis; s. 15(1) and (6) SIO (Pak), although see also s. 15(5); s. 16(1) and (6) SIA (Sing), although see also s. 16(5).

[59] See s. 1(2)(ii) FStIA (SA).

[60] See s. 1603(*a*) FSIA (US); s. 2 SIA (Can); s. 3(3) FStIA (Aus); s. 1 FSIL (Isr).

under Article 2(1)(*b*)(iii) and, indeed, to constituent federal units *qua* separate entities under Article 27(2) ECSI.

(i) 'which are entitled to perform acts in the exercise of sovereign authority'

To qualify as a 'State' under Article 2(1)(*b*)(ii), a constituent unit of a federal State or other political subdivision must first be 'entitled to perform acts in the exercise of sovereign authority'. The choice of the term 'sovereign authority', settled on after heated exchanges of view,[61] is unfortunate. Under the restrictive doctrine of State immunity, it is commonly said that an emanation of a foreign State is entitled to immunity from the jurisdiction of the courts of another State where the proceeding relates to acts performed by it 'in the exercise of sovereign authority'.[62] But the expression 'acts in the exercise of sovereign authority' as used in Article 2(1)(*b*)(ii) does not refer to the acts in respect of which a constituent federal unit or other political subdivision may ultimately be immune. Rather, it merely forms a condition that must be met if the unit or subdivision is to be identified as a 'State'; and, in accordance with Article 5, a 'State' is no more than *prima facie* entitled to immunity. In other words, under Article 2(1)(*b*)(ii), but in contrast to how the descriptor is usually used, establishing that an act is one 'in the exercise of sovereign authority' is a way station, not the endpoint, of the analysis. To compound matters, whether an emanation of a State is acting 'in the exercise of sovereign authority' as the term is usually understood is a question of international law, whereas whether a constituent federal unit or other political subdivision is 'entitled' to perform acts in the exercise of sovereign authority within the meaning of Article 2(1)(*b*)(ii) would appear to be a question of municipal law.

The rational interpretation and application of Article 2(1)(*b*)(ii) is nevertheless not significantly impeded by the infelicity of language. The Convention nowhere relies on the expression 'acts in the exercise of sovereign authority' to limit the scope of the immunity from jurisdiction to which an entity qualifying as a 'State' is entitled. It is sufficiently clear from the context that 'acts in the exercise of sovereign authority' as employed in Article 2(1)(*b*)(ii) denotes no more than acts which the relevant municipal law considers acts in the exercise of public or governmental authority. Indeed, it is worth recalling that the adjective 'governmental' surfaced repeatedly over the course of the provision's drafting.

The real question is whether the requirement that a constituent federal unit or other political subdivision be entitled to perform acts in the exercise of sovereign authority adds anything to Article 2(1)(*b*)(ii). It is not easy to see how such units and subdivisions are not by definition entitled to perform acts in the exercise of sovereign authority within the meaning of Article 2(1)(*b*)(ii), *viz* acts in the exercise of governmental authority. This would seem to be what makes them constituent federal units and other political subdivisions in the first place, rather than merely agencies or instrumentalities of the State, as referred to in Article 2(1)(*b*)(iii). It remains to be seen what courts make of this limb of Article 2(*b*)(ii).

(ii) 'and are acting in that capacity'

To qualify as a 'State' under Article 2(1)(*b*)(ii), a constituent unit of a federal State or other political subdivision must not only be entitled to perform acts in the exercise of

[61] Recall section 2. [62] Recall eg the wording of Art. 27(2) ECSI, as quoted above in the text.

sovereign authority but must also, in relation to the conduct the subject of the proceeding, actually be performing such acts. As with the preceding criterion, it might be asked what this stipulation adds in the context of constituent units of a federal State and other political subdivisions. It is hard to see how such units and subdivisions could act in any other capacity. They are not like individual representatives of the State, as covered by Article 2(1)(*b*)(iv), who can act in a private capacity as well as in their capacity as a representative of the State. Like the 'various organs of government' referred to in Article 2(1)(*b*)(i), constituent federal units and other political subdivisions have no private capacity. They are intrinsically public or, synonymously, governmental. Again, what courts will do with this requirement is at present a matter of speculation.

C. Agencies and instrumentalities of the State and other entities

Article 2(1)(*b*)(iii) brings within the meaning of 'State' as used in the Convention 'agencies or instrumentalities of the State or other entities, to the extent that they are entitled to perform and are actually performing acts in the exercise of sovereign authority of the State'. The ILC commentary is remarkably reticent in relation to this, probably the most difficult sub-subparagraph of Article 2(1)(*b*), stating that '[t]he concept of "agencies or instrumentalities of the State . . . " could theoretically include State enterprises or other entities established by the State performing commercial transactions'.[63] Leaving aside whether such enterprises or entities are to be considered a 'State' when performing commercial transactions, it is undoubtedly the case that, in appropriate circumstances, what are known as 'State enterprises', *viz* corporate entities with legal personality separate from the State and established by it usually with a view to commercial activity, are one category of the agencies or instrumentalities that Article 2(1)(*b*)(iii) has in mind. The provision would also embrace, in certain circumstances, central banks, State utilities, State tourism boards, State commodity boards, sovereign wealth funds, and the like—entities, enjoying a legal personality separate from the State, established by it for a specific purpose and retaining some connection with it. As for the term 'other entities', this is apparently intended to cover private entities not established by the State but nonetheless 'endowed with governmental authority'.[64]

The ILC commentary notes that '[t]here is in practice no [bright] line to be drawn between agencies or instrumentalities of a State and departments of government'.[65] This is perhaps the most difficult problem in relation to Article 2(1)(*b*)(iii)—that is, whether one is dealing with 'an agency or instrumentality of a State or other entity' to begin with, and therefore applying the demanding criteria of Article 2(1)(*b*)(iii), or whether the entity in question is a subsidiary organ of a government department, in which case Article 2(1)(*b*)(i) applies. Article 2(1)(*b*)(iii) itself provides no guidance.

It is unclear on the face of the provision whether Article 2(1)(*b*)(iii) applies to agencies etc of a federal constituent unit or other political subdivision. Given, however, that such units and subdivisions are to be considered a 'State' for the purposes of the Convention when entitled to act and acting in the exercise of sovereign, *viz* governmental, authority, it stands to reason that an agency etc of such a unit or subdivision acting in that capacity is to be considered a representative of the 'State'. At the same time, it is perhaps arguable

[63] ILC commentary, draft art. 2, para. 15.
[64] ILC commentary, draft art. 2, para. 15.
[65] ILC commentary, draft art. 2, para. 16.

that Article 2(1)(*b*)(iii)'s use of the definite article before 'State' is intended to connote the State as such within the meaning of Article 2(1)(*b*)(i).

In a manner similar to Article 2(1)(*b*)(ii) in respect of federal constituent units and other political subdivisions, Article 2(1)(*b*)(iii) characterizes agencies or instrumentalities of a State or other entities as a 'State' for the purposes of the Convention only 'to the extent that they are entitled to perform and are actually performing acts in the exercise of sovereign authority of the State'. Sub-subparagraphs (ii) and (iii) of Article 2(1)(*b*) are not identical, but they refer to the same category of acts, namely acts in the exercise of governmental authority. An agency or instrumentality of the State or other entity, however, unlike a constituent unit or subdivision, does not necessarily act in the exercise of governmental authority in all circumstances, nor is it necessarily entitled in all circumstances to do so. In practice, therefore, these criteria well may be significant, even pivotal, when Article 2(1)(*b*)(iii) is applied.

The application and consequences of the requirements that the agency etc be both entitled to perform and actually performing acts in the exercise of sovereign authority of the State are best illustrated by examples.

It may be that the *raison d'être* of a particular State enterprise is to engage in what is purely commercial activity, in the same manner as a private company. In any proceeding against it in a court of another State in relation to such activity, the enterprise will fall at the first hurdle, since it is not entitled to perform acts in the exercise of sovereign authority.

At the other end of the spectrum, in a proceeding in a foreign court in relation, for example, to the issuance of bonds by a central bank with legal personality distinct from that of the government of the State and with functional independence from the government, the central bank will be considered a 'State' under Article 2(1)(*b*)(iii), and will enjoy at least *prima facie* immunity from jurisdiction by virtue of Article 5. The bank is entitled to perform acts, among them the issuance of bonds, in the exercise of sovereign authority, and was performing such an act in the circumstances in question.

To consider another example, a proceeding may arise in a foreign court in relation to the provision of drinking water, pursuant to statutory authority and in the territory of the State in question, by a water company wholly owned by a State. In such a case, the company is likely to satisfy the criteria of Article 2(1)(*b*)(iii) and be considered a 'State', at least if it has been granted a monopoly. It is entitled to perform acts in the exercise of sovereign authority, namely the provision of drinking water on an exclusive basis throughout the territory of the State which owns it, and, as a matter of fact, it was performing that activity. In contrast, in a foreign proceeding relating to the provision of water by the same company in the territory of a State other than the State which owns it, even if pursuant to the statutory authority of the owner State, the company ought arguably not be to be treated as a 'State' under Article 2(1)(*b*)(iii). While it is entitled to perform acts in the exercise of sovereign authority, namely the provision of drinking water on an exclusive basis within the territory of the owner State, the provision of water in the territory of a foreign State is hard to characterize as the performance of an act in the exercise of the sovereign authority of the owner State, as distinct from that of the territorial State.[66]

[66] See, in this last regard, Report ILC Working Group, 157, para. 20, referring to 'the performance of functions traditionally performed by individual governmental agencies operating within their own national boundaries'.

In all of this, it is worth underlining that the fact that an agency etc qualifies as a 'State' does not necessarily mean that it will be held to be immune in the final analysis. It may be, for example, that the subject-matter of the proceeding is a commercial transaction as defined in Article 2(1)(*c*), bringing into play the exception to immunity from jurisdiction set out in Article 10. In short, qualifying as a 'State' is merely the first step.

D. *Representatives of the State*

Article 2(1)(*b*)(iv), which identifies the only category of natural persons to be treated as a 'State' for the purposes of the Convention, refers to 'representatives of the State acting in that capacity'. The term 'representatives' is not limited to those State officials, such as diplomats, whose functions involve 'representing' the State. The word is intended to refer to all individual State functionaries. The term 'official' might have been better.

To qualify as a 'State' for the purposes of the Convention, representatives of the State must be 'acting in that capacity'. In other words, the conduct the subject of the proceeding instituted against the individual must have been performed in that individual's capacity as a representative of the State, not in a private capacity. This is not, however, the same as saying that the conduct must have been authorized or have been formally within the scope of the representative's official functions. Provided that the individual was acting as a representative of the State at the time, which is often gauged by reference to whether he or she would otherwise have had the opportunity or capability to perform the act, that individual will be considered a 'State' in accordance with Article 2(1)(*b*)(iv).

As with agencies etc, it is unclear on the face of the provision whether Article 2(1)(*b*)(iv) applies to representatives of a federal constituent unit or other political subdivision; but, as with agencies etc, given that such units and subdivisions are to be considered a 'State' for the purposes of the Convention when they are entitled to act and are acting in the exercise of sovereign, *viz* governmental, authority, it stands to reason that a representative of such a unit or subdivision acting in that capacity is to be considered a representative of the 'State'. At the same time, again, it is perhaps arguable that Article 2(1)(*b*)(iv)'s use of the definite article before 'State' is intended to connote the State as such within the meaning of Article 2(1)(*b*)(i).

The ILC commentary suggests that Article 2(1)(*b*)(iv) applies equally to former representatives of the State. It says:

> Such immunities... are not in any way affected by the change or termination of the official functions of the representatives concerned. Thus, no action will be successfully brought against a former representative of a foreign State in respect of an act performed by him in his official capacity. State immunity survives the termination of the mission or the office of the representative concerned.[67]

But while this is undoubtedly the case as a matter of customary international law, it is not self-evident that it flows from Article 2(1)(*b*)(iv). Article 2(1)(*b*) refers to the legal or natural person against which a proceeding is instituted, and, in the case of a former State representative, the person against whom the proceeding is instituted is not a 'representative of the State' but, rather, a former representative of the State. The difficulty is that the words 'representatives of the State acting in that capacity' give rise to a temporal-logical

[67] ILC commentary, draft art. 2, para. 18.

anomaly when substituted for the word 'State' in Article 5, the provision in accordance with which a 'State' is *prima facie* entitled to immunity from the jurisdiction of the court of another State.[68] The statement 'representatives of the State acting in that capacity enjoy immunity', which is how Article 5 reads on substitution, straddles both present (*viz* the enjoyment of immunity from the proceeding in question) and past (*viz* the conduct which is the subject of the proceeding). If one focuses on the present enjoyment of immunity, a former representative of the State is not currently a representative of the State, and so does not enjoy immunity by virtue of the combined operation of Article 2(1)(*b*)(iv) and Article 5. If one focuses, however, on the past conduct, the former representative of the State was indeed a representative of the State when he or she performed the act the subject of the proceeding. The latter is certainly reasonable and plausible, and is the more sensible approach.

As it is, if former State representatives were not, in fact, covered by Article 2(1)(*b*)(iv), the State as such or some organ of government of the State would doubtless be entitled to claim immunity, at least *prima facie*, in accordance with Article 6(2)(*b*). It is surely the case that a proceeding instituted against a former representative of the State in respect of acts which he performed in his capacity as a representative of the State is a proceeding which 'in effect seeks to affect the . . . interests or activities of that . . . State', in the words of Article 6(2)(*b*).

4. Evaluation

Like most compromise texts, Article 2(1)(*a*) and (*b*) are hardly a showcase of the draftsman's art. Sub-subparagraphs (ii) and (iii) of Article 2(1)(*b*) in particular have the potential to cause confusion for courts called on to apply them. But, in the final analysis, the difficulties posed by the text are by no means insurmountable, and there is no reason to think that courts will do any differently than they have always done with imperfect treaty provisions, which is to muddle through. Nor is there much to be gained in thinking it could have been any different. That Article 2(1)(*b*) was settled on at all is a remarkable achievement. As it is, one of the most difficult issues in relation to Article 2(1)(*b*), namely how to distinguish in borderline cases between a department of a government, as will fall under Article 2(1)(*b*)(i), and an agency or instrumentality, as dealt with in Article 2(1)(*b*)(iii), has nothing to do with the text of the provisions but is an inherent problem of appreciation. Interpreted and applied in good faith, which imports reasonableness, Article 2(1)(*b*) may well achieve what has long been needed, which is at least a modicum of consistency in the treatment of federal subdivisions and separate entities.

[68] The same goes, *mutatis mutandis*, for agencies etc under Art. 2(1)(*c*)(iii).

Article 2 (1)(*c*) and (2) and (3)

Stephan Wittich

Article 2

Use of terms

For the purposes of the present Convention:

. . .

(*c*) 'commercial transaction' means:

(i) any commercial contract or transaction for the sale of goods or supply of services;

(ii) any contract for a loan or other transaction of a financial nature, including any obligation of guarantee or of indemnity in respect of any such loan or transaction;

(iii) any other contract or transaction of a commercial, industrial, trading or professional nature, but not including a contract of employment of persons.

2. In determining whether a contract or transaction is a 'commercial transaction' under paragraph (*c*), reference should be made primarily to the nature of the contract or transaction, but its purpose should also be taken into account if the parties to the contract or transaction have so agreed, or if, in the practice of the State of the forum, that purpose is relevant to determining the non-commercial character of the contract or transaction.

3. The provisions of paragraphs 1 and 2 regarding the use of terms in the present Convention are without prejudice to the use of those terms or to the meanings which may be given to them in other international instruments or in the internal law of any State.

1. Introduction

The commercial transaction exception laid down in Article 10, in conjunction with Article 2(1)(*c*), (2), and (3), of the Convention is in practice the most important exception to the general rule of a State's immunity from the jurisdiction of the courts of another State. The basic idea is simple: States do not enjoy immunity from proceedings in respect of acts of a commercial character, these being the archetypal non-sovereign acts.[1] But while the principle and its rationale are well recognized, controversy has persisted for decades over the precise scope of the exception. At the heart of the debate lie two dichotomies. The first is between commercial and sovereign acts. The second, which concerns the appropriate method of distinguishing between the two, is between the nature and purpose of the impugned act.

Because of its complexity, it was felt appropriate to address the concept of a 'commercial transaction' for the purposes of the Convention in the provision dedicated to the use of terms, alongside the equally essential notions of a 'court' and a 'State', as dealt with in

[1] For a brief general account of the restrictive doctrine of State immunity, see section 1 of the commentary to Art. 10.

Article 2(1)(*a*) and (*b*) respectively. So it is that Article 2(1)(*c*) defines the term 'commercial transaction', while Article 2(2) provides guidance on how the commercial character of a transaction is to be identified in those grey areas where the facts resist a priori characterization. Taken together, Article 2(1)(*c*) and (2) provide the key to the application of Article 10, which specifies an exception to a State's immunity from jurisdiction in the case of proceedings arising out of a 'commercial transaction with a foreign natural or juridical person'. For its part, Article 2(3) contains a savings clause according to which the Convention's use of the terms defined in Article 2 is without prejudice to their meaning in other international instruments or in domestic law.

2. Drafting History

The drafting history of Articles 2 and 10 reveals that the basic idea of a commercial transaction exception to the general rule posited in Article 5 of a State's immunity from the jurisdiction of the courts of another State was never seriously in doubt. The devil, throughout the entire evolution of these provisions, was in the details.

2.1 The ILC's first reading

Special Rapporteur Sucharitkul sketched an outline of the commercial transaction exception to a State's immunity from proceedings in his Preliminary Report. He argued that what gave rise to the exception was 'the commercial nature of the transaction, as opposed to the motivation or the aim and purpose of the contract',[2] and he included as commercial transactions 'contracts for the supply of goods or services; loans or other transactions for the provision of finance and any guarantee, or any other financial obligation; and other transactions or activity 'whether of a commercial, industrial, financial, professional or other similar character' concluded by a State 'otherwise than in the exercise of sovereign authority'.[3] But the Special Rapporteur did not reproduce these statements in his proposed text of draft article 2. Instead, his first version of the provision used the term 'trading or commercial activity', and defined it to mean a regular course of commercial conduct or a particular commercial transaction or act.[4] In addition, under the Special Rapporteur's scheme, draft article 2 was to be complemented by a succeeding provision which sought to clarify how to determine the commercial character of a trading or commercial activity. This provision emphasized the nature, rather than the purpose, of the activity.[5]

In response to comments in the Commission, Special Rapporteur Sucharitkul agreed that the definition of 'trading or commercial activity', together with the provision specifying the criterion for characterizing an activity, required refinement. He also conceded, 'having examined in more detail practice and decisions that had caused

[2] Preliminary report Sucharitkul, 241, para. 70.

[3] Preliminary report Sucharitkul, 241, para. 71. The Special Rapporteur noted, however, that government-to-government transactions required separate treatment.

[4] Second report Sucharitkul, 206, para. 33 (draft art. 2(1)(*f*)). This original iteration of draft art. 2 also contained the essence what is now Art. 2(3) UNCSI. See Second report, Sucharitkul, 206, para. 33. As the Special Rapporteur pointed out, Second report, Sucharitkul, 205, para. 28, the concept of commercial transaction extended to an entire series of acts or transactions within the meaning of 'a regular course of commercial conduct' or 'conduct traditionally associated with trade or commerce'.

[5] Second report, Sucharitkul, 211, para. 48.

hardship, particularly to the developing countries', 'that the test of the nature of the act, advocated by the Austrian and German courts, should not be an absolute one'.[6] For the sake of a 'more acceptable compromise',[7] the commercial transaction exception, the definition of 'trading or commercial activity', and the proposed guidance on the characterization of an activity were all referred to the Drafting Committee. The Committee in turn proposed a new draft article 2 which narrowed the scope of the exception, from proceedings arising out of 'trading or commercial activity' to proceedings arising out of a 'commercial contract', with the definition of the latter featuring the three categories of contract or transaction that would eventually appear in Article 2(1)(*c*) of the Convention.[8] In addition, responding to concerns over the emphasis on the nature of the impugned act, the Drafting Committee amended the succeeding provision to refer to both the nature and the purpose of the contract.[9] As adopted on first reading in 1986, the latter draft article stated that, '[i]n determining whether a contract for the sale or purchase of goods or the supply of services is commercial, reference should be made primarily to the nature of the contract, but the purpose of the contract should also be taken into account if, in the practice of that [respondent] State, that purpose is relevant to determining the non-commercial character of the contract'.[10]

2.2 The ILC's second reading

On the basis of written comments and observations by governments and of the reactions of members of the Commission, the second Special Rapporteur, Motoo Ogiso, suggested a number of changes to the texts of the two draft articles as adopted on first reading. The main bone of contention was the provision on the characterization of a contract, the criteria specified in which many governments considered subjective and likely to result in legal uncertainty[11]—a view shared by the Special Rapporteur.[12] Opinion in the Commission was divided.[13]

Faced with divergent views, the Special Rapporteur declared that he had 'no objection to deleting the purpose criterion',[14] as proposed by a number of governments[15] and opposed by others,[16] but that he was well aware that 'the nature test also gives rise to difficulties'.[17] He therefore suggested that the nature of the act should be the primary reference point but that, if an international agreement between the parties stipulated that the contract was for a governmental purpose, 'that purpose should be taken into account

[6] Summary record 1730th ILC meeting, *YILC 1982*, vol. I, 195, 199, para. 28.

[7] Summary record 1730th ILC meeting (n. 6), 199, para. 28.

[8] See summary record 1805th ILC meeting, *YILC 1983*, vol. I, 285, 291, para. 67.

[9] Summary record 1805th ILC meeting (n. 8), 291, para. 68.

[10] Report ILC, thirty-eighth session, 8–9 (draft art. 3(2)).

[11] See Preliminary report Ogiso, 102, para 36.

[12] Report ILC, forty-first session, 100, paras 421–422; Second report Ogiso, 65, para. 19.

[13] See Report ILC, forty-first session, 101, paras 434–435. The views included deleting any reference to the purpose, insisting on the primacy of the nature criterion, treating the purpose test as supplementary to the nature test if the latter did not yield a clear result, and giving both tests equal importance.

[14] Preliminary report Ogiso, 102, para. 39. Elsewhere the Special Rapporteur even stated that he 'basically support[ed] the deletion of the purpose criterion'. See Y. Iwasawa, 'Japan's Interactions with International Law: the Case of State Immunity', in N. Ando (ed.), *Japan and International Law: Past, Present and Future* (The Hague: Kluwer, 1999), 123, 144, fn. 81.

[15] Preliminary report Ogiso, 102, para. 36.

[16] Preliminary report Ogiso, 102 para. 39.

[17] Second report Ogiso, 63 para. 12.

in determining the non-commercial character of the contract'.[18] The proposal met with criticism from certain governments and certain members of a still-divided Commission.[19] In response, the Special Rapporteur proposed next that, while the primary criterion should remain the nature of the transaction, 'the court of the forum State should be free to take a governmental purpose into account also'.[20] In addition, taking up a suggestion by many governments, the Special Rapporteur suggested that what were then draft articles 2 (on use of terms) and 3 (on characterizing a contract) be consolidated.[21] Furthermore, the Special Rapporteur was prepared to replace the term 'contract' with 'activity' or 'transaction', the terms originally proposed by Special Rapporteur Sucharitkul, but stated that he could do so 'only with clear guidance from the Commission'.[22] On the whole, he suggested that all these outstanding questions should, in light of the various proposals made, be referred back again to the Drafting Committee.[23]

The Drafting Committee extended the scope of the exception in what is now Article 10 by replacing 'contract' with 'transaction', which, having a technically less precise meaning, covered a wider range of acts[24] and which was preferred by some members of the ILC and some delegates to the Sixth Committee.[25] The Drafting Committee also reworked a number of other terms relating to the categories of commercial transaction.[26] As for the characterization provision, the Drafting Committee, after much discussion, was 'unable to reach agreement on any other formulation and . . . therefore decided to retain the text adopted on first reading'.[27] The savings clause also remained substantively unchanged.[28]

In the event, draft article 2 as finally adopted on second reading in 1991 read in relevant part:

1. For the purposes of the present articles:

   . . .

   (*c*) 'commercial transaction' means:

   (i) any commercial contract or transaction for the sale of goods or supply of services;

   (ii) any contract of a financial nature, including any obligation of guarantee or of indemnity in respect of any such loan or transaction;

   (iii) any other contract or transaction of a commercial, industrial, trading or professional nature, but not including a contract of employment of persons.

2. In determining whether a contract or transaction is a 'commercial transaction' under paragraph 1(*c*), reference should be made primarily to the nature of the contract or transaction, but its purpose

[18] Second report Ogiso, 100, para. 423 (draft art. 2(3)). See also Second report Ogiso, 65, para. 19 *in fine*.

[19] Third report Ogiso, 8, para. 7. The majority of States pleaded in favour of an exclusive 'nature' test. See 'Comments and observations received from Governments', *YILC 1988*, vol. II(I), 45, 56 para. 5 (Aut), 70, para. 4 (FRG), 73, para. 5 (Ita), 77, para. 2 (Nordic countries), 78, paras 2–7 (Qat), 85, paras 8–10 (UK). See also 'Comments and observations', 80, para. 5 (Spa). On the other hand, see 'Comments and observations', 64, para. 5 (Cze).

[20] Third report Ogiso, 8, para. 8. It is ironic that this is an outcome the Special Rapporteur had wanted in his Preliminary report to avoid and that, while the Commission was unsympathetic to it, it forms the gist of Art. 2(2) of the Convention as eventually adopted.

[21] Third report Ogiso, 100, para. 423. See also Preliminary report Ogiso, 101, para. 29 (draft art. 2).

[22] Third report Ogiso, 102, para. 440.

[23] Third report Ogiso, paras 441–442.

[24] Summary record 2191st ILC meeting, *YILC 1990*, vol. I, 306, 309, para. 34.

[25] See Third report Ogiso, 8, para. 6. See also ILC commentary, draft art. 2, para. 20.

[26] The words 'or purchase' in sub-subparagraph (i) were deleted as superfluous, since every sale necessarily involves a purchase. As for sub-subparagraph (ii), the Committee took account of the fact that an obligation of guarantee or indemnity could exist in respect not only of a loan but also of other transactions of a financial nature. See summary record 2191st ILC meeting (n. 24), 310, paras 35–37.

[27] Summary record 2191st ILC meeting (n. 24), 309, para. 39.

[28] See summary record 2191st ILC meeting (n. 24), 309, para. 40.

should also be taken into account if, in the practice of the State which is a party to it, that purpose is relevant to determining the non-commercial character of the contract or transaction.

3. The provisions of paragraphs 1 and 2 regarding the use of terms in the present articles are without prejudice to the use of those terms or to the meanings which may be given to them in other international instruments or in the internal law of any State.

The baton now passed to the Sixth Committee of the General Assembly.

2.3 Further developments (1991–2004)

When the Commission referred the draft articles to the General Assembly, paragraph 2 of draft article 2 remained one of the major points of disagreement within the Commission and among governments.

In 1992, the Chairman of the open-ended Working Group of the Sixth Committee suggested a streamlined reformulation of the definition of 'commercial transaction', and proposed two alternatives for draft article 2(2).[29] He also drew attention to a proposal on draft article 2(2) communicated to him by former Special Rapporteur Ogiso, which envisaged a peculiar reference to the purpose test in exceptional circumstances relating to the supply of food or medicine.[30] The proposals were discussed in the Working Group the following year, when the Chairman and several delegations proposed further compromises.[31] But agreement remained elusive. In 1994, informal consultations resulted in the suggestion to give States 'the option of indicating the potential relevance of the purpose criterion under their national law and practice either by means of a general declaration in relation to the convention or a specific notification to the other party by whatever means in relation to a particular contract or transaction, or a combination thereof'.[32] This too was rejected.

In 1999, the ILC Working Group established to examine the outstanding issues in relation to the draft articles, having reviewed the work undertaken and the recent case-law, proposed seven alternative solutions to the problem of the definition of a commercial transaction. Given the longstanding differences of opinion, and given that it 'felt that the distinction between the so-called nature and purpose tests might be less significant in practice than the long debate about it might imply', the Working Group considered that the most acceptable course of action would be to delete draft article 2(2) altogether.[33] The idea was not, however, taken up. Over the course of the later efforts of the Working Group of the Sixth Committee, the Chairman put forward a range of alternative proposals and narrowed the choice of options,[34] but again to no avail.

It was not until the informal consultations conducted by Chusei Yamada in 2003 in the context of the Ad Hoc Committee on Jurisdictional Immunities of States and Their Property that a generally acceptable compromise was eventually reached.[35] The

[29] 1992 report Sixth Committee Working Group, 3, para. 13. The proposal attempted to combine the overlapping sub-subparas (i) and (iii) and partly to remove the circular element in the definition.

[30] 1992 report Sixth Committee Working Group, 4, para. 18. The reference was based on ILC commentary, draft art. 2, para. 26.

[31] See 1993 report Sixth Committee Working Group, 7–10, paras 36–48.

[32] Report Sixth Committee informal consultations, 3, para. 6.

[33] 1999 report ILC Working Group, 162, para. 60. See also 1999 report Chairman Sixth Committee Working Group, 3–4, para. 19 and 8, para. 58. In the words of H. Fox, *The Law of State Immunity* (2nd edn) (Oxford: Oxford University Press, 2008), 538, 'there was little that the ILC could do when the issue was referred back to it in 1999 other than to question what the fuss was about. And this is precisely what it did'.

[34] See eg 2000 report Chairman Sixth Committee Working Group, 6, para. 20 and 8, para. 25.

[35] See 2003 report Ad Hoc Committee, 2, para. 9 and 4 (draft art. 2(2)).

'dealmaker' in the final text of what became Article 2(2) of the Convention was that, absent agreement between the parties to the contract or transaction, the precondition to the exceptional additional reference to the purpose criterion was to be the practice of the forum, not respondent, State.

3. Key Points

3.1 Article 2(1)(*c*)

A. Structure and scope

Article 2(1)(*c*) of the Convention offers a three-pronged definition of 'commercial transaction' for the purposes of the Convention. Two of these prongs, namely sub-subparagraph (i) ('any commercial contract or transaction for the sale of goods or supply of services') and sub-subparagraph (ii) ('any contract for a loan or other transaction of a financial nature, including any obligation of guarantee or of indemnity in respect of any such loan or transaction'), deem a specific category of contract or transaction to be a 'commercial transaction'.[36] The third prong, sub-subparagraph (iii), offers a general, residual category of 'any other contract or transaction of a commercial, industrial, trading or professional nature, but not including a contract of employment of persons'. The definition in Article 2(1)(*c*) is supplemented by Article 2(2), which is designed to assist in the characterization of a contract or transaction.

Several types of contract or transaction are to be distinguished, for the purposes of the Convention, from a 'commercial transaction' in the sense of Articles 2(1)(*c*) and 10. Sub-subparagraph (iii) of Article 2(1)(*c*) stipulates that the term 'commercial transaction' does not cover employment contracts, which are the subject of a separate exception to immunity from jurisdiction, as provided for in Article 11.[37] Likewise, acts or omissions alleged to be attributable to the respondent State and giving rise to a claim for pecuniary compensation for death or personal injury or damage to or loss of tangible property lie outside the scope of the term 'commercial transaction', governed as they are by the exception to immunity from jurisdiction specified in Article 12.[38] This rules out reliance on Articles 2(1)(*c*) and 10 to circumvent the territorial condition laid down in Article 12. The same goes, *mutatis mutandis*, for the other exceptions to immunity from jurisdiction enumerated in Articles 13 to 17 of the Convention, all of which have been treated in some of the previous national practice as no more than instantiations of a generic exception in respect of commercial activity.

B. Interpretation and application

(i) General

As noted by at least one State[39] and two members of the ILC,[40] what became Article 2(1)(*c*)(i) and (iii) involve an element of circularity, insofar as the category of contract or

[36] These categories are drawn from those found in s. 3 SIA (UK) and in the corresponding provisions of the Commonwealth State immunity statutes inspired by it. See Third report Ogiso, 8, para. 6. See also ILC commentary, draft art. 2, para. 20, fn. 51; Fox (n. 33), 540.

[37] See the commentary to Art. 11 UNCSI.

[38] See the commentary to Art. 12 UNCSI.

[39] See Preliminary report Ogiso, 101, para. 26, referring to Thailand.

[40] See eg summary record 2115th ILC meeting, *YILC 1989*, vol. I, 135, 142, paras 56–57 (Christian Tomuschat); summary record 2119th ILC meeting, *YILC 1989*, vol. I, 167, 171, para. 41 (Awn Al-Khasawneh).

transaction that each deems a 'commercial transaction' relies on the undefined term 'commercial'. The Commission considered replacing the term 'commercial' in both sub-subparagraphs, but was unable, quite understandably,[41] to find an appropriate substitute.[42] On the other hand, the definition does not use what might be called the 'reverse circular' technique of deeming a transaction 'commercial' on the basis of its non-sovereign character, as is the case with section 3(3)(*c*) SIA (UK) ('otherwise than in the exercise of sovereign authority') and its imitators.[43] That is, Article 2(1)(*c*) does not explicitly rely on the *jure imperii/jure gestionis* distinction.

Article 2(1)(*c*) is important not only for the specific categories of contract or transaction it enumerates but also on account of its implications for the method of ascertaining the character of a contract or transaction, a matter further addressed in Article 2(2). The explicit terms of Article 2(1)(*c*)(ii) and (iii) dictate that the determination whether a contract or transaction is commercial is to be made by reference to the nature of that contract or transaction; and, given the interpretative context provided by sub-subparagraphs (ii) and (iii), the same no doubt applies with respect to sub-subparagraph (i). In other words, notwithstanding Article 2(2), the 'nature' test is embedded in Article 2(1)(*c*)'s definition of a 'commercial transaction'. This raises doubts as to the relevance in practice of Article 2(2).[44]

The definition in Article 2(1)(*c*) is not limited to contracts. The three prongs of the definition speak additionally and disjunctively of a contract 'or transaction', as per sub-paragraphs (i) and (iii), or a contract 'or other transaction', as per sub-subparagraph (ii). Neither the Convention nor the ILC commentary defines a 'transaction'.[45] What is clear, however, is that the term is intended to be broader than the term 'contract'.[46] At the same time, the ordinary meaning of the word 'transaction' implies the limitation of Article 2(1)(*c*) to situations involving some kind of deal or agreement, express or implied, between two or more parties. But neither the ordinary meaning of 'transaction' nor any of the sub-subparagraphs of Article 2(1)(*c*) demands that any benefit as may be conferred need be for consideration.[47]

According to the ILC commentary, the term 'transaction' further includes such non-contractual activities as business negotiations.[48] But the suggestion is not easily

[41] See C. Schreuer, *State Immunity: Some Recent Developments* (Cambridge: Grotius, 1988), 14 and 26.

[42] See ILC commentary, draft art. 2, para. 20.

[43] See also s. 5(3)(*c*) SIO (Pak); s. 4(3)(*c*) FStIA (SA); s. 5(3)(*c*) SIA (Sing). See also, not dissimilarly, s. 1 FSIL (Isr) ('which by its nature does not involve the exercise of governmental power').

[44] See section 3.2 .

[45] The ILC was well aware of the problems raised by the term when it decided to replace 'contract' by 'transaction'. See ILC commentary, draft art. 2, para. 20: 'The term "transaction" presents ... some difficulties of translation into other official languages, owing to the existence of different terminologies in use in different legal systems.'

[46] See ILC commentary, draft art. 2, para. 20. The Special Rapporteur maintained, however, that the replacement of the term 'contract' by 'transaction' 'did not entail any modification of the content of the definition'. See summary record 2158th ILC meeting, *YILC 1990*, vol. I, 61, 65, para. 6.

[47] That no requirement of consideration flows from the ordinary meaning of the word 'transaction' is borne out by the fact that, in many national legal systems of the civil law tradition, legally recognized transactions, of which a contract is a subspecies within the logic of Art. 2(1)(*c*), do not require consideration. Moreover, even in the common law tradition, where contracts require consideration, the broader term 'transaction'—as used in the relevant State immunity legislation alongside the term 'contract'—'arguably encompasses not only contracts but also gifts and non-binding statements such as letters of comfort'. See A. Dickinson, R Lindsay, and J.P. Loonam (eds), *State Immunity: Selected Materials and Commentary* (Oxford: Oxford University Press 2004), 360.

[48] ILC commentary, draft art. 2, para. 20.

reconciled with the text of Article 2(1)(*c*). Such a broad understanding could only be based on the expression 'engages in' as used in Article 10(1) ('If a State engages in a commercial transaction'), which was substituted during the drafting for the earlier expression 'enters into'. 'Engaging in' a transaction is perhaps a more expansive notion than the mere execution of a transaction.[49]

The term 'transaction', while broader than 'contract', is narrower than 'activity', a term frequently used in State immunity legislation and case-law. This is an essential point of distinction with the SIA (UK) and its progeny.[50] It similarly distinguishes Article 2(1)(*c*) of the Convention from the 'commercial activity' exceptions found respectively in section 1605(*a*)(2) FSIA (US), section 5 SIA (Can), and Article 2(*c*) IFSJAC (Arg). This has important consequences in practice.[51] It is not evident from the record why the ILC decided to replace the term 'activity', as originally proposed by Special Rapporteur Sucharitkul, by the phrase 'contract or transaction'.[52] But it is likewise uncertain whether a 'transaction' within the meaning of Article 2(1)(*c*) of the Convention need be accompanied by an intention to create legal relations or to transfer legal title.

As a final general point, it is unlikely that the term 'commercial' requires that the contract or transaction in question be undertaken with a view to profit. It is true that the ILC commentary states that, '[i]n the view of one member [of the Commission], profit-making was the most important criterion for the determination of the commercial character of a contract or transaction, and should have been incorporated in the definition of "commercial transaction"'.[53] Furthermore, the ordinary meaning of the word 'commercial' might be thought to suggest a profit motive.[54] But there are good reasons seriously to doubt whether Article 2(1)(*c*) requires that the contract or transaction be engaged in with an eye to profit.

First, insistence on an intention to make a profit would re-introduce a teleological element reminiscent of the 'purpose' test, which would be at odds with the express reference to the 'nature' of the contract or transaction in Article 2(1)(*c*)(ii) and (iii) and with the explicitly exceptional and ancillary role accorded to the purpose of the contract or transaction by Article 2(2).[55]

Secondly, many examples of what have generally been considered 'commercial' contracts, 'commercial' transactions, or 'commercial' activity have been engaged in by the respondent State with no view to profit. This is especially true as regards procurement contracts[56] and transactions for professional services—contracts and transactions

[49] See the commentary to Art. 10 UNCSI.

[50] See s. 3(3)(*c*) SIA (UK); s. 5(3)(*c*) SIO (Pak); s. 4(3)(*c*) FStIA (SA); s. 5(3)(*c*) SIA (Sing). See too s. 11(3) FStIA (Aus) ('or a like activity in which the State has engaged'); s. 1 FSIL (Isr) ('or activity').

[51] See section 3.1(B)(ii).

[52] See n. 8.

[53] ILC commentary, draft art. 2, para. 20. The issue was raised by several members. See eg summary record 2115th ILC meeting, (n. 40), 142, para. 58 (Christian Tomuschat); summary record 2118th ILC meeting, *YILC 1989*, vol. I, 160, 162, para. 15 (Abdul Koroma). See also Fourth report Sucharitkul, 211, para. 47.

[54] Adopting this line of reasoning, the Supreme Court of the Philippines has stated that if an act is not undertaken for gain or profit it is to be considered as performed in the exercise of sovereign authority. See *Holy See v Starbright Sales Enterprises Inc*, 102 ILR 163, 171 (Phi (SC) 1994).

[55] See 'Comments and observations' (n. 19), 78, paras 2–3 (Qat).

[56] See eg US Congress, House of Representatives (94th Cong., 2d Sess.), Report No. 94-1487, reproduced in (1976) 15 ILM 1398, 1406: 'Such contracts should be considered to be commercial contracts, even if their ultimate object is to further a public function.'

typically engaged in by the State without any thought of profit. Indeed, the judicial practice of States by and large does not support the view that the word 'commercial' in the 'commercial transaction' or equivalent exception to State immunity necessitates a profit motive. For example, in the United States, the Supreme Court has disapproved of making a profit motive a condition of commerciality.[57] Cases in which a view to profit has been considered relevant are the exception.[58] In this light, it would be surprising were the drafters to have intended the position to be different under the commercial transaction exception embodied in Article 2(1)(*c*) of the Convention.

Thirdly, it is telling that, while the ILC commentary mentions that one member of the Commission had proposed to include a profit requirement in the definition of 'commercial transaction', the Commission as a whole, in both the text of and commentary to what became Article 2(1)(*c*), decided not to include such a requirement.

In sum, the better view is that, while a view to profit is an indication of commerciality,[59] it is not a condition of it.

(ii) The relevance of previous national case-law

There is a huge amount of case-law, prior to or otherwise outside the context of the Convention, on what national legislation or courts have styled variously the 'commercial transaction', 'commercial contract', or 'commercial activity' exception to a State's immunity from foreign jurisdiction. This case-law provides the background against which the Convention was elaborated and to this extent remains of interest. But it is critical that this practice be treated with caution when it comes to applying Article 2(1)(*c*) of the Convention, since it is often based on a conception or formulation of the commercial transaction or analogous exception that differs in some significant way from that eventually embodied in the provision.

First, in giving effect to the doctrine of restrictive State immunity, a number of jurisdictions have traditionally not distinguished among the various specific exceptions to immunity from jurisdiction laid down in Part III of the Convention, invoking instead a single, generic commercial exception covering all instances of non-sovereign activity, not just those falling within the commercial transaction exception as framed in Articles 2 and 10 of the Convention. This is particularly true for cases concerning personal injury and property-related rights, as regulated under the Convention by Articles 12 and 13 respectively.

Equally important is the fact that, in much of the case-law preceding or otherwise not based on the Convention, the corresponding exception relates to or embraces commercial 'activity' or 'conduct'.[60] In contrast, and the point merits reiteration, Article 2(1)(*c*)

[57] See *Republic of Argentina and Others v Weltover Inc and Others*, 100 ILR 510, 515 (US (SC) 1992), stating that 'the question is not whether the foreign government is acting with a profit motive'. See also *KJ International and Others v MV Oscar Jupiter*, 131 ILR 529, 535 (SA (SC) 1997), stating that a 'commercial transaction' may not necessarily be one with a 'commercial purpose'; Schreuer (n. 41), 10; Fox (n. 33), 541.

[58] See *Holy See v Starbright Sales Enterprises Inc* (n. 54). In *Judgment 12845/1990* (Gre (CA) 1990), in G. Hafner, M.G. Kohen, and S. Breau (eds), *State Practice Regarding State Immunities* (Leiden: Martinus Nijhoff/Council of Europe, 2006), GR/11, 391, 392, immunity was denied in relation to 'commercial, industrial, financial or other *lucrative* activities' (emphasis added). But 'lucrative' here—which, as it is, is a translation from the original Greek-language judgment—may be intended to mean no more than 'relating to money' (a.k.a. 'lucre'), rather than 'profitable'.

[59] See, in this light, US Congress (n. 56), 1406: 'Certainly, if an activity is customarily carried on for profit, its commercial nature could readily be assumed.'

[60] See s. 1605(*a*)(2) FSIA (US); s. 3(3)(*c*) SIA (UK); s. 5 SIA (Can); s. 5(3)(*c*) SIO (Pak); s. 4(3)(*c*) FStIA (SA); s. 11(3) FStIA (Aus); s. 5(3)(*c*) SIA (Sing); art. 2(*c*) IFSJAC (Arg); s. 1 FSIL (Isr).

nowhere uses the words 'activity', 'conduct', 'act', or the like, preferring instead only the more precise terms 'contract or transaction' or 'contract or other transaction'. In short, the Convention's commercial transaction exception is, at least on its face, narrower than the cognate exception found in some domestic jurisdictions, a difference that may have significant practical consequences. For example, English courts have struggled with whether economic or commercial torts—such as intentional interference with economic or business relationships—are covered by the commercial transaction exception in section 3 SIA (UK).[61] Under the residual category of such transactions recognized in section 3(3)(*c*) SIA (UK), which speaks of 'any other transaction or activity', it could reasonably be argued that they do. But since even the residual category of 'commercial transaction' provided for in Article 2(1)(*c*)(iii) of the Convention restricts the application of Article 10's commercial transaction exception to 'any other contract or transaction', it is unlikely that economic or commercial torts can be brought within it.

Finally, non-Convention case-law may rely for its characterization of the relevant transaction etc not on the 'nature' test but on a version of the 'purpose' test, which Article 2(1)(*c*) and (2) of the Convention treat as subsidiary and ancillary at best.

All these considerations suggest that domestic case-law not based on the wording of Article 2(1)(*c*) and (2) of the Convention is of only limited use in the interpretation and application of these provisions.

(iii) Article 2(1)(*c*)(i)

The first category of commercial transaction enumerated in Article 2(1)(*c*)—and, as previously embodied in customary international law, the ECSI, and national legislation, probably the most commonly litigated—is, in the words of sub-subparagraph (i), 'any commercial contract or transaction for the sale of goods or supply of services'. Comparison of the authentic-language versions of Article 2(1)(*c*)(i) confirms that the adjective 'commercial' qualifies both 'contract' and 'transaction',[62] although it is not apparent what, if anything, the word adds. The better view[63] is that any contract or transaction for the sale of goods or supply of services is *ipso facto* commercial and therefore satisfies Article 2(1)(*c*)(i).

By way of example,[64] the following contracts or transactions for the sale of goods or supply of services have been held to give rise to the commercial transaction or equivalent exception to a State's immunity from foreign jurisdiction: a charter agreement concerning a cargo ship;[65] the purchase of a fishing vessel;[66] the purchase of airline tickets;[67] a contract for repair or building works;[68] a contract for the supply of lumber to a foreign

[61] See Dickinson et al. (n. 47), 360–2.

[62] See eg the French ('Tout contrat ou transaction de caractère commercial') and Spanish versions ('todo contrato o transacción mercantil').

[63] See eg Fox (n. 33), 540.

[64] See also the examples given by Schreuer (n. 41), 18–20.

[65] *Victory Transport Incorporated v Comisaría General de Abastecimientos y Transportes*, 35 ILR 116–17 (US (SDNY) 1964).

[66] *Ocean Transport Co. v Republic of the Ivory Coast*, 63 ILR 11–12 (US (ED Lou) 1967).

[67] *Pakistans Ambassade (Pakistan) v Shah Travel ved Hermunir Hussein Shah* (Dan (SC) 1999), in Hafner et al. (n. 58), DK/4, 310.

[68] *Claim against the Empire of Iran Case*, 45 ILR 57, 81 (FRG (FCC) 1963); *Planmount Limited v Republic of Zaire*, 64 ILR 268, 272 (UK (EWHC) 1980); *Brødrene Smith Entreprenørforretning v South Africa* (2001) 70 *NJIL* 550 (Nor (Eidsivating CA) 1992).

air force base;[69] the provision of public transport services;[70] a contract for the leasing of films;[71] an arms sale commission agreement;[72] the supply of telephone services;[73] a contract for the paid staging of concerts;[74] and a contract for public works.[75]

(iv) Article 2(1)(*c*)(ii)

The second category of 'commercial transaction' within the meaning of Article 2(1)(*c*) comprises, as per Article 2(1)(*c*)(ii), 'any contract for a loan or other transaction of a financial nature, including any obligation of guarantee or of indemnity in respect of any such loan or transaction'. The text of Article 2(1)(*c*)(ii) explicitly lays down that the decisive criterion for the commercial character of the transaction or contract is its financial 'nature'.

States' reliance in recent years on the private money market has increasingly led to private individuals acquiring rights under public loans or other similar financial instruments, while the ILC commentary observes that States not only raise loans in their own names but also guarantee loans raised by others.[76] The discernible judicial practice is nowadays more or less uniform in considering loan contracts, obligations of guarantee, and similar financial transactions in which a State engages to be commercial in character, with the consequence that the State does not enjoy immunity from proceedings in a foreign court in respect of them.[77] The sorts of similar financial transactions in question have included contracts concerning pension rights;[78] the assumption of mortgage obligations, including the obligation to pay interest;[79] a contract on negotiable promissory notes guaranteed by a foreign State;[80] an agreement for the provision of a 'time deposit'

69 *Carried Lumber Company v United States of America*, 64 ILR 661, 665 (Phi (CA) 1974).

70 *Red Nacional de Ferrocariles Espanoles v Mrs Cavaillé and Another*, 65 ILR 41, 42 (Fra (Montpellier CA) 1968).

71 *Arab Republic of Egypt v Cinetelevision International Registered Trust and Another*, 65 ILR 425, 432 (Swi (FT) 1979).

72 *Arms Sales Commission Agreement Case*, 65 ILR 119, 121 (FRG (Koblenz HRC) 1972).

73 *Individu v Consulat des Etats Unis d'Amerique* (Tur (CoC) 1989), in Hafner et al. (n. 58), TK/5, 674–5.

74 *United Euram Company v USSR et al.*, 63 ILR 228, 230 (US (SDNY) 1978).

75 *United States Government v Irsa*, 65 ILR 262, 264 (Ita (CoC) 1963) (construction of drains for military forces of a foreign State).

76 See ILC commentary, draft art. 2, para. 22.

77 See eg *Consorzio Agrario della Tripolitania v Federazione Italiana Consorzi Agrari and Cassa di Risparmio della Libia*, 65 ILR 265, 267 (Ita (CoC) 1966); *Steinmetz v Hungarian People's Republic*, 65 ILR 15, 19 (Aut (SC) 1970); *Central Bank of Nigeria Case*, 65 ILR 131, 136 (FRG (Frankfurt HRC) 1975) and (FRG (Frankfurt HRC) 1976); *Trendtex Trading Corporation v Central Bank of Nigeria*, 64 ILR 111, 132 (UK (EWCA) 1977); *National American Corporation v Federal Republic of Nigeria and Central Bank of Nigeria*, 63 ILR 137, 154–5 (US (SDNY) 1978) (affirmed on a different point by 597 F.2d 314 (US (2nd Cir.) 1979); *Banque Camerounaise de Développement v Société des Etablissement Rolber* (1987) 91 *RGDIP* 773 (Fra (CoC) 1986); *Meadows and Another v Dominican Republic and Another*, 98 ILR 37, 42 (US (9th Cir.) 1987); *Reef Shipping Co Ltd v The Ship Fua Kavenga*, 90 ILR 556, 566 (NZ (HC) 1987); *Yrityspankki Skop Oy v Republic of Estonia* (Fin (Helsinki DC) 1998), in Hafner et al. (n. 58), FIN/16, 335, 336; *Banque Bruxelles Lambert and Others v Republic of Paraguay* (Swi (FT) 1998), in Hafner et al. (n. 58), CH/12, 623, 629. It is worth noting that States often agree to submit to arbitration in these situations, bringing into play, in addition to Arts 2(1)(*c*)(ii) and 10, Art. 17 of the Convention. For details, see the commentary to Art. 17.

78 *Caisse d'Assurance Vieillesse des Non-Salariés v Caisse Nationale des Barreaux Français*, 65 ILR 70, 72 (Fra (CoC) 1977).

79 *Hungarian Embassy Case*, 65 ILR 110, 112 (FRG (FSC) 1969).

80 *Shapiro v Republic of Bolivia*, 98 ILR 110, 115 (US (2nd Cir.) 1991) stating: 'It is self-evident that issuing public debt is a commercial activity within the meaning of Section 1605(*a*)(2) [FSIA].'

as a form of loan;[81] the sale of certificates of deposit;[82] and the sale of shares in a company by a central bank of a foreign State to another bank owned by that State (and taking on the role as that State's new central bank).[83]

One species of financial transaction of particular note in this regard is the issuance of bonds. For the first half of the twentieth century, State loans were mostly[84] considered a matter appertaining to the sovereign power of the State, with the result that State immunity was retained in respect of them.[85] Today, the issuance of State bonds is generally viewed as coming within the purview of the 'commercial transaction' or equivalent exception. In *Republic of Argentina v Weltover Inc*, for example, the US Supreme Court considered the issuance of bonds by a foreign State to be a commercial transaction.[86] Courts of other States have in principle taken the same position.[87]

Many disputes concerning financial transactions and raising questions of State immunity involve the conduct of a foreign State's central bank. In such cases, it can be difficult to draw the line between sovereign and commercial transactions, since the mandate of a central bank can encompass both. It is therefore not surprising that disputes of this sort have led to divergent results. In the majority of cases, foreign national or central banks, when carrying out measures of currency or foreign exchange control, have been considered to be acting in the exercise of sovereign authority, and their conduct has not been characterized as a commercial transaction.[88] Under the Convention the decisive point here is whether the dispute arises out of a commercial contract or other transaction, and this is to be decided by determining the contract or other transaction's nature, according to Article 2(1)(*c*)(ii). It is only where the initial commercial nature of the transaction changes over time that

[81] *Banque Centrale de la République de Turquie v Weston Compagnie de Finance et d'Investissement SA and Another*, 65 ILR 417, 423 (Swi (FT) 1978).

[82] *Callejo v Bancomer*, 84 ILR 106, 114 (US (5th Cir.) 1985).

[83] *Banca Carige SpA Cassa die Risparmio Genova e Imperia v Banco Nacional de Cuba and Another*, 124 ILR 550, 562–3 (UK (CD) 2001).

[84] A few jurisdictions considered State loans commercial. See (1932) 26 *AJIL Supp* 633, referring to cases from Belgium, Italy, and Switzerland.

[85] (1932) 26 *AJIL Supp* 633, referring to cases from the United States, the United Kingdom, and France. It is an irony of history that the Foreign Minister of Argentina argued at the Second Hague Peace Conference that national loans were to be considered sovereign acts. This was an aspect of the 'Drago Doctrine', which resulted in the Convention Respecting the Limitation of the Employment of Force for the Recovery of Contract Debts, The Hague, 18 October 1907, 3 *Martens Nouveau Recueil (sér. 3)* 414 (Drago-Porter Convention or Hague II 1907). See D.J. Hill, 'The Second Peace Conference at the Hague' (1907) 1 *AJIL* 671, 687–8. See also L.M. Drago, 'State Loans in Their Relation to International Policy' (1907) 1 *AJIL* 692, 695, arguing that State bonds 'constitute, in effect, an exceptional class of obligations, not to be confused with any other. They are issued by virtue of the sovereign power of the state, as is its currency, they are authorized by legislation and do not present any of the general characteristics of the contracts of private law'. Some eighty years later, the Argentine financial crisis produced case-law that is unambiguous in classifying financial transactions of this sort as commercial. See also 'Comments and observations' (n. 19), 74, para. 4 (Mex); *Victory Transport Incorporated* (n. 65), 116.

[86] *Republic of Argentina v Weltover* (n. 57), 515. See also the clear statement in *Shapiro v Bolivia* (n. 80). See also *Jackson v Peoples Republic of China*, 84 ILR 133, 138 (US (ND Ala) 1982); *Carl Marks & Co Inc v USSR*, 84 ILR 158, 169 (US (SDNY) 1987).

[87] See *Borri v Argentina*, ILDC 296 (IT 2005) (Ita (CoC) 2005) (although the Court ultimately upheld immunity in view of the subsequent 'sovereign' rescheduling of payments on the bonds); *X v Nauru Finance Corporation (The Republic of Nauru)* (2001) 44 *Japanese Annual of International Law* 204, 206 (Jpn (Tokyo DC) 2000).

[88] This can cause problems where a financial transaction is processed through the central bank for reasons of currency control. See *Blagojevic v Bank of Japan*, 65 ILR 63, 66 (Fra (CoC) 1976); *Banque Centrale de la République de Turquie v Weston* (n. 81), 423–4.

difficulties in characterizing an act may arise. But this goes to the prior question of individuation—that is, of ascertaining what precisely constitutes the 'transaction' for the purposes of the proceeding.[89]

(v) Article 2(1)(*c*)(iii)

The third category of 'commercial transaction' comprises, in the words of Article 2(1)(*c*)(iii), 'any other contract or transaction of a commercial, industrial, trading or professional nature, but not including a contract of employment of persons'. The idea behind sub-subparagraph (iii) of Article 2(1)(*c*) is to provide a relatively open-ended[90] residual category in accordance with which certain contracts or transactions not qualifying as commercial transactions under subparagraphs (i) and (ii) may nonetheless be characterized as such.

It is in sub-subparagraph (iii) of Article 2(1)(*c*) that the circularity of the Convention's definition of a 'commercial transaction' is most noticeable. According to the provision, a commercial transaction includes 'any other contract or transaction of a commercial... nature'. But the further species of commercial transaction cited, namely other contracts or transactions of an 'industrial, trading or professional nature', mitigate this vice. Furthermore, given the relatively clear and comprehensive categories in sub-subparagraphs (i) and (ii), recourse to the residual category in sub-subparagraph (iii) will be necessary only in exceptional circumstances.

An example of this residual category of commercial transaction that has arisen in domestic jurisprudence is the offer of a reward in exchange for information.[91]

C. The necessary prior task of individuation

Article 2(1)(*c*) is premised on the assumption that the contract or other transaction that forms the subject of the proceeding against the State is by nature unalloyed and static—that is, that it is wholly and at all times a 'commercial contract or transaction for the sale of goods or supply of services', as per sub-subparagraph (i); a 'contract for a loan or other transaction of a financial nature', as per sub-subparagraph (ii); or some 'other contract or transaction of a commercial, industrial, trading or professional nature', in the words of sub-subparagraph (iii). In reality, however, contractual relations and other transactions between private parties and States may be of a mixed or dynamic nature or both, so that, depending on which aspect or point of the contractual relation or transaction the court chooses to consider, this nature could be characterized as, variously, commercial, industrial, trading, or professional or, alternatively, something else, the last with the result that the contract or transaction falls outside Article 2(1)(*c*)(iii). In such circumstances, what is usually by far the more difficult task than characterizing and categorizing the contract or transaction is, as a precondition to such characterization and categorization, identifying precisely the subject-matter to which the proceeding, and therefore to which the question of the State's immunity from jurisdiction, is referable[92]—or, putting it another way,

[89] See the discussion at section 3.1(C).

[90] See Schreuer (n. 41), 18 and 26.

[91] *Guevara v Peru*, ILDC 804 (US 2006) (US (11th Cir.) 2006).

[92] Before seeking to identify the relevant conduct, a court will typically isolate the facts on which the claimant's cause of action is founded. As the question of the State's immunity from jurisdiction must be addressed *in limine litis* on the basis of 'manifestly incomplete' evidence, this can be no mean feat. See *I° Congreso del Partido*, 64 ILR 308, 330 (UK (HL) 1981) (Lord Bridge); J. Crawford, 'International Law and Foreign Sovereigns: Distinguishing Immune Transactions' (1983) 54 *BYIL* 75, 96, fn. 80. As suggested in I. Brownlie, *Principles of Public International Law* (7th edn) (Oxford: Oxford University Press, 2008), 332,

determining whether, in the words of Article 10(1)'s embodiment of the commercial transaction exception, the proceeding is one 'arising out of [a] commercial transaction'.[93] This task, performed by courts often 'unconsciously and without much reflection',[94] is referred to in the literature as 'individuation',[95] and requires the court to differentiate between, on the one hand, the immediate or proximate and, on the other, the remote or ulterior aspects of the claim.[96]

Individuation is the feature of proceedings implicating Article 2(*c*)(iii) that is most likely to lead to divergence between courts, even within the same jurisdiction, and (where permitted) among individual judges in the same case. As in some national case-law outside the confines of the Convention, it may be that whether a given contract or, more likely, other transaction is to be considered commercial, industrial, trading, or professional in nature will depend on a sort of preponderance test, according to which the chief aspects of the contract or other transaction are taken to determine its nature. Equally, it may be possible, particularly in cases involving change in the nature of a transaction over time,[97] to tease apart distinct stages or other elements of the transaction and to focus on that stage or element out of which the claimant's cause of action most directly arises. Either way, the Convention itself provides no guidance on the question.

All this said, many of the problems that have arisen in municipal case-law in relation to individuation will likely be avoided under Article 2(1)(*c*), given its relatively restricted scope. It is primarily owing to such broad concepts as commercial 'activity' and commercial 'conduct', terms not used in Article 2(1)(*c*),[98] that difficulties of individuation arise. Under Article 2(1)(*c*), it will be enough in most cases simply to look to the underlying contract or transaction to determine whether or not it comes within the definition of a 'commercial transaction'.

3.2 Article 2(2)

A. Essence, structure, and scope

As the drafting history of Article 2(2) shows, the method of determining the character of a transaction was one of the most disputed questions in relation to the commercial

considerations of causation may assist in delineating the factual basis of the claim. But these will not always be sufficient where the dispute has its origin in a variety of concurrent factors. See *Callejo v Bancomer* (n. 82), 114.

93 Art. 10(1) provides: 'If a State engages in a commercial transaction with a foreign natural or juridical person and, by virtue of the applicable rules of private international law, differences relating to the commercial transaction fall within the jurisdiction of a court of another State, the State cannot invoke immunity from that jurisdiction in a proceeding arising out of that commercial transaction.' Unfortunately the Convention does not clarify what the expression 'arising out of' really means. See D.P. Stewart, 'The UN Convention on Jurisdictional Immunities of States and Their Property' (2005) 99 *AJIL* 194, 199. See also the commentary to Art. 10.

94 Schreuer (n. 41), 15.

95 Crawford (n. 92), 94–9; Fox (n. 33), 515.

96 Crawford (n. 92), 96.

97 In most cases of change of activity over time, courts have focused on the initial commercial character of the transaction, rather than the supervening sovereign intervention. See eg *Josefina Najarro de Sanchez v Banco Central de Nicaragua*, 88 ILR 76 (US (5th Cir.) 1985); *I°Congreso del Partido* (n. 92), 327 (Lord Diplock); *Banque Centrale de la République de Turquie v Weston* (n. 81), 424; *Argentina v Weltover* (n. 57). But see *Borri v Argentina* (n. 87), criticized by B.I. Bonafé, 'State Immunity and the Protection of Private Investors: The Argentine Bonds Case before Italian Courts' (2006) 16 *IYIL* 165 and E. Handl, 'Immunitätsrechtliche Probleme in Zusammenhang mit Argentinienanleihen-Klagen in Deutschland, Italien und den USA', in S. Wittich et al. (eds), *Beiträge zum 33. Österreichischen Völkerrechtstag 2008* (Bern: Peter Lang, 2009) 69, 71–9.

98 See section 3.1(B)(ii).

transaction exception. Two competing approaches have traditionally been adopted, one referring to the purpose of the transaction, the other to its nature. Article 2(2) acknowledges both but does not place them on an equal footing, instead according primacy to the 'nature' test. In this way, the provision departs from the original understanding of restrictive State immunity, which posited that States enjoyed immunity in respect of acts undertaken for a public purpose, but is in line with the majority of subsequent State practice, which, given the subjectivity of the 'purpose' test,[99] has embraced the 'nature' test. The reason for this shift was clearly expressed in the decision of the German Federal Constitutional Court in the *Empire of Iran* case, which rejected the 'purpose' criterion because 'ultimately, activities of the State, if not wholly then to the widest degree, serve sovereign purposes and functions'.[100] The Court concluded that '[a]s a means for determining the distinction between acts *jure imperii* and *jure gestionis* one should rather refer to the nature of the State transaction or the resulting legal relationships, and not to the motive or purpose of the State activity'.[101]

Article 2(2) begins by setting out a general proposition according to which, in determining whether a contract or transaction is a 'commercial transaction' in the sense of Article 2(1)(*c*), 'reference should be made primarily to the nature of the contract or transaction'. It continues, however, that '[the contract or transaction's] purpose should also be taken into account' in two instances: first, if the parties to the contract or transaction have so agreed; and, secondly, 'if, in the practice of the State of the forum, that purpose is relevant to determining the non-commercial character of the contract or transaction'. Comparison with the other authentic-language versions of the text of Article 2(2) fails to clarify whether the word 'primarily' in the general proposition is intended to mean 'in the first place'[102] or 'principally'.[103] Either way, it makes little sense, especially in the light of the exceptions posited. With this caveat, however, the gist of Article 2(2) would seem to be that, unless one of the two exceptions to the general proposition applies, the 'nature' test alone should be employed; and that if either of the exceptions applies, both the 'nature' test and the 'purpose' test should be used.

99 See Schreuer (n. 41), 15: 'The problem with the purpose test is, of course, that once we start inquiring into the underlying motives of the State partner to a transaction we will most probably end up with some political purpose somewhere. No matter how genuinely commercial an activity is, it can always be traced to some aspect of public welfare.' See also the references in Schreuer (n. 41), fn. 12.

100 *Empire of Iran* (n. 68), 80.

101 *Empire of Iran* (n. 68), 80. The Court's reasoning was widely followed by other European and non-European courts. See eg *Société anonyme des chemins de fer liégois-luxemburgois v Netherlands*, in Hafner et al. (n. 58), B/1, 263 (Bel (CoC) 1903); *Société de droit irakien Rafidain Bank et crts v Consarc Corporation*, in Hafner et al. (n. 58), B/6, 267 (Bel (CA) 1993); *Airport Linz v United States of America*, ILDC 3 (AT 2003), (2003) 8 *ARIEL* 423, 432 (Aut (SC) 2003) and S. Wittich, 'International Decisions' (2005) 99 *AJIL* 248; *Société Européenne d'Etudes et d'Entreprises (SEEE) en liquidité volontaire v Yugoslavia* (1972) 3 *NYIL* 290 (Nth (SC) 1973); *Russian Federation v Pied-Rich B.V.* (1994) 25 *NYIL* 512 (Nth (SC) 1993); *Kingdom of Morocco v Stichting Revalidatiecentrum 'De Trappenberg'* (1996) 27 *NYIL* 321 (Nth (SC) 1994); *United Arab Republic v Mrs X*, 65 ILR 385, 390 (Swi (FT) 1960); *I° Congreso del Partido* (n. 92), 314 and 323; *Manuel Ventura Arroja v Bolivia*, in Hafner et al. (n. 58), P/10, 511, 512 (Por (SC) 1997); *Brødrene Smith Entreprenørforretning v South Africa* (n. 68), 550; *X v Mayor of Shibuya Ward* (2008) 51 *JYIL* 533, 537 (Jpn (Tokyo DC) 2007); *Holy See v Starbright Sales* (n. 54), 171; *Barker McCormac Ltd v Kenya*, 84 ILR 18, 35–6 (Zim (HC) 1985); *Republic of Argentina v Weltover* (n. 57), 515–17.

102 See eg the French text ('en premier lieu').

103 See eg the Spanish text ('principalmente').

Article 2(2) is referable, at least in principle, to all three categories of commercial transaction enumerated in Article 2(1)(*c*). That said, in most if not all cases, the application of sub-subparagraphs (i) and (ii) of Article 2(1)(*c*) will yield sufficiently clear results, so that resort to Article 2(2) will be necessary only, if at all, when considering the residual category of commercial transaction in Article 2(1)(*c*)(iii).[104] Even then, however, the role to be played by Article 2(2) is far from clear, given that the 'nature' test is embedded in Article 2(1)(*c*)(iii)'s reference to 'any other contract or transaction of a commercial, industrial, trading or professional nature'.[105] It is perhaps for this reason that the merely hortatory word 'should', rather than the mandatory 'shall', is used throughout Article 2(2).

B. Refining the 'nature' test

Municipal courts sometimes face difficulties in determining the nature of a contract or transaction.[106] Various methods have been suggested, although the extent to which they will remain relevant when it comes to applying Article 2(1)(*c*) of the Convention, as elaborated on by Article 2(2), is a matter of speculation. On the one hand, no particular refinement of the 'nature' test is mentioned in Article 2(1)(*c*) or Article 2(2). On the other hand, past practice suggests that bare reference to the 'nature' of a contract or transaction may prove too abstract to be workable in and of itself. Against this backdrop, the chief refinements of the 'nature' test call for mention.

The most common refinement of the 'nature' test involves asking whether the contract or transaction could have been engaged in by a private party or, synonymously, is of a private-law character.[107] This inquiry may involve subjecting the specific features of the contract or transaction, including individual contractual terms, to detailed scrutiny. For example, one French court, concluding that the transaction at issue in the proceeding was commercial in nature, emphasized that '[t]he parties concluded the lease in the same form and with the same provisions as two ordinary private individuals might have used'.[108]

A second and by no means mutually exclusive method is to take account of 'the whole context in which the claim against the State is made',[109] even where this risks blurring the line between the characterization of the contract or transaction and the prior task of individuation. Lord Wilberforce advocated this contextual approach in *I°Congreso del*

[104] See also Fox (n. 33), 537 and 541.

[105] See also Fox (n. 33), 540, stating that the application of the three categories of Art. 2(1)(*c*)(i) 'is likely to make resort to the controversial criterion of commercial transaction in Article 2(2) largely unnecessary'.

[106] The question, which goes to the characterization of the transaction, is conceptually distinct from the logically prior question of individuation, which involves identifying of what the transaction consists.

[107] See eg the classic statement in *I°Congreso del Partido* (n. 92), 314 (Lord Wilberforce). In addition to the authority cited in Fox (n. 33), 506–7, see also eg *Maria Aparecida Pereira de Melo Cunha Brazão v Brazil*, in Hafner et al. (n. 58), P/14, 515, 516 (Por (Lisbon DC) 2000; *Judgment 13,043/1988*, in Hafner et al. (n. 58), G/12, 392 (Gre (CA Athens) 1988).

[108] *Minister for Public Education of Portugal v Di Vittorio Associates*, 65 ILR 32, 35 (Fra (Casablanca TC) 1955). See, similarly, *United Arab Republic v Mrs X* (n. 101), 390, reasoning that the agreement between the claimant and the respondent State 'evince[d] all the characteristics of an agreement between two private persons'; *Italian Republic, Italian Ministry of Transport and Italian State Railways v Beta Holding SA and Another*, 65 ILR 394, 401 (Swi (FT) 1966), taking the view that 'the transaction ... ha[d] all the characteristics of a contract of purchase of share certificates governed by private law'; *NV Cabolent v National Iranian Oil Co.*, 47 ILR 138, 147 (Nth (The Hague CA) 1968), holding that 'the agreement contains many provisions of a private law nature'.

[109] *I°Congreso del Partido* (n. 92), 318.

Partido,[110] and it has subsequently been applied by the English courts and adopted by other common law jurisdictions.[111]

Some past refinements of the 'nature' test, however, are implicitly ruled out by the terms of the Convention. For example, the Swiss courts regularly weigh the foreign State's interest in benefiting from immunity against the forum State's interest in exercising jurisdiction and the individual's interest in obtaining judicial relief.[112] There is no scope for such an approach under Article 2(1)(*c*) and (2) of the Convention. Equally, some courts have looked to the parties involved in the contract or transaction, drawing a distinction between contracts or transactions engaged in by a State organ and those engaged in by a State agency, instrumentality, or other entity, with the latter indicating commerciality.[113] This approach is manifestly contraindicated for the purposes of the Convention by the definition of 'State' in Article 2(1)(*b*), especially Article 2(1)(*b*)(iii), and by Article 10(3).

C. *The exceptions*

It is not easy to see how additional recourse to the 'purpose' test can be reconciled with the text of Article 2(1)(*c*), which refers expressly in sub-subparagraphs (ii) and (iii) to the nature of the contract or transaction,[114] without mentioning its purpose. Nonetheless, Article 2(2) admits of two exceptional circumstances in which the contract or transaction's purpose may be taken into account alongside its nature.

(i) Agreement between the parties

The first exception to Article 2(2)'s exhortation to refer 'primarily' to the nature of the contract or transaction reflects the principle of party autonomy. Article 2(2) provides that the purpose of the contract or transaction should also be taken into account if the parties to the contract or transaction have so agreed. Practical examples are likely to be rare, if only for the reason that the most the parties can agree to under Article 2(2) is that the 'purpose' test should be applied in addition to the 'nature' test. Party autonomy does not extend to agreeing that the 'purpose' test alone should be employed.

(ii) The practice of the forum State

According to the second exception to the general proposition posited in Article 2(2), the purpose of the contract or transaction should be taken into account in addition to its 'nature' if, 'in the practice of the State of the forum, [it] is relevant to determining the

[110] See *I° Congreso del Partido* (n. 92), 318.

[111] See *Holland v Lampen-Wolfe*, 119 ILR 368, 371–2 (Lord Hope), 375 (Lord Clyde), 381–2 (Lord Millett) (UK (HL) 2000). See also *Littrell v United States (No. 2)*, 100 ILR 438, 459–60 (Rose LJ), 463 (Hoffmann LJ) (UK (EWHC) 1992). For Canada, see *United States of America v Public Service Alliance of Canada and Others (Re Canada Labour Code)*, 94 ILR 264, 280 (Can (SC) 1992). For Australia, see *Reid v Republic of Nauru*, 101 ILR 193, 195–6 (Aus (Victoria SC) 1993); *Victoria Aircraft Leasing v USA*, 218 ALR 640, 646 (Aus (Victoria SC) 2005). For New Zealand, see *Reef Shipping Co Ltd v The Ship Fua Kavenga* (n. 77), 563–4. The contextual approach was also applied in *Commonwealth of Australia v Midford and Another*, 86 ILR 640, 651 (Mal (SC) 1990).

[112] The Swiss courts also rely on 'external indications' such as the place of the transaction, adopting in this way the contextual approach. See *S v Socialist Republic of Romania*, in Hafner et al. (n. 58), CH/11, 619, 623 (Swi (FT) 1987); *R v République d'Irak*, in Hafner et al. (n. 58), CH/5, 597, 599 (Swi (FT) 1994).

[113] See *Senghor v International Bank for West Africa and Republic of Senegal*, 113 ILR 460, 461 (Fra (CoC) 1990); *Arango et al. v Guzman Travel Advisors Corporation et al.*, 63 ILR 467 (US (5th Cir.) 1980); *X v Belgium* (2001) 6 *ARIEL* 288, 296 (Aut (SC) 2001).

[114] Recall section 3.2(A).

non-commercial character of the contract or transaction'. This second exception is of potentially greater significance than the first, given that the courts of a number of States—including those that profess to consider the nature of the contract or transaction the sole or primary criterion—rely in practice on the contract or transaction's purpose when distinguishing the commercial from the non-commercial. The practice of the Italian,[115] French,[116] Japanese,[117] and Austrian[118] courts, among others,[119] is illustrative of this. This practice would seem to reflect the epistemological, perhaps even ontological insight that, at least in certain cases, human acts can be meaningfully characterized only if some account is taken of their purpose or motivation.[120] In other words, in at least certain cases, the purpose of or motivation behind the contract or transaction is difficult to exclude altogether from the characterization calculus.[121]

3.3 Article 3(3)

Article 3(3) comprises a 'commonly used saving[s] clause',[122] according to which what Articles 2(1)(*c*) and 2(2) stipulate as to the use, for the purposes of the Convention, of the relevant terms is 'without prejudice to the use of those terms or to the meanings which may be given to them in other international instruments or in the internal law of any State'. The object of Article 2(3) is, for the avoidance of doubt, explicitly to confine to the Convention itself the meaning of the terms 'court', 'State', and 'commercial transaction', as defined in Article 2(1) and glossed in Article 2(2).[123] Similar provisions can be found in other international instruments.[124]

[115] See *FILT-CGIL Trento and Others v United States of America*, 128 ILR 649 (Ita (CoC) 2000). But Italian case-law on the matter is inconsistent. See S. Wittich, 'The Definition of Commercial Acts', in Hafner et al. (n. 58), 21, 35. Note that, in its observations to the ILC, Italy affirmed that it 'considere[d] the "nature test" to be in principle the sole criterion for determining the commercial character of a contract or transaction'. See UN doc. A/56/291/Add.1, 3, para. 7.

[116] The prevailing approach in the French courts is to look to the nature of the transaction. See eg *Spanish State v Société anonyme de L'Hôtel George V*, 65 ILR 61, 62–3 (Fra (CoC) 1973). See also *Euroéquipement SA v Centre Européen de la Caisse de Stabilisation et de Soutien des Productions agricoles de la Côte d'Ivoire and Another*, 89 ILR 37, 39 (Fra (Paris TdI) 1991), holding that 'the jurisdictional immunity invoked here ... must be examined ... in relation to the nature of the activity performed, which has given rise to the contract at issue'. At the same time, the Court of Cassation has on occasion taken into account that a transaction was motivated by the public interest, as in *Consorts Daninos v Société tunisienne de banque, Banque centrale de Tunisie, Société Banque franco-tunisienne et Etat tunisien* (2003) 92 *Revue critique de droit international privé* 296, 294 (Fra (CoC) 2002), or has invoked both the nature and ultimate aim *(finalité)* of the act, as in *X v Saudi School in Paris and Saudi Arabia*, ILDC 777 (FR 2003).

[117] See *X et al. v United States of America*, in Hafner et al. (n. 58), J/3, 696, and (2003) 46 *Japanese Annual of International Law* 160, 161 (Jpn (SC) 2002), stating that 'judging from the purpose or the nature of these activities, it is clear that they are sovereign acts'. See also *X v Mayor of Shibuya Ward* (n. 101), 537.

[118] See *Airport Linz v United States of America* (n. 101), 436, where the Austrian Supreme Court, while constantly emphasizing the primacy of the nature test, invoked sovereign purposes.

[119] See *Yrityspankki Skop Oy v Republic of Estonia* (n. 77), 336, stating that 'the nature and the purpose of the State transaction had conclusive significance'; *Local Authority of Västerås v Republic of Iceland*, in Hafner et al. (n. 58), S/8, 550 (Swe (SC) 1999); *United States of America v Public Service Alliance of Canada* (n. 111), 278 (La Forest J); *Reid v Republic of Nauru* (n. 111), 195–6; *Victoria Aircraft Leasing v USA* (n. 111), 646.

[120] See Crawford (n. 92), 95; Schreuer (n. 41), 16.

[121] See eg *I° Congreso del Partido* (n. 92), 323 (Lord Wilberforce): 'I agree that the purpose ... is not decisive but it may throw some light upon the nature of what was done.'

[122] Summary record 2191st ILC meeting (n. 24), 310, para. 40.

[123] See ILC commentary, draft art. 2, para. 29.

[124] See eg Art. 2(2) VCLT; Art. 2(2) Vienna Convention on Succession of States in Respect of Treaties: Art. 2(2) Vienna Convention on the Law of Treaties between States and International Organizations or between International Organizations.

This type of savings clause has become less common in recent codifications, no doubt because it is redundant in one respect and ineffective in another. As to its redundancy, it is simply not possible for a treaty's definition of a term used in that treaty—especially a definition explicitly stated to be '[f]or the purposes of' that treaty, as is the case with Article 2 of the Convention—directly to affect the meaning given to the same term as it appears in another international instrument or in a State's internal law. As to its inefficacy, such a clause does nothing to prevent any indirect influence that a treaty's definition of a term may exert, either through its hypothetical contribution to an understanding of the 'ordinary' meaning of that term or through reliance on it by way of persuasive authority by national legislatures or courts.

4. Evaluation

Article 2(1)(*c*) and (2) do not resolve completely the contentious issues raised by the notion of a 'commercial transaction' within the meaning of the commercial transaction exception to a State's immunity from the jurisdiction of the courts of another State, as provided for in the Convention in Article 10. But one may wonder whether any compromise text—for that is what Article 2(1)(*c*) and (2) are—could realistically have achieved this. Flaws notwithstanding, the Convention's definition of 'commercial transaction' is a step towards greater consistency in international practice,[125] even if the 'harmonization' optimistically referred to in the Preamble[126] is distinctly unlikely.

As Hazel Fox observes in relation to sub-subparagraphs (i), (ii), and (iii) of Article 2(1)(*c*), '[t]he listing of these three non-immune categories of transaction is an important clarification of the restrictive rule of immunity and is likely to receive wide recognition and application in national courts'.[127] As for the 'nature' versus 'purpose' debate, the distinction is less important in practice than the long controversy over it might imply.[128] That said, the formula adopted in Article 2(2), while based on previous case-law and a useful means of reconciling developing States with Article 2(1)(*c*), comes at the expense of logical coherence, with its exceptional accommodation of the 'purpose' test being at odds with the text of at least Article 2(1)(*c*)(ii) and (iii). It remains to be seen whether, and how, State practice finds a satisfactory solution to this problem.

[125] In *Svenska Petroleum Exploration AB v Lithuania* [2007] QB 886, 929, para. 132 (Moore-Bick LJ) (UK (EWCA) 2006), Art. 2(1)(*c*) and (2), along with Art. 10, were seen as 'reflecting current international thinking on the subject'.

[126] See Preamble (third recital) UNCSI and the commentary to the Preamble.

[127] Fox (n. 33), 540.

[128] See 1999 report ILC Working Group, 162, para. 60

Article 3

ROGER O'KEEFE

Article 3

Privileges and immunities not affected by the present Convention

1. The present Convention is without prejudice to the privileges and immunities enjoyed by a State under international law in relation to the exercise of the functions of:

   (*a*) its diplomatic missions, consular posts, special missions, missions to international organizations or delegations to organs of international organizations or to international conferences; and

   (*b*) persons connected with them.

2. The present Convention is without prejudice to privileges and immunities accorded under international law to heads of State *ratione personae*.

3. The present Convention is without prejudice to the immunities enjoyed by a State under international law with respect to aircraft or space objects owned or operated by a State.

1. Introduction

Article 3 preserves from the effect of the Convention certain other immunities recognized by international law. What it says ought to be relatively straightforward, but is needlessly complicated by the ILC's commentary to its forerunner. What it does not say makes things messier still.

2. Drafting History

Proposals for a safeguard clause in respect of other immunities owed to a State under international law were first advanced in the early stages of the ILC's work. The original proposal put forward by Special Rapporteur Sucharitkul provided:

The fact that the present articles do not apply to jurisdictional immunities accorded or extended to

(*i*) diplomatic missions under the Vienna Convention on Diplomatic Relations of 1961,
(*ii*) consular missions under the Vienna Convention on Consular Relations of 1963,
(*iii*) special missions under the Convention on Special Missions of 1969,
(*iv*) the representation of States under the Vienna Convention on the Representation of States in Their Relations with International Organizations of a Universal Character of 1975,
(*v*) permanent missions or delegations of States to international organizations in general, shall not affect

   (*a*) the legal status and the extent of jurisdictional immunities recognized and accorded to such missions and representation of States under the abovementioned conventions;

(*b*) the application to such missions or representation of States or international organizations of any of the rules set forth in the present articles to which they would also be subject under international law independently of the articles;

(*c*) the application of any of the rules set forth in the present articles to States and international organizations, non-parties to the articles, in so far as such rules may have the legal force of customary international law independently of the articles.[1]

The Special Rapporteur further proposed an accompanying article entitled 'Immunities of personal sovereigns and other heads of State', which read:

1. A personal sovereign or head of State is immune from the criminal and civil jurisdiction of a court of another State during his office. He need not be accorded immunity from its civil and administrative jurisdiction:
   (*a*) in a proceeding relating to private immovable property situated in the territory of the State of the forum, unless he holds it on behalf of the State for governmental purposes; or
   (*b*) in a proceeding relating to succession to movable or immovable property in which he is involved as executor, administrator, heir or legatee as a private person; or
   (*c*) in a proceeding relating to any professional or commercial activity outside his sovereign or governmental functions.
2. No measures of attachment or execution may be taken in respect of property of a personal sovereign or head of State if they cannot be taken without infringing the inviolability of his person or of his residence.[2]

The ILC's Drafting Committee was not convinced by the complexity of the first provision. Nor did it think it necessary to include a separate provision on head-of-State immunity, suggesting that the two articles be merged so as to deal with head-of-State immunity 'in general terms as a safeguard clause, without going into needless detail'.[3] The Committee's own proposed text provided:

1. The present articles are without prejudice to the privileges and immunities enjoyed by a State in relation to the exercise of the functions of:
   (*a*) its diplomatic missions, consular posts, special missions, missions to international organizations, or delegations to organs of international organizations or to international conferences; and
   (*b*) persons connected with them.
2. The present articles are likewise without prejudice to the privileges and immunities accorded under international law to heads of State *ratione personae.*[4]

The Commission adopted the Drafting Committee's text on first reading.

In response to the Secretary-General's invitation to member States to submit to the ILC written comments and observations on the draft articles as they then stood, Spain suggested 'that not only the privileges of heads of State but also those recognized for heads of Government, ministers for foreign affairs and persons of high rank should be included' in paragraph 2 of draft article 3, while the UK thought that 'certain persons connected with a head of State, e.g. members of his family forming part of his household and his personal servants, should be included'.[5] But Special Rapporteur Ogiso took up

[1] Second report Sucharitkul, 213, para. 54.
[2] Seventh report Sucharitkul, 45, para. 125.
[3] Summary record 1968th ILC meeting, *YILC 1986*, vol. I, 165, 167, para. 26.
[4] Summary record 1968th ILC meeting (n. 3), para. 24.
[5] Preliminary report Ogiso, 103, para. 46.

neither suggestion, since in his view the 'privileges and immunities of members of the family of heads of State, ministers for foreign affairs and persons of high rank [were] accorded rather on the basis of international comity than of established international law'.[6] One ILC member nonetheless questioned whether the confinement of what became Article 3(2) to heads of State was wise, 'since it was highly probable that they were not the only persons to enjoy the privileges and immunities to which the article referred'.[7] It was thought that '[i]t might... be appropriate to add the phrase "or other government officials" after "heads of State", in order to take account of the applicable rules of international law and thus leave open the possibility that there were other persons to whom certain privileges and immunities extended'.[8] Seven other members of the Commission argued for the specific inclusion of heads of government and ministers for foreign affairs,[9] with two of them arguing additionally, like Spain, for 'persons of high rank' or 'high-ranking officials'.[10] In response, the Special Rapporteur, although he did 'not object to the inclusion of a reference in paragraph 2 to those categories of persons whose privileges and immunities were not, strictly speaking, covered by international law', was confident that 'the Drafting Committee would no doubt take account in due course of the subtle difference between international law and international comity in that regard'.[11] In the event, nothing came of the various suggestions.

The Drafting Committee's acceptance of a proposal advanced by Australia and accepted by Special Rapporteur Ogiso to include after the words 'by a State' in the chapeau to paragraph 1 the words 'under international law',[12] along with the Committee's deletion from paragraph 2 of the definite article before the words 'privileges and immunities',[13] completed the text of the draft article as it was finally adopted by the ILC on second reading in 1991. The ILC commentary to draft article 3 explains that the provision was 'intended to preserve the privileges and immunities already accorded to specific entities and persons by virtue of existing general international law and more fully by relevant international conventions in force, which remain[ed] unaffected by the... articles',[14] and it refers in the latter respect to the conventions cited in Special Rapporteur Sucharitkul's original draft.[15]

[6] Preliminary report Ogiso, 103, para. 49.

[7] Summary record 2116th ILC meeting, *YILC 1989*, vol. I, 143, 143, para. 1 (Christian Tomuschat).

[8] Summary record 2116th ILC meeting (n. 7), 143, para. 1 (Christian Tomuschat).

[9] See summary record 2116th ILC meeting (n. 7), 147, para. 40 (Riyadh Al-Qaysi); summary record 2117th ILC meeting, *YILC 1989*, vol. I, 150, 157, para. 71 (Pemmaraju Sreenivasa Rao); summary record 2118th ILC meeting, *YILC 1989*, vol. I, 160, 161, para. 10 (Abdul Koroma), 163, para. 29 (Luis Solari Tudela), 164, para. 45 (Stanislaw Pawlak), 165, para. 56 (Emmanuel Roucounas); summary record 2119th ILC meeting, *YILC 1989*, vol. I, 167, 172, para. 43 (Awn Al-Khasawneh).

[10] Summary record 2118th ILC meeting (n. 9), 161, para. 10 (Abdul Koroma) and 163, para. 29 (Luis Solari Tudela) respectively.

[11] Summary record 2121st ILC meeting, *YILC 1989*, vol. I, 185, 193, para. 67.

[12] See Preliminary report Ogiso, 103, paras 44 and 50, and summary record 2191st ILC meeting, *YILC 1990*, vol. I, 306, 310, para. 42.

[13] See summary record 2191st ILC meeting (n. 12), 310, para. 42. The Chairman of the Drafting Committee explained, not altogether compellingly, that this made the text 'more flexible'.

[14] ILC commentary, draft art. 3, para. 1.

[15] See ILC commentary, draft art. 3, paras 2 and 3.

Draft article 3 as finally adopted in 1991 was left unaltered until 2002, when the Ad Hoc Committee on Jurisdictional Immunities of States and Their Property inserted paragraph 3 into what became Article 3 of the Convention so as to exclude from the instrument's scope the immunities enjoyed by a State in respect of aircraft or space objects owned or operated by that State.[16] The problem of these immunities had been raised late in the day during the ILC's preparation of its draft articles, and the Commission, 'while recognizing the importance of the question, felt that it called for more time and study'.[17] The issue was later discussed in the open-ended Working Group of the Sixth Committee, whose 1993 report recounted that some delegations opposed the inclusion of provisions on aircraft and space objects on the ground that 'this complex subject was governed by existing agreements and long-standing practice' but that others 'felt that the draft would be incomplete if it did not specifically address questions relating to the immunity of aircraft or space objects owned or operated by a State, including issues arising out of the sale, repair or detention of State aircraft'.[18] In the event, the Ad Hoc Committee, believing that the matter 'required substantial attention and appropriate consultations',[19] thought it wise explicitly to exclude such immunity from the scope of the Convention.

3. Key Points

3.1 'Without prejudice to'

'Without prejudice' clauses and analogous textual indicators,[20] a common feature of treaty law, seek to regulate conflict between a provision or provisions of the treaty in which they are included and specified other rules of international law by indicating in effect that the other rules of international law are to prevail in the event of inconsistency between them and the rules provided for in the treaty. Such clauses effectively direct that, should simultaneous application of both the rules in the treaty and the relevant other rules of international law prove logically impossible, the other rules are to be applied in preference to the rules laid down in the treaty. Clauses of this sort do not generate the other international rules to which they refer, the existence of such rules being simply a premise of the priority for which they provide. Should no such other rules in fact exist, the rules provided for in the treaty will apply as normal. Nor do 'without prejudice' and equivalent clauses render void the treaty rules in question. They go merely to the application, not the continued existence, of the inconsistent provisions of the treaty.

[16] See 2002 report Ad Hoc Committee, annex, 4, draft art. 3(3).

[17] Report ILC, forty-third session, 13, para. 24. The Chairman of the Commission's Drafting Committee had noted that the issue was 'a complex one', and, while it was thought likely that aircraft used for military, customs, and police service benefited from immunity, a 'thorough analysis of existing conventions, domestic legislation and case law' was considered necessary before a rule could be formulated. See summary record 2221st ILC meeting, *YILC 1991*, vol. I, 88, 96, para. 83. See also ILC commentary, draft art. 16, para.17.

[18] 1993 report Sixth Committee Working Group, para. 85. For the suggestion to include the issue, see 1992 report Sixth Committee Working Group, para. 35.

[19] 2002 report Ad Hoc Committee, annex, 9, draft art. 16(7) fn. 3.

[20] Other such indicators include clauses specifying that the treaty in question is 'subject to' or is 'not to be considered as incompatible with' certain rules of customary international law or treaty.

3.2 The Immunities Not Affected by the Convention

A. Diplomatic and consular immunities

Article 3(1), which finds more limited forerunners in Article 32 ECSI[21] and in the legislation of certain States,[22] safeguards from the effect of the Convention what are referred to as the privileges and immunities enjoyed by a State under international law in relation to the exercise of the functions of, first, its diplomatic missions, consular posts, special missions, missions to international organizations, delegations to organs of international organizations, and delegations to international conferences,[23] as per subparagraph (*a*); and, secondly, of persons connected with these missions, posts, and delegations, as per subparagraph (*b*). The content of these privileges and immunities is a function of customary international law[24] and, in the case of States parties to them, of the VCDR, the VCCR, the CSM, and the plethora of conventions regulating the privileges and immunities of, *inter alia*, the delegates of States to international organizations.[25] The reference to privileges, as distinct from immunities, in the chapeau to Article 3(1) is in reality otiose, since no provision of the Convention could be taken to impinge on any of the privileges recognized in diplomatic, consular, or cognate international law.

(i) Diplomatic missions, consular posts, etc

No treaty-based or customary rule of diplomatic, consular, or cognate international law provides for the immunity from proceedings in the courts of the receiving State of a diplomatic mission, consular post, special mission, mission to an international organization, delegation to an organ of an international organization, or delegation to an international conference. Nor does any such rule provide for the immunity of the ministry of foreign affairs or the government of the sending State or the sending State as such from proceedings in the courts of the receiving State in respect of the activities or property of any such mission, post, or delegation. While the premises of diplomatic missions, special missions, and missions to international organizations, along with their

[21] Art. 32 ECSI reads: 'Nothing in the present Convention shall affect privileges and immunities relating to the exercise of the functions of diplomatic missions and consular posts and of persons connected with them.'

[22] See s. 16(1), chapeau, SIA (UK); s. 17(1), chapeau, SIO (Pak); s. 19(1) SIA (Sing); s. 6 FStIA (Aus); art. 6 IFSJAC (Arg). See also, subsequently, s. 21 FSIL (Isr); and, in implementation of the Convention, the more general art. 3 ACJJFS (Jpn), which would appear to bring within the one provision the respective savings clauses found in Arts 3, 4 (opening words) and 26 UNCSI.

[23] According to ILC commentary, draft art. 3, para. 4, the expressions 'missions to international organizations' and 'delegations to organs of international organizations' are to be taken to include permanent observer missions and observer delegations.

[24] See ILC commentary, draft art. 3, para. 3. See also, in this connection, preamble (fifth recital) UNCSI, affirming that 'the rules of customary international law continue to govern matters not regulated by the provisions of the . . . Convention'. Most of the relevant provisions of the Vienna Convention on Diplomatic Relations (VCDR), Vienna Convention on Consular Relations (VCCR), and Convention on Special Missions (CSM) are consonant with customary international law, as are many of the relevant provisions of the Vienna Convention on the Representation of States in their Relations with International Organizations of a Universal Character (VCRS) (not in force).

[25] See ILC commentary, draft art. 3, para. 3. To the extent that these treaties provide for jurisdictional immunities, such immunities are also safeguarded by Art. 26 UNCSI ('Other international agreements'), which reads: 'Nothing in the present Convention shall affect the rights and obligations of States Parties under existing international agreements which relate to matters dealt with in the present Convention as between the parties to those agreements.'

furnishings, any other property on such premises[26] or, in the case of special missions, used in the operation of such premises,[27] and the means of transport of such missions, are specified as being immune from attachment and execution in the receiving State, nothing in diplomatic, consular, or analogous international law stipulates that a claimant is barred from bringing an action in the courts of the receiving State against the legal entity of the mission, post, or delegation or against the ministry of foreign affairs or government of the sending State or the sending State *eo nomine* in respect of that mission, post, or delegation.[28] Nor does the inviolability of the premises of diplomatic missions,[29] special missions,[30] and missions to international organizations,[31] let alone the attenuated inviolability of consular posts,[32] have any bearing on the question.[33]

It is true that—in a provision additional to their respective savings clauses for matters covered by the VCDR and VCCR[34]—the SIA (UK), SIO (Pak), and SIA (Sing) each specify that the exception in respect of the ownership, possession, or use of local immovable property to a foreign State's immunity from proceedings 'does not apply to proceedings concerning a State's title to or its possession of property used for the purposes of a diplomatic mission'.[35] As implicitly acknowledged, however, by its existence separate from the VCDR savings clause, this common provision goes beyond the strict requirements of diplomatic law. It is also true that Germany's Federal Constitutional Court held in 1962 that, although diplomatic law did not in all cases bar proceedings against a foreign State in respect of its diplomatic premises, it did bar proceedings that would 'adversely affect the mission in the performance of its diplomatic

[26] See Art. 22(3) VCDR and Art. 23(3) VCRS (not in force), as regards diplomatic missions and missions to international organizations respectively.

[27] See Art. 25(3) CSM, as regards special missions.

[28] See eg *Jurisdiction over Yugoslav Military Mission (Germany) Case*, 38 ILR 162, 163 and 169 (FRG (FCC) 1962), where the German Federal Constitutional Court, after a detailed analysis of State practice and scholarly writings, concluded, 169, that 'no general rule of international law is ascertainable according to which the local courts are precluded in all cases from exercising jurisdiction over actions against foreign States concerning their mission premises'. See also *767 Third Avenue Associates v Permanent Mission of the Republic of Zaire to the United Nations*, 99 ILR 194 (US (2nd Cir.) 1993), in which the appellant State did not appeal, and the US Court of Appeals for the Second Circuit—while overturning the challenged post-judgment measure of constraint in the form of an eviction order—affirmed, the part of the lower court's judgment awarding monetary damages for unpaid rent on the premises of the State's permanent mission to the UN, thereby accepting a fortiori the lower court's exercise of jurisdiction over that State. See too *VČ v Embassy of the Russian Federation to Latvia*, ILDC 1063 (LV 2007); *Guinea v Trovato*, Cass. 10294/1993, 18 October 1993 (Ita (CC) 1993), *Vespignani v Bianchi*, Cass. 13711/2004, 22 July 2004 (Ita (CC) 2004), and *Immobiliare Villa ai Pini srl v China*, Cass. 16461/2006, 19 July 2006 (Ita (CC) 2006), although *cf Italian Ministry of Foreign Affairs v Immobiliare Villa ai Pini srl and China*, ILDC 1371 (IT 2008) (Ita (CC) 2008). See, finally, the many cases cited in the commentary to Art. 11 UNCSI in respect of contracts of employment entered into by foreign States' embassies and consulates, where it is nowhere suggested that a foreign embassy or consulate, or the sending State in respect of the same, is *ipso facto* immune from proceedings in the receiving State.

[29] See Art. 22(1) VCDR.

[30] See Art. 25(1) CSM.

[31] See Art. 23(1) VCRS (not in force).

[32] See Art. 31(1) and (2) VCCR.

[33] See E. Denza, *Diplomatic Law: Commentary on the Vienna Convention on Diplomatic Relations* (3rd edn) (Oxford: Oxford University Press, 2008), 154: 'The modern law . . . draws a clear distinction between inviolability and immunity from jurisdiction . . . Inviolability . . . as elaborated in Article 22 [VCDR] does not in the absence of special provision confer protection from the jurisdiction of the courts of the receiving State.'

[34] See s. 16(1), chapeau, SIA (UK); s. 17(1), chapeau, SIO (Pak); s. 19(1) SIA (Sing).

[35] Section 16(1)(*b*) SIA (UK); s. 17(1)(*b*) SIO (Pak); s. 19(1), second limb, SIA (Sing).

functions'.[36] But it is difficult to see how the vague general principle *ne impediat legatio* can give rise to the immunity of the sending State from proceedings in relation to the mission when, applying the canon of construction *expressio unius exclusio alterius*, the clear implication from the VCDR's explicit provision for the immunity from attachment and execution of certain mission property[37] and for the personal immunity of diplomatic agents from the civil jurisdiction of the receiving State[38]—these rules being the specific instantiations of the general principle—is that no such immunity from proceedings subsists as a matter of customary international law, let alone treaty.

Since no special rule of diplomatic, consular, or cognate international law regulates the immunity from proceedings in the courts of the receiving State of the missions, posts, and delegations specified in Article 3(1)(*a*) of the Convention or of the ministry of foreign affairs or government of the sending State or the sending State sued as such in respect of the same, this immunity is regulated by the Convention. It is a question of restrictive State immunity pure and simple, just as it is under customary international law. That is, diplomatic and equivalent missions, consular posts, and the relevant delegations, when sued as such,[39] as well as any other appropriate legal manifestation of the sending State when sued in respect of the activities or property of any such mission, post, or delegation, enjoy immunity from proceedings in the courts of the receiving State only to the extent provided for in Parts II and III of the Convention.

It is a different story when it comes to the immunity of the immovable property of a mission from pre- and post-judgment measures of constraint in connection with proceedings in the courts of the receiving or indeed another State.[40] As mentioned above, the premises of diplomatic missions, special missions, and missions to international organizations, as well as their furnishings, any other property on such premises[41] or, in the case of special missions, used in the operation of such premises,[42] and the means of transport

[36] *Jurisdiction over Yugoslav Military Mission* (n. 28), 170. See also *Jurisdiction over Yugoslav Military Mission* (n. 28), 169.

[37] Recall Art. 22(3) VCDR.

[38] See Art. 31(1) VCDR. The VCDR and the other relevant conventions, taking account of the characterization by some national legal systems of proceedings in relation to certain matters mentioned in their provisions, speak of the 'civil and administrative' jurisdiction of the receiving State. For the sake of convenience, the following account employs the term 'civil' on its own to encompass all non-criminal proceedings.

[39] Such missions, posts, and delegations are to be considered organs of government within the meaning of Art. 2(1)(*b*)(i) UNCSI, and therefore count as a 'State' for the purposes of the jurisdictional immunities of States recognized in the Convention. See ILC commentary, draft art. 2(1)(*b*)(i), para. 6. See also the commentary to Art. 2(1)(*b*)(i).

[40] While the language of the chapeau to Art. 3(1)—which speaks of 'the privileges and immunities enjoyed by a State . . . in relation to the exercise of the functions of' its missions, etc—could be taken to refer only to the immunity of the State in its various guises from foreign proceedings, *viz* from jurisdiction (in the language of Parts II and III of the Convention), it must be taken also to encompass the immunity of the property of the State's missions, etc, from pre- and post-judgment measures of constraint in connection with any such proceedings, as would otherwise fall within Part IV of the Convention. First, it is clear from the *travaux* that what Art. 3(1)(*a*) safeguards from the effect of the Convention are the special immunity regimes established under the VCDR, VCCR, CSM, and customary international law; and these regimes cover both immunity from proceedings and immunity from measures of constraint in connection with them. Secondly, as it is, while the Convention speaks of the immunity of a State's property, as if the immunity inhered in the property itself, the legally more accurate characterization is that the immunity inheres in the State itself to the procedural benefit of its property.

[41] Recall Art. 22(3) VCDR and Art. 23(3) VCRS (not in force), as regards diplomatic missions and missions to international organizations respectively.

[42] Recall Art. 25(3) CSM, as regards special missions.

of such missions, are specified in the VCDR, CSM, and customary international law as being immune from attachment and execution in the receiving State.[43] In contrast, no rule of consular law serves to protect from attachment or execution the premises or movable property of a consular post.[44]

As it is, however, the Convention itself provides in Article 18 that '[n]o pre-judgment measures of constraint, such as attachment or arrest, against property of a State may be taken in connection with a proceeding before a court of another State unless and except to the extent that . . . the State has expressly consented to the taking of such measures . . . or . . . the State has allocated or earmarked property for the satisfaction of the claim which is the object of that proceeding'.[45] Equally, Article 19, read in combination with Article 21(1)(*a*), specifies that 'property, including any bank account, which is used or intended for use in the performance of the functions of the diplomatic mission of the State or its consular posts, special missions, missions to international organizations or delegations to organs of international organizations or to international conferences'[46] is immune from 'post-judgment measures of constraint, such as attachment, arrest or execution', unless the State has expressly consented to the taking of such measures or has allocated or earmarked property for the satisfaction of the claim the object of the proceedings.[47]

(ii) Persons connected with diplomatic missions, consular posts, etc

Subparagraph (*b*) of Article 3(1) declares the Convention to be without prejudice to the privileges and immunities enjoyed by a State under international law in relation to the exercise of the functions of persons connected with the missions, posts, and delegations mentioned in subparagraph (*a*). The wording of the provision, with its reference to the immunities 'enjoyed by a State under international law in relation to the exercise of the functions of' the persons in question, is infelicitous. Article 3(1)(*b*) could be taken to refer to the immunity of the sending State as such, of its government, or of its ministry of foreign affairs, as the case may be, from proceedings in the receiving State in respect of any conduct by persons connected with its missions, posts, or delegations for which the former may be legally answerable in the courts of the receiving State. Alternatively, it could be read as referring to the immunity *ratione personae* from which serving diplomats[48] benefit, along with the immunities *ratione materiae* from which former diplomats, serving and former consular officers and employees, and certain other persons connected with the sending State's missions or delegations benefit, if sued themselves in the courts of the receiving State—immunities which, even though serving to shield the relevant individuals from proceedings, are ultimately owed to the sending State itself.

[43] Recall Art. 22(3) VCDR; Art. 25(3) CSM; Art. 23(3) VCRS (not in force).

[44] A consular post may, however, operate from the premises of a diplomatic mission.

[45] See the commentary on Art. 18 UNCSI.

[46] Art. 21(1)(*a*) UNCSI. See the commentaries on Arts 19 and 21 UNCSI respectively.

[47] Art. 19 UNCSI. See the commentary on Art. 19 UNCSI.

[48] The term is used henceforth to refer to diplomatic agents within the meaning of Art. 1(*e*) VCDR; to members of the diplomatic staff of a special mission within the meaning of Art. 1(*h*) CSM; and to members of the diplomatic staff of a mission to an international organization within the meaning of the VCRS (not in force). For the sake of convenience, it does not refer to the members of the diplomatic staff of a delegation to an organ of an international organization or to an international conference, the circumscribed immunities posited in respect of which in the VCRS (not in force) are not without controversy.

The ambiguity is compounded by the ILC commentary to draft article 3(1), which reads in relevant part:

> The article is intended to leave existing special regimes unaffected, especially with regard to persons connected with the missions listed. Their immunities may also be regarded, in the ultimate analysis, as State immunity, since the immunities enjoyed by them belong to the State and can be waived at any time by the State or States concerned.[49]

On the one hand, Article 3(1)(*b*) of the Convention, which is identical to the draft version, is supposedly intended to preserve the 'existing special regimes' of immunity with regard to the persons specified, the only such regimes being the regimes of immunity *ratione personae* and *ratione materiae* from which, variously, serving and former diplomats, consular officers and employees, and specified other persons connected with missions and delegations benefit under international law.[50] On the other hand, these same immunities are supposedly capable of being regarded as State immunity—the immunity the subject of the Convention, from the effect of which the 'existing special regimes' of immunity at issue in Article 3(1)(*b*) are avowedly sought to be preserved and as expressions of which at least the immunity *ratione personae* accorded to diplomats can in no way be conceptually characterized.[51] The waters are muddied further by a comparison of the wording of Article 3(1)(*b*) with that of Article 3(2), which refers explicitly to 'privileges and immunities accorded under international law to heads of State *ratione personae*'.

In the final analysis, nonetheless, it is sufficiently evident that what Article 3(1)(*b*) seeks to safeguard from the effect of the Convention are the special regimes of immunity *ratione personae* and *ratione materiae* from which, variously, serving and former diplomats, consular officers and employees, and specified other persons connected with missions and delegations benefit in the event that they are sued in the courts of the receiving State. Whatever the ILC commentary's conceptual confusion, these are the only special regimes of immunity relevant to persons connected with diplomatic missions, consular posts, special missions, missions to international organizations, delegations to organs of international organizations, and delegations to international conferences. The immunity of the sending State as such, of its government and of its ministry of foreign affairs from proceedings in the receiving State in respect of the conduct of such persons is none other than State immunity, the immunity governed by the Convention itself, from the effect of which it is nonsense to seek to preserve it.

[49] ILC commentary, draft art. 3, para. 5.

[50] In relation to serving and former diplomats, see Arts 31, 32, and 39(2) VCDR; Arts 31, 41, and 43 (2) CSM; Arts 30, 31, and 38(2) VCRS (not in force). In relation to serving and former consular officers and employees, see Arts 43–45, 53(4), and 58(2) VCCR. As regards other persons, serving and former, entitled, by virtue of their connection with a mission or delegation, to immunity from proceedings in accordance with diplomatic or cognate international law, see Arts 37(2) to (4) and 39(2) VCDR; Arts 36–38 and 39(2) CSM; Arts 36(2) to (4), 38(2), 66(2) to (4), and 68(2) VCRS (not in force). Not mentioned, for the sake of convenience, in the text are the immunities from jurisdiction enjoyed by members of the family of certain of the above persons, which are also preserved from the effect of the Convention by Art. 3(1)(*b*) of the same. For the beneficiaries and content of these immunities, see Art. 37 (1) and (2) VCDR; Art. 39 CSM; Art. 36(1) and (2); and Art. 66(1) and (2) VCRS (not in force).

[51] In its defence, the commentary's reference to State immunity in this context would appear to have been more by way of rhetorical flourish than formal legal characterization.

Insofar as Article 3(1)(*b*) refers to the privileges[52] and immunities 'enjoyed by a State under international law in relation to the exercise of the functions of' the persons in question, this is to be read as no more than a simple recognition of the legal fact that, even though it is the individual who benefits from the immunity from suit, that immunity is ultimately owed to the sending State, as implicitly acknowledged by the capacity of that State to waive it.[53]

The rationale and effect of Article 3(1)(*b*) is as follows. Representatives of the State—a term used in Article 2(1)(*b*)(iv) of the Convention to refer to all State officials—are, when acting in that capacity, encompassed within the definition of 'State' for the purposes of the Convention, in accordance with the same Article 2(1)(*b*)(iv). As a consequence, in the unlikely event that a serving or former representative of the State were to find himself individually named as a defendant to civil proceedings in the courts of the receiving State in relation to acts performed by him in his capacity as a State representative, the immunity from suit from which he would be entitled to benefit as a combined function of Articles 2(1)(*b*)(iv) and 5 would be subject to the exceptions provided for in the Convention. In other words, State officials acting in that capacity benefit under the Convention, just as under customary international law, from restrictive State immunity and no more. Article 3(1)(*b*), however, is designed to remove serving and former diplomats, consular officers and employees, and the relevant other persons connected with missions and delegations—most of whom, when acting in the relevant capacity, can be characterized as representatives of the State—from the Convention's purview. As a function of Article 3(1)(*b*), the immunity of all such persons from proceedings in the courts of the receiving State is governed not by the Convention but by the pertinent special rules (conventional or customary, as the case may be) of diplomatic, consular, or analogous international law.

The practical consequences of Article 3(1)(*b*) can be illustrated by the improbable scenario of a foreign State functionary who, during official talks in the forum State, loses her temper and punches a local interpreter, breaking his nose. Where that functionary is, say, a visiting minor official not covered by the CSM, the interpreter would not be barred from bringing a claim for damages against her in the courts of the receiving State. Although the official, being a representative of the State acting in that capacity at the time of the impugned conduct, is, through the combination of the definition of 'State' in Article 2(1)(*b*)(iv) and the presumptive immunity from proceedings recognized in Article 5 of the Convention, *prima facie* entitled to immunity from proceedings in the courts of another State, this immunity is, as specified in Article 5, subject to the exceptions enumerated in the Convention; and Article 12 of the Convention provides that a State, again as defined in Article 2(1)(*b*)(iv) to include a representative of the State acting in that capacity,

> cannot invoke immunity from jurisdiction before a court of another State which is otherwise competent in a proceeding which relates to pecuniary compensation for... injury to the person... caused by an act or omission which is alleged to be attributable to the State, if the act or omission

[52] It is also worth bearing in mind that what Art. 3(1) is expressed to safeguard—even if the reference is in fact unnecessary—are 'privileges and immunities', not merely immunities, and that only the regimes of the VCDR, VCCR, CSM, VCRS (not in force), and customary diplomatic, consular, and analogous international law additionally provide for privileges, as distinct from immunities.

[53] See Art. 32(1) VCDR; Art. 45(1) VCCR; Art. 41(1) CSM; Arts 31(1) and 61(1) VCRS (not in force).

occurred in whole or in part in the territory of that other State and if the author of the act or omission was present in that territory at the time of the act or omission.

Where, in contrast, the functionary is, say, a serving diplomatic agent, the interpreter would be barred from bringing his claim against her in the receiving State's courts. As a function of Article 3(1)(*b*) of the Convention, the special regime of diplomatic immunity, rather than the Convention, applies in relation to proceedings against the diplomatic agent herself; and Article 31(1) VCDR, codifying customary international law, provides that a diplomatic agent enjoys immunity from the civil jurisdiction of the receiving State, the exceptions to this immunity specified in subparagraphs (*a*) to (*c*) of Article 31(1) VCDR being irrelevant on the facts of the case. In short, just as under customary international law, the very broad immunity *ratione personae* from the civil jurisdiction of the receiving State from which a serving diplomatic agent benefits would prevail.

This should not be taken to suggest that the practical effect of Article 3(1)(*b*) will always be to bar proceedings in the courts of the receiving State against a serving or former diplomat, consular officer or employee, or relevant other person connected with a mission or delegation. In the case of a serving diplomatic agent, for example, the sorts of civil proceedings specified in subparagraphs (*a*) to (*c*) of Article 31(1) VCDR remain possible. Article 43(2)(*a*) and (*b*) VCCR similarly provide for exceptions to the immunity of a serving consular officer or employee from civil proceedings in the courts of the receiving State. As for former diplomats, former consular officers and employees, and specified other persons formerly connected with a mission or delegation, they are all amenable to suit in the courts of the receiving State in respect of things done by them not as part of their official function, *viz* in a private capacity. In all cases, moreover, any immunity which may serve to shield persons connected with a mission, post, or delegation may be waived by the sending State.[54]

It pays to emphasize too that the special regimes of diplomatic, consular, and cognate immunity preserved from the effect of the Convention by Article 3(1)(*b*) are conversely without prejudice to the immunity of any other appropriate legal manifestation of the sending State, as regulated by the Convention, from proceedings in respect of any conduct of such persons for which it may be legally answerable in the courts of the receiving State.[55] What this means in practice can again be illustrated by the scenario of the serving diplomat sketched above. It will be recalled that, by virtue of Article 3(1)(*b*) of the Convention and Article 31(1) VCDR, the interpreter would be barred from bringing his claim in the courts of the receiving State against the diplomat herself. But by virtue of the exception in Article 12 of the Convention to a foreign State's immunity from proceedings, the interpreter could sue the foreign State (*quâ* the State, its government, or its ministry of foreign affairs, as the case may be[56]) in respect of the wayward conduct of the diplomat.

Finally, it should be noted that specified persons connected with a State's diplomatic or other missions, consular posts, or relevant delegations benefit under the special

[54] Recall n. 53.

[55] Whether, as a matter of substantive law, the receiving State is answerable under the law of the receiving State for any impugned acts of its diplomats will depend on the law of the receiving State, which may answer the question by reference to its municipal law of vicarious liability, agency, or the like or by reference to the customary international rules of State responsibility on the attribution of conduct to a State.

[56] Recall Art. 2(1)(*b*)(i) UNCSI, on the definition of 'State'.

regimes of diplomatic, consular, and similar immunities from such immunity from the jurisdiction of any third State through which they may transit or return 'as may be required to ensure his transit or return'.[57] Article 3(1)(*b*) safeguards this immunity too from the effect of the Convention.

B. Head-of-State immunity

Paragraph 2 of Article 3 provides that the Convention 'is without prejudice to privileges and immunities accorded under international law to heads of State *ratione personae*'. The reference to 'international law' is to customary international law,[58] since no treaty regulates the privileges and immunities of heads of State. As for the formulation 'accorded to heads of State', this should not be taken to alter the legal fact that the immunity *ratione personae* from which a serving head of State benefits is ultimately owed to the State of which he or she is head, with the result that that State may always waive this immunity.

The ILC commentary's view as to the effect of what is now Article 3(2) of the Convention is, regrettably, questionable. It asserts that Article 3(2), which is identical to its draft forerunner, deals with 'the immunities extended under existing international law to foreign sovereigns or other heads of State in their private capacities, *ratione personae*' and that 'article 3, paragraph 2 . . . refers exclusively to the private acts or personal immunities and privileges recognized and accorded in the practice of States'.[59] The suggestion that Article 3(2) relates only to the immunities of heads of State in their private capacities is, however, incorrect—or no longer correct, if it ever was.[60] Article 3(2) specifies, in its own words, that the Convention is 'without prejudice to . . . immunities accorded under international law to heads of State *ratione personae*', and these immunities—at least as they have come to be rationalized by the ICJ since the adoption of the ILC commentary in 1991—are not restricted to heads of State in their private capacity. Moreover, if Article 3(2) were limited, as the commentary suggests, to the immunity from proceedings from which a head of State in her private capacity benefits, the provision would be redundant, since, as made clear in Article 2(1)(*b*)(iv), it is only insofar as individual representatives of the State are acting in their capacity as representatives of the State that the Convention regulates in the first place the immunities from which they do and do not benefit. Although it is not, of course, to be excluded that the provision may have been inserted purely *ex abundante cautela*, the conclusion is not to be drawn lightly, given the canon of treaty interpretation which militates against textual redundancy.

[57] Art. 40(1) VCDR; Art. 42(1) CSM; Art. 54(1) VCCR; Art. 81(1) and (2) VCRS (not in force) ('as may be required to secure his transit').

[58] Recall, in this connection, preamble (fifth recital) UNCSI, affirming that 'the rules of customary international law continue to govern matters not regulated by the provisions of the . . . Convention'.

[59] ILC commentary, draft art. 3, para. 6.

[60] The ILC commentary has been taken at face value by at least one influential scholar. See H. Fox, *The Law of State Immunity* (2nd edn) (Oxford: Oxford University Press, 2008), 668 (implicitly) and 690; I. Roberts (ed.), *Satow's Diplomatic Practice* (6th edn) (Oxford: Oxford University Press, 2009), 176, para. 12.1, in a chapter prepared by Fox. As is clear from the relevant passages cited, Fox bases her agreement with the ILC commentary on the national legislative provisions discussed later in this section.

It is possible,[61] albeit improbable,[62] that the inaccuracy of the commentary stems from a misapprehension as to the meaning of the term 'immunity *ratione personae*'. An immunity *ratione personae*—the Latin being perhaps better translated as 'by reason of the personage', rather than 'by reason of the person', but either way certainly not as 'in a private capacity' or the like—is an immunity from which an individual benefits by mere virtue of her occupancy of a specified office, be it the office of head of State, head of government, or minister for foreign affairs or a diplomatic posting. The term '*ratione personae*' is in contradistinction to '*ratione materiae*', this second label being used to describe an immunity from which an individual benefits by virtue of the subject-matter of the proceedings or, putting it another way, by virtue and in respect of the particular acts performed by that individual. In contrast to an immunity *ratione materiae*, an immunity *ratione personae* serves to shield, for the duration of her tenure, the holder of the specified office from proceedings in the courts of another State irrespective of the subject-matter to which the proceedings relate. That is, an immunity *ratione personae* subsists, for the duration of the individual's term of office, irrespective of whether the acts at issue can be characterized as *acta jure imperii* or *acta jure gestionis*, or were—in a logically precedent question—performed in that person's official or private capacity, or were, for that matter, performed during or before that person's term of office. In short, while the person occupies the office, she cannot be sued.[63] This is not to say that immunity *ratione personae* need be absolute; but, even if an immunity *ratione personae* is circumscribed by reference to excluded categories of proceedings, its gist remains that any immunity available subsists by reason of the beneficiary's office, and not by reason of the acts the subject of the proceedings. All of this is a long way of saying that the expression 'immunity *ratione personae*' does not mean an immunity accorded to persons 'in their private capacities'.[64] That said, it is improbable that the inaccuracy of the ILC commentary has its origins in such a misunderstanding.

Far more likely is that the inaccuracy of the ILC commentary stems from its subscription, based on a consideration of the case-law[65] and State immunity legislation[66] of certain States, to a logical, respectable but now seemingly eclipsed school of thought not as to the concept of immunity *ratione personae* but simply as to the availability of

[61] Consider the formulation 'the immunities extended... to foreign sovereigns or other heads of State in their private capacities, *ratione personae*' and 'the private acts or personal immunities', as employed in ILC commentary, draft art. 3, para. 6. Consider also the following passage from the judgment of the Austrian Supreme Court in *W v Prince of Liechtenstein*, ILDC 1 (AT 2001), para. 13, citations omitted (Aut (SC) 2001): '[F]oreign Heads of State are exempt, by virtue of their office, from the domestic legal order of other States, i.e. judicial authority and coercion, at least for their term of office ("*ratione materiae*"). They are also exempt, however, from such domestic jurisdiction with respect to their private acts ("*ratione personae*"). In this respect they not only enjoy absolute immunity with respect to their function (for their official acts) but also with respect to their acts under private law.'

[62] Seventh report Sucharitkul, 44, para. 119, appears, as one might expect, to evidence a firm grasp of the concept, when it describes the idea of the head of State's immunity *ratione personae* as 'mean[ing], in effect, that immunities follow the person of the head of State only so long as he remains in office'.

[63] See also Fox (n. 60), 666–7 and authors cited therein. See too, albeit in the criminal context, *Arrest Warrant of 11 April 2000 (Democratic Republic of the Congo v Belgium), Judgment*, ICJ Rep 2002, 3, 20–2, paras 53–55.

[64] ILC commentary, draft art. 3, para. 6.

[65] See, in this regard, Seventh report Sucharitkul, 44–5, paras 121–123.

[66] Curiously, none of the legislation adopted at the time is mentioned in the relevant report of Special Rapporteur Sucharitkul or in the later ILC commentary itself. For the former, see Seventh report Sucharitkul, 44–5, paras 119–124.

such immunity to a head of State acting in an official capacity. Section 14(1)(*a*) SIA (UK), as reproduced verbatim or near-verbatim in the legislation of Australia, Canada, Pakistan, Singapore, and South Africa,[67] defines 'State', for the purposes of the restrictive State immunity accorded by the Act, to include 'the sovereign or other head of that State acting in his public capacity'. The result is that the immunity of a foreign head of State from civil proceedings in the courts of the UK in respect of acts performed by him as head of State is limited by the exceptions specified in Part I SIA (UK)—exceptions, based predominantly on the ESCI, which for the most part are substantively the same as those recognized in the Convention. The SIA (UK) goes on to provide in section 20(1)(*a*) that the rules laid down in the VCDR are to apply, subject to the necessary modifications, to a foreign head of State (whether acting in his public or private capacity); but this is qualified by section 20(5), which specifies that the application *mutatis mutandis* of the VCDR to a head of State is to be without prejudice to the exceptions enumerated in Part I of the Act to that head of State's immunity from civil proceedings in respect of acts performed in his public capacity. In short, while foreign heads of State enjoy immunity *ratione personae*, as per Article 31(1) VCDR, from civil proceedings in the UK courts in respect of anything done by them in their private capacity, their immunity in respect of acts done in their official capacity amounts to no more than restrictive State immunity.[68] Equivalent provision is made in the Australian legislation,[69] while the Canadian, Pakistani, Singaporean, and South African State immunity statutes do not specify in the first place that the rules of the VCDR are to apply *mutatis mutandis* to heads of State. Such a doctrinal position is perfectly coherent. The concept of State immunity—or, as it is also known, sovereign immunity or foreign sovereign immunity—originated in the immunity of the person of the sovereign from the jurisdiction of another sovereign, an immunity which in time came to shield not only the sovereign in person but also the State of which she was the metaphysical embodiment. It is therefore logical to suppose that, as the immunity of the legal entity of the State from at least the civil jurisdiction of another State ceased to be absolute, coming instead in its restrictive form to be subject to a range of exceptions, so too did the immunity from foreign civil proceedings of the sovereign or other head of State herself when acting in her capacity as head of State.[70]

But this school of thought has never held uncontested sway. In the US, for example, where the FSIA (US) does not cover head-of-State immunity, on which instead a 'suggestion of immunity' submitted to the court by the executive branch is treated as

[67] See s. 3(3)(*b*) FStIA (Aus); s. 2 SIA (Can); s. 15(1)(*a*) SIO (Pak); s. 1(2)(*a*) FStIA (SA); s. 16(1)(*a*) SIA (Sing).

[68] By virtue of the combined reading of ss. 20(1)(*a*), 20(5), and 16(4) SIA (UK), however, the immunity of a foreign head of State from criminal proceedings in the UK courts is as provided for in Art. 31(1) VCDR in respect of diplomats, *viz* absolute. See also s. 36(1)(*a*) and (3), read in conjunction with the definition of 'proceeding' in s. 3(1) ('does not include a prosecution for an offence'), FStIA (Aus).

[69] See s. 36(1)(*a*) and (3) FStIA (Aus).

[70] Indeed, taking this logic to its conclusion, it would have made more sense still to conclude that a head of State in her private capacity was to be treated no differently from any other representative of the State when acting in a private capacity—namely, that she enjoyed no immunity from civil proceedings whatsoever, rather than the immunity *ratione personae* enjoyed by diplomats in their private capacity. Precisely this position was adopted by the Institut de Droit international at its Vancouver session in 2001, in Art. 3 of its resolution entitled 'Immunities from Jurisdiction and Execution of Heads of State and of Government in International Law' (2000–2001) 69 *Annuaire de l'Institut de Droit international* 743, which reads: 'In civil and administrative matters, the Head of State does not enjoy any immunity from jurisdiction before the courts of a foreign State, unless that suit relates to acts performed in the exercise of his or her official functions.'

conclusive, the immunity of a foreign head of State from civil proceedings in respect of commercial acts performed, it would seem,[71] in his capacity as head of State has been upheld[72]—which could be taken to suggest that the immunity in question was one from which the foreign head of State benefited by mere virtue of his being head of State.[73] The Malaysian courts, in civil proceedings in respect of a foreign head of State's ownership in her official capacity of property in the forum State, have similarly held head-of-State immunity to be absolute, the suggestion being that such immunity subsists by mere virtue of the defendant's position as head of State.[74] The Austrian Supreme Court, which pioneered the restrictive doctrine of State immunity in civil proceedings, has held that the *jure imperii/jure gestionis* distinction does not apply to a foreign head of State.[75] Watts, summing up his account of the immunity of heads of State from foreign civil proceedings in respect of official but non-sovereign acts (*acta jure gestionis*), concluded in 1994 that 'the entitlement of a Head of State's [*sic*] to immunity in respect of his official but commercial acts is still a matter of uncertainty'.[76]

In 2004, however, the ICJ went a long way to dispelling this uncertainty in *Arrest Warrant of 11 April 2000*, a case involving the immunity from criminal jurisdiction of a serving minister for foreign affairs which has implications for the immunity from civil jurisdiction of a serving head of State for acts performed in an official capacity. The Court, assimilating the immunity enjoyed by a serving minister for foreign affairs to that enjoyed by a serving head of State, a serving head of government, and a serving diplomat,[77] rationalized these immunities by reference to the need 'to ensure the effective performance of [these persons'] functions on behalf of their respective States'[78]—the need, that is, 'throughout the duration of his or her office', to 'protect the individual concerned against any act of authority of another State which would hinder him or her in

[71] This is certainly how Watts characterizes the proceedings, dealing with them under the heading 'Official, but non-sovereign, acts'. See A. Watts, 'The Legal Position in International Law of Heads of States, Heads of Governments and Foreign Ministers' (1994) 247 *RdC* 10, 60 and 62–3.

[72] See *First American Corporation v Al-Nahyan*, 121 ILR 577, 586 (US (DDC) 1996).

[73] Although the State Department's 'suggestion of immunity' is unforthcoming as to the conceptual basis of the absolute immunity for which it contends, the tenor of the document is that a foreign head of State is *ipso facto* immune from the civil jurisdiction of the US courts. See United States District Court for the District of Columbia, *First American Corporation v Sheikh Zayed Bin Sultan Al-Nahyan*, Civil Action No. 93–1309, Suggestion of Immunity submitted by the United States of America, 10 October 1996, http://www.state.gov/documents/organization/65794.pdf. That this is the basis on which the State Department proceeds was subsequently made unambiguously clear in United States District Court for the Western District of Oklahoma, *Habyarimana v Kagame*, Civil Action No. 10–437–W, Suggestion of Immunity submitted by the United States of America, 29 August 2011, http://www.state.gov/documents/organization/194076.pdf, which related to a civil claim in respect of acts alleged to have been performed prior to the defendant head of State's assumption of office. Paragraph 7 of the suggestion of immunity reads in relevant part: 'Under the customary international law principles accepted by the Executive Branch, head of state immunity attaches to a head of state's status as the current holder of the office. Thus, acts committed before a sitting head of state assumed that position are not excluded from the scope of his immunity while in office.'

[74] See *Village Holdings Sdn Bhd v Her Majesty the Queen in Right of Canada*, 87 ILR 223, 238 (Mal (HC Malaya) 1987), where the immunity was conceived of as 'the pure absolute doctrine of State immunity', which was an immunity *ratione personae*.

[75] See *Prince of 'X' Road Accident Case*, 65 ILR 13 (Aut (SC) 1964). The case would seem to have involved private conduct. See also *W v Prince of Liechtenstein* (n. 61), paras 13 and 16, where, although the immunity from civil proceedings of a foreign head of State in respect of acts performed in his official capacity was referred to as immunity *ratione materiae*, it was considered, like his immunity in respect of private acts, to be absolute.

[76] Watts (n. 71), 63.

[77] See *Arrest Warrant* (n. 63), 20–2, paras 51–55.

[78] *Arrest Warrant* (n. 63), 21, para. 53.

the performance of his or her duties'.[79] This functional necessity justified, in the Court's view, an immunity for the duration of the individual's office that was without regard to the capacity, public or private, in which the impugned acts were performed or, indeed, to whether they were performed before or during the period of office[80]—in short, an immunity *ratione personae*. Although the Court formally restricted its conclusions to criminal proceedings,[81] it is difficult to see how the rationale for and resultant nature of the immunity of the relevant State officers from foreign civil proceedings could be any different. The implication for the immunity of serving heads of State from civil proceedings in the courts of another State is that such immunity is an immunity *ratione personae* applicable as much to things done in an official capacity as to private conduct.

In short, *pace* the ILC commentary, the immunity from foreign civil proceedings accorded under international law to heads of State *ratione personae*, as preserved from the effect of the Convention by Article 3(2), is—on what today would have to be considered the more accurate view—accorded to heads of State in both their private and public capacities.

As to the precise content of these immunities, it is likely, given the ICJ's assimilation in *Arrest Warrant* of the immunities owed in respect of heads of State and in respect of diplomats, that the immunity *ratione personae* accorded to a serving head of State from civil proceedings in the courts of another State is subject only to those exceptions specified in Article 31(1)(*a*) to (*c*) VCDR.[82] What distinguishes heads of State, however, from diplomats, is that the immunities which serve to shield them, whatever their precise content, are applicable to proceedings in all foreign States, and not just to those in the receiving and transit States.

It should be recalled, however, that—just as with the range of persons covered by Article 3(1)(*b*) of the Convention—none of this affects, as a matter of international law, the procedural capacity of a claimant to sue the State of which the head of State is head in respect of any of the latter's official conduct for which that State may be answerable in the forum State.[83] Whether a claim to this effect is barred by the Convention will depend on whether it falls within one of the exceptions to State immunity recognized in Parts II and III of the instrument.

C. *Other immunities* ratione personae?

It will be recalled that Special Rapporteur Ogiso and the ILC's Drafting Committee declined to include in draft article 3 mention of such immunities *ratione personae* as may be owed in respect of State officials other than the diplomats and heads of State expressly referred to in Article 3(1)(*b*) and (2).[84] The ILC commentary, for its part, was at pains to explain that the draft articles did 'not prejudge the extent of immunities granted by States to heads of Government and ministers for foreign affairs'.[85] At the same time, persons other than heads of State were 'not expressly included' within the scope of draft article 3(2),

[79] *Arrest Warrant* (n. 63), 22, para. 54.

[80] *Arrest Warrant* (n. 63), 22, para. 55.

[81] See *Arrest Warrant* (n. 63), 21, para. 51.

[82] But *cf Village Holdings* (n. 74), 235–6, in which the immunity accorded to a foreign head of State in civil proceedings in the Malaysian courts was said to be absolute.

[83] See section 3.2.A(ii). See also Watts (n. 71), 54.

[84] See section 2.

[85] ILC commentary, draft art. 3, para. 7.

the commentary noted, 'since it would be difficult to prepare an exhaustive list, and any enumeration of such persons would moreover raise the issue of the basis and of the extent of the jurisdictional immunity [enjoyed] by such persons'.[86]

Subsequently,[87] the ICJ in *Arrest Warrant* equated not only diplomats and heads of State but also heads of government and ministers for foreign affairs when discussing the rationale for and, implicitly, the nature of the immunities from foreign jurisdiction from which these respective State representatives were held to benefit; and, even if the Court stressed that it was dealing only with criminal proceedings, its pronouncements cannot but have implications for immunity *ratione personae* from civil proceedings. In short, after *Arrest Warrant*, it would appear that—in addition to serving diplomats and heads of States—at least[88] serving heads of government and serving ministers for foreign affairs benefit from immunity *ratione personae* from civil proceedings in the courts of a State other than their own.[89]

The ICJ's judgment did not, however, lead the Ad Hoc Committee on Jurisdictional Immunities of States and Their Property to amend the text of what became Article 3(2) of the Convention, which refers only to the immunity *ratione personae* from which a head of State benefits. On its face, therefore, the Convention would appear to govern, by virtue of Article 2(1)(*b*)(iv), the immunity from foreign civil proceedings of all other State officials (barring, of course, those specified in Article 3(1)(*b*)).

But in his statement to the Sixth Committee, the Chairman of the Ad Hoc Committee, having noted that 'the general approach of the Convention' was that 'it did not apply where there was a special immunity regime, including immunities *ratione personae*',[90] elaborated:

> Sometimes that was expressly stated in the text, sometimes not. Thus, for example, the express mention of heads of State in article 3 should not be read as suggesting that the immunity *ratione personae* of other state officials was affected by the Convention.[91]

To date two States parties to the Convention, namely Norway and Sweden, have endorsed this position in declarations attaching to their respective instruments of ratification.[92]

[86] ILC commentary, draft art. 3, para. 7.

[87] Recall section 3.2.B.

[88] Since 2002, albeit in the criminal context, magistrates' courts in the UK have applied the ICJ's reasoning in *Arrest Warrant* to accord immunity *ratione personae* to, respectively, a serving minister for defence and a serving minister for commerce and international trade of a foreign State. See *Re Mofaz*, 128 ILR 709 (UK (Bow St MC) 2004) and *Re Barak*, unreported (UK (City of Westminster MC) 2009), re the former; and *Re Bo Xilai*, 128 ILR 713 (UK (Bow St MC) 2005), re the latter. On the other hand, the ICJ indicated in *Certain Matters of Mutual Assistance in Criminal Matters (Djibouti v France), Judgment*, ICJ Rep 2008, 177, 243–4, para. 194, that at least a senior prosecuting magistrate and the head of national security of a foreign State are not entitled to immunity *ratione personae* from foreign criminal jurisdiction. Similarly, in *Bat v Investigating Judge of the German Federal Court*, 147 ILR 633, 653–4, paras 61–62 (UK (EWHC) 2011), a Divisional Court of the High Court of England and Wales held that the head of the executive office of the national security council of a foreign State is not entitled to such immunity.

[89] As with heads of State (see section 3.2.B), but in contrast to diplomats, this immunity serves as a bar to proceedings in any foreign State.

[90] Statement Chairman Ad Hoc Committee, para. 37.

[91] Statement Chairman Ad Hoc Committee, para. 37.

[92] See UNCSI depositary notifications C.N.280.2006.TREATIES–2 (Norway: Ratification), 6 April 2006 ('[A]s . . . noted in the said statement [*viz* 'the statement of 25 October 2004 of the Chairman of the Ad Hoc Committee on Jurisdictional Immunities of States and Their Property introducing the Committee's report'], the Convention does not apply where there is a special immunity regime, including immunities *ratione personae*. Thus, the express mention of heads of State in Article 3 should not be read as suggesting that the

For what it is worth, the UN Secretariat has similarly reiterated the Chairman's words.[93]

Writing in a personal capacity, Gerhard Hafner, who served as Chairman of the Ad Hoc Committee, has since argued that, '[i]n conformity with the general law of treaties, this explanation provides a proper context for purposes of interpretation'[94] in the sense of Article 31(2) VCLT, and has asserted in this light that the Convention does not have the effect of abrogating such immunities *ratione personae* as may be owed under customary international law in respect of other State officers.[95] Going one step further, Fox has suggested that, 'having regard to the International Court's decision in the *Arrest Warrant* case it would seem appropriate to construe this exclusion as including the immunity *ratione personae* of a State's Minister for Foreign Affairs (and possibly other persons entitled to immunity *ratione personae*)'.[96]

Pace Fox, Articles 31 and 32 VCLT grant no licence to read into the unambiguous words of Article 3(2) reference to such other high-ranking State officials as may benefit under international law from immunity *ratione personae* from foreign civil proceedings. On the other hand, it is by no means implausible, in the light of the ICJ's judgment in *Arrest Warrant* and the Convention's preambular recital affirming 'that the rules of customary international law continue to govern matters not regulated by the provisions of the present Convention',[97] to suggest, as did the Chairman of the Sixth Committee and as have both Norway and Sweden, that Article 3 is not to be read *a contrario* so as to subject to the exceptions provided for in the Convention the immunity from foreign civil proceedings of such other officials as may be shielded by immunity *ratione personae* as a matter of customary international law. One could persuasively argue for such an outcome on the basis, in the words of the Chamber of the ICJ in the *ELSI* case, of the difficulty of accepting 'that an important principle of customary international law'—namely immunity *ratione personae*, such as may serve to bar foreign civil proceedings against certain officials not mentioned in Article 3 of the Convention—'should be held to have been tacitly dispensed with, in the absence of any words making clear an intention to do so'.[98] Such a tacit abrogation of other immunities *ratione personae* available under customary international law is even less likely given the ILC's commentary to draft article 3, of which the State representatives who finalized the text of the Convention would have been well aware, as well as the Chairman of the Ad Hoc Committee's statement to the Sixth Committee of the General Assembly just a few weeks before the Convention's adoption by the same General Assembly in plenary.

immunity *ratione personae* of other State officials is affected by the Convention.'); and C.N.912.2009. TREATIES–1 (Sweden: Ratification), 24 December 2009 ('Sweden . . . declares its understanding that the express mention of heads of State in article 3 should not be read as suggesting that the immunity *ratione personae* which other State officials might enjoy under international law is affected by the Convention.')

93 See UN Secretariat, *Immunity of State officials from foreign criminal jurisdiction. Memorandum by the Secretariat*, UN doc. A/CN.4/596 (31 March 2008), 30, para. 45.

94 G. Hafner, 'Accountability and Immunity: The United Nations Convention on Jurisdictional Immunity of States and Their Property and the Accountability of States' (2005) 99 *ASIL Procs* 237, 241.

95 See Hafner (n. 94), 241–2. See also G. Hafner and U. Köhler, 'The United Nations Convention on Jurisdictional Immunities of States and their Property' (2004) 35 *NYIL* 3, 45–6.

96 Fox (n. 60), 404–5.

97 Preamble (fifth recital) UNCSI.

98 *Elettronica Sicula S.p.A. (ELSI) (United States of America v Italy), Judgment*, ICJ Rep 1989, 15, 42, para. 50, referring to the local remedies rule applicable to diplomatic protection claims.

D. *Immunities with respect to aircraft and space objects*

Article 3(3) declares the Convention to be without prejudice to the immunities enjoyed by a State under international law with respect to aircraft or space objects owned or operated by a State.[99] The expression 'the immunities enjoyed by a State . . . with respect to' most obviously embraces any immunity from foreign proceedings enjoyed by the State in respect of aircraft or space objects owned or operated by it—that is, in the terminology of the Convention, the State's immunity from jurisdiction, as regulated by Parts II and III of the Convention. But it can safely be said that the expression also encompasses any immunity from pre- and post-judgment measures of constraint in connection with such proceedings as may serve to shield such aircraft and space objects.[100] Furthermore, the expression most likely comprehends proceedings and related measures of constraint not only in respect of proprietary interests in, liability for damage caused by, etc, such aircraft or space objects themselves but also, as implied by the ILC commentary,[101] in respect of the carriage of goods or persons by them.

A State's immunities in respect of aircraft and space objects owned or operated by it derive in part from customary international law and in part, in the case of States parties to them, from bilateral and multilateral treaties.[102] In this light, it pays to emphasize that the consequence of Article 3(3)'s 'without prejudice' clause is no more than that, in the event of inconsistency between the Convention and another rule of international law in force between the foreign and forum States pertaining to the immunity of the latter from proceedings and measures of constraint with respect to aircraft and space objects owned or operated by it, the other rule of international law is to prevail. Should no such other rule of international law apply as between the foreign and forum States, Article 3(3) is without practical effect and the Convention will apply as normal. In other words, Article 3(3) does not function as a general 'carve-out' from the Convention's application of all proceedings relating to aircraft or space objects owned or operated by a State. It merely safeguards from the effect of the Convention 'the immunities enjoyed by a State' with respect to such aircraft and space objects.

[99] In contrast, the immunity of a State from proceedings against it in the courts of another State in respect of the operation of a ship owned or operated by it is the subject of Art. 16 UNCSI. At the same time, in accordance with Art. 26 UNCSI, the mutual rights and obligations of States parties to the 1926 Brussels Convention or to any other existing international agreement regulating such immunity from foreign jurisdiction and, indeed, the immunity of State ships themselves from foreign measures of constraint remain unaffected by the Convention.

[100] See, similarly, section 3.2.A(i) in relation to the property of the State's diplomatic and equivalent missions, its consular posts, etc.

[101] ILC commentary, draft art. 16, para. 17, fn. 165 cites the Convention for the Unification of Certain Rules relating to International Carriage by Air ('Warsaw Convention'), along with its Hague Protocol and supplementary Guadalajara Convention, as air-law treaties left undisturbed by draft art. 16 (corresponding to Art. 16 UNCSI), on State-owned or -operated ships; and it might be thought to stand to reason that the same treaties fall within the express exclusion with respect to State-owned or -operated aircraft and space objects subsequently included in Art. 3(3) of the Convention. That said, the treaties listed are referred to there simply as '[t]reaties relating to civil aviation' and '[t]reaties relevant to space activities and space objects' respectively, and very few of them impinge in any way on questions of jurisdictional immunities.

[102] To this extent, as is the case with respect to the immunities subsisting as among States parties to the VCDR, VCCR, CSM and so on, Art. 26 UNCSI equally performs, in specific relation to States parties to the Convention that are also parties to the relevant aviation conventions, the function that Art. 3(3) UNCSI performs in relation to all States parties to the Convention. For a list of multilateral treaties on air law and space law of which at least one or two are relevant to questions of State immunity, see ILC commentary, draft art. 16, para. 17, fn. 165.

4. Evaluation

As far as it goes, Article 3 should not prove too difficult to apply. As far as it does not go, it is potentially problematic. It beggars belief that its drafters, even after the ICJ's judgment in *Arrest Warrant*, did not consider it prudent to reformulate paragraph 2 so as to make generic provision for such other immunities *ratione personae* as may be accorded under international law. Nor, at least if one takes seriously Articles 31 and 32 VCLT, could such provision be read into Article 3(2). At the same time, there are persuasive grounds for saying that Article 3(2) cannot be read *a contrario* so as to subject to the exceptions provided for in the Convention the immunity from foreign proceedings of such other State officials as may benefit under customary international law from immunity *ratione personae*.

Article 4

Jean d'Aspremont

Article 4

Non-retroactivity of the present Convention

Without prejudice to the application of any rules set forth in the present Convention to which jurisdictional immunities of States and their property are subject under international law independently of the present Convention, the present Convention shall not apply to any question of jurisdictional immunities of States or their property arising in a proceeding instituted against a State before a court of another State prior to the entry into force of the present Convention for the States concerned.

1. Introduction

Treaties frequently contain a provision on non-retroactivity.[1] More precisely, treaty-makers traditionally decide that the treaty will not apply retroactively. More than a common practice, non-retroactivity is perceived to be a matter of both natural justice and common sense. The ICJ, for example, has effectively presumed that treaties have no retroactive effect unless otherwise specified.[2] Article 28 VCLT, reflecting customary international law[3] or a general principle of law,[4] mirrors this position, providing that, '[u]nless a different intention appears from the treaty or is otherwise established, its provisions do not bind a party in relation to any act or fact which took place or any situation which ceased to exist before the date of the entry into force of the treaty with respect to that party'.

Non-retroactivity nonetheless gives rise to complex questions since it requires the drafters of a treaty clearly to define the period to which the new instrument does not apply.[5] Article 28 VCLT seeks to do so by referring to 'any act or fact which took place or any situation which ceased to exist before the date of the entry into force of the treaty'. It is widely recognized, however, that what constitutes an 'act or fact which took place . . . before the date of the entry into force of the treaty' or a 'situation which ceased to exist before [that date]' is not always straightforward.[6] In this light, it was decided to include in the Convention a specific provision addressing non-retroactivity. The drafters of the ECSI had previously felt a similar need to spell out the temporal scope

[1] See Eighth report Sucharitkul, 31, para. 39.

[2] See *Ambatielos (Greece v United Kingdom), Preliminary Objection*, ICJ Rep 1952, 28, 40.

[3] See eg H.W. Briggs, 'Reflections on Non-Retroactivity of Treaties' (1968) 21 *REDI* 320; H. Fox, 'In Defense of State Immunity: Why the UN Convention on State Immunity is Important' (2006) 55 *ICLQ* 399, 401 and 406; F. Dopagne, 'Article 28 Convention of 1969', in O. Corten and P. Klein (eds), *The Vienna Conventions on the Law of Treaties: A Commentary* (Oxford: Oxford University Press, 2011), 718, 718–20.

[4] See para. 1 of the Resolution of the Institut de Droit international adopted in Wiesbaden, 45 *Annuaire de l'Institut de Droit International* (1973), 536.

[5] See eg Report ILC, thirty-eighth session, 16. See also Summary record 1968th ILC meeting, *YILC 1986*, vol. I, 165, 168, paras 44–45.

[6] Dopagne (n. 3), 720–2.

of application of that instrument and not to rely on the VCLT's general regime, which was still in its infancy.[7]

Article 4 of the Convention specifies the point by reference to which retroactivity is assessed (or 'critical date') with precision: the Convention's regime does not apply to questions of immunity arising in proceedings instituted prior to the Convention's entry into force, even if the proceedings are not aired before the court until after the Convention comes into force for those States. In this way Article 4 supplements the general rule contained in Article 28 VCLT by specifying the application of the principle of non-retroactivity in the particular context of proceedings before a court in which questions of immunity may, *ex hypothesi*, arise.

2. Drafting History

Article 4 goes back to a draft provision introduced by Special Rapporteur Sucharitkul in his Second Report in 1980, which contained the gist of the provision, but envisaged the possibility of States declaring themselves bound by the Convention retroactively.[8] At the instigation of the Special Rapporteur, discussion of the provision was deferred until a full set of draft articles had been elaborated and the Commission could meaningfully discuss their temporal scope of application.[9] Accordingly, towards the end of the first reading, in his Eighth Report, Special Rapporteur Sucharitkul re-introduced his initial draft without amendment.[10] It was considered in the Drafting Committee, which endorsed the proposed text in principle, but gently reformulated the text (for example by deleting the phrase 'States having declared themselves bound thereby' and by framing the provision in the negative).[11] Amended in this way, the provision was adopted on first reading as draft article 5.[12] It attracted few comments by governments[13] and was left untouched during the ILC's second reading. It featured as draft article 4 of the ILC's 1991 draft articles. But for the substitution of the word 'Convention' for the word 'present articles', it carried over into the Convention unchanged.

3. Key Points

3.1 The 'critical date'

Article 4 posits the institution of proceedings as the point at which the Convention must be in force for the States concerned in order for it to apply to the case at hand. Put differently, if the proceedings in question are initiated before the Convention has entered into force between the respondent State and the forum State, the Convention does not apply to them. It is worth noting that, while also precluding retroactivity, the ESCI adopts a different approach. Rather than focusing solely on the point of institution of proceedings, Article 35(3) ECSI also excludes the application of that treaty to

[7] But see section 3.1 for the differences between the ESCI's and UNSCI's approaches.
[8] Second report Sucharitkul, 214, para. 214.
[9] Report ILC, thirty-second session, 139–40.
[10] Eighth report Sucharitkul, 30–1.
[11] See summary record 1968th ILC meeting (n. 5), 168, para. 43.
[12] Report ILC, thirty-eighth session, 16.
[13] Preliminary report Ogiso, 103, paras 51–55.

proceedings 'arising out of, or judgments based on, acts, omissions or facts prior to the date on which the present Convention is opened for signature'. This holds true even where the proceedings are instituted after the ESCI's entry into force.[14] In contrast, the UNCSI is capable of applying to proceedings based on acts, omissions, or facts which predate the Convention's opening for signature, provided that the proceedings are instituted after the Convention's entry into force for the States concerned.

The difference of approach as between the UNCSI and the ECSI is of more than academic interest. It is by no means out of the question that proceedings instituted against a State after the UNCSI's entry into force for that State and the forum State might relate to events predating the Convention's opening for signature on 17 January 2005,[15] and the uncomplicated critical date laid down in Article 4, namely the date of the institution of the proceedings, permits a clear-cut determination of whether the Convention applies or not. Indeed, a potential claimant in a dispute relating to any such events will be in a position to judge before instituting proceedings whether the procedural defence of State immunity will be available. Although the *travaux préparatoires* do not shed much light on the matter, it can reasonably be surmised that a concern for clarity was a factor in the ILC's decision to define retroactivity against the date of the institution of proceedings. In contrast, the ESCI's exclusion of proceedings arising out of past events is not always straightforward to apply.

3.2 The savings clause

The opening words of Article 4 declare the provision to be '[w]ithout prejudice to the application of any rules set forth in the... Convention to which jurisdictional immunities of States and their property are subject under international law independently of the... Convention'.[16] This savings clause, inserted *ex abundante cautela*, refers in practice mainly to rules of customary international law. To this extent it is uncontentious, given that the inapplicability of a treaty provision cannot affect the application of a customary rule of identical content.[17] In addition, Article 4's savings clause would leave undisturbed the application to proceedings instituted prior to the Convention's entry into force for the States concerned of any rules, identical in content to those embodied in the Convention, found in other treaties. Again this is unremarkable, in that the inapplicability of a provision in one treaty can have no bearing anyway on the application of a provision of identical content in another treaty.

[14] See Expl. Rep. ECSI, para. 123, which indicates that the intention was to exclude from the scope of application of the ECSI disputes relating to events in the too-distant past.

[15] Consider, for example, the various proceedings relating to Germany's conduct during World War II which formed the backdrop to *Jurisdictional Immunities of the State (Germany v Italy: Greece intervening), Judgment*, International Court of Justice, 3 February 2012.

[16] Report ILC, thirty-eighth session, 16. See also Fox (n. 3), 401.

[17] See eg *Military and Paramilitary Activities in and Against Nicaragua* (*Nicaragua v United States of America*), *Jurisdiction and Admissibility*, ICJ Rep 1984, 392, 424–5, para. 73. See also Art. 31(3) UNCSI, pursuant to which denunciation of the Convention 'shall not in any way affect the duty of any State Party to fulfil any obligation embodied in the... Convention to which it would be subject under international law independently of the... Convention.'

4. Evaluation

Article 4 is uncontroversial. It usefully supplements the general rule contained in Article 28 VCLT by specifying the date of the institution of proceedings as the 'critical date' for the purposes of retroactivity. The choice of such a straightforward criterion means that the temporal scope of the Convention can be determined easily.

PART II: GENERAL PRINCIPLES

Roger O'Keefe

1. Introduction

The five provisions of Part II of the Convention supposedly lay down what the title of the part calls general principles. But only two of them, namely Articles 5 and 6, have any convincing claim to that rubric, and even then they are 'general' only in relation to the question of immunity from jurisdiction, as regulated by the remaining provisions of Part II and by the provisions of Part III. They are without relevance to the question of immunity from measures of constraint, as regulated by Part IV. Article 5 is the cornerstone of the Convention's scheme of immunity from jurisdiction, positing a general rule of the availability to a State of immunity from the jurisdiction of the courts of another State, a general rule subject only to the exceptions subsequently enumerated in the Convention itself. Article 6 is the concretization of Article 5.

The remaining provisions of Part II, Articles 7 to 9, embody what are effectively the first of the exceptions to the *prima facie* immunity of a State from jurisdiction posited in Article 5. These exceptions give effect to a State's express or implied consent to the exercise of jurisdiction over it. They differ from the exceptions enumerated in Part III of the Convention in that they pertain not to the subject-matter of the proceeding but to the State's conduct in respect of that proceeding or such proceedings. Like, nonetheless, the eight articles of Part III of the Convention, as well as Articles 5 and 6, Articles 7 to 9 concern only a State's immunity from jurisdiction. They do not implicate the immunity of a State's property from measures of constraint. In other words, the fact that, in the application of one of the exceptions provided for in Articles 7 to 9, a State cannot invoke immunity from a court's jurisdiction in a given proceeding does not mean that the court, or indeed any other court, may order pre- or post-judgment measures of constraint against the State's property in connection with that proceeding.

2. Key Points

2.1 Not so 'general'

The title of Part II of the Convention is misleading.

Contrary to what one might expect, the provisions of Part II do not apply in respect of the whole of the remainder of the Convention. Rather, they pertain only to a State's immunity from the jurisdiction of the courts of another State, having no bearing on the immunity of a State's property from pre- or post-judgment measures of constraint. In this way, Parts II and III of the Convention form a pair, while Part IV is a stand-alone part. In this light, instead of having in the Convention a Part II entitled General principles, a Part III entitled 'Proceedings in which State immunity cannot be invoked', and a Part IV entitled 'State immunity from measures of constraint in connection with proceedings before a court', it would have made more sense to have a Part II entitled 'State immunity from jurisdiction' or 'State immunity from proceedings before a court', with a Section A (General principles) and a Section B ('Proceedings in which State immunity cannot be invoked'), followed by a Part III entitled 'State immunity from measures of constraint in connection with proceedings before a court'.

Additionally, it is difficult to see in what sense the exceptions to immunity from jurisdiction posited in Articles 7 to 9 are 'general', unless the term is intended to indicate that—in contrast to the exceptions to immunity from jurisdiction enumerated in Part III, each of which concerns proceedings only in respect of a specific subject-matter—each of the exceptions in Articles 7 to 9 is capable of applying to any and all proceedings, regardless of their subject-matter.

2.2 The nature of the exceptions

Whereas the exceptions to a State's immunity from jurisdiction found in Part III of the Convention all relate to the subject-matter of the proceeding, the exceptions in Articles 7 to 9 relate to the conduct of the State in relation to that proceeding or to that sort of proceeding. More specifically, Articles 7 to 9 are based on the State's consent to that proceeding, whether given in relation to the proceeding itself after the dispute has arisen or in advance in relation to proceedings of that sort.

The descriptive distinction, however, between the conduct of the State in relation to a proceeding or proceedings and the subject-matter of the proceeding is only a very rough one. A State's consent in advance to the exercise of jurisdiction over it in relation to, for example, all disputes arising out of a given contract or, for that matter, on the basis of an international agreement[1] is as much a subject-matter-based exception to immunity from jurisdiction as any of those found in Part III of the Convention. Indeed, it is worth recalling that no national State immunity legislation places the consent-based exceptions to immunity in a different part or section from those more directly linked to the subject-matter of the claim.

2.3 'Exceptions'?

The ILC commentary to draft article 7[2] suggests that the rules embodied in Articles 7 to 9 of the Convention, unlike those in the provisions of Part III, are not exceptions to a State's immunity from jurisdiction at all but, rather, that the absence of the State's consent to the exercise of jurisdiction over it is a precondition to the availability of immunity. The distinction, which is far from universally accepted, has no practical significance for the purposes of the Convention.

3. Evaluation

Like various other aspects of the Convention, the title to Part II was not particularly well thought through, and is apt to confuse at first glance. Indeed, the very structuring of the Convention into Parts II, III, and IV, when the real division is between Parts II and III, on the one hand, and Part IV, one the other, makes the Convention one of the less user-friendly on the market. That said, these particular flaws are no more than cosmetic, and should not stand in the way of a workable application of the instrument.

[1] See, respectively, Art. 7(1)*(b)* and Art. 7(1)*(a)*.

[2] See ILC commentary, draft art. 7, para. 3.

Article 5

TOM GRANT

Article 5

State immunity

A State enjoys immunity, in respect of itself and its property, from the jurisdiction of the courts of another State subject to the provisions of the present Convention.

1. Introduction

Article 5 is the lynchpin of the Convention's provisions on immunity from jurisdiction as set out in Parts II and III. Once a legal or natural person qualifies as a 'State' within the meaning of Article 2(1)(*b*) of the Convention, it is entitled *ipso facto* to the immunity from foreign jurisdiction, in respect of itself and its property, posited in Article 5, subject always to the applicability to the proceedings in question of any of the exceptions to immunity enumerated in Articles 7 to 17. In short, it is Article 5 which, within the scheme of the Convention, effects the grant to a State of immunity from the jurisdiction of the courts of another State.

The broad-brush rule laid down in Article 5 is operationalized through Article 6, on the modalities for giving effect to immunity from jurisdiction, which obliges States to ensure that their courts accord the immunity recognized in Article 5, *proprio motu* if need be.

2. Drafting History

Given the centrality of the provision within the logic of Parts II and III of the Convention, it should perhaps come as no surprise that the drafting of Article 5 proved contentious.[1]

Special Rapporteur Sucharitkul proposed the initial version of the eventual Article 5 in his second report, presented to the Commission in 1980. Having set out, *in extenso*, State practice in respect of the general principle of a State's immunity from the jurisdiction of the courts of another State,[2] the Special Rapporteur put forward in a single provision both this general principle and the consequent rule that States were to give effect to such immunity.

Paragraph 1 of what was then draft article 6 read:

A foreign State shall be immune from the jurisdiction of a territorial State in accordance with the provisions of the present articles.[3]

[1] ILC commentary, draft art. 5, para. 2 notes tersely: 'The formulation of article 5, which expresses the main principle of State immunity, has been difficult, as it is a delicate matter.'

[2] See Second report Sucharitkul, 214–30, paras 65–126.

[3] Second report Sucharitkul, 230, para. 127.

After debate, the references to a 'foreign' State and a 'territorial' State, which at the time also appeared in the draft article on the use of terms,[4] were substituted by the more neutral term 'State',[5] with the Drafting Committee later positing that a State would enjoy immunity 'from the jurisdiction of the courts of another State'.[6] Purporting to adopt a 'neutral' approach that did 'not... take a position on the existing doctrinal theories of the basis for "State immunity"',[7] the Drafting Committee also specified that immunity from jurisdiction would be enjoyed 'subject to the provisions of the present articles and the relevant rules of general international law applicable in the matter'.[8]

The reference to general international law polarized the Commission. Its opponents thought it implied exceptions to the general rule of immunity exceeding those expressly incorporated in the draft articles.[9] One member in particular was 'completely opposed' to the proposed wording, which he believed 'made the whole draft pointless' and the Commission 'look ridiculous'.[10] In contrast, a number of members 'felt very strongly that the article would be acceptable only if it included the words'.[11] The text of draft article 6 adopted by the Commission on first reading[12] reflected this disagreement, with the words '[and the relevant rules of general international law]' being placed in square brackets.[13]

States' comments on the text of draft article 6 adopted on first reading, as well as debate within the Commission on second reading, evidenced continuing disagreement. As a matter of drafting, advocates of the absolutist position—among them Bulgaria, the German Democratic Republic, the USSR, and Brazil[14]—generally favoured deleting the bracketed phrase '[and the relevant rules of general international law]', a proposal endorsed by a number of other States, among them Czechoslovakia[15] and Thailand.[16] In contrast, other States, including the Federal Republic of Germany and the Nordic countries, saw a need for the words, as the rules on immunity were to be interpreted in accordance with existing custom and removing the clause might 'impede further development'.[17]

Faced with this opposition of views, Special Rapporteur Ogiso—who, like his predecessor, found it difficult to avoid extended discussion in the Commission over the theoretical basis of the rule in draft article 6[18]—proposed a number of alternatives. One was to adopt a formula modelled on the ILA's Draft Articles for a Convention on

[4] See the commentary to Art. 2(1)(*a*) and (*b*) UNCSI.

[5] See summary record 1634th ILC meeting, *YILC 1980*, vol. I, 260, 264, para. 43.

[6] Summary record 1968th ILC meeting, *YILC 1986*, vol. I, 169, para. 49.

[7] Summary record 1968th ILC meeting (n. 6), 169, para. 50.

[8] Summary record 1968th ILC meeting (n. 6), 169, para. 50.

[9] See Summary record 1968th ILC meeting (n. 6), 169, para. 52, and summary record 1971st ILC meeting, *YILC 1986*, vol. I, 188, 191, para. 35 (Nikolai Ushakov).

[10] Summary record 1968th ILC meeting (n. 6), 169, para. 52 (Nikolai Ushakov).

[11] Summary record 1970th ILC meeting *YILC 1986*, vol. I, 183, 188, para. 48 (Sir Ian Sinclair).

[12] See *YILC 1986*, vol. II, Part 2, 9.

[13] The words 'applicable in the matter' were, however, deleted. See summary record 1971st ILC meeting (n. 9), 192, paras 51–52.

[14] See eg 'Comments and observations received by Governments', *YILC 1988*, vol. II(1), 45, 82, para. 1 (USSR). For the Special Rapporteur's summary of States' comments, see Preliminary report Ogiso, 104, 57–67.

[15] See 'Comments and observations received by Governments' (n. 14), 64, para. 6 (Cze).

[16] See 'Comments and observations received by Governments' (n. 14), 81, para. 5 (Thai).

[17] 'Comments and observations received by Governments' (n. 14), 70, para. 6 (FRG), and 77, para. 3 (Nordic countries). For further support, see 'Comments and observations received by Governments' (n. 14), 73, para. 6 (Ita), and 84 and 86, paras 2 and 14 (UK).

[18] See Second report Ogiso, 61, para. 3.

State Immunity, adopted at the ILA's Montreal session in 1982, which formulated immunity not as a blanket principle subject to exceptions but as applicable to 'acts performed by it in the exercise of its sovereign authority, i.e. *jure imperii*'.[19] This, however, clashed with the approach in most national State immunity statutes. It was also considered impractical, as it would import into the draft articles' central provision the difficult questions of delineation to which the various, detailed provisions of Part III of the Convention were dedicated. Another suggestion, apparently intended to mollify the supporters of the bracketed phrase, was the inclusion of a new, further provision, a draft article 6 *bis*, which would afford States an opportunity to identify and declare additional exceptions to immunity from jurisdiction not enshrined in the draft articles, to which other States would have thirty days to object.[20] The proposal was poorly received, even among supporters of the general international law clause,[21] and was quickly abandoned.

Compromise solutions having been exhausted, the Drafting Committee no longer could avoid a decision on the retention or deletion of the clause in brackets in draft article 6, and, after further debate, finally decided to delete it.[22] As the ILC commentary explains, in the end supporters accepted that an explicit reference to general international law in what was eventually renumbered draft article 5 was unnecessary, as 'any immunity or exception to immunity accorded under the ... articles would have no effect on general international law and would not prejudice the future development of State practice'.[23] The provision as amended was finally adopted on second reading in 1991.

With the substitution of the word 'Convention' for 'the present articles', the text of draft article 5 passed into the Convention as adopted in 2004.

3. Key Points

Given the significance of Article 5 to Parts II and III of the Convention, it is fortunate that it does not raise major issues of interpretation or application.

3.1 'immunity ... from the jurisdiction of the courts of another State'

Article 5 posits the availability in principle to a State of 'immunity ... from the jurisdiction of the courts of another State'. Three elements of this formulation call for brief note. First, what Article 5 provides for is no more than a procedural immunity, a bar to judicial proceedings, rather than the State's substantive non-liability under the municipal law applied by the court or the exemption from the application of that substantive law to it in the first place.[24] Secondly, although Part II of the Convention, in which Article 5 is

[19] Second report Ogiso, 64, para. 15.

[20] See Second report Ogiso, 64–5, para. 17.

[21] See eg summary record 2115th ILC meeting, *YILC 1989*, vol. I, 135, 141, para 46 (Paul Reuter); summary record 2116th ILC meeting, *YILC 1989*, vol. I, 143, 143, para. 3 (Christian Tomuschat); *YILC 1989*, vol. I, 144, para. 10 (Carlos Calero-Rodrigues); *YILC 1989*, vol. I, 145, para. 22 (Ahmed Mahiou); *YILC 1989*, vol. I, 147, para. 42 (Riyadh Al-Qaysi); summary record 2117th ILC meeting, *YILC 1989*, vol. I, 150, 151, para. 4 (César Sepúlveda Gutiérrez); *YILC 1989*, vol. I, 156, para. 59 (Mohamed Bennouna); *YILC 1989*, vol. I, para. 158, para. 74 (Pemmaraju Sreenivasa Rao); summary record 2118th ILC meeting *YILC 1989*, vol. I, 160, 161, para. 11 (Abdul Koroma).

[22] See summary record 2191st ILC meeting, *YILC 1990*, vol. I, 306, 311, para. 44 (chairman of Drafting Committee).

[23] ILC Commentary, draft art. 5, para. 3.

[24] See eg *Al-Adsani v United Kingdom*, 123 ILR 24, 38, para. 48 (ECtHR (GC) 2001).

found, is entitled 'General principles', it is clear that Articles 5 to 9 pertain only to jurisdiction, and not also to measures of constraint taken against State property.[25] That is, the immunity of the State recognized in Article 5 serves as a bar only to proceedings or, synonymously, suit, and not also to judicially ordered measures against its property, such as arrest, attachment, and execution, the latter being the concern of Part IV of the Convention, in which a general rule of immunity, subject to narrow exceptions, is laid down in Articles 18 and 19 respectively. Thirdly, Article 5 deals with immunity from the jurisdiction of the courts only of another State. Whether a State chooses to provide for the immunity of its various organs of government etc from the jurisdiction of its own courts is a matter for the law of that State.[26]

3.2 'in respect of itself and its property'

The immunity from foreign jurisdiction recognized in Article 5 applies in respect of the State itself and in respect of its property. What the reference to the State's property in Article 5 concerns is not immunity from measures of constraint, a matter addressed under Part IV of the Convention. Article 5's 'property' clause concerns, instead, immunity from proceedings, whether instituted against the State[27] in relation to its rights in or use of property or—Article 18 ('State immunity from pre-judgment measures of constraint') permitting—instituted *in rem* against the property itself.

3.3 'A State enjoys immunity... subject to the provisions of the present Convention'

A. The structure of argument under Parts II and III

Whatever the theoretical and historical foundations of the restrictive doctrine of State immunity, Parts II and III of the Convention are premised on the pragmatic view that 'the principle of State immunity should be taken as a point of departure in any logical treatment of the topic'[28]—in other words, that 'State immunity should be the general rule', with limitations on the availability of this immunity in given proceedings being expressed as exceptions to the rule. This is precisely how Article 5, the cornerstone of Parts II and III of the Convention, is formulated. It posits that a State is entitled to immunity from foreign jurisdiction unless it is not—that is, unless one of the exceptions to immunity enumerated in the remaining provisions of Parts II and III applies in the relevant proceedings.

This argumentative structure, particularly the logic of Article 5 as it relates to Part III, and, more importantly, what some members of the ILC and some States thought it implied about the theoretical basis of State immunity from jurisdiction, was the subject of sharp differences within the ILC.[29] But it is hard to see how else a convention that sought to codify the international rules on a State's immunity from foreign proceedings could be framed. To abandon the general rule and, instead, posit that immunity from the

[25] See the introductory commentary to Part II.

[26] See the commentary to Art. 1.

[27] Note that, in accordance with Art. 6(2) of the Convention, proceedings are taken to be instituted 'against the State' within the meaning of the Convention if the State is either directly or merely indirectly impleaded by them. See the commentary to Art. 6.

[28] Preliminary report Sucharitkul, 240, para. 59.

[29] See the introductory commentary to Part III.

jurisdiction of the courts of another State exists in respect only of *acta jure imperii* would upset the structure in which the exceptions to immunity are indicated in later rules. It would be difficult, in practice, to maintain an orderly application of the rules; and, as the content of the exclusive category would itself be a matter of contention, a text in that form would deprive the main rule of conceptual clarity. It is surely no coincidence in this light that the ECSI, the only binding codification of the law of State immunity at the international level prior to the Convention, and every national State immunity statute, operates by way of a general rule of State immunity from foreign jurisdiction to which subsequent—or, in the case of Chapter I of the ECSI, preceding—rules as to the unavailability of immunity in specific circumstances constitute exceptions.

The practical consequence of this structure for the conduct of proceedings under the Convention is that, once a legal or natural person satisfies the court that it qualifies as a foreign 'State' within the meaning of Article 2(1)(*b*) of the Convention, it is presumed to enjoy immunity from the court's jurisdiction unless the claimant can make out one of the specified exceptions to immunity. In other words, it follows from Article 5, as formulated, that the burden of proof lies on the claimant to prove that the State is not immune from the proceedings. It is not up to the State to establish that it is entitled to immunity.

That said, the onus of proving that the impleaded party is indeed a foreign 'State' lies on that party. As a result, something of a dialectic will play out in proceedings under the Convention, in the same way that it plays out generally in proceedings in which immunity from jurisdiction is pleaded.[30] First the burden lies on the impleaded party to satisfy the court that it is an emanation of a foreign State within the meaning of Article 2(1)(*b*), the default position being that, like any other impleaded party on which process has been served effectively, it is amenable to the court's jurisdiction. Should the court be satisfied on this point, the burden shifts to the claimant to establish that the State is nonetheless not immune from the instant proceedings. In practice, the identity of the impleaded party may be clear enough that extensive argument is unnecessary on the first point; the focus then is principally on the application of the exceptions.

B. *The exhaustiveness of the exceptions*

Article 5 specifies that a State enjoys immunity from the jurisdiction of a court of another State 'subject to the provisions of the . . . Convention'. In other words, the only limitations on a State party's immunity from the jurisdiction of a court of another State party are those enumerated in the Convention itself, by which is meant Parts II and III of the Convention. No other exceptions to the immunity posited in Article 5 are applicable as among States parties. This was a considered choice, as the drafting history of the provision makes clear.[31]

Both the International Court of Justice and a range of national courts have already looked to Article 5 and its relationship with Parts II and especially III of the Convention as persuasive evidence of the unavailability as a matter of customary international law of any exceptions to a State's immunity not specified in those Parts—the specific exception

[30] This includes proceedings under national statute. See eg *Minister of Defense and Support for the Armed Forces of the Islamic Republic of Iran v Elahi*, 546 US 450, 452–3 (*per curiam*) (US (SC) 2006).

[31] See section 2.

alleged in all these cases being an exception in respect of allegations of torture or human rights violations generally or violations of *jus cogens*.[32]

4. Evaluation

Article 5 is of fundamental importance within the Convention's scheme for immunity from jurisdiction. It does not determine whether immunity is to be accorded to a State in a given case, but it structures the argument. The availability to a State of immunity from the jurisdiction of the courts of another State is the 'point of departure'.[33] The specific instances in which a State will be taken to have consented, expressly (as under Article 7) or implicitly (as under Articles 8 and 9), to the exercise of jurisdiction over it and the specific proceedings in which immunity cannot be invoked (as enumerated in Part III of the Convention) represent exceptions to this general rule. It is to the applicability to the instant proceedings of one or more of these exceptions that the submissions of the litigants will be directed.

[32] See *Jurisdictional Immunities of the State (Germany v Italy: Greece intervening), Judgment*, 3 February 2012, International Court of Justice, para. 89; *Jones v Ministry of Interior of the Kingdom of Saudi Arabia*, 129 ILR 629, 727, para. 26 (UK (HL) 2006); *Fang and others v Jiang Zemin and others*, 141 ILR 702, 713–14, para. 49, 716–17, paras 62–63, and 717, para. 65 (NZ (HC) 2006); *Natoniewski v Federal Republic of Germany*, reproduced (2010) 30 *Polish YIL* 299, 302–3, cross-referable to 300 (Pol (SC) 2010); *Islamic Republic of Iran v Hashemi*, 2012 QCCA 1449, paras 54–55 (Can (Quebec CA) 2012). See also also *Carpenter v Republic of Chile*, No. 07-cv-5290, 2009 WL 5255327, *3 (US (EDNY) 2009), affirmed *Carpenter v Republic of Chile*, 610 F.3d 776 (US (2nd Cir.) 2010), where the exhaustiveness of the exceptions specified in the Convention and the absence from them of an exception in respect of alleged violations of *jus cogens* was taken to mean that, contrary to plaintiff's claim, Chile had not expressly or implicitly waived its immunity under the FSIA (US).

[33] Preliminary report Sucharitkul, 240, para. 59.

Article 6

Tom Grant

Article 6

Modalities for giving effect to State immunity

1. A State shall give effect to State immunity under article 5 by refraining from exercising jurisdiction in a proceeding before its courts against another State and to that end shall ensure that its courts determine on their own initiative that the immunity of that other State under article 5 is respected.
2. A proceeding before a court of a State shall be considered to have been instituted against another State if that other State:
   (*a*) is named as a party to that proceeding; or
   (*b*) is not named as a party to the proceeding but the proceeding in effect seeks to affect the property, rights, interests or activities of that other State.

1. Introduction

Article 6 of the Convention operationalizes, as it were, the general rule of a State's immunity from the jurisdiction of the courts of another State posited in Article 5. It stipulates in paragraph 1 that a State party must 'refrain[] from exercising jurisdiction in a proceeding before its courts against another State'. This basic obligation of abstention is furthered by the imposition on a State party of a positive obligation to ensure that its courts not only respect the immunity laid down in Article 5 but, moreover and less self-evidently, that they determine the question of immunity *proprio motu*, if need be. Paragraph 2 of Article 6 clarifies the scope of the obligations embodied in paragraph 1 by specifying when, for the purposes of that provision, a proceeding before a court is to be considered to have been instituted 'against another State'. It makes clear that, under the Convention, a proceeding 'against another State' is not limited to a proceeding in which that other State is named as a party to the proceeding. Rather, as indicated in Article 6(2)(*b*), the immunity from jurisdiction posited in Article 5 extends to situations where the other State is indirectly impleaded—in other words, where the other State 'is not named as a party to the proceeding' but where the proceeding nonetheless 'seeks to affect the property, rights, interests or activities of that other State'.

Although Article 6 stipulates what, for the most part, are no more than natural consequences of Article 5, it is central to the working of Parts II and III of the Convention. It fleshes out the juridical and practical content of Article 5's bare rule, namely by establishing an international legal obligation on the part of the forum State not to exercise jurisdiction, directly or indirectly, over another State. In addition, it operates as a link between the international and domestic legal orders, serving to translate a State party's obligation of abstention into a positive duty on that party to ensure that its legal system is not only capable of but also proactive in giving effect to State immunity.

2. Drafting History

Articles 5 and 6 of the Convention began life as a single draft article. Before adopting a text on first reading, however, the ILC decided to split the provision into two so as to accord separate treatment to, on the one hand, the general rule of the immunity of a State from the jurisdiction of the courts of another[1] and, on the other, the modalities for giving effect to this general rule. The basic idea of the draft article on modalities was agreed at an early stage, although the eventual formulation of paragraphs 1 and 2[2] of what became draft article 6 and in due course Article 6 of the Convention was finalized only towards the end of the Commission's second reading.

In his second report, presented to the ILC in 1980, Special Rapporteur Sucharitkul proposed to render more concrete the general rule of immunity from jurisdiction, then posited in proposed draft article 6(1), by adding a second paragraph to the effect that '[t]he judicial and administrative authorities of the territorial State shall give effect to State immunity recognized in the present articles'.[3] Initial debate within the Commission resulted in a streamlined text,[4] which, together with a provision identifying situations in which a State was obliged to give effect to State immunity, would soon form part of a new, separate draft article 7.[5] Paragraph 1 of this proposed draft article 7 imposed on States an obligation to give effect to State immunity, although a statement that a State was to do so 'notwithstanding its authority under its rules of competence to conduct the proceedings in a given case'[6] was deleted[7] after debate over the meaning of 'competence' and 'authority'.[8]

The eventual Article 6(2) did not appear in Special Rapporteur Sucharitkul's second report. The essence of the provision did, however, form the basis of paragraph 2 of the new draft article 7 proposed the following year.[9] This clarified that a State need not be named as respondent to a proceeding for it to enjoy immunity from the court's jurisdiction but, rather, would still be entitled to immunity if only indirectly impleaded.

[1] For the separate evolution of this limb of the original unitary provision, see the commentary to Art. 5.

[2] On first reading, the Commission posited in addition a draft art. 7(3), listing common instances in which a proceeding was to be considered to have been instituted 'against another State', among them proceedings against State organs, against instrumentalities exercising governmental authority, and so on. As adopted on first reading in 1986, this draft art. 7(3) reproduced the provisions on the meaning of 'State' found in the draft art. on the use of terms. See Report ILC, thirty-eighth session, 9. In their subsequent comments on draft art. 7 as adopted on first reading, several governments drew attention to the overlap, and suggested the deletion of draft art. 7(3). See 'Comments and observations received by Governments', *YILC 1988*, vol. II(1), 45, 90, para. 5 (Ven); Preliminary report Ogiso, 105, para. 74 (Aus, Mex, Swi, and UK). After an attempt by Special Rapporteur Ogiso to salvage the provision in Third report Ogiso, 10, the Drafting Committee conceded defeat. See summary record 2191st meeting, *YILC 1990*, vol. I, 306, 311, para. 49.

[3] Second report Sucharitkul, 230, para. 127.

[4] See Report ILC, thirty-second session, 142. The revised text referred to a 'State' generically, not to the 'territorial' State, and avoided reference to 'judicial and administrative authorities', which had been thought 'unduly restrictive. See summary record 1634th ILC meeting, *YILC 1980*, vol. I, 260, 265, para. 51 (chairman of Drafting Committee).

[5] See summary record 1653rd ILC meeting, *YILC 1981*, vol. I, 55, 58, para. 18.

[6] Summary record 1653rd ILC meeting (n. 5), 58, para. 18.

[7] See summary record 1749th ILC meeting, *YILC 1982*, vol. I, 317, 323, para. 47.

[8] See eg summary record 1653rd ILC meeting (n. 5), 59, para. 29 (Sir Francis Vallat); summary record 1654th ILC meeting, *YILC 1981*, vol. I, 60, 62, para. 12 (Nikolai Ushakov); summary record 1655th ILC meeting, ibid., 65, 66, para. 13 (Milan Šahović); summary record 1715th ILC meeting, *YILC 1982*, vol. I, 97, 99–100, para. 19 (Zhengyu Ni).

[9] See Third report Sucharitkul, 141, para. 44.

Even those ILC members who had initially questioned the need for a draft article specifically on modalities for giving effect to State immunity accepted the need for the clarification. Without it, members acknowledged, a claimant might circumvent a State's immunity from jurisdiction by instituting proceedings which, although implicating the State by affecting its property or other interests, did not name the State as respondent.[10]

The Special Rapporteur put forward alternative proposals for the text of draft article 7(2). No clear preference having emerged in the Commission, the Drafting Committee proposed a compromise formulation according to which a legal proceeding was considered to be one against another State, whether or not that other State is named as a party to the proceeding,

> so long as the proceeding in effect seeks to compel that other State either to submit to the jurisdiction of the court or to bear the consequences of a determination by the court which may affect the rights, interests, properties or activities of that other State.[11]

The provision was adopted in this form on first reading as draft article 7(2).[12]

In its comments on the text as adopted on first reading, Australia expressed concern that draft article 7(2) was formulated too broadly.[13]

On second reading, while Special Rapporteur Ogiso's proposed wording would have left draft article 7(2) largely intact,[14] the Drafting Committee simplified the provision greatly. Considering the formulation 'to bear the consequences of a determination by the court which may affect' to create 'too loose a relationship between the proceeding and the consequences to which it gave rise',[15] the Committee proposed that it be replaced with the simple phrase 'to affect'.[16] The words 'so long as the proceeding in effect seeks to compel that other State either to submit to local jurisdiction', despite having appeared in successive drafts, were also discarded as 'meaningless'.[17] Finally, in the interests of clarity, the distinct scenarios of direct and indirect impleading were 'disentangled' and addressed separately in subparagraphs (*a*) and (*b*) respectively.[18]

In 1990, the Drafting Committee proposed the insertion into draft article 7(1) of an obligation on the State to ensure that its courts gave effect *propio motu* to a foreign State's immunity from jurisdiction.[19] Although concern was expressed by one member that this new, second limb of draft article 7(1) might encourage respondent States not to appear before the court,[20] the proposal was accepted, and the Commission finally adopted draft

[10] See eg summary record 1714th ILC meeting, *YILC 1982*, 92, 94, para. 22 (Stephen McCaffrey) and 96, para. 33 (S.P. Jagota); summary record 1715th ILC meeting, *YILC 1982*, 97, 97, para. 4 (Riyadh Al-Qaysi). But *cf YILC 1982*, 101, para. 35 (Carlos Calero Rodrigues), believing that the second paragraph stated an aspect of the matter that was 'part and parcel' of the obligation laid down in para. 1.

[11] Summary record 1749th ILC meeting (n. 7), 323, para. 47.

[12] See Report ILC, thirty-eighth session, 9.

[13] See Preliminary report Ogiso, 105, para. 73.

[14] See Preliminary report Ogiso, 105, para. 73.

[15] Summary record 2191st ILC meeting, *YILC 1990*, vol. I, 306, 311, para. 48 (chairman of Drafting Committee). The observation was subsequently incorporated into ILC commentary, draft art. 6, para. 13.

[16] Summary record 2191st ILC meeting (n. 15), 311, para. 48.

[17] Summary record 2191st ILC meeting (n. 15), 311, para. 48.

[18] Summary record 2191st ILC meeting (n. 15), 311, para. 47.

[19] See summary record 2191st ILC meeting (n. 15), 311, para. 45.

[20] See summary record 2218th ILC meeting, *YILC 1991*, vol. I, 66, 71, paras 47 and 50 (Stephen McCaffrey). See also, subsequently, 'Convention on Jurisdictional Immunities of States and Their Property: Report of the Secretary-General', UN doc. A/47/326 (4 August 1992), 29, para. 9 (US).

article 6 on second reading.[21] From there it passed unchanged into the Convention as Article 6.

3. Key Points

3.1 Article 6(1)

The first clause of Article 6(1) 'stat[es] the obvious',[22] namely that a State party to the Convention is obliged to give effect to the immunity from the jurisdiction of its courts granted to other States parties by Article 5—subject, that is, to the remaining provisions of Parts II and III of the Convention—'by refraining from exercising jurisdiction in a proceeding before its courts against another State'. It is in its second clause that the added value of Article 6(1) lies. In accordance with the second clause, a State party must see to it that its courts determine the question of, and in appropriate cases grant, State immunity *proprio motu* in the event that a foreign State impleaded by proceedings fails to appear before or otherwise to communicate with the court to claim its immunity. The obligation has antecedents in Article 15 ECSI, which stipulates that 'the court shall decline to entertain . . . proceedings even if the State does not appear', and in numerous national State immunity provisions.[23]

The obligation on a State to ensure that its courts decide *proprio motu* the question of State immunity does not presuppose executive interference with the independence of the judiciary. As has been the case, for example, with the implementation of Article 15 ECSI,[24] it is to be expected that States will legislate to impose such a duty on their courts, as many States not parties to the ECSI have done.[25]

Quite how a determination *proprio motu* of the immunity of a non-appearing and otherwise uncommunicative State works in practice will depend on the court and on the civil procedure of the forum State. It may be, where the State is named as defendant to the proceeding, that the court is compelled by circumstance to invite third-party submissions on the point by an *amicus curiae* or equivalent. Where the State is merely indirectly impleaded, it may be that the court invites submissions from the parties.

The terms 'another State' and 'that other State' in the chapeau to Article 6(2) are obviously cross-referable to the definition of 'State' in Article 2(1)(*b*) of the Convention. That is, whenever a proceeding is against one of the legal or natural persons specified in Article 2(1)(*b*) as falling within the term 'State' for the purposes of the Convention, the State party is obliged to refrain from exercising jurisdiction over it and to ensure that its courts give effect to its immunity.[26]

Although it ought to go without saying, it may be useful to stress that the second clause of Article 6(1) does not mean that courts must conclude that immunity from jurisdiction applies in every case. The foreign State is *prima facie* entitled to immunity as posited in

[21] See summary record 2218th ILC meeting (n. 20), 72, para. 54.

[22] See summary record 1656th ILC meeting, *YILC 1981*, 69, 71, para. 14 (George Aldrich).

[23] See s. 1(2) SIA (UK), given effect to Art. 15 ECSI; s. 27(1)(*b*) and (2) FStIA (Aus); s. 3(2) SIA (Can); s. 14 FSIL (Isr); s. 3(2) SIO (Pak); s. 3(2) SIA (Sing); s. 2(2) FStIA (SA).

[24] See eg s. 1(2) SIA (UK).

[25] Recall references in n. 23.

[26] See ILC commentary, draft art. 6, para. 10.

Article 5, but this remains subject, as Article 5 itself makes clear, to the exceptions enumerated in Articles 7 to 17 of the Convention.

3.2 Article 6(2)

Article 6(1) requires that a State refrain from exercising jurisdiction in a proceeding 'against another State'. Article 6(2) explains when a proceeding is to be considered one 'against another State'. What it provides is that a proceeding is one against another State if it either directly or indirectly impleads that other State.

*A. Article 6(2)(*a*)*

Article 6(2)(*a*) provides that a proceeding is to be considered one 'against another State' for the purposes of Article 6(1) if that other State is 'named as a party to that proceeding'. What 'named as a party to [the] proceeding' means is that the State is named as the respondent (synonymously, defendant) to the case, either individually or jointly.[27] It may be that the State is so named from the outset, having been the object of the service of initiating process, or that the State has intervened in the proceeding to become joined as respondent. Either way, the proceeding is one against that State within the meaning of Article 6(2)(*a*) and therefore within the meaning of Article 6(1).

*B. Article 6(2)(*b*)*

Article 6(2)(*b*) specifies that a State need not be named as a party to the proceeding for that proceeding to be considered one 'against' it. Rather, the obligations of the forum State under Article 6(1) apply also where, in the words of Article 6(2)(*b*), 'the proceeding in effect seeks to affect the property, rights, interests or activities of [the] other State'. This situation is known as 'indirect impleading'. It is not to be confused with the situation where an emanation of the State other than the State by that name is named as a party to the proceeding. A proceeding instituted against, say, a ministry of a State, a federal constituent unit of a State, an agency or instrumentality of a State, or an individual representative of a State is, in accordance with the various sub-subparagraphs of Article 2(1)(*b*) of the Convention, a proceeding against a State, and as such falls for consideration under Article 6(2)(*a*). Indirect impleading within the meaning of Article 6(2)(*b*) is where no legal or natural person qualifying as a 'State' under Article 2(1)(*b*) is named as a party to the proceeding but where that proceeding nonetheless seeks to affect the property, rights, interests, or activities of that person.

The property of a State within the meaning of Article 6(2)(*b*) comprehends all property either owned by a State or possessed or controlled by it. This is in line with the notion of 'property of a State' used in Part IV of the Convention,[28] dealing with immunity from measures of constraint against property of a State.

The classic example of a proceeding in which a State is not named as a party to the proceeding but in which the claimant seeks nonetheless to affect the property, rights, interests, or activities of that State is an action instituted *in rem* against a State ship.[29] An action *in rem* against a ship owned or operated by a State is one in which the ship itself is named as respondent, but such a proceeding clearly seeks to affect the property

[27] See ILC commentary, draft art. 6, para. 8.
[28] See the commentaries to Arts 18 and 19.
[29] See ILC commentary, draft art. 6, paras 11–13.

etc of the owner or operator State.[30] As noted in the ILC commentary, claims involving the seizure or attachment of vessels for maritime liens or collision damages or salvage services have played a considerable role in developing the law of State immunity in general and Article 6 in particular.[31]

A second paradigm case of a proceeding falling under Article 6(2)(*b*) is that in which the parties dispute as between themselves rights or interests in property and a third-party State asserts a right or interest in the same property. In this situation a link exists between Article 6(2)(*b*) and Article 8(2)(*b*). The latter, dealing with implied consent to jurisdiction, provides for the situation in which a State whose property would be affected by proceedings to which the State is not named as a party intervenes 'for the sole purpose of . . . asserting a right or interest in property at issue in the proceeding'.

Depending on the interpretation and application of Article 2(1)(*b*)(iv) of the Convention, dealing with individual State representatives,[32] it may be that another example of indirect impleading for the purposes of Article 6(2)(*b*) is where a former State representative is named as respondent to a claim in respect of acts or omissions during his or her time in office and relating to his or her official capacity. As the respondent to a claim, the former State representative well may say, as the main defence, that he or she for purposes of the proceedings is to be considered a State representative under Article 2(1)(*b*)(iv).[33] As an alternative defence, the former State representative would say that the claim is one that seeks to affect the rights, interests, or activities of the State in whose service he or she once acted, and thus the proceeding is one against the State itself for the purposes of Article 6(2)(*b*).

Two major questions remain unanswered in relation to Article 6(2)(*b*).

First, although the verb 'to affect' was introduced in order to narrow the scope of Article 6(2)(*b*),[34] it is not a verb denoting clear limits. Limits nonetheless are necessary if the provision is to preserve a rational scheme of jurisdiction. In an interconnected society, nearly any proceeding could be said to 'affect' the interests or activities, and even the rights and property, of others, including States. Clearly Article 6(2)(*b*) cannot encompass all actions however ancillary or incidental their relation to a State. In this light, draft article 6(2)(*b*) as finally adopted on second reading attracted the following comment from the US:

> The [ILC] commentary notes . . . that actions involving seizure or attachment of State property have been considered in the practice of States to be proceedings that in effect implicate the foreign sovereign (even though it may not be named as a party to the proceeding). However, paragraph 2(*b*) is not limited to such actions; it also includes proceedings that affect the 'interests' or 'activities' of a foreign State—terms that are sufficiently expansive to reach many other kinds of cases. For example, litigation involving banking, financial or other regulations that may have an impact upon foreign State activities would arguably also be encompassed within this provision. Moreover, it is unclear what obligations the parties to any such proceeding, or the court itself, may have

[30] Note, however, that in most cases under the Convention the institution of actions *in rem* against ships owned or operated by a State will be barred by Art. 18. See the commentary to Arts 16 and especially 18.

[31] See ILC commentary, draft art. 6, para. 12.

[32] Recall commentary to Art. 2(1)(*a*) and (*b*).

[33] In contrast, were the former State representative sued in respect of acts or omissions in an official capacity to be considered a 'State' under Art. 2(1)(*b*)(iv), the proceeding would be one in which the State is named as a party, as per Art. 6(2)(*a*).

[34] Recall section 2.

towards the affected foreign state; for example, must notice be provided to the foreign State, by whom, and within what time period? We believe that further consideration should be given to these issues.[35]

The uncertainty, perhaps, is addressed by saying that the effect with which Article 6(2)(*b*) is concerned is a specifically legal effect, such as the imposition of a lien or a declaration of title, as distinguished from a social, economic, or political effect. Interpreted and applied this way, the provision would afford a meaningful scope of protection to States while also recognizing that immunity from jurisdiction cannot serve as a means by which a foreign State can bar any proceeding the prospective outcome of which may not be to its liking.

The second question in relation to Article 6(2)(*b*) is how, as a procedural matter, a court is to give effect to the immunity of an indirectly impleaded State. The unknown here is whether it is necessary that the State have intervened in the proceedings—not on the merits, but for the purpose of asserting its immunity[36] (and perhaps also, before this, asserting its interest in any property at issue[37]). But this would suggest that the State's participation in the proceedings is a prerequisite to the court applying Article 6(2)(*b*). Given the obligation on the forum State to ensure that another State's immunity from jurisdiction is decided and, where appropriate, accorded by its courts *proprio motu*, the expectation would seem to be that a court will determine the question of the immunity of an indirectly impleaded State notwithstanding the State's absence from the proceedings and the lack of any other communication from the State to the court to assert its immunity. How the court carries out the task of determining the question of immunity in these circumstances presents a procedural puzzle. It may be that the court seeks submissions on the point from either the parties or an *amicus curiae* or the like.[38]

4. Evaluation

To an extent, Article 6 is otiose.[39] Though possibly attractive as a pleading point,[40] it could go without saying that the international legal corollary of the immunity of a State from the jurisdiction of the courts of another State is an obligation on the part of the latter to refrain from exercising the jurisdiction of its courts over the former. It could equally go without saying that States parties to the Convention are obliged to take such action within their respective domestic legal orders as is necessary to make possible their compliance with their obligations under the Convention. Nor does it add great clarity to the matter to say that proceedings in which a State is named as a party are proceedings 'against' that State for the purposes of the immunity from jurisdiction to which it is entitled.

Article 6 nonetheless is significant in two respects. First, it requires States parties to ensure that their courts determine on their own initiative—that is, even if immunity is not raised by the litigants in the proceedings—that the immunity specified in the

35 'Convention on Jurisdictional Immunities of States and Their Property: Report of the Secretary-General', (n. 20), 29–30, para. 10 (US).

36 See, in this regard, Art. 8(2)(*a*) and the commentary thereto.

37 See Art. 8(2)(*b*) and the commentary thereto.

38 Recall section 3.1.

39 Recall summary record 1656th ILC meeting (n. 22), 71, para. 14 (George Aldrich), quoted section 3.1.

40 See *The 'ARA Libertad' Case (Argentina v Ghana), Request for the prescription of provisional measures, Order*, 15 December 2012, para. 49; and Kohen (Arg.), 30 November 2012, ITLOS/PV.12/C20/3., 9, line 20.

Convention is respected under their jurisdiction. Secondly, reflecting a functional rather than formalist approach, the provision specifies that a State's immunity from jurisdiction is to be respected if the proceedings in effect seek 'to affect the property, rights, interests or activities' of that State, even though the State is not named as a party to those proceedings. It is in the light of these rules in particular that the relevance of Article 6 to the interpretation and application of the Convention as a whole is to be seen.

Article 7

Roger O'Keefe

Article 7

Express consent to exercise of jurisdiction

1. A State cannot invoke immunity from jurisdiction in a proceeding before a court of another State with regard to a matter or case if it has expressly consented to the exercise of jurisdiction by the court with regard to the matter or case:
   (*a*) by international agreement;
   (*b*) in a written contract; or
   (*c*) by a declaration before the court or by a written communication in a specific proceeding.
2. Agreement by a State for the application of the law of another State shall not be interpreted as consent to the exercise of jurisdiction by the courts of that other State.

1. Introduction

Article 7 of the Convention, which qualifies a State's immunity from proceedings as recognized in Article 5, is said to embody the general principle[1] that immunity from the exercise of jurisdiction by a foreign court is 'conditional upon the absence or lack of consent on the part of the State against which the exercise of jurisdiction is being sought'.[2] Whether this is the best way of putting it is questionable. What is beyond doubt, however, is that a State's consent to a foreign court's exercise of jurisdiction over it serves in principle to render unavailable to that State in the relevant proceedings the procedural bar of immunity from jurisdiction.

Paragraph 1 of Article 7 provides that a State cannot invoke immunity in proceedings before a court of another State if it has expressly consented to the exercise of jurisdiction by that court, in relation to the matter or case before the court, by way of international agreement, written contract, or either oral declaration before or written communication to the court. Paragraph 2 provides, for the avoidance of doubt, that consent to the application of the law of another State does not constitute consent to the exercise of jurisdiction by the courts of that other State.

Article 7 is the first of a 'trilogy of provisions on . . . consent' in Part II of the Convention, a trilogy completed by Article 8 ('Effect of participation in a proceeding before a court') and Article 9 ('Counterclaims').[3] It is to be read alongside Article 20, which specifies that consent to the exercise of jurisdiction within the meaning of Article 7 does not imply consent to the taking of pre- or post-judgment measures of constraint for the purposes of Articles 18 and 19 of the Convention.

[1] See Part II ('General Principles') UNCSI.
[2] ILC commentary, draft art. 7, para. 3.
[3] ILC commentary, draft art. 9, para. 1.

2. Drafting History

What was originally proposed in the Third Report by Special Rapporteur Sucharitkul as draft article 8 ('Consent of State') was a somewhat inelegant provision.[4] Draft article 8(1) and (2) comprised paired statements to the effect that a State was not permitted to exercise jurisdiction over another State without the latter's consent but that jurisdiction could be exercised over a State which consented to this exercise. Draft article 8(3) detailed the means by which a State could consent to the exercise of jurisdiction over it, namely 'in writing, expressly for a specific case after a dispute has arisen', as per subparagraph (*a*); 'in advance, by an express provision in a treaty or an international agreement or in a written contract in respect of one or more types of cases', as per subparagraph (*b*); or, as provided for in subparagraph (*c*), 'by the State itself, through its authorised representative appearing before the [c]ourt in a proceeding to contest a claim on the merit [*sic*] without raising a plea of State immunity'.[5]

Special Rapporteur Sucharitkul put forward in addition to draft article 8 a draft article 11 dedicated to waiver of immunity.[6] Paragraph 1 of this further provision stated that immunity from jurisdiction could be waived by a State any time prior to or during proceedings against it before a court of another State. Paragraph 2 specified the means by which such waiver could be effected, while paragraphs 3 and 4 had the effect of precluding a State from subsequently claiming immunity if it appeared before the foreign court in the same proceedings for any purpose other than to assert immunity or its rights to property. The ILC, however, dispensed with this proposed additional provision, which in part repeated what was covered in draft article 8 and was in part capable of being merged into draft article 9 ('Voluntary submission').

Draft article 8 was substantially revised by Special Rapporteur Sucharitkul in the light of debate on the topic in the ILC and Sixth Committee. A reformulated provision, adopted by the Drafting Committee, deleted the cumbersome paragraphs 1 and 2 as originally proposed, and posited instead in one simplified and consolidated paragraph the proposition that a State could not invoke immunity in proceedings before a court of another State with regard to any matter in respect of which it had expressly consented to the exercise of jurisdiction. This consent could be manifested in an international agreement, a written contract, or a declaration before the court in a specific case.[7] The Drafting Committee's version of draft article 8 was provisionally adopted by the Commission on first reading in 1982[8] and adopted on first reading with the rest of the draft articles in 1986.[9]

In response to comments by governments,[10] the succeeding Special Rapporteur, Motoo Ogiso, proposed in his Third Report not only to amend draft article 8(*c*) to

[4] See Third report Sucharitkul, 144, para. 58. For further details on the drafting process, see the commentary to Art. 8 UNCSI, section 2.

[5] Third report Sucharitkul, 144, para. 58.

[6] See Third report Sucharitkul, 150, para. 92.

[7] Summary record 1750th ILC meeting, *YILC 1982*, vol. I, 324, 324, para. 3.

[8] See summary record 1750th ILC meeting (n. 7), 325.

[9] See Report ILC, thirty-eighth session, *YILC 1986*, vol. II(2), 9 (draft art. 8): 'A State cannot invoke immunity from jurisdiction in a proceeding before a court of another State with regard to any matter if it has expressly consented to the exercise of jurisdiction by that court with regard to such a matter: *(a)* by international agreement; *(b)* in a written contract; or (*c*) by a declaration before the court in a specific case.'

[10] See Preliminary report Ogiso, 106, paras 85–87 and 90–91.

provide that 'a written express consent given after a dispute between the parties has arisen' sufficed to permit the exercise of jurisdiction by a court of another State but also to insert a second paragraph in the draft article 'to make it clear that an agreement made by one State concerning the application of the law of another State on a certain subject [did] not necessarily signify agreement to the exercise of jurisdiction by the court of the latter State'.[11] On second reading in the Drafting Committee, draft article 8 became draft article 7, and was amended on the basis of discussion in the ILC and comments by governments.[12] The wording of what (with the insertion of a new paragraph 2) was now paragraph 1, which until then had provided that a State could not invoke immunity before a foreign court with regard to any 'matter' in respect of which it had consented to the exercise of jurisdiction, was changed to refer to any 'matter or case'. The amendment was intended to recognize that a State could, if it wished, consent to foreign proceedings strictly in respect of a specific case and that any such consent was without prejudice to the immunity of that State in a different case arising out of the same matter.[13] Secondly, subparagraph (*c*) of paragraph 1 was 'amplified' by the Drafting Committee, as recommended by Special Rapporteur Ogiso, to make allowance for a State's written communication of consent to the exercise of jurisdiction by a foreign court in what—in a further amendment consequent on the use of the inclusive expression 'matter or case' in the chapeau to paragraph 1—was now referred to as 'a specific proceeding'.[14] Lastly, the Drafting Committee endorsed the proposal of the Special Rapporteur to insert in draft article 7 a paragraph 2 stipulating that agreement by a State to the application of the law of another State with regard to a matter or case was not to be interpreted as consent by the former State to the exercise of jurisdiction by the courts of the latter.[15]

It was in this form that draft article 7 was finally adopted by the ILC on second reading in 1991 and that Article 7 of the Convention was adopted by the General Assembly in 2004.

3. Key Points

3.1 The requirement of express consent

The Convention proceeds from the premise that, in the absence of indication to the contrary, a State does not consent to the exercise of jurisdiction over it by a court of another State.[16] In the words of the ILC commentary, consent is not to be 'taken for granted'.[17] A court called on to exercise jurisdiction in accordance with the Convention over an absent foreign State 'cannot . . . assume or presume that there is consent or willingness to consent to jurisdiction'.[18] Rather, a claimant must adduce sufficiently persuasive evidence of the respondent State's consent.[19] The point is underscored by Article 8(4) of

[11] Third report Ogiso, 11.

[12] See summary record 2191st ILC meeting, *YILC 1990*, vol. I, 306, 311, para. 50; ILC commentary, draft art. 7, paras 7, 9, and 13.

[13] See summary record 2191st ILC meeting (n. 12), 311, para. 51; ILC commentary, draft art. 7, para. 7.

[14] See summary record 2191st ILC meeting (n. 12), 311–12, para. 52.

[15] See summary record 2191st ILC meeting (n. 12), 312, para. 53.

[16] See ILC commentary, draft art. 7, paras 3–5.

[17] ILC commentary, draft art. 7, para. 8.

[18] ILC commentary, draft art. 7, para. 4. See also ILC commentary, draft art. 8, para. 1.

[19] See ILC commentary, draft art. 7, para. 4.

the Convention, which provides that '[f]ailure on the part of a State to enter an appearance in a proceeding before a court of another State shall not be interpreted as consent by the former State to the exercise of jurisdiction by the court'.

As a corollary of the Convention's presumption of a lack of consent to jurisdiction on the part of a defendant State, Article 7(1) requires that, for the purposes of the provision, a State's consent to the exercise of jurisdiction over it by a court of another State be express.[20] As the ILC commentary puts it, there is 'no room for implying the consent of an unwilling State which has not expressed its consent in a clear... manner'.[21] Article 7 demands, in short, that '[t]he expression of consent... must be explicit'.[22] 'Any theory of "implied consent" as a possible exception' to State immunity, the commentary elaborates, 'should be viewed not as an exception in itself, but rather as an added explanation or justification for an otherwise valid and generally recognized exception'.[23] In other words, while the notion of implied consent underpins, by way of the most obvious examples, the express exceptions to immunity from jurisdiction specified in Articles 8, 9, and 17, it has no independent purchase.

3.2 The primacy of the terms of consent

It ought to go without saying, but might pay to recall, that the permissible scope of a court's exercise of jurisdiction, in accordance with Article 7(1), over a foreign State which has expressly consented to that exercise will depend on the terms of the State's expression of its consent, including any limitation, condition, or exclusion specified in those terms. This is so regardless of which of the three ways of expressing consent sanctioned by Article 7(1) the State has happened to avail itself. Questions such as the courts and claimants in respect of which the consent to proceedings is effective, whether the consent is revocable, whether the consent is effective in respect of all remedies otherwise available to the court, and so on, are to be answered first and foremost on the basis of interpretation and application of the terms of the international agreement, written contract, declaration before the court or written communication by which the foreign State has conveyed its consent to proceedings.

3.3 Waiver of immunity and submission to jurisdiction

A State's waiver of immunity from hypothetical future proceedings in the courts of another State in respect of a given subject-matter has not always been treated as equivalent, for the purposes of immunity,[24] to that State's submission to the exercise

[20] See, similarly, Art. 2(*b*) and (*c*) ECSI, referring respectively to 'an express term contained in a contract in writing' and 'an express consent given after a dispute between the parties has arisen'. Perhaps curiously, Art. 2(*a*) ECSI, on consent to jurisdiction by way of international agreement, does not specify that such consent be express. But *cf* Exl. Rep. ECSI, para. 21 of which describes Art. 2 ECSI *in toto* as dealing with 'cases in which a Contracting State has expressly undertaken to submit to the jurisdiction of a foreign court'.

[21] ILC commentary, draft art. 7, para. 8.

[22] ILC commentary, draft art. 8, para. 1. The requirement of express consent finds echoes once more in Art. 8(4).

[23] See ILC commentary, draft art. 7, para. 8.

[24] Note that the present discussion pertains solely to the availability or otherwise of immunity from the exercise of such underlying jurisdiction as the court may enjoy according to applicable rules of private international law. Submission to the exercise of the court's jurisdiction in this context should not be confused with submission to jurisdiction for the prior purposes of any such rules.

of jurisdiction by a specific court in respect of a specific claim.[25] But today it tends to be,[26] and Article 7(1) adopts this more flexible approach. Indeed, Article 7(1) dispenses altogether with the potentially confounding language of 'waiver of immunity' and 'submission to jurisdiction', requiring simply that a State have 'expressly consented to the exercise of jurisdiction by the court with regard to the matter or case'.[27] In other words, an express waiver of immunity from such proceedings in relation to a matter as may arise in a court of another State is treated no differently under Article 7(1) from express submission to the exercise of jurisdiction in any specific case that does so arise. The two are merely different ways in which a State can manifest its consent to the exercise of the foreign court's jurisdiction in the proceedings at hand.

It is unclear, however, whether Article 7(1) requires, as the US courts do,[28] that a State's consent to the exercise of jurisdiction with regard to a given matter—as distinct from a given case, in relation to which the answer is obvious—be referable to the courts specifically of the forum State or whether it suffices that the State have consented to the jurisdiction of the courts of another State generically speaking.[29] A State could be said to have 'expressly consented to the exercise of jurisdiction by the court with regard to the matter', in the words of Article 7(1), if it has expressly consented to the exercise of jurisdiction by any foreign court before which the matter might be brought. But it is equally arguable that Article 7(1) is not satisfied unless the State consents to the exercise of jurisdiction expressly by the forum State's courts. The ILC commentary and *travaux préparatoires* are silent on the question, although it is not without relevance that the commentary cites as an example of express consent to proceedings by way of written contract a clause providing unspecifically that, '[f]or the purpose of jurisdiction', the Kingdom of Thailand 'certifies that [it] waives and renounces hereby any right to assert before an arbitration tribunal or court of law or any other authority any defence or exception based on [its] sovereign immunity'.[30] On the other hand, the Explanatory Report to Article 2 ECSI speaks of 'submission to the jurisdiction of... the courts in a specified State to which the dispute may, in this case, be referred'.[31] But Article 2 ECSI's use of the formally narrower term 'submission to the jurisdiction' conceivably imports a difference, and, as it is, the Explanatory Report's position is not uncontested.[32] In the end, the point is one on which the subsequent practice of the States parties to the Convention in the application of Article 7(1) will be determinative. That said, an insistence on the prior stipulation of a specific potential forum State might be thought

[25] See eg H. Fox, *The Law of State Immunity* (2nd edn) (Oxford: Oxford University Press, 2008), 477.

[26] See Third report Sucharitkul, 148–9, paras 82–85.

[27] In contrast, Art. 2 ECSI uses the language of submission to jurisdiction.

[28] See *Argentine Republic v Amerada Hess Shipping Corp.*, 488 US 428 (US (SC) 1989), concerning waiver of immunity for the purposes of s. 1605(*a*)(1) FSIA (US).

[29] For the assertion that consent to the exercise of jurisdiction with regard to a given matter requires express reference to the court—and indeed to the proceedings, which is clearly not true—in question, see Fox (n. 25), 485. It is not apparent on what the author bases her contention.

[30] ILC commentary, draft art. 7, para. 11 note 79.

[31] Expl. Rep. ECSI, para. 21.

[32] See eg A. Dickinson, R. Lindsay, and J.P. Loonam, *State Immunity: Selected Materials and Commentary* (Oxford: Oxford University Press, 2004), 349–50, para. 4.019, referring to s. 2(2) SIA (UK), enacted to implement Art. 2 ECSI.

out of keeping with the provision's apparent aversion to fine distinctions,[33] and would run counter to the contemporary practice of most States.[34]

3.4 The three ways of expressing consent

Subparagraphs (*a*) to (*c*) of Article 7(1) recognize three ways, and three ways only,[35] by which a State may manifest its express consent to proceedings in a court of another State. Consent signalled by any means not enumerated in Article 7(1)(*a*) to (*c*) will be ineffective for the purposes of the Convention, with the result that the State giving such consent will, subject to the other provisions of the Convention, retain its presumptive immunity from the exercise of foreign jurisdiction as embodied in Article 5. Each of Article 7(1)'s three ways of expressing consent merits examination.

A. International agreement

Article 7(1)(*a*) recognizes as potentially effective for the purposes of the Convention a State's expression of consent to the jurisdiction of a court of another State by way of a provision in an international agreement to which the consenting State is party.[36] Provisions to this effect are a common feature of bilateral treaties of friendship, commerce, and navigation.[37] In this classic form, such provisions represent consent, indicated prior to the genesis or crystallization of any relevant dispute, to the exercise of jurisdiction by the foreign court with regard, in the language of Article 7(1), to the 'matter' to which the treaty provision pertains.[38] A recent example of where a State has

[33] In contrast, and although the ILC commentary and preparatory works are once more unenlightening, it stands to reason that consent to the exercise of jurisdiction with regard to a given matter specifically by the courts of a named State other than the forum State is not to be taken as consent 'to the exercise of jurisdiction by the court with regard to the matter'.

[34] See eg, as regards the UK, the Supreme Court's treatment of the submission and waiver clauses in *NML Capital Ltd v Republic of Argentina*, 147 ILR 575 (UK (SC) 2011).

[35] Given that subpara. (*c*) of Art. 7(1) itself recognizes two distinct ways by which a State may signal its consent, it would perhaps be more accurate to speak of the four, not three, ways by which a State may expressly consent, in accordance with Art. 7(1), to the exercise of foreign jurisdiction over it. But given that Art. 7(1) contains only three subparagraphs and that both of the means of expressing consent mentioned in subpara. (*c*) represent consent 'in a specific proceeding', it is less confusing and no less justifiable to refer to the three ways of expressing consent.

[36] See, similarly, Art. 2(*a*) ECSI.

[37] See eg Art. XXIV(6) Treaty of Friendship, Commerce and Navigation between the United States of America and the Italian Republic, Rome, 2 February 1948, 79 UNTS 171; Art. XVIII(3) Treaty of Friendship, Commerce and Navigation between the United States of America and Ireland, Dublin, 21 January 1950, 206 UNTS 269; Art. XIV(5) Treaty of Friendship, Commerce and Navigation between the Kingdom of Greece and the United States of America, Athens, 3 August 1951, 224 UNTS 279; Art. XVIII(3) Treaty of Friendship, Commerce and Navigation between Israel and the United States of America, Washington, 23 August 1951, 219 UNTS 237; Art. XVIII(3) Treaty of Friendship, Commerce and Navigation between the United States of America and the Kingdom of Denmark, Copenhagen, 1 October 1951, 421 UNTS 105; Art. XVIII(2) Treaty of Friendship, Commerce and Navigation between the United States of America and Japan, Tokyo, 2 April 1953, 206 UNTS 143; Art. XVIII(2) Treaty of Friendship, Commerce and Navigation between the United States of America and the Federal Republic of Germany, Washington, 29 October 1954, 273 UNTS 3; Art. XVIII(2) Treaty of Friendship, Commerce and Navigation between the United States of America and the Netherlands, The Hague, 27 March 1956, 285 UNTS 231; Art. XVIII(2) Treaty of Friendship, Commerce and Navigation between the United States of America and the Republic of Korea, Seoul, 28 November 1956, 302 UNTS 281.

[38] That said, there is no reason either in principle or on the face of Art. 7(1) why a State might not equally consent by way of international agreement to the jurisdiction of a foreign court with regard to a specific case, whether while proceedings against it are merely in the contemplation of the claimant or after such proceedings have been initiated. In the latter instance, however, one might expect that an international agreement to this

been held to have expressly submitted to the jurisdiction of the courts of the forum State by way of international agreement is *Government of the Republic of Zimbabwe v Flick*, where the Supreme Court of Appeal of South Africa held that, by becoming party to the Protocol on the Tribunal to the Treaty of the Southern African Development Community, Article 32(3) of which provided that decisions of the Tribunal 'shall be ... enforceable within the territories of the Member States concerned', Zimbabwe 'clearly both waived any immunity it might otherwise have been entitled to claim from the jurisdiction of the courts of member states and agreed that orders of the Tribunal would be enforceable in those courts'.[39]

It is worth reiterating that a State which consents to foreign proceedings by means of an international agreement renders itself amenable to such proceedings to the extent prescribed in the agreement and only to this extent.[40] This, along with the *pacta tertiis* rule of the law of treaties,[41] has implications for the range of claimants to proceedings brought by whom the State can be taken to have consented.

B. *Written contract*

Article 7(1)(*b*) acknowledges as effective in principle for the purposes of the Convention a State's express consent to the exercise of foreign jurisdiction via a term in a written contract to which the consenting State is party.[42] Whether a contractual expression of consent to proceedings is in fact effective will depend on the proper law of the contract[43] and any generally applicable principles of agency or relevant special rules cognizable by the court.[44] An example of such a special rule is section 10(11)(*b*) FStIA (Aus), which provides that 'a person who has entered into a contract on behalf of and with the authority of the State has authority to submit in that contract, on behalf of the State, to the jurisdiction in respect of a proceeding arising out of the contract'. The less precisely worded second limb of section 2(7) SIA (UK)—as well as of section 4(5)

effect would be accompanied by a declaration by the State before the court or its written communication to it, as per subpara. (*c*) of Art. 7(1).

[39] *Government of the Republic of Zimbabwe v Flick and others* [2012] ZASCA 122, para. 44 (SA (SC) 2012). Art. 33 has since been very slightly amended to remove the word 'Member'. See Protocol on the Tribunal and Rules of Procedure thereof, as amended, to the Treaty of the Southern African Development Community, http://www.sadc.int/english/key-documents/protocols/protocol-on-tribunal-and-the-rules-of-procedure-thereof/.

[40] ILC commentary, draft art. 7, para. 10.

[41] See Art. 34 VCLT.

[42] See, similarly, Art. 2(*b*) ECSI. As with consent by international agreement, the classic contractual term of this sort relates to any such proceedings as may in future arise with regard to the matter regulated by the contract, although no dictate of reason or term of Art. 7(1) rules out express contractual consent to jurisdiction in a specific case, even after proceedings have been initiated.

[43] See also Fox (n. 25), 492.

[44] See eg *Donegal International Ltd v Zambia* [2007] EWHC 197 (Comm), paras 431–456 (UK (EWHC) 2007), where the question under s. 2(2) SIA (UK) was framed as being whether the Minister of Finance of Zambia had actual or ostensible authority to enter into a settlement agreement with a private company by which Zambia was said to have waived its immunity and submitted to jurisdiction. It was common ground between the parties, and the court agreed, that the question of actual authority was to be decided by *renvoi* to Zambian law, while the question of ostensible authority was governed by the law of England and Wales. *Cf*, however, *Ahmed v Government of Saudi Arabia* [1996] 2 All ER 248, 255 (UK (EWCA) 1995), where the question appears to have been treated as one of actual authority only, the inquiry being whether 'the person entering into the alleged contract by the letter did so "on behalf of and with the authority of" Saudi Arabia' within the meaning of s. 2(7) SIA (UK). See also Dickinson et al. (n. 32), 353, para. 4.024 ('In such cases, there can be no question of ostensible authority ... ').

SIO (Pak), section 3(6) FStIA (SA), and section 4(7) SIA (Sing), for all of which the UK section provided the template—and of the even terser second limb of section 9(*c*) FSIL (Isr) are intended to be to the same effect.[45]

It is again trite law that a State will be amenable to the exercise of jurisdiction to the extent and only to the extent specified in the contract.

C. Declaration before the court or written communication

Article 7(1)(*c*) recognizes the effectiveness, *ceteris paribus*, as a means of conveying a State's consent to proceedings already initiated in a court of another State an oral declaration before the court on behalf of the respondent State or a written communication on its behalf relayed 'through diplomatic channels or any other generally accepted channels of communication'.[46] By whom such a declaration must be made or from whom such a communication must emanate for it to be treated as an effective expression of the respondent State's consent are questions that Article 7(1)(*c*) leaves unanswered.[47] The ILC commentary speaks of a State's 'declaration before the court properly executed by one of its authorized representatives, such as an agent or counsel', and the emphasis on authorization could be taken to suggest that the matter is to be determined solely by reference to the law of the allegedly consenting State. But the commentary elsewhere explains that the court 'can and must . . . satisfy its own requirements regarding the manner in which such . . . consent could be given with desired consequences'.[48] Moreover, it simply stands to reason that whether a declaration or communication alleged to be binding under the law of the forum State is so binding is a matter for the law of the forum State, be it that law's generally applicable principles of agency—which may recognize, for example, not only actual authority, as logically determined by *renvoi* to the law of the respondent State, but also ostensible authority, as logically determined by

[45] The second limb of s. 2(7) SIA (UK), which is in the vein of Expl. Rep. ECSI, para. 22, provides that 'any person who has entered into a contract on behalf of and with the authority of a State shall be deemed to have authority to submit on its behalf in respect of proceedings arising out of the contract'. The absence, after the word 'submit', of the words '*in that contract*, on behalf of the State' (emphasis added) found in the corresponding Australian provision creates a degree of ambiguity. The respective wordings of the equivalent provisions of the SIO (Pak), FStIA (SA), and SIA (Sing) are closely modelled on s. 2(7) SIA (UK). The second limb of s. 9(*c*) FSIL (Isr) states, in translation: 'and in respect of immunity in a proceeding originating in a contract to which the foreign state is a party, any person who has contracted in the name of the foreign state shall also be so authorized', ie 'authorized to waive the immunity . . . , in the name of the foreign state', in the words of the first limb of the provision.

[46] ILC commentary, draft art. 7, para. 9. The ILC commentary notes that a State might rely on the same means to 'make known its unwillingness or lack of consent' or, as regards the option of written communication, to 'give evidence in writing which tends to disprove any allegation or assertion of consent'. For its part, the equivalent provision of the ECSI, namely Art. 2(*c*), refers unspecifically to 'an express consent given after a dispute between the parties has arisen'.

[47] It may pay to emphasize that whether a declaration or communication alleged to be binding under the law of the forum State is indeed binding under that law is a question of domestic, not international, law, even if international law might—although in the case of Art. 7(1)(*c*) UNCSI does not—oblige the forum State to ensure that its domestic law embodies certain principles. (The same goes for whether a contractual term is binding under the forum State's law for the purposes of Art. 7(1)(*b*) UNCSI.) As such, the international rules specifying which State officials are capable of binding the State by way of unilateral statement are not directly relevant to Art. 7(1)(*c*) UNCSI, even if it is theoretically open to the law of the forum State to draw inspiration from them. Even less directly relevant in this context are the international rules on who is held to represent a State for the purposes of expressing that State's consent to be bound by a treaty, such as would be pertinent to Art. 7(1)(*a*) UNCSI.

[48] ILC commentary, draft art. 7, para. 11.

the legal standards of the forum State—or any special rules on submission by a foreign State to the jurisdiction of the local courts. A pragmatic example of such a special rule is the first limb of section 2(7) SIA (UK), which reads:

> The head of a State's diplomatic mission in the United Kingdom, or the person for the time being performing his functions, shall be deemed to have authority to submit on behalf of the State in respect of any proceedings...

An identical provision, *mutatis mutandis*, forms the first limb of section 4(5) SIO (Pak), section 3(6) FStIA (SA), and section 4(7) SIA (Sing), while an equivalent deeming provision is found in section 10(11)(*a*) FStIA (Aus)[49] and section 9(*c*) FSIL (Isr).[50] (At the same time, both section 10(11) FStIA (Aus) and section 9(*c*) FSIL (Isr) also give explicit effect to actual authority.[51]) The upshot of the silence of Article 7(1)(*c*) of the Convention on the capacity to consent on behalf of a State is the possibility that an oral declaration or written communication by a putative representative of a State could hypothetically lead to different results in different forum States. But this is no different in principle from the situation with regard to the capacity to contract on behalf of the State for the purposes of Article 7(1)(*b*), which is similarly silent. Neither is likely to lead to injustice, even if Convention-dictated harmonization or approximation might have had its advantages.

As with the other expressions of consent sanctioned by Article 7(1), the court will be permitted to exercise its jurisdiction over a respondent State which consents to its jurisdiction by way of oral declaration or written communication as provided for and only as provided for by the terms of the declaration or communication.

3.5 Agreement to the application of foreign law

It is common for contracting parties, including States, to include in the terms of the contract a 'choice of law' clause, *viz* a term specifying that the contract is to be governed by the law of a given State. This does not signify the parties' agreement that any dispute arising out of the contract is to be adjudicated by the courts of the specified State, for the simple reason that it is perfectly possible, according to the rules of private international law typically prevailing in different national jurisdictions, for the courts of one State to apply the law of another. The distinction between choice of law and consent to proceedings is underlined in paragraph 2 of Article 7 of the Convention, which provides that agreement by a State to the application of the law of another State is not to be construed as consent to the exercise of jurisdiction by the courts of that other State.[52]

[49] Section 10(11)(*a*) FStIA (Aus) provides that 'the person for the time being performing the functions of the head of the State's diplomatic mission in Australia has that authority', the latter being a reference to the 'authority to submit, on behalf of a foreign State, to the jurisdiction', in the words of the chapeau to s. 10(11) FStIA (Aus).

[50] The first limb of s. 9(*c*) FSIL (Isr) reads, in translation: 'The head of a diplomatic mission of a foreign state in Israel or any person acting in such capacity is authorized to waive the immunity under this section, in the name of the foreign state...'.

[51] The chapeau to s. 10(11) FStIA (Aus) reads: 'In addition to any other person who has authority to submit, on behalf of a foreign State, to the jurisdiction...'. Section 9(*c*) FSIL (Isr), after respective deeming provisions relating to the head of the foreign State's diplomatic mission in Israel and any person contracting on behalf of that State, states: 'the provisions of this sub-section shall not derogate from an authority conferred on any other person to waive the immunity in the name of the foreign state.'

[52] See, similarly, Expl. Rep. ECSI, para. 24.

3.6 Revocability

Neither the Convention nor the ILC commentary[53] specifies whether a State's unilateral revocation of consent to the exercise of jurisdiction over it by a court of another State will be treated as effective—that is, whether effect will be given to revocation of its consent by the consenting State in circumstances where no express provision has been made for revocation in the international agreement, written contract, oral declaration, or written communication by which the State has previously manifested its consent.[54] The answer will depend on the means by which consent has been expressed.

Whether consent by way of international agreement in accordance with Article 7(1)(*a*) is unilaterally revocable or otherwise capable of later being unilaterally rendered ineffective is a straightforward function of the rules on the invalidity, termination, and denunciation of and withdrawal from treaties laid down in Part V VCLT.

Whether consent by way of written contract, as per Article 7(1)(*b*), and by way of oral declaration or written communication, as per Article 7(1)(*c*), are capable of being unilaterally revoked is for the law of the forum State to determine. In the first context this will be by reference to the relevant rules of contract law (which may, in an application of the proper law of the contract, be the contract law of another State). In the second context it will be by reference to such general or special rules as may be applicable to express submission to the jurisdiction of the forum State's courts.[55] An example of a special rule on submission is section 1605(*a*)(1) FSIA (US), which provides that a foreign State which has waived its immunity shall not be immune from the jurisdiction of the courts of the US or of any of its constituent states 'notwithstanding any withdrawal of the waiver which the foreign [S]tate may purport to effect except in accordance with the terms of the waiver'. Similarly, section 10(5) FStIA (Aus), which provides that '[a]n agreement by a foreign State to waive its immunity... has effect to waive that immunity', goes on to specify that 'the waiver may not be withdrawn except in accordance with the terms of the agreement'.[56] It has also been assumed by one court in the UK that a waiver of immunity for the purposes of section 2 SIA (UK) may not be withdrawn.[57] Again, the standardization via the Convention itself of the unilateral revocability or otherwise of the expressions of consent sanctioned by Article 7(1)(*b*) and (*c*) might have had its benefits, even if the discretion left to the forum State under the Convention as adopted is unlikely to prove scandalous.

[53] The same goes for the ECSI and the Expl. Rep. ECSI.

[54] For an express recognition that consent to the exercise of jurisdiction may be conditional, see s. 10(3) FStIA (Aus): 'A submission... may be subject to a specified limitation, condition or exclusion (whether in respect of remedies or otherwise).'

[55] Note that, as with the capacity to bind the State for the purposes of Art. 7(1)(*c*) UNCSI, the question of the revocability of any consent validly given in accordance with the same provision is a question of domestic, not international, law. As such, the international rules governing the revocability of unilateral statements otherwise binding under international law are not directly relevant, even if it is in principle open to the law of the forum State to draw inspiration from such rules.

[56] This limitation on withdrawal would seem not to apply where the State has submitted to the jurisdiction of the Australian courts otherwise than by agreement, such as by way of oral declaration before the court or written communication to it. See, in this respect, s. 10(2) FStIA (Aus) ('a foreign State may submit to the jurisdiction at any time, whether by agreement or otherwise...').

[57] See *Yendall v Commonwealth of Australia*, 107 ILR 590, 599 (UK (EAT) 1984).

3.7 Appellate proceedings

Although Article 7 itself says nothing on the matter, the ILC commentary to its precursor explains that '[c]onsent to the exercise of jurisdiction in a proceeding before a court of another State covers the exercise of jurisdiction by appellate courts in any subsequent stage of the proceeding up to and including the decision of the court of final instance, retrial and review'.[58] The position accords with the practice of at least certain States.[59] As is apparent from Article 20,[60] however, a respondent State's consent to proceedings is not to be taken to indicate consent also to pre- and post-judgment measures of constraint.

4. Evaluation

That a foreign State can be held to account under domestic law in the event that it declines to rely on its *prima facie* immunity provides proof that State immunity is a procedural and not substantive bar to the exercise of a court's jurisdiction. Article 7 of the Convention, a flexible provision dealing with express consent to the exercise of jurisdiction, is the first of three consecutive articles in accordance with which a State can be taken voluntarily to have rendered itself amenable to proceedings in a court of another State (although not to measures of constraint, for which separate consent is needed). Express consent to proceedings is by no means uncommon. But in a regime of restrictive State immunity its impact is not in practice great, given that the matters to proceedings in respect of which States most frequently consent, especially by way of contract, are the sorts of commercial, employment, proprietary, and cognate acts *jure gestionis* in respect of which they would not enjoy immunity anyway.[61]

[58] ILC commentary, draft art. 7, para. 12. See, similarly, Expl. Rep. ECSI, para. 15 (which adds that submission to the jurisdiction of another State 'covers the case where a court decides, on account of its own lack of competence, to refer the matter to another court in the same State'). Even though the possibility is an extremely remote one, reason suggests that a State's express exclusion of appellate proceedings from the scope of its consent to the exercise of jurisdiction ought to be effective. The better statement of the relevant principle, therefore, is that consent to foreign proceedings is taken to include consent to appellate proceedings in the absence of express intention to the contrary on the part of the consenting State.

[59] See eg s. 4(4) SIO (Pak); s. 4(6) SIA (Sing); s. 3(5) FStIA (SA); s. 2(6) SIA (UK). One might speculate whether it is in implicit recognition of the potential role of any relevant exclusion that s. 10 FStIA (Aus)—the only national legislation explicitly to acknowledge, in s. 10(3), that a State's consent to jurisdiction 'may be subject to a specified limitation, condition or exclusion'—makes no mention of appellate proceedings.

[60] See also ILC commentary, draft art. 7, para. 12.

[61] See Dickinson et al. (n. 32), 348, para. 4.018.

Article 8

Silvia Borelli and Simon Olleson*

Article 8

Effect of participation in a proceeding before a court

1. A State cannot invoke immunity from jurisdiction in a proceeding before a court of another State if it has:
   (*a*) itself instituted the proceeding; or
   (*b*) intervened in the proceeding or taken any other step relating to the merits. However, if the State satisfies the court that it could not have acquired knowledge of facts on which a claim to immunity can be based until after it took such a step, it can claim immunity based on those facts, provided it does so at the earliest possible moment.
2. A State shall not be considered to have consented to the exercise of jurisdiction by a court of another State if it intervenes in a proceeding or takes any other step for the sole purpose of:
   (*a*) invoking immunity; or
   (*b*) asserting a right or interest in property at issue in the proceeding.
3. The appearance of a representative of a State before a court of another State as a witness shall not be interpreted as consent by the former State to the exercise of jurisdiction by the court.
4. Failure on the part of a State to enter an appearance in a proceeding before a court of another State shall not be interpreted as consent by the former State to the exercise of jurisdiction by the court.

1. Introduction

Article 8 of the Convention lays down an exception to the immunity from jurisdiction that a State would otherwise enjoy pursuant to Article 5 of the Convention. Specifically, it regulates the circumstances in which a State is precluded from relying on its immunity from jurisdiction as the result of either having initiated proceedings or having taken some step in proceedings initiated by another party. Article 8 is thus to be distinguished from the provisions of Part III of the Convention, which operate on the basis that the State is not immune from proceedings relating to certain types of conduct. It does not affect the legal regime governing pre- and post-judgment measures of constraint as set out in Part IV.

Having laid down the general principle in paragraph 1 that instituting proceedings, or intervening or otherwise taking a step in proceedings instituted by another party, results in the loss of the State's immunity from jurisdiction in those proceedings, the remainder of Article 8 is devoted to indicating the circumstances in which the State's participation in the proceedings will nevertheless *not* involve its loss of immunity. The second sentence of Article (8)(1)(*b*) makes clear that taking a step in proceedings will not result in the loss

* Sections 1 and 2 of this commentary are to be attributed to Simon Olleson; Sections 3 and 4 are to be attributed to Silvia Borelli.

of immunity if the State is able to satisfy the court that it could not have acquired knowledge of the facts on which a claim to immunity could have been based until after it took the step, provided that the claim to immunity was raised at the earliest possible moment. Article 8(2) specifies that intervention solely for the purpose of invoking immunity or asserting a right or interest in property does not result in the loss of immunity. Article 8(3) stipulates that the mere fact that a representative of a State appears before a court as a witness shall not be interpreted as implying consent to the exercise of jurisdiction over the State, whilst Article 8(4) provides that inaction by a State in the face of a claim (ie, a failure 'to enter an appearance') shall likewise not be interpreted as consent to the exercise of jurisdiction.

Article 8 is closely connected to the provisions immediately preceding and following it. While Article 7 ('Express consent to exercise of jurisdiction') precludes the invocation of immunity where the State has expressly consented to the exercise of jurisdiction over it, whether in advance or after the proceedings have arisen,[1] Article 8 deals with situations in which the State, as a result of its conduct in the proceedings, is taken to have implicitly manifested consent to the exercise of jurisdiction. Although paragraph 1 of Article 8 is not framed explicitly in terms of consent, consent is referred to in paragraphs 2 to 4, which specify the circumstances in which a State is not to be taken to have consented to the exercise of jurisdiction. For its part, Article 9 ('Counterclaims') deals with issues arising from the presentation of counterclaims, laying down rules on the extent of a State's implied consent to the court's exercise of jurisdiction in circumstances in which a counterclaim is brought either against or by that State.

2. Drafting History

Special Rapporteur Sucharitkul proposed the initial precursors to what eventually became Articles 7, 8, and 9 of the Convention in his Third Report, presented to the ILC in 1981.[2] The exceptions to a State's immunity from jurisdiction as a result of its consent, whether express or implied, were scattered across a variety of provisions, namely a draft article 8 ('Consent of States'), a draft article 9 ('Voluntary Submission'), a draft article 10 ('Counter-claims'), and a draft article 11 ('Waiver').

The original draft article 8 laid down in paragraph 1 the basic proposition that jurisdiction was not to be exercised over a State save with its consent, as well as the converse proposition in paragraph 2 that jurisdiction could be exercised where the State had consented. Paragraph 3 then proceeded to enumerate ways in which a State could expressly consent to the exercise of jurisdiction over it by the courts of another State, referring to consent given in writing in respect of a specific case after a dispute had arisen; to consent given in advance by way of express provision in a treaty, international agreement, or contract; and to consent manifest in the appearance before the court of an authorized representative of the State to contest the claim on the merits without raising a plea of immunity.[3]

The initial text of draft article 9 purported to deal with circumstances in which a State was to be taken to have consented to the exercise of jurisdiction over it by virtue of what was referred to as 'voluntary submission'. Voluntary submission was considered to derive

[1] See the commentary to Art. 7.

[2] See Third report Sucharitkul, 125.

[3] Third report Sucharitkul, 144, para. 58.

from a variety of conduct evidencing, with a greater or lesser degree of clarity, the consent of a State to the exercise of jurisdiction over it by the courts of another State in relation to a particular dispute. As originally proposed by the Special Rapporteur, draft article 9 contained three paragraphs. Paragraph 1 provided that jurisdiction could be exercised over a State which had voluntarily submitted by 'instituting or intervening in legal proceedings' before the courts of the other State; by appearing before the court of its own volition or taking a step in connection with proceedings without raising a claim of State immunity; and 'by otherwise expressly indicating its volition to submit to the jurisdiction and to have the outcome of a dispute or question determined' by the court.[4] Paragraphs 2 and 3 set limits on the circumstances in which voluntary submission could be found to exist, providing respectively that a mere failure to appear in proceedings could not be construed as voluntary submission and that appearance or intervention accompanied by 'a contention of lack of jurisdiction on the ground of State immunity, or an assertion of an interest in a property in question', did not amount to voluntary submission for the purposes of draft article 9(1).[5]

While Special Rapporteur Sucharitkul's proposed draft article 10 dealt with the separate and specific consequences of the presentation of counterclaims, whether made by or against a State,[6] his draft article 11 dealt with waiver. Draft article 11(1) laid down the general principle that immunity could be waived at any point in the proceedings. Paragraph 2 listed the ways in which immunity could be waived, these being either expressly in the face of the court or by an express undertaking to submit to the jurisdiction, whether made before or after the dispute had arisen. Paragraph 3 stipulated that a State could not claim immunity after taking a step in proceedings before a court of another State unless it satisfied the court that, first, it could not have acquired knowledge of the facts on which a claim to immunity could have been based until after it had taken that step and, second, that it had thereafter asserted immunity at the earliest possible moment. Finally, draft article 11(4) provided a further limitation on implied waiver, making clear that a State would not be deemed to have waived immunity where it entered an appearance specifically in order to assert immunity or its rights to property.[7]

Draft articles 8 to 11 were all framed around the consent of the foreign State to the exercise of jurisdiction over it.[8] There were obvious overlaps, however, between the various provisions, in particular between 'voluntary submission' and waiver. In addition, there was a degree of inconsistency as to the limits applicable to the different ways in which the right to invoke immunity might be lost.

During consideration in the Commission, these overlaps and inconsistencies were noted.[9] Further, there was general agreement that the provisions of draft article 8, on the effect of consent, should be recast to make clear that they were subject to other exceptions to immunity from jurisdiction, thereby avoiding any impression that draft article 8 created an 'absolute' or 'unqualified' immunity.[10] Finally, as part of a more general criticism of the approach taken by the Special Rapporteur in the draft articles proposed up to that point, it was suggested that the scheme of the ECSI be followed: rather than

[4] Third report Sucharitkul, 146, para. 71, referring to subparagraphs (*a*), (*b*), and (*c*) respectively.
[5] Third report Sucharitkul, 146, para. 71.
[6] See the commentary to Art. 9.
[7] See Third report Sucharitkul, 150, para. 92.
[8] Third report Sucharitkul, 150, para. 92.
[9] See Report ILC thirty-third session, 157, para. 224.
[10] Report ILC thirty-third session, 157, para. 221.

seeking to enumerate the circumstances in which immunity could be invoked, the draft articles, it was argued, should posit a general principle of immunity, which would be subject only to narrowly formulated exceptions.[11]

In response to these comments, the Special Rapporteur reformulated his proposed draft articles 8 to 11 for consideration by the Drafting Committee. His new draft article 8 ('Consent of States'), although clarifying that it was subject to any other exception to immunity, maintained the twin propositions that jurisdiction could not be exercised against a State without its consent and that jurisdiction could be exercised against a State which consented. The Special Rapporteur's new draft article 9 grouped together all the ways in which consent to the exercise of jurisdiction could be given—namely express consent, voluntary submission, and waiver—into a single provision, entitled 'Expression of consent'.[12] The new draft article 10 dealt with counterclaims.[13]

In the event, the outcome of the consideration by the Drafting Committee was the deletion of the revised draft article 8 on the ground that its statement of general principle was superfluous.[14] In addition, the omnibus draft article 9 proposed by the Special Rapporteur was re-divided into separate articles: the first (which became the new draft article 8) dealt with express consent to the exercise of jurisdiction, while the second (numbered draft article 9) covered conduct implying consent to the exercise of jurisdiction, although under the 'more neutral' title of 'Effect of participation in a proceeding before a court'.[15]

In parallel with the approach taken in the new draft article 8, the new draft article 9 made no mention of waiver, and was framed in the negative, setting out situations in which a State was precluded from invoking immunity from jurisdiction in proceedings before the courts of another State.[16] Draft article 9(1) indicated that a State could not invoke immunity from jurisdiction if it had instituted the proceedings, intervened, or taken any step in relation to the merits. Draft article 9(2) stipulated that intervention would not result in loss of immunity where it was solely for the purpose of invoking immunity or asserting a right or interest in property the subject of the proceedings. Paragraph 3 of draft article 9 maintained the principle that the mere failure to enter an appearance could not be taken to constitute consent to the exercise of jurisdiction. While the previous draft provisions had distinguished between, on the one hand, institution and intervention and, on the other, appearance before the courts or the taking of other steps in the proceedings, the Drafting Committee's draft article 9 treated the State's institution of proceedings as particular, and dealt with intervention together with the taking of 'other steps' in the proceedings.

The report of the Drafting Committee recounted that a further provision had been proposed in the course of its deliberations to deal with the situation in which a State official appeared before a court of another State simply to make a statement or to give evidence. The report noted, however, that opinions had differed as to whether such an

[11] Report ILC thirty-third session, 157, para. 222.
[12] Report ILC thirty-third session, 157–8, para. 226, fn. 670.
[13] Report ILC thirty-third session, 157–8, para. 226, fn. 670.
[14] See summary record 1750th ILC meeting, *YILC 1982*, vol. I, 324, 324, para. 1.
[15] Summary record 1750th ILC meeting (n. 14), para. 2.
[16] Summary record 1750th ILC meeting (n. 14), 325, para. 6.

appearance would constitute submission to the jurisdiction, with the result that the issue was left over for future consideration.[17]

What had been paragraph 7 of the Special Rapporteur's revised draft article 9—stipulating that questions of immunity could be raised at any stage of the proceedings, but that a State was precluded from invoking immunity after it had taken a step relating to the merits unless it was unaware at the time of the facts giving rise to the plea of immunity—was deleted by the Drafting Committee, for reasons which are not entirely clear.[18] As a consequence, in the subsequent debate in the Commission, one member proposed, in terms echoing the SIA (UK), that the Commission's commentary should clarify that, if a State did not have the requisite knowledge at the relevant time, it retained the right to invoke immunity if, first, the facts could not reasonably have been ascertained and, second, that immunity was invoked as soon as practicable.[19] In the event, the commentary accompanying the draft article provisionally adopted on first reading included a short statement to this effect, with reference to the SIA (UK).[20]

After the adoption in 1986 on first reading of a complete set of draft articles, which included draft article 9 as proposed by the Drafting Committee,[21] substantive comments on that provision were received from only Mexico and the UK.[22] The UK observed, with reference to Article 3(1) ECSI, that further consideration ought to be given to the qualification that immunity was not lost where a State took a step in relation to the merits of a proceeding before it had knowledge of facts on which a claim to immunity might be based.[23] Mexico proposed the insertion of an explicit statement that the appearance of a representative of a State before a court for the purpose, *inter alia*, of giving evidence should not be deemed to constitute consent to the exercise of jurisdiction over the State.[24] Special Rapporteur Ogiso agreed with both points.[25] The proposed addition to cover a State's lack of knowledge was favourably received in the Commission,[26] as was, by and large, the proposed additional paragraph dealing with the giving of evidence by representatives of the State.[27]

Draft article 9, together with the additions proposed by the Special Rapporteur,[28] was subject to a number of minor changes of formulation at the hands of the Drafting

[17] Summary record 1750th ILC meeting (n. 14), 325, para. 7.

[18] Summary record 1750th ILC meeting (n. 14), 325, para. 6.

[19] Summary record 1750th ILC meeting (n. 14), 325, para. 11 (Sir Ian Sinclair).

[20] See Report ILC thirty-fourth session, 111 (commentary to draft art. 9, para. 10).

[21] See Report ILC thirty-eighth session, 8, para. 20.

[22] See 'Comments received from Governments', *YILC 1988*, vol. II, Part 1, 45, 75 (Mexico, paras 17 and 18) and *YILC 1988*, vol. II, Part 1, 45, 86 (United Kingdom, para. 17). In addition, France thought (*YILC 1988*, vol. II, Part 1, 45, 66 (France, para. 22)) that further clarification of draft art. 9 was necessary to make clear, for instance, that a State which submitted a defence on the merits in the alternative to a simultaneous plea of immunity could not be regarded as having waived its immunity.

[23] See *YILC 1988*, vol. II, Part 1, 45, 86 (United Kingdom, para. 17); notably, no mention was made of the SIA (UK) by the United Kingdom. In addition, Mexico raised a slightly different point, suggesting that immunity should not be regarded as having been lost 'where the State has not been properly impleaded', on the basis that if the suit was not transmitted through the proper channels, there was a risk that the rights of the State to invoke immunity might not be satisfactorily asserted on its behalf (*YILC 1988*, vol. II, Part 1, 45, 75 (Mexico, para. 17).

[24] See *YILC 1988*, vol. II, Part 1, 45, 75 (Mexico, para. 18).

[25] See Preliminary report Ogiso, 107, paras 98–100.

[26] See Report ILC forty-first session, 106, para. 480.

[27] See Report ILC forty-first session, 106–7, para. 480.

[28] See Third report Ogiso, 11.

Committee in 1990, at which time it was renumbered draft article 8.[29] It was adopted on second reading, together with the rest of the draft articles, the following year and passed unaltered into the Convention as Article 8.

3. Key Points

Consent by a State to the exercise of jurisdiction over it by a court of another State precludes the State's invocation of immunity from that jurisdiction. Such consent may be expressed explicitly in a statement, whether in writing or in the face of the court (as per Article 7) or may be deduced from conduct (as per Article 8). In the latter case, it must be possible to point to positive conduct. As the ILC commentary makes clear, '[c]onsent [...] cannot be presumed to exist by sheer implication, nor by mere silence, acquiescence or inaction'.[30] This fundamental principle is reflected in Article 8(4), which indicates that a State's mere failure to enter an appearance cannot be taken to disclose its consent to the exercise of jurisdiction over it.

Article 8 posits in paragraph 1 a precisely worded general rule in respect of which paragraphs 2 to 4 are not, strictly speaking, exceptions, but rather specifications or clarifications included merely for the avoidance of doubt. The only exception to the rule posited in Article 8(1) is found in the provision itself, and specifically in the second sentence of Article 8(1)(*b*).

3.1 Article 8(1)

Article 8(1) provides that a State which either institutes proceedings in a court of another State or intervenes, or takes any other step on the merits, in proceedings instituted by another party is precluded from invoking immunity from the jurisdiction of the court in question. The essence of the provision is that, by taking steps to participate in a case without raising its immunity, a State implicitly waives any immunity to which it may otherwise have been entitled in those proceedings. The ILC commentary elaborates:

> Consent [can] be evidenced by positive conduct of the State [...] A clear instance of conduct or action amounting to the expression of assent, concurrence, agreement, approval or consent to the exercise of jurisdiction is illustrated by entry of appearance by or on behalf of the State contesting the case on the merits.[31]

The commentary speaks similarly of the institution of, or intervention or the taking of any other step on the merits in foreign proceedings as constituting 'voluntary submission by a State to the jurisdiction'.[32] Indeed, despite the changes in formulation present in the ILC's draft article 8 as adopted on second reading by the ILC as compared to the original proposal by Special Rapporteur Sucharitkul in his Third Report, the ILC's commentary

[29] See summary record 2191st ILC meeting, *YILC 1990*, vol. I, 306, 312, paras 54–58. In addition to the insertion of what became paragraphs 1(*b*) and 3 of Art. 8, the most significant reformulation was the modification of the chapeau to para. 2 so that the latter was not expressly tied to para. 1(*b*) but referred in general terms to the circumstances in which a State was not to be considered to have consented to the exercise of jurisdiction.

[30] ILC commentary, draft art. 8, para. 1.

[31] ILC commentary, draft art. 8, para. 1.

[32] ILC commentary, draft art. 8, para. 1.

substantially adopts wholesale and unmodified large parts of his discussion of the question.[33]

It ought to go without saying that the State's loss of immunity pertains only to the proceeding it has instituted or in which it has intervened or taken some other step relating to the merits. The State will remain entitled to claim immunity in relation to pre- or post-judgment measures of constraint,[34] as well as from the jurisdiction of the courts of the forum State in relation to any other proceedings that may arise in those courts.

A. Subparagraph (a)

In accordance with Article 8(1)(*a*), when a State institutes proceedings, *viz* brings a claim, before the courts of another State, it forgoes any right it may otherwise have to invoke immunity from the jurisdiction of that court in respect of those proceedings. The institution of foreign proceedings by a State is the paradigm case of its implied consent to the exercise of jurisdiction over it. In the words of the ILC commentary to draft article 8, '[b]y becoming a plaintiff before the judicial authority of another State, the claimant State, seeking judicial relief or other remedies, manifestly submits to the jurisdiction of the forum'.[35] Instances of claims brought by States before the courts of other States are far from uncommon.[36]

Neither in Article 8(1)(*a*), nor anywhere else in Article 8, is it specified which officials or organs of a State should be taken to have authority to take a step in proceedings which would result in the loss of the right to invoke immunity. Further, in parallel with the situation under Article 7 as regards express consent to the exercise of jurisdiction, no indication is given in Article 8 as to the identity of the official or organ of the State which has authority to authorize the participation in litigation before the courts of another State. The matter depends on the applicable laws of the forum State, whether its generally applicable rules on agency and representation, or any special rules specifically addressing a foreign State's submission to jurisdiction. In that latter regard, it is worth noting that a number of national statutes, starting with the SIA (UK), expressly provide that only the head of the State's diplomatic mission (or the person for the time being performing those functions) has the power to submit to the jurisdiction on behalf of the State.[37] Such a stipulation, although somewhat rigid and formalistic, has the advantage of providing a bright line rule, rather than provoking endless litigation as to whether any particular official had sufficient authority to take any particular step resulting in the loss of immunity.[38]

[33] In particular, compare Third report Sucharitkul, 145 (paras 62–65) with ILC Commentary, draft art. 8, paras 4–6 and 9, including the discussion of 'Entering an appearance on a voluntary basis'.

[34] ILC commentary, draft art. 8, para. 1.

[35] ILC commentary, draft art. 8, para. 4.

[36] See eg *Mbasogo and Republic of Equatorial Guinea v Logo Ltd and Others* [2007] 2 WLR 1062 (UK (EWCA) 2006); *Islamic Republic of Iran v Barakat Galleries Ltd* [2009] QB 22 (UK (EWCA) 2007).

[37] See eg s. 2(7) SIA (UK); s. 10(11) FStIA (Aus); s. 4(7) SIA (Sing); s. 9(c) FSIL (Isr).

[38] Conversely, such provisions, if applied in an overly-formalistic manner, may provide an opportunity for a State effectively to take steps in relation to the proceedings on the merits, only then to raise the lack of authority of the official who had taken those steps (or who had authorized the instruction of local lawyers who had taken such steps on behalf of the State): for examples of the application of s. 2(7) SIA (UK), see eg *Arab Republic of Egypt v Gamal-Eldin and another* [1996] 2 All ER 237; [1996] ICR 13 (UK (EAT) 1995); *Aziz v Embassy of Republic of Yemen* [2005] EWCA Civ 745; [2005] ICR 1391 (UK (EWCA) 2005). *Cf* FStIA (Aus), which, in addition to s. 10(11) which provides that only the head of mission or equivalent has authority to

*B. Subparagraph (*b*)*

(i) The rule

The first limb of Article 8(1)(*b*) stipulates that a State is precluded from invoking immunity from the jurisdiction of a court of another State in relation to a particular proceeding if it has 'intervened in the proceeding or taken any other step relating to the merits'. The reference to any 'other' step necessarily implies that the intervention referred to is itself a step relating to the merits. In other words, the sort of intervention to which Article 8(1)(*b*) refers is specifically intervention on the merits. The rationale for the rule in Article 8(1)(*b*) is a familiar one: as the ILC commentary puts it, '[a]ny positive action by way of participation in the merits of a proceeding by a State on its own initiative and not under any compulsion is inconsistent with a subsequent contention that the volunteering State is being impleaded against its will'.[39]

Depending on the procedural rules of the forum, intervention, in the technical sense, may be permissible in a variety of forms. A third party might formally apply to be joined to the proceedings as a party, whether or not presenting a claim. Alternatively, it may seek merely to present observations, for instance as an *amicus curiae*. The ILC commentary, as well as Special Rapporteur Sucharitkul's Third Report (on which the commentary is substantially based), strongly suggests that the reference to intervention in what became Article 8(1)(*b*) (and also in Article 8(2)) was not intended to be limited to the technical procedural sense of the term but, rather, was used generically to denote the taking of any step in proceedings before a court.[40] It is, in effect, a synonym for the term 'participation' as used in the title to Article 8. This construction may pose the question as to what independent meaning, if any, is to be attributed to the words 'any other step relating to the merits' in Article 8(1)(*b*),[41] given that any such step will necessarily itself constitute 'intervention' by the State. There are however other instances in the Convention of what in strict terms may be semantic redundancy, all of them intended, *ex abundante cautela*, to forestall the exclusionary potential inherent in terms, such as 'intervention', with both a general and a specific, technical meaning.

All this said, it is still useful to distinguish between intervention in the technical sense of an application by a third party to be joined as a party to proceedings, or otherwise to take part in the proceedings, and in the more general sense of the taking of steps in proceedings by a party. As with the institution of proceedings, if a State itself applies to be joined as a party to proceedings in a court of another State, there can be little doubt that it has evidenced its consent to the court's exercise of jurisdiction over it in those proceedings. The same is arguably true if the State otherwise attempts formally to intervene, unless the intervention is strictly limited to raising the question of immunity, or to asserting a right or interest in property at issue, as envisaged by Article 8(2). As to intervention in the more general sense, it is again proper that a State taking any step in

submit to the jurisdiction, provides in s. 10(9) that immunity will not be lost where the 'intervention or step was taken by a person who did not know and could not reasonably have been expected to know of the immunity' and the immunity is then asserted without unreasonable delay.

[39] ILC commentary, draft art. 8, para. 5.

[40] See eg ILC commentary, draft art. 8, paras 5 and 6. *Cf* ILC commentary, draft art. 9, para. 6, from which it would appear that the term 'intervene' in draft art. 9(2) was intended as something closer to the technical procedural sense: see further the commentary to Art. 9.

[41] Consider also the similar use of the term 'any other step' in Art. 8(2).

relation to a claim before a foreign court without raising the question of its immunity from the court's jurisdiction should be taken to have expressed its consent to the exercise by the court of jurisdiction over it in those proceedings.[42] Such a step may comprise the writing of a letter to the court, if not accompanied by a reservation of the State's position as to its immunity; the filing of a defence addressing the substance of the claim; the making of an application for the summary dismissal of the claim as without foundation; or any one of a number of analogous acts.[43]

For its part, the ILC commentary states that, 'by choosing to become a party to [...] litigation before the court of another State, a State clearly consents to the exercise of such jurisdiction, regardless of whether it is a plaintiff or a defendant'.[44] Although it is perhaps unclear whether the reference to becoming 'a party' to litigation is intended in the technical sense of being joined as a party or in the more general sense of participating or playing a part in the litigation, the same essential point holds good. By voluntarily engaging with a claim without raising its immunity from the court's jurisdiction, a State is taken to have consented to the exercise by the court of jurisdiction over it in relation to the merits of the claim, and is precluded from subsequently raising a plea of immunity from jurisdiction.

(ii) The exception

The second sentence of Article 8(1)(*b*) posits an exception to the rule contained in the first sentence. It provides that, 'if the State satisfies the court that it could not have acquired knowledge of facts on which a claim to immunity can be based until after it took such a step, it can claim immunity based on those facts, provided it does so at the earliest possible moment'. Surprisingly, the ILC's commentary to draft article 8 appears to envisage that the exception applies to all instances in which a State has implicitly consented to the exercise of jurisdiction, including where it has itself instituted proceedings.[45] Yet any such interpretation is contradicted by both the text and context of the provision. It ignores the fact that the second sentence of Article 8(1)(*b*) runs on directly from the first, rather than starting on a new line, and also fails to appreciate that the phrase 'took such a step' arguably refers back to the phrase 'taken any [...] step', which appears in the first sentence of Article 8(1)*(b),* but not in Article 8(1)*(a).* Both elements suggest that, if a State institutes proceedings itself, it loses its right to invoke immunity from jurisdiction even it lacks 'knowledge of facts on which a claim to immunity can be based'. And this makes sense. It is one thing to suggest that a State might not have

[42] Although, alone among national State immunity legislation, s. 1605(*a*)(1) FSIA (US) provides that the immunity of a foreign State from the jurisdiction of the US courts may be waived 'by implication', the US courts are slow to imply from conduct an intent to waive, even where the State fails to raise a defence of State immunity in good time. They insist on 'a conscious decision to take part in the litigation and a failure to raise sovereign immunity despite the opportunity to do so': *Foremost-McKesson Inc. v Islamic Republic of Iran,* 101 ILR 536, 544 (US (DC Cir.) 1990). On the other hand, positively seeking the assistance of the US courts against the plaintiff may be sufficient to constitute waiver of immunity: see *Siderman de Blake v Republic of Argentina,* 103 ILR 454 (US (9th Cir.) 1992).

[43] Note, however, that the presentation of a counterclaim is expressly dealt with in Art. 9(3).

[44] ILC commentary, draft art. 8, para. 3. *Cf* ILC commentary, draft art. 8, para. 6, which refers to 'entering an appearance on a voluntary basis' in terms which suggest an intention to cover some instances of application to be joined as a party.

[45] See ILC commentary, draft art. 8, para. 5: 'there might be circumstances in which a State would not be familiar with certain facts on the basis of which it could invoke immunity. It could happen that the State *instituted proceedings* or intervened in a case before it had acquired knowledge of such facts' (emphasis added).

participated in proceedings had it known it could have claimed immunity, but quite another to argue that it might not have sued had it known.

A more difficult question is whether the exception pertains to all instances of participation referred to in the first sentence of Article 8(1)*(b)*, or whether it is only applicable to a State which had taken 'any other step relating to the merits' (for instance, a State which, when a claim was brought against it, filed a defence or took some other step in relation to the merits of the claim). The reference in the second sentence of Article 8(1)*(b)* to 'such a step' could plausibly be read as referring back to references to intervention and other steps in the first sentence (thereby excluding only the institution of proceedings under Article 8(1)(a) from its coverage), or as limited to a State which takes 'any other step in relation to the merits' other than intervening. If a distinction is to be drawn between a State which has 'intervened in the proceeding' and one which has 'taken any other step relating to the merits', the better arguments suggest that the exception should only apply to the latter, more limited, case. If intervention in Article 8 is to be understood in the narrow, technical meaning (although the drafting history of the ILC's draft Article 8 and the accompanying commentary suggests it should not), as a matter of principle, it is, at the very least, open to question whether a State which has intervened by becoming a party to existing proceedings should subsequently be able to claim that it was unaware of the basis on which it could claim to be immune. In any case, in practice, such a situation is only likely to arise in circumstances in which the State intervenes to bring a claim, and is then met with a substantial counterclaim. In such a situation, it may be expected that a plea of ignorance of the basis for any immunity subsequently invoked is likely to be met with some scepticism by the courts. In this regard, it is notable that Article 3(1) ECSI, on which the exception in the second sentence of Article 8(1)(*b*) is purportedly based, is clearly on its face only concerned with knowledge at the time of the taking of 'any step in the proceedings relating to the merits'. By contrast, the institution of proceedings and intervention are both treated by Article 1(1) ECSI as constituting a submission to the jurisdiction of the courts of the forum State.[46]

On analysis, these interpretative difficulties in the ILC's draft article 8(1), which was carried through unchanged to the Convention, ultimately derive from the fact that the notion of 'submission to the jurisdiction', on which the ECSI is premised, was not adopted by the ILC. As a consequence, the transposition or transplant from Article 3(1) ECSI to the draft articles of the exception for lack of knowledge is not fully compatible with the different notion of 'consent to the exercise of jurisdiction' on the basis of which the ILC approached the same issue.

3.2 Article 8(2)

Article 8(2) is the first of three paragraphs specifying forms of conduct that cannot be regarded as amounting to consent to the exercise of jurisdiction by a court of another State which would result in the loss of the right to invoke any immunity a State would otherwise enjoy.

[46] In this context, it is clear from the ECSI Explanatory Report that the term 'intervenes' in Art. 1(1) ECSI is used in the technical procedural sense, rather than the general sense of 'participation' (Expl. Rep. ECSI, paras 14 and 18). See also SIA (UK), s. 2(3) and (5) which distinguishes between, on the one hand, the institution of proceedings by the State and on the other, intervention and the taking of any step in the proceedings, and excludes the plea of ignorance of relevant facts going to immunity where the State has instituted proceedings.

A. *Subparagraph* (a)

Article 8(2)(*a*) makes clear that a State which takes a step in proceedings before the courts of another State is not to be taken to have consented to the exercise of jurisdiction if the intervention is made solely in order to invoke its immunity. As the invocation of immunity is intended to preclude the exercise of jurisdiction, this is indeed a fairly straightforward proposition.

It should be noted that, in proceedings before the courts of England and Wales, the position is slightly complicated by the fact that a State which intends to rely on its immunity from jurisdiction is required to apply to the court for a declaration that the court has no jurisdiction or should not exercise its jurisdiction,[47] and, before doing so, is required to first file an acknowledgment of service.[48] However, the relevant procedural rules make clear that, by filing an acknowledgment of service, a defendant does not lose any right to dispute the jurisdiction of the court.[49]

B. *Subparagraph (*b*)*

Under Article 8(2)*(b)*, which draws on similar provisions in the ECSI and the legislation of a number of States,[50] a State will not be taken to have consented to the exercise of jurisdiction insofar as it intervenes merely in order to assert a right or interest in the property at issue in the proceedings. That provision must be read in the light of the definition of what will be taken to constitute a proceeding 'instituted against another State' as set out in Article 6 for the purposes of the obligation to give effect to any immunity possessed by a foreign State. In that regard, Article 6(2)*(b)* makes clear that proceedings are to be considered as 'instituted' against a State not only if the State is named as a party to the proceedings, but also where the foreign State is indirectly impleaded, because the proceeding 'in effect seeks to affect the property, rights, interests or activities of that other State'.[51]

As a consequence, if proceedings concern property over which the State asserts a right or interest, the State may as a minimum be required—and, conversely, is entitled, without losing its right to invoke immunity—to intervene to the extent necessary to prove the existence of that interest. The Convention, in common with the ILC draft, is silent as to the precise extent of the evidence which is required in order to show the existence of the right or interest, although the ILC's commentary proceeds on the basis that at least *prima facie* evidence of the State's interest is required.[52]

It should be noted that the practical effects of the limitation are reduced to a certain extent by reason of the absence of immunity in any event under Article 13 of the

[47] Civil Procedure Rules (England and Wales, SI 1998/3132, as amended), r. 11.1.

[48] See Civil Procedure Rules 1998 (n. 47), r. 11.2; as to the consequences of failure to file an acknowledgement of service, see Civil Procedure Rules 1998 (n. 46), r. 10.1.

[49] See Civil Procedure Rules 1998 (n. 47), r. 11.3.

[50] See eg Art. 13 ECSI; s. 2(4)(b) SIA (UK), s. 10(8) FStIA (Aus). Art. 13 ECSI excludes from the category of interventions by a State which will be deemed to constitute a submission to the jurisdiction any intervention for the purpose of asserting that the State 'has a right or interest in property which is the subject-matter of the proceedings' and if the circumstances are such that the State would have been entitled to immunity if the proceedings had been brought directly against it.

[51] See the commentary to Art. 6, section 3.2(B).

[52] ILC commentary to draft art. 8, para. 7; and see also the various older English cases cited, inexplicably, in fn 85.

Convention as regards the rights or interests of a State in or over immovable property situated in the forum State; any right or interest of a State in movable or immovable property which arises by way of succession, gift, or *bona vacantia*; and any right or interest of the State in the administration of property.[53]

3.3 Article 8(3)

Article 8(3) posits that '[t]he appearance of a representative of a State before a court of another State as a witness' shall not be interpreted as consent to jurisdiction. As noted above, the provision was inserted during the course of second reading upon the suggestion of Mexico.[54] Although Mexico's principal concern in suggesting the addition appears to have been appearances made before foreign courts by consular officials in the context of performance of consular protection functions, the exception inserted by the ILC during the course of second reading is (or at least was intended to be) substantially narrower. The ILC's commentary makes clear that the provision was intended to be limited to the situation in which a representative of a State appears as a witness, 'for instance to affirm that a particular person is a national of the State' and 'does not relate to all appearances of a State or its representatives in a foreign proceeding in the performance of the duty of affording protection to nationals of that State'.[55]

As such, the provision is arguably of extremely limited scope and therefore of questionable utility. In the hypothesis given, the State will not normally be a party to the proceedings, or the target of any claim therein. Accordingly, in practice there would appear to be little scope for immunity being held to have been lost in any case.

Fox comments that the provision is 'misleading' and that '[u]nless accompanied by limitation of the appearance for a stated specific purpose it would seem that an unqualified appearance or tender of evidence by an authorised State representative, such as the filing of an affidavit by a serving head of state in support of a claim brought in another State's national court, would constitute waiver of immunity'.[56] Although in an appropriate case that analysis may well be correct, as framed, the observation appears to be stated in an overly broad manner. First, the decision of the English court cited, apparently in support,[57] contains no explicit discussion relating to the proposition stated.[58] Second, much will depend upon the precise circumstances of the case, including, in particular, the identity of the parties to the litigation and the manner in which (if at all) it is sought to implead the State in those proceedings.

Whatever the precise scope of Article 8(3), as stipulated by Article 3, the Convention as a whole is without prejudice to the privileges and immunities enjoyed by members of the diplomatic mission or consular posts of a State. As the ILC's commentary to draft article 8(3) notes, those privileges and immunities include specific immunities relating to appearance as a witness under Article 31(2) of the 1961 Vienna Convention on Diplomatic Relations (unqualified immunity from being compelled to give evidence as

[53] See the commentary to Art. 13. [54] See section 2.

[55] ILC commentary to draft art. 8, para. 8.

[56] H. Fox, *The Law of State Immunity* (2nd edn) (Oxford: Oxford University Press, 2008), 494.

[57] Fox (n. 56), citing *Tajik Aluminium Plant v Ermatov and others* [2006] EWHC 2374 (Comm) (UK (EWHC) 2006).

[58] Indeed, the judgment was one arising from an application to amend the pleadings so as to *remove* any references to alleged wrongdoing by the head of state so as to avoid objections on the basis of act of State and/or non-justiciability.

a witness) and Article 44(1) of the 1963 Vienna Convention on Consular Relations (imposing an international obligation on States parties that (with certain specified exceptions) their consular officers should give evidence when requested by the receiving State, coupled with an immunity of individual consular officers from any measures of coercion or application of penalties in the event of refusal).[59]

4. Evaluation

Article 8 contains an overly detailed but useful application of the principle of implied consent and a necessary addition to the basic rule of Article 7. As regards the types of conduct which may justify a conclusion of implied consent to jurisdiction, the general rule of paragraph 1, the exception laid down in the second sentence of subparagraph 1(*b*), and the different clarifications introduced by paragraphs 2–4 provide guidance on many issues, even though a number of interpretative difficulties, largely the result of differences between the provision and the ILC's commentary, exist. However, the fact that the provision, notwithstanding its detail, fails to spell out what officials or representatives can bind the State is a significant lacuna; it means that in one crucial respect the Convention will not contribute to the 'harmonization of domestic practice'.[60]

Given the potential consequences, where the Convention is applicable, a State faced with a claim before the courts of another State may well be best advised simply not to respond in any way, and to rely upon the obligation imposed on States parties by Article 6 of the Convention to ensure that questions of immunity are examined by their courts *sua sponte*, as well as the requirement under Article 23 which preconditions the entry of a default judgment against a State upon verification that the State does not in fact benefit from immunity.

[59] ILC commentary, draft art. 8, para. 8 and fn 88.

[60] See the Convention's Preamble, third recital.

Article 9

Silvia Borelli and Simon Olleson*

Article 9

Counterclaims

1. A State instituting a proceeding before a court of another State cannot invoke immunity from the jurisdiction of the court in respect of any counterclaim arising out of the same legal relationship or facts as the principal claim.
2. A State intervening to present a claim in a proceeding before a court of another State cannot invoke immunity from the jurisdiction of the court in respect of any counterclaim arising out of the same legal relationship or facts as the claim presented by the State.
3. A State making a counterclaim in a proceeding instituted against it before a court of another State cannot invoke immunity from the jurisdiction of the court in respect of the principal claim.

1. Introduction

Article 9 of the Convention deals with the availability to a State of immunity from foreign jurisdiction in the context of counterclaims. It is the last of three consecutive provisions (Articles 7 to 9) addressing questions of consent.

A counterclaim ('*demande reconventionelle*') is a claim presented by a party to proceedings in response—whether by way of set-off, defence, or otherwise—to a claim by another party, most often the principal claimant, *viz* the party that initiated the proceedings. Article 9 covers two distinct situations. Paragraphs 1 and 2 deal with counterclaims brought against a State that has either instituted proceedings before a court of another State or intervened to present a claim in such proceedings. Paragraph 3 deals with the converse situation, namely counterclaims brought by a State in response to a claim brought against it by another party before the courts of another State.

The principle underlying Article 9 is that a State is not entitled to immunity where it has consented to the exercise of jurisdiction by the courts of the forum State. But while that principle, which also underlies Articles 7 and 8, is relatively unproblematic and uncontroversial, its application in relation to counterclaims is less straightforward. The issues raised do not as such relate to whether the State should be taken to have consented to some exercise of jurisdiction over it by the courts of the forum State. Insofar as the State has initiated proceedings before a foreign court, intervened to present a claim in such proceedings, or made a counterclaim in response to a claim presented against it, there can be little doubt that it is to be taken to have sufficiently manifested its consent to the exercise by the foreign court of jurisdiction over it in relation to the claim or

* Sections 1 and 2 of this commentary are to be attributed to Simon Olleson; Sections 3 and 4 are to be attributed to Silvia Borelli.

counterclaim it has itself advanced.[1] The difficulty relates, rather, to the scope of that consent, and whether it is also to be taken to extend to the exercise of jurisdiction by the foreign court over the State in relation to any counterclaim or claim advanced in the same proceedings by an opposing party.

In the case of proceedings before the courts of one State initiated by another State, or in which a State intervenes to present a claim, the question is the extent to which, by putting forward a claim of its own before the foreign court, the State thereby consents to the exercise by that court of jurisdiction over it in respect of any counterclaims brought by the defendant (or, conceivably, by any other party subsequently joined to the proceedings). As a subsidiary issue, the question also arises whether any such consent extends only to counterclaims closely related to the subject-matter of the State's own claim, or whether it also extends to any other, unrelated counterclaims another party may raise against the State.

Where, on the other hand, the proceedings before the foreign court concern a claim against a State, and the State submits a counterclaim in response, the question is whether the submission of the counterclaim necessarily implies the consent of the State to the exercise of jurisdiction over it by the foreign court, such that it is not immune in relation to that principal claim.

Article 9(1) answers the first two questions by specifying that a State instituting proceedings before a court of another State cannot invoke immunity from the exercise of jurisdiction over it by that court in respect of any counterclaim arising out of the same legal relationship or facts as the principal claim. Article 9(2) provides the same, *mutatis mutandis*, in relation to a counterclaim against a State that intervenes to present a claim in proceedings before a court of another State. Article 9(3), dealing with the third and converse question, stipulates that a State making a counterclaim in proceedings instituted against it in a court of another State cannot invoke immunity from the court's exercise of jurisdiction over it in respect of the principal claim.

2. Drafting History

2.1 The ILC's first reading

An inelegant provision on immunity in respect of counterclaims, numbered draft article 10, was put forward by Special Rapporteur Sucharitkul in his Third Report as part of a suite of provisions (draft articles 8 to 11) dealing with the consent of a State to the exercise of jurisdiction over it by a court of another State.[2]

As regards counterclaims against a State, draft article 10(1) as initially proposed[3] provided that, where foreign proceedings had been instituted by a State or the State had intervened in such proceedings, jurisdiction could be exercised over the State 'in respect of any counter-claim' if jurisdiction could have been exercised had separate proceedings been instituted against it (draft article 10(1)(*a*)), or if, in the formulation of draft article 10(1)(*b*), the counterclaim 'arose out of the same legal relationship or facts as the principal claim'. In both cases, however, it was proposed that jurisdiction could be exercised only insofar as the counterclaim did not seek relief 'exceeding in amount or

[1] As to the first situation, see Art. 7(1) and the commentary on that provision. As to the latter situation, see Art. 8(1)(*b*) and the commentary on that provision, as well as the discussion of Art. 9(3) in this chapter.

[2] Third report Sucharitkul, 146–8, paras 72–81.

[3] Third report Sucharitkul, 148, para. 81.

differing in kind from that sought by the State in the principal claim' (draft article 10(1)(*c*)). In that latter regard, draft article 10(2) went on to specify that any counterclaim going beyond the amount referred to in paragraph 1(*c*) was to operate 'as a set-off only'.[4]

Draft article 10(3) provided that, notwithstanding 'voluntary submission' by a State in accordance with the proposed draft article 9,[5] jurisdiction could not be exercised against that State 'in respect of any counter-claim exceeding in amount or differing in kind from the relief sought by the State in the principal claim'.[6]

As regards the making of a counterclaim by a State in foreign proceedings brought against it, draft article 10(4) clarified that, in presenting a counterclaim, the State thereby submitted voluntarily to the jurisdiction of the foreign courts 'with respect not only to the counter-claim but also to the principal claim'.[7]

As noted by Special Rapporteur Sucharitkul,[8] the effect of his proposed draft article 10(1) to (3) would have been that a State was in a privileged position when instituting or intervening in proceedings in a court of another State, insofar as it was not amenable to jurisdiction to the extent that any counterclaim against it exceeded the amount of its principal claim. This stood in contrast to the position under draft article 10(4), pursuant to which the jurisdiction of the foreign court in respect of a counterclaim brought by a State was not so limited.

Although it was questionable whether the State practice relied on by the Special Rapporteur supported the proposed limitations on counterclaims against a State,[9] no criticism was raised on this basis within the ILC. Indeed, comments on draft article 10 were comparatively few. Some members questioned the appropriateness of restricting counterclaims against a State to a set-off.[10] Others suggested that draft article 10(4) be amended to provide that immunity was lost in the case of a counterclaim made by a State only to the extent that the principal claim against the State arose out of the 'same transaction or legal relationship' as the counterclaim it raised.[11] Additionally, it was doubted whether, conceptually, all of the situations falling within draft article 10 could properly be regarded as manifestations of consent to the exercise of jurisdiction; in particular, the view was expressed by one member that a State's consent to jurisdiction in respect of future counterclaims was a fiction, since the State could not know when it instituted proceedings whether any counterclaim would be brought.[12]

In the light of these criticisms, the Special Rapporteur reformulated and greatly simplified draft article 10,[13] the new version consisting of only two paragraphs, dealing

[4] Third report Sucharitkul, 148, para. 81.

[5] Draft art. 9, the origin of what is now Art. 7 of the Convention, dealt with a State's submission to the jurisdiction by means of instituting or intervening in proceedings, entering an appearance or taking a step in the proceedings without raising the question of immunity, or otherwise expressly submitting to the jurisdiction.

[6] Third report Sucharitkul, 148, para. 81.

[7] Third report Sucharitkul, 148, para. 81.

[8] Third report Sucharitkul, 148, para. 80.

[9] See section 3.1(C).

[10] Summary record 1657th ILC meeting, *YILC 1981*, vol. I, 75, 78, para. 22 (George Aldrich) and see *YILC 1981*, vol. I, 80, para. 34 (Willem Riphagen).

[11] Summary record 1665th ILC meeting, *YILC 1981*, vol. I, 120, 122, para. 16 (Laurel Francis).

[12] Summary record 1663rd ILC meeting, *YILC 1981*, vol. I, 110, 112, para. 19 (Willem Riphagen). But *cf* summary record 1664th ILC meeting; *YILC 1981*, vol. I, 115, 118, para. 27 (Sir Francis Vallat).

[13] See Report ILC, thirty-third session, 157–8, para. 226 and n. 671; see also summary record 1716th ILC meeting, *YILC 1982*, vol. I, 102, 104, para. 17. The Commission had actually already decided to refer the original draft art. 10 to the Drafting Committee. See Report ILC, thirty-third session, 155, para. 221. The

with counterclaims against and by a State respectively. As regards counterclaims against a State, the new draft article 10(1) provided that, in any proceedings either instituted by a State 'or in which a State has taken part or a step relating to the merits', jurisdiction could be exercised in respect of any counterclaim 'arising out of the same legal relationship or facts as the principal claim' or 'if, in accordance with the provisions of the present articles, jurisdiction could be exercised had separate proceedings been instituted'. As regards counterclaims by a State, the new draft article 10(2) provided that, by making a counterclaim, a State was 'deemed to have given consent to the exercise of jurisdiction' over both the counterclaim and the principal claim against the State, although only to the extent that the principal claim arose 'out of the same legal relationship or facts [as the counter-claim]'.[14]

When the ILC's Drafting Committee eventually came to examine the revised proposal two years later, the draft article 10 that emerged was markedly different from either version put forward by Special Rapporteur Sucharitkul.[15] In order to make the various rules 'more easily understandable', the Drafting Committee separated out the three situations 'mixed together in the two paragraphs of the original text', by which was meant the Special Rapporteur's revised proposal.[16] As a result, the Committee's draft article 10 consisted of three paragraphs dealing with, respectively, counterclaims against a State in proceedings instituted by it, counterclaims against a State in proceedings in which the State had intervened to present a claim, and counterclaims by a State in proceedings instituted against it. The requirement that, in order for a State's immunity to be lost, a counterclaim should arise 'out of the same legal relationship or facts', was retained in relation to counterclaims against a State, as dealt with in the first two paragraphs. No such requirement was, however, stipulated in relation to a counterclaim made by a State. The Drafting Committee's text of draft article 10 was provisionally adopted in 1983[17] and was adopted by the ILC on first reading with the complete set of draft articles in 1986.[18]

2.2 The ILC's second reading and beyond

In its comments on draft article 10 as adopted on first reading, Thailand suggested the insertion of an additional paragraph stipulating that a State was precluded from invoking immunity from foreign jurisdiction 'only to the extent that the claim or counterclaim against it [did] not seek relief exceeding in amount or differing in kind from that sought by that State itself'.[19] Perhaps not coincidentally, the Thai proposal was similar to the

Drafting Committee, however, had insufficient time to consider the revised provision during what remained of the thirty-third session.

[14] The square brackets form part of the text proposed by the Special Rapporteur.

[15] See summary record 1805th ILC meeting, *YILC 1983*, vol. I, 285, 290, para. 61. Curiously, the Drafting Committee insisted in its report that the text resulting from its deliberations 'corresponded substantially' to the revised draft art. 10 proposed by the Special Rapporteur and that 'minor drafting changes had been introduced only to make the text clearer and more precise'. *YILC 1983*, vol. I, 285, 290, paras 61 and 63, respectively.

[16] Summary record 1805th ILC meeting (n. 15), 290, para. 62.

[17] Report ILC, thirty-fifth session, 20, para. 95.

[18] Report ILC, thirty-eighth session, 8, para. 20.

[19] 'Comments and observations received from Governments', UN doc. A/CN.4/410 and Add. 1–5, *YILC 1988*, vol. II(1), 45, 81, para. 8. For its part, Australia, the only other State to comment on draft art. 10 as adopted on first reading, proposed the merging of paras 1 and 2 back into a single provision: *YILC 1988*, vol. II(1), 51, para. 22.

limitation proposed by the now former Special Rapporteur Sucharitkul, a Thai, in his initial text of draft article 10. However, the proposed amendment went substantially further, insofar as it would also have circumscribed the court's exercise of jurisdiction over the principal claim in the event that the State brought a counterclaim. In response to a request to explain the rationale for Thailand's proposal, the new Special Rapporteur, Motoo Ogiso, stated that the suggested amendment was intended to address the situation where 'a claimant or counter-claimant, utilizing the circumstances in which the State could not claim immunity, collected or purchased debts attributable to the State and would present a claim or counter-claim far exceeding the original claim'.[20]

Although initially supported by Special Rapporteur Ogiso and by a number of members of the ILC, others doubted Thailand's proposal.[21] After further consideration, the Special Rapporteur withdrew his support, and sought guidance on the broader question of whether a State might invoke immunity in respect of a counterclaim that either exceeded, or was unrelated to, its own claim.[22] On the Drafting Committee's consideration of draft article 10 on second reading, Thailand's proposed amendment quietly sank without trace.[23] The Drafting Committee made no more than minor amendments to the formulation of the draft provision adopted on first reading,[24] which was by now renumbered draft article 9.[25] It was in this form that the Commission finally adopted the provision on second reading in 1991.[26]

Draft article 9 as adopted by the ILC on second reading remained unchanged throughout the subsequent drafting process, save that, in the final *toilettage* prior to the adoption of the draft Convention by the Ad Hoc Committee on Jurisdictional Immunities of States and Their Property, the hyphen was removed from the word 'counter-claim' throughout,[27] so that what the General Assembly adopted in late 2004 was an Article 9 of the Convention on 'Counterclaims'.

3. Key Points

3.1 Counterclaims against a State

A. Overview

The first two paragraphs of Article 9 deal with a State's immunity from jurisdiction in respect of a counterclaim brought by another party to foreign proceedings either instituted by the State itself (Article 9(1)), or in which the State has intervened to present

[20] Report ILC, forty-first session, 107, para. 486 and see summary record 2122nd ILC meeting, *YILC 1989*, vol. I, 194, 194–5, paras 1–2 (Motoo Ogiso).

[21] See the various comments made at the 2114th to 2122nd ILC meetings, *YILC 1989*, vol. I, 128–97. The observations of a number of members appear to indicate that they misunderstood the provision, insofar as they seem to have proceeded on the basis that it was aimed at claims and counterclaims between two States.

[22] Third report Ogiso, 11–12.

[23] As did the (non-substantive) proposal for reformulation made by Australia.

[24] Report ILC, forty-second session, 32, para. 167; for the report of the Drafting Committee, see UN doc. A/CN.4/L.444 and summary record 2191st ILC meeting, *YILC 1990*, vol. I, 306, 312, para. 59.

[25] See the Report of the Drafting Committee, UN doc. A/CN.4/L.444 and summary record 2191st ILC meeting (n. 24), 308, para. 26.

[26] For the report of the Drafting Committee, see A/CN.4/L.457 and summary record 2218th ILC meeting, *YILC 1991*, vol. I, 66, 72, para. 57. See also Report ILC, forty-third session, 12, para. 23.

[27] Compare the text of draft art. 9 as annexed to 2003 report Ad Hoc Committee with that of art. 9 Draft UNCSI as annexed to 2004 report Ad Hoc Committee.

a claim (Article 9(2)). In both cases, where the counterclaim arises out of 'the same legal relationship or facts' as the claim made by the State, the State cannot, in respect of that counterclaim, invoke any immunity from jurisdiction it would have enjoyed were the counterclaim to have been brought as a claim against that State. In keeping with the overall approach of Parts II and III of the Convention, pursuant to which a State's general entitlement to immunity from jurisdiction is subject to enumerated exceptions, both paragraphs (1) and (2) of Article 9, comprising as they do exceptions to immunity, provide that a State 'cannot invoke immunity' in respect of the counterclaims specified.

The scheme of Parts II and III of the Convention, as well as the drafting history of Article 9 and the ILC commentary,[28] indicate that Article 9(1) and (2) posit exceptions to a State's immunity from jurisdiction in their own right. Although it would not have hurt to have made the point explicitly, as is, in effect, the case with Article 1(2)(*b*) ECSI,[29] it goes without saying that, insofar as the subject-matter of a counterclaim against a State falls within one of the exceptions to the State's immunity from jurisdiction enumerated in Part III of the Convention, the relevant exception is applicable to proceedings in respect of the counterclaim such that the State in any case enjoys no immunity. In such circumstances, recourse to Article 9(1) and (2) is unnecessary. The point of the exceptions to immunity in Article 9(1) and (2) is that, as is the case with Articles 7(1) and 8(1), they apply where the State would otherwise be entitled to invoke immunity—that is, where the subject-matter of the counterclaim does not fall within one of the exceptions to immunity from jurisdiction provided for in Part III of the Convention.

B. *Relationship to Article 8(1)*

Article 9(1) goes hand-in-hand with Article 8(1)(*a*) of the Convention. Under Article 8(1)(*a*), a State which institutes proceedings before a foreign court is taken by so doing to have manifested its consent to the court's exercise of jurisdiction over it in respect of the claim or claims which form the subject of the proceedings. Accordingly, it cannot invoke in relation to those claims any immunity from the court's jurisdiction that it would have enjoyed had proceedings arising out of the same subject-matter been instituted against it in the same court. In that regard, Article 9(1) simply clarifies that a State which institutes proceedings before a foreign court is thereby taken also to have manifested its consent to the exercise of jurisdiction over it also in respect of any counterclaim by the respondent to the principal claim made by the State which arises out of the same legal relationship or facts as the principal claim.

When it comes to participation by a State in order to present a claim other than by instituting proceedings, the relationship between Article 9 and 8 is more complex. Despite the superficial similarity of the terms used in Articles 8(1)(*b*) and 9(2), respectively ('intervened' and 'intervening'), there is in fact no parallelism between the two provisions equivalent to that between Article 8(1)(*a*) and 9(1).

[28] ILC commentary, draft art. 9, para. 5.

[29] Article 1(2) ECSI provides: '[A] Contracting State [which institutes or intervenes in proceedings before a court of another Contracting State] cannot claim immunity from the jurisdiction of the courts of the other Contracting State in respect of any counterclaim: (*a*) arising out of the legal relationship or the facts on which the principal claim is based; (*b*) if, according to the provisions of this Convention, it would not have been entitled to invoke immunity in respect of that counterclaim had separate proceedings been brought against it in those courts.'

The two provisions are concerned with different questions. Article 8(1)(*b*) is concerned with situations in which a claim is brought directly against a State, or in which, although the State is not named as a party, the proceedings are deemed to have been so brought because the claim concerns property in which the State has a right or interest so that it is deemed to have been indirectly impleaded.[30] The provision thus regulates the circumstances in which a State will be held to have lost its right to invoke immunity as a response to such a claim by reason of the fact that it has participated in those proceedings, either because it has 'intervened' or (which appears to be the same thing), it has 'taken some other step in relation to the merits', with knowledge of its entitlement to immunity from jurisdiction.[31]

By contrast, Article 9(2) circumscribes the situations in which a State, by 'intervening' to present a claim in foreign proceedings, loses its entitlement to invoke any immunity it would otherwise have in respect of any further counterclaim brought against it by another party, and, in that regard, restricts the situations in which immunity will be held to have been lost *in respect of such a counterclaim.* It does so by limiting the loss of immunity to circumstances in which the counterclaim arises from the same legal relationship or facts as the claim presented by the State by way of intervention.

On its clear wording, and when read in the context of Article 9 as a whole, Article 9(2) deals only with loss of immunity in respect of counterclaims *against a State* consequent upon (and subsequent to) a claim made by way of intervention and is not concerned with loss of immunity by a State in relation to a principal claim against it. The situation in which a State, in response to a claim made against it, presents a counterclaim falls squarely within the scope of Article 9(3).[32] In any case, the claim against the State in such a case (ie the 'principal claim') cannot plausibly be described as a 'counterclaim' in the sense in which that term was understood by the ILC (ie 'a claim brought by a defendant in response to an original or principal claim') for the purposes of Article 9(2).[33]

As such, the function of Article 9(2), and the factual situations to which it is intended to apply, are extremely limited and in no way correspond to those covered by Article 8(1)(*b*).

As a consequence, it is also clear there is a difference in the scope and meaning of the terms 'intervened' and 'intervening' in Articles 8 and 9, respectively. As noted in the context of the discussion of Article 8, the term 'intervened' in draft article 8 of the ILC's Draft Articles and in Article 8 of the Convention appears to have been used to denote any conduct constituting active participation in proceedings in response to a claim which is inconsistent with an intention to invoke immunity, rather than in the narrower, procedural sense of an application by a third party formally to become a party to the proceedings (or to otherwise take a part in the proceedings in some other manner, for instance as *amicus curiae*).[34] The sole exceptions envisaged in this regard are, on the one

[30] *Cf* Art. 6(2)(b).

[31] See the commentary to Art. 8.

[32] Further, in such a situation, any immunity in relation to the principal claim by the original claimant against the State will in any case normally necessarily be lost under Art. 8(1)(*b*) as the presentation of a counterclaim by the State will constitute 'intervention' or the taking of a step in relation to the merits of that claim. See further below.

[33] *Cf* ILC commentary, draft art. 9, para. 3. The ILC also observed that 'the notion of "counter-claims" presupposes the prior existence or institution of a claim'.

[34] ILC commentary, draft art. 9, para. 6.

hand, the narrow carve-outs set out in Article 8(2), ie intervention or the taking of steps solely in order to invoke immunity, and intervention by the State as a non-party to assert a right or interest in property, and, on the other, the specific situation dealt with in Article 8(3), ie appearance in proceedings of a representative of the State as a witness on limited factual matters.

By contrast, the use of the term 'intervening' in Article 9(2) must be read in light of the words which immediately follow (ie 'intervening *to present a claim*') and as such can only be interpreted as being used in the narrower sense, ie as referring to a situation in which a State, not being a party, intervenes in order to become a party for the purpose of making a claim.[35] This follows necessarily from the ILC's use of the term 'counterclaim' (a claim brought by a defendant in response to an original or principal claim),[36] taken with the consideration that if the State is already a party and a claim has been made against it, any claim which it makes is necessarily a counterclaim, which falls within Article 9(3).

This narrower meaning to be attributed to the term 'intervening' in Article 9(2) is substantially confirmed by the ILC's commentary on draft article 9, although the question is not entirely free from doubt. The ILC, in discussing counterclaims in general, distinguished between three situations covered by the different constituent paragraphs of Article 9, namely: counterclaims against a State where it has instituted proceedings; counterclaims against a State where it has 'interven[ed] in a proceeding to present a claim'; and the making of a counterclaim by a State 'in a proceeding instituted against it'.[37] In similar fashion, it observed 'there appear to be two possible circumstances in which counter-claims could be brought against a State', referring on the one hand to the situation in which a State institutes proceedings and, on the other, to that in which 'a State has not itself instituted a proceeding but has intervened in a proceeding to present a claim'.[38] Finally, and most clearly, in discussing Article 9(2), the ILC noted that that provision deals with the situation in which 'a State intervenes in a proceeding before a court of another State not as an *amicus curiae*, but as an interested party, in order to present a claim. It is only in this sense that it is possible to conceive of a counter-claim being brought against a State which has intervened as a claimant, and not as a mere witness or merely to make a declaration'.[39] It will be noted that all of the examples of 'intervention' to which the ILC referred in that latter passage consist of conduct taken by a non-party.

As a consequence, the situation covered by Article 9(2) is that in which the State, not being a party to the proceedings, formally applies to be joined as a party in order to present a claim (whether against an original party, or against some third party which is

[35] Art. 1(1) ECSI provides that '[a] Contracting State which institutes or intervenes in proceedings before a court of another Contracting State submits, for the purpose of those proceedings, to the jurisdiction of the courts of that State.'; as discussed in relation to Art. 8, it appears to be relatively clear from Expl. Rep. ECSI, para. 18, as well as from the separate provision of Art. 3 ECSI in relation to the circumstances in which the conduct of a State in proceedings results in the loss of immunity, that the term 'intervenes' is there used in the technical, procedural sense, rather than in the general sense of 'participation'.

[36] See ILC commentary, draft art. 9, para. 3.

[37] ILC commentary, draft art. 9, para. 2.

[38] ILC commentary, draft art. 9, para. 3.

[39] ILC commentary, draft art. 9, para. 6; *cf* similarly para. 3, in which the ILC distinguished intervention to present a claim, from 'intervention as *amicus curiae*, or in the interest of justice, or in order to make a suggestion, or in order to give evidence on a point of law or of fact without itself consenting to the exercise of jurisdiction against it in respect of the entire proceeding'.

joined for these purposes), and is then in turn faced with a counterclaim (again potentially either by an original party, or by the newly joined defendant to its own claims). In such situations, provided the counterclaim in response by another party arises out of the same legal relationship or facts as the claim presented by the State, the State will not be able to invoke any immunity it would otherwise possess. By contrast, as the ILC's commentary makes clear, other, lesser, forms of intervention by a State in proceedings are insufficient to result in the loss of immunity in relation to any such counterclaim brought against it by another party.[40]

As such, although there is a substantial correlation between the situation covered by Article 9(3) and the situations in which a State will lose its right to invoke immunity under Article 8(1)(*b*) by taking a step in proceedings (most evidently, in circumstances in which a claim is brought directly against the State, and the State is named as a party),[41] there is no such correlation as regards loss of immunity in respect of a related counterclaim presented in response to a claim made by the State by way of intervention. Nevertheless, the logic of Article 9(2) follows inexorably from that of Article 9(1): having presented a claim, the State cannot complain if it is held not to be entitled to immunity in respect of any counterclaim arising out of the same legal relationship or facts.

C. *'any counterclaim arising out of the same legal relationship or facts'*

Both Article 9(1) and (2) limit the extent to which a State that has instituted proceedings or intervened to present a claim is amenable to jurisdiction with respect to any counterclaim by requiring that the counterclaim be one 'arising out of the same legal relationship or facts' as the claim brought by the State.

The requirement that the counterclaim against the State arise out of the same legal relationship or facts as the principal claim or a claim presented by way of intervention was inspired by Article 1(2)(*a*) ECSI, which provides that a Contracting State which institutes or intervenes in proceedings before a court of another Contracting State 'cannot claim immunity from the jurisdiction of the courts of the other Contracting State in respect of any counterclaim . . . arising out of the legal relationship or the facts on which the principal claim is based'.[42] Similar provisions are found in the State immunity legislation of a number of States.[43]

Article 9(1) and (2), like Article 1(2)(*a*) ECSI and the vast majority of the pre-Convention national legislation, are silent as to whether a State that institutes or intervenes to present a claim in foreign proceedings is entitled to invoke immunity from jurisdiction to the extent that any counterclaim against it arising out of the same legal relationship or facts as its claim exceeds the claim in amount or differs from it in the nature of the relief sought. Proposals to this effect having been rejected in the course of the drafting of Article 9,[44] it is clear that paragraphs (1) and (2) of Article 9 do not

[40] ILC commentary, draft art. 9, paras 3 and 6.

[41] For discussion of the correct characterization of the situation of a State which is indirectly impleaded and presents a claim, see below.

[42] Art. 1(2)(*a*) ECSI itself draws on Art. 11(2) Convention on the Recognition and Enforcement of Foreign Judgments in Civil and Commercial Matters, The Hague, 1 February 1971, 1144 UNTS 249, as explained in Expl. Rep. ECSI, para. 18.

[43] See s. 2(6) SIA (UK), enacted to give effect to Art. 2(1)(a) ECSI, along with s. 4(4) SIO (Pak), s. 3(5) FStIA (SA), and s. 4(6) SIA (Sing), all modelled on the UK legislation. See also, not dissimilarly, s. 1607(*b*) FSIA (US); s. 4(4) SIA (Can); s. 10(10) FStIA (Aus).

[44] See section 2.

circumscribe in this way the exception to a State's immunity from jurisdiction that they embody. A State that institutes or intervenes to present a claim in foreign proceedings is taken, as far as Article 9(1) and (2) are concerned, to have consented to the court's exercise of jurisdiction over it with respect to any counterclaim arising out of the same legal relationship or facts as that State's claim, regardless of its extent or the nature of the relief sought.

In this last regard, it is worth noting parenthetically section 1607(*c*) FSIA, which provides that a foreign State instituting or intervening in proceedings in a US court shall not, with respect to any counterclaim against it, be accorded immunity from jurisdiction 'to the extent that the counterclaim does not seek relief exceeding in amount or differing in kind from that sought by the foreign state'. This might be thought to suggest, as the ILC commentary thinks it does, that '[i]n some jurisdictions' the abrogation of a foreign State's immunity from proceedings in respect of a counterclaim is 'limited in amount, which cannot exceed that of the principal claim'.[45] But this would be to take section 1607(*c*) FSIA out of context. Section 1607(*c*) is framed as one of three alternative exceptions to a foreign State's immunity from US jurisdiction. Another of those exceptions, section 1607(*b*), applies, without limitation, 'with respect to any counterclaim . . . arising out of the transaction or occurrence that is the subject matter of the claim of the foreign state'. In contrast, section 1607(*c*), which does impose a limitation as to the extent and kind of relief sought, applies only to counterclaims that do not 'aris[e] out of the transaction or occurrence that is the subject matter of the claim of the foreign state'—ie it is applicable only to unrelated counterclaims. In short, section 1607(*c*) FSIA, with which the subsequent section 10(*a*) and (*c*) FSIL (Isr) are analogous, provides no support for the assertion in the ILC commentary.[46] As it is, the musings in the ILC's commentary to draft article 9 should be taken to have no bearing on paragraphs (1) and (2) of Article 9 of the Convention, which impose no restrictions on the amount or nature of the relief sought by way of counterclaim against a State that institutes or intervenes to present a claim in foreign proceedings.

Whether a particular counterclaim brought against a State arises out of 'the same legal relationship or facts' as the State's claim obviously depends on the circumstances. In this regard, the ILC commentary is singularly unilluminating.[47] However, some guidance in this regard may be derived from decisions of the US federal courts under section 1607(*b*) FSIA; despite the difference in formulation ('arising out of the transaction or occurrence that is the subject matter of the claim of the foreign state', as opposed to 'arising out of the same legal relationship or facts as the principal

[45] ILC commentary, draft art. 9, para. 4.

[46] In addition, the ILC commentary refers to a number of older English authorities in which cross-claims or counterclaims were permitted to be brought against a sovereign claimant up to the amount of its principal claim 'in order for complete justice to be done', in support of the proposition that, in some jurisdictions, a counterclaim against a State may not 'go beyond "the point where affirmative relief is sought"': ILC commentary, draft art. 9, para. 4, citing *inter alia Strousberg v Republic of Costa Rica* (1881) 44 *Law Times Reports* 199 (UK (EWCA) 1881), *South African Republic v La Compagnie franco-belge du chemin de fer du Nord* [1898] 1 Ch. 190 (UK (EWHC) 1897), and *USSR v Belaiew* [1925] All ER 369 (UK (EWHC) 1925). However, in doing so, it appears to have failed to have taken account of the specific reasoning of those cases, and further that those authorities have in any case been superseded as a matter of the law of England and Wales by the enactment of s. 2(6) SIA (UK).

[47] See ILC commentary, draft art. 9, paras 4 and 6.

claim'), the two tests are broadly similar, and appear to have been treated by the ILC as disclosing no substantive difference.[48]

In *Kunstsammlungen zu Weimar and others v Elicofon*,[49] a dispute in which multiple parties asserted conflicting claims of ownership of two valuable works of fine art, the Court of Appeals for the 2nd Circuit held (perhaps unsurprisingly) that a collateral cross-claim brought by one of the various parties asserting ownership against another such party for payment of annuities under an agreement dating from 1921 did not arise out of the 'same transaction or occurrence' as the principal dispute in relation to ownership of the works of art.

In *Cabiri v Ghana*,[50] the claimant, an ex-trade representative of Ghana, alleged that he had been lured back to Ghana where he had then been tortured and imprisoned. He attempted, originally by way of counterclaims in proceedings relating to eviction from the house he and his family had occupied whilst he had been in post, to raise various counterclaims against the State. The Court of Appeals for the 2nd Circuit held that there was no immunity in relation to the claim relating to breach of contract based on the termination of his employment, since use of the residence in question had been incidental to his employment, and both the claim for breach of contract and the eviction therefore turned upon the valid termination of that employment, and thus arose out of the 'same transaction', namely the claimant's contract of employment and its termination.[51] However, the Court of Appeals affirmed the finding of the District Court that the remaining claims, relating to the manner in which the claimant had been lured back to Ghana and his alleged subsequent detention and mistreatment at the hands of the authorities in Ghana, did not arise out of his employment, and therefore did not fall within the exception.[52]

Finally, although decided at common law, prior to the adoption of the SIA (UK), a further clear illustration of a counterclaim against a State which is not sufficiently connected with the principal claim is provided by the facts of *High Commissioner for India v Ghosh*.[53] In that case, the Court of Appeal of England and Wales held that, in bringing a claim for debt or damages for breach of contract, India had not submitted to the jurisdiction of the English courts as regards a counterclaim for alleged slander by State officials which was unrelated to and independent of the subject-matter of its own claim. There can be little doubt that a similar conclusion would be reached applying the 'same legal relationship or facts' test applicable under section 2(6) SIA (UK).

D. *Extent of loss of immunity*

As the ILC commentary observes, a State instituting foreign proceedings 'is deemed to have consented to the jurisdiction of the court for all stages of the proceedings, including trial and judgment at first instance, appellate and final adjudications and the award of

[48] ILC commentary, draft art. 9, para. 4. Nevertheless, it is perhaps open to question whether the ILC's implicit assumption that the two tests are in substance identical is correct, and whether given the difference in terminology, application of the two tests would produce the same results in all cases.

[49] *Kunstsammlungen zu Weimar and others v Elicofon*, 94 ILR 133 (US (2nd Cir.) 1982).

[50] *Cabiri v Government of the Republic of Ghana*, 165 F.3d 193 (US (2nd Cir.) 1999).

[51] *Cabiri v Government of the Republic of Ghana* (n. 50), 198.

[52] *Cabiri v Government of the Republic of Ghana* (n. 50), 198–9.

[53] *High Commissioner for India v Ghosh*, 28 ILR 150 (UK (EWCA) 1960).

costs where such lies within the discretion of the deciding authority';[54] but the State does not consent, merely by instituting proceedings, to the taking of pre- or post-judgment measures of constraint against its property.[55] Nor, self-evidently, does a State, by instituting proceedings, indicate its consent to the exercise of jurisdiction over it in 'relation to all other civil actions against the State which happen to be justiciable or subject to the jurisdiction of the same court or another court of the State of the forum'.[56] Logically, the same ought to be the case under Article 9 in respect of any counterclaim against the State arising out of the same legal relationship or facts as a claim made by the State, independently of whether that claim is made by the State instituting proceedings, or by way of intervention by the State in already extant proceedings.[57]

3.2 Counterclaims by a State

Article 9(3) is concerned with the converse of the situation regulated by Article 9(1) and (2), namely the instances in which a State advances a counterclaim in proceedings in a foreign court in response to a claim brought against it by another party to the proceedings. Article 9(3), which is essentially an instantiation of Article 8(1)(*b*) of the Convention, provides that a State making a counterclaim 'in a proceeding instituted against it before a court of another State' cannot invoke immunity from the court's jurisdiction 'in respect of the principal claim'. In that regard, the ILC commentary indicates that, by bringing a counterclaim, a State takes a step in relation to the merits of the proceedings within the meaning of Article 8(1)(*b*),[58] which stipulates that a State cannot invoke immunity from jurisdiction in proceedings before a court of another State if it has intervened in the proceedings 'or taken any other step relating to the merits'. As a consequence, by making a counterclaim in proceedings brought against it before a foreign court, a State is taken to consent to the court's exercise of jurisdiction over it in respect not only of its counterclaim but also, as per Article 9(3), in respect of the claim against it.[59]

In light of the fact that it essentially confirms the outcome dictated by the rule laid down in Article 8(1)(*b*), Article 9(3) gives rise to fewer interpretative problems than Article 9(2); nevertheless there are certain issues which are not entirely clear.

First, in the light of Article 6(2) of the Convention, it is strongly arguable that the term 'proceeding instituted against it' in Article 9(3) should be understood as encompassing both the situation in which the State is named as a party to the proceedings and the situation in which it is not named as a party but in which it is indirectly impleaded because 'the proceeding in effect seeks to affect [its] property, rights, interests or activities'. However, in such circumstances, a question arises as to whether a State that is only indirectly impleaded but then presents a claim against the party which has initiated the proceedings must necessarily be regarded as making a counterclaim under Article 9(3), or whether it might in an appropriate case be regarded as intervening in

[54] ILC commentary, draft art. 9, para. 4, referring, for reasons which are not altogether apparent, to draft art. 8(1)(*a*); the intended reference appears to be to ILC commentary, draft art. 8, para. 1. See also ILC commentary, draft art. 9, paras 2 and 8.

[55] See ILC commentary, draft art. 9, para. 4. See also ILC commentary, draft art. 8, para. 1.

[56] ILC commentary, draft art. 9, para. 4.

[57] See ILC commentary, draft art.9, paras 2 and 8.

[58] See ILC commentary, draft art. 9, para. 7.

[59] See ILC commentary, paras 7 and 8.

order to present a claim within the meaning of Article 9(2), with the result that the State is to be regarded as having lost immunity in respect of any related counterclaim brought against it by another party. If the latter approach were held to be correct, the difference in outcome compared to treating the situation as compared to Article 9(3) would be relatively minor: by presenting a claim in such circumstances, the State will normally be regarded as having intervened or taken some other step in relation to the merits of the proceedings for the purposes of Article 8(1)(*b*). As a result, any right to invoke immunity which might have existed in relation to the principal claim by which the State was indirectly impleaded would in any case be lost.

A further interpretative issue concerns the phrase 'the principal claim', which is used in both Article 9(1) and (3). In the context of Article 9(1), there can be no doubt that those words refer to the claim made by the State which has instituted proceedings, and that it is this 'principal claim' which is to be taken as constituting the relevant comparator for the purposes of assessing whether the counterclaim arises out of the 'same legal relationship or facts'. By contrast, in Article 9(3), the words are used for a different purpose, namely so as to identify the claim (or claims) against the State in relation to which immunity is lost by reason of the presentation by the State of a counterclaim. However, there is no basis in the work of the ILC to support the view that the notion of 'principal claim' as used in Article 9(3) should be understood as limited to claims made by the party instituting proceedings as is the case in Article 9(1). The term should thus arguably be understood as extending to any claim made against the State in response to which the State presents a counterclaim, including a claim made by a party which has intervened in order to present a claim, or which has been subsequently joined and presented a claim once proceedings have been commenced. It is entirely consistent with the underlying scheme of Article 9 (and the more general principal contained in Article 8(1)(*b*)) that a State, if it makes a counterclaim in response to a claim made against it by another party, should be regarded as losing immunity from jurisdiction in respect of that claim. This is so irrespective of whether that principal claim is one made by the party which has instituted the proceedings, or by some other party. What is important is that, when faced with a claim, the consent of the State that the court should exercise jurisdiction over the claim should be clearly discernible; the making of a counterclaim in response undoubtedly constitutes sufficiently clear evidence in this regard.

Finally, it should be emphasized that, in contradistinction to Article 9(1) and (2), there is no requirement in Article 9(3) that the counterclaim made by the State should be one which 'arises out of the same legal relationship or facts' as the 'principal' claim to which it responds. The absence of any such condition is a reflection of the fact that, in the situation covered by Article 9(3), it is the State which is making the counterclaim, rather than being the entity against which the counterclaim is made; as a result, there is no requirement, as is the case under Article 9(1) and (2), to limit the circumstances in which the State will be held to have lost an immunity it would otherwise enjoy. Consequently, Article 9(3) is not simply the inverse or mirror image of Article 9(1) and (2), but permits a State, by presenting a counterclaim, to evidence its consent to the exercise of jurisdiction over any principal claim, even if there is no connection with its counterclaim. Once again, the underlying philosophy is broadly the same as that contained in Article 8(1)(*b*), namely, that once a State has taken steps in proceedings involving claims against it, it evidences its consent to the exercise of jurisdiction over it not only in relation to its own claims, but also in relation to claims made against it by other parties.

As is the case under Article 9(1) and (2), the consent to the exercise of jurisdiction by the courts of the forum State over a principal claim evidenced by the bringing of a counterclaim must be understood as extending to any related appellate proceedings. But as is the case with Articles 7 to 9 in their entirety, such consent to the exercise of jurisdiction does not imply or encompass consent to pre- or post-judgment measures of constraint against the State's property.[60]

4. Evaluation

As discussed above, Article 9 presents a certain number of relevantly significant issues of interpretation, both internally and in terms of consistency of the use of specific terms in other provisions of the Convention. However, those interpretative problems are likely to be of little practical significance given that the circumstances in which Article 9 may be relevant are comparatively limited.

First, many of the circumstances in which one would expect issues of counterclaims to arise are subject areas in relation to which States in any case enjoy no immunity. This is the case most notably as regards commercial transactions,[61] torts occasioning death or physical harm or damage to property committed within the jurisdiction of the forum State,[62] and disputes relating to any right or interest relating to ownership, possession, or use of immovable property located within the jurisdiction of the forum State.[63]

Second, the question of whether or not a counterclaim may be presented by or against a State may well be disposed of on other grounds under the domestic procedural rules relating to joinder of parties and the circumstances in which counterclaims may be presented in response to a claim. By way of example, in the English decision of *Commonwealth of Australia v Peacekeeper International*,[64] Australia started interpleader proceedings in order to determine to which of two companies which had laid competing claims it should return armoured vehicles it had leased for the purposes of peacekeeping operations in Iraq. Subsequently, one of the competing claimants to the vehicles (and respondent to the interpleader proceedings) made an application for permission, *inter alia*, to add claims against Australia relating to a continued obligation to pay hire charges until such time as the vehicles were returned to it. All concerned (including the court) appear to have proceeded on the basis that, by having itself instituted the interpleader proceedings, Australia had submitted to the jurisdiction and was thus unable to invoke immunity from jurisdiction in respect of any counterclaims against it.[65] Given their

[60] ILC commentary, draft art. 9, para. 7; *cf* ILC commentary, draft art. 8, para. 1. Although Art. 20 of the Convention explicitly specifies that this is the case only in relation to express consent in accordance with Art. 7, it is clear that the same principle applies in respect of the implied consent by a State to the exercise of jurisdiction by the court over it deriving from participation in the proceedings on the merits, including by the making of a counterclaim.

[61] Art. 10.

[62] Art. 12.

[63] Art. 13(*a*).

[64] *Commonwealth of Australia v Peacekeeper International FZC UAE & Anor* [2008] EWHC 1220 (QB) (UK (EWHC) 2008).

[65] Although there is some discussion in the judgment of 'submission to the jurisdiction' (in particular *Commonwealth of Australia v Peacekeeper International* (n. 64), paras 45–55) this was not in the context of examination of whether there had been submission to the jurisdiction for the purposes of the SIA. Rather, the issue arose in relation to the parallel but separate question of whether Australia and one of the claimants, as

nature, the claims undoubtedly arose out of the 'same legal relationship or facts' as the principal claim for the purpose of section 2(6) SIA (UK). However, the claims against Australia were not permitted to be brought in the context of the interpleader proceeding, the court reasoning that, given the specific nature of interpleader proceedings under English law, which are limited to the resolution of questions of disputed title, it was not possible to advance substantive claims of the type sought to be added in those proceedings.[66]

To the extent that it applies, Article 9 sets out a somewhat complex regime. By providing that immunity is lost in respect of counterclaims against a State only to the extent that those counterclaims arise out of the same legal relationship or facts as the claim made by the State, Article 9(1) and (2) adopt a relatively narrow approach. However, such a limitation is undoubtedly justified in order to protect States which submit to the jurisdiction of the courts of another State by making a claim against the risk of thereby being held to have consented to the exercise of jurisdiction over multiple claims having no relationship to the specific dispute for which they have submitted. The narrow approach in Articles 9(1) and (2) may be contrasted to the situation under Article 9(3) (which deems the State to have consented to the principal claim against it even where it makes an unrelated counterclaim), where no such considerations apply. While complex and not without problems, Article 9 is generally in line with the approach adopted in Article 8 and its underlying logic, and—depending on the willingness of States to join the Convention regime—has the potential of contributing to 'the harmonization of practice in this area'.

parties located outside the jurisdiction and therefore otherwise outwith the jurisdiction of the English courts, had submitted so that the court was able to exercise jurisdiction over them.

66 *Commonwealth of Australia v Peacekeeper International* (n. 64), paras 36–42.

PART III: PROCEEDINGS IN WHICH STATE IMMUNITY CANNOT BE INVOKED

Rosanne van Alebeek

1. Introduction

The eight provisions of Part III of the Convention enumerate a range of what the title of the part calls 'proceedings in which State immunity cannot be invoked'. These provisions differ from the three in Part II of the Convention that specify circumstances in which a State cannot invoke immunity from the jurisdiction of a court of another State, namely Articles 7 to 9, in that they relate solely to the subject-matter of the proceeding. Articles 7 to 9, which give effect to a State's express or implied consent to the exercise of jurisdiction over it, pertain to the State's conduct in respect of that proceeding or such proceedings.[1]

Like Articles 7 to 9, nonetheless, the eight articles detailed in Part III of the Convention concern only a State's immunity from jurisdiction, *viz* from proceedings. They do not implicate the immunity of a State's property from measures of constraint, which forms the subject of Part IV of the Convention. In other words, the fact that, in an application of one of the exceptions provided for in Part III, a State cannot invoke immunity from a foreign court's jurisdiction in a given proceeding does not mean that the foreign court may order pre- or post-judgment measures of constraint against the State's property in connection with that proceeding.

The circumstances specified in Parts II and III of the Convention in which a State cannot invoke immunity from foreign jurisdiction are, for the purposes of the Convention, the only circumstances in which a State cannot invoke such immunity. What this means specifically for Part III is that, for the purposes of the Convention, the 'proceedings in which State immunity cannot be invoked' laid down in that part are the only proceedings in which, by virtue solely of the subject-matter of the proceeding, a State is not entitled to invoke immunity from foreign jurisdiction. This, perhaps needless to say, is formally without prejudice to the availability to a claimant in proceedings not governed by the Convention of such further subject-matter-based exceptions to State immunity from foreign jurisdiction as may hypothetically exist as a matter of customary international law. At the same time, it remains to be seen whether Part III of the Convention exerts, through the imitative practice of States not parties to the Convention, an influence on the content of the relevant customary rules.

Part III represents the heart of the restrictive doctrine of State immunity whose embodiment in multilateral treaty form is the gist of the Convention.

[1] More fundamentally, it has been suggested that Arts 7 to 9 of the Convention, unlike the provisions of Part III, are not exceptions to a State's immunity from foreign jurisdiction, but, rather, that the absence of the State's consent to the exercise of foreign jurisdiction over it is a precondition to the availability of immunity. See ILC commentary, draft art. 7, para. 3. The distinction, which is far from universally accepted, has no practical significance for the purposes of the Convention.

2. Key Points

2.1 The title of Part III

Part III of the Convention is entitled 'Proceedings in which State immunity cannot be invoked'. The title reflects an attempt to bridge the doctrinal differences that characterized the drafting of Part II and especially of Part III of the ILC's draft articles. When all is said and done, however, what Part III embodies within the structural logic of the Convention is effectively a set of exceptions to the immunity of a State from foreign jurisdiction recognized in Article 5.[2] The same structural logic is adopted in the ECSI[3] and in all national State immunity legislation.

The ILC commentary acknowledges that, even among proponents of the restrictive doctrine of State immunity, there was no consensus, at least during the preparation of the draft articles, on the theoretical underpinnings of such immunity. Some considered a State's immunity from the jurisdiction of the courts of another State to be 'an exception to the principle of territorial sovereignty of the State of the forum and as such [to] be substantiated in each case'.[4] Others saw it as 'as a general rule or principle of international law' subject to exceptions.[5] Others still considered such immunity to be 'a unitary rule' that was 'inherently subject to existing limitations'.[6]

In his Preliminary Report, Special Rapporteur Sucharitkul outlined the choice facing the Commission, and expressed a preference for the statement of a general rule of immunity from jurisdiction subject to specific exceptions:

> Two approaches are open for the determination of the precise limits of the application of the doctrine of State immunity. One possible solution is to state the circumstances in which a State is entitled to sovereign immunity by listing the types of activities covered by the doctrine, thereby leaving out the uncovered areas of activities as lying outside the province of its application. Another would be to specify the types of activities, or the private or commercial nature of the transactions, or the non-governmental functions or capacities assumed by the State which will be subject to the territorial jurisdiction of another State. Both approaches could be pursued simultaneously. However, the Special Rapporteur is more inclined towards a more convenient approach: stating the general rule of State immunity, followed by the suggestion and discussion of possible exceptions.[7]

Others, however, favoured the so-called 'dual approach' to the formulation of the rule, as supported by at least one representative in the Sixth Committee:

> Without having to predetermine the existence of a general rule of State immunities, it would not be impossible to proceed to examine State practice which could provide definite evidence of the two types of circumstances: cases where State immunity operates and cases of non-immunity. In other

[2] See also, among many others, G. Hafner and U. Köhler, 'The United Nations Convention on Jurisdictional Immunities of States and their Property' (2004) 35 *NYIL* 3, 10; D.P. Stewart, 'The UN Convention on Jurisdictional Immunities of States and Their Property' (2005) 99 *AJIL* 194, 195 and 197; H. Fox, 'In Defence of State Immunity: Why the UN Convention on State Immunity is Important' (2006) 55 *ICLQ* 399, 400.

[3] The difference between the UNCSI and the ECSI in this regard is merely that the ECSI posits the exceptions first, before providing in Art. 15 that '[a] Contracting State shall be entitled to immunity from the jurisdiction of the courts of another Contracting State if the proceedings do not fall within Articles 1 to 14'.

[4] ILC commentary, draft art. 5, para. 2.

[5] ILC commentary, draft art. 5, para. 2.

[6] ILC commentary, draft art. 5, para. 2.

[7] Preliminary report Sucharitkul, 241, para. 69.

words, a search could be made at the same time to identify activities which are *acta jure imperii*, where State immunity applies, and activities which are *acta jure gestionis*, where State immunity is not applicable.[8]

This second approach paralleled that adopted around the same time by Ian Brownlie in his capacity as rapporteur for the Institut de Droit international on Contemporary Problems concerning the Jurisdictional Immunity of States. Brownlie would later state:

There is a complete absence of reference [in the literature] to the indicia which favour 'immunity *ratione materiae*' . . . Indeed, one may suspect that some lawyers have the curious assumption that it is heretical to study the legal geography on *both* sides of the line between immunity and no immunity.[9]

But the Special Rapporteur was not convinced. He considered the dual approach inconsistent with State practice, and he feared that the two sets of criteria would overlap or that there would be a gap between them, giving rise to a 'twilight zone or borderland where existing uncertainties would not only linger but would continue to be preserved and even to grow'.[10] Instead, he proposed to include an introductory provision in Part III of the draft articles that would clarify the link between Parts II and III.[11] The Commission, however, considered the proposed provision unnecessary.[12]

The controversy over the theoretical underpinnings of a State's immunity from the jurisdiction of the courts of another State crystallized in the debate over the title to be given to Part III of the ILC's draft articles. Special Rapporteur Sucharitkul proposed 'Exceptions to State Immunity'.[13] Several ILC members argued instead for a title that would cast the 'exceptions' as inherent limitations on a State's immunity from foreign jurisdiction.[14] Against this backdrop, the title to Part III adopted on first reading was '[Limitations on][Exceptions to] State Immunity', the Commission having decided 'to consider the matter further on second reading in the light of the comments and observations of Governments'.[15] While the Commission stressed that 'the title of part III [was] not intended to express any preference between the divergent doctrinal interpretations of the immunities of States',[16] States nonetheless divided along doctrinal

[8] Fourth report Sucharitkul, 206, para. 24.

[9] I. Brownlie, 'Contemporary Problems Concerning the Jurisdictional Immunity of States, Definitive Report', in 62 *Annuaire de l'Institut de Droit international* (1987), vol. I, 45, 49, original emphasis. Art. 2 of the Institut's eventual resolution on the topic lays down criteria indicative of both the incompetence and competence of the relevant organs of the forum State to determine the substance of a claim against a foreign State. See 'Contemporary Problems Concerning the Immunity of States in Relation to Questions of Jurisdiction and Enforcement' (Basel session, 2 September 1991), in 64 *Annuaire de l'Institut de Droit international* (1992), vol. II, 388.

[10] Fourth report Sucharitkul, 206, paras 25–26.

[11] See Fourth report Sucharitkul, 207, para. 29. The proposed draft article, entitled 'Scope of the present part', read: 'Except as provided in the following articles of the present part, effect shall be given to the general principles of State immunity as contained in part II of the present articles.'

[12] Summary record 1711th ILC meeting, *YILC 1982*, vol. I, 73, 77, para. 27 (José Manuel Lacleta Muñoz); summary record 1712th ILC meeting, *YILC 1982*, vol. I, 80, 85, para. 35 (Mikuin Balanda); summary record 1728th ILC meeting, *YILC 1982*, vol. I, 181, 183, para. 8 (Chafic Malek); Report ILC, thirty-fourth session, 98, para. 193.

[13] Fourth report Sucharitkul, 202.

[14] See summary record 1971st ILC meeting, *YILC 1986*, vol. I, 188, 192–3, para. 57 (Sir Ian Sinclair), recounting the discussion within the Drafting Committee.

[15] Report ILC, thirty-eighth session, 16.

[16] Report ILC, thirty-eighth session, 17.

lines.[17] In an attempt 'to reconcile these two positions',[18] the Commission opted in the event for a third, avowedly neutral title, namely 'Proceedings in which State immunity cannot be invoked'.

But however they are labelled, the rules specified in what became Part III of the Convention are clearly framed within the overarching structure of Parts II and III as exceptions to the general availability to a State of immunity from the jurisdiction of the courts of another State recognized in Article 5. Whether this is merely 'a matter of legislative convenience'[19] or says something about the conceptual foundations on which State immunity rests is ultimately of no significance to the application of the operative provisions of Part III.

2.2 The rationale for the exceptions

Throughout the drafting process, Special Rapporteurs Sucharitkul and Ogiso emphasized that 'the method and techniques employed in the preparation of reports and draft articles [were] inductive in the sense that conclusions and propositions of law [were] drawn from the practice of States'.[20] In other words, the ILC's draft articles and the eventual Convention did not proceed from an agreed theory of restrictive State immunity but sought instead simply 'to remain faithful . . . to the existing realities of emerging State practice'.[21] In particular, so as 'to avoid unnecessary theoretical controversies',[22] Part III of the Convention eschews explicit reference to the 'distinction between acts performed *jure imperii* and acts performed *jure gestionis*'.[23] This is not, however, to deny that the distinction could be taken to inform all bar one of the exceptions to immunity from jurisdiction specified in Part III,[24] even if, in relation to over half of these exceptions, it is not alone in grounding the court's exercise of jurisdiction, which rests additionally on some link, usually but not always territorial, between the conduct

[17] See Preliminary report Ogiso, 108, para. 109.

[18] ILC commentary, draft Part III, para. 1.

[19] C.H. Schreuer, *State Immunity: Some Recent Developments* (Cambridge: Grotius, 1988), 7.

[20] Fourth report Sucharitkul, 203, para. 10.

[21] Summary record 1762nd ILC meeting, *YILC 1983*, vol. I, 43, 44, para. 6 (Sompong Sucharitkul).

[22] Summary record 1762nd ILC meeting (n. 21), 44, para. 6 (Sompong Sucharitkul).

[23] Summary record 1762nd ILC meeting (n. 21), 44, para. 6 (Sompong Sucharitkul).

[24] See, in this regard, *Jurisdictional Immunities of the State (Germany v Italy: Greece intervening), Judgment*, 3 February 2012, International Court of Justice, para. 59: '[T]he Court notes that many States . . . now distinguish between *acta jure gestionis*, in respect of which they have limited the immunity which they claim for themselves and which they accord to others, and *acta jure imperii*. That approach has also been followed in the United Nations Convention . . .' The odd exception out is Art. 12, dealing with proceedings relating to 'pecuniary compensation for death or injury to the person, or damage to or loss of tangible property, caused by an act or omission which is alleged to be attributable to the State, if the act or omission occurred in whole or in part in the territory of that other State and if the author of the act or omission was present in that territory at the time of the act or omission'. Art. 12 is not restricted to acts or omissions *jure gestionis*. See, in this regard, ILC commentary, draft art. 12, para. 8; *Jurisdictional Immunities of the State*, para. 64. See also, less directly, *Letelier v Republic of Chile*, 63 ILR 378, 386–7 (US (DDC) 1980); *Schreiber v Canada (Attorney General)*, 2002 SCC 62, paras 32 and 35–36 (Can (SC) 2002); *Prefecture of Voiotia v Federal Republic of Germany (Distomo Massacre Case)*, 129 ILR 513, 517–19 (Gre (CoC) 2002). Whether, however, Art. 12 and the rest of the Convention apply specifically in respect of military activities remains an open question. See Hafner, 'Historical Background to the Convention' and the commentary to the 'general understandings' in this volume.

impugned and the forum State[25] or, in one case, on the implied consent of the impleaded State to the exercise of jurisdiction over it.[26]

2.3 The exhaustiveness of the exceptions

The subject-matter-based exceptions to immunity from jurisdiction specified in Part III are the only subject-matter-based exceptions[27] available under the Convention to a State's immunity from proceedings in a foreign court. Putting it another way, Part III is exhaustive as to the range of proceedings in which, by virtue solely of the subject-matter to which the proceeding relates, a State party to the Convention cannot invoke immunity from the jurisdiction of a court of another State party. This does not mean, obviously, that other such exceptions may not in principle exist as a matter of customary international law and be relied on in proceedings to which the Convention does not apply[28]—that is, in proceedings in the courts of or against a State not party to the Convention. But in proceedings under the Convention, Articles 10 to 17, along with the consent-based Articles 7 to 9, comprise a *numerus clausus.* In the words of Article 5, a State party enjoys immunity from the jurisdiction of the courts of another State party 'subject to the provisions of the . . . Convention'.

It was not always so during the ILC's work on the draft articles. As adopted on first reading, what was then draft article 6 provided that a State enjoyed immunity from the jurisdiction of the courts of another State 'subject to the provisions of the present articles [and the relevant rules of general international law]'.[29] The bracketed text was included on the insistence of some ILC members, who, seemingly conflating two distinct issues, thought it 'essential that the future development of State practice be left unfrozen and undeterred'.[30] A few other members thought the bracketed text 'unnecessary but tolerable'.[31] Others, however, were adamant that it 'would only serve to encourage unilateral restrictions of the immunity of a State and leave room for different interpretations',[32] thereby 'render[ing] the entire draft articles useless'.[33] In the latter light, Special Rapporteur Ogiso proposed in his Preliminary Report to delete the bracketed phrase,[34] drawing attention to the possibility of stating instead in the preamble to any future convention that 'the rules of general international law continue[d] to govern questions not expressly regulated' by the convention.[35]

25 See Arts 11(1), 13(*a*), 14, and 15(1) UNSCI. In the case of the exception laid down in Art. 12, the territorial link between the impugned conduct and the forum State is the sole justification for the forum State's exercise of jurisdiction, as made clear in ILC commentary, draft art. 12, para. 8.

26 See Art. 17 UNCSI.

27 As to the solely consent-based exceptions, or 'exceptions', to a State's immunity from foreign jurisdiction, see Arts 7 to 9 UNCSI.

28 Recall, reiterating this axiom of the relationship between treaty and custom, Preamble (fifth recital) UNCSI, which affirms 'that the rules of customary international law continue to govern matters not regulated by the provisions of the present Convention'. See section 2.7(B) for more.

29 Report ILC, thirty-eighth session, 16.

30 ILC commentary, draft art. 6, para. 3.

31 Report ILC, thirty-eighth session, 16.

32 Preliminary report Ogiso, 104, para. 63.

33 Report ILC, thirty-eighth session, 16.

34 Preliminary report Ogiso, 104, para. 67.

35 Preliminary report Ogiso, 104, paras 65 and 67. See also Preliminary report Ogiso, 121–2, paras 267 and 273.

In his Second Report, however, Special Rapporteur Ogiso conceded that the deletion of the bracketed phrase 'might restrict the jurisdiction of some States whose courts [were] already applying the rule of restrict[ive] immunity', and suggested that, '[i]n view of the recent developments supporting the doctrine of restrictive immunity, the retention of the phrase would not be illogical, as it would allow for the future development of the law on th[e] subject'.[36] But rather than retaining the phrase as was, the Special Rapporteur proposed a new draft article 6 *bis*, according to which a State party to any future convention modelled on the draft articles could, when signing or expressing its consent to be bound, 'make a declaration of any exception to State immunity, in addition to the cases falling under articles 11 to 19, according to which the court of that State [would] be able to entertain proceedings against another State Party, unless the latter State raise[d] objection within thirty days after the declaration was made'.[37]

But the Special Rapporteur's proposed draft article 6 *bis* was poorly received[38] and promptly abandoned, the bracketed clause in what was to become Article 5 of the Convention was deleted,[39] and Part III, along with Articles 7 to 9 in Part II, finally emerged as an enumeration of—not a mere starting point in relation to—the circumstances in which a State party is not entitled to invoke immunity from the jurisdiction of the courts of another State party.

2.4 The elements common to the exceptions

A. Rules on the exercise, not existence, of jurisdiction

Part III of the Convention, like the Convention as a whole, relates to the exercise of jurisdiction by a court. The existence of such jurisdiction in the first place is, in contrast, a matter for the law of the forum State. Putting it another way, Articles 10 to 17, in conjunction with Article 5, regulate whether a court may exert over a foreign State any jurisdiction it may enjoy with regard to the proceeding. Whether it in fact enjoys jurisdiction with regard to the proceeding is a question of domestic law into which the Convention does not enter.

All of this is evident in the respective texts of the provisions, which are premised on the underlying competence under the law of the forum State of the court before which the proceeding is brought. Articles 11 to 17 speak of 'a court of another State which is otherwise competent'. To identical effect, Article 10 refers to where, 'by virtue of the applicable rules of private international law, differences relating to the commercial transaction fall within the jurisdiction of a court of another State'.

It is important to emphasize in this regard that, insofar as the exceptions to State immunity specified in Articles 11(1), 12, 13(*a*), 14, and 15(1) respectively of the

[36] Second report Ogiso, 64, para. 16.

[37] Second report Ogiso, 64, para. 17. See, similarly, albeit subject to a crucial limitation, Art. 24(1) ECSI, an optional clause: 'Notwithstanding the provisions of Article 15, any State may, when signing this Convention or depositing its instrument of ratification, acceptance or accession, or at any later date, by notification addressed to the Secretary General of the Council of Europe, declare that, in cases not falling within Articles 1 to 13, its courts shall be entitled to entertain proceedings against another Contracting State to the extent that its courts are entitled to entertain proceedings against States not party to the present Convention. Such a declaration shall be without prejudice to the immunity from jurisdiction which foreign States enjoy in respect of acts performed in the exercise of sovereign authority *(acta jure imperii).*'

[38] See Report ILC, forty-first session, 104, para. 461.

[39] Third report Ogiso, commentary to art. 6, para 3.

Convention each require a nexus between the conduct the subject of the proceeding and the forum State, this requirement does not concern the jurisdictional basis on which the court seised of the proceeding depends for its underlying competence to entertain the claim. It is simply a precondition to the availability in that proceeding of the relevant exception to the immunity from jurisdiction of the State against which the proceeding is brought. The nexus on which the court seised of the proceeding relies for any jurisdiction it may wield to begin with is, to reiterate, a matter for the law of the forum State.

B. *Provision for derogation by mutual consent of States*

Articles 11, 12, 13, 14, and 16(1) and (3) all begin with the words 'Unless otherwise agreed between the States concerned', the 'States concerned' being the State against which the proceeding is brought and the forum State. Equally, the first limb of Article 15(2) permits a State to invoke immunity in the sorts of proceedings dealt with in Article 15(1) 'if the States concerned have so agreed'. In this way, the relevant provisions permit derogation from the rules specified therein by mutual consent of the impleaded and forum States. This facility for agreed derogation is formally distinct from Article 26's savings clause concerning 'the rights and obligations'—'as between the parties to those agreements'—'of States Parties under existing international agreements which relate to matters dealt with in the . . . Convention'. In practice, however, there is a large measure of overlap between the two. But the proviso in the various articles of Part III relating to agreement otherwise between the impleaded and forum States goes further than Article 26 by taking into account agreements not capable of characterization as 'existing' within the meaning of the latter, including any ad hoc agreement in relation to a specific case, perhaps reached after proceedings have been initiated.

While there is no question but that any such agreement between the impleaded and forum States will be effective for the purposes of the Convention to displace the exception to State immunity otherwise provided for in the relevant provision of Part III, it is worth speculating where such a derogation would leave a forum State that was a contracting party to the European Convention on Human Rights. It might well be argued that a contracting party to the ECHR whose court holds a claim falling within a pertinent provision of Part III UNCSI barred by State immunity on the basis of an agreement between the forum State and the impleaded State to opt out of the relevant exception to immunity from jurisdiction violates the claimant's right of access to a court guaranteed by Article 6(1) ECHR.[40] The European Court of Human Rights, emphasizing that the exercise of the right of access to a court may be subject to such limitations as are proportionate to a legitimate aim, has reiterated in a string of cases not only that 'the grant of sovereign immunity to a State in civil proceedings pursues the legitimate aim of complying with international law'[41] but also that, crucially, 'measures taken by a High Contracting Party which reflect generally recognized rules of public international law on

[40] For the enunciation of the right of access to a court as a function of the right to fair trial guaranteed by Art. 6(1) ECHR, see *Golder v United Kingdom*, 57 ILR 200, 218, para. 36 (ECtHR 1975).

[41] *Al-Adsani v United Kingdom*, 123 ILR 24, 40, para. 54 (ECtHR (GC) 2001); *Fogarty v United Kingdom*, 123 ILR 53, 65, para. 34 (ECtHR (GC) 2001); *McElhinney v Ireland*, 123 ILR 73, 85, para. 35 (ECtHR (GC) 2001); *Kalogeropoulou v Greece and Germany*, 129 ILR 537, 546 (ECtHR 2002); *Cudak v Lithuania*, application no. 15869/02, Judgment (Merits and Just Satisfaction), ECtHR (GC), 23 March 2010, para. 60; *Sabeh El Leil v France*, application no. 34869/05, Judgment (Merits and Just Satisfaction), ECtHR (GC), 29 June 2011, para. 49.

State immunity cannot in principle be regarded as imposing a disproportionate restriction on the right of access to [a] court embodied in Article 6(1)'.[42] In short, it comes down to whether 'generally recognized rules of public international law on State immunity' require the forum State to accord State immunity in any given case. And it is certainly arguable that the grant of State immunity not by virtue of a generally recognized rule of international law embodied in a codificatory provision of a multilateral convention open to all States but courtesy of a bilateral agreement providing for the impleaded State's immunity from suit above and beyond what would otherwise be necessitated by international law is not required by international law. While the bilateral agreement binds the forum State to ensure that its courts accord the greater immunity, no rule of international law compels the forum State to conclude such an agreement. Much, however, may depend in this regard on whether the bilateral agreement providing for immunity despite the existence of a relevant exception in Part III of the Convention is part and parcel of the establishment by the States concerned of some sort of alternative forum for the adjudication or other processing of the claims in question[43] or perhaps even of some sort of settlement entered into by the forum State on behalf of, *inter alia*, the claimant.[44]

2.5 The burden of proof

The fact that the provisions of Part III, however they be labelled, are framed as exceptions to the general rule of a State's immunity from foreign jurisdiction posited in Article 5 has at least one practical consequence. It means that it falls to the claimant in proceedings against a State under the Convention to establish to the satisfaction of the court the applicability of the relevant provision of Part III, rather than to the respondent to prove the availability to it of a positively circumscribed immunity. All the respondent need do to establish its procedural defence to the claim is to satisfy the court that it[45] qualifies as a 'State' within the meaning of Article 2(1)(*b*) of the Convention. Should it succeed in this, it will, by mere virtue of its being a 'State' for the purposes of the Convention, enjoy *prima facie* immunity from the jurisdiction of the court—that is, immunity from jurisdiction 'subject to the provisions of the . . . Convention', in the words of Article 5. It is then up to the claimant to prove to the relevant standard (be it the balance of probabilities or some other test applicable under the law of the forum State) that some provision of the Convention operates to abrogate that immunity in the instant proceeding; and when the claimant's argument goes to the subject-matter to which the proceeding relates, it is up to that claimant to prove to the relevant standard that the apposite provision of Part III of the Convention applies.

[42] *Al-Adsani v United Kingdom* (n. 41), 40, para. 56; *Fogarty v United Kingdom*, (n. 41), 65, para. 36; *McElhinney v Ireland* (n. 41), 85, para. 37; *Kalogeropoulou v Greece and Germany* (n. 41), 546; *Cudak v Lithuania* (n. 41), para. 57; *Sabeh El Leil v France* (n. 41), para. 52.

[43] See, by analogy, *Waite and Kennedy v Germany*, 118 ILR 121, 135–7, paras 67–73 (ECtHR (GC) 1999); *Beer and Regan v Germany* (2001) 33 EHRR 3, paras 54–63 (ECtHR (GC) 1999).

[44] See *Natoniewski v Federal Republic of Germany* (2010) 30 *Polish YIL* 299 (Pol (SC) 2010).

[45] The 'it' may in fact be a 'she' or 'he', in accordance with Art. 2(1)(*b*)(iv) of the Convention.

2.6 Exceptions discussed but not included

A. Fiscal matters

As adopted by the ILC on first reading, Part III of the draft articles embodied an exception to a State's immunity from foreign jurisdiction in relation to what were referred to as 'fiscal matters'. What was then draft article 16 provided:

> Unless otherwise agreed between the States concerned, the immunity of a State cannot be invoked before a court of another State which is otherwise competent in a proceeding which relates to the fiscal obligations for which it may be liable under the law of the State of the forum, such as duties, taxes or other similar charges.[46]

But the provision was 'not considered to have its proper place in the draft articles',[47] dealing as it did with relations between the impleaded and forum States, rather than between the impleaded State and a private natural or juridical person. Some ILC members, on the other hand, opposed its deletion, pointing to national State immunity legislation in which a narrower version of the exception featured.[48] It was finally decided to delete the article 'on the understanding that the commentary to article 10 would clarify that its deletion [was] without prejudice to the law with respect to fiscal matters'.[49]

B. Violations of human rights and/or jus cogens

In an appendix to its 1999 report, the ILC Working Group tasked with considering outstanding issues in relation to the Commission's draft articles considered it 'necessary to draw to the attention of the Sixth Committee'[50] a matter 'not specifically dealt with in the draft articles on jurisdictional immunities of States and their property',[51] namely 'the argument increasingly put forward that immunity should be denied in the case of death or personal injury resulting from acts of a State in violation of human rights norms having the character of *jus cogens*, particularly the prohibition on torture'.[52] The Working Group suggested that this was 'a recent development relating to immunity which should not be ignored'.[53] Briefly surveying State practice in this regard, the Working Group observed that, while '[n]ational courts, in some cases, had shown some sympathy for th[e] argument',[54] 'in most cases, the plea of sovereign immunity ha[d] succeeded'.[55] The Working Group did, however, highlight two developments that lent 'further support to the argument that a State may not plead immunity in respect of gross human rights violations'.[56] The first was the exception to State immunity inserted into the FSIA (US) by the Antiterrorism and Effective Death Penalty Act of 1996.[57] The

46 Report ILC, thirty-eighth session, 11.

47 ILC commentary, draft art. 10, para. 12.

48 ILC commentary, draft art. 10, para. 12. See, in this regard, s. 11 SIA (UK); s. 12 SIO (Pak); s. 12 FStIA (SA); s. 13 SIA (Sing). See also, not wholly dissimilarly, s. 20 FStIA (Aus).

49 ILC commentary, draft art. 10, para. 12.

50 1999 report ILC Working Group, appendix, para. 3.

51 1999 report ILC Working Group, appendix, para. 13.

52 1999 report ILC Working Group, appendix, para. 3.

53 1999 report ILC Working Group, appendix, para. 13.

54 1999 report ILC Working Group, appendix, para. 6, citation omitted.

55 1999 report ILC Working Group, appendix, para. 7, citation omitted.

56 1999 report ILC Working Group, appendix, para. 8.

57 1999 report ILC Working Group, appendix, paras 9–10. Formerly under s. 1605(*a*)(7) FSIA (US), originally introduced by s. 221 Antiterrorism and Effective Death Penalty Act of 1996, and now under s. 1605A FSIA (US), inserted by way of s. 1083(*b*)(1) National Defense Authorization Act for Fiscal Year

second was the judgment in *R v Bow Street Metropolitan Stipendiary Magistrate, ex parte Pinochet Ugarte*,[58] which, although 'expressly stat[ing] that it [did] not affect the correctness of decisions upholding the plea of sovereign immunity in respect of civil claims, as it was concerned with a criminal prosecution', had 'generated support for the view that State officials should not be entitled to plead immunity for acts of torture committed in their own territories in both civil and criminal actions'.[59]

When the open-ended Working Group of the Sixth Committee convened later the same year, it considered whether the Sixth Committee, whose decision it would be, ought to take up 'the question of the existence or nonexistence of immunity in the case of violation by a State of *jus cogens* norms of international law'.[60] 'It was generally agreed', however, by the delegates to the Working Group 'that this issue, although of current interest, did not really fit into the . . . draft articles'.[61] In addition, and perhaps more to the point, the question 'did not seem to be ripe enough for the Working Group to engage in a codification exercise over it'.[62] The chairman of the Working Group concluded:

> In the light of the discussions held in the Working Group of the Sixth Committee, it does not seem advisable to include this matter among the issues to be covered by the forthcoming considerations on the topic.[63]

No objection to this manner of proceeding was subsequently raised in the Sixth Committee itself, and the Japanese delegate who introduced the draft of what became General Assembly resolution 54/101 of 9 December 1999 ('Convention on jurisdictional immunities of States and their property') explicitly supported the exclusion of future discussion of the matter in the drafting of the proposed Convention.[64]

In 2001, a Grand Chamber of the European Court of Human Rights—noting, *inter alia*, 'as the [ILC] Working Group itself acknowledged, [that] while national courts had in some cases shown some sympathy for the argument that States were not entitled to plead immunity where there had been a violation of human rights norms with the character of *jus cogens*, in most cases . . . the plea of sovereign immunity had succeeded'—concluded in *Al-Adsani v United Kingdom* that there was '[not] yet acceptance in international law of the proposition that States are not entitled to immunity in respect of civil claims for damages for alleged torture committed outside the forum State'.[65] The following year, in *Kalogeropoulou v Greece and Germany*, the Court's First Section came to the same conclusion in relation to civil claims for crimes against humanity.[66]

2008, the immunity from proceedings to which a foreign State designated as a State sponsor of terrorism would otherwise be entitled under the FSIA (US) is abrogated in respect of actions for damages for personal injury or death caused to a US national or, now under s. 1605A FSIA (US), to a member of the US armed forces or US government employee or contractor acting within the scope of their employment by that foreign State's act of torture, extrajudicial killing, aircraft sabotage, or hostage-taking or by its provision of material support or resources for any such act.

[58] 1999 report ILC Working Group, appendix, paras 11–12, referring to *R v Bow Street Metropolitan Stipendiary Magistrate, ex parte Pinochet Ugarte*, 119 ILR 135 (UK (HL) 1999).

[59] 1999 report ILC Working Group, appendix, para. 12.

[60] 1999 report Sixth Committee Working Group, para. 46.

[61] 1999 report Sixth Committee Working Group, para. 47.

[62] 1999 report Sixth Committee Working Group, para. 47.

[63] 1999 report Sixth Committee Working Group, para. 67.

[64] See UN doc. A/C.6/54/SR.36 (24 April 2000), para. 9.

[65] *Al-Adsani v Government of Kuwait* (n. 41), 43, para. 66.

[66] See *Kalogeropoulou v Greece and Germany* (n. 41), 147.

In December 2004, the General Assembly adopted the Convention without a 'human rights' or '*jus cogens*' exception to a State's immunity from the jurisdiction of the courts of another State.

Writing later in a personal capacity, the chairman of the Sixth Committee's Working Group and later of the Ad Hoc Committee on Jurisdictional Immunities of States and Their Property, Gerhard Hafner, recounts:

> [I]t became clear during the negotiations that the inclusion of such a restriction of immunity in the Convention would have precluded any possibility of achieving a broadly acceptable text. The negotiations were confronted with only two alternatives: either a text without such a restriction of immunity or no text at all. The states unanimously preferred the first alternative to the second. No other alternative existed.[67]

In this light, the decision not to include a human rights or *jus cogens* exception in the Convention was a 'wise' one.[68]

2.7 Part III and customary international law

A. Part III as evidence pro

There is no doubt that the broad contours of Part III of the Convention reflect customary international law. That is, it is almost certainly the case that each of the exceptions provided for in Articles 10 to 17 exists as a matter of custom in some form or other. Indeed, the indirect involvement of States, via their comments and observations, in the ILC's work on the draft articles on jurisdictional immunities of States and their property, along with their direct involvement via the Sixth Committee in the post-1991 drafting of the Convention, have in themselves made an influential contribution to State practice and *opinio juris* in this regard, as acknowledged by the ICJ in *Jurisdictional Immunities of the State*.[69]

The real question, however, is whether the precise formulation of each provision is also consonant with custom. To this the answer is at present very likely to be no, even if one or two of them may well be. But it remains to be seen, of course, whether Articles 10 to 17 eventually shape custom in their own image, being looked to in time sufficiently often by the courts of a sufficient number of sufficiently representative States not parties to the Convention as persuasive indices of the internationally preferred formulation of each exception as to inspire the crystallization of the customary wording.

B. Part III as evidence contra

It ought to go without saying, as acknowledged in the Preamble,[70] that the Convention, like any treaty, is formally without prejudice to customary international law. But there is nonetheless the possibility in practice that any evidence of custom drawn from the Convention may serve to cement the position that prevailed when the Convention was adopted. This has already happened in relation to one exception not included in Part III,

[67] G. Hafner, 'Accountability and Immunity: The United Nations Convention on Jurisdictional Immunities of States and Their Property and the Accountability of States' (2005) 99 *ASIL Procs* 237, 242.

[68] I. Pingel, 'Observations sur le convention du 17 janvier 2005 sur les immunités juridictionnelles des États et leurs biens' (2005) 132 *JDI* 1045, 1054.

[69] See *Jurisdictional Immunities of the State* (n. 24), para. 55.

[70] Recall Preamble (fifth recital) UNCSI, '[a]ffirming that the rules of customary international law continue to govern matters not regulated by the provisions of the ... Convention'.

namely the 'human rights' or '*jus cogens*' exception argued for on normative grounds by its proponents.

On ratification of the Convention in 2009, Sweden, in words which reproduce almost verbatim Norway's declaration of 2006,[71] declared its understanding that 'the Convention is without prejudice to any future international legal development concerning the protection of human rights'.[72] Similarly, on acceding to the Convention in 2010, Switzerland declared its understanding that the Convention 'is without prejudice to developments in international law' regarding 'pecuniary compensation for serious human rights violations which are alleged to be attributable to a State and are committed outside the State of the forum'.[73] But these declarations have proved to be wishful thinking. It is now apparent that the non-inclusion in Part III of the Convention of a 'human rights' or '*jus cogens*' exception to a State's immunity from foreign jurisdiction has been influential in ensuring that no such exception emerges for the foreseeable future.

In the landmark UK case of *Jones v Saudi Arabia*, the House of Lords drew support from the Convention for its conclusion that customary international law did not recognize an exception to State immunity along such lines. Lord Bingham, describing the Convention as 'the most authoritative statement available on the current international understanding of the limits of state immunity in civil cases', held that 'the absence of a torture or *jus cogens* exception [was] wholly inimical to the claimants' contention'.[74] Randerson J in the New Zealand High Court case of *Fang v Jiang*[75] and Latham J in the New South Wales Supreme Court case of *Zhang v Jiang*[76] subsequently quoted Lord Bingham's dictum with approval. The former, referring to the Convention as 'a very recent expression of the consensus of nations on this topic', expressly 'agree[d] with the House of Lords that the absence of a torture or *jus cogens* exception to state immunity in the UN Immunities Convention 2004 speaks powerfully against the plaintiffs' argument'.[77] It was similarly on the basis of, *inter alia*, the Convention that the Supreme Court of Poland later came to an analogous conclusion in relation to the more general purported exception to State immunity in respect of violations of human rights.[78]

Far more significantly, in its judgment of February 2012 in *Jurisdictional Immunities of the State*, the International Court of Justice drew heavily on the Convention for evidence of the non-existence under customary international law of an exception to a State's immunity from foreign jurisdiction in proceedings alleging particularly serious

[71] See UNCSI depositary notification C.N.280.2006.TREATIES–2 (Norway: Ratification), 6 April 2006.

[72] UNCSI depositary notification C.N.912.2009.TREATIES–1 (Sweden: Ratification), 24 December 2009.

[73] UNCSI depositary notification C.N.223.2010.TREATIES–2 (Switzerland: Accession), 20 April 2010.

[74] *Jones v Ministry of Interior of the Kingdom of Saudi Arabia*, 129 ILR 629, 727, para. 26 (UK (HL) 2006). See also at 733, para. 47 and 741, para. 71 (Lord Hoffmann).

[75] *Fang and others v Jiang Zemin and others*, 141 ILR 702, 713–14, para. 49, 716–17, paras 62–63, and 717, para. 65 (NZ (HC) 2006).

[76] *Zhang v Jiang Zemin and others*, 141 ILR 542, 551–2, paras 35–36 (Aus (NSWSC) 2008).

[77] *Fang v Jiang* (n. 75), 717, para. 65.

[78] See *Natoniewski v Federal Republic of Germany* (n. 44), 302–3, where '[t]he Supreme Court observes that, on the basis of the materials referred to above, there is no sufficient legal ground to declare that tort claims resulting from . . . a violation of human rights constitute an exception to State immunity'. The cross-reference is to *Natoniewski v Federal Republic of Germany* (n. 44), 300, where the court explains that '[t]he relevant legal materials . . . include the provisions of the European Convention on state immunity ("Basle Convention") and UN conventions [*sic*]'.

violations of international human rights law or international humanitarian law or, insofar as they may be factually distinguishable, violations of *jus cogens*. The Court stated:

> It is... noticeable that there is no limitation of State immunity by reference to the gravity of the violation or the peremptory character of the rule breached in the European Convention [on State Immunity], the United Nations Convention [on Jurisdictional Immunities of States and Their Property] or the draft Inter-American Convention [on Jurisdictional Immunities of States]. The absence of any such provision from the United Nations Convention is particularly significant, because the question whether such a provision was necessary was raised at the time that the text of what became the Convention was under consideration. In 1999 the International Law Commission established a Working Group which considered certain developments in practice regarding some issues of State immunity which had been identified by the Sixth Committee of the General Assembly. In an appendix to its report, the Working Group referred, as an additional matter, to developments regarding claims 'in the case of death or personal injury resulting from acts of a State in violation of human rights norms having the character of *jus cogens*' and stated that this issue was one which should not be ignored, although it did not recommend any amendment to the text of the International Law Commission's Articles. The matter was then considered by the Working Group established by the Sixth Committee of the General Assembly, which reported later in 1999 that it had decided not to take up the matter as 'it did not seem to be ripe enough for the Working Group to engage in a codification exercise over it' and commented that it was for the Sixth Committee to decide what course of action, if any, should be taken. During the subsequent debates in the Sixth Committee no State suggested that a *jus cogens* limitation to immunity should be included in the Convention. The Court considers that this history indicates that, at the time of the adoption of the United Nations Convention in 2004, States did not consider that customary international law limited immunity in the manner now suggested by Italy.[79]

Nor did the Convention condition a State's entitlement to immunity from foreign jurisdiction in cases involving grave violations of international law and/or violations of *jus cogens* on the availability to the claimant of effective alternative means of redress.[80]

In August 2012, the Court of Appeal of Quebec, holding unanimously in *Islamic Republic of Iran v Hashemi* that no exception to a foreign State's immunity from jurisdiction existed in respect of 'a *jus cogens* protection of human rights', characterized the ICJ's reference to the Convention as part of the Court's 'conclusive refutation' of arguments for such an exception.[81]

[79] *Jurisdictional Immunities of the State* (n. 24), para. 89.

[80] *Jurisdictional Immunities of the State* (n. 24), para. 101.

[81] *Islamic Republic of Iran v Hashemi*, 2012 QCCA 1449, paras 54–55, quote at para. 55 (Can (Quebec CA) 2012). It is perhaps worth further noting, however, the intervention of the Canadian legislature earlier the same year in the form of s. 5 Safe Streets and Communities Act 2012 (S.C. 2012, c.1) (SSCA). (Section 5 falls within Part I of the SSCA, an 'Act within an Act' entitled the Justice for Victims of Terrorism Act, which in turn is divided into a sub-part entitled 'Enactment of the Act', comprising s. 2 SSCA, and a sub-part entitled 'Amendments to the State Immunity Act', comprising ss. 3 to 9 SSCA.) S. 5 SSCA inserts into the SIA (Can) a new s. 6.1 SIA (Can), which provides in relevant part as follows: '6.1 (1) A foreign state that is set out on the list referred to in subsection (2) is not immune from the jurisdiction of a court in proceedings against it for its support of terrorism on or after 1 January 1985. (2) The Governor in Council may, by order, establish a list on which the Governor in Council may, at any time, set out the name of a foreign state if, on the recommendation of the Minister of Foreign Affairs made after consulting with the Minister of Public Safety and Emergency Preparedness, the Governor in Council is satisfied that there are reasonable grounds to believe that the foreign state supported or supports terrorism.... (11) Where a court of competent jurisdiction has determined that a foreign state, set out on the list in subsection (2), has supported terrorism, that foreign state is also not immune from the jurisdiction of a court in proceedings against it that relate to terrorist activity by the state.' S. 5 SSCA—the amendments to the SIA (Can) introduced by which are modelled on what was formerly s. 1605(*a*)(7) and is now s. 1605A FSIA (US)—and the rest of the SCCA received assent on 13 March 2012, just over a month after

3. Evaluation

Part III is the centrepiece of the Convention, embodying as it does the restrictive doctrine of State immunity from foreign proceedings. In many ways it represents a lowest common denominator, which in turn reflects a strategy on the part of its drafters of avoiding controversy wherever possible. In a world where it still cannot be taken as read that a State's immunity from foreign proceedings is not absolute,[82] this conservatism makes pragmatic sense, and may already have paid dividends,[83] although perhaps at the cost of the progressive development of international law.

the judgment of the ICJ in *Jurisdictional Immunities of the State*. But the Safe Streets and Communities Bill (Bill C-10), which on enactment became the SSCA, was tabled in the Parliament of Canada on 20 September 2011, before the ICJ's judgment.

[82] See eg *Democratic Republic of the Congo v FG Hemisphere Associates LLC*, FACV Nos 5, 6 & 7 of 2010, 8 June 2011, para. 226 (Chan and Ribeiro PJJ and Mason NPJ) (PRC (HKSAR CFA) 2011), ruling that it was not open to the Court as a matter of constitutional law to apply a doctrine of State immunity different from the policy practised by the Central People's Government of the People's Republic of China, held that '[t]he doctrine of state immunity which presently applies in the HKSAR is the doctrine of absolute immunity'. The technically provisional decision was declared final in *Democratic Republic of the Congo v FG Hemisphere Associates LLC*, FACV Nos 5, 6 & 7 of 2010, 8 September 2011 (PRC (CFA HKSAR) 2011).

[83] The PRC signed the Convention on 14 September 2005. It is yet to ratify it.

Article 10

Stephan Wittich

Article 10

Commercial transactions

1. If a State engages in a commercial transaction with a foreign natural or juridical person and, by virtue of the applicable rules of private international law, differences relating to the commercial transaction fall within the jurisdiction of a court of another State, the State cannot invoke immunity from that jurisdiction in a proceeding arising out of that commercial transaction.
2. Paragraph 1 does not apply:
   (*a*) in the case of a commercial transaction between States; or
   (*b*) if the parties to the commercial transaction have expressly agreed otherwise.
3. Where a State enterprise or other entity established by a State which has an independent legal personality and is capable of:
   (*a*) suing or being sued; and
   (*b*) acquiring, owning or possessing and disposing of property, including property which that State has authorized it to operate or manage,

is involved in a proceeding which relates to a commercial transaction in which that entity is engaged, the immunity from jurisdiction enjoyed by that State shall not be affected.

Understanding with respect to Article 10

The term 'immunity' in article 10 is to be understood in the context of the present Convention as a whole.

Article 10, paragraph 3, does not prejudge the question of 'piercing the corporate veil', questions relating to a situation where a State entity has deliberately misrepresented its financial position or subsequently reduced its assets to avoid satisfying a claim, or other related issues.

1. Introduction

Pursuant to Article 10 of the Convention, a State cannot invoke immunity from foreign proceedings 'arising out of [a] commercial transaction'. Article 10 must be read in conjunction with the definition of a 'commercial transaction' laid down in Article 2(1)(*c*), guidance on the application of which is in turn offered by Article 2(2). Together, Article 10 and Article 2(1)(*c*) and (2) provide for an exception to the immunity of a State from proceedings in a court of another State recognized in Article 5 of the Convention.

Paragraphs 1 and 2 of Article 10 are relatively straightforward. Stripped down to its essentials, Article 10(1) stipulates that a State 'cannot invoke immunity from [the] jurisdiction [of a court of another State] in a proceeding arising out of [a] commercial transaction'. Article 10(2), for its part, specifies two situations in which the commercial transaction exception to a State's immunity from foreign proceedings laid down in Article 2(1) does not apply, namely 'in the case of a commercial transaction between States', as per subparagraph (*a*), and 'if the parties to the commercial transaction have expressly agreed otherwise', as per subparagraph (*b*).

The gist of paragraph 3 of Article 10 is more difficult to grasp at first blush. The provision addresses the impact on a State's immunity from the jurisdiction of a court of another State of the involvement of a State enterprise or other State-created entity with legal personality separate from that of the State and capable of suing or being sued and of acquiring, owning or possessing, and disposing of property in a proceeding in that court arising out of a commercial transaction entered into by that enterprise or entity. Article 10(3) is intended to make it clear that the State's immunity from the jurisdiction of the court of the other State is unaffected by such proceedings.

Annexed to the Convention is an 'understanding' with respect to Article 10, with two separate limbs, one an elaboration on the term 'immunity' as used in the provision, the other a form of savings or 'without prejudice' clause pertaining to Article 10(3).

While the commercial transaction exception is only one among the various exceptions to a State party's immunity from the jurisdiction of the courts of other States parties enumerated in Parts II and III of the Convention, it is arguably[1] the most important in practice. It may also be the 'most complex of all problems in the field of State immunity'.[2] Within the scheme of the Convention, however, any such complexities as may exist in this regard are far more likely to pertain to the definition of a 'commercial transaction' laid down in Article 2(1)(*c*), guidance on the application of which is provided by Article 2(2), than to Article 10 as such.

2. Background

The rationale most commonly advanced for the commercial transaction exception to a State's immunity from foreign jurisdiction is the rationale most commonly advanced for the restrictive doctrine of State immunity more generally, a rationale neatly summarized by the Austrian Supreme Court in 1950 in the leading case of *Dralle v Republic of Czechoslovakia*:

> [The] subjection of... *acta gestionis* to the jurisdiction of States has its basis in the development of the commercial activity of States. The classic doctrine of [absolute] immunity arose at a time when all the commercial activities of States in foreign countries were connected with their political activities, either by the purchase of commodities for their diplomatic representatives abroad, or by the purchase of war material for war purposes, *etc.* Therefore there was no justification for any distinction between private transactions and acts of sovereignty. Today the position is entirely different; States engage in commercial activities and, as the present case shows, enter into competition with their own nationals and with foreigners. Accordingly, the classic doctrine of immunity has lost its meaning and, *ratione cessante*, can no longer be recognised as a rule of international law.[3]

[1] It may share this title with the exception in relation to contracts of employment recognized in Art. 11. See the commentary to Art. 11 UNCSI.

[2] C.H. Schreuer, *State Immunity: Some Recent Developments* (Cambridge: Grotius, 1988), 14.

[3] *Dralle v Republic of Czechoslovakia*, 17 ILR 155, 163 (Aut (SC) 1950). See also *Claim against the Empire of Iran*, 45 ILR 57, 61 (FRG (FCC) 1963); *Victory Transport Inc. v Comisaria General de Absteciementos y Transportes*, 35 ILR 110, 112 (US (2nd Cir.) 1964); *Société Européenne d'Etudes et d'Entreprises en liquidité volontaire (SEEE) v Socialist Federal Republic of Yugoslavia*, in G. Hafner, M.G. Kohen, and S. Breau (eds), *State Practice regarding State Immunities* (Leiden: Martinus Nijhoff/Council of Europe, 2006), 466, 469 (Nth (SC) 1973); *Carried Lumber Company v United States of America*, 64 ILR 661, 665 (US (7th Cir.) 1974).

In short, the commercial transaction exception, according to the received wisdom, is no more than a specific application of the general distinction drawn by the modern, restrictive doctrine of State immunity between *acta jure imperii*, or acts of an inherently sovereign character, and *acta jure gestionis*, or acts that, although performed by a State in the instant case, are the sort of thing a private party could do. Other explanations advanced over the years for the commercial transaction exception have proceeded from a different premise. On one outdated view, a State, by entering into a commercial contract governed by private law rules, implicitly waived its immunity and voluntarily consented to the jurisdiction of the forum State.[4] On another view, the commercial transaction exception is not an exception in the proper sense of the word; rather, State immunity is said never to have extended to commercial activities in the first place.[5]

The deep historical background to Article 10 of the Convention is in many ways a history of the rise of the restrictive doctrine of State immunity itself—a vast topic that it is unnecessary for present purposes to recall in detail.[6] What is of immediate relevance is no more than that, prior to and in the course of the ILC's work on jurisdictional immunities of States and their property, the commercial transaction exception to State immunity found its way into a number of important international and national instruments, to which the ILC looked when deciding whether to include and how to formulate an analogous exception in its draft articles. The ECSI, which predates the start of the ILC's work by six years, contains two separate provisions on what might be called—loosely, in this context, since no such term, let alone such an expansive exception, is to be found in the treaty—the 'commercial transaction' exception. Article 4(1) ECSI provides:

> [A] Contracting State cannot claim immunity from the jurisdiction of the courts of another Contracting State if the proceedings relate to an obligation of the State, which, by virtue of a contract, falls to be discharged in the territory of the State of the forum.

Article 7, which borrows from the 1932 Harvard Law School draft convention,[7] provides:

1. A Contracting State cannot claim immunity from the jurisdiction of a court of another Contracting State if it has on the territory of the State of the forum an office, agency or other establishment through which it engages, in the same manner as a private person, in an industrial, commercial or financial activity, and the proceedings relate to that activity of the office, agency or establishment.
2. Paragraph 1 shall not apply if all the parties to the dispute are States, or if the parties have otherwise agreed in writing.

[4] For a long time this approach enjoyed considerable support, since waiver of immunity could be reconciled with the doctrine of absolute State immunity. That is, the exercise of jurisdiction over a foreign State in proceedings arising out of commercial transaction engaged in by that State was not, on this view, an exception in the true sense to the State's immunity from the jurisdiction of the forum State but simply a recognition by the court of the respondent State's voluntary submission to jurisdiction.

[5] See eg summary record 1728th ILC meeting, *YILC 1982*, vol. I, 181, 186–7, para. 38 (Stephen McCaffrey).

[6] For a thumbnail sketch, see G. Hafner, 'Historical Background to the Convention' in this volume. For more in-depth accounts, see H.Fox, *The Law of State Immunity* (2nd edn) (Oxford: Oxford University Press, 2008), chaps 8 and 9; Y. Xiaodong, *State Immunity in International Law* (Cambridge: Cambridge University Press, 2012); Schreuer (n. 2); S. Wittich, 'The Definition of Commercial Acts', in Hafner et al. (n. 3), 21–7.

[7] (1932) 26 *AJIL Supp* 633.

Versions of more general exceptions to a State's immunity from foreign proceedings in respect of commercial transactions or activity can be found in the State immunity legislation[8] and case-law[9] of a wide variety of States, some of it predating and some of it contemporaneous with the ILC's work on jurisdictional immunities of States and their property.

3. Drafting History

As might have been expected, given the uneven and at times contested evolution of the commercial transaction exception in State practice, what became Article 10 of the Convention gave rise to considerable debate during the drafting process, even if it was clear from the start that some version of the exception to immunity from jurisdiction that it came to embody should feature in the ILC's draft articles.

Although Special Rapporteur Sucharitkul sketched in his Preliminary Report an outline of what would become the commercial transaction exception, he focused mainly on the delineation and definition of the conduct in respect of which the exception would arise,[10] rather than on the formulation of the exception as such. He turned to address the exception itself only in his Fourth Report, in which he offered a survey of State practice and suggested a draft article 12 on 'trading or commercial activity', as follows:

1. In the absence of agreement to the contrary, a State is not immune from the jurisdiction of another State in respect of proceedings relating to any trading or commercial activity conducted by it, partly or wholly in the territory of that other State, being an activity in which private persons or entities may there engage;
2. Paragraph 1 does not apply to transactions concluded between States, nor to contracts concluded on a government-to-government basis.[11]

The Commission referred the Special Rapporteur's proposed draft, together with those of the definitional and associated provisions, to the Drafting Committee,[12] which put forward a new and appreciably different text of what it renumbered draft article 11,[13] partly consequential on its changes to what became Article 2(1)(*c*) of the Convention, the

[8] As regards commercial 'transactions', see s. 3 SIA (UK) ('Commercial transactions and contracts to be performed in the United Kingdom'); s. 5 SIO (Pak) ('Commercial transactions and contracts to be performed in Pakistan'); s. 5 SIA (Sing) ('Commercial transactions and contracts to be performed in Singapore'); s. 11 FStIA (Aus) ('Commercial transactions'); s. 4 FStIA (SA) ('Commercial transactions'). See also now s. 3 FSIL (Isr) ('Commercial transactions'). As regards commercial 'activity', see s. 1605(*a*)(2) FSIA (US); s. 5 SIA (Can); art. 2(1)(*c*) IFSJAC (Arg) ('commercial or industrial activity').

[9] See eg *Société anonyme des chemins de fer liégeois-luxembourgeois v Etat néerlandais* (1904) RDI 417 (Fra (CoC) 1903); *Nederlands Rijnbank v Mühlig Union, Teplitz-Schönau*, 14 AD 77, 78 (Nth (CRLR–DJD) 1947); *Guggenheim v State of Viet Nam* (1962) 66 *RGDIP* 654 (Fra (CoC) 1961); *Yrityspankki Skop Oy v Republic of Estonia*, in Hafner et al. (n. 3), FIN/16, 335, 336 (Fin (Helsinki DC) 1998); *Den Franske Republik v Intra ApS*, in Hafner et al. (n. 3), DK/2, 309 (Den (SC) 1992); *A v USA*, in Hafner et al. (n. 3), N/4, 496 (Nor (Eidsivating CA) 1989); *Judgment 12845/1990*, in Hafner et al. (n. 3), GR/11, 391, 392 (Gre (Athens CA) 1990); *Kramer Italo Limited v Government of the Kingdom of Belgium*, 103 ILR 299, 309–10 (Nga (CA) 1988). See also the survey in Report ILC, forty-third session, 36–8 paras 14–18 (commentary to draft art. 10).

[10] Recall the commentary to Art. 2(1)(*c*), (2), and (3) UNCSI.

[11] Fourth report Sucharitkul, 211–29.

[12] Summary record 1730th ILC meeting, *YILC 1982*, vol. I, 195, 199, para. 29.

[13] Summary record 1805th ILC meeting, *YILC 1983*, vol. I, 285, 290, paras 63–65.

definitional provision. What was at that point referred to as the 'commercial contracts' exception read, as adopted on first reading:

1. If a State enters into a commercial contract with a foreign natural or juridical person and, by virtue of the applicable rules of private international law, differences relating to the commercial contract fall within the jurisdiction of a court of another State, the State is considered to have consented to the exercise of that jurisdiction in a proceeding arising out of that commercial contract, and accordingly cannot invoke immunity from jurisdiction in that proceeding.
2. Paragraph 1 does not apply:
   (*a*) in the case of a commercial contract concluded between States or on a Government-to-Government basis;
   (*b*) if the parties to the commercial contract have otherwise expressly agreed.[14]

In the course of the second reading of draft article 11, the Drafting Committee, on the suggestion of Special Rapporteur Ogiso and in the light of comments by governments, made several minor changes to the text. In consequence of the changes made to the definitional provision in draft article 2, the term 'contracts' was replaced by 'transactions', while the phrase 'enters into' was substituted with 'engages in'.[15] In addition, '[f]or reasons of consistency and clarity',[16] the reference in draft article 11(1) to the implied consent of the State to the exercise of jurisdiction was amended to provide simply that 'the State cannot invoke immunity'.[17]

A dispute was to arise, however, over so-called 'segregated' property, *viz* property—separate as a matter of domestic law from the property of the State—held by State enterprises with legal personality distinct from that of the State.[18] According to some States of what was still the communist bloc, such property was to be treated as distinct from the property of the State for the purposes of immunity from the jurisdiction of the courts of another State.[19] In response, Special Rapporteur Ogiso proposed a new draft article 11 *bis* according to which a State's immunity from foreign jurisdiction was to be unaffected by a commercial contract entered into by a State enterprise with separate legal personality 'unless the State enterprise, being a party to the contract on behalf of the State, with a right to possess and dispose of segregated property, [was] subject to the same rules of liability relating to a commercial contract as a natural or juridical person'.[20] But the proposed provision was criticized in principle for allowing States in effect to avoid liability by undercapitalizing State enterprises,[21] while the Special Rapporteur's text raised further problems.[22] In the event, Special Rapporteur Ogiso reformulated draft

[14] Report ILC, thirty-fifth session, 25, draft art. 12 and commentary. See also Report ILC, thirty-eighth session, 10 (renumbered draft art. 11) and 'Comments and observations received from Governments', UN doc. A/CN.4/410 and Add. 1–5, *YILC 1988*, vol. II(1), 45, 47–51.

[15] Summary record 2218th ILC meeting, *YILC 1991*, vol. I, 66, 72, para. 58.

[16] ILC commentary, draft art. 10, para. 2.

[17] Summary record 2218th ILC meeting (n. 15), 72, para. 58.

[18] See Preliminary report Ogiso, 100, para. 12.

[19] See 'Comments and observations' (n. 14), 60, para. 3 (BSSR), 83, para. 6 (USSR).

[20] Preliminary report Ogiso, 109, para. 122 (draft art. 11 *bis*).

[21] See eg summary record 2218th ILC meeting (n. 15), 73, para. 64 (Stephen McCaffrey); statement of the UK in the Sixth Committee (1991) 62 *BYIL* 607, 609–10 (Derek Bowett).

[22] For a start, it referred to 'liability', a question for the applicable law of the forum, not for the draft articles on jurisdictional immunities. To make matters worse, the relationship between the treatment of State enterprises in the proposed draft art. 11 *bis* and the definition of a 'State' in draft art. 2 was far from clear. See Fox (n. 6), 448–9.

article 11 *bis*, deleting all reference to segregated property.[23] For its part, the Drafting Committee agreed that enterprises created by a State to perform commercial transactions and enjoying a separate legal personality should be addressed in the context of the commercial transaction exception;[24] but it favoured doing so in a new paragraph 3 of what was by then renumbered draft article 10.[25]

After minor drafting changes, draft article 10 ('Commercial transactions') was finally adopted by the ILC on second reading as follows:

1. If a State engages in a commercial transaction with a foreign natural or juridical person and, by virtue of the applicable rules of private international law, differences relating to the commercial transaction fall within the jurisdiction of a court of another State, the State cannot invoke immunity from that jurisdiction in a proceeding arising out of that commercial transaction.
2. Paragraph 1 does not apply:
   (*a*) in the case of a commercial transaction between States; or
   (*b*) if the parties to the commercial transaction have expressly agreed otherwise.
3. The immunity from jurisdiction enjoyed by a State shall not be affected with regard to a proceeding which relates to a commercial transaction engaged in by a State enterprise or other entity established by the State which has an independent legal personality and is capable of:
   (*a*) suing or being sued; and
   (*b*) acquiring, owning or possessing and disposing of property, including property which the State has authorized it to operate or manage.

But the question of State enterprises was subsequently placed among the outstanding issues calling for resolution after the Commission's final adoption of the draft articles.

When the Working Group of the Sixth Committee examined these outstanding issues in 1992 and 1993, it discussed a range of questions in relation to the application of the commercial transaction exception to State enterprises,[26] among them the problem of under-capitalization, especially in circumstances where the State deliberately misled the private party as to the financial position of the enterprise or stripped its assets in anticipation of a claim, and the effect of the distinction between the State and State enterprises on the immunity of State property from measures of constraint.[27] But little came of this.

Another problem was that, conceptually, the outstanding question of the entire draft article 10(3) was closely associated with the likewise unresolved problem of the definition of 'State' in draft article 2(1)(*b*). The main bone of contention concerned the debate over whether and to what extent agencies, instrumentalities, and other entities of a State were to be considered the 'State' for the purposes of immunity under the Convention.[28]

[23] Third report Ogiso, 13.

[24] Summary record 2218th ILC meeting (n. 15), 69, para. 25.

[25] Summary record 2218th ILC meeting (n. 15), 72, para. 58.

[26] The Chairman of the Working Group, Carlos Calero-Rodrigues, proposed in 1992 that draft art. 10(3) be deleted and that an equivalent provision, which consciously did not address the under-capitalization of State enterprises or the closely related issue of 'piercing the corporate veil', be inserted either in draft art. 5 or in a new draft article in Part V. See 1992 report Sixth Committee Working Group, 6–7, paras 31–34.

[27] See 1993 report Sixth Committee Working Group, 10–12, paras 49–61. The relationship between the State and State enterprises and the possibility of recourse to measures of constraint against segregated property arose as well in the context of what eventually became Art. 19(*c*) of the Convention. See the commentary to Art. 19 UNCSI.

[28] The relationship between Art. 10(3) and Art. 2(1)(*b*)(iii) remains problematic. See section 4.3.

When the matter was referred to it in 1999, the ILC's Working Group on jurisdictional immunities of State and their property suggested, as had been floated in informal consultations in the Sixth Committee in 1994,[29] that draft article 10(3) be clarified by indicating that immunity from jurisdiction could not be invoked by a State where a State enterprise 'engage[d] in a commercial transaction as an authorized agent of the State' or where the State 'act[ed] as a guarantor of liability of the State enterprise'.[30] It also considered a third possible ground for State liability, again suggested previously, namely where the State enterprise had deliberately misrepresented its financial position or subsequently reduced its assets to avoid satisfying a claim.[31] But the ILC Working Group concluded that this third suggestion went beyond the scope of draft article 10(3); that it conflated immunity from jurisdiction, immunity from execution, and the propriety of piercing the corporate veil of a State enterprise in special cases; and that it ignored whether the State entity, in acting as it did, had acted on instructions from the State or on its own.[32]

In the ensuing debates in the reconvened Working Group of the Sixth Committee, the chairman, Gerhard Hafner, suggested that agreement on the matter might be facilitated, first, by keeping the issue of the legal capacity of a State enterprise or other entity separate from questions arising in connection with, among other things, the enterprise or entity's under-capitalization or the misrepresentation of its financial position; and, secondly, by dealing separately with the various other issues raised by the relationship between the State and the State enterprise or other entity.[33] Over the following years, Chairman Hafner, who from 2002 was Chairman of the Ad Hoc Committee on Jurisdictional Immunities of States and Their Property, put forward a range of options, which in time were narrowed down to either deleting paragraph 3 of Article 10 altogether or maintaining it in revised form.[34]

In the event, the Ad Hoc Committee agreed in 2003 on a final, revised version of what would be adopted by the General Assembly in late 2004 as Article 10(3) of the Convention. This specified that the immunity from jurisdiction of a State as such was not to be affected by proceedings against a State enterprise or similar entity with independent legal personality and capable of suing or being sued and acquiring, owning or possessing, and disposing of property where such proceedings arose out of a commercial transaction engaged in by that enterprise or entity. In something of a breakthrough, the eventual Article 10(3) was to be elaborated on by one of the 'understandings' that the Ad Hoc Committee proposed for the first time in 2003 to annex to the draft articles and, as of the following year, to the draft convention.[35] The relevant statement, a savings clause of sorts eventually adopted in 2004 as the second limb of the understanding with respect to Article 10 annexed to the Convention, specifies that Article 10(3) 'does not

[29] See Report Sixth Committee informal consultations, 3–4.

[30] 1999 report ILC Working Group, 164, para. 80. The ILC Working Group noted at 165, para. 80, that the clarification could be achieved either through the textual characterization of the relevant acts as commercial or through an understanding to this effect at the time of the adoption of the article.

[31] 1999 report ILC Working Group, 164, para. 81.

[32] 1999 report ILC Working Group, 164, para. 82. The ILC Working Group also took the view, at para. 83, that the question of piercing the corporate veil, which implicated substantive issues as well as issues of immunity, went beyond its mandate.

[33] 1999 report Chairman Sixth Committee Working Group, 8–9, paras 59–61.

[34] 2000 report Chairman Sixth Committee Working Group, 9–11; 2002 report Ad Hoc Committee, 6–7.

[35] 2003 report Ad Hoc Committee, 7 and 14.

prejudge the question of "piercing the corporate veil", questions relating to a situation where a State entity has deliberately misrepresented its financial position or subsequently reduced its assets to avoid satisfying a claim, or other related issues'.

The first limb of the understanding with respect to Article 10, which provides that '[t]he term 'immunity' in article 10 is to be understood in the context of the present Convention as a whole', also refers to Article 10(3) and was inserted on the proposal of the UK delegation.

4. Key Points

4.1 Article 10(1)

A. General

Article 10(1) posits the essence of Article 10, namely that a State cannot invoke immunity from the jurisdiction of a court of another State in a proceeding arising out of a commercial transaction engaged in by that State with a foreign natural or juridical person. The rule embodied in Article 10(1) constitutes an exception to the immunity of a State from foreign jurisdiction recognized, 'subject to the provisions of the . . . Convention', in Article 5. Like all the other exceptions to immunity enumerated in Part III of the Convention, Article 10(1) relates to the immunity of a State from jurisdiction—synonymously, from proceedings or from suit—and not to the immunity of that State's property from measures of constraint, which is the subject of Part IV of the Convention.

B. 'commercial transaction'

The key term 'commercial transaction' in Article 10(1) is defined not in Article 10(1) itself but in Article 2(1)(*c*) of the Convention, guidance to the application of which is provided in Article 2(2).[36] Any difficulties as may exist under the Convention in the application of the commercial transaction exception are more likely to exist in connection with Article 2(1)(*c*) and (2) than with Article 10(1) as such. That is, it is more likely that what is contested in a proceeding pursuant to Article 10 is whether the conduct which is the subject of the claim is a 'commercial transaction' to begin with, rather than whether the State's immunity in respect of what is incontestably a 'commercial transaction' otherwise falls within Article 10.

C. 'immunity'

According to the first limb of the understanding with respect to Article 10 annexed to the Convention, the term 'immunity' in the provision 'is to be understood in the context of the . . . Convention as a whole'. The import of this odd statement is far from clear. What is apparent, however, is that it is not intended to qualify the meaning of the term 'immunity' in paragraph 1. Rather, the statement seems to have been included in order to clarify the relationship between the immunity of a State as such and that of the sort of State enterprise or entity mentioned in Article 10(3).[37] It is highly doubtful whether it achieves this aim.

[36] See the commentary to Art. 2(1)(*c*) and (2) UNCSI.

[37] Fox (n. 6), 547. See section 4.3.

D. *'and, by virtue of the applicable rules of private international law, differences relating to the commercial transaction fall within the jurisdiction of a court of another State'*

Like the other exceptions to a State's immunity from foreign jurisdiction enumerated in Part III of the Convention, Article 10(1) is premised on the underlying competence under the law of the forum State of the court before which the proceeding is brought.[38] That is, the provision does not purport to restrict or otherwise specify the jurisdictional basis on which the court may rely in proceedings under the Convention. It regulates not the existence but the exercise of that jurisdiction.

The relevant phrasing in Article 10(1), however, differs markedly from that in the other provisions of Part III of the Convention. Whereas the latter refer simply to 'a court of another State which is otherwise competent', the former speaks wordily of situations where, 'by virtue of the applicable rules of private international law, differences relating to the commercial transaction fall within the jurisdiction of a court of another State'. In 1992, the Chairman of the Sixth Committee Working Group proposed replacing the formula employed in Article 10(1) with that used in the other exceptions to immunity from jurisdiction laid down in Part III,[39] but—perhaps out of a reluctance to reopen to debate unimportant aspects of an article on which enough work remained to be done—the proposal failed to gain the necessary support. Whatever the explanation, however, for the defeat of the proposal, there is no appreciable substantive difference between the relevant wording of Article 10 and that of its fellow provisions in Part III.

E. *'arising out of'*

For a State's immunity from foreign jurisdiction to be precluded by Article 10(1), the proceeding brought against the State must be one 'arising out of' a commercial transaction. Again, this wording is a point of distinction between Article 10(1) and all the other exceptions to immunity from jurisdiction enumerated in Part III of the Convention, which refer instead to a proceeding 'which relates to' the subject-matter of the exception in question. But again it is a distinction without a difference.

Like the other exceptions specified in Part III, Article 10(1) does not elaborate further on the required link between the commercial transaction and the proceeding. The matter can be of some difficulty, especially in disputes involving 'mixed' transactions and transactions the nature of which might be viewed as having changed over time.[40]

F. *'foreign natural or juridical person'*

Article 10(1) applies only in respect of commercial transactions between a State and a 'foreign' natural or juridical person. As its position in the wording of the provision makes clear,[41] the word 'foreign' is opposable to the State that engages in the transaction, not the State of the forum. The requirement that the claimant not be a national of the

[38] ILC commentary, draft art. 10, paras 3–5.

[39] 1992 report Sixth Committee Working Group, 5–6, paras 27–28.

[40] See section 3.1(C) of the commentary to Art. 2(1)(*c*) UNCSI.

[41] The only State mentioned in Art. 10(1) before the appearance of the word 'foreign' is the State engaging in the transaction. Reference to the forum State via the phrase 'a court of another State' comes later.

respondent State was inserted by the ILC's Drafting Committee in 1983,[42] but the *travaux préparatoires* do not clarify why,[43] and the limitation has been criticized as 'arbitrary' and 'superfluous'.[44]

It is worth noting that draft article 11(2)(*d*) as adopted in 1991 had contained a similar requirement, but the provision was later amended and now, as Article 11(2)(*e*), allows proceedings to be brought if the employee 'has the permanent residence in the State of the forum'.[45] The change was seemingly intended to take account of the forum State's overriding public policy interest in affording protection to its local labour force.[46] This social welfare imperative was considered to justify a broader exception to State immunity in relation to contracts of employment to be performed in whole or in part in the forum State's territory. But such compelling considerations of domestic public policy are not necessarily present in the case of commercial transactions between individuals and foreign States.[47]

G. No requirement of performance in the forum State's territory

As well as containing a limitation that other versions of the commercial transaction exception lack, Article 10(1) lacks a limitation that a few other versions of the exception contain. In contrast to Articles 4(1) and 7(1) ECSI and some national case-law,[48] although in accordance with all national State immunity legislation,[49] Article 10(1) does not condition the availability of the commercial transaction exception on the

[42] Summary record 1805th ILC meeting (n. 13), 291, para. 65. The summary records reveal only that the newly proposed draft article 'specified that one of the parties to the contract had to be a foreign natural or juridical person'. The same limitation is found in Art. 17 ('Effect of an arbitration agreement') of the Convention. See the commentary to Art. 17 UNCSI.

[43] Presumably it was felt that a national of the respondent State should be required to bring any claim he or she may have against the latter in the latter's own courts. But the bringing of a claim this way may not always be possible. For comment, see C. Kessedjan and C. Schreuer, 'Le projet d'articles de la Commission du droit international des Nations Unies sur les immunités des Etats' (1992) 96 *RGDIP* 299, 319; Fox (n. 6), 543, who argues that this limitation 'may arise from treating State immunity as an aspect of protection of aliens and hence not applicable where the claimant is a national of the forum State'.

[44] See Kessedjan and Schreuer (n. 43), 319; H. Fox, 'The Merits and Defects of the 2004 UN Convention on State Immunity: Gerhard Hafner's Contribution to its Adoption by the United Nations', in I. Buffard et al. (eds), *International Law between Universality and Fragmentation:* Festschrift *in Honour of Gerhard Hafner* (Leiden: Martinus Nijhoff, 2008), 412, 417.

[45] See section 3.2(E) of the commentary to Art. 11.

[46] See Report Sixth Committee informal consultations. It was feared that the earlier version of subpara. (*c*) would have left nationals of third States without any legal protection. See 1993 report Chairman Sixth Committee Working Group, 13, para. 66.

[47] This is especially so as Art. 10(1)—as will be noted immediately below—does not require that the transaction be performed in whole or in part in the territory of the forum State.

[48] See eg *United Arab Republic v Mrs X*, 65 ILR 384, 389 (Swi (FT) 1960). But *cf* eg *Société Européenne d'Etudes et d'Entreprises en liquidité volontaire (SEEE) v Socialist Federal Republic of Yugoslavia* (n. 3), 469.

[49] The SIA (UK) and the legislation of other States that it has inspired do not follow the approach of the ECSI, providing instead for an exception to immunity from jurisdiction if the subject of the proceeding is either a commercial transaction entered into by a foreign State or an obligation of a foreign State which by virtue of a contract falls to be performed wholly or partly in the forum State. See s. 3(1) SIA (UK); s. 5(1) SIO (Pak); s. 5(1) SIA (Sing); s. 4(1) FStIA (SA). As for the US, s. 1605(*a*)(2) FSIA (US) speaks of 'a commercial activity carried on in the United States by the foreign State;... an act performed in the United States in connection with a commercial activity of the foreign State elsewhere; or... an act outside the territory of the United States in connection with a commercial activity of the foreign State elsewhere [if] that act causes a direct effect in the United States'. For their part, s. 5 SIA (Can), s. 11 FStIA (Aus), art. 2(1)(*c*) IFSJAC (Arg), and s. 3 FSIL (Isr) make no reference whatsoever to the territory of the forum State.

performance of, or the requirement to perform, the transaction, whether in whole or in part, in the territory of the forum State.[50]

H. No effect of agreement otherwise between the States concerned

Articles 11, 12, 13, 14, and 16(1) and (3) of the Convention all begin with the words 'Unless otherwise agreed between the States concerned', the 'States concerned' being the State against which the proceedings are brought and the forum State. Similarly, the first limb of Article 15(2) permits a State to invoke immunity in the sorts of proceedings dealt with in Article 15(1) 'if the States concerned have so agreed'. In contrast, neither paragraph 1 nor paragraph 2 of Article 10 makes provision for derogation by agreement between the impleaded and forum States—as distinct from as between the parties to the commercial transaction[51]—from the application of the provision. In this way, Article 10 is on a par with Article 17 of the Convention.

If the States concerned do make such an agreement, the legal situation is somewhat complicated, even if, in the final analysis, any such agreement must be considered ineffective as a waiver of the applicability of Article 10's commercial transaction exception. It is true that, as a matter of general international law, any specific agreement of this sort would exclude the application of any more general agreement to the contrary, in this case the agreement between all State parties to the Convention, manifest in Article 10, to recognize the commercial transaction exception. But since it is clear from the contrast with the other provisions of Part III of the Convention that the drafters of Article 10 made a deliberate choice to exclude for the purposes of this provision the effectiveness of such bilateral 'contracting-out' agreements between the impleaded State and the forum State, this agreement to exclude such special agreements constitutes *lex specialis* to the usual position under general international law, with the result that any such bilateral agreement must indeed be treated as ineffective for the purposes of Article 10.

4.2 Article 10(2)

A. Subparagraph (a)

In stipulating that Article 10(1) 'does not apply... in the case of a commercial transaction between States', Article 10(2)(*a*) sets out the first of two exceptions to the commercial transaction exception for the purposes of the Convention. Since the phrase 'foreign and juridical person' in Article 10(1) could be taken to include States, the ILC felt it necessary expressly to exclude the possibility that a court of one State might exercise jurisdiction in relation to a commercial transaction between two other States.[52] In preserving a State's immunity from foreign proceedings in relation to a commercial contract or other commercial transaction between it and another State or among it and other States, the Commission sought to protect in particular the interests of developing States, which tended at the time to conclude trading contracts with other States. By way

[50] Note that such a requirement is not one as to the jurisdictional basis on which the court relies for its underlying competence to entertain the claim. Rather, it is a precondition to the availability of the commercial transaction exception to what would otherwise be the bar to the exercise of the court's underlying competence over the respondent State.

[51] See Art. 10(2)(*b*), discussed in section 4.2(B).

[52] ILC commentary, draft art. 10, para. 6.

of example, the ILC commentary mentions tripartite transactions for the more efficient administration of food aid programmes, especially in areas suffering from famine.[53]

Some scholars have criticized this exception to the commercial transaction exception as unjustified and illogical, given that a commercial contract between States governed by municipal law is in principle no different from a commercial contract, governed by municipal law, between a State and a private party.[54]

While State practice does not disclose examples of the kind mentioned in the commentary, it is worth noting that Swiss, Swedish, and Austrian courts have on occasion upheld a State's immunity in proceedings arising from a commercial transaction between States.[55] Their reasoning, however, has tended to elide a respondent State's immunity *in personam* from proceedings arising out of a municipal law transaction between it and another State and the conceptually distinct question of what is usually the municipal non-justiciability of inter-State transactions governed by public international law.[56] More on a par with Article 10(2)(*a*) is Article 4(2)(*a*) ECSI, which excludes the application of the 'commercial contract' exception 'in the case of a contract concluded between States'. An analogous provision can be found in the State immunity legislation of a range of States.[57]

The text of Article 10(2)(*a*) limits the inapplicability of the exception set forth in Article 10(1) to transactions 'between States'. On the face of it, this suggests that commercial transactions between States and international organizations or, for that matter, between States and other legal persons under public international law fall within the scope of Article 10(1), and as such do not attract immunity. At the same time, the ILC commentary to draft article 10, referring to the administration of food aid programmes, explains that the acquisition of food supplies 'could be financed by another State or a group of States, either directly or through an international organization or a specialized agency of the United Nations, by way of purchase from a developing food-exporting country on a State-to-State basis as a consequence of tripartite or multilateral negotiations'.[58] In this light, it may at least be arguable that the omission of reference to international organizations is an unintended oversight, although even the situation mentioned in the commentary is ultimately that of a State-to-State contract.

A final question is whether Article 10(2)(*a*) applies only where both States engaged in the transaction are parties to the Convention or simply where the State impleaded by the proceeding is a State party. The answer is the latter. No limitation to the former effect is to be found in Article 2(2)(*a*). Nor is the *pacta tertiis* rule of the law of treaties in any way infringed by a treaty provision whose effect is to render procedurally unamenable to

[53] ILC commentary, draft art. 10, para. 7.

[54] See Kessedjan and Schreuer (n. 43), 312; P.-M. Dupuy and Y. Kerbrat, *Droit international public* (10th edn) (Paris: Dalloz, 2010), 145. For criticism within the ILC, see eg summary record 1728th ILC meeting (n. 5), 185, para. 27 (Mikuin Balanda).

[55] See *Italian Republic, Italian Ministry of Transport and Italian State Railways v Beta Holding SA and Another*, 65 ILR 394 (Swi (FT) 1966); *Municipality of Västerås v Iceland*, 128 ILR 705 (Swe (SC) 1999) and S. Mahmoudi, 'International Decisions' (2001) 95 *AJIL* 192; *Airport Linz v United States of America* (2003) 8 *ARIEL* 430 (Aut (SC) 2003) and S. Wittich, 'International Decisions' (2005) 99 *AJIL* 248.

[56] It might, however, be noted that the distinct concept of non-justiciability is unknown to many civil law jurisdictions.

[57] See s. 3(2) SIA (UK); s. 5(2) SIO (Pak); s. 5(2) SIA (Sing); s.4(2) FStISA (SA); s. 11(2)(*a*) FStISA (Aus).

[58] ILC commentary, draft art. 10, para. 7.

adjudication in the courts of a State party a transaction between another State party and a State not party.

B. *Subparagraph (b)*

The second exception specified in Article 10(2) to the commercial transaction exception laid down in Article 10(1) is where, in accordance with Article 10(2)(*b*), 'the parties to the commercial transaction have expressly agreed otherwise'. This situation is to be distinguished from any agreement between the impleaded and forum States to set aside Article 10(1), an agreement that would be ineffective for the purposes of the provision.[59] Article 10(2)(*b*), which is akin to Articles 11(2)(*f*) and 17,[60] pertains only to agreements between the parties to the relevant transaction.

Article 10(2)(*b*) flows from the principle of party autonomy, which the Convention, as a general rule, respects. There is in principle no reason to prohibit a State and a private party with which it engages in a commercial transaction from agreeing between themselves that the State should be entitled to avail itself of immunity from the jurisdiction either of national courts generally, of specific courts, or of a specific court. The most likely situations in which they might wish to do this are where they opt to resolve any dispute arising out of the transaction in a specific domestic forum or by non-judicial means such as arbitration.[61] Limitations on party autonomy in respect of Article 10 might be warranted in cases where there is an overwhelming disparity of bargaining power between the parties, but this is not addressed by the Convention.[62]

Article 10(2)(*b*), while demanding that the agreements to which it refers be express, does not, in contrast to Articles 11(2)(*f*) and 17, require that they be in writing, although the usual practice as far as contracts are concerned would be to specify any such agreement in the contract.[63] Nor, unlike Article 11(2)(*f*) but like Article 17, does Article 10(2)(*b*) subject such agreements to 'any considerations of public policy conferring on the courts of the State of the forum exclusive jurisdiction by reason of the subject-matter of the proceeding'. The distinction in this regard between Articles 10(2) and 11 (2)(*f*) would appear to stem again[64] from the special social welfare considerations attaching to employment in the territory of the forum State.

4.3 Article 10(3)

A. *General*

Article 10(3) addresses the effect on the immunity of a State from the jurisdiction of a court of another State of proceedings brought in that court by or against an enterprise or other entity established by that State. What it provides is that the State's immunity from the jurisdiction of a court of another State is unaffected by the involvement of a State

[59] Recall section 4.1(H).

[60] See the commentaries to Arts 11(2)(*f*) and 17 respectively. Note that the second limb of Art. 15(2) UNCSI permits derogation by way of agreement between the parties to the dispute, as distinct from to the contract, agreement, or other transaction. See the commentary to Art. 15(2) UNCSI.

[61] ILC commentary, draft art. 10, para. 8.

[62] This would be a case of mandatory public policy restrictions comparable to those generally prevailing in employment contracts. Recall section 4.1(F).

[63] ILC commentary, draft art. 10, para. 8, stating that '[a]ny such express agreement would normally be in writing'.

[64] Recall section 4.1(F).

enterprise or other State-created entity with legal personality separate from that of the State and capable of suing or being sued and of acquiring, owning or possessing, and disposing of property in a proceeding in that court arising out of a commercial transaction entered into by that enterprise or entity. Related to Article 10(3) is the savings clause, for want of a better term, which forms the second limb of the understanding with respect to Article 10 annexed to the Convention. This specifies that Article 10(3) 'does not prejudge the question of "piercing the corporate veil", questions relating to a situation where a State entity has deliberately misrepresented its financial position or subsequently reduced its assets to avoid satisfying a claim, or other related issues'. Seemingly also connected with Article 10(3) is the first limb of the understanding with respect to Article 10,[65] which says that the term 'immunity' in Article 10 'is to be understood in the context of the . . . Convention as a whole'.

B. Scope

The term 'State enterprise' is not defined in the Convention. It is usually used, however, to refer to a juridical person, generally a corporation or the like, created by a State, commonly for commercial purposes, and endowed by municipal law with legal personality separate from that of the State. That this meaning is the one ascribed to the term by Article 10(3) is implied by the chapeau's further, alternative reference to any 'other entity established by a State which has an independent legal personality' and by the fact that the provision relates to commercial transactions engaged in by such enterprises or other entities. That the enterprise or other entity be established by a State and enjoy legal personality independent of that of the State are, indeed, preconditions to the application of Article 10(3), as is the engagement of that enterprise or entity in a commercial transaction within the meaning of Article 2(1)(*c*) of the Convention.

The application of Article 10(3) is subject to the further, cumulative conditions stipulated in subparagraphs (*a*) and (*b*) of the provision. Subparagraph (*a*) requires that the State enterprise or other entity be capable of suing or being sued, while subparagraph (*b*) requires that it be capable of 'acquiring, owning or possessing and disposing of property, including property which that State has authorized it to operate or manage'. The added value of these two subparagraphs is doubtful, given that the capabilities cited are inherent incidents of the enjoyment by the enterprise or entity of legal personality in its own right.[66]

C. Effects

The import of Article 10(3) is a question calling for close textual analysis within the hermeneutical context of the Convention as a whole. The term 'State', as used in Article 10(3) and, for that matter, everywhere else in the Convention, is defined in Article 2(1)(*b*). Article 2(1)(*b*)(iii) defines 'State' to include 'agencies or instrumentalities of the State or other entities, to the extent that they are entitled to perform and are actually performing acts in the exercise of sovereign authority of the State'; and a classic example of the sort of 'agencies', 'instrumentalities', and 'other entities' mentioned in Article 2(1)(*b*)(iii) is what, in common parlance, would be called a State enterprise—that is, an entity established by a State for commercial purposes, endowed with independent

[65] See section 4.1(C).

[66] See ILC commentary, draft art. 10, para. 11.

legal personality and capable of suing or being sued and of acquiring, owning or possessing, and disposing of property.

At the same time, Article 10(3) posits a terminological distinction between, on the one hand, a State and, on the other, 'a State enterprise or other entity established by a State which has an independent legal personality and is capable of... suing or being sued... and... acquiring, owning or possessing and disposing of property'. In this light, the only way of making sense of Article 10(3)'s terminological distinction is to construe the provision's reference to 'a State enterprise or other entity established by State which has independent legal personality' etc so as not to encompass State enterprises and analogous State-established entities 'to the extent that they are entitled to perform and are actually performing acts in the exercise of sovereign authority of the State', in the words of Article 2(1)(*b*)(iii). Put differently, the only coherent meaning capable of being ascribed to Article 10(3)'s reference to State enterprises etc in the context of the Convention as a whole is one restricted, first, to those State enterprises etc that are not entitled to perform acts in the exercise of sovereign authority of the State and, secondly, to those State enterprises etc that are entitled to perform but are not, as regards the conduct out of which the proceeding arises, actually performing acts in the exercise of sovereign authority of the State.

On the basis of the foregoing, it should be apparent that Article 10(3) is without practical consequence. All the provision says is that where a State enterprise etc that does not qualify as the State under Article 2(1)(*b*)(iii) 'is involved in a proceeding which relates to a commercial transaction in which that [enterprise etc] is engaged, the immunity from jurisdiction enjoyed by that State shall not be affected'. But this ought to go without saying. If a State enterprise etc does not qualify as the State to begin with, it is a truism that its involvement in a proceeding relating to a commercial transaction in which it is engaged does not affect the immunity of the State.

There is no convincing logical reason, moreover, why Article 10(3) should make explicit in relation to the involvement of a State enterprise etc in a proceeding relating to a commercial transaction what it is not made explicit, but is no less true, in relation to, for example, the involvement of such an enterprise etc in a proceeding in which it has submitted to the jurisdiction of the court. Indeed, all the explicit reference in Article 10(3) serves to do, given the canon of construction *expressio unius exclusio alterius*, is to suggest, wrongly, that the involvement of a State enterprise etc in a proceeding relating to a commercial transaction raises a unique problem in terms of the immunity of a State from foreign proceedings.

D. *The understanding*

The second limb of the annexed understanding with respect to Article 10, included to accommodate the concerns of some western States over the possible implications of Article 10(3), is also of dubious value. It is difficult to see in the first place how Article 10(3), which purports to relate to no more than a State's immunity from jurisdiction, could be taken to prejudge the question of 'piercing the corporate veil' or the other questions and issues to which the understanding refers, all of which are questions of substantive law to be answered by reference to whatever body of municipal law falls to be applied by the court in which the proceeding is heard.

The first limb of the annexed understanding, according to which the 'term "immunity" in Article 10 is to be understood in the context of the present Convention as a whole', was inserted in order to make it clear *ex abundante cautela* that the reference in Article 10(3) to the immunity from jurisdiction enjoyed by the State does not imply the availability to that State of any greater immunity than it would otherwise enjoy under the Convention. The fear was that the words 'the immunity from jurisdiction enjoyed by that State shall not be affected' might be taken to suggest that, when the conditions specified in Article 10(3) obtain, the immunity granted to the State by Article 5 is subject to no exception, including the exception provided for in Article 10(1). But this fear was purely fanciful. No good-faith reading of Article 10(3) in context could be taken to accord the State in question any greater immunity than it would otherwise enjoy under the Convention.

5. Evaluation

The text of Article 10 is the outcome of a protracted and difficult drafting process. Together with the definition of a 'commercial transaction' in Article 2(1)(*c*), as elaborated on in Article 2(2), it represents something of a compromise between opposing views as to the scope of the commercial transaction exception, and this trio of provisions raises almost as many questions as it answers. It would be foolish to suggest that the Convention addresses the commercial transaction exception in a completely satisfactory manner, and it is unlikely that the States parties will apply the exception uniformly. But at least Article 10, combined with Article 2(1)(*c*) and (2), will narrow the scope of divergence.

As for States not parties to the Convention, the latter's embodiment and, to a lesser extent, formulation of the commercial transaction exception may help to approximate their practice as well, accelerating what was already the trend, resulting in part from the drafting debates over Article 10, towards the exception's more consistent application. At the very least, as noted by the Supreme Court of Japan, the adoption of Article 10 makes it difficult for a national court to uphold, on the alleged basis of customary international law, a State's immunity from civil proceedings arising out of a commercial transaction engaged in by that State.[67] Indeed, one can confidently say that some form of the commercial transaction exception reflects customary international law. The real question is whether the customary definition of a 'commercial transaction', if there is any, accords with Article 2(1)(*c*) and (2).

The redundant Article 10(3), for its part, reflects astute drafting politics. Its inclusion brought the developing States on board, but, on close reading, it is actually without formal legal significance. That said, given its complexity, it has the potential to cause trouble when applied by domestic courts which might not appreciate the strategic reason for its inclusion.

[67] *Case no 1231* [2003], reported and commented on by C.P.A. Jones, 'International Decisions' (2006) 100 *AJIL* 908, 909 (Jpn (SC) 2006).

Article 11

Joanne Foakes and Roger O'Keefe

Article 11

Contracts of employment

1. Unless otherwise agreed between the States concerned, a State cannot invoke immunity from jurisdiction before a court of another State which is otherwise competent in a proceeding which relates to a contract of employment between the State and an individual for work performed or to be performed, in whole or in part, in the territory of that other State.
2. Paragraph 1 does not apply if:
   (*a*) the employee has been recruited to perform particular functions in the exercise of governmental authority;
   (*b*) the employee is:
      (i) a diplomatic agent, as defined in the Vienna Convention on Diplomatic Relations of 1961;
      (ii) a consular officer, as defined in the Vienna Convention on Consular Relations of 1963;
      (iii) a member of the diplomatic staff of a permanent mission to an international organization or of a special mission, or is recruited to represent a State at an international conference; or
      (iv) any other person enjoying diplomatic immunity;
   (*c*) the subject-matter of the proceeding is the recruitment, renewal of employment or reinstatement of an individual;
   (*d*) the subject-matter of the proceeding is the dismissal or termination of employment of an individual and, as determined by the head of State, the head of Government or the Minister for Foreign Affairs of the employer State, such a proceeding would interfere with the security interests of that State;
   (*e*) the employee is a national of the employer State at the time when the proceeding is instituted, unless this person has the permanent residence in the State of the forum; or
   (*f*) the employer State and the employee have otherwise agreed in writing, subject to any considerations of public policy conferring on the courts of the State of the forum exclusive jurisdiction by reason of the subject-matter of the proceeding.

Understanding with respect to article 11

The reference in article 11, paragraph 2(*d*), to the 'security interests' of the employer State is intended primarily to address matters of national security and the security of diplomatic missions and consular posts.

Under article 41 of the 1961 Vienna Convention on Diplomatic Relations and article 55 of the 1963 Vienna Convention on Consular Relations, all persons referred to in those articles have the duty to respect the laws and regulations, including the labour laws, of the host country. At the same time, under article 38 of the 1961 Vienna Convention on Diplomatic Relations and article 71 of the 1963 Vienna Convention on Consular Relations, the receiving State has a duty to exercise its jurisdiction in such a manner as not to interfere unduly with the performance of the functions of the mission or the consular post.

1. Introduction

Contracts of employment are expressly excluded from the ambit of the term 'commercial transaction' as defined in Article 2(1)(*c*) of the Convention.[1] A State's immunity from foreign proceedings relating to such contracts falls to be considered solely under Article 11 ('Contracts of employment') and not under Article 10 ('Commercial transactions') of the Convention.[2]

Until comparatively recently, States enjoyed complete immunity from foreign proceedings in respect of contracts of employment to which, in their capacity as employer, they were party.[3] This was consistent with the privileged treatment accorded by most municipal legal systems to public-sector employment disputes.[4] It was also thought to reflect the structural principle of the international legal order whereby the organization of a State's internal apparatus is a matter exclusively for that State.[5]

Under the restrictive doctrine of State immunity, however, an exception to a State's immunity from jurisdiction began to emerge, at least in certain circumstances, in respect of those contracts of employment between the State and an employee that fell to be performed in the forum State.[6] This development was prompted by the increasing number of persons employed by States in the territory of other States and by the increasing interest of those other States in the protection of their local labour forces.[7] These factors stimulated a growing recognition that a foreign State's sovereign discretion as to the recruitment, appointment, and dismissal of those who represented it ought to be weighed against the forum State's legitimate interest, as a matter of domestic public policy, in ensuring compliance with its labour law.[8] Article 11 of the Convention seeks to reflect this delicate balance.[9] The perceived justification for the forum State's exercise of jurisdiction in proceedings falling within the exception to State immunity recognized in Article 11 is twofold, namely the connection between the contract of employment and the forum State[10] (in the form of the performance of the contract in whole or in part in the territory of the forum State[11] and the nationality or permanent residence of the contracted employee[12]) and the *jure gestionis* character of the functions that the employee was recruited to perform.[13]

Under Article 11(1), unless the States concerned agree otherwise, a State enjoys no immunity from foreign proceedings relating to a contract of employment for work to be performed for it wholly or partly in the forum State. This exception is itself subject to a

1 See Art. 2(1)(*c*)(iii) UNCSI.

2 See ILC commentary, draft art. 11, para. 1, observing that contracts of employment are 'different in nature from commercial transactions'.

3 See R. Garnett, 'State Immunity in Employment Matters' (1997) 46 *ICLQ* 81, 83; H. Fox, *The Law of State Immunity* (2nd edn) (Oxford: Oxford University Press, 2008), 547.

4 Fox (n. 3), 547.

5 See eg, in the diplomatic and consular contexts respectively, Art. 7 Vienna Convention on Diplomatic Relations, Vienna, 18 April 1961, 500 UNTS 95 (VCDR) and Art. 19(1) Vienna Convention on Consular Relations, Vienna, 24 April 1963, 596 UNTS 261 (VCCR).

6 See ILC commentary, draft art. 11, para. 14.

7 Garnett (n. 3), 83.

8 As regards the latter, see ILC commentary, draft art. 11, para. 4.

9 See ILC commentary, draft art. 11, paras 5 and 8.

10 See ILC commentary, draft art. 11, para. 4.

11 See Art. 11(1) UNCSI.

12 See Art. 11(2)(*e*) UNCSI.

13 See, *a contrario*, Art. 11(2)(*a*) UNCSI. See also 1999 report ILC Working Group, 166, para. 98.

number of exceptions, as exhaustively listed in Article 11(2), and two of these exceptions to the exception are in turn subject to further exceptions. Annexed to the Convention, in addition, is an understanding with respect to Article 11, the first paragraph of which relates specifically to Article 11(2)(*d*).

It is difficult to assess whether Article 11 of the Convention comports with customary international law, although the Grand Chamber of the ECtHR has in recent years twice held that it does.[14]

2. Background

It may be useful to set the drafting of Article 11 of the Convention against the backdrop of the analogous provision in the ECSI and the judicial and legislative practice of States.

2.1 European Convention on State Immunity

The ECSI, like the later UNCSI, makes a distinction between contracts of employment and other contracts, dealing with the former in a separate provision that in 1972 reflected the emerging trend towards a discrete exception to State immunity in this area. The relevant provision of the ECSI, Article 5, reads:

1. A Contracting State cannot claim immunity from the jurisdiction of a court of another Contracting State if the proceedings relate to a contract of employment between the state and an individual where the work has to be performed on the territory of the State of the forum.
2. Paragraph 1 shall not apply where:
   (*a*) the individual is a national of the employing State at the time when the proceedings are brought;
   (*b*) at the time when the contract was entered into the individual was neither a national of the State of the forum nor habitually resident in that State; or
   (*c*) the parties to the contract have otherwise agreed in writing unless, in accordance with the law of the State of the forum, the courts of that State have exclusive jurisdiction by reason of the subject-matter.
3. Where the work is done for an office, agency or other establishment referred to in Article 7, paragraph 2(*a*) and (*b*) of the present article apply only if, at the time the contract was entered into, the individual had his habitual residence in the Contracting State which employs him.

The distinction drawn between contracts of employment within the meaning of Article 5 ECSI and those contracts in respect of which State immunity is abrogated by Article 4 ECSI[15] is explained in the Explanatory Report by reference to the argument that, in the case of contracts of employment, it may be justified in certain circumstances—for example, where the employee is a national of the employer State or a foreign worker who was not locally recruited by the employer State—to accord immunity from suit to a

[14] See *Cudak v Lithuania*, application no. 15869/02, Judgment (Merits and Just Satisfaction), ECtHR (GC), 23 March 2010, para. 67 and *Sabeh El Leil v France*, application no. 34869/05, Judgment (Merits and Just Satisfaction), ECtHR (GC), 29 June 2011, paras 54 and 57. See also the view of the Colombian Supreme Court of Justice (Chamber of Labour Cassation) in *García de Borrosow v Embassy of Lebanon*, ILDC 1009 (CO 2007), paras 25–26 (Col (SCJ) 2007).

[15] Art. 4(1) ECSI provides: 'Subject to the provisions of Article 5, a Contracting State cannot claim immunity from the jurisdiction of the courts of another Contracting State if the proceedings relate to an obligation of the State, which, by virtue of a contract, falls to be discharged in the territory of the State of the forum.'

foreign State respondent. In such cases, the Report elaborates, the links between the employee and the employer State may be far closer that those between the employee and the forum State.[16]

Unlike Article 11 UNCSI, Article 5 ECSI contains no express exclusion relating to the employment of members of staff of diplomatic or consular missions. The Explanatory Report, however, states that, '[a]s regards contracts of employment with diplomatic missions or consular posts, Article 32 [ECSI] shall also be taken into account'.[17] Article 32 has the effect of preserving those generally recognized privileges and immunities relating to the exercise of the functions of diplomatic missions and consular posts and of persons connected with them, as codified in the VCDR and VCCR.

2.2 Judicial and legislative practice of States

The ILC commentary to what became Article 11 UNCSI characterizes the contract-of-employment exception as 'recently emerged'.[18] In contrast to the extensive State practice that existed in relation to the commercial activities of foreign States, when the ILC commenced its work on the draft articles there was scant evidence on which to base firm conclusions with regard to contracts of employment, and such evidence as did exist derived from only a limited number of jurisdictions.[19] The employment of local personnel by foreign States, although becoming more frequent, was a relatively recent phenomenon; and even where it had occurred, disputes had proved infrequent and recorded instances of judicial settlement few.[20] Although both judicial and legislative practice have proliferated since, there remain significant differences among jurisdictions with regard to the immunity of foreign States from suit in respect of employment matters. Although a reasonably consistent pattern of upholding immunity is apparent as regards personnel employed to perform acts in the exercise of sovereign authority, State practice is more mixed in relation to other types of employment.[21]

In giving effect to an exception to immunity from jurisdiction in respect of proceedings relating to contracts of employment, States have adopted a variety of often-overlapping approaches.[22]

The most common approach, both judicial and legislative, has been to look first for some nexus between the contract of employment and the employee, on the one hand,

[16] See Expl. Rep. ECSI, para. 30. [17] Expl. Rep. ECSI, para. 30.

[18] ILC commentary, draft art. 11, para. 1. [19] Fifth report Sucharitkul, 34, para. 39.

[20] Fifth report Sucharitkul, 34, para. 40.

[21] See 1999 report ILC Working Group, 166, paras 99–100; Garnett (n. 3), 124.

[22] See, generally, Garnett (n. 3), 83–100 and 105–20. Note, as far as national legislation goes, that the distinction between contracts of employment and other contracts is made in SIA (UK), enacted to give effect to the ECSI, and in legislation based on or influenced by it. See ss. 3(3) and 4 SIA (UK); ss. 5(1) and 6 SIA (Sing); ss. 5(2) and 6 SIO (Pak); ss. 4(3) and 5 FStIA (SA); ss. 11(3) and 12 FStIA (Aus). See also, not dissimilarly, art. 2(*c*) and (*d*) IFSJAC (Arg). S. 4(*c*) FSIL (Isr) is particularly striking. It provides: 'In an action by an employee . . . where the conditions specified in this section are not fulfilled, the foreign state shall have immunity from jurisdiction, even where the cause of action is a commercial transaction as provided in section 3.' In contrast, there is no special provision for employment contracts in either the FSIA (US) or the SIA (Can), with the consequence that employment claims against foreign States must be brought under the commercial activity exception to State immunity provided for in s. 1605(*a*)(2) FSIA (US) and s. 5 SIA (Can) respectively. In this regard, the legislative report on the FSIA (US) comments, not altogether helpfully: 'Also public or governmental and not commercial in nature would be the employment of diplomatic, civil service, or military personnel, but not the employment of American citizens or third country nationals by the foreign state in the United States.' See US Congress, House of Representatives (94th Congress, 2nd session), Report No. 94-1487 (1976), reproduced in 15 ILM 1398, 1407 (1976).

and the State of the forum, on the other. National courts have been prepared, at least as a threshold matter, to exercise jurisdiction over a foreign State in cases where the employment contract falls to be performed wholly or partly in the territory of the forum State and where the employee is a national or permanent resident of that State.[23] This school of thought is also reflected in national legislation.[24] But even where the requirement of a nexus has been satisfied, it has usually been thought necessary to apply in addition the *jure imperii/jure gestionis* distinction and to analyse whether the foreign State, in its capacity as employer, was acting in an inherently sovereign capacity.

In seeking to resolve this second question, courts in some jurisdictions have emphasized the importance of the setting or context of the contracted employment. If an employee is employed at whatever level by an establishment, such as an embassy, consulate, or the like, where a foreign State is engaged in sovereign activities, it has been held that immunity from suit should be retained, on the basis that any inquiry into the foreign State's conduct as employer in relation to such an establishment would impinge on its sovereignty.[25] Similarly, in the legislative realm, the SIA (UK), the SIO (Pak), and the FStIA (SA) provide expressly that the statutory exception to immunity in respect of proceedings relating to contracts of employment does not apply to proceedings concerning the employment of the members of a diplomatic mission or consular post,[26] these terms being defined in the relevant international instruments to include everyone from the head of the mission or post down to the members of the service staff.[27] In contrast, foreign-State educational institutions and trading corporations have been regarded by some courts as no different from equivalent entities in the private sector, with the result that the court's inquiry into the foreign State's conduct as employer in this context would involve no infringement of sovereignty.[28] Likewise, the SIA (UK), which

[23] See the cases referred to later in this chapter.

[24] See s. 4(1) and (2) SIA (UK); s. 6(1) and (2) SIA (Sing); s. 6(1) and (2) SIO (Pak); s. 5(1) FStIA (SA); s. 12(1) and (3) FStIA (Aus); art. 2(*d*) IFSJAC (Arg); s. 4 FSIL (Isr).

[25] See eg *Conrades v United Kingdom*, 65 ILR 205 (FRG (Hanover LC) 1981), re a receptionist/switchboard operator/clerk/interpreter at a consulate; *X v Argentina*, 114 ILR 502 (FRG (FLC) 1996), re a member of the administrative and technical staff of a consulate; *Muller v United States of America*, 114 ILR 512 (FRG (Hesse RLC) 1998), re a financial assistant at a consulate; *Government of Canada v Employment Appeals Tribunal and Burke*, 95 ILR 467 (Ire (SC) 1981), re an ambassador's chauffeur; *Sengupta v Republic of India*, 64 ILR 352 (UK (EEAT) 1982), re a clerk at the Indian High Commission (*viz* embassy) in London; *Arab Republic of Egypt v Gamal-Eldin*, 104 ILR 673 (UK (EAT) 1995), re drivers at the medical office of an embassy; *Brazilian Embassy Employee Case*, 116 ILR 625 (Por (SC) 1984), re an administrative functionary at an embassy (although see n. 30 for the current Portuguese position); *Heusala v Republic of Turkey*, ILDC 576 (FI 1993) (Fin (SC) 1993), re a secretary/translator at an embassy; *Governor of Pitcairn v Sutton*, 104 ILR 508 (NZ (CA) 1994), re a typist/clerk in the Auckland office of the governor of a UK dependent territory; *A v B*, ILDC 23 (NO 2004) (Nor (SC) 2004), re a driver at an embassy.

[26] See s. 16(1)(*a*) SIA (UK); s. 17(1)(*a*) SIO (Pak); s. 5(2)(*b*) FStIA (SA), referring more specifically, although neither more inclusively nor restrictively, to 'the head of a diplomatic mission or any member of the diplomatic mission or any member of the diplomatic, administrative, technical or service staff of the mission' and to 'the head of a consular post or any member of the consular, labour, trade, administrative, technical or service staff of the post'.

[27] See Art. 1(*b*) and (*c*) VCDR; Art. 1(1)(*g*) VCCR. Private servants—that is, persons in the domestic service of a member of the mission who are not employees of the sending State—are not encompassed by the respective definitions.

[28] See eg *Mallaval v French Ministry of Foreign Affairs*, 65 ILR 303 (Ita (Rome Ex. Mag.) 1974) (but see nn. 37 and 38 for the approach subsequently taken by the Italian Court of Cassation), re a teacher at a French lycée in Rome; *Gazder v Air India*, 574 F.Supp 134 (US (SDNY) 1983), re an employee of a foreign State-owned airline; *Starrett v Iberia Airlines of Spain*, 756 F.Supp 292 (US (SD Tex) 1989), again re an employee of a foreign State-owned airline.

in this regard gives effect to Article 5(3) ECSI, and the SIO (Pak) and SIA (Sing), which were modelled on the SIA (UK), specify that the contract-of-employment exception to State immunity continues to apply, as a general rule, where the work performed by the employee in the forum State is for an office, agency, or establishment maintained by the foreign State for commercial purposes.[29]

In other jurisdictions, courts have instead focused the *jure gestionis/jure imperii* inquiry on the nature of the particular employee's functions. On this basis it has been held that the immunity of a foreign State from jurisdiction should be upheld only where an employee is engaged in inherently sovereign activities. Employees engaged in menial duties, wherever they may have been employed, have been permitted to sue.[30] The same distinction is evident in some legislation.[31] The FStIA (Aus) disapplies the exception to immunity from suit otherwise applicable in respect of contracts of employment only where the claim relates to the employment of a member of the diplomatic staff of a mission or of a consular officer[32] or, at least in general, to the employment of a member of the administrative and technical staff of a mission or of a consular employee,[33] within the meanings given to these terms by the pertinent international instruments.[34] That is, the exception to immunity from proceedings recognized by the FStIA (Aus) in respect of contracts of employment remains applicable where the claim relates to the employment of a member of the service staff of a mission or post.[35] The Australian Law Reform Commission report which led to the adoption of the FStIA (Aus) explains that, whereas the relationship between foreign States and their diplomatic and consular personnel is a sensitive one, 'there seems no reason why locally recruited staff employed on routine administrative, clerical or maintenance functions should not be able to sue their foreign state employer'.[36]

29 See s. 4(3) SIA (UK); s. 6(3) SIO (Pak); s. 6(3) SIA (Sing). This is not the case, however, where the employee was, at the time the employment contract was made, habitually resident in the foreign State.

30 See eg *British Embassy Driver Case*, 65 ILR 20 (Aut (Vienna SPC) 1978), re a driver at an embassy, unsurprisingly; *S v Republic of India*, 82 ILR 13 (Swi (FT) 1984), re a radio-telegrapher/clerk at an embassy; *Landano v United States of America*, 116 ILR 636 (Swi (Geneva LC) 1987), re a telephonist at an embassy; *M v Arab Republic of Egypt*, 116 ILR 656 (Swi (FT) 1994), re a chauffeur at a permanent mission to an international organization; *R v Republic of Iraq*, 116 ILR 664 (Swi (FT) 1994), re an interpreter/translator at a permanent mission to an international organization; *MK v Republic of Turkey*, 94 ILR 350 (Nth (Hague SDC) 1985), re a secretary at an embassy (but see n. 37 for the approach subsequently taken by the Netherlands Supreme Court); *De Guieros Magalhaes Abrantes v Republic of Portugal* (1992) 27 *RBDI* 698 (Bel (Brussels LC) 1991), re a language teacher at an embassy; *Sawas v Kingdom of Saudi Arabia*, ILDC 1146 (BE 2007) (Bel (Brussels LT) 2007), re a telephonist/secretary at an embassy; *Coco v State of Argentina*, 113 ILR 491 (Fra (CoC) 1996), re an assistant in the press section of an embassy; *Saignie v Embassy of Japan*, 113 ILR 492 (Fra (CoC) 1997), re a caretaker at an embassy; *Barrandon v United States of America*, 116 ILR 622 (Fra (CoC) 1998), re a nurse/medical secretary at an embassy; *El Hadad v Embassy of the United Arab Emirates*, 216 F 3rd 29 (US (DC Cir.) 2000), re an auditor at an embassy; *AA v Austrian Embassy*, ILDC 826 (PT 2007) (Por (SCJ) 2007), re an administrative secretary at an embassy.

31 In addition to the explicit provisions of the FStIA (Aus), query also s. 19(1) SIA (Sing), which provides that the exceptions to a foreign State's immunity from proceedings specified in Part II of the Act do not affect 'any immunity or privilege applicable in Singapore to diplomatic and consular agents', the reference to 'consular agents' presumably being to consular officers within the meaning of Art. 1(1)(*d*) VCCR. But the provision almost certainly refers solely to the immunities *ratione personae* and *ratione materiae* from which serving and former diplomatic agents and consular officers benefit by virtue of the VCDR and VCCR, and not to any immunity of their State from proceedings relating to their employment.

32 See s. 12(5) FStIA (Aus).

33 See s. 12(6) FStIA (Aus). This is not the case where the employee was, at the time the employment contract was made, a permanent resident of Australia.

34 See Art. 1(*d*) and (*f*) VCDR; Art. 1(1)(*d*) and (*e*) VCCR.

35 It also remains applicable a fortiori to claims relating to the employment of a private servant.

36 Australian Law Reform Commission, *Foreign State Immunity* (ALRC report no. 24, 1984), 58, para. 100.

Finally, the courts in yet other States have sought to resolve the *jure imperii/jure gestionis* issue by reference to the subject-matter of the claim. According to this approach, if adjudicating the merits of the claim would require the court to examine the organizational or security policies of a foreign State to an extent incompatible with that State's sovereignty, immunity should be upheld.[37] If, however, the claim relates purely to remuneration and other financial aspects of the employment contract, an example being a claim for unpaid wages, it should be allowed to proceed.[38]

3. Drafting History

The terms of the contract-of-employment exception to a State's immunity from foreign proceedings—or, to be precise, the terms of the exceptions to the exception—proved to be one of the most difficult issues in the drafting of the Convention. It was identified in 1999 by the ILC's Working Group on Jurisdictional Immunities of States and Their Property as one of the five problems outstanding after agreement had been reached on all else.[39] The eventual wording of the provision, which had featured in some form in the ILC's work since 1983,[40] was agreed only in the final text of the draft convention adopted in 2004 by the Ad Hoc Committee on Jurisdictional Immunities of States and Their Property.[41]

3.1 Paragraph 1

Paragraph 1 of the draft article adopted on first reading by the ILC in 1986, the gist of which corresponded to Article 5(1) ECSI, removed a State's immunity from foreign proceedings in respect of contracts of employment where the work was to be performed in whole or in part in the territory of the forum State and where the employee was both recruited in the forum State and covered by any social security provisions in force in that State.[42] In his subsequent Preliminary Report, however, Special Rapporteur Ogiso proposed in the light of comments from States that the social security requirement be deleted as unduly restrictive.[43] The proposal received a mixed response, but the requirement was eventually dropped on this basis.[44] The reference to recruitment in the territory of the forum State was also deleted.[45] Draft article 11(1) as finally adopted by the ILC on second reading in 1991 passed unchanged into the Convention as Article 11(1).

[37] See eg *Van der Hulst v United States of America*, 94 ILR 373 (Nth (SC) 1989); *Norwegian Embassy v Quattri*, 114 ILR 525 (Ita (CoC) 1991); *Canada v Cargnello*, 114 ILR 559 (Ita (CoC) 1998).

[38] See eg *British Consulate-General in Naples v Toglia*, 101 ILR 379 (Ita (CoC) 1989); *Norwegian Embassy v Quattri* (n. 37); *Schmidt v Goethe Institut*, ILDC 1616 (IT 2008) (Ita (CoC) 2008); *X v Saudi School in Paris and Kingdom of Saudi Arabia*, 127 ILR 163 (Fra (CoC) 2003); *Bah v Libyan Embassy*, 142 ILR 167 (Bot (IC) 2005).

[39] 1999 report ILC Working Group, 155, para. 7. See also 1999 report Chairman Sixth Committee Working Group, part III.

[40] See Fifth report Sucharitkul, 32–8, paras 28–62.

[41] See draft art. 11 UNCSI.

[42] See Report ILC, thirty-sixth session, 59, para. 206, and 62. The provision was at that point numbered draft art. 13.

[43] See Preliminary report Ogiso, 110, para. 131. The provision was by this stage numbered draft art. 12.

[44] See ILC commentary, draft art. 11, para. 6.

[45] See ILC commentary, draft art. 11, para. 6.

3.2 Paragraph 2

For their part, the exceptions in paragraph 2(*a*) to (*f*) to the general exception to immunity from jurisdiction laid down in paragraph 1 of what is now Article 11 of the Convention underwent numerous changes over the protracted course of their drafting, not least in the period between the ILC's final adoption of draft article 11(2) and the eventual adoption of Article 11(2) of the Convention, which differs noticeably from its ILC forebear.

A. Subparagraph (a)

Subparagraph (*a*) of Article 11(2), which finds no counterpart in the ECSI and was not found in Special Rapporteur Sucharitkul's original version of the draft article,[46] was included in a revised version presented by the Special Rapporteur to the Drafting Committee,[47] was amended by the Drafting Committee the following session,[48] and was provisionally adopted on first reading by the Commission in the course of the same,[49] going on to be adopted on first reading along with the rest of the draft articles in 1986.[50] But the wording of the provision, in accordance with which immunity continued to subsist if the employee 'ha[d] been recruited to perform services associated with the exercise of governmental authority', was subsequently criticized in the Commission and in comments by States as open to 'unduly extensive interpretation'.[51] The version of draft article 11(2)(*a*) finally adopted by the ILC on second reading accordingly spoke of the performance of 'functions closely related to the exercise of governmental authority'.

The ILC's Working Group, however, recommended in 1999 that the scope of the subparagraph be restricted even further by amending the key phrase to refer to 'functions in the exercise of governmental authority',[52] a view which divided the delegations to the Sixth Committee's Working Group.[53] By the 2002 report of the Ad Hoc Committee, however, the formulation eventually adopted as Article 11(2)(*a*) of the Convention, *viz* 'the employee has been recruited to perform particular functions in the exercise of governmental authority', had been settled on.[54]

B. Subparagraph (b)

In his third and final report, Special Rapporteur Ogiso, concerned at what he saw as the overly broad drafting of subparagraph (*a*) of paragraph 2 as it then stood, had proposed as an alternative the foreign State's retention of immunity from suit where the employee was a member of the administrative or technical staff of a diplomatic mission or consular post who was associated with the exercise of governmental authority.[55] Although the proposal did not make its way into the ILC's draft articles, the idea of specifying in

[46] See Fifth report Sucharitkul, 38, para. 62, the relevant provision being the proposed draft art. 13(2)(*b*).

[47] See Report ILC, thirty-fifth session, 20, para. 96, fn. 58.

[48] See summary record 1868th ILC meeting, *YILC 1984*, vol. I, 320, 321–2, paras 7, 8, and 10.

[49] See Report ILC, thirty-sixth session, 59, para. 206, and 62.

[50] See Report ILC, thirty-eighth session, 10.

[51] ILC commentary, draft art. 11, para. 9.

[52] 1999 report ILC Working Group, 167, paras 104 and 105.

[53] See 1999 report Chairman Sixth Committee Working Group, 5, para. 29; 2000 report Chairman Sixth Committee Working Group, 11–13, paras 42–52.

[54] See 2002 report Ad Hoc Committee, 7.

[55] See Third report Ogiso, 13.

greater detail in draft article 11(2)(*a*) the functionaries in respect of whose employment a foreign State should remain immune was taken up in 1999 by the ILC's Working Group, which suggested adding specific but non-exhaustive reference to the diplomatic staff of a mission and consular officers, as defined in the VCDR and VCCR respectively, as well as the diplomatic staff of permanent missions to international organizations and of special missions, and '[o]ther persons enjoying diplomatic immunity, such as persons recruited to represent a State in international conferences'.[56] The suggestion was largely welcomed by States, although different views were expressed as to the precise content of the list of specified functionaries.[57]

In its First Report, in 2002, the Ad Hoc Committee—hiving the list of functionaries off from draft article 11(2)(*a*), placing it in a separate provision, and wording it as exhaustive, rather than merely illustrative—put forward alternative proposals for a draft article 11(2)(*a*) *bis*.[58] The first excluded from the exception to immunity laid down in draft article 11(1) any contract for the employment of, *inter alia*, a member of a diplomatic mission or consular post, as defined in the VCDR and the VCCR respectively—that is, in relation to a diplomatic mission, of members of the administrative and technical staff and service staff of the mission as much as of its diplomatic agents;[59] and, in relation to consular posts, of not only consular officers but also consular employees (*viz* those employed in the administrative or technical service of the post) and members of the service staff.[60] The second proposal excluded from the scope of draft article 11(1) employment claims relating only to diplomatic agents and consular officers. It was the second, narrower alternative which found greatest favour in the Sixth Committee, with many delegations stressing that the scope of a foreign employer State's immunity in respect of contracts for the employment of persons other than its nationals and of permanent residents of the receiving State should, in line with what they believed to be State practice, be limited.[61] In response, the Ad Hoc Committee included the following year the second, more restrictive alternative as two elements of what was by then numbered draft article 11(2)(*b*),[62] elements which ended up unaltered as Article 11(2)(*b*)(i) and (ii) of the Convention.

As for Article 11(2)(*b*)(iii) and (iv), these derive, with only organizational changes, from the suggestion of the ILC Working Group in 1999. But the organizational changes may have unintended consequences. The ILC Working Group had proposed exceptions to draft article 11(1) in respect of contracts for the employment of—in addition to

56 1999 report ILC Working Group, 167, para. 105.

57 See 2000 report Chairman Sixth Committee Working Group, 12, paras 43–46.

58 See 2002 report Ad Hoc Committee, annex, 7.

59 See Art. 1(*c*) VCDR.

60 See Art. 1(1)(*e*) and (*g*) VCCR.

61 See Sixth Committee, fifty-seventh session, summary record 18th meeting, UN doc. A/C.6/57/SR.18, 6, para. 47 (Gre), 7, para. 53 (Por), 8, para. 65 (SA); Sixth Committee, fifty-seventh session, summary record 19th meeting, UN doc. A/C.6/57/SR.19, 3, para. 14 (Rus). Only one State expressed a preference for the first, broader alternative. See Sixth Committee, fifty-seventh session, summary record 18th meeting, 8, para. 60 (Aus).

62 See 2003 report Ad Hoc Committee, annex I, 8. Note, as stated in E. Denza, *Diplomatic Law* (3rd edn) (Oxford: Oxford University Press, 2008), 66, that the freedom of the sending State to appoint and dismiss members of the staff of a diplomatic mission, as recognized in Art. 7 VCDR, 'includes the freedom to specify the functions they are to perform and, accordingly whether they are to be classified as diplomatic staff, administrative and technical staff, or service staff'. Short of declaring individuals *persona non grata* under Art. 9 VCDR or limiting the size of the mission as per Art. 11 VCDR, the receiving State has only a limited capacity to influence this classification. See Denza (n. 62), 67. The same goes, *mutatis mutandis*, for consular posts.

diplomatic staff and consular officers within the meaning of the VCDR and VCCR respectively—the following categories of person:

(*b*) Diplomatic staff of permanent missions to international organizations and of special missions;
(*c*) Other persons enjoying diplomatic immunity, such as persons recruited to represent a State in international conferences.[63]

But the text drafted by the Ad Hoc Committee, which became Article 11(2)(*b*)(iii) and (iv), provides a contract-of-employment exception to Article 11(1) in respect of an employee who is:

(iii) a member of the diplomatic staff of a permanent mission to an international organization or of a special mission, or is recruited to represent a State at an international conference; or
(iv) any other person enjoying diplomatic immunity...

The formulation is problematic, as will be seen.[64]

C. Subparagraph (c)

Subparagraph (*c*) of Article 11(2), another provision without analogue in the ECSI, has its origins in the earliest draft article put forward by Special Rapporteur Sucharitkul, in which the relevant subparagraph preserved the employer State's immunity if the proceedings 'relate[d] to failure to employ an individual or dismissal of an employee'.[65] The Drafting Committee redrafted the provision 'to indicate clearly that a State would be immune in a proceeding that was intended to force an employer State to recruit, reinstate or renew the contract of employment of an individual',[66] with the draft subparagraph as provisionally adopted on first reading retaining immunity if 'the proceeding relate[d] to the recruitment, renewal of employment or reinstatement of an individual'.[67]

For his part, sharing the fear expressed by the Federal Republic of Germany that the subparagraph as then worded 'could give rise to unduly wide interpretations, which could lead to confusion in the implementation of the future convention', Special Rapporteur Ogiso recommended its deletion.[68] But the suggestion proved unpopular in some quarters. '[S]uch a step', certain ILC members believed, 'would be contrary to the clearly established rules', with one member being 'particularly concerned about the [proposed] deletion of subparagraph (*b*)', which 'could lead to a situation in which a foreign State might be compelled by the forum State, for example, to employ a particular individual'.[69] In response, the Special Rapporteur expressed his own concern that the subparagraph 'had the effect of substantially narrowing the scope of application of local labour regulations to protect the position of employees',[70] a view shared by some other ILC members and some governments.[71] 'The reference to "recruitment"', moreover, 'raised a particularly difficult problem', in that, 'where there was a requirement under local labour law for non-discrimination in respect of recruitment,

[63] 1999 report ILC Working Group, 167, para. 105.
[64] See section 4.2(B).
[65] Fifth report Sucharitkul, 38, para. 62, the relevant provision being the proposed draft art. 13(2)(*a*).
[66] Summary record 1868th ILC meeting (n. 48), 322, para. 11.
[67] Summary record 1868th ILC meeting (n. 48), 321, para. 7.
[68] Preliminary report Ogiso, 110, para. 132.
[69] Report ILC, forty-first session, 110, para. 512.
[70] Report ILC, forty-first session, 110, para. 513.
[71] See Report ILC, forty-second session, 34, para. 177.

the State of the forum might have an overriding interest in determining the violation of that requirement in the local court'.[72] In this light, one suggestion made both in the ILC and in the Sixth Committee was that 'appointment' be substituted for 'recruitment'.[73] Once again, however, some members of the Commission 'insisted on the retention of [the] subparagraph..., including the word "recruitment", which, it was maintained, was consistent with the established rules of international law'.[74] In the event, Special Rapporteur Ogiso proposed keeping the provision, which was referred to the Drafting Committee.

The Drafting Committee, retaining the provision, 'tried to make the text... more precise in order to prevent unduly extensive interpretation... which would reduce the rule stated in paragraph 1 to nothing'.[75] It replaced the words 'the proceeding relates to' with the formulation 'the subject of the proceeding is', since '[e]ven a proceeding concerning the performance of a contract of employment could be regarded as "relating to" the contract, and that would defeat the purpose of the exception stated in paragraph 1':[76]

> The words 'the subject of the proceeding is' made it clear that the scope of the exception was restricted to the specific acts which were referred to in [the] subparagraph... and which were legitimately within the discretionary power of the employer State. Moreover, paragraph (12) of the commentary explained that the rule... was without prejudice to the possible recourse which might still be available in the forum State for compensation for wrongful dismissal, for example.[77]

The subparagraph finally adopted by the ILC on second reading as draft article 11(2)(*b*) preserved the employer State's immunity from suit if 'the subject of the proceeding is the recruitment, renewal of employment or reinstatement of an individual'. With the subsequent amendment of the word 'subject' to 'subject-matter'[78] and the subparagraph's renumbering (or, rather, relettering), the provision passed into the Convention as Article 11(2)(*c*).

D. Subparagraph (d) *and accompanying understanding*

No provision corresponding to subparagraph (*d*) of Article 11(2) was included in the ILC's draft articles as finally adopted on second reading in 1991. What became Article 11(2)(*d*), along with the accompanying first paragraph of the understanding with respect to Article 11 annexed to the Convention, first featured, without recorded explanation, in the 2003 report of the Ad Hoc Committee.[79] Both the subparagraph and the first paragraph of the understanding passed unaltered and without recorded discussion into the Convention.

E. Subparagraph (e)

The provision embodied in subparagraph (*e*) of Article 11(2) to the effect that the employer State's immunity is preserved if the employee is a national of the employer

[72] Report ILC, forty-second session, 34, para. 177.
[73] Report ILC, forty-second session, 34, para. 177.
[74] Report ILC, forty-second session, 34, para. 181.
[75] Summary record 2191st ILC meeting, *YILC 1990*, vol. I, 306, 314, para. 71.
[76] Summary record 2191st ILC meeting (n. 75), 314, para. 72.
[77] Summary record 2191st ILC meeting (n. 75), 314, para. 72.
[78] See Statement Chairman Ad Hoc Committee, 6, para. 34.
[79] See 2003 report Ad Hoc Committee, annex I, 8, and annex II, 14.

State at the time proceedings are instituted—a provision inspired by Article 5(2)(*a*) ECSI—appeared in Special Rapporteur Sucharitkul's earliest proposed draft of the article.[80] But it did so without the eventual qualification as to the employee's permanent residence in the forum State. Nor did the qualification feature in what was finally adopted by the ILC in 1991 as draft article 11(2)(*d*). When later, in 1999, the Working Group of the Sixth Committee considered the provision, 'a number of delegations expressed the view that the provision might [...] present some problems with regard to the principle of non-discrimination based on nationality, in particular regarding employees permanently residing in the forum State'.[81] While '[t]here was general agreement [...] that [sub]paragraph (*d*) should be retained', it was also agreed 'that wording should be added to meet the concerns of delegations regarding employees residing permanently in the forum State'.[82] The words in question were inserted during the following year's session of the Working Group,[83] from where the whole provision passed unchanged into the Convention.

Special Rapporteur Sucharitkul's earliest proposed draft[84] and what was finally adopted by the ILC as draft article 11(2)(*c*) had both contained a provision specifying that a foreign State's immunity from suit would be preserved if the employee was neither a national nor a resident of the forum State at the time the contract of employment was concluded. Both conditions were taken from Article 5(2)(*b*) ECSI. Both, on later examination by the ILC's Working Group, were agreed to be discriminatory,[85] and it was proposed that both be deleted,[86] which they were.[87] The result is that, provided such individuals do not fall foul of any of the other exceptions to the contract-of-employment exception to immunity from suit, Article 11(2) of the Convention does not serve to bar proceedings against a foreign employer State brought by persons who, at the time of their entry into the employment contract, were third-State nationals resident abroad.

F. Subparagraph (f)

In his Fifth Report, Special Rapporteur Sucharitkul, drawing on Article 5(2)(*c*) ECSI, proposed that the exception posited in the first paragraph of what was then draft article 13 to the employer State's immunity from proceedings be inapplicable where 'the employee has otherwise agreed in writing, unless, in accordance with the law of the State of the forum, the courts of that State have exclusive jurisdiction by reason of the subject-matter'.[88] After minor alteration by the Drafting Committee, the subparagraph, recognizing an exception to the exception to immunity from proceedings where 'the employee and the employer State have otherwise agreed in writing, subject to any considerations of public policy conferring on the courts of the State of the forum exclusive jurisdiction by reason of the subject-matter of the proceeding', was adopted on first reading as draft

[80] See Fifth report Sucharitkul, 38, para. 62, the relevant provision being the proposed draft art. 13(2)(*b*).

[81] 1999 report Chairman Sixth Committee Working Group, 5, para. 34.

[82] 1999 report Chairman Sixth Committee Working Group, 5, para. 34.

[83] See 2000 report Chairman Sixth Committee Working Group, 12–13, paras 48–49.

[84] See Fifth report Sucharitkul, 38, para. 62, the relevant provision being the proposed draft art. 13(2)(*c*).

[85] See 1999 report ILC Working Group, 165, para. 87.

[86] See 1999 report ILC Working Group, 167, para. 106.

[87] 1999 report Chairman Sixth Committee Working Group, 5, para. 33; 2000 report Chairman Sixth Committee Working Group, 12–13, paras 42, 47, and 49.

[88] Fifth report Sucharitkul, 38, para. 62.

article 11(2)(*e*).[89] The order of reference to the employee and the employer State being subsequently reversed, the provision, finally adopted on second reading by the ILC again as draft article 11(2)(*e*), passed without amendment into the Convention as the eventual Article 11(2)(*f*).

3.3 Second paragraph of understanding

Like the first, the second paragraph of the understanding with respect to Article 11 annexed to the Convention entered the frame in the 2003 report of the Ad Hoc Committee.[90] No explanation for it is to be found in the drafting records, although it is evident that its inclusion was closely connected with the inclusion the same year, in its final form, of subparagraph (*b*) of Article 11(2), in accordance with which an employer State remains immune from proceedings relating to contracts for the employment of, on the hand, diplomatic agents and their equivalents and consular officers but not, on the other, of members of the administrative and technical staff and of the service staff of a diplomatic mission or consular post, at least insofar as the latter are not nationals of the employer State permanently resident abroad[91] and the proceedings do not fall within some other provision of Article 11(2). The first sentence of the second paragraph of the understanding, which recalls that, as per Article 41 VCDR and Article 55 VCCR, diplomatic agents and consular officers respectively 'have the duty to respect the laws and regulations, including the labour laws, of the host country', would seem to have been included with an eye to mollifying those States suspicious of any retention of the foreign employer State's immunity from proceedings in respect of its alleged breach of the forum State's labour laws. The second sentence, which recalls that, pursuant to Article 38 VCDR and Article 71 VCCR respectively, the receiving State 'has a duty to exercise its jurisdiction [over certain non-diplomatic and non-consular employees] in such a manner as not to interfere unduly with the performance of the functions of the mission or the consular post', would appear, conversely, to have been by way of consolation to those States which opposed any inroad into the immunity of a foreign employer State from proceedings relating to the employment of members of the staff of its diplomatic missions or consular posts.

4. Key Points

Article 11 of the Convention raises a range of issues. Insofar as these consist of uncertainties as to the proper interpretation and application of its various provisions, they are best answered by focusing on the respective texts. Unless they are referable specifically to Article 11 or, any subsequent modifications being borne in mind, to earlier draft versions of it, State practice and international judicial pronouncements on the contract-of-employment exception, and on the exceptions to that exception, are at best of limited use and at worst misleading.

89 See Report ILC, thirty-eighth session, 10.

90 See 2003 report Ad Hoc Committee, annex I, 8, and annex II, 14.

91 See Art. 11(2)(*e*) UNCSI, as discussed in section 3.2(E) and section 4.2(E).

4.1 Article 11(1): The exception

Article 11(1) lays down the general exception in respect of contracts of employment to a foreign State's immunity from proceedings.

A. *'Unless otherwise agreed between the States concerned'*

The exception to a State's immunity from foreign proceedings posited in Article 11(1), like most of the other exceptions provided for in Part III of the Convention, permits of derogation by mutual consent of the impleaded and forum States. As the ILC commentary elaborates, it remains open to the foreign State and the forum State to adopt by agreement 'a different solution' from that stipulated as a general rule by the contract-of-employment exception to State immunity, thereby 'waiving local labour jurisdiction in favour of immunity'.[92] No equivalent provision is found in Article 5 ECSI. Moreover, it would appear that no such agreement has ever publicly been reached between States.

The opt-out clause in Article 11(1) is to be distinguished from the opt-out clause in Article 11(2)(*f*). The former concerns agreement between the foreign State and the forum State, whereas the latter relates to an agreement between the foreign State and the employee. Unlike under Article 11(2)(*f*), there is no requirement on the face of Article 11(1) that any agreement reached between the foreign and forum States be in writing. Nor, given the premised consent of the forum State, does Article 11(1) make any agreement within the meaning of the provision 'subject to any considerations of public policy conferring on the courts of the State of the forum exclusive jurisdiction by reason of the subject-matter of the proceeding', as is the case with Article 11(2)(*f*).

B. *'before a court of another State which is otherwise competent'*

The exception to immunity from proceedings provided for in Article 11(1) presupposes that the national court before which the claim against the foreign State is brought 'is otherwise competent' to adjudicate the claim. The same words appear in every other exception to immunity from jurisdiction enumerated in Part III of the Convention bar Article 10's commercial transaction exception, in which the same idea is conveyed by a different linguistic formula. Whether or not the court enjoys this underlying competence is a question for the domestic law of the forum State. It is, moreover, a question logically distinct from and precedent to the territorial precondition to the internationally lawful exercise of that competence specified in Article 11(1).

C. *'a proceeding which relates to a contract of employment'*

At first blush, the words 'a proceeding which relates to a contract of employment' might be taken to suggest that the exception to a foreign State's immunity from suit recognized in Article 11(1) relates solely to contractual claims—that is, to proceedings brought by an employee alleging breach of contract by the employer State. The impression is, unfortunately, scarcely dispelled by the injudiciously worded ILC commentary, which explains that the identically worded forerunner to Article 11(1) 'applie[d] to matters arising out of

[92] ILC commentary, draft art. 11, para. 7. The commentary adds cryptically, by way of justification for this opt-out clause, that '[r]espect for treaty regimes and for the consent of the States concerned is of paramount importance, since they are decisive in solving the question of waiver or of exercise of jurisdiction by the State of the forum or of the maintenance of jurisdictional immunity of the employer State'.

the terms and conditions contained in the contract of employment'.[93] *Pace* the commentary, the scope of Article 11(1) is wider than this. The State practice on which Article 11(1) is based, both general and specifically pursuant to the contract-of-employment exception to immunity embodied in Article 5(1) ECSI, makes it clear that, subject to the exemptions specified in Article 11(2)(*c*) and (*d*),[94] Article 11(1) applies to all employment claims, whether under the private law of contract or under relevant employment legislation.[95] The same is plainly evident from the drafting history of the provision and, indeed, from the ILC commentary, both of which manifest a consistent concern 'to maintain a delicate balance between the competing interests of the employer State with regard to the application of its law and the overriding interests of the State of the forum for the application of its labour law'.[96] (Labour law is mentioned twice more in the commentary.[97]) In short, all other conditions being met, a foreign employer State is not immune from any proceedings in the courts of another State which relate to its role as employer, including proceedings for breach of any relevant employment legislation, for example involving allegations of workplace racial or sexual discrimination or harassment or of breach of statutory maximum hours of work or minimum rates of pay.

D. 'for work performed or to be performed, in whole or in part, in the territory of that other State'

Even leaving aside inter-State agreement to the contrary and the exceptions to the exception specified in paragraph 2 of Article 11, the exception to immunity laid down in Article 11(1) does not apply to every contract of employment between an individual and a foreign State. For a respondent State's immunity from proceedings to be excluded under Article 11(1), the contract of employment that is the subject of the claim must be 'for work performed or to be performed, in whole or in part, in the territory of [the forum] State'. The words 'in whole or in part' represent an advance over the formulation found in Article 5(1) ECSI, which relates to individual–State contracts of employment 'where the work has to be performed on the territory of the State of the forum', although section 5(1) SIA (UK), while enacted to give effect to Article 5(1) ECSI, is more precise in applying 'where the work is to be performed wholly or partly in the United Kingdom'. The UK wording has been reproduced, *mutatis mutandis*, in the legislation of five other States.[98] It is on this State practice that Article 11(1) draws.

On the face of the provision there is no *de minimis* requirement as to the proportion of the contracted work which need be performed in the territory of the forum State in order for Article 11(1) to apply. If, after the application of domestic doctrines of private international law such as *forum non conveniens*, the court is competent, the contract-of-employment exception to State immunity is available, subject to inter-State agreement otherwise and to the exceptions to the exception specified in Article 11(2).

[93] ILC commentary, draft art. 11, para. 2.

[94] See sections 4.2(C) and 4.2(D).

[95] See eg s. 4(6) SIA (UK); s. 6(1), explanation, SIO (Pak); s. 6(5) SIA (Sing); s. 12(2)(*a*) FStIA (Aus).

[96] ILC commentary, draft art. 11, para. 5.

[97] See ILC commentary, draft art. 11, paras 11 and 12.

[98] See s. 6(1) SIA (Sing); s. 6(1) SIO (Pak); s. 5(1)(*a*) FStIA (SA); s. 12(1) FStIA (Aus). See also s. 4(*a*)(2) FSIL (Isr) ('the subject matter of the action is labour, all or a part of which has been performed, or is to be performed, in Israel').

4.2 Article 11(2): The exceptions to the exception

The exception to immunity from jurisdiction provided for in Article 11(1) is itself subject to exceptions. These are set out in Article 11(2), which exhaustively[99] lists six instances in which, even though the requirements of Article 11(1) might be fulfilled, the foreign State can nonetheless rely on immunity from jurisdiction. These exceptions to the exception, which are arranged somewhat haphazardly, are stated in the alternative[100]—that is, only one of them need be satisfied in order for a foreign employer State to avail itself of immunity.

A. Employee 'recruited to perform particular functions in the exercise of governmental authority'

Pursuant to Article 11(2)(*a*), the contract-of-employment exception to a foreign State's immunity from proceedings does not apply if 'the employee has been recruited to perform particular functions in the exercise of governmental authority'. Not covered by this provision are employment disputes relating to diplomatic agents, consular officers, and the like, who form a special category of employee recruited to perform sovereign acts which was carved out late in the drafting process[101] and is treated separately in Article 11(2)(*b*).[102] The general exception to non-immunity in Article 11(2)(*a*), which as a logical matter would have been better placed after the special exception to non-immunity in Article 11(2)(*b*), deals with a residual pool of employees recruited to perform sovereign acts. It is important to bear in mind, however, that reliance on neither Article 11(2)(*a*) nor Article 11(2)(*b*) is necessary if, as per Article 11(2)(*e*), the employee is a national of the employer State at the time the proceedings are instituted, unless he or she is permanently resident in the forum State.

The concern of the drafters of Article 11(2)(*a*), an extensively debated and successively narrowed provision, was to ensure that it was not open to inappropriately extensive interpretation.[103] The gist of Article 11(2)(*a*) is to keep intact the immunity of a foreign State from proceedings in relation to contracts for the employment of persons whose duties involve the performance of acts *jure imperii*. It is in relation to such employees and to such employees alone that a foreign State, in its capacity as employer, is considered to act in a sovereign vein and not in the manner of a private entity. The problem, as ever with the *jure imperii/jure gestionis* distinction, is where to draw the line. The ILC commentary to draft article 11(2)(*a*), which applied more broadly to situations where the employee was recruited to perform functions 'closely related to' the exercise of governmental authority, gives as examples of such employees 'private secretaries, code clerks, interpreters, translators and other persons entrusted with functions related to State security or basic interests of the State'[104]—in short, members of the administrative and technical staff of at least certain foreign State-run establishments in the territory of the

[99] See eg *Sabeh El Leil v France* (n. 14), para. 60.

[100] See the word 'or' after Art. 11(2)(*e*) UNCSI.

[101] Recall section 3.2(A).

[102] See section 4.2(B).

[103] Recall section 3.2(A).

[104] ILC commentary, draft art. 11, para. 9. Draft art. 11(2)(*a*) applied in addition to all '[o]fficials of established accreditation', *viz* diplomatic agents and consular officers, groups now treated in Art. 11(2)(*b*)(i) and (ii) UNCSI respectively.

forum State.[105] Whether the replacement of the words 'closely related to the exercise of governmental authority' with the phrase 'in the exercise of governmental authority' has the effect of narrowing the field remains at present an open question.

Two judgments of the Grand Chamber of the ECtHR evidence a restrictive approach to the interpretation and application of Article 11(2)(*a*) of the Convention. The 2011 case of *Sabeh El Leil v France* centred on the termination of employment of the head accountant at the Kuwaiti embassy in Paris, a matter held by the French courts to be one concerning which Kuwait was entitled to rely on immunity from suit. The Grand Chamber, in seeking to ascertain whether the limitation placed by the French courts on the applicant's right of access to a court as guaranteed by Article 6(1) ECHR was proportionate, described the customary rule reflected in Article 11(2)(*a*) of the Convention as 'clearly irrelevant' on the facts, in that the applicant, recruited as an accountant, 'was not employed to perform any particular duties in the exercise of governmental authority'.[106] Similarly, in *Cudak v Lithuania* the previous year, the Grand Chamber, seemingly oblivious to the fact that the wording of the ILC's draft article 11(2)(*a*) differs from that of Article 11(2)(*a*) of the Convention, held, in reliance on the former but in an apparent departure from the ILC commentary on it, that a Lithuanian switchboard operator employed by the Polish embassy in Vilnius did not perform 'any particular functions closely related to the exercise of governmental authority'.[107] The Court observed that it had not been shown that the applicant's main duties—namely 'recording international conversations, typing, sending and receiving faxes, photocopying documents, providing information and assisting with the organisation of certain events'—'could objectively have been related to the sovereign interests of the Polish Government'.[108]

A restrictive approach to the interpretation and application of what became Article 11(2)(*a*) of the Convention was also taken, for what it is worth, by the Advocate-General to the French Court of Cassation in *X v Saudi School in Paris and Kingdom of Saudi Arabia*.[109] The case involved an Egyptian national hired by the Kingdom of Saudi Arabia as a language teacher at the Saudi school in Paris who, having later acquired French nationality by marriage, sued for the right to affiliate to the French national insurance body and for damages in respect of loss resulting from her non-affiliation. The Advocate-General—basing his reasoning on the Ad Hoc Committee's 2003 text of draft article 11(2)(*a*), which is identical to the text of Article 11(2)(*a*) of the Convention, as 'the final state of public international law on the matter'—'propose[d] that the Court of Cassation should apply the criteria contained in Article 11(2)(*a*) of the Draft Articles and conclude that the teaching activity of the claimant was not such that she was recruited to perform particular functions in the exercise of governmental authority'.[110]

[105] See, in this regard, Third report Ogiso, 14, para. 3.

[106] *Sabeh El Leil v France* (n. 14), para. 61.

[107] *Cudak v Lithuania* (n. 14), para. 69.

[108] *Cudak v Lithuania* (n. 14), para. 70. The Court added, seemingly ignoring the words 'has been recruited to perform' in Art. 11(2)(*a*) UNCSI, that although 'the schedule to the employment contract stated that the applicant could have been called upon to do other work at the request of the head of mission', it did not appear 'that she actually performed any functions related to the exercise of sovereignty by the Polish State'.

[109] See n. 38.

[110] *X v Saudi School in Paris and Kingdom of Saudi Arabia* (n. 38), 165. In the event, the Court, although dismissing Saudi Arabia's claim to immunity from suit, reasoned instead, at 166, that the conduct of the Saudi

In the final analysis, the text of Article 11(2)(*a*) of the Convention, with its reference to 'particular functions in the exercise of governmental authority', suggests that a restrictive approach to the interpretation and application of the provision which focuses on the character of the duties that the employee was recruited to perform, as distinct from the setting or context of the employment, is more appropriate. This conclusion is supported by recourse to the drafting history of the provision, which reveals successive attempts to narrow the scope of this exception to the exception to immunity in respect of employment contracts.[111]

B. *Employee a diplomatic agent, consular officer, etc*

Article 11(2)(*b*), sub-subparagraphs (i) to (iv), which by and large reflect State practice, have the effect of maintaining a foreign State's immunity from proceedings in relation to an employment contract for work to be performed in whole or in part in the forum State where the employee is, respectively, a diplomatic agent, as defined in the VCDR; a consular officer, as defined in the VCCR; a member of the diplomatic staff of a permanent mission to an international organization or of a special mission, or has been recruited to represent a State at an international conference; or any other person enjoying diplomatic immunity. Where at the time the proceedings are instituted the employee is not a national of the employer State (in which case, unless the employee is permanently resident in the forum State, the employer State will retain its immunity by simple virtue of Article 11(2)(*e*) of the Convention), Article 11(2)(*b*) ought logically to be the first port of call in any claim which centres on a contract for the employment of an individual by an embassy, consular post, permanent mission to an international organization, special mission, or delegation to an international conference. It is only if an individual falls outside all the categories of employee enumerated in Article 11(2)(*b*), the *lex specialis*, that recourse by a foreign State employer to Article 11(2)(*a*), the *lex generalis*, need be contemplated. Putting it another way, what Article 11(2)(*b*) does in effect is to deem those employees referred to in sub-subparagraphs (i) to (iv) to have been recruited to perform particular functions in the exercise of governmental authority.

A diplomatic agent, as per Article 11(2)(*b*)(i) of the Convention, is defined in Article 1(*e*) VCDR as the head of a permanent diplomatic mission or a member of the diplomatic staff of such a mission, the latter being defined in Article 1(*d*) VCDR as a member of the staff of the mission having diplomatic rank. A consular officer, as per Article 11(2)(*b*)(ii) of the Convention, is defined in Article 1(1)(*d*) VCCR as 'any person, including the head of a consular post, entrusted in that capacity with the exercise of consular functions'; and, as acknowledged in Article 1(2) VCCR, there exist career consular officers and honorary consular officers. As for Article 11(2)(*b*)(iii) of the Convention, a member of the diplomatic staff of a permanent mission to an international organization is a member of the staff of the mission with diplomatic status,[112] while a member of the diplomatic staff of a special mission is a member of the staff of the special mission who has diplomatic status for the

school forming the subject-matter of the claim, namely the school's failure to notify the claimant's employment to the French national insurance body for the purposes of her affiliation, was an act *jure gestionis*.

[111] Recall section 3.2(A).

[112] See eg Art. 1(1)(28) Vienna Convention on the Representation of States in their Relations with International Organizations of a Universal Character, Vienna, 14 March 1975, UN doc. A/CONF.67/16 (not in force).

purposes of the special mission.[113] The further reference in Article 11(2)(*b*)(iii) to a person 'recruited to represent a State at an international conference' would appear, applying the *ejusdem generis* canon of construction and having regard to the *travaux préparatoires*,[114] to be to any such person enjoying diplomatic status.

As for the 'any other person[s] enjoying diplomatic immunity' within the meaning of Article 11(2)(*b*)(iv), it is here that the divergence between the proposal of the ILC Working Group and the eventual text of Article 11(2)(*b*)(iii) and (iv)[115] becomes problematic.

On its face, the expression 'any other person enjoying diplomatic immunity' in Article 11(2)(*b*)(iv) could be taken to refer to the categories of employee of a diplomatic mission covered by Article 37(2) and (3) VCDR, which accord diplomatic immunity to members of a mission's administrative and technical staff and to members of its service staff respectively, although only insofar as they are neither nationals nor permanent residents of the receiving State. Indeed, the expression might be thought further to embrace, first, those private servants of members of a diplomatic mission who are neither nationals nor permanent residents of the receiving State and who have been freely conceded diplomatic immunity by that State in accordance with Article 37(4) VCDR; and, secondly, those members of the mission's administrative and technical staff and service staff who, although nationals or permanent residents of the receiving State, have been freely conceded diplomatic immunity by that State in accordance with Article 38(2) VCDR.

But such an expansive reading would fly in the face of the *travaux préparatoires*. When confronted with the choice in 2002 of including in what became Article 11(2)(*b*)(i) either all the members of a diplomatic mission—that is, not only diplomatic agents but also administrative and technical staff and service staff—or only those members of the mission qualifying as diplomatic agents, the delegates to the Sixth Committee, it will be recalled,[116] opted unequivocally for the second, narrower alternative so as to keep to a minimum the range of employment proceedings involving nationals or permanent residents of the forum State (and, indeed, of third States) in respect of which a foreign employer State would remain immune. In short, any reading of Article 11(2)(*b*)(iv) which encompassed the administrative and technical staff and service staff of a diplomatic mission would run plainly contrary to the rationale for the restrictive wording of Article 11(2)(*b*)(i). It will also be recalled, moreover, that the original proposal of the ILC Working Group, from which there is no evidence that the Ad Hoc Committee or the Sixth Committee intended to depart, was to preserve the employer State's immunity from proceedings in respect of contracts for the employment of '[o]ther persons enjoying diplomatic immunity, such as persons recruited to represent a State in international conferences',[117] the clear intention being to limit the residual category of employees in

[113] See eg Art. 1(*b*) Convention on Special Missions, New York, 8 December 1969, 1400 UNTS 231 (CSM).

[114] Recall from section 3.2(B) that the proposal of the ILC Working Group in 1999, which the Ad Hoc Committee took up, albeit in modified form, in 2002, was for the retention of the employer State's immunity in respect of contracts for the employment of '(*b*) Diplomatic staff of permanent missions to international organizations and of special missions; (*c*) Other persons enjoying diplomatic immunity, such as persons recruited to represent a State in international conferences.' See Report ILC Working Group, 167, para. 105.

[115] Recall section 3.2(B).

[116] See section 3.2(B).

[117] 1999 report ILC Working Group, 167, para. 105.

what became Article 11(2)(*b*)(iv) to miscellaneous persons of diplomatic status not already mentioned in Article 11(2)(*b*).

A construction limiting Article 11(2)(*b*)(iv) to miscellaneous, not aforementioned employees of diplomatic status is also suggested by the second sentence of the second paragraph of the understanding with respect to Article 11 annexed to the Convention,[118] which, forming as it does an integral part of the text of the Convention,[119] constitutes an element of the context in which Article 11(2)(*b*)(iv) is to be interpreted.[120] This sentence recalls that, pursuant to Article 38 VCDR and Article 71 VCCR respectively, the receiving State 'has a duty to exercise its jurisdiction in such a manner as not to interfere unduly with the performance of the functions of the [diplomatic] mission or the consular post'. The jurisdiction referred to is the receiving State's jurisdiction over, first, those non-diplomatic members of the staff of a diplomatic mission, as well as private servants, who are nationals of or permanently resident in the receiving State, as mentioned in Article 38(2) VCDR; and, secondly, those non-consular members of a consular post who are nationals of or permanently resident in the receiving State, as mentioned in Article 71(2) VCCR. In other words, the second sentence of the second paragraph of the understanding strongly suggests that, by virtue of Article 11, the courts of the receiving State are not barred—subject, that is, to any other relevant provision of Article 11(2)(*b*)—from entertaining employment proceedings brought against a foreign employer State by nationals or permanent residents of the receiving State employed as other than diplomatic agents or the equivalent or consular officers.

In conclusion, Article 11(2)(*b*)(iv) applies only to miscellaneous employees of diplomatic status not previously listed in Article 11(2)(*b*).

In practice, it is highly probable that the nationality exception in Article 11(2)(*e*) to the contract-of-employment exception to State immunity will mean that Article 11(2)(*b*) is rarely determinative of a foreign employer State's immunity from suit insofar as the latter provision applies, via sub-subparagraphs (i), (iii), and (iv), to persons of diplomatic status.[121] Article 11(2)(*b*) may stand more chance of making a difference in the consular context, as per sub-subparagraph (ii), although in practice only in relation to honorary consular officers, who are likely to be permanently resident in, and perhaps nationals of, the forum State.

C. Subject-matter of proceedings recruitment, renewal of employment, or reinstatement

Article 11(2)(*c*) excludes from the scope of Article 11(1) proceedings against a foreign State the subject-matter of which is the recruitment, renewal of employment, or reinstatement of an individual. The ILC commentary to Article 11(2)(*c*)'s forerunner, draft article 11(2)(*b*), explains that the exclusion in relation to recruitment is 'designed to confirm the existing practice of States in support of the rule of immunity in the exercise of the discretionary power of appointment or non-appointment by the State of an individual

[118] See section 4.3.

[119] See Art. 25 UNCSI.

[120] See Art. 31(1) and (2) VCLT.

[121] See, in this regard, Art. 8(1) VCDR ('Members of the diplomatic staff of a mission should in principle be of the nationality of the sending State.') and Art. 10(1) CSM ('The representatives of the sending State in the special mission and the members of its diplomatic staff should in principle be of the nationality of the sending State.')

to any official post or employment position'.[122] (The obvious might also be noted, namely that no contract of employment will exist in the first place where an individual has not been appointed to a post or position.) As the text of the provision makes clear, subparagraph (*c*) of Article 11(2) also covers 'cases where the employee seeks the renewal of his employment or reinstatement after untimely termination of his engagement'.[123]

The ILC commentary suggests that the exception to non-immunity where the subject-matter of the proceedings is recruitment, renewal of employment, or reinstatement has no application to claims against a foreign employer State for such damages as may be available for its breach of any legal obligation to recruit or to renew employment or for wrongful dismissal or other termination of employment by it.[124] On this reading, Article 11(2)(*c*) serves to bar only proceedings by which claimants seek to compel foreign States to appoint them, to renew their employment, or to reinstate them. While this construction is not apparent on the face of the sub-subparagraph itself, it is supported by the provision's context, in that the following sub-subparagraph, Article 11(2)(*d*), deals with cases where the subject-matter of the proceedings is the dismissal or other termination of employment of an individual. It is also confirmed by the *travaux préparatoires*, insofar as the ILC deliberately replaced the words 'the proceeding relates to' provisionally adopted on first reading with the words 'the subject of the proceeding is' (which later became 'the subject-matter of the proceeding is') 'to make it clear that the scope of the exception is restricted to the specific acts which are referred to in the subparagraph and which are legitimately within the discretionary power of the employer State'.[125] The reading suggested by the ILC commentary was effectively endorsed by the Grand Chamber of the ECtHR in *Cudak v Lithuania*, a case centring on the allegedly wrongful dismissal of an embassy employee, where the Court necessarily implied that Article 11(2)(*c*) does not apply to proceedings in respect of dismissal.[126] It is also supported by the only national legislation to date in implementation of the Convention.[127]

That at least the appointment aspect of what became Article 11(2)(*c*) of the Convention is consonant with customary international law was affirmed in 2001 by the Grand Chamber of the ECtHR in *Fogarty v United Kingdom*.[128] The applicant, whose claim in the UK courts alleged that her non-appointment by the US embassy in London was a result of sex discrimination, argued that section 16(1)(*a*) SIA (UK)'s upholding of State immunity in all proceedings concerning the employment of a member of a diplomatic mission represented a violation by the UK of the right of access to a court secured to her by Article 6(1) ECHR. In concluding that section 16(1)(*a*) SIA (UK), which was held to pursue a legitimate aim, constituted a proportionate restriction on the applicant's right of access to a court, the Grand Chamber—having already found that 'it cannot be said that the United Kingdom . . . falls outside any currently accepted international standards'[129]—stated by way of further observation:

[122] ILC commentary, draft art. 11, para. 10.

[123] ILC commentary, draft art. 11, para. 10.

[124] See ILC commentary, draft art. 11, para. 10. A fortiori it does not apply to claims for the recovery of unpaid salary or wages, as made clear in 1999 report ILC Working Group, 166, para. 101.

[125] ILC commentary, draft art. 11, para. 10.

[126] See *Cudak v Lithuania* (n. 14), para. 69 cross-referenced with para. 72.

[127] See Art. 9(2)(iii) ACJJFS (Jpn).

[128] *Fogarty v United Kingdom*, 123 ILR 53 (ECtHR (GC) 2001).

[129] *Fogarty v United Kingdom* (n. 128), 65, para. 37.

[T]he proceedings which the applicant wished to bring did not concern the contractual rights of a current embassy employee, but instead related to alleged discrimination in the recruitment process. Questions relating to the recruitment of staff to missions and embassies may by their very nature involve sensitive and confidential issues, related, *inter alia,* to the diplomatic and organisational policy of a foreign State. The Court is not aware of any trend in international law towards a relaxation of the rule of State immunity as regards issues of recruitment to foreign missions. In this respect, the Court notes that it appears clearly from the materials referred to above [*viz* draft article 11 and the ILC's commentary thereto] that the International Law Commission did not intend to exclude the application of State immunity where the subject of proceedings was recruitment, including recruitment to a diplomatic mission.[130]

The general reference in the final sentence of the Grand Chamber's dictum to 'recruitment', of which recruitment to a diplomatic mission is expressed to be only one example, is in line not only with the exception to draft article 11(1) embodied in draft article 11(2)(*b*) but, more importantly, with the eventual exception to Article 11(1) of the Convention embodied in Article 11(2)(*c*), which is not limited in its application to employment by a foreign State's diplomatic mission, consular post, or the like.

D. Subject-matter of proceedings dismissal or termination of employment

Article 11(2)(*d*) exempts from Article 11(1)'s contract-of-employment exception to immunity situations where 'the subject-matter of the proceeding is the dismissal or termination of employment of an individual and, as determined by the head of State, the head of Government or the Minister for Foreign Affairs of the employer State, such a proceeding would interfere with the security interests of that State'. While Article 11(2)(*c*) does nothing to bar claims against a foreign employer State for any damages that may be available for wrongful dismissal or other termination of employment by it, the barring of a subset of such claims is the very essence of Article 11(2)(*d*).[131]

The first paragraph of the understanding with respect to Article 11 annexed to the Convention relates specifically to Article 11(2)(*d*). It reads:

The reference in article 11, paragraph 2(*d*), to the 'security interests' of the employer State is intended primarily to address matters of national security and the security of diplomatic missions and consular posts.

This limb of the understanding is intended to shape the exercise by the foreign employer State's head of State, head of government, or minister for foreign affairs of his or her discretion to determine, as per Article 11(2)(*d*), and to notify the court that given proceedings in relation to the dismissal or termination of employment of an employee of that State would interfere with the State's security interests. Whether or not it will make a difference remains to be seen. The fact remains, moreover, that the determination

[130] *Fogarty v United Kingdom* (n. 128), 65–6, para. 38. See also the joint concurring opinion of Judges Calflisch, Costa, and Vajić, at 67: 'The selection of a State's diplomatic and consular staff must be dictated by that State's interests, laws and procedures. It is inconceivable that a State, when appointing those who will represent it abroad—including clerical staff—would have to submit to the standards set by the laws and procedures of another State, in particular those of their host country. Accordingly, when selecting its foreign service officers, the first State is evidently acting within its public authority, *jure imperii,* and, in so doing, is covered by sovereign immunity.'

[131] But *cf,* curiously, Art. 11(2)(iv) ACJJFS (Jpn), explicitly excluding actions or petitions seeking compensation from the scope of the relevant exception to the contract-of-employment exception to immunity from proceedings.

whether or not proceedings whose subject-matter is the dismissal or termination of employment of a foreign-State employee would interfere with the security interests of the employer State is, in accordance with Article 11(2)(*d*), for that State—via its head of State, head of government, or minister for foreign affairs—and that State alone to determine. It is not a question for the court, for which Article 11(2)(*d*) envisages that the employer State's executive determination will be conclusive.[132] So, for example, in *Sabeh El Leil v France*, the Grand Chamber of the ECtHR, applying the rule embodied in Article 11(2)(*d*) of the Convention in its perceived quality as customary international law, and holding the rule not to apply to the proceedings before the Court of Appeal of Paris which the applicant argued violated her right of access to a court, reasoned:

> [I]t has not been established that there was any risk of interference with the security interests of the State: the judgment of the Paris Court of Appeal makes no reference to any claim by the State of Kuwait that the head of State, the head of Government or the Minister for Foreign Affairs (the authorities enumerated in that provision), were of the opinion that such a risk existed.[133]

Article 11(2)(*d*) has been criticized for 'grant[ing] to the defendant employer State a broad discretion to characterize any unfair dismissal claim as one which interferes with its security interests and so [to] remove the matter from the forum State's jurisdiction'.[134] Whether the exception to non-immunity is used this way obviously remains to be seen.

E. Employee a national of employer State, without permanent residence in forum State, when proceedings instituted

Article 11(2)(*e*) serves to preserve the immunity of a foreign State from proceedings concerning a contract of employment in cases where the employee is a national of the employer State when the proceedings are instituted, unless at that time the employee is permanently resident in the forum State. The provision is seemingly as applicable to cases of dual or multiple nationality as it is to the more common situation of single nationality.

The nationality exception to a foreign State's amenability to suit in respect of contracts of employment, which finds echoes in one form or another not only in Article 5(2)(*a*) ECSI but also in the practice of many States, is justified in the ILC commentary on the ground that '[r]emedies and access to courts exist in the employer State'.[135] This too readily assumes, however, that either the employment law of the employer State will apply extraterritorially[136] or, as is highly unlikely, that the courts of the employer State

[132] As a consequence, nothing is to be gained in the context of Art. 11(2)(*d*) UNCSI by considering the previous practice of national courts in relation to proceedings against a foreign State employer for wrongful dismissal or other termination of employment in circumstances where it is alleged that the proceedings would jeopardize the security interests of that State.

[133] *Sabeh El Leil v France* (n. 14), para. 61.

[134] R. Garnett, 'The Precarious Position of Embassy and Consular Employees in the United Kingdom' (2005) 54 *ICLQ* 705, 717. See also I. Pingel, 'Observations sur la Convention du 17 janvier 2005 sur les immunités juridictionelles des Etats et de leurs biens' (2005) 132 *JDI* 1045, 1050–1.

[135] ILC commentary, draft art. 11, para. 12.

[136] For a graphic illustration of how the combination of State immunity and the strictly territorial application of national employment law can leave a foreign-State employee of the employee State's nationality without an employment claim in either State, see *Bryant v Foreign and Commonwealth Office*, Case No. EAT/174/02/RN, Judgment, Employment Appeal Tribunal (UK), 10 March 2003 (UK (EAT) 2003). The claimant, a UK national employed by the British embassy in Rome, had no claim in any UK court under the UK's Employment Rights Act, Equal Pay Act, or Sex Discrimination Act, none of which had extraterritorial application on the facts of her case.

will sanction the application of foreign employment law; and while the situation may be more promising as regards contractual claims,[137] this cannot be taken for granted either. Moreover, there exist States in which the government is not amenable to suit in any form. As for the caveat relating to permanent residence, this is likely to help only locally-recruited nationals of the foreign employer State, since it is improbable in practice that persons permitted to reside in the forum State on the basis, and usually on the condition, of their employment by their State of nationality will be granted indefinite leave to remain.[138] And while the same criticisms could be levelled at other exceptions to the non-immunity provided for in Article 11(1), persons not of the employer State's nationality who find their claims barred in the forum State by Article 11(2) will at least have the theoretical possibility of recourse to an inter-State claim in diplomatic protection.[139]

F. Employer State and employee otherwise agreeing in writing

Under Article 11(2)(*f*), the contract-of-employment exception to immunity will not apply where the employer State and the employee have otherwise agreed in writing. The Explanatory Report on the ECSI explains that the analogous Article 5(2)(*c*) ECSI 'enables a Contracting State to invoke immunity where the contract of employment contains a clause in writing providing for the settlement of disputes by a court other than that of the State of the forum, for example a court of the employing State or an arbitral tribunal'.[140] But the ability to opt out of Article 11(1) by way of Article 11(2)(*f*) UNCSI is itself 'subject to any considerations of public policy conferring on the courts of the State of the forum exclusive jurisdiction by reason of the subject-matter of the proceeding'. The Explanatory Report on the ECSI elaborates on the equivalent provision in Article 5(2)(*c*) ECSI as follows:

[137] It may be that the contract of employment was concluded in the territory of the employer State, that the employer State's contract law can apply to contracts concluded abroad or that the employer State's courts sanction the application of foreign contract law. The last enabled the claimant in *Bryant v Foreign and Commonwealth Office* (n. 136) to proceed with a claim for breach of contract in the English courts.

[138] See eg the facts of *X v Morocco*, ILDC 548 (NL 2007) (Nth (The Hague CA) 2007), in which a Moroccan recruited in Morocco as a driver for the Moroccan consulate-general in Rotterdam was not a permanent resident of the Netherlands, despite having worked there from 1986 to 1993 and from 1994 to 2005.

[139] Nor would the employee's change of nationality so as to facilitate a claim against the employer State by the new State of nationality be to any avail, given the customary international rules reflected in paras 1–3 of Art. 5 ('Continuous nationality of a natural person') Articles on Diplomatic Protection, UN doc. A/RES/62/67, Annex, 8 January 2008. The possibility of a claim in diplomatic protection in cases of dual or multiple nationality will depend on the application of the customary rules codified in Arts 6 and 7 Articles on Diplomatic Protection.

[140] Expl. Rep. ECSI, para. 30. For its part, ILC commentary, draft art. 11, para. 13, elaborates that the exclusion of non-immunity embodied in what is now Art. 11(2)(*f*) UNCSI 'provides for the freedom of contract, including the choice of law and the possibility of a chosen forum or *forum prorogatum*'. The statement is, with respect, odd. First, in the words of Art. 7(2) UNCSI, '[a]greement by a State for the application of the law of another State shall not be interpreted as consent to the exercise of jurisdiction by the courts of that other State'. That is, a choice of law clause in a contract of employment would not amount, for the purposes of Art. 11(2)(*f*) UNCSI, to an agreement between the employer State and the employee that the former should not be subject to the jurisdiction of the courts of the forum State in the event of a dispute between the parties. As for *forum prorogatum*, it is hard to see how this might be agreed on in advance in writing, although perhaps some appropriate formula could be found.

[Article 5(2)(c)'s opt-out] clause would not have the effect of making the employing State immune from the jurisdiction of the State of the forum where that State's law on employment confers exclusive jurisdiction on its own courts.[141]

The Report adds that '[j]urisdiction is not exclusive for this purpose if resort may be had to arbitration'.[142]

4.3 Second paragraph of understanding

The second paragraph of the understanding with respect to Article 11 annexed to the Convention has no intended[143] bearing on the interpretation and application of any of the article's provisions.[144] Its respective sentences were included merely as political sops to States not altogether happy with, variously, the principle or precise formulation of Article 11(2)(*b*).

The first sentence, which, recalling Article 41 VCDR and Article 55 VCCR, emphasizes that diplomatic agents and consular officers respectively 'have the duty to respect the laws and regulations, including the labour laws, of the host country', is somewhat curious, in that it is surely the sending State as employer, rather than the diplomatic or consular employee, which stands in need of reminding of its duty to abide by the labour laws of the receiving State. It can only be assumed that the diplomatic agents and consular officers alluded to by way of reference to Article 41 VCDR and Article 55 VCCR are those with line-management responsibility for more junior members of the diplomatic or consular staff, in respect of whose contracts of employment (like those of their superiors) the sending State remains immune from suit in the courts of the receiving State.

The second sentence of the second paragraph of the understanding is just as odd. This recalls that, pursuant to Article 38 VCDR and Article 71 VCCR respectively, the receiving State 'has a duty to exercise its jurisdiction [over those non-diplomatic members of the staff of the mission and private servants and those non-consular members of the staff of the post who are nationals of or permanently resident in the receiving State] in such a manner as not to interfere unduly with the performance of the functions of the [diplomatic] mission or the consular post'. The idea would seem to be to urge that, in those circumstances where the foreign employer State is not immune from proceedings in the courts of the receiving State in respect of the employment of persons at or in connection with a diplomatic mission or consular post, such proceedings should be conducted in such a way as to interfere with the functions of the mission or post no more than is absolutely necessary for the determination of the merits of the case. But the reliance for this exhortation on Article 38 VCDR and Article 71 VCCR is strange. Taking Article 38 VCDR, the relevant provision is paragraph 2, which specifies that 'the receiving State must

141 Expl. Rep. ECSI, para. 30. ILC commentary, draft art. 11, para. 13, states less informatively: '[The freedom of contract recognized in Article 11(2)(*f*)] is not unlimited. It is subject to considerations of public policy or *ordre public* or, in some systems, "good moral and popular conscience" whereby exclusive jurisdiction is reserved for the courts of the forum State by reason of the subject-matter of the proceeding.'

142 Expl. Rep. ECSI, para. 30.

143 As for the probably unintended bearing of its second sentence on the interpretation of Art. 11(2)(*b*)(iv), recall section 4.2(B).

144 See also, as regards the second sentence, T. Treves, 'Some Peculiarities of the UN Convention on Jurisdictional Immunities of States and Their Property: a Footnote on the Codification Technique', in I. Buffard et al. (eds), *International Law between Universalism and Fragmentation: Festschrift in Honour of Gerhard Hafner* (Leiden: Martinus Nijhoff, 2008), 503, 504.

exercise its jurisdiction over those persons in such a manner as not to interfere unduly with the performance of the functions of the mission'. This stipulation clearly pertains to the relevant persons in their capacity as potential defendants to a civil or criminal action in the courts of the receiving State, not as potential claimants, let alone as claimants against the sending State. The same goes, *mutatis mutandis*, for Article 71 VCCR. But be that as it may. Despite the confusing references to Articles 38 VCDR and 71 VCCR, the gist of the sentence is apparent enough.

5. Evaluation

The labyrinthine technical complexity of Article 11 bespeaks the finely poised balance the provision seeks to strike between the sovereign discretion and interests of the foreign employer State and the domestic public policy of the State of the forum. The article's structural convolution need not, however, result in difficulty of application. The only provision liable to lead to the scratching of judicial heads is Article 11(2)(*a*), with its recourse to the unhelpfully general distinction between acts *jure imperii* and acts *jure gestionis*—precisely the unhelpfully general distinction on which the codification of restrictive State immunity represented by the Convention was intended to improve.

Article 12

Joanne Foakes and Roger O'Keefe

Article 12

Personal injuries and damage to property

Unless otherwise agreed between the States concerned, a State cannot invoke immunity from jurisdiction before a court of another State which is otherwise competent in a proceeding which relates to pecuniary compensation for death or injury to the person, or damage to or loss of tangible property, caused by an act or omission which is alleged to be attributable to the State, if the act or omission occurred in whole or in part in the territory of that other State and if the author of the act or omission was present in that territory at the time of the act or omission.

1. Introduction

Article 12 is the 'odd one out' among the exceptions to a State's immunity from foreign jurisdiction enumerated in Part III of the Convention. Whereas all the other exceptions reflect, at least in part, the non-sovereign character of the conduct forming the subject of proceedings, the exception provided for in Article 12 is justified solely by reference to the place where the impugned act or omission took place, namely in the territory of the forum State. What Article 12, often referred to for convenience as the 'territorial tort' exception or principle,[1] provides is that a State is not immune from foreign proceedings in which pecuniary compensation is claimed for death or personal injury or damage to or loss of tangible property caused by that State's act or omission 'if the act or omission occurred in whole or in part in the territory of that other State and if the author of the act or omission was present in that territory at the time of the act or omission'.

The most significant unanswered question in relation to Article 12 has nothing to do with the text of the provision itself. Rather, it is whether the Convention as a whole applies in respect of military activities or at least of the activities of a State's armed forces while present in the territory of another State. The answer, on which the effective scope of application of Article 12's 'territorial tort' exception depends, hangs on whether the alleged 'general understanding' among States that the Convention does not so apply can be substantiated.[2]

[1] See eg *Jurisdictional Immunities of the State (Germany v Italy: Greece intervening), Judgment*, International Court of Justice, 3 February 2012, paras 62–79, including the subsection's heading ('Italy's argument: the territorial tort principle').

[2] Recall the commentary to the 'general understandings'. So far two States parties to the Convention, Norway and Sweden, have declared on ratification their understanding that the Convention 'does not apply to military activities, including the activities of armed forces during an armed conflict, as those terms are understood in international humanitarian law, and activities undertaken by military forces of a State in the exercise of their official duties'. See UNCSI depositary notifications C.N.280.2006.TREATIES–2 (Norway: Ratification), 6 April 2006; C.N.912.2009.TREATIES–1 (Sweden: Ratification), 24 December 2009. On the other hand, the sole State party to have enacted legislation so far to implement the Convention, namely Japan, has excluded neither military activities nor situations involving armed conflicts from the scope of application of either its statute as a whole or of the 'territorial tort' exception. See ACJJFS (Jpn).

2. Background

As far back as 1891, the Institut de Droit international proposed an exception to a State's immunity from foreign jurisdiction in proceedings relating to delictual and quasi-delictual acts committed by that State in the territory of the forum State.[3] But subsequent State practice in this regard has been 'neither uniform nor consistent'.[4]

The 'territorial tort' exception was initially recognized in the context of proceedings concerning personal injury occasioned by negligent driving for which the foreign State was answerable under local law. The justification advanced by continental courts for the exercise of jurisdiction over the foreign State in such cases was that the driving of a motor vehicle, including for governmental purposes, was by nature an act *jure gestionis*.[5] The first international legal embodiment of the exception, however, was and is not limited to this sort of unintentional, insurable tort or delict, being instead posited in general terms capable of application to intentional harm and even to harm inflicted in the exercise of sovereign authority, provided two territorial criteria are met. Article 11 ECSI, the wording of which borrows from Article 10(4) Convention on the Recognition and Enforcement of Foreign Judgments in Civil and Commercial Matters,[6] provides:

> A Contracting State cannot claim immunity from the jurisdiction of a court of another Contracting State in proceedings which relate to redress for injury to the person or damage to tangible property, if the facts which occasioned the injury or damage occurred in the territory of the State of the forum, and if the author of the injury or damage was present in that territory at the time when those facts occurred.[7]

The various national State immunity statutes, all bar one of which include an exception to the same effect,[8] similarly premise the exercise of jurisdiction over the foreign State not on the character of the impugned act but solely on some nexus with the territory of the forum State, usually[9] in the form of the place of commission of, or of the failure to perform, the relevant act. Indeed, the courts of two such legislating States have expressly

[3] See 'Projet de règlement international sur la compétence des tribunaux dans les procès contre les Etats, souverains ou chefs d'Etat étrangers' (Hamburg session, 11 September 1891), reproduced in Institut de Droit international, *Tableau général des résolutions (1873–1956)* (Basel: Karger, 1957), 14, art. 4(6).

[4] Fifth report Sucharitkul, 41, para. 76.

[5] See *Collision with Foreign Government-Owned Motor Car (Austria) Case*, 40 ILR 73 (Aut (SC) 1961); *Ciniglio v Indonesian Embassy and Compagnia di Assicurazioni Intercontinentali*, 65 ILR 268, 269 (Ita (Ex. Mag. Rome) 1966).

[6] Expl. Rep. ECSI, para. 47, referring to Convention on the Recognition and Enforcement of Foreign Judgments in Civil and Commercial Matters, The Hague, 1 February 1971, 1144 UNTS 249, Art. 10(4) of which provides that '[t]he court of the State of origin shall be considered to have jurisdiction for the purposes of this Convention . . . in the case of injuries to the person or damage to tangible property, if the facts which occasioned the damage occurred in the territory of the State of origin, and if the author of the injury or damage was present in that territory at the time when those facts occurred'.

[7] See also, along similar lines, art. III(F) ILA Draft Articles and art. III(F) ILA Revised Draft Articles.

[8] See s. 5 SIA (UK), enacted to give effect to Art. 11 ECSI; s. 6 FStIA (SA); s. 13 FStIA (Aus); s. 7 SIA (Sing); art. 2(*e*) IFSJAC (Arg); s. 5 FSIL (Isr). The odd statute out is the SIO (Pak).

[9] But *cf* s. 1605(*a*)(5) FSIA and s. 6 SIA (Can), requiring only that the harm the subject of the claim occur within the territory. The US courts, however, have construed s. 1605(*a*)(5) narrowly to require that both the harm and the causal act or omission occur in US territory. See *McKeel v Islamic Republic of Iran*, 81 ILR 543 (US (9th Cir.) 1983); *Persinger v Islamic Republic of Iran*, 90 ILR 586 (US (DC Cir.) 1984); *Frolova v Union of Soviet Socialist Republics*, 85 ILR 236, 246–7 (US (7th Cir.) 1985); *Amerada Hess Shipping Corporation v Argentine Republic*, 830 F.2d 421 (US (2nd Cir.) 1987). In Canada, the Court of Appeal of Quebec has taken the opposite view in relation to s. 6 SIA (Can). See *Hashemi v Islamic Republic of Iran*, 2012 QCCA 1449, para. 66 (Can (CA Quebec) 2012).

held that the 'territorial tort' exception as statutorily embodied is without regard to the *jure imperii/jure gestionis* distinction.[10]

At the same time, several of the statutes in question provide elsewhere that the statute does not apply to proceedings relating to anything done by or in relation to the armed forces of a State while present in the forum State and/or does not affect the application of legislation pertaining to visiting forces.[11] The former echoes Article 31 ECSI, which, in a savings clause of significance to the effective scope of application of Article 11 ECSI, states:

> Nothing in this Convention shall affect any immunities or privileges enjoyed by a Contracting State in respect of anything done or omitted to be done by, or in relation to, its armed forces when on the territory of another Contracting State.

That said, the fact that foreign armed forces present in the forum State's territory are not subject to the specific State immunity regimes in question cannot be taken necessarily to imply that these forces are immune from the jurisdiction of the forum State's courts in all circumstances.[12]

In some States without a statutory 'territorial tort' exception, the courts have declined to extend the exception to acts *jure imperii* committed in the territory of the forum State.[13] What is more, in the case of *McElhinney v Ireland*, decided ten years after the final adoption of the ILC's draft articles and three years before the adoption of the Convention, a Grand Chamber of the European Court of Human Rights—noting that, as it was, the recognition of a 'territorial tort' exception to a foreign State's immunity from jurisdiction was 'by no means universal'—declared that 'the present state of the development of international law' did not enable it to conclude that a State which accorded another State immunity from jurisdiction in proceedings in respect of personal

[10] See *Letelier v Republic of Chile*, 63 ILR 378, 386–7 (US (DDC) 1980) and *Schreiber v Canada (Attorney General)*, 2002 SCC 62, paras 32 and 35–6 (Can (SC) 2002). As for States without legislation, see *Prefecture of Voiotia v Federal Republic of Germany (Distomo Massacre Case)*, 129 ILR 513, 517–519 (Gre (CoC) 2002).

[11] See s. 16(2) SIA (UK), enacted to give effect to Art. 31 ESCI; s. 16 SIA (Can); s. 6 FStIA (Aus); s. 19(2)(*a*) SIA (Sing); s. 22 FSIL (Isr).

[12] This is particularly the case with regard to those statutory provisions which apparently exclude foreign armed forces only to the extent that they are covered by a status of forces agreement (SOFA). See eg s. 16 SIA (Can); s. 6 FStIA (Aus); s. 22 FSIL (Isr). Note, however, that in February 2012, in *Jurisdictional Immunities of the State* (n. 1), para. 78, the ICJ held that 'customary international law continues to require that a State be accorded immunity in proceedings for torts allegedly committed on the territory of another State by its armed forces and other organs of State in the course of conducting an armed conflict'. See section 4 for a fuller discussion.

[13] See *McElhinney v Williams and Her Majesty's Secretary of State for Northern Ireland*, 104 ILR 691, 703 (Ire (SC) 1995). In addition, as specifically regards the activities of foreign armed forces in the forum State's territory, see *McElhinney v Williams* (n. 13), 701; *FILT-CGIL Trento v United States of America*, 128 ILR 644 (Ita (CoC) 2000); *AA*, Up-13/99, 8 March 2001, paras 13–14 (Slo (CC) 2001); *Margellos v Federal Republic of Germany*, 129 ILR 525, 533 (Gre (Special SC) 2002); *Greek Citizens v Federal Republic of Germany (Distomo Massacre Case)*, 129 ILR 556, 561 (FRG (Fed. SC) 2003) (holding limited to military action in wartime). For what it is worth, one might also note that the draft Inter-American Convention on Jurisdictional Immunity of States contains no exception to immunity from jurisdiction in respect of proceedings for death or personal injury, or damage to or loss of tangible property, caused by an act or omission in the forum State. It does, however, contain an idiosyncratic provision, Art. 6(*e*), according to which a State may not invoke immunity from foreign jurisdiction 'in proceedings for losses and damages on tort liabilities arising from the activities mentioned in Article 5, paragraph one', the latter in turn relating to 'trade or commercial activities undertaken in the State of the forum'.

injury caused by an act or omission *jure imperii* in the territory of the forum State fell 'outside any currently accepted international standards'.[14]

3. Drafting History

Pointing to what he suggested was 'an emerging trend' to restrict the availability to a State of immunity from foreign jurisdiction along such lines,[15] Special Rapporteur Sucharitkul proposed in his Fifth Report a draft article 14, entitled 'Personal injuries and damage to property', which provided:

> Unless otherwise agreed, a State is not immune from the jurisdiction of the courts of another State in respect of proceedings relating to injury to the person or death or damage to or loss of tangible property, if the act or omission which caused the injury in the State of the forum occurred in that territory, and the author of the injury or damage was present therein at the time of its occurrence.

The proposal provoked lively discussion within the ILC. Some members opposed the draft article on the grounds that 'it was premature to deal with the exceptions envisaged therein'[16] and that it 'might open a floodgate of litigation in cases where the alternative method of peaceful settlement of disputes by negotiations through diplomatic channels would be more suitable'.[17] Others, recalling the Institut's suggestion of 1891, countered that draft article 14 'proposed nothing new',[18] and pointed out that 'the territorial State did not always come to the assistance of injured private parties, particularly when other valid legal remedies were available apart from negotiations through diplomatic channels'.[19] Indeed, some members argued for an expansion of the scope of the proposed exception to a State's immunity from foreign jurisdiction to cover 'cases of transfrontier torts, including time bombs or letter-bombs', by deleting the requirement as to the presence in the forum State's territory of the author of the act or omission.[20]

In the event, draft article 14 was referred to the Drafting Committee,[21] to which the Special Rapporteur, on the basis of the discussions within the Commission, submitted a narrower and more prolix-revised proposal,[22] which the Drafting Committee proceeded

[14] *McElhinney v Ireland*, 123 ILR 73, 85, para. 38 (ECtHR (GC) 2001).

[15] Fifth report Sucharitkul, 45, para. 99.

[16] Report ILC, thirty-fifth session, 19, para. 88.

[17] Report ILC, thirty-fifth session, 19, para. 91.

[18] Report ILC, thirty-fifth session, 19, para. 88.

[19] Report ILC, thirty-fifth session, 19–20, para. 91.

[20] Report ILC, thirty-fifth session, 19, para. 90.

[21] See Report ILC, thirty-fifth session, 20, para. 94.

[22] See Report ILC, thirty-fifth session, 20, para. 96. The proposal (UN doc. A/CN.4/L.367), reproduced at fn. 59, provided:

'1. Unless otherwise mutually agreed between the States concerned, a State which, through one of its organs, or agencies or instrumentalities acting in the exercise of governmental authority, maintains an office, agency or establishment in another State or occupies premises therein, or engages therein in the transport of passengers or cargoes either by air or by rail or road, or by waterways, is considered to have consented to the exercise of jurisdiction by a court of that other State in a proceeding relating to compensation for death or injury to the person or damage to a loss of tangible property, if the act or omission which caused the injury or damage in the State of the forum occurred in that territory, and the person responsible for or contributing to that injury or damage was present therein at the time of its occurrence.

2. Paragraph 1 is without prejudice to the rights and duties of individuals in one State vis-à-vis another State which are specifically regulated by treaties, or other bilateral agreements, or regional arrangements, or international conventions specifying or limiting the extent of liabilities or compensation.'

effectively to ignore. The Drafting Committee's only additions of substance to the version of draft article 14 originally put forward in the Special Rapporteur's Fifth Report were, first, to clarify that the act or omission could occur 'in whole or in part' in the territory of the forum State[23] and, secondly, to qualify the reference to the act or omission with the words 'which is alleged to be attributable to the State'.[24] In relation to the second of these amendments, the Chairman of the Drafting Committee clarified that, '[o]f course, the question of attribution was distinct from that of immunity, in that it related to merits, and would be determined in due course in accordance with local law'.[25] Although several members of the Commission, including the Chairman of the Drafting Committee, continued to oppose the draft article,[26] it was provisionally adopted on first reading, as amended by the Drafting Committee, in 1984.[27] After 'certain drafting adjustments . . . to ensure consistency in terminology and substance and correspondence between the draft articles and between the different language versions',[28] the draft article, by now renumbered 13, was adopted along with the rest of the draft articles on first reading in 1986 as follows:

> Unless otherwise agreed between the States concerned, the immunity of a State cannot be invoked before a court of another State which is otherwise competent in a proceeding which relates to compensation for death or injury to the person or damage to or loss of tangible property if the act or omission which is alleged to be attributable to the State and which caused the death, injury or damage occurred in whole or in part in the territory of the State of the forum and if the author of the act or omission was present in that territory at the time of the act or omission.[29]

Along with the other draft articles adopted on first reading, draft article 13 was circulated among States for comment.

Although the USSR, the Byelorussian Soviet Socialist Republic and the German Democratic Republic all opposed draft article 13 in principle, the new Special Rapporteur, Motoo Ogiso, defended in his Preliminary Report a national court's exercise of jurisdiction in cases where an act or omission in the territory of the forum State which caused death, personal injury, or damage to or loss of tangible property was 'attributable to [a] foreign State in accordance with the municipal law of the forum State'.[30] He also agreed—doubting as he did whether the proviso could 'legitimately be viewed as a necessary criterion for exclusion of State immunity'[31]—with a suggestion by Australia, the Federal Republic of Germany, and Thailand, all of which were 'in favour of extending the scope of application of the draft article to transboundary injury or damage',[32] to delete from draft article 13 as adopted on first reading the requirement

[23] See summary record 1868th ILC meeting, *YILC 1984*, vol. I, 321, 324, para. 28, where the Chairman of the Drafting Committee describes the addition as deriving from the Special Rapporteur's revised proposal. But, at least as reproduced in Report of the ILC, thirty-fifth session, 20, para. 96, fn. 59, the revised proposal contained nothing to this effect.

[24] Summary record 1868th ILC meeting (n. 23), 324, para. 28.

[25] Summary record 1868th ILC meeting (n. 23), 324, para. 28.

[26] Summary record 1868th ILC meeting (n. 23), 325, paras 30–36.

[27] Summary record 1868th ILC meeting (n. 23), 325, para. 37. The text of the draft article as provisionally adopted is reproduced at summary record 1868th ILC meeting (n. 23), 324, para. 25.

[28] Report ILC, thirty-eighth session, 8, para. 18.

[29] Report ILC, thirty-eighth session, 10.

[30] Preliminary report Ogiso, 111, para. 140.

[31] Preliminary report Ogiso, 111, para. 141.

[32] Preliminary report Ogiso, 111, para. 137.

that the author of the relevant act or omission be present in the territory of the forum State at the time of the act or omission.[33] In his Second Report, however, Special Rapporteur Ogiso clarified that, although he supported the deletion of the words in question, this would not, in his view, make the exception to State immunity provided for in draft article 13 'applicable to tort[s] committed abroad or to other transboundary injurious acts', since there would remain the requirement that the act or omission occur in whole or in part in the territory of the forum State.[34] He also reiterated his understanding that the question whether the act or omission was alleged to be 'attributable' to the State concerned was not referable to the law of State responsibility.[35] Finally, when introducing within the ILC the discussion of draft article 13 on second reading, the Special Rapporteur 'suggested that the Commission might, for the sake of compromise, consider narrowing the scope of the article to cover only traffic accidents'.[36]

The ILC's discussion of draft article 13 on second reading revealed what was by then a predictable division between those members opposed to the provision in its entirety and those in favour of it. On balance, although some 'stressed that the [draft] article required substantial redrafting',[37] 'the views expressed by members generally indicated a preference [for] retain[ing] the text of the article as adopted on first reading'.[38] In particular, and although the criticism missed the point, '[t]he deletion of the second territorial criterion, as proposed by the Special Rapporteur, was not considered appropriate, since transboundary damage normally gave rise to international disputes which had to be settled by recourse to international law and not to the law applicable in a forum State'.[39] On the question of limiting draft article 13 to traffic accidents, the Commission was divided, with some members remarking that 'the general practice of settlement through insurance would diminish the practical need' for an exception to immunity from jurisdiction restricted in this way,[40] although it was further noted that insurance 'did not always cover the full risk involved'.[41] In the light of all these views, the Special Rapporteur submitted to the Commission for final consideration the text of draft article 13 as adopted on first reading, 'without change'.[42]

On final consideration, only a single ILC member favoured deleting draft article 13 as a whole.[43] The text was referred once more to the Drafting Committee, which, in addition to rewording the provision's principal clause in line with what had emerged as the standard formulation employed in Part III of the Convention ('a State may not invoke'), inserted the adjective 'pecuniary' before 'compensation', *ex abundante cautela*.[44] The provision, renumbered draft article 12, was finally adopted in this form on second reading, and passed unaltered into the eventual Convention as Article 12.

[33] For the suggestion and the Special Rapporteur's agreement, see Preliminary report Ogiso, 111, paras 137 and 141 respectively.
[34] Second report Ogiso, 65–6, para. 20.
[35] See Second report Ogiso, 66, para. 21.
[36] Report ILC, forty-first session, 111, para. 519.
[37] Report ILC, forty-first session, 111, para. 523.
[38] Report ILC, forty-first session, 111, para. 524.
[39] Report ILC, forty-first session, 111, para. 524.
[40] Report ILC, forty-first session, 111, para. 525.
[41] Third report Ogiso, 14.
[42] Third report Ogiso, 14.
[43] See Report ILC, forty-second session, 35, para. 187.
[44] See ILC commentary, draft art. 12, para. 10.

4. Key Points

4.1 Extrinsic limits on Article 12's scope of application

There are certain exclusions from Article 12's effective scope of application—'carve outs', as they are sometimes called—that are not apparent on the face of the provision. Article 3 of the Convention specifies a range of special immunity regimes under international law to which the Convention as a whole is without prejudice, namely diplomatic, consular, and cognate immunities; the immunity *ratione personae* of a head of State; and the immunities enjoyed by a State with respect to aircraft or space objects owned or operated by that State.[45] These exclusion clauses have particular significance in the context of Article 12, in accordance with which, were it not for Article 3, foreign diplomats or heads of State—both of them qualifying as the 'State' under Article 2(1)(*b*)(iv) of the Convention—would be personally amenable to civil proceedings in the receiving State in respect of any acts performed or omitted to be performed by them in their official capacity in the territory of that State which give rise to death or personal injury or damage to or loss of tangible property. The same would otherwise be the case as regards the amenability of a foreign State, in any of its relevant emanations, to proceedings in respect of death, personal injury, or property damage or loss caused by, for example, the negligent operation of an aircraft in the territory of the forum State. Article 3 ensures that Article 12 does not apply in relation to any and all such proceedings.

At the same time, it is crucial to recall what Article 3 does not exclude from the scope of the Convention.[46] In the field of diplomatic, consular, and cognate law, and in relation to the head of State, it does not exclude the amenability of the State sued as such or in the guise of its government or ministry for foreign affairs, as the case may be, to civil proceedings alleging its vicarious liability for death or personal injury or damage to or loss of tangible property caused by the acts or omissions in the territory of the forum State of its diplomats or head of State or alleging its tortious liability as the occupier of its diplomatic, consular, or cognate premises. None of these sorts of proceedings is barred by the special immunity regimes of diplomatic, consular, or cognate law or by the immunity *ratione personae* of a head of State.

The question left unanswered when it comes to exclusions from the scope of Article 12 not apparent on the provision's face is whether the Convention applies in respect of military activities or at least of the activities of foreign armed forces present in the territory of the forum State.[47] Should the purported 'general understanding' concerning such activities be established, this would clearly have the effect of removing proceedings relating to the latter from the purview of the 'territorial tort' exception in Article 12.

4.2 'Unless otherwise agreed between the States concerned'

Like most of the other exceptions to immunity from jurisdiction provided for in Part III of the Convention, but in contrast to Article 11 ECSI, the exception to a State's immunity from foreign proceedings embodied in Article 12 permits of derogation by mutual consent of the impleaded and forum States. A classic example of where the States

[45] Recall the commentary to Art. 3 UNCSI.
[46] Recall, again, the commentary to Art. 3 UNCSI.
[47] Recall the commentary to the 'general understandings'.

concerned might agree not to apply the 'territorial tort' exception in a given case or cases is where they have agreed to establish some form of international claims commission to adjudicate on or otherwise process compensation claims by private parties against one of the States in respect of death or personal injury or damage to or loss of tangible property caused by that State's act or omission in the territory of the other State.

4.3 'a court of another State which is otherwise competent'

The exception to immunity from jurisdiction provided for in Article 12 presupposes that the national court before which the claim against the foreign State is brought 'is otherwise competent' to adjudicate the claim. The same words appear in every other exception to immunity from jurisdiction enumerated in Part III of the Convention barring Article 10's commercial transaction exception, in which the same idea is conveyed by a different linguistic formula. Whether or not the court enjoys this underlying competence is a question for the domestic law of the forum State. It is, moreover, a question logically distinct from and precedent to the territorial preconditions to the internationally lawful exercise of that competence specified in Article 12.

4.4 'a proceeding which relates to pecuniary compensation for death or injury to the person, or damage to or loss of tangible property, caused by an act or omission'

A. Formal legal character of claim

Although the exception to a State's immunity from foreign proceedings specified in Article 12 is popularly referred to as the 'territorial tort' exception, the reference to tort derives not from Article 12 itself but from the much earlier and better known section 1605(*a*)(5) FSIA (US).[48] In the context of Article 12, any reference to tort—or, in the language of the civil law, delict—is merely for the sake of convenience, being intended as no more than shorthand for any proceedings, however formally characterized under the applicable municipal law, which relate to pecuniary compensation for death or personal injury or damage to or loss of tangible property allegedly caused by the respondent State's act or omission.

B. 'pecuniary compensation'

The exception to a State's immunity from foreign jurisdiction recognized in Article 12 applies only in respect of proceedings relating to 'pecuniary compensation'. This has several implications.

First, Article 12's restriction to proceedings relating to compensation makes it clear, *ex abundante cautela*, that the provision does not apply in respect of criminal proceedings against individual State representatives or, in jurisdictions where corporate criminal

[48] S. 1605(*a*)(5) FSIA (US) reads in relevant part: 'A foreign state shall not be immune from the jurisdiction of courts of the United States or of the States in any case . . . in which money damages are sought against a foreign state for personal injury or death, or damage to or loss of property, occurring in the United States and caused by the tortious act or omission of that foreign state or of any official or employee of that foreign state while acting within the scope of his office or employment . . . '. Prior to the enactment in 2008 of s. 5 FSIL (Isr) ('A foreign state shall not have immunity from jurisdiction in an action in tort where personal injury or damage to tangible property has occurred, provided the tort was committed in Israel.'), s. 1605(*a*)(5) FSIA (US) was the only national State immunity provision to specify the formal legal character of the claim against the State.

responsibility is recognized, against other emanations of a foreign State. That is, proceedings seeking only the imposition of a custodial sentence, a fine, forfeiture, or any other form of punitive sanction for the foreign State's occasioning of death or personal injury or damage to or loss of property within the forum State's territory do not fall within Article 12's exception to immunity from foreign jurisdiction. As it is, even leaving aside Article 12, there exists a 'general understanding' that the Convention as a whole does not relate to criminal proceedings.[49]

Whether, however, Article 12 permits civil proceedings against a foreign State to the extent that the claimant seeks, over and above purely compensatory damages, what are variously termed 'exemplary' or 'punitive' damages is not so clear. The more persuasive view, based on the drafters' choice of the term 'compensation' over 'damages', is that it does not. Either way, the judicial practice of those States that have given legislative effect to a 'territorial tort' exception to State immunity provides no guidance, since the respective formulations of the relevant provisions are crucially different.[50]

Secondly, the restriction of Article 12 to proceedings relating to compensation further means that the exception to a State's immunity from foreign jurisdiction embodied in the provision does not apply to the extent that the claimant seeks a non-compensatory remedy like restitution or a declaratory judgment.

Finally, Article 12's application only in respect of proceedings relating specifically to 'pecuniary' compensation means that, at least when it comes to Article 12, a State remains immune from foreign proceedings insofar as some non-pecuniary form of compensation, such as compensation in kind, is sought. The ILC commentary indicates that the word 'pecuniary' was added on second reading precisely to remove from the scope of Article 12 any proceedings in which compensation other than damages is claimed.[51]

C. 'for death or injury to the person, or damage to or loss of tangible property'

For the exception to immunity from jurisdiction specified in Article 12 to apply, the pecuniary compensation sought in the proceedings against the State must be for 'death or injury to the person' or for 'damage to or loss of tangible property'. Claims alleging, for example, damage to reputation, loss of amenity, interference with privacy, or economic loss not consequential upon death or personal injury or damage to or loss of tangible property do not fall within Article 12.[52] As a result, as far as Article 12 goes, a State remains immune from foreign proceedings alleging, for example, defamation, nuisance, misrepresentation, or interference with contractual rights, incorporeal hereditaments, or choses in action. At the same time, it is important to highlight that the ILC commentary may be misleading when it states, in relation specifically to injury to the person, that 'Article 12 does not cover cases where there is no physical damage'.[53] There is no clear

[49] Recall, again, the commentary to the 'general understandings'.

[50] S. 5 SIA (UK) refers simply to 'proceedings in respect of' death, personal injury, etc. See also, identically or closely analogously, s. 6 FStIA (SA); s. 13 FStIA (Aus); s. 6 SIA (Can); s. 7 SIA (Sing). S. 1605(*a*)(5) FSIA (US) refers to 'any case . . . in which money damages are sought . . . for' personal injury, death, etc. See also, not dissimilarly, art. 2(*e*) IFSJAC (Arg) ('[c]uando fueren demandados por daños y perjuicios').

[51] See ILC commentary, draft art. 12, para. 10.

[52] See ILC commentary, draft art. 12, para. 5.

[53] ILC commentary, draft art. 12, para. 5.

warrant for this assertion in the text of Article 12, which refers simply to 'injury to the person'.

If the pecuniary compensation sought in the proceedings against the State is indeed for death or injury to the person or for damage to or loss of tangible property, the particulars do not matter for the purposes of Article 12.[54] In the case of death, it is immaterial whether the claim constitutes the notionally surviving claim of the deceased or a claim by the deceased's dependents or, as regards those dependents, whether the claim is for loss of economic support, bereavement, funeral expenses, or the like. In the case of injury to the person, it is irrelevant whether the claim relates specifically to medical costs, pain and suffering, loss of earnings, or what have you, provided that the pecuniary compensation sought can be considered to be 'for injury to the person'.[55] The same goes, *mutatis mutandis*, for proceedings relating to compensation for damage to or loss of tangible property.[56]

Whether a claim for pecuniary compensation is considered to be one for 'injury to the person', a term not defined in the Convention, will probably depend on the applicable domestic law. In many jurisdictions, the development of a recognized psychiatric illness as a result of another's act or omission is deemed in and of itself to constitute injury to the person, while in other jurisdictions it may not be. Conversely, while in many jurisdictions mere pain and suffering or emotional distress not amounting to a recognized psychiatric condition are not compensable unless consequential upon some form of physical injury, other jurisdictions may class these things as injury to the person in their own right.[57] Article 12 does not on its face dictate such legal characterizations of fact. The same goes, *mutatis mutandis*, for whether the proceedings against the State relate to damage to or loss of 'tangible property'.

D. *'by an act or omission'*

Article 12 does not stipulate that the proceedings relate to the respondent State's allegedly negligent act or omission. As made clear in the ILC commentary, claims in respect of intentionally or recklessly inflicted harm are equally encompassed by the provision, as are claims based on a standard of strict or even absolute liability.[58]

Nor does the applicability of Article 12 depend on whether the impugned act was performed by the State, or the impugned omission not performed by it, *jure gestionis*—that is, otherwise than in the exercise of sovereign authority. Whereas all the other exceptions in Part III of the Convention to a State's immunity from foreign jurisdiction rest, wholly or partly, on the implicit notion that the State conduct the subject of the proceedings is the sort of thing a private party could do, the exception posited in Article 12 applies even in respect of conduct performed *jure imperii*, as emphasized in the ILC

[54] It should go without saying that whether any particular head of damages is open to the claimant in the first place is a question of domestic law. Art. 12, like the rest of the Convention, relates only to whether a court may exercise jurisdiction over a foreign State in relation to any substantive claim as may subsist.

[55] See also, as regards Art. 11 ECSI, Expl. Rep. ECSI, para. 48: 'Where there has been injury to the person or damage to property, the rule of non-immunity applies equally to any concomitant claims for non-material damage resulting from the same acts, provided of course that a claim for such damage lies under the applicable law (eg in respect of *pretium doloris*).'

[56] See Expl. Rep. ECSI, para. 48.

[57] See eg *Hashemi v Islamic Republic of Iran* (n. 9), paras 82–84.

[58] See ILC commentary, draft art. 12, paras 3, 4, and 8.

commentary[59] and highlighted by the International Court of Justice in *Jurisdictional Immunities of the State.*[60] The rationale for Article 12 is solely the *locus* of the impleaded State's act or omission.[61] To this extent, Article 12 is on all fours with the various national State immunity statutes.[62]

It is worth noting the misleading character of another, related sentence of the ILC commentary, which states that Article 12 'appears to be confined principally to insurable risks'.[63] The expression 'confined principally to' simply makes no sense. The injury[64] to the person or damage to tangible property encompassed by Article 12 is either confined to insurable risks or it is not. And it is perfectly clear from the text of the provision that it is not. Indeed, the relevant passage of the ILC commentary goes on to say precisely this. After continuing at length to the effect that Article 12 is 'mainly concerned with . . . traffic accidents, such as [those involving] moving vehicles, motor cycles, locomotives or speedboats'[65] (*viz* 'most areas of accidents involved in the transport of goods and passengers by rail, road, air or waterways'[66]), the commentary adds, abruptly:

> In addition, the scope of article 12 is wide enough to cover also intentional physical harm such as assault and battery, malicious damage to property, arson or even homicide, including political assassination.[67]

In short, while in practice most proceedings falling within the exception to a State's immunity from foreign jurisdiction specified in Article 12 might be expected to relate to 'accidents occurring routinely within the territory of the State of the forum' (in other words, insurable risks such as liability for traffic accidents and, as the ILC commentary overlooks, occupiers' liability), the scope of the provision is in no way confined to such mundane acts and omissions.

4.5 'which is alleged to be attributable to the State'

If a State is sued in respect of an act or omission, it ought to go without saying that the claimant alleges that State to be legally answerable under the applicable municipal law for

[59] See ILC commentary, draft art. 12, para. 8.

[60] See *Jurisdictional Immunities of the State* (n. 1), para. 64. In this regard, the Fifth Section of the ECtHR plainly took no account of Art. 12 of the Convention when it stated as follows in *Grosz v France*, application no. 14717/06, Decision on admissibility, 16 June 2009 (available only in French): 'L'immunité de juridiction des Etats est régie par le droit international coutumier, dont la codification a été réalisée par la Convention des Nations Unies du 2 décembre 2004 sur l'immunité juridictionnelle des Etats et de leurs biens. L'article 5 de cette Convention prévoit que «[u]n État jouit, pour lui-même et pour ses biens, de l'immunité de juridiction devant les tribunaux d'un autre État». Elle repose sur la distinction entre acte de souveraineté ou d'autorité (*acte jure imperii*) et acte de commerce ou de gestion (*acte jure gestionis*). Ainsi, sauf son consentement, un Etat ne peut être jugé par des juridictions nationales étrangères pour tout acte effectué dans l'exercice de son autorité souveraine.'

[61] See ILC commentary, draft art. 12, para. 8. See also J. Crawford, 'International Law and Foreign Sovereigns: Distinguishing Immune Transactions' (1983) 54 *BYIL* 75, 111.

[62] Recall, in this regard, *Letelier v Republic of Chile* (n. 10), 386–7, re s. 1605(*a*)(5) FSIA (US); *Schreiber v Canada (Attorney General)* (n. 10), paras 32 and 35–36, re s. 6 SIA (Can).

[63] ILC commentary, draft art. 12, para. 4.

[64] It might additionally be noted that the adjective 'physical', as inserted before the word 'injury' by the Special Rapporteur, is not found in Art. 12 of the Convention.

[65] ILC commentary, draft art. 12, para. 4.

[66] ILC commentary, draft art. 12, para. 4.

[67] ILC commentary, draft art. 12, para. 4, citation omitted. The reference to political assassination is to *Letelier v Republic of Chile* (n. 10).

the act or omission. That is, it should be taken as read when one of the emanations of a State cited in Article 2(1)(*b*) of the Convention is named as respondent to proceedings pertaining to a given act or omission that the claimant submits that any liability as may arise in respect of that act or omission can, in accordance with the relevant domestic law, be ascribed to whichever emanation of the State is named as respondent. This is no more than common sense. If the claimant does not allege the respondent to be liable for the act or omission, he or she would not have instituted proceedings against the latter to begin with. It is for this reason that neither Article 11 ECSI nor any of the corresponding national State immunity provisions refers, as Article 12 of the Convention unnecessarily refers, to proceedings in respect of an act or omission 'which is alleged to be attributable to the State'.[68] And in saying more than is necessary, the text of Article 12 ends up confusing matters.

The choice of the expression 'attributable to the State' is unfortunate, given the association of the terminology of 'attribution' with those rules of the international law of State responsibility codified in Chapter II ('Attribution of conduct to a State') of Part One of the ILC's Articles on Responsibility of States for Internationally Wrongful Acts. The misleading impression given by Article 12's reference to the attribution of the act or omission to the State is that the question is governed by the international law of State responsibility. As made clear, however, over the course of the provision's drafting,[69] whether or not the act or omission the subject of the foreign proceedings is, in the language of the provision, 'attributable' to the respondent State is a matter for the applicable municipal law.[70] In this context, the word 'attributable' reflects no more than the drafters' clumsy attempt at a generic term, not restricted in its application to any single national legal tradition, for what the common law would refer to as vicarious liability—that is, the liability of one natural or juridical person for the act or omission of another. This usage goes hand-in-hand with Article 12's later, again somewhat maladroit reference to 'the author of the act or omission'. Both are intended to take account of the likely distinction between, on the one hand, the individual State functionary who, as a matter of fact, performed or failed to perform the relevant act and, on the other, the State as such or the organ of government or the State agency, instrumentality, or other entity

[68] In a similar way, no provision of the ECSI, national legislation or, indeed, the Convention specifies, for example, that any commercial contract the subject of proceedings against a State under the 'commercial contract'/'commercial activity'/'commercial transaction' exception to immunity from jurisdiction be allegedly entered into by a person with the capacity to bind the State contractually. It is simply assumed, given that the claimant has instituted proceedings against the State on a contract between the two parties, that the former alleges the latter to be bound by that contract.

[69] Recall from section 2 the statement on first reading by the chairman of the ILC's Drafting Committee, summary record 1868th ILC meeting (n. 23), 324, para. 28, that 'the question of attribution . . . would be determined . . . in accordance with local law'; the reference on second reading by Special Rapporteur Ogiso, Preliminary report Ogiso, 111, para. 140, to acts or omissions 'attributable to [a] foreign State in accordance with the municipal law of the forum State'; and the latter's reiteration, Second report Ogiso, 66, para. 21, of his understanding that whether the act or omission was alleged to be 'attributable' to the State concerned was not referable to the law of State responsibility.

[70] It may well be, as is perhaps worth pointing out for the avoidance of doubt, that the applicable municipal law goes about answering this question by reference to the international rules on the attribution of conduct to a State. The point here is simply that whether, in municipal proceedings against a State in tort/delict or some other related branch of private law, a court applies the usual private law rules on the ascription of conduct to a natural or legal person or whether judicial recourse is had by way of *renvoi* to the international rules on the attribution of conduct to a State is a matter for the relevant municipal law, not for Art. 12 of the Convention.

which is named as respondent to the claim and to which, as a matter of municipal law, conduct engaged in by that functionary may be ascribed.[71]

4.6 'if the act or omission occurred in whole or in part in the territory of that other State and if the author of the act or omission was present in that territory at the time of the act or omission'

Article 12 imposes two cumulative territorial conditions on the availability of the exception to State immunity in respect of proceedings for pecuniary compensation for death or injury to the person, or damage to or loss of tangible property, caused by an act or omission alleged to be attributable to a foreign State. Not only must the act or omission have occurred in whole or in part in the territory of the forum State but, in addition, its 'author' must have been present in the territory of the forum State at the time. It is this necessary territorial nexus between, on the one hand, the impugned act or omission and its author and, on the other, the forum State that is the very gist of the 'territorial tort' exception.

According to the ILC commentary, the reference in Article 12 to the 'author' of the act or omission is to the individual representative of the State who actually does or does not do the relevant thing, as distinct from 'the State itself as a legal person'.[72] Putting it another way, the author of the act will not necessarily be the same as the respondent to the proceedings.[73] It may well be—and is most likely to be, given what is usually the deeper pocket of the legal person in comparison with the natural—that, while an individual representative of the State is the author of the impugned act or omission within the meaning of Article 12, the respondent to the proceedings is the State as such or its government or some ministry or department thereof, as vicariously liable or the equivalent for the acts and omissions of its officers and employees in accordance with such municipal legal principles as may apply.

With the exception of the phrase 'in whole or in part', Article 12's first stipulation, namely that the impugned act or omission have occurred in the territory of the forum State, corresponds to the sole territorial condition imposed by all bar two of the pre-Convention State immunity statutes.[74] With the same exception, it also corresponds to the first limb of the twofold territorial requirement specified in Article 11 ECSI, the different formulation of which probably does not import a substantive difference.[75] As for the extent to which the words 'or in part' widen the availability of the 'territorial tort' exception, this is circumscribed by Article 12's second requirement that the author of the act or omission be present at the time of that act or omission in the territory of the forum State. The ILC commentary elaborates on this further stipulation as follows:

[71] It might be noted that the posited distinction takes no account of the possibility that the 'State' named as respondent to the claim may well be, as per Art. 2(1)(*b*)(iv) of the Convention, the individual State functionary the 'author' of the act or omission—in other words, that no question of the 'attribution' of the act or omission to the respondent may in fact arise.

[72] ILC commentary, draft art. 12, para. 10.

[73] See, as regards Art. 11 ECSI, Expl. Rep. ECSI, para. 49.

[74] See s. 5 SIA (UK); s. 6 FStIA (SA); s. 13 FStIA (Aus); s. 7 SIA (Sing); art. 2(*g*) IFSJAC (Arg); s. 5 FSIL (Isr).

[75] The first territorial stipulation in Art. 11 ECSI is that 'the facts which occasioned the injury or damage occurred in the territory of the State of the forum'.

The second condition, namely the presence of the author of the act or omission causing the injury or damage within the territory of the State of the forum at the time of the act or omission, has been inserted to ensure the exclusion from the application of this article of cases of transboundary injuries or trans-frontier torts or damage, such as export of explosives, fireworks or dangerous substances which could explode or cause damage through negligence, inadvertence or accident. It is also clear that cases of shooting or firing across a boundary or of spill-over across the border of shelling as a result of an armed conflict are excluded from the areas covered by article 12.[76]

But while it is obvious that the requirement of the contemporaneous presence of the author of the act or omission rules out the application of Article 12's 'territorial tort' exception to proceedings concerning transboundary acts or, insofar as it is conceivable, omissions initiated by their author outside the territory of the forum State and culminating within it, it would seem not to preclude the application of the exception to proceedings concerning the author's initiation in the forum State of an act or omission consummated in the territory of another State. That is, from the perspective of the forum State, the requirement of the territorial presence of the author precludes proceedings regarding the 'import' of a transboundary civil wrong but not, *pace* the ILC commentary, regarding their 'export'. Even less does the presence requirement preclude the application of Article 12 to acts or omissions occurring in whole in the territory of the forum State but causing relevant harm in the territory of another State. In this connection, it pays to note that Article 12 contains no requirement like that in section 1605(*a*)(5) FSIA (US) and section 6 SIA (Can) that the death or personal injury or damage to or loss of tangible property caused by the act or omission be sustained in the territory of the forum State.

It has to be said that it is not entirely clear what could be meant by the occurrence of the act or omission 'in part' in the territory of the forum State, at least when the reference to 'the author' of that act or omission is taken into account. It is one thing to say that the author's act or omission occurred in the territory of one State but that the resultant death, personal injury, or damage to or loss of tangible property was sustained in the territory of another. Depending on how the body of private international law applied by the court characterizes the matter, it may even be one thing to say that the alleged municipal legal wrong occurred in part in one State and in part in another. But it is difficult to see how the author's act or omission could be taken to occur 'in part' within the State of the forum and 'in part' without; and it is telling in this regard that the ILC commentary speaks apparently synonymously, and consequently imprecisely, of 'transboundary injuries or trans-frontier torts or damage'.[77]

5. Evaluation

It is not self-evident why in principle a discrete exception to a foreign State's immunity from jurisdiction should exist in relation to those of its acts or omissions in the forum State that give rise to death or personal injury or damage to or loss of tangible property but not in relation to those that give rise to other, intangible harm. The answer may be that there is, in fact, no principled reason for the distinction but that there is no compelling practical call for an exception to immunity in relation specifically to

[76] ILC commentary, draft art. 12, para. 7.
[77] ILC commentary, draft art. 12, para. 7.

intangible types of harm given that proceedings in respect of at least pure economic loss—in practice the most significant species of such harm—occasioned by a foreign State's act or omission in the territory of the forum State will most likely already be permitted by reference to one of the other exceptions to immunity from jurisdiction laid down in Part III of the Convention. In this light, Article 12 does not seek to privilege certain forms of harm over others but, rather, insofar as they are both caused by a foreign State's act or omission in the forum State's territory, serves merely to place non-economic forms of harm on effectively the same footing as economic ones.

When it comes to whether the 'territorial tort' exception as embodied in Article 12 or in some comparable form exists as a matter of customary international law, the Supreme Court of Poland has held that it does, concluding as follows:

> [O]n the basis of the above materials, there is no international duty, on the part of States, to grant immunity to other States in matters of torts, if the actions leading to a tort occurred in the territory of the forum State, and if the author of the injury or damage was present in that territory at the time when those actions occurred.[78]

The reference to 'the above materials' embraces the Convention.[79] Subsequently, however, the ICJ held in *Jurisdictional Immunities of the State* that 'customary international law continues to require that a State be accorded immunity in proceedings for torts allegedly committed on the territory of another State by its armed forces and other organs of State in the course of conducting an armed conflict'.[80] The Court reasoned:

> ... State practice in the form of judicial decisions supports the proposition that State immunity for *acta jure imperii* continues to extend to civil proceedings for acts occasioning death, personal injury or damage to property committed by the armed forces and other organs of a State in the conduct of armed conflict, even if the relevant acts take place on the territory of the forum State. That practice is accompanied by *opinio juris*, as demonstrated by the positions taken by States and the jurisprudence of a number of national courts which have made clear that they considered that customary international law required immunity. The almost complete absence of contrary jurisprudence is also significant, as is the absence of any statements by States in connection with the work of the International Law Commission regarding State immunity and the adoption of the United Nations Convention or, so far as the Court has been able to discover, in any other context asserting that customary international law does not require immunity in such cases.[81]

The ICJ was not called on in the case to decide the more general question 'whether there is in customary international law a "[territorial] tort exception" to State immunity applicable to *acta jure imperii* in general'.[82] It did, however, venture the view—referable once more to situations narrower than those encompassed by Article 12 but broader than the focus of the dispute before it, which the Court stressed was confined to the context of armed conflict—that various national judicial decisions, along with the judgment of the Grand Chamber of the ECtHR in *McElhinney*, 'suggest that a State is entitled to

[78] *Natoniewski v Federal Republic of Germany*, reproduced in (2010) 30 *Polish YIL* 299, 300 (Pol (SC) 2010).

[79] See *Natoniewski v Federal Republic of Germany* (n. 78), 300, where the court explains that '[t]he relevant legal materials ... include the provisions of the European Convention on state immunity ("Basle Convention") and UN conventions [*sic*]'.

[80] *Jurisdictional Immunities of the State* (n. 1), para. 78.

[81] *Jurisdictional Immunities of the State* (n. 1), para. 77.

[82] *Jurisdictional Immunities of the State* (n. 1), para. 65.

immunity in respect of *acta jure imperii* committed by its armed forces on the territory of another State'.[83] If the suggestion is correct, it becomes all the more important to ascertain whether the Convention applies to military activities or at least to the activities of a foreign State's armed forces while they are present in the territory of the forum State. Should the Convention apply in either circumstance, the blanket application of Article 12 to all territorial acts or omissions alleged to be ascribable to a foreign State would represent a not insignificant departure from the customary position.

That said, it pays to bear in mind, as it does when pondering transboundary wrongs, that the vast majority of proceedings under Article 12 can be expected to concern quotidian accidents and incidents—diplomatic car crashes, slips and falls on consular premises, the occasional scuffle with a visiting minor official—which promise to raise no problems as to either the interpretation or application of the provision.

By way of epilogue, it is perhaps worth noting the assertion recently advanced in the distinct but related context of criminal proceedings that there exists an exception akin to the 'territorial tort' exception to the immunity *ratione materiae* (synonymously, State immunity) from which foreign State officials otherwise benefit in respect of acts performed in their official capacity. In his second report, the ILC's first Special Rapporteur on immunity of State officials from foreign criminal jurisdiction—while suggesting that, as a general rule, 'state officials enjoy immunity *ratione materiae* from foreign criminal jurisdiction, i.e., immunity in respect of acts performed in an official capacity'[84]—described as a 'special case', in respect of which 'there are sufficient grounds to talk of an absence of immunity', '[a] situation where criminal jurisdiction is exercised by a state in whose territory an alleged crime has taken place, [where] this state has not given its consent to the performance in its territory of the activity which led to the crime and to the presence in its territory of the foreign official who committed [that] crime'.[85] The Special Rapporteur's statement was subsequently relied on in the English extradition case of *Khurts Bat v Investigating Judge of the German Federal Court*,[86] where the court held that an exception along the lines alleged by the Special Rapporteur existed as a matter of customary international law to the immunity *ratione materiae*, or State immunity, from which a State official would otherwise benefit in criminal proceedings in the courts of another State. Whether the conclusion is accurate remains to be seen.

[83] *Jurisdictional Immunities of the State* (n. 1), para. 72.

[84] 'Second report on immunity of State officials from foreign criminal jurisdiction, by Roman Anatolevich Kolodkin, Special Rapporteur', UN doc. A/CN.4/631 (10 June 2001), 58, para. 94(*b*).

[85] 'Second report . . . by Roman Anatolevich Kolodkin, Special Rapporteur' (n. 84), 59–60, para. 94(*p*).

[86] 147 ILR 633, 662, para. 96 and 663, para. 99 (UK (EWHC) 2011).

Article 13

Jörg Philipp Terhechte

Article 13

Ownership, possession and use of property

Unless otherwise agreed between the States concerned, a State cannot invoke immunity from jurisdiction before a court of another State which is otherwise competent in a proceeding which relates to the determination of:

(*a*) any right or interest of the State in, or its possession or use of, or any obligation of the State arising out of its interest in, or its possession or use of, immovable property situated in the State of the forum;

(*b*) any right or interest of the State in movable or immovable property arising by way of succession, gift or *bona vacantia*; or

(*c*) any right or interest of the State in the administration of property, such as trust property, the estate of a bankrupt or the property of a company in the event of its winding up.

Understanding with respect to articles 13 and 14

The expression 'determination' is used to refer not only to the ascertainment or verification of the existence of the rights protected, but also to the evaluation or assessment of the substance, including content, scope and extent, of such rights.

1. Introduction

Article 13 precludes a State's immunity from foreign proceedings relating to the determination of its rights or interests in certain property or, in the case of immovable property situated in the State of the forum, of certain obligations incumbent on the State in respect of that property. Notwithstanding what might be considered the commercial character of many property-related rights, interests, and the like, Article 13 operates independently of Article 10's exception to a State's immunity from foreign proceedings in relation to commercial transactions. That is, when determining whether a State enjoys immunity from the jurisdiction of a court of another State in proceedings relating to the determination of its rights, interests, etc in property, there is no need to consider whether any transaction as may underlie such right, interest etc is a 'commercial transaction' within the meaning of Article 2(1)(*c*) of the Convention. Article 13 constitutes an exception to immunity in its own right.

Annexed to the Convention and considered an integral part of it[1] is an 'understanding' with respect to Article 13. This understanding, which relates also to Article 14, clarifies that the term 'a proceeding which relates to the determination of' a State's rights, interests, etc in property—in respect of which a State party is not immune from the jurisdiction of a court of another State party—encompasses not only proceedings for 'the ascertainment or verification of the existence of the rights protected' but also proceedings for 'the evaluation or assessment of the substance, including content, scope and extent, of such rights'.

[1] See Art. 25 UNSCI.

2. Background

The holding of rights or interests in and the possession and use of property are classic *acta jure gestionis*. In this light, Article 13 is in line with the restrictive doctrine of State immunity, which precludes immunity from proceedings in respect of non-sovereign acts. But while based on the logic of what might be called commerciality, the exception to State immunity in the case of property-related proceedings has traditionally been treated as a freestanding exception. The recognition of this exception was facilitated by the fact that, even prior to the gradual recognition of the restrictive doctrine, the forum State's interest in exercising jurisdiction in the sorts of property-related proceedings covered by Article 13 was widely accepted. In proceedings relating to immovable property situated in the forum State, as per subparagraph (*a*) of Article 13, the territorial link provided a strong justification for the exercise of jurisdiction.[2] With respect to subparagraphs (*b*) and (*c*), which demand no territorial link, the foreign State acquires rights or interests gratuitously or in relation to assets owned by others. This in turn could explain why its international law does not recognize its interest in upholding immunity.[3]

This dual justification—the act's commercial character plus the forum State's overarching interest in the exercise of jurisdiction—may explain why exceptions to State immunity in respect of property-related proceedings met with relatively little opposition. The Institut de Droit international's Hamburg resolution of 1891 contained a precursor to Article 13(*a*),[4] while the Harvard Research in International Law's draft treaty recognized exceptions akin to Article 13(*a*) and (*b*).[5] Even in States that only cautiously embraced the restrictive approach to State immunity, the courts tended to exercise jurisdiction in cases relating to the determination of a State's rights or interests in immovable property or trust funds.[6] Writing in 1951, Lauterpacht noted that there was 'uniform authority' supporting an exception as regards a State's rights in immovable

[2] In his Fifth report, Special Rapporteur Sucharitkul noted that 'the State of the *situs* exercises supreme authority as part and parcel of its sovereignty' and that this 'predominant authority' was a factor in accepting the exercise of jurisdiction. See Fifth report Sucharitkul, 46–7, paras 107–108. See also Harvard Research on International Law, 'Competence of Courts in Regard to Foreign States' (1932) 26 *AJIL Supp* 455, 578 ('indissoluble link' between land and the *situs*).

[3] The point is stressed in R.F. Lengelsen, *Aktuelle Probleme der Staatenimmunität im Verfahren vor den Zivil- und Verwaltungsgerichten* (Frankfurt: Peter Lang, 2011), 119. Others have suggested that in relation to subparagraphs (*b*) and (*c*) 'the rights claimed are confined to those created and dependent on the local law of the forum State' (H. Fox, *The Law of State Immunity* (2nd edn) (Oxford: Oxford University Press, 2008), 591), but this would seem to be based on an assumption as to applicable rules of private international law, which the Convention otherwise avoids.

[4] 'Projet de règlement international sur la compétence des tribunaux dans les procès contre les Etats, souverains ou chefs d'Etat étrangers' (Hamburg session, 11 September 1891), reproduced in Institut de Droit international, *Tableau général des résolutions (1873–1956)* (Basel: Karger, 1957), 14, art. 4(1).

[5] Harvard Research on International Law (n. 2), 572–97, arts 9 and 10, with commentaries.

[6] For example, with respect to Japan, see *Limbin Hteik Tin Lat v Union of Burma*, 32 ILR 124 (Jpn (Tokyo DC) 1966). As regards the UK, some form of 'trust fund exception' was recognized from the middle of the nineteenth century. See *Duke of Brunswick v King of Hanover* (1844) 6 Beav 1. Whether there should be a separate exception for disputes relating to immovable property was left open by the House of Lords in *Sultan of Johore v Abubakar Tunku Aris Bendahar*, 19 ILR 182 (UK (HL) 1952). But in his judgment for the Privy Council in *The Philippine Admiral*, 64 ILR 90, 108 (UK (PC) 1975), which otherwise did not recognize the restrictive doctrine of State immunity in respect of actions *in personam*, Lord Cross considered the exceptions for immovable property and trust funds to be '[t]he only possible exceptions to the generality of the rule that no proceedings *in personam* can be brought against a sovereign or a sovereign State or a body which is a department (or equivalent to a department) of a sovereign State of which there is any trace in the English authorities brought to their Lordships' attention'. The commentary to draft art. 9 of the Harvard Research

property.[7] Practice along the lines of subparagraphs (*b*) and (*c*) of Article 13 was less common, but this would seem to reflect the narrow scope of the two exceptions[8] and the fact that some jurisdictions have traditionally treated them as manifestations of the 'commercial transaction' exception.[9]

In formulating Article 13 of the Convention, the drafters could draw on Articles 9 and 10 ECSI, as well as on national legislation, notably section 6 SIA (UK), section 7 SIO (Pak), section 8 SIA (Sing), section 7 FStIA (SA), section 14 FStIA (Aus), and, to some extent, section 8 SIA (Can) and section 1605(*a*)(3) and (4) FSIA (US). Article 13 is in line with these earlier codifications in that, first, it recognizes an exception for property-related proceedings and, secondly, it formulates this exception as a freestanding one that operates independently of Article 2(1)(*c*) and (2) and Article 10.[10]

3. Drafting History

For the most part, the drafting of Article 13 proved uncontroversial.

An early version of the provision was proposed by Special Rapporteur Sucharitkul in 1983,[11] was discussed by the Drafting Committee the same year,[12] and was adopted on first reading as draft article 14(1) in 1986.[13] This first reading version recognized exceptions to a State's immunity from foreign jurisdiction in proceedings relating to the determination of, among other things, its rights, interests, etc in immovable property and its rights and interests in property acquired by succession, gift or *bona vacantia*. These elements of the draft article were generally approved of by governments in their comments on the 1986 text, did not give rise to serious concern in the ILC's subsequent debates, and were finally adopted on second reading as draft article 13(*a*) and (*b*). They carried over into the Convention without change.

Additionally, and even though the matter was considered relevant to common law countries in the main, there was support[14] from the outset for the inclusion of a further exception covering proceedings relating to the determination of any right or interest of a State in the administration of property. The formulation of this exception underwent considerable change over the course of its drafting. What was adopted on first reading as draft article 14(1) encompassed—in addition to the sorts of proceedings eventually

draft treaty (n. 5) provides an instructive analysis of many early twentieth-century (and some nineteenth-century) decisions.

[7] H. Lauterpacht, 'The Problem of Jurisdictional Immunities of Foreign States' (1951) 28 *BYIL* 220, 244.

[8] See eg *Re Russian Bank for Foreign Trade*, 7 ILR 151 (UK (EWHC) 1933); *Nizam of Hyderabad v Jung* [1957] 1 All ER 257 (UK (EWCA) 1957).

[9] See Fifth report Sucharitkul, 49, paras 122–123.

[10] See J.W. Dellapenna, *Suing Foreign Governments and their Corporations* (2nd edn) (New York: Transnational Publishers, 2003), 84. Unlike with respect to contracts of employment (another specific exception based on commerciality), the Convention does not spell this out as such. *Cf* Art. 2(1)(*c*), pursuant to which the term 'commercial transaction' (in respect of which Art. 10 precludes immunity from jurisdiction) comprises 'any other contract or transaction of a commercial, industrial, trading or professional nature, but not including a contract of employment of persons'.

[11] See Fifth report Sucharitkul, 52.

[12] See summary record 1805th ILC meeting, *YILC 1983*, vol. I, 285, 291–2.

[13] See Report ILC, thirty-eighth session, 10.

[14] But see 'Comments and observations received from Governments,' UN doc. A/CN.4/410 and Add. 1–5, *YILC 1988*, vol. II(1), 45, 82, para. 14 (USSR).

covered by Article 13(*a*) and (*b*)—proceedings relating to the determination of a State's rights or interests in a range of specific instances of the administration of property, namely the administration of the estate of a deceased person, person of unsound mind, or bankrupt; the administration of a company in the event of its dissolution or winding up; and the administration of trust property or property otherwise held on a fiduciary basis.[15] This formulation was considered unnecessarily complicated by governments and a number of ILC members alike.[16] What on second reading was finally adopted as draft article 13(*c*) responded to these concerns, framing the exception in general terms ('the determination of... any right or interest of the State in the administration of property') and giving no more than three common examples of property in administration ('trust property, the estate of a bankrupt or the property of a company in the event of its winding up'). No further changes were made to subparagraph (*c*) between 1991 and the adoption of Article 13(*c*) of the Convention.[17]

After the completion of the ILC's second reading, the term 'determination' used in the chapeau to draft article 13—which had been criticized by the UK in its comments on the first reading text on the ground that it might have been taken to suggest that only disputes relating to the existence or extent of a right or interest were covered[18]—began to attract debate. In the 2002 report of the Ad Hoc Committee on Jurisdictional Immunities of States and Their Property, the words 'the determination of' in the chapeau were placed in square brackets. But rather than amending the provision itself, the Committee decided to address the issues raised by means of one of the 'understandings' proposed in 2003 and eventually annexed to the Convention as adopted.

Along with what was then draft article 14, Special Rapporteur Sucharitkul had originally proposed a draft article 15 containing a clause safeguarding the 'immunities of States in respect of their property from attachment and execution, or the inviolability of premises of diplomatic or special missions or consular premises'.[19] As the draft articles took shape, however, it became clear that these were matters of more general relevance, not limited in their application to what became draft article 13 and eventually Article 13 of the Convention. A 'without prejudice' clause in relation to 'the privileges and immunities enjoyed by a State under international law in relation to the exercise of the functions of... its diplomatic missions, consular posts, special missions, missions to international organizations or delegations to organs of international organizations or to international conferences' is found instead in Article 3(1)(*a*) of the Convention.[20]

[15] See Report ILC, thirty-eighth session, 10.

[16] See Preliminary report Ogiso, 47, para. 156.

[17] Note that draft art. 14(2) as adopted on first reading in 1986 had specifically addressed proceedings that, while brought against 'a person other than a State', affected State property. This, however, was found to be unnecessary in the light of Art. 6(2)(*b*). See Report ILC, thirty-eighth session, 10 for the proposed wording and summary record 1770th ILC meeting, *YILC 1983*, vol. I, 93, 94 (Ahmed Mahiou) and 96 (Sir Ian Sinclair) for background. See also ILC commentary, draft art. 13, para. 7.

[18] See 'Comments and observations received from Governments' (n. 14), 88, para. 22 (UK).

[19] Fifth report Sucharitkul, 52, paras 141–142.

[20] See the commentary to Art. 3(1)(*a*).

4. Key Points

4.1 Chapeau

The chapeau to Article 13, in addition to formulating the consequence of satisfying the provision ('a State cannot invoke immunity from jurisdiction before a court of another State'), makes a number of basic points. First, as in most of the other exceptions to a State's immunity from jurisdiction enumerated in Part III of the Convention, the words '[u]nless otherwise agreed between the States concerned' permit derogation from Article 13 by agreement between the State impleaded and the forum State. Next, and again as with nearly all of the other enumerated exceptions to immunity, the reference in Article 13 to 'a court of another State which is otherwise competent' presupposes the existence, in accordance with the law of the forum State, of the relevant underlying jurisdiction, without seeking to regulate or pass judgment on any question of private international law in relation to that jurisdiction.[21] As for the term 'a proceeding which relates to the determination of' the various rights, interests, etc referred to in Article 13, the scope of which was considered uncertain by some of the drafters,[22] the understanding with respect to Article 13 makes it clear that this embraces proceedings not only for 'the ascertainment or verification of the existence of the rights protected' but also for 'the evaluation or assessment of the substance, including content, scope and extent, of such rights'. Putting it another way, a State may not, by virtue of Article 13, avail itself of immunity from foreign jurisdiction either where the proceeding pertains to whether it actually enjoys the right, interest, etc that it asserts in the property or where it pertains to the content of any right, interest, etc that it asserts or is acknowledged to enjoy in the property. That the understanding with respect to Article 13 mentions only 'rights' and not also 'interests', 'possession', 'use', and 'obligations', as referred to as well in Article 13(*a*), would seem to be negligent drafting, rather a deliberate choice to omit mention of these other terms. The same goes, *mutatis mutandis,* for the overproliferation of terms in the expressions 'evaluation or assessment' and 'content, scope and extent,' the semantic redundancy in both of which ought to have been apparent.

4.2 Article 13(*a*)

Subparagraph (*a*) of Article 13 concerns proceedings relating to the determination of 'any right or interest of the State in, or its possession or use of, or any obligation of the State arising out of its interest in, or its possession or use of, immovable property situated in the State of the forum'. Immovable property, the term from the civilian legal tradition for what is referred to in the common law as 'real property,' is property that cannot be removed without its alteration, and comprises land, buildings, and fixtures. The application of Article 13(*a*), as the text makes clear, is restricted to proceedings concerning immovable property situated in the forum State. The provision does not cover proceedings relating to immovable property located elsewhere, even where these

[21] ILC commentary, draft art. 13, para. 3, expressly notes that draft art. 13 'does not confer jurisdiction on any court where none exists'.

[22] Recall section 3.

proceedings pertain to the use of that property[23] and this use has effects in the forum State.[24]

The exception to a State's immunity from foreign jurisdiction provided for in Article 13(*a*) extends to three categories of proceeding relating to immovable property situated in the forum State, namely proceedings in relation to an alleged or acknowledged right or interest in such property on the part of the first State; proceedings in relation to that State's possession or use of such property; and proceedings in relation to any obligation alleged or acknowledged to arise for that State out of its interest in, or its possession or use of, such property. The convoluted wording of Article 13(*a*) was considered necessary to do justice to the various national legal traditions. The concept of a 'right' in immovable property, deemed sufficient on its own for the purposes of Article 9 ECSI, is complemented by the notion of an 'interest' so as to ensure that any legal entitlements in respect of such property not characterized under domestic law as rights are still covered.[25] Similarly, 'possession' receives express mention, given that some domestic legal systems do not, or do or not generally, treat it as a legal right or interest in property, characterizing it instead as a question of fact.[26] All told, Article 13(*a*) covers, among other things,[27] proceedings relating to a State's ownership of immovable property, to the respective rights of the claimant and the State as co-owners of any such property, and to the boundary between any such property owned by a State and adjoining property; proceedings relating to a lease, tenancy, or licence agreement, whether the State be in the position of lessor or lessee or of landlord or tenant or licensee;[28] proceedings relating to a mortgage or other charge on immovable property; and proceedings relating to the use of immovable property, including in respect of nuisances emanating from it or accidents caused by its dilapidated state.[29]

Article 13(*a*) refers to immovable property *tout court.* The exception it posits to a State's immunity from foreign proceedings applies in respect of any immovable property in the forum State in which the first State has or purports to have a right or interest or which it possesses or uses. No special provision is made for diplomatic, consular, or cognate premises, which are therefore covered by Article 13(*a*) just like any other type of immovable property. Nor do proceedings relating to the determination of any right, interest, etc of a State in diplomatic, consular, or cognate premises implicate, in the words of Article 3(1)(*a*), the privileges and immunities enjoyed by a State under international law in relation to the exercise of the functions of its variety of missions, its consular posts, and its delegations.[30]

[23] Under the rules of private international rule applied by most States, the courts would have no competence to entertain proceedings relating to rights or interests in, or the possession or use of, immovable property situated in another territorial jurisdiction.

[24] For instance, the Austrian litigation relating to the operation of a Czech nuclear power plant located in the territory of the former Czechoslovakia would not come within the scope of Art. 13(*a*). See *Nuclear Power Plant Injunction Case (No. 1)*, 86 ILR 575 (Aut (SC) 1991).

[25] See ILC commentary, draft art. 13, para. 4.

[26] See ILC commentary, draft art. 13, para. 4.

[27] A useful survey of relevant property-related disputes can be found in Hafner et al. (eds), *State Practice Regarding State Immunities* (Leiden: Martinus Nijhoff/Council of Europe, 2006), 199–205.

[28] Examples include proceedings concerning rights to possession, rights of access, increases in rent, and the termination of a lease, tenancy, or licence.

[29] The latter example may also come within the scope of Art. 12's 'territorial tort' exception.

[30] See the commentary to Art. 3(1)(*a*).

Article 13, like any other of the exceptions to a State's immunity from proceedings enumerated in Parts II and III, may be invoked not only in a proceeding in which a State respondent to a claim asserts its immunity from the jurisdiction of the court of another State but also in a proceeding in which the immunity to be overcome is that of an indirectly impleaded State—that is, where the State 'is not named as a party to the proceeding but the proceeding in effect seeks to affect the property, rights, interests or activities' of the State concerned, in the words of Article 6(2)(*b*) of the Convention.[31] In this regard, the word 'activities' in Article 6(2)(*b*) is capable of encompassing the possession and use of property, as both referred to in Article 13(*a*).[32]

4.3 Article 13(*b*)

Article 13(*b*) posits an exception to a State's immunity from jurisdiction where the proceeding relates to the determination of 'any right or interest of the State in movable or immovable property arising by way of succession, gift or *bona vacantia*'. In contrast to Article 13(*a*), Article 13(*b*), as the text makes clear, covers both immovable and movable property, and it is not restricted to property situated in the forum State.[33] The common feature of the three legal modalities by which the State is purported to have acquired the right or interest in the property is that they do not involve reciprocal engagement.

The terms used in Article 13(*b*) are intended generically. Their meaning is not limited to the meaning accorded the same terms by any single national legal tradition. 'Succession' in this light denotes no more than the transmission of a legal right or interest in property on the death of the former holder of that right or interest. 'Gift' describes the transmission of a right or interest without consideration. '*Bona vacantia*' comprises property that has no legal owner, because, for instance, it has been abandoned or forms an undistributed part of an estate or of the property of a company that has been wound up. The acquisition of rights and interests in *bona vacantia* is characterized as an instance of succession in some legal systems and as a combination of forfeiture and acquisition in others. This divergent legal characterization made separate reference to it prudent.[34]

Article 13(*b*) does specify the conditions under which rights or interests in property can be acquired in accordance with the three modalities of acquisition mentioned. This is a matter for the applicable domestic law.

Article 13(*b*) covers proceedings relating to the determination of 'any right or interest' in property acquired by way of any of the three specified modalities. Just as in Article 13(*a*), the expression 'right or interest' is intended to cover a broad range of proprietary entitlements not limited to ownership, although it does not include mere possession or use.[35]

[31] See the commentary to Art. 6(2)(*b*).

[32] As for the obligations of a State 'arising out of its interest in, or its possession or use of, immovable property', it is hard to see how they could be the subject of indirect impleading in the first place, which is probably why no mention of a State's obligations is made in Art. 6(2)(*b*).

[33] Where a State acquires by way of succession or gift a right or interest in immovable property located abroad, there may be, depending on the precise subject-matter of the proceedings, an overlap between subparas (*a*) and (*b*) of Art. 13.

[34] See Fifth report Sucharitkul, 51, para. 135.

[35] This would seem to follow from subparagraph (*a*), which provides interpretative context for subparagraph (*b*). In the text of the former, 'use' and 'possession' are mentioned alongside 'rights and interests,' indicating a terminological differentiation.

4.4 Article 13(*c*)

Article 13(*c*) posits an exception to a State's immunity from jurisdiction where the proceeding relates to the determination of 'any right or interest of the State in the administration of property'. As with subparagraph (*b*), the provision does not qualify the location of the property and applies to movable as well as immovable property. It is intended to accommodate the situation, typical in common-law jurisdictions, in which a court exercises 'some form of supervisory jurisdiction or other functions with regard to the administration of trust property or property otherwise held on a fiduciary basis',[36] and it applies irrespective of whether the court administers the property itself or merely supervises its administration. The exercise of jurisdiction pursuant to Article 13(*c*) may affect the foreign State only incidentally, as the proceeding may involve the determination or ascertainment of the rights or interests of a range of interested parties.[37]

Article 13(*c*) is formulated broadly. It encompasses 'any right or interest' in property under administration. Equally the term 'the administration of property' is deliberately general. The examples of administered property mentioned (trust property, the estate of a bankrupt, and the property of a company in the event of its winding up) are merely illustrative. '[A]dministration' is intended to cover the full range of actions that a court may be required to perform in the discharge of its protective jurisdiction.[38] This may include the distribution of assets. It may, depending on the applicable domestic law, also include prohibiting or permitting the sale or use of property.

5. Evaluation

Article 13 is among the more straightforward provisions of Part III of the Convention. Article 13(*a*) codifies one of the earliest exceptions to a State's immunity from the jurisdiction of the courts of another State. Article 13(*b*) and (*c*) are less significant in practice, although their relatively uneventful drafting history suggests their general acceptability.

[36] ILC commentary, draft art. 13, para. 6.

[37] See ILC commentary, draft art. 13, para. 6.

[38] Note that the Special Rapporteur's initial draft art. 15(1)(*c*) had referred to 'the distribution of assets in connection with the estates of deceased persons'. See Fifth report Sucharitkul, 52, para. 142. This was criticized as too narrow. See summary record 1767th ILC meeting, *YILC 1983*, vol. I, 74, 79, para. 37 (Sir Ian Sinclair).

Article 14

JÖRG PHILIPP TERHECHTE

Article 14

Intellectual and industrial property

Unless otherwise agreed between the States concerned, a State cannot invoke immunity from jurisdiction before a court of another State which is otherwise competent in a proceeding which relates to:

(*a*) the determination of any right of the State in a patent, industrial design, trade name or business name, trademark, copyright or any other form of intellectual or industrial property which enjoys a measure of legal protection, even if provisional, in the State of the forum; or

(*b*) an alleged infringement by the State, in the territory of the State of the forum, of a right of the nature mentioned in subparagraph (*a*) which belongs to a third person and is protected in the State of the forum.

Understanding with respect to articles 13 and 14

The expression 'determination' is used to refer not only to the ascertainment or verification of the existence of the rights protected, but also to the evaluation or assessment of the substance, including content, scope and extent, of such rights.

1. Introduction

Article 14 of the Convention precludes a State's immunity from foreign proceedings relating to intellectual and industrial property rights protected in the forum State. The provision distinguishes between proceedings relating to the determination of any such rights on the part of a State, as dealt with in subparagraph (*a*), and proceedings relating to the alleged infringement by a State of the rights of others, as dealt with in subparagraph (*b*).

Disputes relating to intellectual and industrial property ('intangible property') typically arise out of commercial transactions, and thus might well have been treated under Article 10. However, just as with respect to other property-related rights,[1] the Convention addresses proceedings relating to intangible property separately, in a specific provision. It follows that when determining whether a State enjoys immunity from the

[1] See Art. 13 UNCSI, dealing with rights, interests, etc in immovable property located in the forum State, rights or interests in property acquired by gift, succession or *bona vacantia*, and rights or interests in the administration of property. In addition, Art. 12, under certain conditions, precludes immunity from suit in proceedings relating to damage to or loss of tangible property caused by an act of omission in the territory of the forum State.

jurisdiction of a court of another State in proceedings relating to intellectual or industrial property, there is no need to consider whether the right in question, or the conduct allegedly resulting in its infringement, is of a commercial character within the meaning of Article 2(1)(*c*) of the Convention.[2]

Article 14 is complemented by an 'understanding' pursuant to which the expression 'a proceeding which relates to the determination of', as also used in Article 13, encompasses not only proceedings for 'the ascertainment or verification of the existence of the rights protected' but also proceedings for 'the evaluation or assessment of the substance, including content, scope and extent, of such rights'.

2. Background

Article 14 addresses a category of conduct that will typically be *jure gestionis*. The provision's recognition of an exception in this regard to a State's immunity from foreign jurisdiction is therefore in line with the restrictive doctrine of State immunity, which precludes a State's immunity from foreign proceedings in respect of its non-sovereign acts. Some jurisdictions—typically those without legislation governing the availability of State immunity, but also the United States and Canada[3]—have treated proceedings relating to intellectual and industrial property under the general exception to State immunity for commercial activities/transactions. Indeed, the *Dralle* case—one of the '*causes célèbres* [of the law of State immunity] . . . well known throughout the world for the thoroughness with which the court examined . . . judicial practice and jurisprudence'[4] and influential in paving the way for the restrictive doctrine generally—concerned the use of trade marks.[5] Most jurisdictions and relevant international texts, however, have sought to regulate immunity from jurisdiction in respect of intellectual and industrial property via a freestanding exception, rationalized not just as a variation on the theme of commerciality but also as the price to be paid for the effective protection of intangible property.[6] In this light, the inclusion in the Convention of Article 14 met with little opposition.

In formulating the terms of the provision, the drafters could draw on, and appear to have been influenced by, Article 8 ECSI and provisions of domestic law such as section 7 SIA (UK), section 8 SIO (Pak), section 9 SIA (Sing), and section 8 FStIA (SA).[7]

[2] For comment, see V. Morris, 'Sovereign Immunity: The Exception for Intellectual or Industrial Property' (1986) 19 *Vanderbilt Journal of Transnational Law* 83, 91–2; ILC commentary, draft art. 14, para. 2 (giving examples of 'non-commercial' infringements).

[3] Unlike other national State immunity legislation, neither the FSIA (US) nor the SIA (Can) contains a specific provision on proceedings relating to intangible property.

[4] Sixth report Sucharitkul, 18, para. 65.

[5] See *Dralle v Republic of Czechoslovakia*, 17 ILR 155 (Aut (SC) 1950). See also *X v Spanish Government Tourist Bureau*, 65 ILR 141 (FRG (Frankfurt HRC) 1977).

[6] Morris (n. 2), 93. See Sixth report Sucharitkul, 17–18, paras 53–63, for a range of explanations. Among these, the argument that by seeking the protection of the law of the forum State on intangible property a State submits to the jurisdiction of the forum State, while flawed for a number of reasons, is particularly popular: see eg S. Breau, 'Ownership, Possession and Use of Property', in G. Hafner et al. (eds), *State Practice Regarding State Immunities* (Leiden: Martinus Nijhoff/Council of Europe, 2006), 113, 124.

[7] S. 15 FStIA (Aus) is different insofar as it excludes the application of the intangible property exception where the tangible property to which the copyright, patent, trademark, or design relates has not been imported into or used in Australia in the course or for the purposes of a commercial transaction.

3. Drafting History

The drafting of Article 14 proved largely uncontroversial, although the ILC's early debates were at times marked by ideological differences over about the substantive scope of intangible property rights (a matter not addressed in what became Article 14) and the effect of their protection on developing countries.[8]

A version of the provision was first proposed by Special Rapporteur Sucharitkul in 1984 as draft article 16.[9] This embodied the gist of what is now Article 14, but provided a long list of specific intellectual and industrial property rights, which it sought to distinguish from trade or business names.[10] Additionally, in mentioning questions of 'attribution', it seemed to address issues of substantive law.[11] During the Commission's debates, members generally[12] endorsed the essence of the provision, but suggested simplifying its wording, which was felt to be 'unduly detailed'.[13] Taking up a proposal by Motoo Ogiso,[14] the Drafting Committee agreed on a revised version which did not treat trade or business names separately and which condensed the list of protected rights while also making clear that it was non-exhaustive. This revised version was adopted on first reading as draft article 15.[15]

Draft article 15 as adopted on first reading attracted very few comments and observations by governments.[16] The United Kingdom, however, proposed defining the categories of intellectual and industrial property covered more precisely, and asked for clarification on whether novel forms of intangible property (such as rights relating to plants or to computer-generated works) would be included. On second reading, the Commission deleted the word 'similar', referring to other categories of intellectual or industrial property not specifically mentioned, with the commentary clarifying that the generic terms employed 'intended to include the whole range of forms of intellectual or industrial property..., including, for example, a plant breeder's right and a right in computer-generated works'.[17] With one other, purely technical amendment, the provision was adopted on second reading in 1991 as draft article 14.[18]

[8] See especially summary record 1834th ILC meeting, *YILC 1984*, vol. I, 116, 118, para. 17 (Chief Richard Akinjide), 120, paras 29–30 (Sir Ian Sinclair), 121, para. 39 (Nikolai Ushakov); summary record 1835th ILC meeting, *YILC 1984*, vol. I, 121, 124, para. 13 (Zhengyu Ni), 125, para. 26 (Mikuin Balanda).

[9] Sixth report Sucharitkul, 21, para. 80.

[10] Sixth report Sucharitkul, 21, para. 80. Within each paragraph, a separate subpara. (*b*) addressed questions relating to the use of a trade or business name in the forum State.

[11] See notably Sixth report Sucharitkul, 21, para. 80, subpara. 2(*b*) ('an alleged infringement by or attributable to a State').

[12] But see summary record 1833rd ILC meeting, *YILC 1984*, vol. I, 110, 114, paras 27–29 (Nikolai Ushakov); summary record 1834th ILC meeting (n. 8), 117–18, paras 9–17 (Chief Richard Akinjide); summary record 1836th ILC meeting, *YILC 1984*, vol. I, 128, 134, para. 43 (Edilbert Razafindralambo).

[13] Summary record 1834th ILC meeting (n. 8), 116, para. 1 (Motoo Ogiso). For similar observations, see eg summary record 1837th ILC meeting, *YILC 1984*, vol. I, 135, 137, para. 11 (Stephen McCaffrey) ('could be simplified'), 141, para. 37 (Ahmed Mahiou) (could be 'condensed').

[14] Summary record 1834th ILC meeting (n. 8), 117, para. 3.

[15] Report ILC, thirty-eighth session, 10.

[16] See the summary of comments in Preliminary report Ogiso, 113, paras 157–160.

[17] ILC commentary, draft art. 14, para. 3. See also, previously and see already Preliminary report Ogiso, 113, para. 161.

[18] Report ILC, forty-third session, 47.

Draft article 14 carried over into the Convention unchanged as Article 14. However, taking up another point initially raised by United Kingdom,[19] the Ad Hoc Committee on Jurisdictional Immunities of States and Their Property took steps to clarify the term 'determination' in Article 14(*a*). Having placed the words 'The determination of' in square brackets in its 2002 report,[20] the Committee agreed in 2003 to an 'understanding' with respect to Articles 13 and 14 which explained that the word 'determination' referred not only to the 'ascertainment or verification of the existence' of intellectual and industrial property rights but also to the 'evaluation or assessment of [their] substance'. The understanding was eventually annexed to and became an integral part[21] of the Convention as adopted.

4. Key Points

4.1 Chapeau

The chapeau to Article 14 follows the typical pattern of the exceptions to a State's immunity from jurisdiction enumerated in Part III of the Convention. It sets out the consequence of satisfying the provision ('a State cannot invoke immunity from jurisdiction before a court of another State'); it clarifies that the forum State and the impleaded State can agree not to apply the exception laid down in the provision ('[u]nless otherwise agreed between the States concerned'); and it presupposes the existence, in accordance with the law of the forum State, of jurisdiction on the part of the domestic court ('a court of another State which is otherwise competent').[22]

4.2 Article 14(*a*)

Article 14(*a*) concerns proceedings relating to the determination of any right on the part of a foreign State in any form of intellectual or industrial property which enjoys a measure of legal protection in the forum State. It follows from Article 6(2)(b) of the Convention that, just as a State may invoke Article 5's prima facie immunity from foreign jurisdiction not simply in a proceeding to which it is named as a party but in any proceeding which 'seeks to affect the property, rights, interests or activities' of that State,[23] so may a private claimant invoke Article 14(a)'s exception to State immunity in the latter instance. Judging from the paucity of relevant jurisprudence, in practice Article 14(*a*) is likely to be the less significant of Article 14's two subparagraphs.

Article 14(*a*) lists common forms of intellectual and industrial property (patents, industrial designs, trade names or business names, trademarks, and copyright) by way of illustration of the general category of intangible property, *viz* 'any . . . form of intellectual

[19] See 'Comments and observations received from Governments', UN doc. A/CN.4/410 and Add. 1–5, *YILC 1988*, vol. II(1), 45, 88, para. 24.

[20] 2002 report Ad Hoc Committee, 8.

[21] See Art. 25 UNCSI.

[22] See ILC commentary, draft art. 10, paras 3–5 and draft art. 13, para. 3.

[23] See Art. 6(2)(*b*) UNCSI.

or industrial property', to which the subparagraph pertains. The provision does not define the terms 'intellectual [property]' and 'industrial property', but, the ILC commentary describes them as 'broad and generic expressions intended to cover existing and future forms, types, classes or categories of intellectual or industrial property'. While noting that the lines may be blurred, the commentary goes on to suggest a broad division between 'the three principal types of property' covered by Article 14, namely 'patents and industrial designs' (as industrial property); 'trade marks and trade names' (which are said to 'pertain more to the business world'); and copyright and any other form of intellectual property.[24] But notwithstanding this grouping of the different property rights covered by the provision into categories, Article 14(*a*) applies to all forms of intangible (or 'incorporeal') property capable of ownership, possession, and use. This includes novel forms of intangible property such as rights relating to databases and domain names, as well as indigenous intellectual property.[25] Especially in light of the drafters' reference to the international protection of the rights covered by Article 14,[26] relevant international conventions can be used to aid the interpretation and application of the provision.[27]

Article 14(*a*) requires that the rights at issue in the proceeding 'enjo[y] a measure of legal protection, even if provisional, in the State of the forum'. What 'measure of legal protection' is enjoyed will depend on the applicable domestic law.[28] For Article 14(*a*) to apply, it is sufficient that some measure of protection is granted. For the avoidance of doubt, the provision expressly mentions 'provisional protection', which under many domestic legal systems is enjoyed for the duration of the process of registration of a trademark, patent, design, geographical indication, or the like.

Article 14(*a*) does not require a State party to the Convention to ensure any particular level of protection or, indeed, any protection to intellectual or industrial property under its domestic law.[29] Obligations of this sort may derive from one or other of the various multilateral treaties addressing substantive questions of intellectual property law (such as the (Revised) Berne Convention for the Protection of Literary or Artistic Works, the Nairobi Treaty on the Olympic Symbol, or the Singapore Treaty on Trademarks[30]); but Article 14 does not add to them.[31]

[24] ILC commentary, draft art. 14, para. 3, referring additionally to 'the whole range of forms of intellectual or industrial property which may be identified under the groups of intellectual or industrial property rights'.

[25] Recall from sections 1 and 2 that—unlike s. 15 FStIA (Aus)—Art. 14 of the Convention applies to intangible property irrespective of any nexus with commercial transaction.

[26] See ILC commentary, draft art. 14, para. 4.

[27] See eg Art. 2(vii) Convention Establishing the World Intellectual Property Organization, Stockholm, 14 July 1967, 828 UNTS 3 (listing protected intellectual property rights); Art. 3 Patent Law Treaty, Geneva, 1 June 2000, 39 ILM 1047 (seeking to clarify the term 'patent').

[28] ILC commentary, draft art. 14, para. 4, expressly notes: 'The protection provided by States within their territorial jurisdiction varies according to the type of industrial or intellectual property in question and the special regime or organized system for the application, registration or utilization of such rights for which protection is guaranteed by domestic law.'

[29] See further Morris (n. 2), 108–9.

[30] See Berne Convention for the Protection of Literary and Artistic Works, Berne, 9 September 1886, as revised at Stockholm, 14 July 1967, 828 UNTS 299; Nairobi Treaty on the Protection of the Olympic Symbol, Nairobi, 26 September 1981, 1863 UNTS 367; Singapore Treaty on the Law of Trademarks, Singapore, 27 March 2006, UKTS No. 32 (2012).

[31] See ILC Commentary, draft art. 14, para. 10: 'The State of the forum is . . . free to tolerate or permit . . . infringements or to deny remedies thereof in the absence of an internationally organized system of protection for the rights violated or breached in its own territory.'

Article 14(*a*) applies to proceedings that 'relate' to determination of a foreign State's intangible property rights. As indicated in the understanding to Articles 13 and 14 annexed to the Convention, this encompasses not only proceedings relating the 'ascertainment or verification of the existence of' such rights but also proceedings relating to the 'evaluation or assessment of the substance, including content, scope and extent, of' those rights. Precisely what sorts of proceedings the provision envisages is not immediately apparent, given that it cannot embrace proceedings instituted by the foreign State, those in which the State has intervened on the merits, or those involving relevant counterclaims by or against the State.

4.3 Article 14(*b*)

Article 14(*b*) precludes the availability to a foreign State of immunity from proceedings relating to the alleged infringement by that State, in the territory of the forum State, of any intellectual or industrial property right of another protected in the latter State. Judging from State practice it is likely to prove the more significant of Article 14's two subparagraphs.

Article 14(*b*) covers the types of rights referred to in Article 14(*a*), *viz* all forms of intellectual and industrial property. Just as under subparagraph (*a*), these rights must be 'protected in the State of the forum'. In the light of subparagraph (*a*), such protection includes provisional protection.

Article 14(*b*) precludes immunity from proceedings related to 'an alleged infringement by the State' of the intellectual or industrial property rights of another. The term 'infringement' covers all violations of intellectual or industrial property law. Examples might include the distribution by a State's tourism board of videos making unlicensed use of copyrighted music;[32] the use of copyrighted photographs by a State organ in violation of stipulated conditions;[33] the unlicensed use of a patent by a State enterprise;[34] and the unlawful acquisition and dissemination of trade secrets by a State enterprise.[35] The motive behind the infringement is irrelevant. Nor is there any need for the State to have acted out of commercial interest.

As the word 'alleged' makes clear,[36] for Article 14(*b*) to apply it is sufficient that an infringement is claimed to have taken place. Whether an infringement has in fact occurred is a question for the merits.

Article 14(*b*) requires that the infringement must be alleged to have taken place in the territory of the State of the forum.[37] Article 14(*b*) does not apply to a State's alleged infringement of intangible property rights in its own or a third State's territory.[38]

[32] See *X v Spanish Government Tourist Bureau* (n. 5).

[33] See *Henry Leutwyler v Office of Her Majesty Queen Rania Al Abdullah*, 184 F.Supp. 2d 277 (US (SDNY) 2001).

[34] See *James K. Gilson v Republic of Ireland and Gaeltarra Eireann*, 682 F.2d 1022 (US (DC Cir) 1982).

[35] See *BP Chemicals Ltd v Jiangsu Sopo Corporation Ltd et al.*, 285 F.3d 677 (US (8th Cir.) 2002).

[36] See Art. 14(*b*) ('an alleged infringement by the State').

[37] Compare, in this light, Art. 12 UNCSI.

[38] See ILC commentary, draft art. 14, para. 10 Morris (n. 2), 88 and 96–7.

5. Evaluation

In formulating Article 14 of the Convention, the drafters could not draw on a substantial body of domestic jurisprudence or legislation. But the provision's rapid acceptance suggests general support for it among States. Given the growing concern worldwide for the protection of intellectual and industrial property, Article 14 is likely to be of considerable importance in the future.

Article 15

Andrew Dickinson

Article 15

Participation in companies or other collective bodies

1. A State cannot invoke immunity from jurisdiction before a court of another State which is otherwise competent in a proceeding which relates to its participation in a company or other collective body, whether incorporated or unincorporated, being a proceeding concerning the relationship between the State and the body or the other participants therein, provided that the body:
   (*a*) has participants other than States or international organizations; and
   (*b*) is incorporated or constituted under the law of the State of the forum or has its seat or principal place of business in that State.
2. A State can, however, invoke immunity from jurisdiction in such a proceeding if the States concerned have so agreed or if the parties to the dispute have so provided by an agreement in writing or if the instrument establishing or regulating the body in question contains provisions to that effect.

1. Introduction

Article 15 of the Convention, a provision whose complexity outweighs its likely practical significance, governs the immunity of a State in its capacity as a participant in a company or other collective body in respect of proceedings in a foreign court concerning the State's relations with the body or with other participants in it. The provision addresses, in other words, dealings by a State which, by and large, could aptly be characterized as commercial in nature, although it must be considered separately from the rules on commercial transactions in Article 10.[1]

Article 15(1), which specifies an exception to the presumptive immunity from proceedings in the courts of another State provided for in Article 5 of the Convention, is limited in scope. It covers only certain relationships internal to the company or other collective body, and does not concern itself with the rights and obligations of a State otherwise than as a participant in a company etc (for example, as an ordinary creditor or debtor[2] or as a regulator or company registrar[3]) or with relations between the State or relevant body and third parties (such as creditors,[4] public authorities,[5] or regulators). Moreover, the Article 15(1) exception applies only if the body in question involves participants other than States or international organizations and if it is either incorporated or constituted under the law of the forum State or has its seat or principal place of business in that State. Accordingly, and in contrast to Article 10, Article 15(1) requires

[1] As to the relationship between the two provisions, see sections 4.1(B)(ii) and (iv) and 4.3.

[2] See eg *Re Rafidain Bank*, 101 ILR 332 (UK (EWHC) 1991).

[3] See eg *Richard A. Week v Cayman Islands*, 983 F.2d 1074 (US (7th Cir.) 1992).

[4] See eg *Banca Carige SpA Cassa di Risparmio di Genova e Imperia v Banco Nacional de Cuba*, 124 ILR 550 (UK (EWHC) 2001).

[5] See eg *State of Georgia v City of Chattanooga, Tennessee*, 264 US 472 (US (SC) 1924).

specific territorial connecting factors to exist before a court may exercise jurisdiction in a proceeding falling within its scope. In addition, the exception to immunity from proceedings within Article 15(1) may be excluded by agreement, as Article 15(2) makes clear.

2. Background

Article 15 bears a number of similarities to Article 6 ECSI,[6] which appears to have been influential in the drafting process.[7] It also echoes an exception to immunity from proceedings found in the State immunity legislation of certain States,[8] in particular Australia,[9] Pakistan,[10] Singapore,[11] South Africa,[12] and the United Kingdom.[13] That said, not all State immunity statutes[14] or, for that matter, non-binding international[15] and non-governmental texts,[16] contain an exception to the same effect as Article 15(1), with other instruments instead addressing its subject-matter within a broad exception for commercial activities. For example, the Institut de Droit international's 1991 resolution on State immunity cites 'incorporated bodies, unincorporated bodies and associations, and partnerships' as examples of those 'relationships of a private law character to which a foreign State . . . is a party' which indicate competence under international law to determine a claim against a foreign State.[17]

[6] Art. 6 ECSI provides:

'1. A Contracting State cannot claim immunity from the jurisdiction of a court of another Contracting State if it participates with one or more private persons in a company, association or other legal entity having its seat, registered office or principal place of business on the territory of the State of the forum, and the proceedings concern the relationship, in matters arising out of that participation, between the State on the one hand and the entity or any other participant on the other hand.

2. Paragraph 1 shall not apply if it is otherwise agreed in writing.'

[7] The significance as a precedent of Art. 6 ECSI appears, however, to have been overlooked by the ILC's first Special Rapporteur on Jurisdictional Immunities of States and Their Property, Sompong Sucharitkul, when he suggested in his Sixth report that the ECSI had accommodated the exception now found in Art. 15 UNCSI under the broader heading of trade or commercial activities conducted or undertaken in the State of the forum. See Sixth report Sucharitkul, 27, para. 116. (It may be that Special Rapporteur Sucharitkul had in mind Art. 7 ECSI.) This comment was carried forward into a footnote to the ILC's commentary to its draft arts. See ILC commentary, draft art. 15, para. 8, note 159. But *cf* ILC commentary, draft art. 15, para. 6, citing Art. 6 ECSI as a source of inspiration for the text of Art. 15 UNCSI.

[8] This legislation was cited in Special Rapporteur Sucharitkul's Sixth report, as well as in the ILC commentary. See, respectively, Sixth report Sucharitkul, 26, paras 114–115 (not including the Australian, Israeli, or Japanese legislation, which postdates the report) and ILC commentary, draft art. 15, para. 8, note 159.

[9] See s. 16 FStIA (Aus).

[10] See s. 9 SIO (Pak).

[11] See s. 9 SIA (Sing).

[12] See s. 9 FStIA (SA).

[13] See s. 8 SIA (UK). See also Art. 14 ACJJFS (Jpn), adopted in 2009 in anticipation of Japan's ratification of the UNCSI.

[14] See SIA (Can) and FSIA (US), as referred to in Sixth report Sucharitkul, 26, para. 115. See also, subsequently, FSIL (Isr). Reliance must be placed instead on the commercial activity or transaction exception found in s. 5 SIA (Can), s. 1605(*a*)(2) FSIA (US), and s. 3 FSIL (Isr) respectively.

[15] See Inter-American Draft Convention, as referred to in ILC commentary, draft art. 15, para. 8, note 159. It must be assumed that the drafters envisaged reliance instead on the exception in Art. 5 Inter-American Draft Convention in respect of trade or commercial activities in the forum State.

[16] See Institut resolution and ILA Revised Draft Articles. For alternative, more general exceptions, see Art. 2(2)(*b*) Institut resolution and Art. III(B)(i) ILA Revised Draft Articles.

[17] Art. 2(2)(*b*) Institut resolution.

3. Drafting History

3.1 The Special Rapporteur's proposed exception

In his preliminary report, delivered in 1979, Special Rapporteur Sucharitkul identified, under the heading 'Shareholdings and membership of bodies corporate', the following possible exception to the immunity of a State from proceedings in the courts of another State:

> In respect of its membership of a body corporate, or an uncorporated [*sic*] entity or a partnership, a State is not immune from suits against it in the country where jurisdiction is being exercised, whether the subject matter relates to the dispute with that body or its other members or partners. Proceedings relating to the operation of a trading corporation or commercial enterprise in which the State has an interest as shareholder or stockholder, or to its interests in the shares or stock in that body, lie outside the scope of application of the rule of State immunity.[18]

Developing the proposition in his Sixth Report, the Special Rapporteur suggested a draft article 18 framed as follows and under the same heading as before:

1. A State cannot invoke immunity from the jurisdiction of a court of another State in a proceeding relating to the determination of its rights and obligations arising from its shareholdings or membership of a body corporate, an unincorporated body or a partnership between the State and the body or its other members or, as the case may be, between the State and the partnership or the other partners, provided that the body or partnership:
   (*a*) has members other than States; and
   (*b*) is incorporated or constituted under the law of the State of the forum or is controlled from or has its principal place of business in that State.
2. Paragraph 1 does not apply if provision to the contrary has been made by an agreement in writing between the parties to the dispute or by the constitution or other instrument establishing or regulating the body or partnership in question.[19]

As will be seen, this proposed exception was carried forward in essence into the final text, although a number of important technical changes were made.

3.2 The work of the Drafting Committee prior to adoption on first reading

The tenor of the proposed exception was generally well received in the Commission.[20] The text of the Special Rapporteur's proposed draft article was, however, substantially amended by the Drafting Committee before its provisional adoption on first reading. The Committee's ostensible objective in these revisions was to formulate a rule 'in more general terms, so as to take account of the various kinds of legal persons and forms of association under different legal systems'.[21] To this avowed end, the Committee made a

[18] Preliminary report Sucharitkul, 242, para. 79.

[19] Sixth report Sucharitkul, 27, para. 118. For the Rapporteur's justification of the provision, see section 4.1.A.

[20] See summary record 1833rd to 1838th ILC meetings, *YILC 1984*, vol. I, 110–45 and summary record 1869th ILC meeting, *YILC 1984*, vol. I, 330, 332–4, paras 16–35. A notable exception to the consensus on first reading was the Soviet representative, Nikolai Ushakov, who declared his strong opposition to draft art. 18 and criticized its wording as containing 'several enigmas'. See eg summary record 1869th ILC meeting, *YILC 1984*, vol. I, 333, paras 25–28, quote para. 25. Note also the reservations expressed in the ILC's commentary to draft article 18 as provisionally adopted on first reading. See Report ILC, thirty-sixth session, 72 (para. 13 of commentary to draft art. 18).

[21] Summary record 1869th ILC meeting (n. 20), 332, para. 16.

range of changes. First, the words 'Unless otherwise agreed between the States concerned' were introduced at the beginning of paragraph 1 as an indication of the residual nature of the rule.[22] Secondly, the words 'the determination of its rights and obligations arising from' were deleted as surplusage.[23] Thirdly, the term 'participation' (also used in the French-language version) was chosen instead of 'membership' and the term 'participants'[24] substituted elsewhere for 'members'.[25] Consequently, the reference to shareholdings was deleted, it being thought that this was implicit in the term 'participation' in the case of an incorporated body and inapplicable in the case of other bodies.[26] Fourthly, the reference to 'a body corporate, an unincorporated body or a partnership'[27] was replaced by the less specific expression 'company or other collective body, whether incorporated or unincorporated'.[28] The Chairman of the Drafting Committee explained the reasoning behind this series of terminological changes as follows:

> In order to overcome the virtually insurmountable difficulties of transposing terms and concepts specific to a particular language and legal system, the Committee... sought to arrive at a more general form of wording and to find an expression that would command sufficiently broad acceptance to cover the various types of legal persons and forms of association under the various legal systems.[29]

Similar difficulties led, fifthly, to the replacement of the original description of the parties to the proceedings in question (namely 'the State and the body or its other members or, as the case may be, ... the State and the partnership or the other partners') by a more concise reference to proceedings concerning 'the relationship between the State and the body or the other participants therein'.[30] Sixthly, when it came to subparagraph (*a*) of paragraph 1, the words 'or international organizations' were added to make clear that States could combine with international organizations in the formation of companies or other collective bodies without losing their immunity.[31] Finally, while the English-language text of subparagraph (*b*) of paragraph 1 was left intact, in the French- and

[22] See summary record 1868th ILC meeting, *YILC 1984*, vol. I, 320, 321, para. 6.

[23] See summary record 1869th ILC meeting (n. 20), 332, para. 17.

[24] The term used in the French text of the draft article provisionally adopted on first reading, as well as of the eventual Art. 15, is '*parties*'.

[25] See summary record 1869th ILC meeting (n. 20), 332, para. 22.

[26] See summary record 1869th ILC meeting (n. 20), 332n. 25, para. 17.

[27] The French text of the original proposal referred to '*une société dotée de la personnalité juridique ou... une société en participation*'.

[28] See summary record 1869th ILC meeting (n. 20), 332, para. 18. The expression used in the French text provisionally adopted on first reading and of the eventual Art. 15 is '*une société ou un groupement ayant ou non la personnalité juridique*'.

[29] Summary record 1869th ILC meeting (n. 20), 332, para. 18.

[30] See Summary record 1869th ILC meeting (n. 20), 332, para 19. The French version of the Drafting Committee's text ('*une procédure... concernant les rapports sociétaires*') as provisionally adopted on first reading was even more concise, but the text eventually adopted on first reading in 1986 ('*une procédure... concernant les rapports entre l'Etat et la société ou le groupement ou les autres associés*') was more closely aligned with the English. See, respectively, Report ILC, thirty-sixth session (French version), 65 and 72, draft art. 18(1) and Report ILC, thirty-eighth session (French version), 11, draft art. 17(1). The eventual text of Art. 15 refers to '*les rapports entre l'Etat et la société ou le groupement ou les autres parties*'.

[31] See summary record 1838th ILC meeting (n. 20), 144, paras 20–21 and summary record 1869th ILC meeting (n. 20), 332, para. 22.

Spanish-language versions the references to the source of 'control' over a company etc were replaced by references to the location of the 'seat'.[32]

3.3 The subsequent drafting history

The provision which became Article 15 of the Convention passed largely unchanged through the remaining drafting stages, and a few points only are of note.

First, in line with amendments to other provisions, the requirement that the court seized be 'otherwise competent' was inserted prior to the adoption on first reading of what was by then draft article 17.[33] Secondly, certain adjustments, mostly of a technical nature, were made to the French-language version.[34] Thirdly, substantive comments on the draft article as adopted on first reading were received from a few States,[35] most notably Austria and the Federal Republic of Germany. Austria suggested the deletion of the words 'or is controlled from' in subparagraph (*b*) of paragraph 1.[36] The Federal Republic of Germany suggested that the connecting factors cited in the same subparagraph should be placed in order of precedence,[37] by which it apparently sought to give jurisdictional priority, in the event of concurrent proceedings in different States, to the courts of the State in which the principal place of business of the company etc was located.[38] The German proposal was rejected by the new Special Rapporteur, Motoo Ogiso, who noted that neither Article 6 ECSI nor section 8 SIA (UK) gave precedence to the principal place of business.[39] Fourthly, prior to the provisional adoption on second reading of the then draft article 16, the Drafting Committee made further changes to clarify what its Chairman described as 'a few ambiguities' in the text.[40] In particular, in order to delineate more clearly between the exception to immunity from proceedings laid down in paragraph 1 and the possibilities for derogating from it specified in paragraph 2, the words 'Unless otherwise agreed between the States concerned' were deleted from the former and the words 'if the States concerned have so agreed' inserted in the latter.[41] Paragraph 2 was also reformulated, with its new opening words ('A State can, however, invoke immunity from jurisdiction in such a proceeding'[42]) suggesting that it was now

[32] See summary record 1869th ILC meeting (n. 20), 332, para. 22. In French, the phrase '*soit contrôlée à partir de cet Etat*' became '*ait le siège de sa direction ... dans cet Etat*'. In the Spanish, '*sea controlada desde ese Estado*' became '*tenga la sede de su dirección ... en ese Estado*'. As to the Drafting Committee's general approach to correspondence between the different language texts and the need for close attention to the question on second reading, see summary record 1869th ILC meeting (n. 20), 332, paras 20–21.

[33] See Report ILC, thirty-eighth session, 8, para. 18.

[34] See Report ILC, thirty-eighth session, 8, para. 18. Recall in particular the change discussed in n. 30.

[35] See UN doc. A/CN.4/410 and Add. 1–5, reproduced *YILC 1988*, vol. II(1), 45, 56 (Austria, para. 12), 63 (Chile, para. 13), 71 (FRG, para. 18), 75 (Mexico, para. 26), and 82 (Thailand, para. 15).

[36] See *YILC 1988*, vol. II(1), 56 (para. 12). See, further below section 4.2.B(vi).

[37] See *YILC 1988*, vol. II(1), 71 (para. 18).

[38] The approach reflected German private international law rules for corporate matters, under which the law of the place where a company's actual centre of administration is located ('*Sitztheorie*' or real seat theory) is applied in preference to the law of the State of incorporation ('*Gründungstheorie*' or incorporation theory). See Case C-208/00, *Überseering BV v Nordic Construction Company Baumanagement GmbH* [2002] ECR I-9919, para. 4, where certain aspects of the '*Sitztheorie*' were held to violate EU rules on free movement. See also section 4.1.A.

[39] See Preliminary report Ogiso, 114, para. 176. See also Third report Ogiso, 15.

[40] Summary record 2219th ILC meeting, *YILC 1991*, vol. I, 75, 78, para. 50.

[41] Summary record 2219th ILC meeting (n. 40), 78, para. 51.

[42] See Summary record 2219th ILC meeting (n. 40), 78, para. 49 for the text, the commas around 'however' in fact being added between provisional and final adoption on second reading.

concerned solely with arrangements enhancing the protection afforded to the State. At the same time, the wording of the second connecting factor in subparagraph (*b*) of paragraph 1 of the English text was changed from 'is controlled from' to make reference instead to the 'seat' of the entity, in line with the French and Spanish texts and with Article 6 ECSI.[43]

The provision was finally adopted on second reading as article 15 of the ILC's draft articles. It was carried forward without further amendment or renumbering to become Article 15 of the Convention.

4. Key Points

4.1 Article 15(1)

A. Rationale

In the view of Special Rapporteur Sucharitkul, the exception to a State's immunity from proceedings in the courts of another State now found in Article 15 of the Convention was justified, despite the paucity of case-law and international opinion supporting its existence,[44] both by the legislative practice of States[45] and by arguments based on consent and necessity.[46]

As to the argument based on consent, the Rapporteur, having addressed himself to the treatment of company law and similar matters under private international law rules, reasoned:

> If the only applicable law coincides with the sole jurisdiction of the State of incorporation and customary international law requires other States to respect the applicable local law of the place of incorporation or of the place of business operation, as the case may be, the presumption is almost irrebuttable that any extraterritorial State acquiring shares in a company or membership of a body corporate established under the law of another State must have understood and consented to be bound by the very same law which creates the legal obligations contracted and, failing other available jurisdictions, also agreed to the exercise of jurisdiction by the competent court of that legal system in all matters relating to or arising out of the legal relationship connected with the company or body corporate in question. No other explanation makes any sense.[47]

With respect, this argument, which links Article 15(1)'s exception to immunity to private international law concepts, rests on questionable foundations. In the field of private international law, State practice concerning questions of jurisdiction and identification of the applicable law with respect to the affairs of corporate and unincorporated bodies is diverse.[48] In particular, there is a continuing divide between those legal systems which

[43] See Summary record 2219th ILC meeting (n. 40), 78, para 52. The French and Spanish texts, which had previously referred to '*le siège de sa direction*' and '*la sede de su dirección*' respectively (see n. 32) were also amended to refer simply to '*le siège*' and '*la sede*'.

[44] Sixth report Sucharitkul, 26–7, paras 112 and 117. In response, Paul Reuter observed (summary record 1833rd ILC meeting, *YILC 1984*, vol. I, 110, 115, paras 38–39) that, '[i]n fact, practice was abundant, but it was not known', a possible reference to Swiss practice concerning 'the presence in Switzerland of numerous private companies wholly owned by foreign States'.

[45] Sixth report Sucharitkul, 26, paras 113–115. See the references to legislation in section 2, nn. 9–14.

[46] Sixth report Sucharitkul, 25–6, paras 105–111. See also ILC commentary, draft art. 15, paras 7–8.

[47] Sixth report Sucharitkul, 26, para. 110.

[48] For an admirably detailed survey of the landscape in the middle of the twentieth century, see E. Rabel, *The Conflict of Laws: A Comparative Study* (Chicago: Callaghan & Co., 1947), vol. II, part 6. See also, more

focus on the place of incorporation or formation, a theory associated with the common law world, and those jurisdictions which focus on the 'real seat' of the company, *viz* the place where its central administration is established.[49] In its private international law, a State may associate itself with the 'incorporation theory' or the 'real seat theory' or adopt its own solutions to questions of jurisdiction and applicable law for 'corporate matters'. Although, by treaty or other international instrument, a State adopting one theory may bind itself to accept the jurisdiction of a State founded on a different theory,[50] it does not follow that a State which becomes, for example, a shareholder in a foreign company can in any meaningful sense be said to consent to the exercise of jurisdiction by a foreign court which may take a very different view from that State's own courts as to the most appropriate basis of jurisdiction with respect to company law matters.[51] The Rapporteur's reference to 'the very same law which creates the legal obligations contracted' hides this complexity. Further, insofar as the exception refers to the State where a company or other collective body has its seat or its principal place of business, it must be recognized that a State as shareholder etc will likely have only a limited ability to control or predict the location of these connecting factors. The State may have only a minority stake, and it is in any event the entity's management that will make the day-to-day decisions that will shape the entity's geographical profile and, in particular, where its places of business are located. Although this observation, of itself, does not necessarily preclude a theory of implied consent as the basis for exercise of jurisdiction over the State as a participant in the affairs of a body corporate, it makes such an argument substantially less persuasive.

As to the argument based on necessity, the Rapporteur reasoned:

> It is . . . becoming increasingly clear that, in this particular area of 'shareholdings and membership of bodies corporate', the principle of State immunity does not and cannot truly apply without creating a legal vacuum which can never be filled. This area may be said to have acquired a rightful place in the current stage of legal developments as an inevitable and uncontested exception to the doctrine of State immunity.[52]

Again, the reasoning based on the existence of a 'legal vacuum' appears inadequate.[53] State immunity, operating as a bar to the jurisdiction of domestic courts in civil proceedings, does not require that there be another available forum before which the claimant can seek a judicial remedy, and in practice there may be cases in which the claimant is left without

recently, S. Rammeloo, *Corporations in Private International Law: A European Perspective* (Oxford: Oxford University Press, 2001), chaps 4–5; P. Paschalidis, *Freedom of Establishment and Private International Law for Corporations* (Oxford: Oxford University Press, 2012), esp. chaps 1–2.

[49] In addition to the works cited in n. 48, see Case C-208/00, *Überseering BV v Nordic Construction Company Baumanagement GmbH* (n. 38).

[50] See eg Art. 22(2) Regulation (EC) No. 44/2001 of 22 December 2000 on jurisdiction and the recognition and enforcement of judgments in civil and commercial matters, OJ L12, 16.1.200, 1, 1–23, relating to proceedings concerning corporate and unincorporated bodies, which confers jurisdiction on the courts of the place of the seat but permits each Member State to apply its own rules of private international law to determine the location of the seat in each case.

[51] For example it could not meaningfully be said that the Federal Republic of Germany, a State which subscribes in its private international law rules to the 'real seat' theory (see n. 38), impliedly consents to the jurisdiction of the courts of the State of incorporation of a company in which it becomes a shareholder, whether or not the company's central administration is also located in that State.

[52] Sixth report Sucharitkul, 26, para. 111.

[53] For a similar argument, based on the practical consequences of according immunity, see the text to n. 58.

such a remedy.[54] Even in these cases, however, it does not follow that there is a 'legal vacuum'. The immunity which the Convention recognizes is procedural, not substantive, in character.[55] Thus, even if it were entitled to assert immunity from jurisdiction, the State would remain subject to any laws affecting the company or other body in which it invests, and those laws may be given effect in such a way as to affect the State's position without the need for judicial proceedings which would engage the provisions of the Convention. (For example, the rights and obligations of the State may be affected as a consequence of resolutions passed at a general meeting or of entries made in the company's register.) A State may also choose to waive its immunity. Accordingly, the likely absence of a judicial remedy if a State is permitted to, and does, assert immunity from the jurisdiction of any courts which may consider themselves competent to determine disputes on a particular subject-matter does not render the conferral of that immunity illogical or unjustifiable.

Instead, it is submitted, the exception in Article 15(1) can be rationalized on a different and more straightforward basis. When participating in a company or other body established under domestic law, a State typically performs acts *jure gestionis*, in the sense of acts 'of a private law character such as a private citizen might have entered into'.[56] This being the case, the removal of the State's immunity in respect of such acts accords with the modern, restrictive doctrine of State immunity which underpins most of the other provisions of Part III of the Convention, including the commercial transaction exception in Article 10.[57] An explanation to this effect accords, furthermore, with the requirement in subparagraph (*a*) of Article 15(1) that the body have participants other than States or international organizations, a requirement which emphasizes that the State, through its involvement in a company etc, is descending from the international plane and engaging in an activity alongside, and on the same level as, one or more non-international actors.

In policy terms, removing the State's immunity from jurisdiction not only removes an unjustifiable procedural inequality between participants in a company etc but also serves an important practical purpose, as explained by one of the members of the ILC's Drafting Committee:

> There was, of course, good reason for such a provision, since the alternative would be the enactment of legislation stipulating that States could not participate in commercial organizations. In other words, article [15] was merely saying that, when it came to investing in, or participating in the control of, a commercial organization in another country, a State could not have its cake and eat it. It could hardly be otherwise, for a rule of immunity would not only adversely affect the organizations themselves, but would also frustrate the implementation and enforcement of the statutory schemes that governed the way in which such companies operated. Article [15], therefore, was a logical and necessary element of the draft.[58]

[54] Consider in the context of the Council of Europe, however, the possible impact of Art. 6(1) ECHR. See, in this regard the commentary to Art. 6.

[55] On the purely procedural nature of the immunity conferred under the Convention, see the commentary to Art. 6. See also *Dickinson v Del Solar*, 5 ILR 29 (UK (CA) 1929); *United States v Nolan* [2010] EWCA Civ 1223, [2011] IRLR 40 (UK (EWCA) 2010); *Jurisdictional Immunities of the State (Germany v Italy: Greece intervening), Judgment*, International Court of Justice, 3 February 2012, paras 58 and 93.

[56] *I° Congreso del Partido*, 64 ILR 307, 314 (Lord Wilberforce) (UK (HL) 1982).

[57] For a discussion of whose rationale see the commentary to Art. 10, section 1.

[58] Summary record 1837th ILC meeting, *YILC 1984*, vol. I, 135, 137, para. 13 (Stephen C. McCaffrey). Earlier in the paragraph, the speaker appears to suggest that the basis of the provision might lie in the supposed

This reasoning, if taken to its logical conclusion, would be capable of supporting a wider exception than that recognized in Article 15(1), without the restrictions set out in subparagraphs (*a*) and (*b*). The further limits to be found in Article 15(1)(*a*) and (*b*) respectively can, however, be explained in terms which seem consistent with the above proposition that the Article 15(1) exception is a specific application of the principle of non-immunity for acts *jure gestionis*. First, as noted above, the situation of a company or other collective body populated solely by States and international organizations is one where the relevant relationships, although arising from domestic law, retain a sufficient link to the international plane to justify giving priority to the claim of immunity. Secondly, the requirement of a connecting link to the forum State (whether it be the company etc's place of incorporation, its seat, or its principal place of business) would seem to mark an apparent, albeit imprecise, attempt to reflect the range of private international law practice in allocating jurisdiction with respect to disputes pertaining to corporate matters.

B. Application

As its opening words indicate, Article 15(1) constitutes an exception to the immunity of a State from foreign proceedings recognized in Article 5 of the Convention. Its application depends on several requirements being satisfied with respect to the proceedings in which the question of immunity arises. As the provision makes clear, it applies only to proceedings which relate to the 'participation' of a State in a 'company or other collective body, whether incorporated or unincorporated' and which concern either the relationship between the State and the body itself or the relationship between the State and one or more other participants in the body. Article 15(1) does not concern itself with the rights and obligations of a State otherwise than as a participant in a company or collective body or with relations between the State or the body itself and third parties. Further, Article 15(1) applies only if the relevant body has participants other than States or international organizations, as required by subparagraph (*a*), and is incorporated or constituted under the law of the forum State or has its seat or principal place of business in that State, as required by subparagraph (*b*). These elements raise further questions, which, although to a degree interlinked, will be addressed by examining, in the order in which it appears in the text, the particular wording of Article 15(1) to which each question principally relates.

(i) The concept of a 'State'

It should first be noted for the avoidance of doubt that the term 'State' is used in Article 15(1), wherever it appears, in accordance with the definition given to the term in Article 2(1)(*b*) of the Convention. In other words, Article 15(1) applies where the proceedings relate to the participation in a company or other collective body not only of the State as such but also of one or more of its various organs of government or, in specified circumstances, of its constituent federal units or other political subdivisions, of its agencies, instrumentalities, or other separate entities, or of its individual representatives;[59] and it applies where those proceedings concern the relationship between, on the one hand, either the body or one or

agreement of the State ('the price of admission was in effect agreement not to claim immunity'), but the passage quoted here does not depend on such reasoning.

[59] See Art. 2(*b*)(i)–(iv) UNCSI, noting the conditions stipulated in sub-subparagraphs (ii) to (iv).

more other participants in the body and, on the other, the 'State' in any one or more of these manifestations. In addition, as with all operative provisions of the Convention, Article 15 (1) applies as much to proceedings in which one of those emanations is named as defendant, or in which the property, rights, interests, or activities of the State are affected, as to proceedings against the State itself.[60]

(ii) A State's 'participation' in a company etc

Article 15(1) applies only in respect of foreign proceedings against a State which relate to the 'participation' of that State in a company or other collective body. It is obviously essential, therefore, when approaching the provision to have a clear idea as to the meaning of the term 'participation' and what it means for a proceeding to 'relate to' it.

Taken out of context, at least the English word 'participation', and as a consequence 'participants', could be read widely so as to include, for example, the involvement of a State as creditor or debtor, contractual counterparty, functionary, or regulator of a company or other collective body. It is submitted, however, that a narrower reading, referring only to a right of ownership of or in a company etc, is the correct one. First, it should be recalled[61] that the reason why the terms 'participation' and 'participants' were preferred by the ILC's Drafting Committee to the more specific references to 'shareholdings or membership' and 'members' favoured by the Special Rapporteur in his original draft was not to extend the situations to which the draft article applied but simply to avoid using terminology specific to some legal systems only. It seems clear from the ILC commentary to the eventual draft article 15 that shareholding was seen as the paradigm example of 'participation'.[62] Secondly, the corresponding terms for 'participation' in the French ('*participation*') and Spanish ('*participación*') versions are more closely aligned with this narrower, legal meaning. Thirdly, if the term 'participants' were to be given the wider interpretation, the requirement in subparagraph (*a*) of paragraph 1 that the company etc have 'participants other than States or international organizations'[63] would be rendered redundant to all intents and purposes, as it is highly improbable that a company or other collective body's roll-call of creditors, debtors, contractual counterparties, officers, functionaries, regulators, and so on would ever consist solely of States and/or international organizations. Fourthly, it seems highly relevant as part of the interpretative context of Article 15(1), which includes other provisions of the Convention,[64] that the position of the State in its role as one of these other sorts of putative 'participants' (creditors, debtors, contractual counterparties, officers, and functionaries[65]) would plainly be dealt with under different exceptions to immunity, notably the exception in Article 10 for commercial transactions, as defined in Article 2(1)(*c*), and the

[60] See Art. 6(2)(*b*).

[61] See section 3.

[62] See ILC commentary, draft art. 15, para. 7.

[63] See section 4.1.B(iv).

[64] See Art. 31(2) VCLT.

[65] As to the position of the State as regulator (which plainly falls outside the definition of 'commercial transaction' in Art. 2(1)(*c*) UNCSI), there seems no good reason to interpret Art. 15(1), in the light of its object and purpose (as per Art. 31(1) VCLT), as extending this far. While the precise details of the doctrine can be debated, it is submitted that the statutory regulation of a company represents a very clear example of a sovereign act (an act *jure imperii*) and that clear words would be required to bring such cases within the ambit of a provision such as Art. 15(1), the main focus of which is private or commercial acts (acts *jure gestionis*). See *Richard A. Week v Cayman Islands* (n. 3), para. 39 ('[t]he chartering, oversight and regulation of companies are core governmental functions').

exception in Article 11 for contracts of employment. Overlap and possible inconsistencies between the exceptions, as would very arguably be created by interpreting Article 15(1) to include cases in which the State becomes involved in the life of a company in one of these ways, should be avoided, so far as possible. Accordingly, in summary, a 'participant' should be understood as a person holding a 'participation', a term which in turn means a right of ownership of or in a company or other collective body. Article 15(1) is not concerned with proceedings insofar as they relate to the involvement of a State, or any other person, in the affairs of a company etc as creditor or debtor[66] or in any other capacity apart from as a holder of a right of ownership in that body.

It remains inevitable, however, that the diversity of collective bodies to which Article 15(1) may apply[67] and of the types of interest recognized under national law will present difficulties in ascertaining the limits of the terms 'participation' and 'participants'. For example, is a State which as a creditor has the right in future to convert some of the debt into equity to be treated as a 'participant', even though it has not exercised the right? What about a State which has contracted to purchase, or has taken security over, shares from an existing member and which has contractual or other legal rights over the shares as a result? There appears no ready answer to these questions. It would not, however, appear necessary that the State have a controlling interest, or even that it should actively participate in the affairs of the company etc. Thus, for example, a limited partnership interest (which, in systems where this type of partnership is recognized, may expressly preclude involvement in the management of the partnership as a condition of limited liability[68]) would constitute a 'participation' for the purposes of Article 15(1). It is the fact that the State holds an interest in a company or other collective body which is the same, or which is of the same character,[69] as an interest held by one or more private persons which appears decisive.

(iii) A State's participation 'in a company or other collective body, whether incorporated or unincorporated'

Article 15(1) relates to a State's participation 'in a company or other collective body, whether incorporated or unincorporated'. These words are not to be given a narrow or technical meaning, as indicated by the ILC's commentary to draft article 15:

> The expression 'company or other collective body, whether incorporated or unincorporated', used in article 15, has been deliberately selected to cover a wide variety of legal entities as well as other bodies without legal personality. The formulation is designed to include different types or categories of bodies, collectivities and groupings known under different nomenclatures, such as corporations, associations, partnerships and other similar forms of collective bodies which may exist under various legal systems with varying degrees of legal capacity and status.[70]

The entity need not exist for a commercial or profit-making purpose: Article 15 may apply to a State's participation in a non-profit making body, 'such as a learned society, a

[66] To the same effect, see Expl. Rep. ECSI, para. 31, commenting on Art. 6 ECSI.

[67] See section 4.2.B(ii).

[68] See, eg, s. 6(1) Limited Partnerships Act 1907 (UK).

[69] Thus the fact that special rights may attach to the State's participation (eg a 'golden share') should not take the situation outside the scope of Art. 15(1).

[70] ILC commentary, draft art. 15, para. 2.

temple, a religious congregation, a charity or charitable foundation, or any other similar philanthropic organization'.[71]

Unfortunately, neither the Convention nor the ILC commentary to draft article 15(1) provides a clear answer to the question whether international organizations or other bodies established under a treaty (an instrument governed, by definition, by international law,[72] rather than by the municipal law of any State) may fall within the category of 'other collective body', in particular one which is 'unincorporated'. This question will not need to be decided in most cases, given the requirement in subparagraph (*a*) that, in order to bring the case within Article 15(1), the relevant entity must have participants other than States or international organizations.[73] That requirement would not be satisfied by the large majority of organizations established by treaty whose members consist only of States or other international organizations. In a limited number of cases, however, the 'other participants' in the international organization or similar body will include private sector entities or other entities distinct from States and international organizations. International organizations which may fall into this category include those whose membership extends to non-State territorial entities[74] and those recognizing a class of membership, such as associate or affiliate membership, which extends to non-governmental or private sector entities.[75] If so, this opens up the possibility that Article 15(1) may be argued to apply.

There is circumstantial evidence that Article 15(1) may extend this far. Addressing subparagraph (*a*)'s requirement that the relevant bodies have members other than States and international organizations, the ILC commentary provides:

> [I]nternational organizations and other forms of collectivity which are composed exclusively of States and/or international organizations without participation from the private sector are excluded from the scope of article 15.[76]

This might be taken to imply that Article 15(1) encompasses at least those international organizations whose members include private sector entities. Further, during debate in the ILC, Motoo Ogiso (who would later take on the role of Special Rapporteur) noted that there were international organizations with non-State members, expressed the opinion that 'organizations of that kind should remain outside the scope of paragraph 1(*a*)', and sought the views of other members and of Special Rapporteur Sucharitkul on

[71] ILC commentary, draft art. 15, para. 3. A suggestion that the exception be restricted to commercial activities was not taken up. See summary record 1836th ILC meeting, *YILC 1984*, vol. I, 128, 131, para. 22.

[72] See Arts 2(1)(*a*) and 5 VCLT.

[73] See section 4.1.B(v).

[74] For example, the membership of the International Monetary Fund is open to 'countries', rather than 'states', in accordance with Art. 2, s. 2 Articles of Agreement of the International Monetary Fund, Washington, 27 December 1945, 2 UNTS 39, as amended. The term is taken to extend to dependent or *sui generis* special territories of existing member countries, and the IMF's current membership includes, in their own right, the Hong Kong Special Administrative Region and the Macao Special Administrative Region (PRC), Anguilla and Monserrat (UK), and Aruba, Curaçao, the Netherlands Antilles, and Sint Maarten (Nth). As to the Convention definition of 'State', see above section 4.1.B(i) and below, text to n. 94.

[75] See eg affiliate membership of the World Tourism Organization, as per Arts 4 and 7 Statutes of the World Tourism Organization, Mexico City, 27 September 1970, 985 UNTS 350, as amended (see now <http://unwto.org/en/about/statutes>). This class of membership extends, in accordance with Art. 7(1) Statutes of the World Tourism Organization, to non-governmental international bodies 'concerned with specialized interests in tourism' and to 'commercial bodies and associations whose activities are related to the aims of the Organization or fall within its competence'.

[76] ILC commentary, draft art. 15, para. 5.

the subject.[77] A similar query was raised by Thailand in its comments on the draft articles as adopted on first reading.[78] However, no changes were made to Article 15(1) as a result of these interventions.[79]

The position is further complicated by the approach of some municipal legal systems, for example those within the United Kingdom, whereby recognition of the legal personality of an international organization is considered a matter of local law (taking into account, where appropriate, any relevant rules of private international law) and does not follow automatically from the establishment by treaty of the relevant organization and recognition of its personality under international law. For example, in *Arab Monetary Fund v Hashim (No. 3)*, the leading English decision on this point, Lord Templeman reasoned:

> [T]he international organisation for which recognition is sought must have acquired legal personality and capacity under the laws of one or more member states or the state wherein it has its seat or permanent location. This requirement is necessary because the courts of the United Kingdom cannot enforce treaty rights but they can recognise legal entities created by the laws of one or more sovereign states. A treaty cannot create a corporation but a sovereign state which is party to a treaty can, in pursuance of its obligations accepted under the treaty, create a corporation which will be recognised in the United Kingdom. A member state can create a corporation by signing and ratifying the treaty if in that member state a treaty is self-executing and becomes part of domestic law on signature and ratification.[80]

Against this background, the temptation to characterize international organizations as but one species of 'collective body' may be a strong one. Indeed, in one of the series of English cases arising from the financial collapse in the 1980s of the International Tin Council, one of the members of the Court of Appeal inclined towards the view that the ITC was an 'unincorporated body' for the purposes of the exception in section 8 SIA (UK), which corresponds to Article 15.[81]

This temptation, however strong, should be resisted. Article 15(1) should not be taken to apply to international organizations or other collective bodies established by treaty, even if their membership extends beyond States and other such organizations.[82] This conclusion accords with both the wording and rationale of the provision.[83]

[77] Summary record 1834th ILC meeting, *YILC 1984*, vol. I, 116, 117, para. 6. The example given was INTELSAT, which at the time was an international organization whose 'signatories' included telecommunications organizations. See Art. I(*g*) Agreement relating to the International Telecommunications Satellite Organization 'INTELSAT', Washington, 28 August 1971, 1220 UNTS 21. In 2001, INTELSAT became a private company incorporated in Luxembourg.

[78] See *YILC 1988*, vol. II(1) (n. 35), 82. The Thai comment suggested that the issue could be addressed by reverting to the terms 'membership' and 'members', instead of 'participation' and 'participants'. It is to be doubted whether, even if the suggestion had been accepted, it would have sufficed to address the ambiguity.

[79] See Preliminary report Ogiso, 114, para. 177.

[80] 85 ILR 1, 8–9 (UK (HL) 1991). See also *J. H. Rayner (Mincing Lane) Ltd v Department of Trade and Industry*, 81 ILR 670 (UK (HL) 1989); *Westland Helicopters Ltd v Arab Organization for Industrialization*, 108 ILR 564 (UK (EWHC) 1994). For a discussion, see C.F. Amerasinghe, *Principles of the Institutional Law of International Organizations* (2nd edn) (Cambridge: Cambridge University Press, 2005), 69–77.

[81] See *Maclaine Watson & Co. Ltd v International Tin Council*, 80 ILR 191, 207 (Ralph Gibson LJ) (UK (EWCA) 1988). The point did not, however, arise for decision in that case. The learned judge also acknowledged that this construction might be thought to yield a 'surprising result', unintended by the draftsman.

[82] To the same effect, see Expl. Rep. ECSI, para. 31, commenting on Art. 6 ECSI.

[83] For discussion in the context of the immunities of international organizations themselves, see A. Reinisch, *International Organizations before National Courts* (Cambridge: Cambridge University Press),

In terms of the wording of Article 15(1), it should be noted that subparagraph *(a)* refers expressly to 'international organizations' as being in the same position as States for the purposes of the participation requirement set out in that subparagraph. Accordingly, a domestic company in which the only shareholders are a State and an international organization is treated no differently from a domestic company in which the only shareholders are two States—Article 15(1) will apply to neither situation. Within this framework, it appears curious (indeed absurd) to subject a State's membership of an international organization to the scrutiny of national courts solely because the organization, by its founding treaty, admits persons other than States or other international organizations as members. Further, it is also worth noting that the first connecting factor in subparagraph (*b*), namely that the body is 'incorporated or constituted under the law of the State of the forum' cannot, at least without artificiality, be applied to an international organization.[84] Although the alternative connecting factors cited in the subparagraph, namely the body's 'seat or principal place of business', could be so applied without such difficulty,[85] the possibility of reliance on the body's incorporation or constitution *under the law of the forum State* may be thought to indicate, by way of context, that Article 15(1) is not intended to apply to collective bodies (such as international organizations) whose origins lie in a treaty and not in an act of incorporation under domestic law.

As for the rationale for Article 15(1), it will readily be apparent—whether the provision is rationalized in terms of consent or, as suggested above,[86] in terms of the State's engagement in acts of a private law character (acts *jure gestionis*)—that participation in an international organization constituted by way of treaty is of a wholly different character to participation in an entity incorporated or constituted under domestic law, and cannot support the inference that the State has consented to the jurisdiction of the courts of the seat or headquarters of the organization or has performed acts *jure gestionis*. As Millett J noted in another case arising from the collapse of the International Tin Council:

> Sovereign states are free, if they wish, to carry on a collective enterprise through the medium of an ordinary commercial company incorporated in the territory of one of their number. But if they choose instead to carry it on through the medium of an international organisation, no one member state, by executive, legislative or judicial action, can assume the management of the enterprise and subject it to its own domestic law. For if one could, then all could; and the independence and international character of the organisation would be fragmented and destroyed.[87]

233–43, 324–6 and 377–82, and the materials cited therein. See also *Westland Helicopters Ltd v Arab Organization for Industrialization* (n. 80). As to the relationship between the broader principle of sovereign equality and the constitutional framework of international organizations, see J. Kokott, 'States, Sovereign Equality', in R. Wolfrum (ed.), *Max Planck Encyclopedia of Public International Law* (Oxford: Oxford University Press, 2012), vol. IX, 571, paras 70–77.

[84] *Cf*, however, the views of Lord Templeman and Lord Lowry in *Arab Monetary Fund v Hashim (No. 3)* (n. 80), 5 (Lord Templeman) and 26–8 (Lord Lowry) as to whether the Fund had been 'incorporated' by domestic legislation of the United Arab Emirates.

[85] If Art. 15(1) were to apply, one could plausibly characterize the organization's headquarters as the 'seat' and/or 'principal place of business' of the organization, giving jurisdiction to the courts of the location of the headquarters to determine disputes as against members of the organization other than the forum State (to which the UNCSI would not apply). The immunities and privileges of the organization itself would, of course, need to be separately determined.

[86] See section 4.1.A.

[87] *Re International Tin Council*, 77 ILR 18, 36 (UK (EWHC) 1987), rejecting the submission that UK insolvency legislation should be read as applying to an international organization such as the ITC.

A narrow reading of Article 15(1) in this respect protects the independence of international organizations and is to be preferred.

(iv) A proceeding 'concerning the relationship between the State and the body or the other participants therein'

In order for the exception to immunity from proceedings embodied in Article 15(1) to apply, the proceedings must concern the relationship either, first, between the defendant State and the company or other collective body in question or, secondly, between that State and the other participants in the company etc. It has been suggested above that the term 'participants' in a company or other collective body, as used in Article 15(1), should be taken to refer to persons holding a 'participation', meaning a right of ownership of or in a company etc.[88] Article 15(1) also requires that the proceedings relate to the defendant State's participation. The requirement that the proceedings in question concern 'the relationship between the State and the body or the other participants therein' narrows Article 15(1) still further. The focus of the exception is on relationships which are internal to the company etc, namely the vertical relationship between the company etc and its shareholders or other participants and the horizontal relationship among the participants themselves. Put another way, Article 15(1) is not concerned with proceedings which do not have as their subject-matter the rights and obligations of the State as a participant in the body vis-à-vis the body itself or one or more other participants, where those rights and obligations arise from their respective participations.

Consequently, it seems clear that Article 15(1) would not apply to proceedings between a State and another participant (or former or aspiring participant) in a company etc where the proceedings are brought for the purpose of enforcing the provisions of a share purchase agreement. The relationship between the parties in question would not be one between participants in the company etc with respect to their rights and obligations as participants, but between the parties to a commercial contract the subject-matter of which happens to be rights of participation. This dispute would fall not within Article 15 but within the exception for commercial transactions in Article 10, to which reference has already been made. A fortiori, Article 15 would also not appear material to any question as to whether a State is entitled to assert immunity from proceedings which call into question, for example by way of a title claim, a State's purported acquisition of shareholdings or other interests in a company etc by means of expropriation or otherwise by operation of law, for example as a result of bankruptcy.[89] In such cases, although the dispute between the rival parties may be said to concern, indirectly, the relationship between the State and the company etc, its direct focus is on events which preceded the

[88] See section 4.1.B(ii).

[89] See eg the 'international takings exception' to immunity in s. 1605(3) FSIA (US), concerning proceedings in respect of property taken in violation of international law, as was at issue in *Siderman de Blake v Republic of Argentina*, 103 ILR 454, 467–9 (US (9th Cir.) 1992). Note that the recognition in such situations of the State's proprietary interest may raise private international law issues of jurisdiction and applicable law, as well as the question of the justiciability of a claim founded on a 'foreign act of state'. For a discussion, see P. Adriaanse, *Confiscation in Private International Law* (The Hague: Martinus Nijhoff, 1956); Lord Collins of Mapesbury (ed.), *Dicey, Morris & Collins: The Conflict of Laws* (15th edn) (London: Sweet & Maxwell, 2012), rules 3 and 137 and commentary; M. Ooi, *Shares and Other Securities in the Conflict of Laws* (Oxford: Oxford University Press, 2003), 20–2, paras 2.21–2.27. The leading English case on this subject is *Williams & Humbert Ltd v W & H Trade Marks (Jersey) Ltd* [1986] AC 468 (UK (HL) 1985), noted F.A. Mann (1986) 102 *LQR* 191. In such cases, the question of immunity from proceedings is a logically prior one.

State's acquisition of its participation, and should be considered to be separate from it. The exclusion of 'expropriation' disputes from Article 15 would also be consistent with the reasoning underlying Article 15(1), whether the provision be explained on the basis of State consent or, as suggested above,[90] in terms of the State's engagement in an act *jure gestionis, viz* an act of a private law character. A State which expropriates property by legislative or other governmental act cannot, by this action,[91] be said to have performed an act *jure gestionis* or to have consented to the jurisdiction of the courts of the State of incorporation, seat, or headquarters of the entity expropriated.[92] If, however, the State continues to hold the acquired interest following expropriation or acquisition by any other means, the nature of its conduct changes. Its interest becomes more closely aligned with that of a private participant, and in these circumstances it should—subject to the other requirements of Article 15(1)—no longer be entitled to rely on the immunity from jurisdiction recognized in Article 5 with respect to that later conduct.

Again, however, difficult cases will no doubt arise. For example, it is unclear whether Article 15(1) would apply to disputes concerning agreements between shareholders or promoters which are legally separate from the instrument establishing the body or to disputes between current and past participants in relation to their rights and obligations as such. In principle, there appears no reason why Article 15 should not apply to a dispute of the latter kind. In the case of a shareholders' agreement, the precise nature of the right relied on and its relationship to the parties' rights under company etc law will need to be more closely examined.

(v) A body which 'has participants other than States or international organizations'

Article 15(1)(*a*) indicates that, in order for Article 15(1) to apply, the company or other collective body in question must have at least one[93] participant which is neither a State nor an international organization. Here, as elsewhere in Article 15, the reference to a State must be understood, in accordance with Article 2(1)(*b*) of the Convention, to embrace not only the State as such but also its several emanations,[94] and may here include the forum State (including its emanations). As to international organizations,

[90] See section 4.1.A.

[91] Other, factually associated conduct of the expropriating State may, of course, have implications for the availability of State immunity. See eg *I° Congreso del Partido* (n. 56), 319–20 (Lord Wilberforce).

[92] *Cf* draft art. 20 as adopted on first reading, Report ILC, thirty-eighth session, 17: 'The provisions of the present articles shall not prejudge any question that may arise in regard to extraterritorial effects of measures of nationalization taken by a State with regard to property, movable or immovable, industrial or intellectual.' The draft commentary to the provision stated, Report ILC, thirty-eighth session, 17: 'It is generally understood that nationalization, within the context of this article, is a measure taken by a State in the exercise of its sovereign authority.' Draft art. 20 as adopted on first reading received a mixed reaction and was deleted on second reading, although it was reiterated (Report ILC, forty-second session, 39, paras 214–215) that 'measures of nationalization, as sovereign acts, were not subject to the jurisdiction of another State and could not be considered as representing an exception to the principle of State immunity'.

[93] The reference to 'participants' should be read as embodying the singular as well as the plural. See *YILC 1988*, vol. II(1), para. 5 ('without participation from the private sector') and Sixth report Sucharitkul, 26, para. 113 (noting the requirement in earlier national legislative provisions that 'another member (or members) must not be a State'). *Cf*, however, the suggestion by ILC member Paul Reuter (summary record 1869th ILC meeting, *YILC 1984*, vol. I, 110, 116, para. 39) that '[t]he Special Rapporteur required that at least two members should not be States'.

[94] See section 4.1.B. Consider also para. 13 of the ILC's commentary to art. 2 of its draft Articles on Responsibility of International Organizations, Report ILC, sixty-third session, 77, which makes clear that the presence of States as members of an international organization may take the form of membership 'by individual State organs or agencies'.

draft article 2(*a*) of the ILC's draft articles on responsibility of international organizations, as finally adopted on second reading in 2011,[95] provides a useful point of departure,[96] defining an international organization as 'an organization established by a treaty or other instrument governed by international law and possessing its own international legal personality'. The provision adds that international organizations 'may include as members, in addition to States, other entities'. This definition would not extend, however, to transnational non-governmental organizations (NGOs) or inter-State enterprises established solely under the law of one or more[97] States.[98]

The requirement in Article 15(1)(*a*) of participation in the company or other collective body by at least one entity other than a State or international organization is likely to exclude very few companies etc from the scope of Article 15(1), since most companies etc created under municipal law have some private sector ownership. It may be, however, that the requirement will become increasingly important as the constitutional and procedural imperatives implicated by the conclusion of treaties, as well as the management of international organizations, lead cooperating States to consider more efficient and economical solutions to problems requiring common action. A recent, significant example is the European Financial Stability Fund (EFSF), established in 2010 as a private law company under Luxembourg law for the purpose of providing financial support to the member States of the eurozone.[99] Its shareholders consist exclusively of those member States. Accordingly, the Article 15(1) exception would not apply in proceedings between the EFSF and a member State or between member States in their capacity as shareholders.

(vi) A body which is 'incorporated or constituted under the law of the State of the forum or has its seat or principal place of business in that State'

Article 15(1)(*b*) requires that, for Article 15(1) to apply, the company or other collective body in question be incorporated or constituted under the law of the forum State or have either its 'seat' or principal place of business in that State. The requirement of incorporation or constitution under the forum State's law is unlikely to present significant difficulties of interpretation, the terms 'incorporated' and 'constituted' being intended to refer generically to the formation of a collective body under municipal law.[100] In the case of States comprising more than one legal system, it will suffice that the company etc has been formed under the law of any legal system within that State. Enterprises

[95] Report ILC, sixty-third session, 54, para. 87.

[96] That the definition is not necessarily to be taken as definitive for all international legal purposes is emphasized in the ILC's commentary to draft art, 2, para. 1. For more on the concept of an international organization, see eg P. Sands and P. Klein (eds), *Bowett's Law of International Institutions* (6th edn) (London: Sweet & Maxwell, 2009), para. 1–028; Amerasinghe (n. 80), 10–11; H.G. Schermers and N. Blokker, *International Institutional Law: Unity within Diversity* (4th edn) (Leiden: Martinus Nijhoff, 2004), paras 29–47.

[97] See eg The Arab Investment Company SAA (TAIC) (<http://www.taic.com>), established in 1974 as a 'pan-Arab joint-stock company' and owned by the governments of 17 Arab States.

[98] See Sands and Klein (n. 96), para. 1–029; D. Akande, 'International Organizations' in M.D. Evans (ed.), *International Law* (3rd edn) (Oxford: Oxford University Press, 2010), 252, 253–4.

[99] The statutes of the EFSF are available at <http://www.efsf.europa.eu/about/legal-documents/index.htm>. For another example, see the Asia-Europe Foundation (<http://www.asef.org>), established in 1997 as a company limited by guarantee under the laws of Singapore.

[100] See ILC commentary, draft art. 15, para. 8, referring to a State's 'system of incorporation, charter or other type of constitution' of a company or other collective body.

incorporated or constituted under the laws of more than one State will *semble* fulfil the requirement in Article 15(1)(*b*) in the event of proceedings in any of those States. As to the other two connecting factors cited in Article 15(1)(*b*), the ILC commentary to draft article 15—borrowing without acknowledgment from the Explanatory Report to the ECSI, whose Article 6 cites the same two factors—explains that '[t]he seat is normally the place from which the entity is directed; and the principal place of business means the place where the major part of its business is conducted'.[101] The enquiry required of the court would appear largely factual in character. The ILC commentary suggests that the verb 'directed' is concerned with the acts of those in day-to-day control of the entity's affairs and not of those by which the State exercises such control as it may have over the company's affairs.[102]

4.2 Article 15(2)

Article 15(1)'s exception to the immunity from foreign proceedings accorded to a State by Article 5 of the Convention is subject to derogation as specified in Article 15(2). In accordance with this provision, a State may, notwithstanding Article 15(1), successfully assert immunity from jurisdiction in any of three situations, each of which calls for brief examination.

A. 'the States concerned have so agreed'

In accordance with paragraph 2 of Article 15, a State may invoke immunity from the jurisdiction of a court of another State in proceedings of the sort stipulated in paragraph 1 'if the States concerned have so agreed'. The reference to the States concerned is to the forum State and the defendant State. In contrast with an agreement between the parties to the dispute to disapply paragraph 1 of Article 15,[103] there is no requirement on the face of paragraph 2 that an agreement between States to do the same be in writing.

B. 'the parties to the dispute have so provided by an agreement in writing'

Article 15(2) further provides that a State is entitled to rely on immunity from jurisdiction even in the circumstances specified in Article 15(1) 'if the parties to the dispute have so provided by an agreement in writing'. The reference to the parties to the dispute is to the defendant State and either the claimant or the person whose right is asserted by the claimant.

C. 'if the instrument establishing or regulating the body in question contains provisions to that effect'

Finally, Article 15(2) provides that the exception to jurisdictional immunity in Article 15(1) may be set aside 'if the instrument establishing or regulating the body in question contains provisions to that effect'. The ILC commentary explains that '[t]he phrase "the instrument establishing or regulating the body in question" should be understood as intending to apply only to the two fundamental instruments of a corporate body and not

[101] *YILC 1988*, vol. II(1), para. 6, drawing without acknowledgment on Expl. Rep. ECSI, para. 32.

[102] See n. 100, noting that '[t]he reference to the place of control which appeared in the English text of paragraph 1*(b)* provisionally adopted on first reading ha[d] been deleted, as it was felt that the issue of determination of how a State is in control of a corporate entity was a very controversial one'. See also section 3 for the drafting history of Art. 15(1)(*b*).

[103] See section 4.2.B.

to any other type of regulation'.[104] The reference here is to the memorandum and articles of association (by-laws) or equivalent documents. In other words, Article 15(1) cannot be set aside by way of provisions in, for example, a shareholders' agreement.

4.3 Relationship to Article 10[105]

A State's participation in a company or other collective body could, without straining the use of language, be characterized as a 'transaction of a commercial, industrial, trading or professional nature' and could, therefore, be classified as a 'commercial transaction' within the meaning of Article 2(1)(*c*) of the Convention. If, however, this analysis were to be adopted, there would be a substantial overlap between Article 15 and the exception to immunity in Article 10 in respect of commercial transactions, as the term is defined in Article 2(1)(*c*). The consequence of such an overlap would be that Article 10, which contains no restrictions corresponding to those in subparagraphs (*a*) and (*b*) of Article 15(1), would render Article 15 largely ornamental. Although the question is not specifically addressed in the Convention,[106] the need to render effective the additional requirements in subparagraphs (*a*) and (*b*) of Article 15(1) and the objectives that they serve[107] supports a reading of 'commercial transaction' in Article 2(1)(*c*), as relied on in Article 10, so as to exclude from the scope of Article 10 the relationships between a company etc and its participants and among those participants which are specifically dealt with in Article 15. In short, the exceptions to immunity from proceedings in Articles 10 and 15 should be treated as mutually exclusive.

5. Evaluation

The several restrictions on the scope of Article 15, and the lack of a significant body of State practice with respect to claims of these kinds prior to the adoption of the Convention, suggest that the article's overall significance will be limited, at least in terms of the case-law and academic comment that it will generate. It may be, however, that a greater willingness of international actors to cooperate in new ventures otherwise than through traditional, treaty-based vehicles will lead to Article 15 and similar exceptions in existing national legislation having a more prominent role to play in the future. If that proves to be the case, national courts which are required, directly or indirectly, to apply the exception will, regrettably, also have to grapple with the many uncertainties in its formulation. Article 15 may not be the worst drafted rule in the Convention, but it has no claim to be the best.

[104] ILC commentary, draft art. 15, para. 9.

[105] See also above section 4.1.B(ii) and (iv).

[106] Note, however, Art. 2(1)(*c*)(iii)'s exclusion of contracts of employment, as dealt with in Art. 11, from the definition of 'commercial transaction' in Art. 2(1)(*c*), as relied on in Art. 10. The lack of a similar carve-out for corporate participation is notable, but it cannot resolve the logically prior question whether Arts 10 and 15 should, absent such a provision, be read as containing overlapping exceptions.

[107] See section 4.1.A.

Article 16

Douglas Guilfoyle

Article 16

Ships owned or operated by a State

1. Unless otherwise agreed between the States concerned, a State which owns or operates a ship cannot invoke immunity from jurisdiction before a court of another State which is otherwise competent in a proceeding which relates to the operation of that ship if, at the time the cause of action arose, the ship was used for other than government non-commercial purposes.
2 Paragraph 1 does not apply to warships, or naval auxiliaries, nor does it apply to other vessels owned or operated by a State and used, for the time being, only on government non-commercial service.
3. Unless otherwise agreed between the States concerned, a State cannot invoke immunity from jurisdiction before a court of another State which is otherwise competent in a proceeding which relates to the carriage of cargo on board a ship owned or operated by that State if, at the time the cause of action arose, the ship was used for other than government non-commercial purposes.
4. Paragraph 3 does not apply to any cargo carried on board the ships referred to in paragraph 2, nor does it apply to any cargo owned by a State and used or intended for use exclusively for government non-commercial purposes.
5. States may plead all measures of defence, prescription and limitation of liability which are available to private ships and cargoes and their owners.
6. If in a proceeding there arises a question relating to the government and non-commercial character of a ship owned or operated by a State or cargo owned by a State, a certificate signed by a diplomatic representative or other competent authority of that State and communicated to the court shall serve as evidence of the character of that ship or cargo.

1. Introduction

Article 16 of the Convention sets out general rules in paragraphs 1 and 3 whereby a State which owns or operates a ship may not invoke immunity from the jurisdiction of a competent foreign court in proceedings relating to the operation of that ship or to the carriage of cargo on board it if, at the time the cause of action arose, the ship 'was used for other than government non-commercial purposes'. The general rule in paragraph 1 as to proceedings in respect of the operation of State-owned or -operated vessels does not apply, as specified in paragraph 2, to warships or naval auxiliaries, or to other State-owned or -operated ships 'used, for the time being, only on government non-commercial service'. Nor, correspondingly, in accordance with paragraph 4, does the general rule in paragraph 3 in relation to cargo on board State-owned or -operated ships apply to cargo on board the ships mentioned in paragraph 2 or, regardless of the owner or operator of the ship, to State-owned cargo 'used or intended for use exclusively for government non-commercial purposes'. Paragraph 5 of Article 16 confirms that, in proceedings permitted by paragraphs 1 and 3, States may plead all 'measures of defence, prescription and limitation of liability' available to private parties.

The criterion of use for 'government non-commercial' purposes or service is clearly critical to the application of Article 16 and to the scope of immunity from proceedings preserved. In this connection, paragraph 6 of Article 16 provides that the 'government and non-commercial character' of a ship or cargo in relevant proceedings may be evidenced by 'a certificate signed by a diplomatic representative or other competent authority' of the State claiming immunity. Such a certificate need not, however, be treated as conclusive.

2. Drafting History

In his Sixth Report, delivered to the ILC in 1984, Special Rapporteur Sucharitkul highlighted what he called 'a clear and unmistakable trend', which he further described as 'undeviating',[1] in favour of the absence of a State's immunity from foreign proceedings relating to 'vessels employed by States exclusively on commercial non-governmental service',[2] adding that '[w]hat ha[d] been said of vessels [was] also applicable to cargo belonging to the State'.[3] He based his assessment on a range of State practice, from the Brussels Convention[4] and its 1934 Additional Protocol[5] through to the State immunity legislation enacted in the 1970s and early 1980s by a range of States.[6] In the light of this perceived trend, the Special Rapporteur proposed, in two alternative forms, a draft article, originally numbered 19, to the effect that a State did not enjoy immunity from the jurisdiction of a court of another State in proceedings relating to such matters,[7] although he withdrew one of these alternatives after debate in the Commission and submitted a heavily revised text of the other.[8]

A range of issues arose during the drafting of what would become Article 16 of the Convention. The major concerns were, first, whether developing States should be subject to the provision's exception to a State's immunity from foreign proceedings as recognized in Article 5; secondly, how to formulate precisely the scope both of the exception and of the exception to the exception; and, finally, how to find terms general enough to encompass both common law and civil law proceedings in the field of maritime law.

[1] The use of the word is open to doubt, given Art. 30 ECSI, which excludes the application of the ECSI to 'proceedings in respect of claims relating to the operation of seagoing vessels owned or operated by a Contracting State or to the carriage of cargoes and of passengers by such vessels or to the carriage of cargoes owned by a Contracting State and carried on board merchant vessels'.

[2] Sixth report Sucharitkul, 53, para. 229.

[3] Sixth report Sucharitkul, 53, para. 231(*f*).

[4] International Convention for the Unification of Certain Rules relating to the Immunity of State-owned Vessels, Brussels, 10 April 1926, 176 LNTS 199 (1926 Brussels Convention). The 1926 Brussels Convention currently has only 24 States parties.

[5] Brussels, 24 May 1934, 176 LNTS 214.

[6] See s. 1605(*b*) FSIA (US), along with, as inserted by way of amendment in 1988, s. 1605(*c*) and (*d*) FSIA (US), although none of these provisions precludes reliance on s. 1605(*a*) FSIA (US); s. 10 SIA (UK); s. 11 SIO (Pak); s. 11 FStIA (SA). See also, subsequently, s. 18 FStIA (Aus); s. 7 SIA (Can); s. 12 SIA (Sing); s. 8 FSIL (Isr).

[7] See Sixth report Sucharitkul, 53–4, para. 232 (draft art. 19, 'alternative A') and 54, para. 233 (draft art. 19, 'alternative B').

[8] See summary record 1915th ILC meeting, *YILC 1985*, vol. 1, 227, 227–8, para. 2.

2.1 State immunity and developing States

As with the rest of the Convention, controversy surfaced during the drafting of Article 16 between developed and developing States over immunity from proceedings in respect of State trading or other economic activity. 'The thrust of the [developing States'] argument', in the words of one commentator, 'was that immunity should be available with respect to ships used by developing countries for the carriage of commercial cargoes in connection with technical assistance or emergency aid programmes'.[9] One ILC member went even further, contending:

[I]n developing countries, it was the State that engaged in the bulk of development activities. Such States owned a number of ships operated by para-State enterprises, which carried out commercial activities to foster development. In such cases, it was difficult to argue that those ships, used exclusively for commercial purposes, could not enjoy the jurisdictional immunity of the State... [which should therefore encompass] ships which belonged to the State and were used for governmental commercial service, and ships which, even if they did not belong to the State, were used for commercial purposes in order to help development.[10]

This expansive view did not, however, prevail in either the ILC's draft articles or in Article 16(1) or (3) of the eventual Convention. The preservation, nonetheless, in Article 16(4) of immunity from proceedings relating to the carriage of State-owned cargo intended for government non-commercial purposes—a category automatically including, in the view of the Commission, 'food relief or transport of medical supplies'[11]—addresses in part the concerns expressed.

2.2 The scope of the exception to immunity in respect of the operation of State-owned and State-operated ships

A. 'government non-commercial purposes'

Something of a developed/developing State divide was similarly evident when it came to formulating in precise terms the exception to a State's presumptive immunity from proceedings, and the exception to that exception, in cases relating to the operation of State-owned and State-operated ships. The formulation of the relevant draft article, then numbered 18(1), adopted by the ILC on first reading was as follows:

Unless otherwise agreed between the States concerned, a State which owns or operates a ship engaged in commercial [non-governmental] service cannot invoke immunity from jurisdiction before a court of another State which is otherwise competent in any proceeding relating to the operation of that ship provided that, at the time the cause of action arose, the ship was in use or intended exclusively for use for commercial [non-governmental] purposes.[12]

The word 'non-governmental' was left in square brackets in light of debate over the possible *a contrario* implication that there was such a thing as 'commercial governmental' service or purposes,[13] on the basis of which the provision could have been interpreted 'to

[9] D.W. Greig, 'Specific Exceptions to Immunity under the International Law Commission's Draft Articles: Part 2' (1989) 38 *ICLQ* 560, 579–80.

[10] Summary record 1917th ILC meeting, *YILC 1985*, vol. I, 241, 244–5, para. 24 (Mikuin Balanda).

[11] ILC commentary, draft art. 16, para. 15.

[12] Report ILC, thirty-eighth session, 11 (draft art. 18(1)).

[13] Eighth report Sucharitkul, 28, para. 24.

mean that a ship owned by a State and used in commercial service [or for commercial purposes] enjoys immunity from the jurisdiction of another State'.[14] The result of such a reading would have been that, while 'a commercial ship operating under the free-market system would be subject to local jurisdiction', 'all commercial ships in service under [or used for the purposes of] a State trading system might invoke immunity'.[15] 'Such an uneven legal consequence', Special Rapporteur Ogiso later explained, was 'quite unacceptable to a significant number of States'.[16] A formula stressing that only ships in 'government non-commercial' service or being used for 'government non-commercial' purposes would enjoy immunity was thought to eliminate this ambiguity,[17] as well as perhaps emphasizing that the 'government' and 'non-commercial' criteria were cumulative.

The final choice of words in Article 16(1) of the Convention was also thought more consistent with treaty law. The 1926 Brussels Convention subjects, as among States parties to it, all State-owned and -operated ships to 'the same rules of liability and the same obligations' as private ships, with the exception of 'vessels owned or operated by a State and employed exclusively at the time when the cause of action arises on Government and non-commercial service'.[18] That is, it classifies seagoing vessels entitled to immunity 'not according to ownership but according to the nature of their operation (*exploitation*) or their use, whether in "governmental and non-commercial" or in "commercial" service' at the time the cause of action arises.[19] For their part, the treaty-based regimes of the territorial sea and high seas refer respectively to the immunities of 'government ships operated for non-commercial purposes' and of ships used only on 'government non-commercial service'.[20] The expression 'government non-commercial purposes' as eventually included in Article 16(1) UNCSI, as well as in the exception in Article 16(3) relating to the carriage of cargo on such ships, was seemingly first used in the High Seas Intervention Convention.[21]

The discussion within the ILC tended, in line with the preceding treaty law, to use the terms 'purposes' and 'service' interchangeably. It may be that the word 'purposes' was eventually settled on in Article 16(1) and (3) in the interests of terminological consistency with what became Articles 19(*c*) and 21. Whatever the explanation, the reason for

[14] Second report Ogiso, 66, para. 24.

[15] Second report Ogiso, 66, para. 24.

[16] Second report Ogiso, 66, para. 24.

[17] See ILC commentary, draft art. 16, paras 6–8.

[18] Arts 1 and 3 respectively 1926 Brussels Convention.

[19] ILC commentary, draft art. 16, para. 5.

[20] Arts 32 and 96 respectively United Nations Convention on the Law of the Sea, Montego Bay, 10 December 1982, 1833 UNTS 3 (UNCLOS). See also Art. 22(2) Convention on the Territorial Sea and Contiguous Zone, Geneva, 29 April 1958, 516 UNTS 205 (subject to exceptions, nothing in the specified articles affecting the immunities of 'government ships operated for non-commercial purposes', as referred to in Art. 22(1)) and Art. 9 Convention on the High Seas, Geneva, 29 April 1958, 450 UNTS 82 ('[s]hips owned or operated by a State and used only on government non-commercial service shall, on the high seas, have complete immunity from the jurisdiction of any State other than the flag State'). See too the discussion in *Philippines Embassy Bank Account Case*, 65 ILR 146, 177–8 (FRG (FCC) 1977). Note, in addition, the reference to 'government vessels . . . engaged in non-commercial service' in Art. 298(1)(*b*) UNCLOS, dealing with an optional exception to the dispute settlement procedures specified in Part XV section 2 UNCLOS.

[21] See Art. I International Convention relating to Intervention on the High Seas in Cases of Oil Pollution Casualties, Brussels, 29 November 1969, 970 UNTS 212.

the disconsonant retention in Article 16(2) of the word 'service', taken from the 1926 Brussels Convention, is unclear.

B. Actual versus intended use of ship

As adopted on first reading, the first paragraph of the relevant draft article, like some of the national legislation by which it was inspired,[22] referred to a ship 'in use or intended . . . for use for commercial [non-governmental] purposes'. The criterion of intended use was dropped on second reading in favour of exclusive reference in Article 16(1) to use 'at the time the cause of action arose', both because the eventual Article 16(1) 'presupposed the existence of a cause of action relating to the operation of the ship and it was difficult to imagine that such a cause of action could arise if the ship was not actually in use' and because 'the criterion of intended use was very vague and likely to give rise to difficulties in practice'.[23] The deletion was also consistent with the language used in Article 3 1926 Brussels Convention, which refers to use at the time the cause of action arises. Article 16(1)'s criterion of actual use at the time the cause of action arose, in addition to being reproduced verbatim in Article 16(3), is reiterated in the exception to Article 16(1) provided for in Article 16(2), which refers to use 'for the time being'. The words were inserted into the eventual Article 16(2) during the first session of the Ad Hoc Committee on Jurisdictional Immunities of States and Their Property,[24] presumably in the interests of conceptual, albeit not terminological consistency with Article 16(1).

C. The 'operation' of a ship

The revised draft article 19 proposed by Special Rapporteur Sucharitkul to the Drafting Committee restricted the 'commercial shipping' exception to a State's immunity from jurisdiction to proceedings relating to 'the operation of [a] ship'.[25] The restriction was not in itself controversial. The debate within the ILC focused instead on what proceedings relating to the 'operation' of a ship encompassed. On first reading, what was by then draft article 18 contained a paragraph 3 which provided:

> For the purposes of this article, the expression 'proceeding relating to the operation of that ship' shall mean, *inter alia*, any proceeding involving the determination of:
>
> (a) a claim in respect of collision or other accidents of navigation;
> (b) a claim in respect of assistance, salvage and general average;
> (c) a claim in respect of repairs, supplies or other contracts relating to the ship.[26]

The three subparagraphs were taken from Article 3 1926 Brussels Convention.

On second reading, the Drafting Committee, in light of suggestions made in the Sixth Committee the previous session, added a subparagraph (*d*) to what had become draft article 17(3), as follows:

> (d) [loss or damage resulting from] pollution of the marine environment.

[22] See s. 10(2) to (4) SIA (UK); s. 11(2) to (4) SIO (Pak); s. 11(1) and (2) FStIA (SA). See also, subsequently, s. 7(1) and (2) SIA (Can); s. 12(2) to (4) SIA (Sing). But *cf* s. 18 FStIA (Aus); s. 8(*a*) FSIL (Isr).

[23] Summary record 2219th ILC meeting, *YILC 1991*, vol. I, 75, 79, para. 57.

[24] See 2002 report Ad Hoc Committee, annex, 9. The formulation 'used, for the time being, only on government non-commercial service' echoes Art. XI(1) International Convention on Civil Liability for Oil Pollution Damage, Brussels, 29 November 1969, 973 UNTS 3 and Art. 236 UNCLOS.

[25] See summary record 1915th ILC meeting, (n. 8), 227–8, para. 2.

[26] *YILC 1986*, vol. II(2), 11.

Although the Committee took care to reiterate that the proceedings mentioned in draft article 17(3) were purely illustrative, it 'felt that, in view of the importance attached by the international community to environmental questions and the increase in the number of cases of pollution of the sea by ships, there was merit in making special mention of claims arising from the pollution of the marine environment'.[27] Some members of the Drafting Committee, however, had pushed for the insertion of the words 'loss or damage resulting from' before 'pollution of the marine environment', fearing 'frivolous claims or claims in the service of mankind not involving specific loss or damage'.[28] Others in turn considered the insertion of the reference to loss or damage not only unnecessary but also undesirable, lending itself to implication *a contrario* in relation to subparagraphs (*a*) to (*c*).[29] Unable to reconcile these divergent points of view, the Drafting Committee had left the reference to loss or damage in square brackets when presenting draft article 17 to the Commission.[30] The ensuing debate was polarized, with the Commission eventually agreeing that the contested phrase be replaced by the words 'consequences of'.[31] As finally adopted on second reading, what became draft article 16(3) read:

For the purposes of this article, 'proceeding relating to the operation of that ship' means, *inter alia*, any proceeding involving the determination of a claim in respect of:

(*a*) collision or other accidents of navigation;
(*b*) assistance, salvage and general average;
(*c*) repairs, supplies or other contracts relating to the ship;
(*d*) consequences of pollution of the marine environment.

The ILC commentary recalled the divide within the Commission over the wording of subparagraph (*d*).[32]

In the event, however, and without any record of why, draft article 16(3) as finally adopted by the ILC in 1991 was deleted in its entirety in 2002 by the Ad Hoc Committee.[33]

2.3 The avoidance of terminology confined to the common law tradition

When drafting what became Article 16, the ILC was obliged to confront the problem that, in the field of maritime law, certain expressions 'may be in current usage in the terminology of [the] common law but are unknown to and have no equivalents in other legal systems'.[34] Special Rapporteur Sucharitkul's initial drafts were criticized as 'reflect[ing] unduly the principles of English and United States law, which used somewhat esoteric terms such as "suits in admiralty" or "actions *in rem* and *in personam*"',[35] which had 'little or no meaning in the context of civil law or other non-common-law systems'.[36]

27 Summary record 2219th ILC meeting (n. 23), 79–80, para. 61.
28 Summary record 2219th ILC meeting (n. 23), 80, para. 61.
29 See summary record 2219th ILC meeting (n. 23), 80, para. 61.
30 See summary record 2219th ILC meeting (n. 23), 80, para. 62.
31 See summary record 2219th ILC meeting (n. 23), 80–2, paras 73–86; summary record 2220th ILC meeting (n. 27), 83, 85–8, paras 25–58; summary record 2220th ILC meeting, *YILC 1991*, vol. I, 88, 89, paras 1–8 and 95–96, paras 75–81.
32 See ILC commentary, draft art. 16, para. 14.
33 See 2002 report Ad Hoc Committee, annex.
34 ILC commentary, draft art. 16, para. 3.
35 Summary record 1915th ILC meeting (n. 8), 229, para. 8.
36 ILC commentary, draft art. 16, para. 3.

Expressions of this sort were deleted from the revised text put to the Commission,[37] and were replaced by words capable of 'a more general application'.[38]

3. Key Points

3.1 Article 16(1)

In accordance with Article 16(1), unless otherwise agreed between the States concerned, a State which owns or operates a ship 'cannot invoke immunity from jurisdiction before a court of another State which is otherwise competent in a proceeding which relates to the operation of that ship if, at the time the cause of action arose, the ship was used for other than government non-commercial purposes'. The various elements of this exception to the immunity from jurisdiction accorded States by Article 5 of the Convention call for unpacking.

A. 'Unless otherwise agreed between the States concerned'

Like the great majority of the exceptions to State immunity enumerated in Part III of the Convention, the rule in Article 16(1) abrogating a State's immunity from certain proceedings pertaining to the operation of a ship owned or operated by that State is capable of being opted out of by agreement between the forum State and the State the owner or operator of the ship. The ILC commentary notes a number of treaties to equivalent effect concluded between the former Soviet Union and other States.[39]

B. 'a ship'

Article 16(1) applies to proceedings relating to the operation of a State-owned or -operated 'ship'. But 'ship' is not defined in the Convention.[40] Nor is there any universal definition of the term in public international law.[41] Various international instruments offer different definitions for different purposes,[42] most of which are either over- or under-inclusive as candidates for a general definition.

Dispute may arise in practice over the status of certain floating structures incapable of movement unless towed, as well as over structures, such as mobile offshore drilling units, capable of either being fixed in place or moving under their own power.[43] Similarly, while a seaplane may be thought clearly not to be a 'ship', the appropriate characterization of hovercraft has at times been controversial.[44]

The ILC's Special Rapporteur on the regime of the high seas, J.P.A. François, defined a 'ship', perhaps more succinctly than clearly, as 'a device capable of traversing the sea but not the airspace, with the equipment and crew appropriate to the purpose [for] which she

[37] See summary record 1915th ILC meeting (n. 8), 229, para. 8.

[38] ILC commentary, draft art. 16, para. 3.

[39] See ILC commentary, draft art. 16, para. 1 n. 160.

[40] That said, one would not expect it to have been.

[41] See D.P. O'Connell, *The International Law of the Sea* (Oxford: Clarendon Press, 1984), vol. 2, 747–8.

[42] See O'Connell (n. 41), 748–50.

[43] See O'Connell (n. 41), 748–50. See also R. Churchill and A.V. Lowe, *The Law of the Sea* (3rd edn) (Manchester: Manchester University Press, 1999), 154–5.

[44] See O'Connell (n. 41), 749. Note eg the specific reference to hovercraft in s. 11 SIO (Pak).

is used'.[45] This definition was not included, however, in the Articles concerning the Law of the Sea as finally adopted by the Commission.[46] Nor does either the Convention on the High Seas or UNCLOS include any such definition.

To the extent that the term might be thought unclear, the ILC commentary suggests that 'ship', as used in Article 16, 'should be interpreted as covering all types of seagoing vessels, whatever their nomenclature and even if they are engaged only partially in seagoing traffic'.[47] A more precise definition than 'seagoing vessel' may not be possible, and the apparent intention of the drafters was that Article 16's reference to a 'ship' is to be interpreted broadly.

C. *'owns or operates'*

In contrast to section 10(2) SIA (UK) and other national State immunity provisions modelled closely on it, which provide an exception to a foreign State's immunity from proceedings only in respect of ships 'belonging to' that State',[48] Article 16(1) of the Convention, like section 7(1) SIA (Can) and section 8(*a*) FSIL (Isr), encompasses proceedings concerning the operation of a ship which a foreign State 'owns or operates'.[49] The formulation 'owns or operates' obviously indicates that a State which owned but was not operating the ship at the time the cause of action arose is nonetheless not entitled to invoke immunity from such foreign proceedings instituted against it in relation to the ship's operation as the applicable municipal law may in substance allow.[50]

Like 'ship', the word 'operates' is, it seems, to be interpreted inclusively.[51] The ILC suggests that the term encompasses 'the "possession", "control", "management" and "charter" of ships by a State, whether the charter is for a time or voyage, bare-boat or otherwise'.[52] This accords with the Additional Protocol to the 1926 Brussels Convention, which confirms, after doubts had arisen, that the words 'operated by a State' ('*exploités par lui*') found in Article 3 1926 Brussels Convention—against the background of which Article 16(1) UNCSI must, at least according to the ILC commentary,[53] be read—includes vessels chartered by a State either for time or for voyage.[54]

D. *'before a court of another State which is otherwise competent'*

As with the rest of the Convention, Article 16, with its reference to 'a court of another State which is otherwise competent', leaves the existence of the court's underlying jurisdiction to the applicable municipal law;[55] and, as the ILC commentary to what

45 'Regime of the high seas. Sixième rapport de J.P.A. François, rapporteur special', *YILC 1954*, vol. II, 7, 9 (proposed draft art. 6) ('Un navire est un engine apte à se mouvoir dans les espace maritimes à l'exclusion de l'espace aérien, avec l'armament et l'equipage qui lui sont propres en vue des services que comporte l'industrie à laquelle il est employé.'). The translation is from O'Connell (n. 41), 750.

46 See *YILC 1956*, vol. II, 256.

47 ILC commentary, draft art. 16, para. 1.

48 See s. 10(2) and (3) SIA (UK); s. 11(2) and (3) SIO (Pak); s. 11(1) FStIA (SA); s. 11(2) and (3) SIA (Sing).

49 For their part, s. 18(1) and (2) FStIA (Aus) avoid the question altogether.

50 ILC commentary, draft art. 16, para. 10, suggests that it should not be necessary in such cases to bring proceedings against the owner State, given that the claimant can sue the operator. The suggestion is unlikely to correspond to the realities of litigation where the operator has limited assets.

51 See ILC commentary, draft art. 16, para. 9.

52 ILC commentary, draft art. 16, para. 9.

53 See ILC commentary, draft art. 16, para. 9.

54 See Art. 1 Additional Protocol to the 1926 Brussels Convention.

55 See Sixth report Sucharitkul, 30, paras 134–135; H. Fox, *The Law of State Immunity* (2nd edn) (Oxford: Oxford University Press, 2008), 568.

became Article 16 elaborates, this law 'may recognize a wide variety of causes of action and may allow a possible choice of proceedings, such as *in personam* against the owner and operator or *in rem* against the ship itself'.[56] This non-prescriptive approach to the municipal legal basis of the court's jurisdiction is particularly apt in the context of Article 16, given that certain species of common law proceedings in the field of shipping law, notably the action *in rem*, lack direct equivalents in other legal systems. The essence of the common law action *in rem* is the pre-judgment arrest of a ship, the latter comprising the '*res*' in the expression '*in rem*'—that is, the placing of the ship 'under judicial detention pending adjudication of the claim'.[57] Such detention may serve one or more of three purposes, namely 'provid[ing] pre-judgment security for the claim, found[ing] the jurisdiction of the court, and usually secur[ing] the appearance of the ship-owner'.[58] A variation on this theme noted by the ILC commentary is the recognition in most common law States of 'the possibility of arrest or seizure of a sister ship *ad fundandam jurisdictionem*'.[59] 'Sister ship' or 'surrogate ship' jurisdiction is jurisdiction founded on the arrest not of 'the particular ship in respect of which the maritime claim arose' but of 'any other ship which is owned by the person who was, at the time when the maritime claim arose, the owner of the particular ship'.[60]

It is important to emphasize, however, that the various municipal procedures that allow for the court's jurisdiction over maritime claims on the basis of the arrest or seizure of a ship are of significantly less relevance in the context of State-owned or -operated ships and, more specifically, in the context of the Convention than they may be in other contexts. Article 18 ('State immunity from pre-judgment measures of constraint') of the Convention expressly prohibits the taking, 'in connection with a proceeding before a court of another State', of all 'pre-judgment measures of constraint, such as attachment or arrest, against property of a State', unless that State has expressly consented to such measures by one of the means specified in Article 18(*a*) or, as per Article 18(*b*), has allocated or earmarked the property for the satisfaction of the claim the object of the proceeding.[61] Unlike Article 19, and in contrast with the position under the law of more than a few States when it comes to pre-judgment arrest or attachment of State ships in use for commercial ends,[62] this prohibition extends to property of a State—which is taken to

[56] ILC commentary, draft art. 16, para. 13.

[57] W. Tetley, 'Arrest, Attachment, and Related Maritime Law Procedures' (1999) 73 *Tulane Maritime Law Review* 1895, 1898. For more detailed treatments, see S. Derrington and J.M. Turner, *The Law and Practice of Admiralty Matters* (Oxford: Oxford University Press, 2007), chap. 2; D.C. Jackson, *Enforcement of Maritime Claims* (4th edn) (Richmond: LLP, 2005), chaps 10 and 15.

[58] Tetley (n. 57), 1907.

[59] ILC commentary, draft art. 16, para. 13.

[60] Art. 3(1) International Convention for the Unification of Certain Rules relating to the Arrest of Sea-going Ships, Brussels, 10 May 1952, 439 UNTS 193 (1952 Brussels Convention).

[61] See the commentary to Art. 18 UNCSI.

[62] See eg s. 13(2)(4) SIA (UK) ('in use or intended for use for commercial purposes'), which constitutes an exception to s. 13(2)(*b*)'s prohibition on the arrest, detention or sale of a State ship in an action *in rem*; s. 14(2)(*b*) SIO (Pak); s. 14(3) FStIA (SA); s. 32(2) FStIA (Aus); s. 12(1)(*b*) SIA (Can); s. 15(4) SIA (Sing); s. 16(1) FSIL (Isr). See also s. 1610(*a*)(2) FSIA (US), along with, on other grounds, s. 1610(*b*)(2) and (*e*) FSIA (US). The jurisprudence of certain other States permits similarly the pre-judgment attachment of State-owned commercial property, including ships. See eg *Szczesniak v Backer and Others*, 65 ILR 23 (Bel (CA Brussels) 1955); *Société Paul Liegard v Captain Serdjuk and Magne*, 65 ILR 38 (Fra (Trib. de Comm.) 1964); *The Philippine Admiral (Owners) v Wallem Shipping (Hong Kong) Limited and Another*, 64 ILR 90, 109 (HK (PC) 1975); *Romanian Maritime Navigation Company (Navrom) v Buenamar Compania Naviera*, 82 ILR 93 (Fra (CoC) 1988); *Russian Federation v Pied-Rich BV* (1994) 25 *NYIL* 512 (Nth (SC) 1993).

mean any property owned or possessed or controlled by a State[63]—in use 'for other than government non-commercial purposes'.[64] Given this explicit prohibition on all pre-judgment arrest of State property, the effect of Article 18 is that proceedings *in rem* may not be instituted against a State-owned or -operated ship unless the State has expressly consented to this as specified in Article 18(*a*). In other words, proceedings pursuant to Article 16 will, it appears, be limited in practice to actions *in personam* against a foreign State in its capacity as either the owner or operator of the ship.

At the same time, it is worth noting that Article 18 will not bar all actions *in rem* against State-owned or -operated vessels as among States parties to the 1926 Brussels Convention, rights and obligations under which are, in accordance with Article 26 UNCSI, preserved from the effect of the UNCSI.[65] Proceedings *in rem* against any State-owned or -operated ships that are not 'employed exclusively at the time when the cause of action arises on Government and non-commercial service' will remain possible among such States,[66] with the consequence that the exception to immunity from foreign jurisdiction provided for in Article 16 will, to this extent, be of greater practical significance to them.

E. 'a proceeding which relates to the operation of that ship'

The exception to a State's immunity from foreign jurisdiction provided for in Article 16(1) applies only insofar as the proceedings against the State relate to the operation of a ship owned or operated by it. The exception does not extend to proceedings relating to possession over or ownership of a ship operated by a State or purportedly owned by it. At the same time, the expression 'a proceeding which relates to the operation of [a] ship' is clearly capable of encompassing a wide range of claims. In this regard, the fact that what was adopted by the ILC on second reading as draft article 16(3) was subsequently deleted from what emerged as Article 16 should in no way be taken to mean that the illustrative species of proceedings mentioned in the excised provision are not the sorts of proceedings that would, all other things being equal, fall within Article 16(1).

None of the pre-Convention State immunity statutes limits the 'commercial shipping' exception to proceedings relating to the operation of a ship. Most abrogate immunity from foreign jurisdiction in relation to any action *in rem* against a relevant ship and any action *in personam* for enforcing a claim in connection with a relevant ship.[67] For its part, the FSIA (US) expressly permits suits in admiralty against a foreign State to enforce against a vessel of that State any maritime lien based on a commercial activity, as well as actions brought to foreclose a preferred mortgage.[68]

[63] See the commentary to Art. 18 UNCSI.

[64] See Art. 19(*c*) UNCSI and the commentary thereto.

[65] See the commentary to Art. 26 UNCSI. Recall from n. 1 that, for its part, Art. 30 ECSI excludes the ECSI's application to 'proceedings in respect of claims relating to the operation of seagoing vessels owned or operated by a Contracting State or to the carriage of cargoes and of passengers by such vessels or to the carriage of cargoes owned by a Contracting State and carried on board merchant vessels'. See, in this regard, Expl. Rep. ECSI, para. 115: 'The purpose of this article is to exclude matters covered by the Brussels Convention . . . and [its] Protocol . . . These instruments are in force between a fairly large number of member States of the Council of Europe. The expressions used in Article 30 should be interpreted in accordance with the interpretation generally given to them in these two instruments.'

[66] See, by necessary implication, Art. 3 1926 Brussels Convention.

[67] See s. 10(2) SIA (UK); s. 11(2) SIO (Pak); s. 11(1) FStIA (SA); s. 18(1) FStIA (Aus); s. 7(1) SIA (Can); s. 12(2) SIA (Sing); s. 8(*a*) FSIL (Isr).

[68] See s. 1605(*b*) and (*d*) respectively FSIA (US).

Given the breadth of the term 'the operation of the ship', there is likely in practice to be a degree of overlap between the situations giving rise to the 'commercial shipping' exception to immunity from jurisdiction provided for in Article 16(1) and the 'commercial transaction' exception to the same recognized in Article 10; and it is perhaps worth noting in this regard that Congress has made clear and the US courts have affirmed that the shipping exceptions recognized in section 1605(*b*) and (*d*) FSIA (US) are not exclusive means by which to bring claims in admiralty against a foreign State.[69]

F. 'if, at the time the cause of action arose, the ship was used for other than government non-commercial purposes'

Article 16(1) posits the unavailability to a State of immunity from foreign proceedings in respect of ships 'used for other than government non-commercial purposes', the criterion being actual, not intended use, as assessed by reference to the time the cause of action arose. The adjectives 'government' and 'non-commercial' are cumulative, with the consequence that, all other things being equal, a State is not immune from proceedings arising out of the use of a State-owned or -operated ship for either non-government or commercial purposes.

The test is one as to the purpose, rather than the nature, of a ship's use. This stands in apparent contrast with the emphasis on the nature, rather than the purpose, of a transaction in the definition of a 'commercial transaction' specified in Article 2(1)(*c*) of the Convention, as elaborated on in Article 2(2) and applied in Article 10's 'commercial transaction' exception to immunity from jurisdiction. But any inconsistency is merely apparent, for the reason that a commercial transaction and commercial use are different, albeit closely related concepts, the latter being at one remove from the former. Interpreting Article 16(1) against the backdrop of Article 2(1)(*c*), which forms part of the former's context,[70] it is logical to construe the term 'non-commercial purposes' in Article 16(1) to mean 'purposes other than a "commercial transaction" as defined in Article 2(1)(*c*)'. In short, a ship is used for 'other than . . . non-commercial purposes' within the meaning of Article 16(1) when—stating it in the positive—it is used for the purpose of a commercial transaction as understood by the Convention. Recourse to the *travaux préparatoires* confirms this interpretation. Special Rapporteur Sucharitkul explicitly drew in his original and revised drafts of the eventual Article 16(1) on the provisions of national legislation[71] which elsewhere defines the term 'commercial purposes' by reference to the 'commercial transaction' or 'commercial activity' exception to immunity also found in the legislation.[72]

3.2 Article 16(2)

Article 16(2) provides that the exception to immunity from proceedings laid down in Article 16(1) 'does not apply to warships, or naval auxiliaries, nor does it apply to other

[69] See HR Rep. No. 94-1487, *Jurisdiction on the United States in Suits Against Foreign States*, 94th Cong. (9 September 1976), 22; *Velidor and Others v L/P/G Benghazi (Appeal of Compagnie Algéro-Libyenne de Transport Maritime)*, 63 ILR 622, 627–8 (US (3rd Cir.) 1981).

[70] See Art. 31(1) and (2) VCLT. See also R. Gardiner, *Treaty Interpretation* (Oxford: Oxford University Press, 2008), 185–6.

[71] See Sixth report Sucharitkul, 46–7, paras 194–197 and 53, para. 231, the former citing s. 10 SIA (UK), s. 11 SIO (Pak), s. 12 SIA (Sing), and s. 7 SIA (Can), as well as what became s. 18 FStIA (Aus).

[72] See s. 17(1) SIA (UK); s. 7(1) SIA (Can). See also s. 1(1) FStIA (SA).

vessels owned or operated by a State and used, for the time being, only on government non-commercial service'. A degree of ambiguity is perhaps occasioned by the words 'apply to', which could be taken to suggest, falsely, that State immunity vests in the ship itself, as distinct from in the State to which that ship belongs. Such a reading might result in the application of Article 16(2)'s 'exception to the exception' only to proceedings *in rem, viz* instituted against the ship itself, and not also to proceedings *in personam, viz* instituted against the State in respect of the operation of its ship. This would be manifestly contrary to the intention of Article 16's drafters, who sought to obviate reliance on such procedural distinctions; would run counter to the well-established customary immunity of a State from foreign proceedings in respect of its warships[73] and other vessels in use only on government non-commercial service;[74] and would be disconsonant with the scope of application *ratione personae* of Article 16(1), in accordance with which 'a State may not invoke immunity' from foreign proceedings which relate to the operation of a ship owned or operated by it. In this combined light, the words 'apply to' in Article 16(2) are better interpreted to mean 'apply with respect to' or 'apply in respect of'.

Article 29 of UNCLOS defines a warship as:

> a ship belonging to the armed forces of a State bearing the external marks distinguishing such ships of its nationality, under the command of an officer duly commissioned by the government of the State and whose name appears in the appropriate service list or its equivalent, and manned by a crew which is under regular armed forces discipline.[75]

The definition has been applied in at least one national State immunity case.[76] Naval auxiliaries will in practice satisfy the same definition, which does not insist on offensive capability.

Insofar as Article 16(2) refers to 'other vessels owned or operated by a State and used, for the time being, only on government non-commercial service', it is redundant, strictly speaking, positing as it does simply the converse of Article 16(1), for the avoidance of doubt. The ILC commentary suggests that this limb of the provision was included to preserve immunity for 'other government ships such as police patrol boats, customs inspection boats, hospital ships, oceanographic survey ships, training vessels and dredgers, owned or operated by a State and used... in government non-commercial service'.[77] The specification of use 'for the time being' picks up Article 16(1)'s criterion of use 'at the time the cause of action arose'. As for Article 16(2)'s reference to government non-commercial 'service', in comparison with the government non-

[73] See eg, among many others, *Allianz Via Insurance v United States of America*, 127 ILR 148, 152 (Fra (CA Aix-en-Provence) 1999), 152 ('Assigned to the public service of national defence, a warship is the very expression of the sovereignty of the State whose flag it flies, on the high seas or in territorial waters... In the event... this public service mission may give rise to... a judicial proceeding of any kind..., the State whose flag the warship is flying should be recognised as enjoying absolute sovereign immunity before the courts of another State.'). See also, classically, *The Schooner Exchange v McFaddon*, 11 US (7 Cranch) 116, 144 (US (SC) 1813). See too Arts 32 and 95 UNCLOS, codifying customary international law, and *The 'ARA Libertad' Case (Argentina v Ghana), Request for the prescription of provisional measures, Order*, 15 December 2012, para. 98.

[74] See eg, reasoning *a contrario*, s. 1605(b) FSIA (US); s. 10(2) SIA (UK); s. 11(2) SIO (Pak); s. 11(1) FStIA (SA); s. 18(1) FStIA (Aus); s. 7(1) SIA (Can); s. 12(2) SIA (Sing); s. 8(*a*) FSIL (Isr). Countless examples could be given from the case-law of States without equivalent legislation.

[75] See also, similarly, Art. 8(2) High Seas Convention.

[76] See *Allianz Via Insurance v United States of America* (n. 73), 152.

[77] ILC commentary, draft art. 16, para. 11.

commercial 'purposes' mentioned in Article 16(1), this is a distinction without a difference. UNCLOS, the most important inspiration for the expression 'used, for the time being, on government non-commercial service' found in Article 16(2), uses the two words interchangeably.[78] So does the ILC commentary,[79] which further indicates that a proposal to change the word 'service' in draft article 16(2) to 'purposes'—so as to avoid any confusion caused by the terminological inconsistency with draft article 16(1), on which draft article 16(2) was consequential—was not taken up,[80] suggesting that the Commission was content that no confusion resulted from the use of the two synonyms.

Article 16(2) will not apply, in accordance with Article 26 UNCSI, as between States parties to the 1926 Brussels Convention to the extent that Article 3(1) of the latter abrogates a State's immunity from foreign proceedings relating to its 'ships of war, State owned yachts, patrol vessels, hospital ships, fleet auxiliaries, supply ships and other vessels owned or operated by a State and employed exclusively at the time when the cause of action arises on Government and non-commercial service' in three alternative cases. These are claims 'in respect of collision or other accidents of navigation'; claims 'in respect of salvage or in the nature of salvage and in respect of general average'; and claims 'in respect of repairs, supplies or other contracts relating to the ship'.

3.3 Article 16(3)

Article 16(3) does for proceedings relating to the carriage of cargo on a State-owned or State-operated ship what Article 16(1) does for proceedings relating to the operation of the ship. It provides that, subject to agreement otherwise between the States concerned, the impleaded State may not invoke immunity from the jurisdiction of a competent court of the forum State 'in a proceeding which relates to the carriage of cargo on board a ship owned or operated by that State if, at the time the cause of action arose, the ship was used for other than government non-commercial purposes'. Many of the key elements of Article 16(3) are identical to those of Article 16(1). Only a few further elements call for elaboration.

First, in line with Article 1 1926 Brussels Convention, the exception to State immunity provided for in Article 16(3) applies only where it is the carriage of the cargo that is the subject-matter of the proceedings. The emphasis on the cargo's carriage might, on first impression, be taken to imply that Article 16(3) encompasses no more than proceedings arising out of, for example, the non-delivery or spoilage of the cargo, leaving the State as the owner or operator of the ship immune from foreign proceedings pertaining to the cargo's possession or ownership. But, for example, the proceedings in detinue and conversion in *I° Congreso del Partido*—discussed and quoted from at some length in Special Rapporteur Sucharitkul's Sixth Report,[81] which considered '[t]he rules of State immunity as applied to vessels owned or operated by States' to have been 'restated with

[78] See Art. 32 ('operated for non-commercial purposes') and Art. 96 ('used only on government non-commercial service') UNCLOS. Similarly, where Art. 3(1) 1926 Brussels Convention refers to 'Government and non-commercial service', s. 10 SIA (UK), enacted in implementation of the provision, uses 'commercial purposes' throughout. See also s. 11 SIO (Pak); s. 12 SIA (Sing); s. 11 FStIA (SA); s. 18 FStIA (Aus); s. 8 FSIL (Isr) ('a commercial purpose').

[79] See ILC commentary, draft art. 16, paras 2, 5, 6, and 7.

[80] See ILC commentary, draft art. 16, para. 11.

[81] See Sixth report Sucharitkul, 36, paras 155–156 and 44, para. 183.

accuracy' in the judgment of Lord Wilberforce in the case[82]—could be said, with no violence to language, to have been 'relate[d] to the carriage of cargo on board a ship' within the meaning of Article 16(3); and it certainly seems unlikely that the ILC intended to exclude from the scope of the provision the sorts of causes of action that gave rise to the judicial practice of States on which the rule specified in Article 16(3) draws. In this respect, whereas the focus on the operation of the ship in Article 16(1) would seem to narrow that particular exception, the focus on the carriage of the cargo in Article 16(3) may make no, or at least very little, difference to the pre- or extra-Convention situation.

Secondly, it is immaterial under Article 16(3) to whom the cargo belongs. It most definitely need not belong to the respondent State.[83] Indeed, if, according to the logic of Article 16(3), it is the State owner or operator of the ship that is being sued in respect of the carriage of that cargo, it stands to reason that the cargo belongs either to the claimant or to a third party.[84] That said, the ownership of the cargo is relevant to the exception provided for in the second limb of Article 16(4) to the exception to immunity from jurisdiction laid down in Article 16(3).[85]

Next, the relevant use for the purposes of Article 16(3) is that of the ship, not of the cargo.[86] Indeed, it is difficult to conceive of the cargo being used for any purpose at the time the cause of action arises.[87] What is relevant under Article 16(3) is whether, at that time, the ship is being 'used for other than government non-commercial purposes'. As with the ownership of the cargo, however, the use of that cargo is germane to the exception to Article 16(3) posited in the second limb of Article 16(4).

Finally, as with Article 16(1),[88] there is likely to be overlap between the circumstances giving rise to the exception under Article 16(3) and those underlying proceedings pursuant to the commercial transaction exception to a State's immunity from foreign jurisdiction.

3.4 Article 16(4)

A. 'Paragraph 3 does not apply to any cargo carried on board the ships referred to in paragraph 2'

Just as Article 16(2) safeguards from the effect of Article 16(1) a State's immunity from foreign proceedings relating to the operation of warships, naval auxiliaries, and 'other

[82] See Sixth report Sucharitkul, 44, para. 183.

[83] ILC commentary, draft art. 16, para. 15 is manifestly incorrect when it states that the forerunner to Art. 16(3) 'provides for the rule of non-immunity applicable to a cargo belonging to a State'. It is also inconsistent with ILC commentary, draft art. 16, para. 2, which observes, correctly, that what became Art. 16(3) 'enunciates the rule of non-immunity in proceedings relating to the carriage of cargo on board a ship owned or operated by a State'.

[84] In the latter case, the claimant might be someone with a contractual right in relation to or beneficial interest in the cargo.

[85] See section 3.4.

[86] Again, ILC commentary, draft art. 16, para. 15 is obviously wrong when it states that the precursor to Art. 16(3) 'provides for the rule of non-immunity applicable to a cargo . . . used or intended for use for commercial non-government purposes'. It also again contradicts ILC commentary, draft art. 16, para. 2, which correctly notes what became Art. 16(3) 'enunciates the rule of non-immunity in proceedings relating to the carriage of cargo on board a ship . . . used for other than government non-commercial service'.

[87] See, further section 3.4

[88] Recall section 3.1(E).

vessels owned or operated by a State and used...only on government non-commercial service', so Article 16(4) safeguards from the effect of Article 16(3) a State's immunity from foreign proceedings relating to the carriage of any cargo aboard such ships.

B. 'nor does it apply to any cargo owned by a State and used or intended for use exclusively for government non-commercial purposes'

In addition to its preservation of a State's immunity from proceedings in respect of the carriage of any cargo aboard the ships mentioned in Article 16(2), Article 16(4) preserves a State's immunity from proceedings in respect of the carriage of any cargo owned by that State 'and used or intended for use exclusively for government non-commercial purposes'. This retention of immunity is irrespective of the owner or operator of the ship on which the cargo is conveyed—although this must, in accordance with the logic of Article 16(3), to which Article 16(4) constitutes an exception, be a State—and of the character of that ship's service.

The words 'or intended for use' may at first seem anomalous, since it will be recalled that previous references to intended use in what are now paragraphs 1, 2, and 3 of Article 16—these references having derived from the original alternative drafts put forward by Special Rapporteur Sucharitkul,[89] who in turn would appear to have taken them from section 10(2)(*b*) SIA (UK) and its imitators[90]—were deleted from the relevant draft article on second reading. The ILC commentary notes that the words were retained in what is now Article 16(4) 'because the cargo is not normally used while it is on board the ship and it is therefore its planned use which will determine whether the State concerned is or is not entitled to invoke immunity'.[91] The provision, the commentary continues, preserves a State's immunity in respect of, 'inter alia, cargo involved in emergency operations such as food relief or transport of medical supplies'.[92]

More problematic is the alternative concept of the use of the cargo, which presumably refers to its use at the time the cause of action arises. Given that proceedings under Article 16(3), to which Article 16(4) posits an exception, relate to the cargo's carriage, the cargo is not used for anything at the time the cause of action arises. It is simply sitting on board the ship. The point is acknowledged, half-heartedly, in the ILC commentary, which, as already seen, concedes that 'the cargo is not normally used while it is on board the ship'.[93]

More difficult still is to conceive of a situation in which the second limb of Article 16(4) might in practice apply. The proceedings permitted by Article 16(3), to which the second limb of Article 16(4) provides an exception, are limited to those instituted against a State owner or operator of the ship on board which the cargo—the carriage of which constitutes the subject-matter of the proceedings—is being carried at the time the cause of action arises. That is, the only possible circumstance in which the second limb of Article 16(4) might have purchase is where, at the time the cause of action in relation to the cargo's carriage arises, the State-owned cargo in question is being carried on board a ship owned or operated by a State. That State might conceivably be the State the owner of the cargo

89 See Sixth report Sucharitkul, 53–4, paras 232–233.
90 Consider in this light Sixth report Sucharitkul, 46–7, paras 194–197.
91 ILC commentary, draft art. 16, para. 15.
92 ILC commentary, draft art. 16, para. 15.
93 ILC commentary, draft art. 16, para. 15.

itself or some other State. Since, in the first scenario, it is absurd to imagine that the State would sue itself in relation to the carriage of its own cargo, Article 16(4) will apply only where a third party with, for example, contractual rights in relation to or a beneficial interest in the State-owned cargo sues the State the owner of the cargo in its capacity not as owner of the cargo but as owner or operator of the ship on which it is carried. But it is not easy to envisage circumstances in which a third party might enjoy contractual rights in relation to or a beneficial interest in a cargo owned by a State and 'used or intended for use exclusively for government non-commercial purposes', although presumably such circumstances exist. Where, on the other hand, the State sued as owner or operator of the ship on which the State-owned cargo is carried is, as per the second scenario, some other State, the claimant might be a third party or it might equally be the State the owner of the cargo. Either way, the upshot of Article 16(4) would be the respondent State's immunity from the proceedings in respect of the carriage of the cargo, a perverse result which suggests that Article 16(4) should not be taken to apply in this context.

3.5 Article 16(5)

Article 16(5) provides that a State may plead 'all measures of defence, prescription and limitation of liability' as are available to private ships and cargoes and their owners. In referring to the State's pleading of substantive and non-immunity-based procedural defences, paragraph 5 of Article 16 is clearly dealing with situations in which, by virtue of paragraphs 1 and 3, the State is not entitled to invoke immunity from the proceedings in question. The wording would appear to have been drawn from Article 4 1926 Brussels Convention.[94]

The ILC commentary observes that the rule enunciated in Article 16(5) 'is not limited in its application to proceedings relating to ships and cargoes'; rather, 'States may plead all available means of defence in any proceedings in which State property is involved'.[95] Given, however, that no corresponding provision is found elsewhere in the Convention, Article 16(5) remains somewhat anomalous.

3.6 Article 16(6)

Article 16(6) makes evidentiary provision for proceedings where 'there arises a question relating to the government and non-commercial character of a ship owned or operated by a State or cargo owned by a State'. It specifies that, in such cases, 'a certificate signed by a diplomatic representative or other competent authority of that State and communicated to the court shall serve as evidence of the character of that ship or cargo'. Article 16(6) affords one possible means by which evidence of the character of a ship or cargo may be furnished.[96] A similar provision appears in Article 5 1926 Brussels Convention,[97] from which Article 16(6) of the Convention would seem to draw its inspiration. But in

[94] Art. 4 1926 Brussels Convention reads: 'States shall be entitled to rely on all defences, prescriptions and limitations of liability available to privately-owned ships and their owners.'

[95] ILC commentary, draft art. 16, para. 16.

[96] See ILC commentary, draft art. 16, para. 16.

[97] Art. 5 1926 Brussels Convention provides: 'If in any proceedings to which Article 3 applies there is . . . a doubt on the question of the Government and non-commercial character of the ship or the cargo, a certificate signed by the diplomatic representative of the Contracting State to which the ship or the cargo belongs . . . shall

contrast with Article 5 1926 Brussels Convention,[98] Article 16(6) of the Convention does not stipulate that the evidence provided by such a certificate be regarded by a national court as irrebuttable.[99] Similar provisions in national State immunity legislation, albeit relating not to the State's immunity from proceedings in respect of its ships but to the immunity of State property from execution, tend not to specify the conclusiveness of certificates of this sort,[100] although they may deem them to give rise to a rebuttable presumption.[101]

The reference in Article 16(6) to the 'character' of a State-owned or -operated ship jars with Article 16(1) and (3), the provisions to which it pertains, neither of which has recourse to the idea of a ship's 'character', speaking instead of a ship 'used', 'at the time the cause of action arose', 'for other than government non-commercial purposes'. Similar contrasts are evident between Article 16(6) and Article 16(2), the latter referring to a ship on 'government non-commercial service', and between Article 16(6) and Article 16(4)'s reference to cargo 'used or intended for use exclusively for government non-commercial purposes'. It is clear, however, from the context provided by Article 16 as a whole that the word 'character' in Article 16(6) means, in relation to Article 16(1) and (3), 'character as a ship used, at the time the cause of action arose, for other than government non-commercial purposes' and, in relation to Article 16(4), 'character as a cargo used or intended for use exclusively for government non-commercial purposes'. The word 'character' in Article 16(6) is the product of no more than the drafters' unthinking verbatim lifting of the phrase 'government and non-commercial character' from Article 5 1926 Brussels Convention.

4. Evaluation

Article 16 of the Convention, although presenting a few, ultimately unproblematic drafting infelicities, is broadly in line with customary international law, existing national law, and past treaty practice. A few divergences nonetheless deserve mention. First, Article 16(1) and (3) extend the 'commercial shipping' exception to immunity from foreign jurisdiction to proceedings against the State as mere operator of the ship. Although this accords with Article 1 1926 Brussels Convention, it is a point on which national legislation is at best equivocal. That said, there is nothing under existing national law to prevent a claimant from instituting under some other exception to immunity, notably the commercial transaction or commercial activity exception, proceedings against a foreign State in its capacity as operator of a ship. Secondly, while the focus under Article 16(1) to (3) on the use of a ship at the time the cause of action arose has the virtue of clarity, much current national legislation includes an 'intended use' criterion. Thirdly, insofar as the exception provided for in Article 16(1) applies to proceedings in respect of the operation, and not also the possession or ownership, of a

be conclusive evidence that the ship or the cargo falls within the terms of Article 3, but only for the purpose of obtaining the discharge of any seizure, arrest or detention effected by judicial process.'

[98] See Art. 5 1926 Brussels Convention, referring to 'conclusive' evidence.

[99] ILC commentary, draft art. 16, para. 16. Contrast the rebuttable character of the evidence furnished by a certificate under Art. 16(5) with the conclusiveness of the certificate referred to in Art. 11(2)(*d*) UNCSI.

[100] See s. 13(5) SIA (UK); s. 14(4) SIO (Pak); s. 15(5) SIA (Sing); s. 41 FStIA (Aus).

[101] See s. 13(5) SIA (UK); s. 14(4) SIO (Pak); s. 15(5) SIA (Sing).

ship, it introduces a subject-matter limitation that does not presently obtain under national legislation. The most notable difference between Article 16 and the 1926 Brussels Convention is that, whereas Article 3 1926 Brussels Convention abrogates a State's general immunity from foreign proceedings in respect of its warships and other ships on government non-commercial service when the claim relates to certain specified matters such as accidents of navigation, salvage, and contractual issues relating to the ship's repairs and supplies,[102] Article 16(2) of the Convention does not.[103]

In policy terms, Article 16 generally strikes an appropriate balance between State and private interests when it comes to foreign proceedings arising from the commercial operation of State-owned or -operated ships and the commercial carriage of cargoes on them. It should prove a workable arrangement.

[102] Art. 3 1926 Brussels Convention.

[103] Recall, however, from section 3.2 that, as per Art. 26 UNCSI, the regime of immunities established under the 1926 Brussels Convention remains applicable as between those States parties to UNCSI that are also States parties to the 1926 Brussels Convention.

Article 17

KATE PARLETT

Article 17
Effect of an arbitration agreement

If a State enters into an agreement in writing with a foreign natural or juridical person to submit to arbitration differences relating to a commercial transaction, that State cannot invoke immunity from jurisdiction before a court of another State which is otherwise competent in a proceeding which relates to:
(*a*) the validity, interpretation or application of the arbitration agreement;
(*b*) the arbitration procedure; or
(*c*) the confirmation or setting aside of the award,
unless the arbitration agreement otherwise provides.

Understanding with respect to article 17

The expression 'commercial transaction' includes investment matters.

1. Introduction

Where two parties have agreed to settle a dispute by arbitration, one or both of them may end up bringing proceedings in the courts of the seat of the arbitration or of another jurisdiction in relation to the validity, interpretation, or application of the arbitration agreement, to the arbitration procedure, or to the confirmation or setting aside of the award.[1] But where the other party to the arbitration agreement is a State, the first party may be confronted in the domestic proceedings with a plea of State immunity. Article 17 of the Convention stipulates, however, that the State may not invoke immunity in such proceedings unless the arbitration agreement provides otherwise.

Article 17 applies where a State has entered into an agreement with a foreign natural or legal person to submit differences 'relating to a commercial transaction' to arbitration. The term 'commercial transaction' is defined in Article 2(1)(*c*) of the Convention.[2] This definition is supplemented by an understanding with respect to Article 17 annexed to the Convention, which indicates that the term 'commercial transaction' includes 'investment matters'. The term 'investment matters' is not itself defined in the Convention.

2. Background

A provision analogous to Article 17 of the Convention is found in the earlier Article 12 ECSI, which reads:

[1] The party may allege, for example, that the arbitration agreement was procured by fraud or that the tribunal was not properly constituted.
[2] See the commentary to Art. 2(1)(*c*).

1. Where a Contracting State has agreed in writing to submit to arbitration a dispute which has arisen or may arise out of a civil or commercial matter, that State may not claim immunity from the jurisdiction of a court of another Contracting State on the territory or according to the law of which the arbitration has taken or will take place in respect of any proceedings relating to:
   (*a*) the validity or interpretation of the arbitration agreement;
   (*b*) the arbitration procedure;
   (*c*) the setting aside of the award, unless the arbitration agreement otherwise provides.
2. Paragraph 1 shall not apply to an arbitration agreement between States.[3]

Unlike Article 17(*c*) of the Convention, Article 12(1)(*c*) ECSI makes no reference to proceedings relating to the confirmation of the award. Nor is Article 12(1) ECSI as a whole restricted to differences arising out of a matter itself the subject of the equivalent of the 'commercial transaction' exception,[4] the preferred term in the chapeau being the less prescriptive 'civil or commercial matter'.

A provision corresponding to Article 17 is also found in most pre-Convention State immunity legislation. In contrast, however, to both Article 17 UNCSI and Article 12 ECSI, most of these national provisions refer simply to proceedings arising out of an arbitration agreement, without specifying to what such proceedings must relate.[5] Moreover, only one of these national provisions[6] stipulates, as Article 17 of the Convention does, that the arbitration agreement must concern differences relating to a 'commercial transaction'.

3. Drafting History

The original draft of what became Article 17 of the Convention was introduced to the ILC by Special Rapporteur Sucharitkul in his Sixth Report, in which he surveyed the various types of arbitration (including international commercial arbitration, arbitration of investment disputes, and inter-State arbitration) and examined, in summary form, the practice of States with respect to judicial proceedings relating to a State's agreement to arbitrate.[7] The Special Rapporteur contended that a State's agreement to arbitrate gave rise to an 'irresistible implication of consent', which he framed as a waiver of immunity:

Once a State agrees in a written instrument to submit to arbitration disputes which have arisen or may arise between it and other private parties to a transaction, there is an irresistible implication, if not an almost irrebuttable presumption, that it has waived its jurisdictional immunity in relation to all pertinent questions arising out of the arbitral process, from its initiation to judicial confirmation and enforcement of the arbitral awards. A crucial point is the existence of available jurisdiction which is competent to consider the subject-matter, whether it be the appointment or challenging of arbitrators, arbitral procedures, the setting aside or confirmation of an award, or judicial supervision of the arbitral process.[8]

[3] Expl. Rep. ECSI, para. 50, indicates that the circumstances mentioned in Art. 12(1)(*a*) to (*c*) ECSI are merely the 'most important', rather than an exhaustive list, of the cases in which a party to an arbitration agreement may be required to appear before a national court.

[4] See Art. 4 ECSI, embodying a narrower exception to immunity where 'the proceedings relate to an obligation of the State, which, by virtue of a contract, falls to be discharged in the territory of the State of the forum'.

[5] See eg s. 9 SIA (UK); s. 10 SIO (Pak); s. 11 SIA (Sing); s. 10 FStIA (SA); s. 11 FSIL (Isr). But *cf* Art. 2(*h*) IFSJAC (Arg); s. 17 FStIA (Aus); s. 1605(*a*)(6) FSIA (US), enacted by way of amendment to the FSIA in 1988.

[6] See Art. 2(*h*) IFSJAC (Arg).

[7] See Sixth report Sucharitkul, 54–8, paras 234–256.

[8] Sixth report Sucharitkul, 57–8, para. 255.

Special Rapporteur Sucharitkul's proposed draft article, numbered article 20, provided in paragraph 1 that a State which agreed in writing with a foreign person to submit to arbitration an existing or potential dispute arising out of a 'civil or commercial matter' was considered to have consented to the exercise of jurisdiction by a court of the 'State on the territory or according to the law of which the arbitration has taken or will take place'.[9] As a consequence, the State could not invoke immunity before that court in proceedings relating to the validity or interpretation of the arbitration agreement, to the arbitral process, or to the setting aside of the award.[10] A proposed draft article 20(2) provided that paragraph 1 was to have effect subject to any contrary provision in the arbitration agreement, and did not apply to an arbitration agreement between States.[11]

The Commission modified the draft article proposed by the Special Rapporteur. As provisionally adopted by the Commission on first reading, draft article 20 left open the kind of disputes falling within its scope, did not specify the courts to which it applied, and did not expressly exclude arbitration agreements between States,[12] reading as follows:

> If a State enters into an agreement in writing with a foreign natural or juridical person to submit to arbitration differences relating to a [commercial contract] [civil or commercial matter], that State cannot invoke immunity from jurisdiction before a court of another State which is otherwise competent in a proceeding which relates to:
> (*a*) the validity or interpretation of the arbitration agreement;
> (*b*) the arbitration procedure,
> (*c*) the setting aside of the award,
> unless the arbitration agreement otherwise provides.[13]

The draft commentary indicated that the phrase 'a court [...] which is otherwise competent' referred to a court of the seat of the arbitration, a court of the State of the chosen applicable law, or a court of the State where the property to be seized or attached was situated; and that the relevant competence was the competence to exercise supervisory jurisdiction.[14]

Following the adoption of the draft articles on first reading in 1986, the ILC sought comments and observations from States, which it assimilated in 1988.[15] The few comments received in respect of what was by then draft article 19 were mixed, with some States arguing expressly or effectively that the provision was too broad, and others that it was too narrow.[16] These comments were taken into account in the work of Special Rapporteur Ogiso, who dealt with draft article 19 in his Second Report. Of the alternative expressions bracketed in paragraph 1 of draft article 19, the Special Rapporteur preferred

[9] Sixth report Sucharitkul, 58, para. 256.

[10] Sixth report Sucharitkul, 58, para. 256.

[11] See Sixth report Sucharitkul, 58, para. 256.

[12] The draft commentary to draft art. 19 noted that the article applied only to disputes between States and foreign natural and juridical persons, the implication being that express exclusion of inter-State arbitration was superfluous. See Report ILC, thirty-seventh session, 64, para. 7 of draft commentary.

[13] Report ILC, thirty-seventh session, 63.

[14] Report ILC, thirty-seventh session, 63–4, para. 3 of draft commentary.

[15] See UN doc. A/CN.4/410 and Add. 1–5, *YILC 1988*, vol. II(1), 45–91.

[16] See eg *YILC 1988*, vol. II(1) (n. 15), comments on draft articles received from Australia (para. 37), Austria (para. 13), Bulgaria (para. 12), Cameroon (para. 5), France (para. 36), the Nordic countries (para. 7), and the UK (para. 32).

'civil or commercial matter'.[17] He also favoured changing the phrase 'a court of another State which is otherwise competent' to 'a court of another State on the territory or according to the law of which the arbitration has taken or will take place'.[18]

More significantly, Special Rapporteur Ogiso favoured distinguishing between the execution of an arbitral award, which would effectively be addressed in the draft articles dealing with measures of constraint against State property, and the recognition and enforcement of the award, by which was meant 'turning the award into a judgment or a title equivalent to a judgment by providing it with an *exequatur* or some similar judicial certificate'.[19] He elaborated:

> If one approaches the question from the view that 'an application for enforcement serves no useful purpose except as a first step towards execution', the plea of State immunity would be allowed in that proceeding to obtain the preliminary order in so far as the State's consent has not been given to the jurisdiction of the courts relating to actual execution. On the other hand, if one considers that—distinguishing the recognition of an award from its execution—recognition is 'the normal complement of the binding character of the arbitration agreement and should not be affected by considerations of sovereign immunity', the immunity would apply to the process of execution but not to the preceding recognition of the arbitral award.[20]

Implicitly favouring the second approach, the Special Rapporteur suggested adding to draft article 19(1) a subparagraph (*d*) providing for an exception to a State's immunity where the proceedings related to the recognition of the award, subject to an understanding that this did not imply waiver of immunity from execution.[21]

The Commission did not, in the event, take up the proposed subparagraph (*d*) of draft article 19(1). Moreover, in the light of its revision of what would become draft article 2(1)(*c*),[22] the Commission opted for the expression 'commercial transaction' over 'civil or commercial matter'. As finally adopted on second reading, what was by then renumbered draft article 17 read as follows:

> If a State enters into an agreement in writing with a foreign natural or juridical person to submit to arbitration differences relating to a commercial transaction, that State cannot invoke immunity from jurisdiction before a court of another State which is otherwise competent in a proceeding which relates to:
> (*a*) the validity or interpretation of the arbitration agreement;
> (*b*) the arbitration procedure;
> (*c*) the setting aside of the award,
> unless the arbitration agreement otherwise provides.

The words 'confirmation or' as appear in Article 17(*c*) of the Convention were added later, first appearing, without recorded explanation, in the 2002 report of the Ad Hoc Committee on Jurisdictional Immunities of States and Their Property.

17 Second report Ogiso, 68, para. 32.
18 Second report Ogiso, 69, para. 33.
19 Second report Ogiso, 70, para. 38.
20 Second report Ogiso, 71, para. 39, quoting respectively F.A. Mann, 'State contracts and international arbitration' (1967) 42 *BYIL* 1, 18 and G.R. Delaume, *Transnational Contracts: Applicable Law and Settlement of Disputes*, binder II, booklet 16 (Dobbs Ferry: Oceana Publications, 1990), chap. XIV, 19, para. 14.03.
21 Second report Ogiso, 71, para. 40.
22 See the commentary to Art. 2(1)(*c*).

As for the understanding with respect to Article 17 annexed to the Convention, this, along with the other understandings, was introduced by the Ad Hoc Committee in 2003,[23] again without recorded explanation. It was included unchanged in the Annex to the eventual Convention.

4. Key Points

4.1 'unless the arbitration agreement provides otherwise'

Unlike most of the other exceptions to a State's immunity from foreign jurisdiction specified in Part III of the Convention,[24] Article 17 does not provide for derogation from its provisions by way of agreement between the potential respondent State—within the scheme of Article 17, the State that is party to the arbitration agreement—and the forum State. Article 17 may, however, be set aside by the mutual consent, expressed in the arbitration agreement, of the State party to the agreement and the private counterparty.[25]

4.2 'an agreement in writing with a foreign natural or juridical person'

Article 17 is limited to proceedings in respect of 'an agreement in writing with a foreign natural or juridical person'. The requirement that the counterparty to the arbitration agreement be a foreign national makes it clear that Article 17 does not cover an arbitration agreement entered into by a State and its own national. Nor, as the ILC's commentary to draft article 17 indicates, does Article 17 cover agreements between States or between States and international organizations.[26]

4.3 'differences relating to a commercial transaction'

Article 17 is restricted to proceedings in respect of an agreement to submit to arbitration 'differences relating to a commercial transaction'.[27] The term 'commercial transaction' is defined in Article 2(1)(*c*) to mean any commercial contract or transaction for the sale of goods or supply of services; any contract for a loan or other transaction of a financial nature, including any obligation of guarantee or of indemnity in respect of any such loan or transaction; and any other contract or transaction of a commercial, industrial, trading, or professional nature, excluding contracts of employment of persons.[28] In this light, Article 17 would not encompass, for example, proceedings in relation to an arbitration agreement included in a contract of employment between an individual and a foreign State, but it would embrace proceedings relating to an arbitration agreement included in a contract for the supply of professional services.

The expression 'commercial transaction' is further stated in the understanding with respect to Article 17 annexed to the Convention to include 'investment matters'. But the term 'investment matters' is not itself defined. On its face, it would appear to cover any

[23] See 2003 report Ad Hoc Committee, annex II.

[24] See Arts 11, 12, 13, 14, 15(2), and 16(1) and (3) UNCSI.

[25] See also, *mutatis mutandis*, Arts 10(2)(*b*), 11(2)(*f*), and 15(2) UNCSI.

[26] See ILC commentary, draft art. 17, para. 7. For the extent to which dispute resolution clauses contained in investment treaties may be covered by Art. 17 of the Convention, see section 4.4.

[27] *Cf* Art. 12 ECSI, referring, arguably more broadly, to 'a dispute which has arisen or may arise out of a civil or commercial matter'.

[28] See Art. 2(1)(*c*)(i), (ii), and (iii) UNCSI respectively. See also the commentary to Art. 2(1)(*c*).

matters relating to any investment. On the other hand, the relevant limbs of the definition of 'commercial transaction' found in Article 2(1)(*c*),[29] which form part of the context of the understanding with respect to Article 17, are limited to contracts and other transactions. Were the understanding to be read in the latter light, Article 17 would provide an exception to a State's immunity from foreign proceedings in the investment context only insofar as the investment to which the arbitration the subject of the proceedings relates is pursuant to a contract between the State and the other party or could otherwise be considered a transaction between the two (for example, because it arises out of a transaction in which the other party obtained a licence or other concession from the State). As to which of the two views is the more persuasive, it is worth emphasizing that the Annex gives no indication that the inclusion of 'investment matters' within the concept of a 'commercial transaction' for the purposes of Article 17 was intended to expand the use of the latter term so broadly as to disregard the existing criteria posited in Article 2(1)(*c*). On this basis, the understanding with respect to Article 17 is better taken to indicate that proceedings concerning an agreement to submit to arbitration differences relating to a contract or other transaction pertaining to investment are covered by the exception to immunity from jurisdiction provided for in Article 17 but that proceedings concerning an agreement to arbitrate differences relating to other 'investment matters' are not.

The restriction of Article 17 to proceedings regarding an agreement to submit to arbitration 'differences relating to a commercial transaction' may reflect the reality that most arbitration agreements between States and private parties concern commercial matters.[30] But if the exception to State immunity as regards supervisory proceedings in relation to arbitration stems in principle from the State's implicit submission, via its agreement with the counterparty to submit to arbitration, to a measure of supervisory jurisdiction in relation to that arbitration, the subject-matter of the arbitration agreement ought logically to be immaterial. This would seem to explain why all bar one[31] of the corresponding national State immunity provisions make no mention of the subject-matter of the arbitration.

4.4 'arbitration'

The ILC commentary suggests obliquely that what became Article 17 of the Convention was intended to cover only agreements to submit to 'commercial arbitration'[32] and not arbitration agreements pursuant to an investment treaty.[33] There are compelling reasons to believe, however, that supervisory proceedings in a national court in relation to non-ICSID investment treaty arbitration do indeed fall with the scope of Article 17 of the Convention, at least insofar as the investment is pursuant to a contract or other transaction within the meaning of Article 2(1)(*c*) of the Convention.

It should first be borne in mind that the understanding annexed to the Convention with respect to Article 17, which makes clear that the expression 'commercial transaction'

[29] See Art. 2(1)(*c*)(ii) and (iii).

[30] See also, in this light, Art. 12 ECSI ('a dispute which has arisen or may arise out of a civil or commercial matter').

[31] Recall art. 2(*h*) IFSJAC (Arg).

[32] See ILC commentary, draft art. 17, paras 3, 5, 6, and 9.

[33] ILC commentary, draft art. 17, paras 7 and 8.

used in the provision includes 'investment matters', was introduced only in 2003, by the Ad Hoc Committee, twelve years after the ILC commentary was finalized. In this light, it is distinctly arguable that the commentary, insofar as it might be taken to suggest that Article 17 of the eventual Convention does not extend to investment arbitration per se, is not a reliable guide to the provision's interpretation and application, as elaborated by the annexed understanding. Given that the concept of a 'commercial transaction' as employed in Article 17 now expressly embraces investment matters, there is no cogent reason to exclude from the provision's purview an agreement to submit to arbitration any differences relating to an investment contract or other transaction on the sole ground that the differences do not relate to a 'commercial transaction'.

On the other hand, the express indication in the ILC commentary that Article 17 does not encompass investment arbitration specifically pursuant to the Convention on the Settlement of Investment Disputes between States and Nationals of Other States (ICSID Convention)[34] makes sense. As the commentary notes,[35] arbitration under the ICSID Convention is not subject to the supervisory jurisdiction of any national legal system.[36] ICSID has its own regime for the supervision of awards through the annulment process, and such awards are enforceable pursuant to the terms of the ICSID Convention itself. In this light, an agreement to submit to ICSID arbitration does not imply submission to supervisory proceedings in a national court. Indeed, there can never be supervisory proceedings in a national court in relation to ICSID arbitration.

The question remains, however, whether an agreement to submit to non-ICSID investment arbitration—whether administered by the International Chamber of Commerce (ICC), under the UNCITRAL Rules, or ad hoc—falls within the scope of Article 17 if it is pursuant to a dispute resolution clause in an investment treaty. The issue here, as highlighted in the ILC commentary,[37] is whether the agreement can be considered 'an agreement in writing with a foreign natural or juridical person' within the meaning of Article 17 UNCSI; and in this regard the ILC commentary betrays a misunderstanding of the nature of an agreement to arbitrate pursuant to a dispute resolution clause in an investment treaty. Such an agreement is not perfected in the treaty itself (which is not an agreement between a State and 'a foreign natural or juridical person'). A dispute resolution clause in an investment treaty represents no more than a standing offer to arbitrate, and is considered to have been accepted only when an investor protected by the treaty files a request for arbitration.[38] The result is an agreement to arbitrate concluded in two parts,[39] with the offer being made by the State via the clause in the treaty and acceptance being signalled by the investor via its request for arbitration. In short, such an agreement to arbitrate is between a State and a 'foreign natural or juridical person'. It is also, it might be noted, in writing. Moreover, if the clause provides for non-ICSID arbitration, the consequent agreement can logically be taken to constitute waiver by the

[34] ILC commentary, draft art. 17, paras 7 and 8.

[35] ILC commentary, draft art. 17, paras 2 and 7.

[36] See Art. 26 ICSID Convention.

[37] See ILC commentary, draft art. 17, para. 7.

[38] See eg *Lanco International Inc. v Argentina (Preliminary Decision on Jurisdiction)*, 8 December 1998, 5 ICSID Reports 367, 383–94, paras 43–44; *American Manufacturing and Trading, Inc. v Republic of Zaire (Award)*, 21 February 1997, 5 ICSID Reports 11, 25–6, paras 5.18–5.23.

[39] See C. Schreuer et al.(eds), *The ICSID Convention: A Commentary* (2nd edn) (Oxford: Oxford University Press, 2009), 211–13, paras 25–447 to 25–449.

State concerned of immunity from the supervisory jurisdiction of any domestic court competent to exercise that jurisdiction in relation to the arbitration. In such cases, therefore, there can be no objection either on the wording of Article 17 or in principle to Article 17's abrogation of the State's immunity in supervisory proceedings.

In sum, the better view is that supervisory proceedings in a domestic court in relation to non-ICSID investment treaty arbitration fall within the scope of Article 17, at least where the investment is pursuant to a contract or other transaction within the meaning of Article 2(1)(*c*) of the Convention.

4.5 'a proceeding which relates to ... the validity, interpretation or application of the arbitration agreement; ... the arbitration procedure; or ... the confirmation or setting aside of the award'

The exception to a State's immunity from foreign jurisdiction provided for in Article 17 is limited to proceedings relating to the validity, interpretation, or application of the arbitration agreement, to the arbitration procedure, or to the confirmation or setting aside of the award. That is, Article 17 pertains only to proceedings in the exercise of the court's supervisory jurisdiction in respect of the arbitration. It does not concern proceedings for the recognition and enforcement of an arbitral award.[40]

Proceedings relating to the validity of the arbitration agreement might concern matters such as the capacity of the individuals who concluded the agreement to bind the respective parties and whether the agreement was procured by fraud or coercion or was based on a legally relevant mistake, while proceedings relating to the application of the agreement might involve questions such as whether the agreement has been discharged on the ground of frustration. Proceedings relating to the arbitration procedure include proceedings in which a court order is sought to compel the attendance of witnesses[41] or the production[42] of evidence before the arbitral tribunal or to ensure the preservation of evidence of potential relevance to the arbitration.[43] Proceedings relating to the confirmation of the award can comprehend not only proceedings on an application specifically to confirm the award[44] but also proceedings on an application to challenge any award of the tribunal as to its substantive jurisdiction[45] and on an appeal on a question of law arising out of the award.[46] Finally, proceedings relating to the setting aside of the award can comprise those, again, on an application to challenge an award of the tribunal as to its substantive jurisdiction[47] and on an appeal on a question of law arising out of the award,[48] as well as those on an application to challenge an award on the ground of serious irregularity affecting the tribunal, the proceedings, or the award.[49]

40 See later in this section for details.

41 See eg s. 43 Arbitration Act 1996 (UK); s. 7 Federal Arbitration Act (US).

42 See eg s. 43 Arbitration Act (UK); art. 184(2) Private International Law Act 1987 (Swi); s. 7 Federal Arbitration Act (US).

43 See eg s. 44(2)(*b*) Arbitration Act (UK).

44 See eg s. 9 Federal Arbitration Act (US).

45 See eg s. 67(1)(*a*) and (3)(*a*) Arbitration Act (UK).

46 See eg s. 69(1) and (7)(*a*) Arbitration Act (UK).

47 See eg s. 67(1)(*a*) and (3)(*c*) Arbitration Act (UK).

48 See eg s. 69(1) and (7)(*d*) Arbitration Act (UK).

49 See eg ss. 68(1)(*a*) and (3)(*b*) Arbitration Act (UK).

Article 17 does not on its face encompass proceedings relating to the variation of an award. It remains to be seen, however, at least in those State parties where a court is empowered to vary an award in response to an application to set that award aside,[50] whether Article 17(*c*)'s abrogation of a foreign State's immunity from jurisdiction in 'a proceeding which relates to . . . the . . . setting aside of the award' is taken to extend to an order for variation. Nor, on first impression, does Article 17 cover proceedings on an application for an order to require the arbitral tribunal to set out its reasons in sufficient detail to enable the court to determine an application or appeal in relation to the award.[51] But proceedings on an application to this end might be considered part and parcel of, again, 'a proceeding which relates to . . . the . . . setting aside of the award' or of 'a proceeding which relates to . . . the confirmation . . . of the award' within the meaning of Article 17(*c*).

Like Article 12 ECSI, Article 17 UNCSI definitely does not embrace proceedings relating to the recognition and enforcement of an arbitral award.[52] This is in contrast with section 9 SIA (UK), section 10 SIO (Pak), section 11 SIA (Sing), section 10 FStIA (SA), and section 11 FSIL (Isr), which do not limit the range of proceedings to which the arbitration exception to immunity from jurisdiction applies, with the result, at least in the UK, that the State 'will enjoy no immunity in proceedings . . . to enter judgment on an award . . . or to register an award for enforcement'.[53] Article 17 of the Convention is also in contrast with section 1605(*a*)(6) FSIA (US), inserted by way of amendment in 1988, which says, in effect, that in certain defined instances 'an agreement to arbitrate constitutes a waiver of immunity in an action to enforce that agreement or the resultant award'.[54] Article 17 differs too from section 17(2) FStIA (Aus), which provides that where, in certain defined instances and subject to any contrary provision in the agreement, a foreign State is a party to an agreement to submit to arbitration a dispute about a relevant transaction or event, that State is not immune 'in a proceeding concerning the recognition as binding for any purpose, or for the enforcement, of an award made pursuant to the arbitration, wherever the award was made'.[55] In short, under

[50] See eg s. 67(1)(*a*) and (3)(*b*) and s. 69(1) and (7)(*b*) Arbitration Act (UK).

[51] See eg s. 70(4)(*b*) Arbitration Act (UK).

[52] See also H. Fox, *The Law of State Immunity* (2nd edn) (Oxford: Oxford University Press, 2008), 498 and 501. Nor, *a fortiori*, does Art. 17 extend to post-judgment measures of constraint, such as execution, against State property in connection with an arbitral award. These remain governed by Art. 19 UNCSI, as elaborated on by Art. 21 UNCSI.

[53] A. Dickinson, R. Lindsay, and J. Loonam, *State Immunity: Selected Materials and Commentary* (Oxford: Oxford University Press, 2004), 378, para. 4.069, referring to s. 9 SIA (UK). See, in this regard, *Svenska Petroleum Exploration AB v Government of the Republic of Lithuania (No. 2)* [2007] QB 886. Any measure of execution against the State's property will, in contrast, continue to be governed by the rules on immunity from execution. See, in this regard, s. 13(2)(*b*) SIA (UK); s. 14(2)(b) SIO (Pak); s. 15(2)(*b*) SIA (Sing); s. 14(*b*)(ii) FStIA (SA). See also s. 15(*a*) FSIL (Isr), where the absence of reference to the enforcement of an arbitral award is presumably on account of the fact that what is enforced is technically, upon its recognition, 'a judgment or other decision of a court in Israel'.

[54] *Cargill International SA v M/T Pavel Dybenko*, 991 F 2d 1012, 1018 (US (11th Cir.) 2000), quoting 131 Cong. Rec. S5369 (daily edn 3 May 1985) (Sen. Mathias). S. 1610(*a*)(6) FSIA (US) provides that the property in the US of a foreign State, 'used for a commercial activity in the United States, shall not be immune from attachment in aid of execution, or from execution, upon a judgment entered by a court of the United States or of a State . . . if . . . the judgment is based on an order confirming an arbitral award rendered against the foreign state, provided that attachment in aid of execution, or execution, would not be inconsistent with any provision in the arbitral agreement'.

[55] The rules on execution remain, however, unchanged. See, in this regard, s. 30 FStIA (Aus).

Article 17 of the Convention, as under the legislation of Argentina,[56] the exception to a State's immunity from foreign proceedings in cases concerning an agreement to arbitrate relates only to the supervisory jurisdiction of the court.

5. Evaluation

Article 17 of the Convention is consistent with the accepted principle that valid consent to arbitration implies consent to a measure of supervisory jurisdiction over that arbitration by a competent foreign court, a principle endorsed in the ILC's commentary to draft article 17:

> [C]onsenting to a commercial arbitration necessarily implies consent to all the natural and logical consequences of the commercial arbitration contemplated. In this limited area only, it may therefore be said that consent to arbitration by a State entails consent to the supervisory jurisdiction by a court of another State, competent to supervise the implementation of the arbitration agreement.[57]

But if the arbitration exception to a State's immunity from foreign proceedings is ultimately justified by the consent to supervisory jurisdiction implicit in the State's submission to arbitration, it is curious that Article 17 should be restricted to proceedings concerning the arbitration of differences relating to a 'commercial transaction'. In the same way that the exceptions to immunity embodied in Articles 8 and 9 of the Convention—which are similarly based on the respondent State's implied consent to the exercise of jurisdiction over it—are without regard to the *jure imperii/jure gestionis* distinction, so too should the character of the transaction out of which the arbitration arises be immaterial to the availability of an exception to immunity in respect of a foreign court's supervisory jurisdiction over that arbitration.

Two important questions as to the scope of Article 17 remain to be answered. The first is whether the provision relates to the arbitration of differences over any investment matter or only over what Article 2(1)(*c*) of the Convention would understand as contracts and other transactions pertaining to investment. The second is whether Article 17 embraces supervisory proceedings in relation to non-ICSID investment treaty arbitration. The answers to these questions will determine the practical impact of Article 17 on the immunity of States parties from the jurisdiction of the courts of other States parties. They will also determine whether certain States, in the event that they become parties to the Convention, will need to amend their currently more expansive legislation to bring it into line with Article 17. A restriction of immunity from proceedings relating to an arbitration agreement to an extent greater than that required by Article 17 will leave the State party of the forum in breach of Article 5 vis-à-vis the State party the respondent to the proceedings, except in those cases where the latter State and the private counterparty have provided in the arbitration agreement for the application of this more restrictive immunity in any supervisory proceedings that may arise. In the interests—in the words of the Convention's preamble—of 'legal certainty, particularly in dealings of States with natural or juridical persons', and of 'the harmonization of practice in this area', it can only be hoped that these answers are forthcoming sooner rather than later.

[56] See art. 2(*h*) IFSJAC (Arg).

[57] ILC commentary, draft art. 17, para. 6. The commentary is at pains to emphasize, however, that consent to arbitration is 'no waiver of immunity from the jurisdiction of a court which would otherwise be competent to decide the dispute or difference on the merits'.

PART IV: STATE IMMUNITY FROM MEASURES OF CONSTRAINT IN CONNECTION WITH PROCEEDINGS BEFORE A COURT

CHESTER BROWN AND ROGER O'KEEFE*

1. Introduction

Just because an exception exists in given proceedings to the immunity of a State from the jurisdiction of a court of another State does not mean that any judgment on the merits obtained by the claimant against the State can be executed against that State's property. Nor does the State's established or prospective amenability to the court's jurisdiction mean that a claimant can obtain conservatory measures against the State's property or an injunction against the State in relation to its use of the property. As emphasized by the International Court of Justice in *Jurisdictional Immunities of the State*, customary international law posits a fundamental distinction between a State's immunity from proceedings in a foreign court and the immunity of its property—or, more accurately, the immunity of the State in respect of its property[1]—from attachment, arrest, execution, and all cognate judicially ordered measures.[2]

The Convention reflects this cardinal distinction between immunity from jurisdiction, as dealt with in Parts II and III of the instrument, and 'immunity from measures of constraint', as dealt with in Part IV.[3] The conceptual and practical divide is reiterated in the final provision of Part IV, Article 20 ('Effect of consent to jurisdiction to [*sic*] measures of constraint'), which specifies that consent to the exercise of jurisdiction for the purposes of Article 7 of the Convention is not to be taken to imply consent to measures of constraint for the purposes of Articles 18 and 19.

In turn, Part IV of the Convention distinguishes between what it calls 'pre-judgment measures of constraint', the more expansive immunity from which is dealt with in Article 18 ('State immunity from pre-judgment measures of constraint'), and 'post-judgment measures of constraint', immunity from which is regulated by Article 19 ('State immunity from post-judgment measures of constraint'). The latter provision is linked, via its paragraph (*c*), to Article 21 ('Specific categories of property'), which elaborates on it.

* The authors would like to thank Ashique Rahman, LLM (Syd), for his valuable assistance in the preparation of this chapter.

[1] Recall the commentary to Art. 1 UNCSI.

[2] See *Jurisdictional Immunities of the State (Germany v Italy: Greece intervening), Judgment*, 3 February 2012, International Court of Justice, para. 113.

[3] For more on the distinction, see M. Wood, 'Immunity from Jurisdiction and Immunity from Measures of Constraint' in this volume.

2. Key Points

2.1 The two distinctions

A. Immunity from jurisdiction and immunity from measures of constraint

The ILC Working Group established in 1978 to determine the scope of the Commission's future work on the topic of jurisdictional immunities of States and their property recognized at the outset that immunity from the execution of court orders, judgments, and any other 'measures of constraint' against a State's property was a question separate from that of immunity from jurisdiction. The Working Group observed:

> Immunities from execution form a different dimension of State immunities, requiring special attention and distinct treatment. Waiver of immunities from jurisdiction does not, as a general rule, extend to waiver of execution.[4]

Although practice had progressively developed towards a restrictive doctrine of State immunity, this development was far more pronounced in relation to immunity from jurisdiction than in relation to immunity from measures of constraint.[5] This led the ILC to remark in 1986 that, in a claim against a State, '[i]mmunity from execution may be viewed... as the last fortress, the last bastion of State immunity'.[6]

That said, not all States have treated immunity from execution as distinct from and more plenary than immunity from jurisdiction. The Swiss courts, for example, have traditionally considered immunity from jurisdiction and immunity from measures of constraint as a unified regime, so that, where there is no immunity from jurisdiction, any resulting judgment or award can be executed,[7] subject to the condition, *inter alia*, that measures of execution may not be taken against property used for sovereign purposes.[8] The Supreme Court of the Netherlands has held that international law is not 'opposed to any execution against foreign State-owned property situated in the territory of another State',[9] seemingly leaving little room for immunity from measures of constraint. But this permissive approach has never found general favour. The far more common view traditionally was that, except for where the State consented to the taking of such measures, all measures of constraint against foreign State property were barred by State immunity.

Initial steps on the wider path towards a more restrictive doctrine of immunity in relation to measures of constraint were taken in the 1970s and 1980s in the legislation and judicial practice of some States, which provided for an exception to the immunity of

[4] Report ILC, thirtieth session, 154, para. 23.

[5] See eg H. Fox, *The Law of State Immunity* (2nd edn) (Oxford: Oxford University Press, 2008), 600–9; X. Yang, *State Immunity in International Law* (Cambridge: Cambridge University Press, 2012), 343–422. See also G. Hafner, 'Historical Background to the Convention' and M. Wood, 'Immunity from Jurisdiction and Immunity from Measures of Constraint' in this volume.

[6] Report ILC, thirty-eighth session, 17. See also ILC commentary, draft art. 18, para. 2.

[7] See eg *Kingdom of Greece v Julius Bär & Co.*, 23 ILR 195 (Swi (FT) 1956); *Arab Republic of Egypt v Cinetelevision International Registered Trust and Another*, 65 ILR 425, 430 (Swi (FT) 1979). See also 'Comments and Observations Received from Governments', *YILC 1988*, vol. II(1), 45, 92, para. 5 (Swi). See too, generally, P. Lalive, 'Swiss Law and Practice in relation to Measures of Execution against the Property of a Foreign State' (1979) 10 *NYIL* 153.

[8] See eg *Arab Republic of Egypt v Cinetelevision International* (n. 7), 434–5.

[9] *Société Européenne d'Etudes et d'Entreprises en liquidité volontaire (SEEE) v Socialist Federal Republic of Yugoslavia*, 65 ILR 356, 362 (Nth (SC) 1973).

foreign State property from measures of constraint where the property was in use or intended for use for commercial purposes.[10] For its part, Article 26 ECSI, an optional provision, stipulates that a judgment rendered in an industrial or commercial case may, if certain conditions are met, be enforced against any property of a foreign State used exclusively in connection with the industrial or commercial activity. At the other end of the spectrum, however, the German Democratic Republic, for one, stridently declared as late as 1988 that it 'strictly rejected' the '[c]ompulsory enforcement of court decisions against a State'.[11]

The divergence in State practice on immunity from measures of constraint inevitably informed the drafting of the Convention. Reaching agreement on the content of such immunity proved one of the drafters' greatest challenges.[12]

B. *Immunity from pre- and post-judgment measures of constraint*

With a view to narrowing the grounds of disagreement over immunity from measures of constraint, the decision was taken to distinguish in Part IV of the Convention between immunity from pre-judgment measures of constraint and immunity from post-judgment measures.[13] The essence of the distinction is that 'State immunity should be broader in respect of pre-judgment measures of constraint than in respect of measures taken with a view to executing a judgment'.[14] The conviction would appear to be premised on a reluctance, necessarily absent in the context of execution, to restrain a State's free use of its property unless and until its liability on the merits has been established. The rationale is hardly compelling, going as it does to the merits of any application for pre-judgment measures of constraint against the property rather than to any principle underpinning the law of State immunity.

The practical reflection of the differentiation between immunity from pre-judgment measures and immunity from post-judgment measures of constraint in Part IV of the Convention is that, whereas Article 19 does not prohibit post-judgment measures against State property located in the territory of the forum State and in use or intended for use by the State 'for other than government non-commercial purposes',[15] Article 18 prohibits pre-judgment measures unless the State against whose property the measures are to be taken has expressly consented to them by one of several specified means or, alternatively, has allocated or earmarked the property for the satisfaction of the claim the object of the proceedings. In short, State immunity is more restrictive in relation to post-judgment measures than in relation to pre-judgment measures.

This difference in the restrictiveness of the immunity of State property as between the pre-judgment and post-judgment contexts is by no means as prevalent in State practice as the more essential difference in restrictiveness between immunity from jurisdiction and immunity from measures of constraint. For example, while the FSIA (US) recognizes a

[10] See the commentaries to Arts 18 and 19 UNCSI respectively.

[11] 'Comments and Observations Received from Governments' (n. 7), 69, para. 25 (GDR).

[12] See the commentaries to Arts 18 and 19 UNCSI respectively.

[13] See, again, the commentaries to Arts 18 and 19 UNCSI respectively.

[14] 1999 report Chairman Sixth Committee Working Group, 6, para. 35.

[15] Art. 19(*c*) UNCSI. The proviso is that the property must have a connection with the specific emanation of the State against which the proceeding on the merits was directed.

broader immunity from pre-judgment than from post-judgment measures,[16] the SIA (UK), SIA (Can), SIO (Pak), FStIA (SA), FStIA (Aus), SIA (Sing), and FSIL (Isr) do not.[17]

2.2 Immunity from measures of constraint

A. Terminology

The expression 'measures of constraint' used in Part IV of the Convention is not one found in the legal lexicon of many, if any, national legal systems. This is the point, as explained in the ILC commentary to Part IV of its draft articles on jurisdictional immunities of States and their property:

> The expression 'measures of constraint' has been chosen as a generic term, not a technical one in use in any particular internal law. Since measures of constraint vary considerably in the practice of States, it would be difficult, if not impossible, to find a term which covers each and every possible method or measure of constraint in all legal systems. Suffice it, therefore, to mention by way of example the more notable and readily understood measures, such as attachment, arrest and execution. The problem of finding readily translatable terms in the official languages is indubitably multiplied by the diversity of State practice in the realm of procedures and measures of constraint.[18]

Equally generic are the terms 'pre-judgment' and 'post-judgment'.

More familiar terms used in connection with measures of constraint include 'immunity from execution' and 'immunity from enforcement'. Neither is incorrect or devoid of value. But both have their problems, and the ILC was wise to avoid them.

'Immunity from execution' might be taken, and is often used, to refer specifically to immunity from measures against State property in execution of a judgment or arbitral award—that is, in the language of Part IV of the Convention, to immunity solely from post-judgment measures of constraint. The term 'execution', however, might equally be taken in this context, and is again often used, to embrace the execution of any court order, including interlocutory orders, thereby encompassing both post- and pre-judgment measures of constraint.

'Immunity from enforcement', for its part, is liable to lead to confusion in the specific context of the enforcement of foreign judgments or arbitral awards between immunity from jurisdiction and immunity from what the Convention calls post-judgment measures of constraint. Proceedings for the 'enforcement', or for the 'recognition and enforcement', of a foreign judgment are judicial proceedings in their own right, which as such implicate immunity from jurisdiction rather than immunity from measures, specifically post-judgment measures, of constraint.[19] The same goes for proceedings for the recognition and enforcement of an arbitral award. In each case, it is only after the

[16] See s. 1610(*a*) and (*b*) versus s. 1610(*d*) FSIA (US), although see also s. 1610(*e*), on the immunity of State vessels.

[17] See s. 13(2) to (4) SIA (UK); ss. 11–12 SIA (Can); s. 14(2) to (3) SIO (Pak); s. 14(1) to (3) FStIA (SA); ss. 30–33 FStIA (Aus); s. 15(2) to (4) SIA (Sing); ss. 15–18 FSIL (Isr). As for the ECSI, the immunity accorded by Art. 23 ECSI is the same as between 'measures of execution' and 'preventive measures'. At the same time, Art. 26, an optional provision, seeks to restrict immunity from execution only.

[18] ILC commentary, draft Part IV, para. 2.

[19] See *Jurisdictional Immunities of the State* (n. 2), paras 128 and 130.

judgment or award has been recognized and enforced by the court that the successful claimant can apply for execution—that is, for post-judgment measures of constraint.

The term 'measures of constraint' was picked up by the ICJ in *Jurisdictional Immunities of the State*.[20] Perhaps unfortunately, however, the Court also referred repeatedly in the same context to 'immunity from enforcement'.[21]

B. Property of the State as such and property of separate entities

When it comes to the content of immunity from measures of constraint, Part IV of the Convention draws no distinction between the property of the State as such—that is, as a juridical person separate as a matter of municipal law from any political subdivisions and from any State agencies, instrumentalities, or other entities (known in some jurisdictions as 'separate entities') as may exist and enjoy independent legal personality—and the property of any separate entities. Provided a separate entity, such as a State enterprise, qualifies as a 'State' under Article 2(1)(*b*)(iii) of the Convention, Part IV of the Convention places its property on the same footing as the property of the State *eo nomine* in terms of its immunity from foreign measures of constraint. Articles 18 and 19 apply equally to both. This is in contrast to the State immunity legislation of a range of States.[22]

Differentiation for the purposes of immunity from measures of constraint between the property of a State as such and the property of a separate entity, such as a State enterprise, was in fact considered by the ILC. In 1990, in his Third Report, Special Rapporteur Ogiso proposed a wholly new provision, intended to follow what ultimately became Article 21 of the Convention, which was to provide that, '[i]f a State property including a segregated State property is entrusted by the State to a State enterprise for commercial purposes, the State cannot invoke immunity from a measure of constraint before a court of a forum State in respect of that State property'.[23] One member of the Commission suggested in response that the wording be changed to provide more straightforwardly that a State 'cannot invoke immunity from measures of constraint, including measures of attachment, arrest and execution, in respect of the property of a State enterprise'.[24] The majority of the Commission, on the other hand, did not think the proposed provision necessary, given what was then the definition of the term 'State' in draft article 2, which provided that a State enterprise established for commercial purposes was not to be considered a 'State'.[25] If a State enterprise established for commercial purposes could never be a State, 'it fell outside the topic of jurisdictional immunities of States and the new draft article . . . should therefore be deleted'.[26] But in the event it transpired that State enterprises—'agencies or instrumentalities of the State or other entities', in the words of the eventual Article 2(*b*)(iii) of the Convention—do fall within the definition of 'State' as used in the Convention, including in Part IV of the Convention, 'to the extent

[20] See *Jurisdictional Immunities of the State* (n. 2), Part IV ('The measures of constraint taken against property belonging to Germany located on Italian territory') and paras 110, 112–114, and 118–119.

[21] See *Jurisdictional Immunities of the State* (n. 2), paras 110, 113, and 114.

[22] See the commentary to Arts 18 and 19 UNCSI.

[23] Third report Ogiso, 19. The provision was intended to go hand-in-hand with a provision on the immunity of State enterprises from jurisdiction.

[24] Report ILC, forty-second session, 42, para. 228.

[25] Report ILC, forty-second session, 42, para. 228.

[26] Report ILC, forty-second session, 42, para. 228.

that they are entitled to perform and are actually performing acts in the exercise of sovereign authority of the State'.[27]

In practice, however, any variation between State practice and Part IV of the Convention in the treatment of the immunity of the property of separate entities from measures of constraint may not be as great as it may appear. In many circumstances, separate entities will simply not qualify as a 'State' under Article 2(1)(*b*)(iii) of the Convention, either because they are not entitled to perform or because they are not actually performing acts in the exercise of sovereign authority of the State. And, as pointed out by the ILC, if they are not a 'State', their property is not 'property of a State' for the purposes of Part IV, and will not be immune.

Whether Part IV's equal treatment of the property of the State as such and the property of State enterprises means that 'the (commercial) assets of either [are] liable to be taken in execution by the creditors of the other'[28] is a separate question, and is regulated by the proviso in Article 19(*c*) that 'post-judgment measures of constraint may only be taken against property that has a connection with the entity against which the proceeding was directed'. It is also the subject of two limbs of the 'understanding' with respect to Article 19 annexed to the Convention.

3. Evaluation

The immunity of foreign State property from measures of constraint has traditionally been the poor relation in the doctrinal and pedagogical treatment of the law of State immunity. Indeed, 'State immunity' has tended in these contexts to mean 'State immunity from jurisdiction'. In part perhaps this is because the immunity of the property of a foreign State from attachment, arrest, execution, and all cognate judicially ordered measures of constraint does not fit neatly within the story of the move from the absolute to the restrictive doctrine of State immunity. In part perhaps it is because there has been comparatively little to say. Whatever the explanation, the result has been somewhat misleading. The impression has been that the claimant's successful reliance on an exception to the immunity of the State from jurisdiction is the beginning, middle, and end of the story. But the story begins when the claimant seeks to prevent the State from moving its assets abroad, and it ends when the judgment debtor wants her money.

Part IV of the Convention—a discrete, complete part dedicated to immunity from measures of constraint—usefully lends some balance. The distinction and the significance of the distinction it embodies and highlights between the immunity of the State from jurisdiction and the immunity of its property from measures of constraint has been underlined in *Jurisdictional Immunities of the State*, in which the respondent State invoked Article 19, on post-judgment measures of constraint, as evidence of the customary international rules on point.[29] It is not the last that will be heard of Articles 18 to 21 of the Convention.

[27] See the commentary to Art. 2(1)(*a*) and (*b*) UNCSI.

[28] *La Générale des Carrières et des Mines v F.G. Hemisphere Associates LLC* [2002] UKPC 27, para. 3 (UK (PC Jersey) 2012).

[29] See *Jurisdictional Immunities of the State* (n. 2), para. 115.

Article 18

Chester Brown and Roger O'Keefe*

Article 18

State immunity from pre-judgment measures of constraint

No pre-judgment measures of constraint, such as attachment or arrest, against property of a State may be taken in connection with a proceeding before a court of another State unless and except to the extent that:

(*a*) the State has expressly consented to the taking of such measures as indicated:
  (i) by international agreement;
  (ii) by an arbitration agreement or in a written contract; or
  (iii) by a declaration before the court or by a written communication after a dispute between the parties has arisen; or

(*b*) the State has allocated or earmarked property for the satisfaction of the claim which is the object of that proceeding.

1. Introduction

Article 18 is the first of the two main provisions in Part IV of the Convention dealing with immunity from measures of constraint against State property taken in connection with proceedings before a foreign court. In contrast to Article 19, which deals with post-judgment measures of constraint, Article 18 deals with pre-judgment measures, such as conservatory attachment and pre-judgment arrest. In further contrast to Article 19, which does not prohibit post-judgment measures against State property located in the territory of the forum State and in use or intended for use by the State 'for other than government non-commercial purposes',[1] Article 18 prohibits pre-judgment measures of constraint unless the State against whose property the measures are to be taken has expressly consented to them by one of several specified means or, alternatively, has allocated or earmarked the property for the satisfaction of the claim the object of the proceedings.

2. Drafting History

2.1 The ILC's first reading

It was not until his Seventh Report, in 1985, that Special Rapporteur Sucharitkul first proposed to the ILC the texts of draft provisions on State immunity from foreign measures of constraint.[2] The relevant rules were initially presented in the form of a

* The authors would like to thank Ashique Rahman, LLM (Syd), for his valuable assistance in the preparation of this chapter.

[1] Art. 19(*c*) UNCSI. The proviso is that the property must have a connection with the specific emanation of the State against which the proceedings on the merits were directed.

[2] See generally Seventh report Sucharitkul, 23–44, paras 4–117.

draft article 21 ('Scope of the present part'), a draft article 22 ('State immunity from attachment and execution'), a draft article 23 ('Modalities and effect of consent to attachment and execution'), and a draft article 24 ('Types of State property permanently immune from attachment and execution').[3] Article 18 of the eventual Convention has its origins in Special Rapporteur Sucharitkul's proposed draft articles 22 and 23, which treated as one pre-judgment and post-judgment measures of constraint.

As proposed by the Special Rapporteur, what was then draft article 22(1)[4] laid down a general rule that 'State property, or property in the possession or control of a State, or property in which a State has an interest,' was not to be subject to 'attachment, arrest and execution by order of a court of another State, as an interim or precautionary pre-judgment measure, or as a process to secure satisfaction of a final judgment of such a court'.[5] Four subparagraphs then enumerated exceptions to this presumptive immunity. In accordance with State practice and as foreshadowed in the Special Rapporteur's Preliminary Report of 1979,[6] consent was recognized in subparagraph (*a*) as grounding an exception. Next, subparagraph (*b*) provided that property 'in use or intended for use by the State in commercial and non-governmental service' was not to benefit from immunity. As for subparagraph (*c*), the Special Rapporteur proposed that immunity from measures of constraint not be available where what was at issue in the proceedings was the State's ownership, possession, or use of the property 'or any right or interest arising for the State by way of succession, gift or *bona vacantia*'. Finally, subparagraph (*d*) reflected the view of the Special Rapporteur that State property[7] set aside specifically 'for satisfaction of judgment debts, or plainly for payment of the claim, must be regarded as attachable by consent expressly given or indicated by clear conduct'.[8]

The Special Rapporteur's proposed draft article 22(2) stipulated the availability to a State of immunity 'in respect of its property, or property in its possession or control or in which it has an interest,' from 'an interim or final injunction or specific performance order' by a foreign court 'which [was] designed to deprive the State of its enjoyment, possession or use of the property or other interest, or otherwise to compel the State . . . to vacate the property or to surrender it to another person'.[9] The proposal was premised on the belief that measures of constraint could not be 'forcibly ordered' against a sovereign State, 'since physical compulsion against a foreign State, even with judicial sanction, [was] still unwelcome'.[10]

When the Commission came to consider the Special Rapporteur's text, some members expressed concern that the terms used to describe the various measures regulated by draft

[3] Of these four provisions, the proposed draft art. 21 was not retained, while the substance of the proposed draft art. 24 is found today, in amended form, in Art. 21 of the Convention.

[4] See Seventh report Sucharitkul, 38, para. 84.

[5] Seventh report Sucharitkul, 38, para. 84.

[6] See Preliminary report Sucharitkul, 243, para. 87.

[7] Note that, unless found in direct quotation, the term 'State property' is used in section 2 of the present commentary as shorthand for whatever description of the relevant property was current at the time, be it 'State property, or property in the possession or control of a State, or property in which a State has an interest', as proposed by the Special Rapporteur; 'its'—meaning the State's—'property or property in its possession or control [, or property in which it has a legally protected interest]', as adopted on first reading by the ILC; or 'property of a State', as adopted on second reading and in the eventual Article 18 of the Convention. In contrast, the term 'State property' is used in section 3 as shorthand for 'property of a State', the expression found in Art. 18 of the Convention.

[8] Seventh report Sucharitkul, 38, para. 84.

[9] Seventh report Sucharitkul, 38, para. 84.

[10] Seventh report Sucharitkul, 36, para. 77.

article 22 might have different meanings in different national legal systems.[11] It was suggested that a more generic formulation, 'such as "judicial measures of constraint against the use of such property, including attachment, arrest or execution"', be relied on.[12] A 'general reference' like this 'would also include all other measures of judicial constraint under domestic law, including certain types of interlocutory injunctions that might not be strictly considered as attachment, arrest or execution',[13] which in turn would do away with the need for paragraph 2 of draft article 22. When it came to what property was to be covered by the provision, the formulation 'or property in which a State has an interest' was the subject of debate.[14] In the event, the Special Rapporteur revised draft article 22 in response to discussion within the Commission, and his new text—which spoke simply of 'judicial measures of constraint upon the use of such property, including attachment, arrest or execution'—was referred to the Drafting Committee for consideration.[15]

The simplified revised draft article proposed to the Commission by the Drafting Committee, entitled 'State immunity from measures of constraint', set out a general rule of immunity from measures of constraint subject to a commercial use exception (which further required that the property have a connection with the object of the claim) and an exception for where the property had been allocated or earmarked for the satisfaction of the claim.[16] The Committee further amended the Special Rapporteur's revised reference to the measures regulated by draft article 22, dropping the qualifier 'judicial' to speak solely of 'measures of constraint, including any measure of attachment, arrest and execution';[17] and in the light of the use of this generic label, it proposed, as suggested within the Commission, the deletion of paragraph 2 of the draft article. As for the property properly the subject of the provision, this generated conflicting opinions in the Drafting Committee, with some members expressing the view that immunity should not be extended to property in which a State had merely a 'legally protected interest', as distinct from property owned or possessed or controlled by the State.[18] In the event, the text proposed by the Committee spoke of 'its'—meaning the State's—'property or property in its possession or control [, or property in which it has a legally protected interest]', the square brackets designating text on which agreement could not be reached.[19] It was this version of the draft article, by then renumbered 21, that was adopted by the ILC on first reading in 1986.[20]

Together with what had been his draft article 22, Special Rapporteur Sucharitkul had originally proposed a draft article 23 dealing with the modalities and effect of State consent to attachment and execution.[21] This draft article 23 provided in paragraph 1 that a State could undertake in writing, in a treaty or contract concluded by it or by one of its State agencies, not to invoke immunity from measures of constraint in respect of any of

[11] See Report ILC, thirty-seventh session, 55, para. 230.
[12] Report ILC, thirty-seventh session, 55, para. 230.
[13] Report ILC, thirty-seventh session, 55, para. 230.
[14] See Report ILC, thirty-seventh session, 55, para. 231.
[15] See Report ILC, thirty-seventh session, 55, para. 230, 57, para. 247, text of revised provision, fn. 206.
[16] See summary record 1968th ILC meeting, *YILC 1986*, vol. I, 165, 171, para. 82.
[17] Summary record 1968th ILC meeting (n. 16), 171, para. 82.
[18] Summary record 1968th ILC meeting (n. 16), 171, para. 84.
[19] Summary record 1968th ILC meeting (n. 16), 171, para. 82.
[20] See Report ILC, thirty-eighth session, 17.
[21] See Seventh report Sucharitkul, 41–2, para. 103.

its property forming part of a commercial transaction or the like and situated in the territory of the forum State.[22] In formulating the provision this way, the Special Rapporteur recognized that State practice was yet to suggest a consistent set of rules in relation to the expression of consent to measures of attachment and execution against State property.[23] Such rules were often negotiated on a bilateral basis, with the result that the content and scope of the waiver of immunity could vary.[24]

Issues were raised during the Commission's consideration of draft article 23 as proposed.[25] As a consequence, this provision too was revised and referred to the Drafting Committee.[26] The Drafting Committee further amended the text of what was by then renumbered draft article 22(1) to provide that a State could not invoke immunity from measures of constraint against 'its property, or property in its possession or control [, or property in which it has a legally protected interest,]' if and to the extent that it had 'expressly consented to the taking of such measures in respect of that property' in an international agreement or written contract or by declaration before the court.[27] Draft article 22(2) confirmed that consent to jurisdiction did not imply consent to the taking of measures of constraint. The ILC adopted on first reading in 1986 the text of draft article 22 proposed by the Drafting Committee.[28]

2.2 The ILC's second reading

States' comments on the draft articles as adopted on first reading were considered by the new Special Rapporteur, Motoo Ogiso, whose Third Report proposed alternative formulations of draft articles 21 and 22.[29] The first iteration of the two provisions was identical to the versions adopted on first reading. The second combined the two draft articles into a single provision, and proposed some changes of wording. Discussion in the Commission revealed 'general support' for combining draft articles 21 and 22,[30] although there remained disagreement on issues of substance.

The UK, the Federal Republic of Germany, Belgium, and the five Nordic countries considered the phrase 'or property in which it has a legally protected interest' in the proposed consolidated draft article to be 'vague in itself and uncertain in its effect', the concern being that 'it might permit a broadening of the [then] present scope of State immunity from execution'.[31] A few other States, among them Thailand and Venezuela, proposed that the wording be retained.[32] For his part, Special Rapporteur Ogiso proposed instead a radically simplified reference to 'property of a foreign State'.[33] Supporters of this formulation considered it 'absurd to grant to third parties complete

[22] For details as to the 'commercial use' aspect of the provision as proposed by the Special Rapporteur and its evolution over the course of the drafting process, see the commentary to Art. 19 UNCSI.

[23] See Seventh report Sucharitkul, 40–1, para. 97.

[24] See Seventh report Sucharitkul, 40–1, para. 97.

[25] See Report ILC, thirty-seventh session, 54–7, paras 222–240.

[26] See Report ILC, thirty-seventh session, 57, para. 247, text of revised provision at fn. 206.

[27] See Report ILC, thirty-seventh session, 57, para. 247, fn. 206.

[28] See Report ILC, thirty-eighth session, 18.

[29] See Third report Ogiso, 18.

[30] Report ILC, forty-second session, 42, para. 222. The proposal also had the support of States. See ILC commentary, draft art. 18, para. 3.

[31] Preliminary report Ogiso, 117, para. 211.

[32] See Preliminary report Ogiso, 117, para. 211.

[33] Third report Ogiso, 18.

protection from measures of constraint simply because a foreign State had an interest in the property concerned'.[34] Opponents continued to oppose the deletion of the more expansive formula.[35] In the event, when the Commission referred the entirety of the draft articles to the Drafting Committee, together with the Special Rapporteur's proposals and those put forward by individual ILC members,[36] an even simpler variation on the formulation proposed by Special Rapporteur Ogiso won out.

On the basis of the Drafting Committee's report, the ILC finally adopted on second reading a single draft article 18 ('State immunity from measures of constraint'), as follows:

1. No measures of constraint, such as attachment, arrest and execution, against property of a State may be taken in connection with a proceeding before a court of another State unless and except to the extent that:
   (*a*) the State has expressly consented to the taking of such measures as indicated:
      (i) by international agreement;
      (ii) by an arbitration agreement or in a written contract; or
      (iii) by a declaration before the court or by a written communication after a dispute between the parties has arisen;
   (*b*) the State has allocated or earmarked property for the satisfaction of the claim which is the object of that proceeding; or
   (*c*) the property is specifically in use or intended for use by the State for other than government non-commercial purposes and is in the territory of the State of the forum and has a connection with the claim which is the object of the proceeding or with the agency or instrumentality against which the proceeding was directed.

2. Consent to the exercise of jurisdiction under article 7 shall not imply consent to the taking of measures of constraint under paragraph 1, for which separate consent shall be necessary.

The initiative then passed to the Sixth Committee.

2.3 From draft article 18 to Article 18 of the Convention

Article 18 proved controversial in the ensuing debates in the Sixth Committee's Working Group, where the idea of attaching different conditions to pre-judgment and post-judgment measures of constraint against State property—specifically, the condition that commercial property the subject of such measures have a 'connection with the claim which is the object of the proceeding or with the agency or instrumentality against which the proceeding was directed', as per draft article 18(1)(*c*)—was first mooted in 1992.[37] Despite the best efforts of the Chairman of the Working Group to reach consensus the following year, there remained lively disagreement, with some States maintaining that the immunity of State property from measures of constraint was absolute and others considering it possible to take such measures in certain circumstances.[38] It proved equally

[34] Report ILC, forty-second session, 42, para. 223.

[35] See Report ILC, forty-second session, 42, para. 223.

[36] See Report ILC, forty-second session, 32, para. 166.

[37] See 1992 report Sixth Committee Working Group, 4–5. A modified form of the proposed condition features in Art. 19(*c*) UNCSI. See section 3.2(C) of the commentary to Art. 19 UNCSI. The view had previously been expressed in the literature that no distinction should be drawn between pre- and post-judgment measures of constraint. See J. Crawford, 'Execution of Judgments and Foreign Sovereign Immunity' (1981) 75 *AJIL* 820, 820.

[38] See eg 1993 report Sixth Committee Working Group, 13, para. 67 (Carlos Calero-Rodrigues).

impossible to achieve agreement during the informal consultations in 1994 within the framework of the Sixth Committee.[39]

In 1999, the ILC Working Group established under the chairmanship of Gerhard Hafner to examine outstanding issues in relation to the draft articles suggested that the distinction between pre-judgment and post-judgment measures could help to resolve the difficulties over the immunity of State property from measures of constraint.[40] The Working Group suggested that pre-judgment measures against State property should be possible only where the State had expressly consented, either ad hoc or in advance, to their taking; where the State had designated the property to satisfy the claim the subject of the relevant proceedings; where such measures were provided for under a special regime, such as that relating to the arrest of State ships; or where the property was that of an agency having separate legal personality, provided it was the respondent to the claim.[41]

The Working Group of the Sixth Committee, also chaired by Gerhard Hafner, was reconvened later the same year similarly to consider outstanding issues in relation to the draft articles. As expected, there were mixed reactions to the proposal to distinguish between pre-judgment and post-judgment measures of constraint,[42] the idea behind which was that 'State immunity should be broader in respect of pre-judgment measures of constraint than in respect of measures taken with a view to executing a judgment'.[43] When the Sixth Committee's Working Group met again in 2000, Chairman Hafner offered a variety of alternative proposals for the articles on measures of constraint.[44] Following prolonged discussion during which a consensus eventually coalesced around the proposal to split the former draft article 18, the Chairman recommended a 'New article XY (preceding article 18)' dedicated exclusively to pre-judgment measures of constraint.[45]

In 2002, the Ad Hoc Committee on Jurisdictional Immunities of States and Their Property, again under the chairmanship of Gerhard Hafner, accepted the proposal to divide the former draft article 18 into an 'article XY', on pre-judgment measures of constraint,[46] the text of which corresponded verbatim to that proposed by Chairman Hafner in his last capacity, and a new draft article 18, dedicated to post-judgment measures.[47] The chapeau (apart from an additional illustrative reference in the latter to execution) and paragraphs (*a*) and (*b*) of each were the same, *mutatis mutandis*; and to this extent both simply reproduced, again *mutatis mutandis*, draft article 18(1) as finally adopted by the ILC in 1991.

Draft article XY was eventually numbered, and in 2004 was adopted unchanged by the General Assembly as Article 18 of the Convention.

[39] See Report Sixth Committee informal consultations, 4–5, paras 11–13.

[40] See 1999 report ILC Working Group, 171, para. 126.

[41] See 1999 report ILC Working Group, 171, para. 127.

[42] See 1999 report Chairman Sixth Committee Working Group, 6, paras 35–37 and 9, para. 66; 2000 report Chairman Sixth Committee Working Group, 15, paras 55–56 and 18–19, paras 65 and 67.

[43] 1999 report Chairman Sixth Committee Working Group, 6, para. 35.

[44] See 2000 report Chairman Sixth Committee Working Group, 13–22, paras 53–83.

[45] 2000 report Chairman Sixth Committee Working Group, 27–8.

[46] See 2002 report Ad Hoc Committee, annex, 10.

[47] See 2002 report Ad Hoc Committee, annex, 10–11.

3. Key Points

3.1 Article 18, chapeau: the general rule of immunity

The chapeau to Article 18 lays down a general rule, subject only to the exceptions subsequently enumerated in paragraphs (*a*) and (*b*), that '[n]o pre-judgment measures of constraint, such as attachment or arrest, against property of a State may be taken in connection with a proceeding before a court of another State'. This is consonant with Article 23 ECSI, which, absent consent in writing to the contrary, prohibits what it calls 'preventive measures' against the property of a Contracting State in the territory of another Contracting State. It also accords with State practice, which, either absolutely or *prima facie*, posits the immunity of State property from foreign measures of constraint taken prior to judgment.[48] That said, Article 27(1) ECSI[49] and numerous States do not forbid the taking of such measures against the property of State agencies, instrumentalities, or other entities established by the State and enjoying municipal legal personality separate from it (known in some jurisdictions as 'separate entities').[50] But the difference in this regard with Article 18 may not be as great in practice as it may appear, given that in many instances separate entities will not qualify as a 'State' to begin with under Article 2(1)(*b*)(iii) of the Convention.[51]

The rule enunciated in the chapeau to Article 18 is straightforward, even if several elements of it are worthy of further consideration. The ILC commentary is not always helpful in this regard, since the draft article 18 to which it refers, which covered in a single provision both pre-judgment and post-judgment measures of constraint, was not the same as the eventual Article 18 of the Convention. At the same time, much of the commentary to draft article 18 retains whatever value it had to begin with.

A. *'property of a State'*

Article 18's key term 'property of a State' is potentially ambiguous, and the ILC commentary sheds no real light on the point.[52] The preposition 'of' could, as a matter of ordinary meaning,[53] be taken to mean 'belonging to'—that is, to denote ownership alone. But it could equally be taken to comprehend possession or control. Recourse to the *travaux préparatoires* to resolve the ambiguity[54] indicates plainly that the second reading is the correct one. The words 'property of a State', having been proposed as

[48] See, as only the most easily identifiable of this practice, s. 1609 FSIA (US); s. 13(2) SIA (UK); ss. 11(1) and 12(1) chapeau SIA (Can); s. 14(2) SIO (Pak); s. 14(1) FStIA (SA); s. 30 FStIA (Aus); s. 15(2) SIA (Sing); s. 15(*a*) FSIL (Isr).

[49] Art. 27(1) ECSI provides: 'For the purposes of the present Convention, the expression "Contracting State" shall not include any legal entity of a Contracting State which is distinct therefrom and is capable of suing or being sued, even if that entity has been entrusted with public functions.'

[50] See eg s. 14(1) SIA (UK), declaring a separate entity not to be included within references to a 'State' (including for the purposes of the *prima facie* prohibition on post-judgment measures of constraint against State property). But see also s. 14(3) SIA (UK), prohibiting such measures against the property of a separate entity if it submits to the jurisdiction of the UK courts in a case where it would otherwise enjoy immunity by virtue of s. 14(2); and s. 14(4), second limb, preventing the taking of post-judgment measures of constraint against a State's central bank or other monetary authority in the event that it is a separate entity. See also s. 11(3) SIA (Can); s. 15(1), (3) and (4) SIO (Pak); ss. 1(2) and 15(2) and (3) FStIA (SA); ss. 3(3) and 35 FStIA (Aus); s. 16(1), (3) and (4) SIA (Sing); s. 18 FSIL (Isr).

[51] See the commentaries to Art. 2(1)(*a*) and (*b*) and Part IV UNCSI.

[52] See ILC commentary, draft art. 18, para. 5.

[53] See Art. 31(1) VCLT.

[54] See Art. 32(*a*) VCLT.

shorthand for the formulation 'its property or property in its possession or control' adopted on first reading,[55] are to be construed as referring to any property that a State owns or that it possesses or controls. On the other hand, any property in which a State has some lesser species of right or interest is excluded from the purview of Article 18, the bracketed words '[, or property in which it has a legally protected interest]' adopted on first reading having been deleted on second reading.[56]

It is important to note that nothing in Article 18 specifies that the State whose property benefits from the immunity from pre-judgment measures of constraint laid down in the chapeau need be named as a party to the foreign proceeding in connection with which the measure or measures are to be taken. Article 18 stipulates simply that '[n]o pre-judgment measures of constraint... against property of a State may be taken in connection with a proceeding before a court of another State'. Moreover, Article 6(2)(*b*) of the Convention indicates that a State enjoys immunity from jurisdiction in respect of itself and its property even when it is not named as a party to the proceeding, provided that 'the proceeding in effect seeks to affect the property... of that... State'; and it stands to reason that the same goes for the immunity of the State's property from pre-judgment measures of constraint in connection with such a proceeding.

B. 'pre-judgment measures of constraint... against property of a State'

The expression 'pre-judgment measures of constraint' used in Article 18 is a generic term intended to embrace all measures of a judicial and related executive character capable of being taken against or in relation to property in connection with, and prior to the handing down of judgment in, court proceedings, with a view to restraining the use or disposal of that property.[57] The illustrative examples in Article 18 itself, namely attachment and arrest, give a useful and obviously non-exhaustive[58] indication of the sorts of measures to which the provision relates. The ILC commentary elaborates further, explaining that the measures of constraint referred to in the pre-judgment context in draft article 18 covered not only attachment and arrest but also 'other forms of *saisie*, ... including... interlocutory and all other prejudgement conservatory measures, intended sometimes merely to freeze assets in the hands of the defendant'.[59] Elsewhere it speaks of 'interlocutory measures or pre-trial or prejudgment measures of attachment, or seizure of property *ad fundandam jurisdictionem*'.[60]

The pre-judgment measures of constraint against State property prohibited as a general rule by Article 18 include, as the provision's express mention of arrest and the ILC commentary's reference to seizure *ad fundandam jurisdictionem* make clear, the arrest of ships.[61] That is, subject to the exceptions in paragraphs (*a*) and (*b*) of the provision (which in practice means paragraph (*a*) in this context), Article 18 prohibits proceedings *in rem*—the defining characteristic of which is their institution by means of

[55] Recall sections 2.1 and 2.2.

[56] Recall sections 2.1 and 2.2. See also, to this extent usefully, ILC commentary, draft art. 18, para. 5.

[57] See ILC commentary, introduction to draft Part IV, para. 2. Recall also the commentary to Part IV. As argued in section 3.1(C), the term as used in Article 18 should be taken to extend to the same measures when taken in connection with arbitral proceedings—that is, to what might be called 'pre-award' measures of constraint.

[58] See ILC commentary, draft art. 18, para. 4.

[59] ILC commentary, draft art. 18, para. 4.

[60] ILC commentary, introduction to draft Part IV, para. 3.

[61] See, further, Seventh report Sucharitkul, 29, para. 34.

the arrest of the ship the subject of the proceedings—against State ships. In contrast with the laws of numerous States on the pre-judgment arrest or attachment of State ships, no exception is made in Article 18 for State ships in use for commercial purposes.[62]

As among those State parties to the Convention, however, that are also States parties to the 1926 Brussels Convention[63] (rights and obligations under which are safeguarded from the effect of Article 18 of the Convention by Article 26 of the same[64]), Article 18 will not bar all proceedings *in rem* against State ships. The institution of proceedings *in rem* against any State ship not 'employed exclusively at the time when the cause of action arises on Government and non-commercial service' will remain possible.[65]

The formulation 'pre-judgment measures of constraint . . . against property of a State' might be taken at first glance to exclude from the ambit of Article 18 those pre-judgment measures of constraint directed not, like attachment and arrest, against a State's property as such but against the State itself in relation to its use or disposal of that property—that is, measures of constraint *in personam* such as a *Mareva* injunction (or 'freezing order'), which compels the enjoined party to refrain from dissipating its assets in anticipation of judgment. But such an exclusion would be unreasonable, first, in that the applicability of Article 18 would arbitrarily depend on the formal characterization of a measure under municipal law and, secondly, in that Article 18 would run counter to the State practice it seeks to codify, which expressly or by necessary implication prohibits (subject to exceptions) the giving of relief against a State by way of injunction or order.[66] In this light, interpretive recourse to the *travaux préparatoires* is permitted,[67] and these reveal clearly that the words 'pre-judgment measures of constraint . . . against property of a State' are to be taken to encompass 'all . . . measures of judicial constraint under domestic law, including certain types of interlocutory injunctions'.[68]

[62] See eg s. 13(2)(4) SIA (UK) ('in use or intended for use for commercial purposes'), which constitutes an exception to s. 13(2)(*b*)'s prohibition on the arrest, detention, or sale of a State ship in an action *in rem*; s. 14(2)(*b*) SIO (Pak); s. 14(3) FStIA (SA); s. 32(2) FStIA (Aus); s. 12(1)(*b*) SIA (Can); s. 15(4) SIA (Sing); s. 16(1) FSIL (Isr). See also s. 1610(*a*)(2) FSIA (US), along with, on other grounds, s. 1610(*b*)(2) and (*e*) FSIA (US). See too *Szczesniak v Backer and Others*, 65 ILR 23 (Bel (Brussels CA) 1955); *Société Paul Liegard v Captain Serdjuk and Magne*, 65 ILR 38 (Fra (TdC) 1964); *The Philippine Admiral (Owners) v Wallem Shipping (Hong Kong) Limited and Another*, 64 ILR 90, 109 (HK (PC) 1975); *Romanian Maritime Navigation Company (Navrom) v Buenamar Compania Naviera*, 82 ILR 93 (Fra (CoC) 1988); *Russian Federation v Pied-Rich BV* (1994) 25 *NYIL* 512 (Nth (SC) 1993).

[63] International Convention for the Unification of Certain Rules relating to the Immunity of State-owned Vessels, Brussels, 10 April 1926, 176 LNTS 199 (1926 Brussels Convention). See also the Additional Protocol to the 1926 Brussels Convention, Brussels, 24 May 1934, 176 LNTS 214. The 1926 Brussels Convention currently has only 24 States parties.

[64] See the commentary to Art. 26 UNCSI. For its part, Art. 30 ECSI excludes the ECSI's application to 'proceedings in respect of claims relating to the operation of seagoing vessels owned or operated by a Contracting State or to the carriage of cargoes and of passengers by such vessels or to the carriage of cargoes owned by a Contracting State and carried on board merchant vessels'. See, in this regard, Expl. Rep. ECSI, para. 115: 'The purpose of this article is to exclude matters covered by the Brussels Convention . . . and [its] Protocol . . . These instruments are in force between a fairly large number of member States of the Council of Europe. The expressions used in Article 30 should be interpreted in accordance with the interpretation generally given to them in these two instruments.'

[65] See, by necessary implication, Art. 3 1926 Brussels Convention.

[66] See eg *S & S Machinery Co. v Masinexportimport*, 706 F.2d 411, 418 (US (2nd Cir.) 1983), re s. 1609 FSIA (US); s. 13(2)(*a*) SIA (UK); s. 11(1) SIA (Can); s. 14(2)(*a*) SIO (Pak); s. 14(1)(*a*) FStIA (SA); s. 30 FStIA (Aus); s. 15(2)(*a*) SIA (Sing).

[67] See Art. 32(*b*) VCLT.

[68] Report ILC, thirty-seventh session, 55, para. 230.

C. *'pre-judgment measures . . . in connection with a proceeding before a court of another State'*

Article 18's reference to 'pre-judgment' measures of constraint against State property in connection with 'a proceeding before a court of another State' would appear, on the face of it, to exclude the application of the provision to measures of constraint taken by a court in support of arbitral proceedings. At the same time, however, Article 18(*a*)(ii) provides that a State's consent to the taking of 'pre-judgment' measures of constraint against its property can be expressed in an arbitration agreement.

Special Rapporteur Sucharitkul referred several times in his Seventh Report to the execution of arbitral awards;[69] cited in support of his proposed draft articles section 13(2)(*b*) SIA (UK) and section 14(2)(*b*) SIO (Pak), *inter alia*, which both provide that 'the property of a State shall not be subject to any process for the enforcement of a judgment or arbitration award',[70] the formulation being taken to encompass pre-judgment measures of constraint; and originally proposed texts of draft articles 22 and 23 which made no mention of proceedings before a court of another State. The execution of arbitral awards was also mentioned in the ensuing discussion in the ILC.[71] The words 'in connection with a proceeding before a court of another State' first appeared in the Special Rapporteur's revised version of his proposed draft article 22,[72] and there is no indication that the insertion or its endorsement by the Drafting Committee[73] was motivated by an intention to exclude from the application of the proposed provisions measures of constraint in connection with pending or ongoing arbitration. It would seem, rather, to have been an instance of inattentive drafting, the potential implications of which were not divined at any point between 1985 and the adoption of the Convention in 2004. Paragraph 1(*a*)(ii) of draft article 18 referred, as Article 18(*a*)(ii) of the Convention refers, to a State's grant of express consent to measures of constraint 'by an arbitration agreement'; and the ILC commentary to draft article 18 refers repeatedly to questions of immunity from measures of constraint taken in connection with arbitration.[74] The oversight was eventually compounded by the decision of the Ad Hoc Committee to refer, on the splitting of former draft article 18, to 'pre-judgment' and 'post-judgment' measures of constraint, thereby failing once more to take into account arbitral 'awards'.

It is certainly reasonable to argue—in light of the interpretative context provided by Article 18(*a*)(ii)'s reference to arbitration agreements, of the *travaux préparatoires*, and of the requirement of interpretation in good faith[75]—that what seems to have been the unwitting omission of any reference to arbitral awards or arbitral proceedings in the chapeau to Article 18 should not be taken to indicate *a contrario* that measures of constraint taken by a court against the property of a foreign State in support of arbitral

[69] See Seventh report Sucharitkul, 34, paras 68 and 71, 35, para. 74, 36, para. 75, 39, para. 91, 41, para. 99, and 41, paras 99 and 100.

[70] See also, subsequently, s. 14(1)(*b*)(ii) FStIA (SA); s. 30 FStIA (Aus); s. 15(2)(*a*) SIA (Sing). The first two are cited in ILC commentary, draft art. 18, para. 7, fn. 171. S. 12(1) SIA (Can) refers simply to 'attachment and execution', without mention of either judgments or arbitral awards.

[71] See Report ILC, thirty-seventh session, 55–6, para. 235.

[72] See Report ILC, thirty-seventh session, 57, para. 247, fn. 206.

[73] See summary record 1968th ILC meeting (n. 16), 171, paras 82 and 83.

[74] See ILC commentary, draft art. 18, paras 4, 7, including fn. 171, and 9.

[75] See Art. 31(1) and (2) and Art. 32 VCLT.

proceedings do not fall within the ambit of Article 18.[76] In this light, the expression 'pre-judgment measures of constraint . . . taken in connection with a proceeding before a court of another State' should be construed as shorthand for 'pre-judgment or pre-award measures of constraint taken in connection with a proceeding before a court of another State or an arbitral tribunal'. It remains to be seen whether future States parties to the Convention enter interpretative declarations on this point. The absence of any such declarations to date may suggest that at least the current State parties see no real issue here.

Article 18's encompassing of pre-award measures of constraint taken by a court against the property of a foreign State in support of arbitral proceedings would, it might be added, accord with principle; with Article 23 ECSI, which provides unspecifically that '[n]o . . . preventive measures against the property of a Contracting State may be taken in the territory of another Contracting State'; and with certain national legislation, which either mentions arbitral awards alongside judgments or refers to neither.[77]

On a separate but related note, the ILC commentary to draft article 18 asserts that '[t]he word "State" in the expression "proceeding before a court of another State" refers to the State where the property is located, regardless of where the substantive proceeding takes place'.[78] The statement is manifestly unsound. The 'State' referred to in the words 'in connection with a proceeding before a court of another State' is clearly the State where the substantive proceeding takes place, wherever that may be. The ILC's comment appears to be a garbled version of the Chairman of the Drafting Committee's acknowledgment that the State in whose courts an application for measures of constraint against property of another State located in the territory is made may not be the State in whose courts the substantive proceeding takes place.[79]

3.2 The exceptions to the general rule of immunity

*A. Article 18(*a*): express consent*

The first of the two exceptions in Article 18 to the general rule of the immunity of a State's property from pre-judgment measures of constraint is, as provided for in Article 18(*a*), where and to the extent that the State whose property it is has expressly consented to such measures, whether by 'international agreement', by 'an arbitration agreement or in a written contract', or by 'a declaration before the court or by a written communication after a dispute between the parties has arisen'. The exception is based on State

[76] Were, however, pre-award measures of constraint taken by a court against the property of a foreign State in support of arbitral proceedings to be held not to be regulated by the Convention, their lawfulness as among States parties to the Convention would instead be governed by customary international law. As it happens, the present content of customary international law most likely accords with Art. 18, serving to prohibit all pre-judgment measures of constraint against the property of a State unless that State has consented expressly or, by allocating or earmarking the property for the satisfaction of the claim, implicitly to the taking of such measures. See section 4. Time will tell, however, whether custom moves towards a more restrictive immunity for State property from pre-judgment measures of constraint, coming perhaps to recognize the 'commercial use' exception found in some national legislation and, in relation to post-judgment measures of constraint, in Art. 19(*c*) of the Convention.

[77] Recall s. 13(2)(*b*) SIA (UK); s. 12(1) SIA (Can); s. 14(2)(*b*) SIO (Pak); s. 14(1)(*b*)(ii) FStIA (SA); s. 30 FStIA (Aus); s. 15(2)(*a*) SIA (Sing).

[78] ILC commentary, draft art. 18, para. 6.

[79] See summary record 1968th ILC meeting (n. 16), 171, para. 83.

practice.[80] It is also in principle in line with Article 23 ECSI, which abrogates the immunity of State property from foreign 'preventive measures' only 'where and to the extent that the State has expressly consented thereto in writing'. But Article 18(*a*) UNCSI differs from Article 23 ECSI insofar as the latter goes on to require that express consent be given 'in any particular case', which could be taken to mean that consent can be given for the purposes of Article 23 ECSI only by means of a written communication after a dispute between the parties has arisen, to borrow the words of Article 18(*a*)(iii) UNCSI. In contrast, for the purposes of Article 18(*a*)(i) and (ii) UNCSI, an express grant of consent to pre-judgment measures of constraint given in advance of the genesis of any dispute between the parties is to be considered effective.

The general considerations relevant to the express grant of consent to pre-judgment measures of constraint in accordance with Article 18 are the same, *mutatis mutandis*, as those relevant to the express grant of consent to the exercise of jurisdiction in accordance with Article 7.[81] On the specific question of whether a State's express consent to the taking of pre-judgment measures of constraint against its property can be revoked, it suffices for present purposes to say that there is reason to doubt the restrictiveness of the ILC's conclusions on this point,[82] for which there is no basis in the text of draft article 18(1)(*a*), let alone in Article 18(*a*) of the Convention.

A historically significant example of States' consent by international agreement to pre-judgment measures of constraint against their property is Article 1 1926 Brussels Convention.[83] As among States parties to that convention, Article 1 subjects all seagoing ships owned or operated by a State 'to the same rules of liability and the same obligations' as those applicable to privately owned ships, with the exception, as provided for in Article 3, of ships, among them warships and patrol boats, 'employed exclusively at the time when the cause of action arises on Government and non-commercial service'. Despite its misleading reference to 'liability', Article 1 is taken, in the light of the object and purpose of the 1926 Brussels Convention as manifest in its formal title ('International Convention for the Unification of Certain Rules relating to the Immunity of State-owned Vessels'), to refer to immunity from proceedings and, more importantly for present purposes, to immunity from 'seizure, arrest or detention by any legal process, [and] any proceedings *in rem*', in the words of Article 3.

A classic contractual provision in accordance with which a State patently consented to the taking of, *inter alia*, pre-judgment measures of constraint against its property was the dispute-settlement provision in the fiscal agency agreement that was at issue before the

[80] See eg 1610(*d*)(1) FSIA (US); s. 13(3) SIA (UK); s. 14(3) SIO (Pak); s. 12(1)(*a*) SIA (Can); s. 14(2) FStIA (SA); s. 31 FStIA (Aus); s. 15(3) SIA (Sing); s. 17(*a*) and (*b*) FSIL (Isr).

[81] For a full discussion, subject to the necessary modifications, see section 3 of the commentary to Art. 7 UNCSI.

[82] See ILC commentary, draft art. 18, para. 9: 'Once consent has been given under paragraph . . . (*a*), any withdrawal of that consent may only be made under the terms of the international agreement (subparagraph (i)) or of the arbitration agreement or the contract (subparagraph (ii)). However, once a declaration of consent or a written communication to that effect (subparagraph (iii)) has been made before a court, it cannot be withdrawn. In general, once a proceeding before a court has begun, consent cannot be withdrawn.' For a full discussion of the general question of the revocability of a State's waiver of State immunity, see section 3.6 of the commentary to Art. 7 UNCSI.

[83] See eg Seventh report Sucharitkul, 39, para. 90. Note, however, that, for the purposes of the UNCSI, the 1926 Brussels Convention represents an existing international agreement within the meaning of Art. 26 UNCSI (rights and obligations under which are unaffected by the Convention), rather than an international agreement referable to Art. 18(*a*)(i).

UK Supreme Court in *NML Capital Ltd v Republic of Argentina*[84] (a case concerning immunity from jurisdiction, rather than from pre-judgment measures of constraint). This provided in relevant part:

> To the extent that the Republic or any of its revenues, assets or properties shall be entitled, in any jurisdiction in which any specified court is located, in which any related proceeding may at any time be brought against it or any of its revenues, assets or properties, or in any jurisdiction in which any specified court or other court is located in which any suit, action or proceeding may at any time be brought solely for the purpose of enforcing or executing any related judgment, to any immunity . . . from attachment prior to judgment . . . or from any other legal or judicial . . . remedy, and to the extent that in any such jurisdiction there shall be attributed such an immunity, the Republic has hereby irrevocably agreed not to claim and has irrevocably waived such immunity to the fullest extent permitted by the laws of such jurisdiction . . . provided further that such agreement and waiver, in so far as it relates to any jurisdiction other than a jurisdiction in which a specified court is located, is given solely for the purpose of enabling the fiscal agent or a holder of securities of this series to enforce or execute a related judgment.[85]

Obviously the permissibility of pre-judgment measures of constraint in such circumstances will depend on the terms of the contract or arbitration agreement, as the case may be. So, taking the example of the fiscal agency agreement in *NML Capital*, pre-judgment measures of constraint against Argentine State property in 'any jurisdiction other than a jurisdiction in which a specified court is located' would not be permissible if the substantive proceedings were not 'for the purpose of enabling the fiscal agent or a holder of securities of [the relevant] series to enforce or execute a related judgment'.

*B. Article 18(*b*): the allocation or earmarking of property to satisfy the claim*

The second exception to the general rule of the immunity of a State's property from pre-judgment measures of constraint is where and to the extent that 'the State has allocated or earmarked property for the satisfaction of the claim which is the object of that proceeding', in the words of Article 18(*b*). Such a situation clearly represents implied consent by the State to the taking of pre-judgment measures of constraint against the property so allocated or earmarked.[86] The ILC commentary explains that the rule in what became Article 18(*b*) 'should have the effect of preventing extraneous or unprotected claimants from frustrating the intention of the State to satisfy specific claims or to make payment for an admitted liability'.[87] It adds that 'the question whether particular property has or has not been allocated for the satisfaction of a claim may in some situations be ambiguous and should be resolved by the court'.[88]

3.3 Immunity from pre-judgment measures of constraint and from jurisdiction

The ILC commentary to draft article 18, which, it will be recalled, combined in a single provision what are now the distinct questions of immunity from pre-judgment measures (Article 18) and immunity from post-judgment measures (Article 19) of constraint

[84] *NML Capital Ltd v Republic of Argentina*, 147 ILR 575 (UK (SC) 2011).
[85] *NML Capital Ltd v Republic of Argentina* (n. 84), 611–12.
[86] See eg Seventh report Sucharitkul, 38, para. 83(*c*).
[87] ILC commentary, draft art. 18, para. 10.
[88] ILC commentary, draft art. 18, para. 10.

against State property, remarks that 'the question of immunity from execution does not arise until after the question of jurisdictional immunity has been decided in the negative and until there is a judgment in favour of the plaintiff'.[89] If the term 'execution' as used here is limited, as it is clearly intended to be, to post-judgment measures of constraint, the ILC's statement is self-evident. In the context of pre-judgment measures, however, it is equally obvious that the question of the immunity of a State's property from measures of constraint may arise before the court has been called on to consider whether the State is immune from the substantive proceedings in connection with which the pre-judgment measures of constraint are sought.

Nowhere is the last point more obvious than in situations where it is the desired pre-judgment measure of constraint that founds the court's jurisdiction over those proceedings in the first place, for example in maritime actions *in rem* against State ships. But it is also apparent in relation to conservatory measures such as freezing orders, for which claimants may have strategic cause to apply long before the court has ruled on the question of the State's immunity from the substantive proceedings.

Indeed, it is precisely because pre-judgment measures of constraint tend to be applied for prior to the determination of the immunity or otherwise of the State from the substantive proceedings that they are more controversial than post-judgment measures[90] and are subject under the Convention to an even stricter regime of State immunity, not being available, in contrast to post-judgment measures, even as against property 'in use or intended for use by the State for other than government non-commercial purposes'.[91]

4. Evaluation

Article 18 of the Convention is probably consonant with customary international law. The practice of States reveals clearly that immunity from pre-judgment or pre-award measures of constraint against foreign State property in connection with judicial or arbitral proceedings is to be treated separately from and more stringently than the foreign State's immunity from jurisdiction. The more difficult question, however, is whether the foreign State's customary immunity from pre-judgment or pre-award measures of constraint against its property is subject only to its express or, via the allocation or earmarking of that property for the satisfaction of the claim, implicit consent to the taking of such measures or whether, as is the case under Article 19(*c*) of the Convention and customary international law[92] in relation to post-judgment measures, custom recognizes in addition a 'commercial use' exception in the pre-judgment context. In *Jurisdictional Immunities of the State*, the ICJ stated:

> [T]here is at least one condition that has to be satisfied before any measure of constraint may be taken against property belonging to a foreign State: that the property must be in use for an activity not pursuing government non-commercial purposes, or that the State which owns the property has

[89] ILC commentary, draft art. 18, para. 2.

[90] See eg Seventh report Sucharitkul, 29, paras 35–37.

[91] Art. 19(*c*) UNCSI.

[92] See *Jurisdictional Immunities of the State (Germany v Italy: Greece intervening), Judgment*, 3 February 2012, International Court of Justice, para. 118.

expressly consented to the taking of a measure of constraint, or that that State has allocated the property in question for the satisfaction of a judicial claim.[93]

The Court's reference to 'any measure of constraint' might be taken to suggest that its statement applies as much to pre-judgment as to post-judgment measures of constraint, with the result that a 'commercial use' exception to immunity from pre-judgment measures is to be considered a part of customary international law. Given, however, the immediate context of the Court's dictum, namely a question relating to post-judgment measures and Article 19, it would be rash to read too much into this wording.

As for Article 18 itself, while the discontinuity between the chapeau's reference to 'pre-judgments measures of constraint... taken in connection with proceedings before a court of another State' and paragraph (*a*)(ii)'s reference to arbitration agreements is a major drafting oversight, the interpretation of the chapeau in good faith and in context, as confirmed by recourse to the *travaux préparatoires*, ought to result in its embrace of measures of constraint taken by a court in support of arbitral proceedings. Apart from this issue, which deserves to prove no more than an irritation, the interpretation and application of Article 18 should pose few problems of international law.

[93] *Jurisdictional Immunities of the State* (n. 92), para. 118.

Article 19

Chester Brown and Roger O'Keefe*

Article 19

State immunity from post-judgment measures of constraint

No post-judgment measures of constraint, such as attachment, arrest or execution, against property of a State may be taken in connection with a proceeding before a court of another State unless and except to the extent that:

(*a*) the State has expressly consented to the taking of such measures as indicated:
  (i) by international agreement;
  (ii) by an arbitration agreement or in a written contract; or
  (iii) by a declaration before the court or by a written communication after a dispute between the parties has arisen; or

(*b*) the State has allocated or earmarked property for the satisfaction of the claim which is the object of that proceeding; or

(*c*) it has been established that the property is specifically in use or intended for use by the State for other than government non-commercial purposes and is in the territory of the State of the forum, provided that post-judgment measures of constraint may only be taken against property that has a connection with the entity against which the proceeding was directed.

Understanding with respect to article 19

The expression 'entity' in subparagraph (*c*) means the State as an independent legal personality, a constituent unit of a federal State, a subdivision of a State, an agency or instrumentality of a State or other entity, which enjoys independent legal personality. The words 'property that has a connection with the entity' in subparagraph (*c*) are to be understood as broader than ownership or possession.

Article 19 does not prejudge the question of 'piercing the corporate veil', questions relating to a situation where a State entity has deliberately misrepresented its financial position or subsequently reduced its assets to avoid satisfying a claim, or other related issues.

1. Introduction

Article 19 is the second of the two main provisions in Part IV of the Convention dealing with immunity from measures of constraint against State property taken in connection with proceedings before a foreign court. In contrast to Article 18, which deals with pre-judgment measures of constraint, Article 19 deals with post-judgment measures, such as arrest or attachment in aid of execution and execution itself. In further contrast to Article 18, under which the only circumstances in which pre-judgment measures of constraint against State property are not prohibited are where the State has expressly consented to their taking or has allocated or earmarked the property for the satisfaction of the claim

* The authors would like to thank Ashique Rahman, LLM (Syd), for his valuable assistance in the preparation of this chapter.

the object of the proceedings, Article 19, which acknowledges the same two exceptions in relation to the immunity of State property from post-judgment measures, provides for a third, key exception. This is where property located in the territory of the forum State is in use or intended for use 'for other than government non-commercial purposes' and has a connection with the specific emanation of the State against which the proceedings on the merits were directed.

Article 19 is the subject of a threefold understanding annexed to the Convention. The first limb explains the meaning of the term 'entity' in Article 19(*c*); the second extends the meaning of 'connection' as used in the same paragraph beyond ownership and possession; and the third, which (numbering aside) reproduces verbatim the second limb of the understanding with respect to the 'commercial transaction' exception to immunity from jurisdiction embodied in Article 10 of the Convention, provides that Article 19 'does not prejudge the question of "piercing the corporate veil", questions relating to a situation where a State entity has deliberately misrepresented its financial position or subsequently reduced its assets to avoid satisfying a claim, or other related issues'.

Article 19 is linked closely to Article 21, which specifies certain categories of State property that, for the purposes of the exception to immunity from post-judgment measures of constraint laid down in Article 19(*c*), are deemed not to be in use or intended for use for other than government non-commercial purposes.

2. Drafting History

The drafting history of Article 19 of the Convention tracks that of Article 18 to a very large extent, given that what the ILC finally adopted on second reading in 1991 as draft article 18 combined in a single provision what would later be treated textually as the distinct questions of immunity from pre-judgment measures of constraint against State property, the subject of Article 18, and of immunity from post-judgment measures, the subject of Article 19. Indeed, it was only in 2000 that the former draft article 18 was split into two provisions. Moreover, what emerged as the chapeau to Article 19 is simply a '*mutatis mutandis*' version of the chapeau to Article 18, while paragraphs (*a*) and (*b*) of each article are identical. The only aspect of Article 19 whose drafting history warrants separate examination is paragraph (*c*),[1] the forerunners to which were the subject of tortuous debate between 1985, when Special Rapporteur Sucharitkul initially proposed texts for draft articles on immunity from measures of constraint, and the adoption of the Convention in 2004.

2.1 The ILC's draft articles

What would become Article 19(*c*) of the Convention has its origins in the draft articles 22(1)(*b*) and 23 first put forward by Special Rapporteur Sucharitkul in his Seventh Report. The Special Rapporteur's draft article 22(1)(*b*) specified an exception to the immunity of State property[2] from 'attachment, arrest and execution by order of a court

[1] For the drafting history of the remainder of Art. 19, see the commentary to Art. 18 UNCSI.

[2] Note that, unless found in direct quotation, the term 'State property' is used in section 2 of the present commentary as shorthand for whatever description of the relevant property was current at the time, be it 'State

of another State' as, *inter alia*, 'a process to secure satisfaction of a final judgment of such a court' where that property was 'in use or intended for use by the State in commercial and nongovernmental service'.[3] Draft article 23 provided in paragraph 1 that a State could undertake in writing, in a treaty or contract concluded by it or by one of its State agencies, not to invoke immunity from measures of constraint in respect of any of its property which, as per paragraph (*a*), 'form[ed] part of a commercial transaction or [was] used in connection with commercial activities, or [was] otherwise in use for non-public purposes unconnected with the exercise of governmental authority of the State' and, as per paragraph (*b*), was 'identified as being situated in the territory of the State of the forum'.[4]

No consensus was apparent when the Special Rapporteur's proposed text of draft article 22(1)(*b*) was discussed in the Commission. Some members expressed concern that the provision as proposed failed adequately to take into account developing States, where 'trade with foreign entities' fell by law to the government, the purpose being not to profit but to satisfy 'the basic needs of their population'.[5] It was argued that the 'commercial activities of Governments in such circumstances should . . . not be treated on the same footing as the commercial activities of private entities'.[6] Other members, however, considered the fact that draft article 22(1)(*b*)'s exception to immunity from post-judgment measures of constraint applied only where State property was used or intended for use in both 'commercial' and 'nongovernmental' service to be sufficient to safeguard the interests of developing States.[7] Still other members thought that draft article 22(1)(*b*) went too far in the other direction by not abrogating the immunity from post-judgment measures of constraint of State property in use or intended for use for an activity which, although characterizable as 'governmental service', was 'solely "commercial" in nature'.[8] As for draft article 23(1), there was general agreement that it should be limited to the modalities of expressing consent, with the result that the provisos specified in subparagraphs (*a*) and (*b*) should be deleted.[9] The Special Rapporteur revised his proposals in this light, before both draft articles as revised[10] were referred to the Drafting Committee.

The following year, disagreement within both the Drafting Committee[11] and the Commission[12] as to the desirability of retaining both 'commercial' and 'nongovernmental'

property, or property in the possession or control of a State, or property in which a State has an interest', as proposed by the Special Rapporteur; 'its'—meaning the State's—'property or property in its possession or control [, or property in which it has a legally protected interest]', as adopted on first reading by the ILC; or 'property of a State', as adopted on second reading and in the eventual Article 19 of the Convention. In contrast, the term 'State property' is used in section 3 as shorthand for 'property of a State', the expression found in Art. 19 of the Convention.

3 Seventh report Sucharitkul, 38, para. 84.

4 Seventh report Sucharitkul , 41–2, para. 103.

5 Report ILC, thirty-seventh session, 55, para. 225.

6 Report ILC, thirty-seventh session, 55, para. 225.

7 Report ILC, thirty-seventh session, 56, para. 237.

8 Report ILC, thirty-seventh session, 56, para. 237.

9 See Report ILC, thirty-seventh session, 56, para. 240.

10 See Report ILC, thirty-seventh session, 57, para. 247, fn. 206 for the Special Rapporteur's revised texts. The revisions to draft art. 22 did not alter the wording of what had formerly been paragraph 1(*b*).

11 See summary record 1968th ILC meeting, *YILC 1986*, vol. I, 165, 171, para. 86.

12 See summary record 1968th ILC meeting (n. 11), 171–2, paras 88 (Nikolai Ushakov) and 94 (Abdul Koroma).

in draft article 22(1)(*b*) led to the provisional adoption,[13] and later adoption,[14] on first reading of a text of a renumbered draft article 21—a provision representing a merger of the former draft articles 22(1)(*b*) and 23(1)(*a*)—which spoke in paragraph (*a*) of property 'specifically in use or intended for use by the State for commercial [non-governmental] purposes'.[15] No territorial requirement along the lines of the former draft article 23(1)(*b*), which in the Special Rapporteur's revised text of draft article 22 had become the adjectival clause 'being located in the State of the forum', was included.

As adopted on first reading, draft article 21(*a*), in contrast to the original and revised texts proposed by the Special Rapporteur, also required that the property have 'a connection with the object of the claim, or with the agency or instrumentality against which the proceeding was directed'. The requirement was inserted, without recorded explanation, by the Drafting Committee,[16] and was not to the liking of all, with one member of the Commission arguing that it 'excessively limited the property subject to measures of constraint, particularly with respect to tort cases'.[17]

In their comments on the draft articles as adopted on first reading, the UK and Australia both considered that the use of the term 'non-governmental' in addition to 'commercial' in draft article 21(*a*) might 'impose [an] additional restriction on the scope of the provision[] and thereby unwarrantably broaden the circumstances in which States [could] claim immunity in respect of their commercial activities'.[18] At the other end of the spectrum, the German Democratic Republic favoured the deletion from the provision of any restriction on the immunity of State property from measures of constraint, while the USSR observed more cautiously that draft article 21(*a*) 'significantly limit[ed] the principle of the inadmissibility of measures of constraint against a State'.[19] As for the requirement that the property have a connection with the object of the claim or with the agency or instrumentality against which the proceeding was directed, the UK, Australia, Canada, the five Nordic countries, Qatar, and Switzerland all thought that 'its inclusion might impose an unnecessary limitation upon the cases in which property may be legitimately subject to measures of constraint'.[20]

For his part, Special Rapporteur Ogiso proposed, in his Preliminary Report, the deletion of 'non-governmental', which was 'ambiguous and could become an unnecessary source of controversy',[21] and of the 'connection' requirement, since 'further limitation' beyond that imposed by the commercial use criterion 'did not seem necessary'.[22] In his Second Report, however, he floated the possibility that the 'connection' criterion be retained but that the draft article as a whole be introduced with the words 'Unless otherwise agreed between the States concerned';[23] and ultimately, in the second of the alternative proposals offered in his Third Report, he included the 'connection' criterion in

[13] See summary record 1968th ILC meeting (n. 11), 172, para. 96.
[14] See Report ILC, thirty-eighth session, 8, para. 17.
[15] See Report ILC, thirty-eighth session, 11.
[16] See summary record 1968th ILC meeting (n. 11), 171, para. 82.
[17] See summary record 1968th ILC meeting (n. 11), 172, para. 95 (Christian Tomuschat).
[18] Preliminary report Ogiso, 117, para. 218, cross-referable to 115, para. 180.
[19] Preliminary report Ogiso, 117, para. 216.
[20] Preliminary report Ogiso, 117, para. 213.
[21] Preliminary report Ogiso, 117, para. 218, cross-referable to 115, para. 191.
[22] Preliminary report Ogiso, 117, para. 219.
[23] See Second report Ogiso, 73, para. 46.

square brackets without alluding to the possibility of agreement otherwise.[24] This second version also re-introduced the proviso, originally included in paragraph 1(*b*) of Special Rapporteur Sucharitkul's initial draft article 23, that the property be in the territory of the forum State.[25]

Opinion within the Commission on the Special Rapporteur's proposals was divided.[26] By this point, debate over the 'connection' requirement had become intertwined with the controversy, in the context of the drafting of the 'commercial transaction' exception to immunity from jurisdiction, over so-called 'segregated' property, namely property, separate as a matter of domestic law from the property of the State, held by State agencies and enterprises with legal personality distinct from that of the State.[27] This, in turn, was entangled with the unresolved issue of the definition of a 'State'.[28] Against this backdrop, '[m]ost speakers argued that the ["connection" requirement] was of crucial importance and should be retained', in particular so as to 'avoid confusion between State property, on the one hand, and property of other agencies and of public enterprises, on the other'.[29] Some members, in contrast, supported the deletion of the criterion, 'for it was often hard, if not impossible, in practice to establish a link between the claim and the property against which execution was sought, especially where financial claims were concerned'.[30]

In the event, the Commission retained the requirement of a connection between the property and either the object of the claim or the agency or instrumentality against which the proceeding was directed, only slightly adjusting its formulation. In contrast, it changed the expression 'commercial [non-governmental] purposes' adopted on first reading to 'other than government non-commercial purposes', the wording used in draft article 16 in relation to immunity from proceedings concerning State-owned or -operated ships.[31] Framing the provision in the negative, the Commission finally adopted on second reading draft article 18 ('State immunity from measures of constraint'), as follows:

1. No measures of constraint, such as attachment, arrest and execution, against property of a State may be taken in connection with a proceeding before a court of another State unless and except to the extent that:
   (*a*) the State has expressly consented to the taking of such measures as indicated:
      (i) by international agreement;
      (ii) by an arbitration agreement or in a written contract; or
      (iii) by a declaration before the court or by a written communication after a dispute between the parties has arisen;
   (*b*) the State has allocated or earmarked property for the satisfaction of the claim which is the object of that proceeding; or
   (*c*) the property is specifically in use or intended for use by the State for other than government non-commercial purposes and is in the territory of the State of the forum and has a

24 See Third report Ogiso, 18. 25 See Third report Ogiso, 18.

26 See Report ILC, forty-first session, 177, paras 576 and 577; Report ILC, forty-second session, 42, paras 224–226.

27 See section 3 of the commentary to Art. 10 UNCSI.

28 See section 2 of the commentary to Art. 2(1)(*a*) and (*b*).

29 Report ILC, forty-second session, 42, para. 224.

30 Report ILC, forty-second session, 42, para. 224.

31 See ILC commentary, draft art. 18, para. 11.

connection with the claim which is the object of the proceeding or with the agency or instrumentality against which the proceeding was directed.

2. Consent to the exercise of jurisdiction under article 7 shall not imply consent to the taking of measures of constraint under paragraph 1, for which separate consent shall be necessary.

The matter was now in the hands of the Sixth Committee.

2.2 From draft article 18 to Article 19 of the Convention

Draft article 18, considered one of the five outstanding issues in relation to the draft articles, was re-examined the following year by the Sixth Committee's Working Group, where the Chairman suggested that the requirement of a connection between the property and either the claim the object of the proceeding or the agency or instrumentality against which the proceeding was directed might be imposed on pre-judgment measures of constraint alone.[32] But agreement could not be reached on the matter over the course of either 1992 or 1993,[33] with some concern being expressed, as it was in the context of draft article 10 (the 'commercial transaction' exception to immunity from jurisdiction), as regards 'the absence of a provision with regard to the under-capitalized State agency or instrumentality'.[34]

When the ILC's Working Group examined the problem in 1999 under the chairmanship of Gerhard Hafner, it suggested three possible alternatives in relation to post-judgment measures of constraint where there was no express consent to their taking and where the property had not been allocated or earmarked, the third of these being to delete draft article 18(1)(*c*) in its entirety 'because of the delicate and complex aspects of the issues involved'.[35]

When the Sixth Committee's Working Group, also chaired by Gerhard Hafner, reconvened later that year, support was expressed variously for draft article 18 as finally adopted by the ILC in 1991 and for all three alternatives presented by the ILC Working Group, including the third.[36] 'Other delegations', however, 'found this last alternative unacceptable', since, unless rules on immunity from execution formed 'an integral part of the draft articles', 'the recognition of exceptions to State immunity [from jurisdiction] in the draft articles, and the judgments against a State resulting therefrom, would constitute a futile exercise'.[37] The following year, when the Working Group met again, Chairman Hafner, after prolonged and inconclusive debate,[38] offered as his final recommendation two alternative formulations of draft article 18,[39] both dealing solely with post-judgment measures of constraint, which he proposed to hive off from a separate draft article on pre-judgment measures provisionally labelled 'New article XY (preceding article 18)'.[40] The first version of the new draft article 18 reproduced, *mutatis mutandis*, the text as finally adopted by the ILC on second reading, although paragraph (*c*)'s contentious final words

[32] See 1992 report Sixth Committee Working Group, 4–5, paras 21–22.
[33] See 1993 report Sixth Committee Working Group, 14, paras 70–76.
[34] 1999 report ILC Working Group, 169, para. 115, recalling the debate in the Sixth Committee Working Group.
[35] 1999 report ILC Working Group, 171, para. 129.
[36] See 1999 report Chairman Sixth Committee Working Group, 6–7, paras 38–45.
[37] 1999 report Chairman Sixth Committee Working Group, 7, para. 44.
[38] See 2000 report Chairman Sixth Committee Working Group, 13–22, paras 53–83.
[39] See 2000 report Chairman Sixth Committee Working Group, 28–9.
[40] See 2000 report Chairman Sixth Committee Working Group, 27–8.

'and has a connection with the claim that is the object of the proceeding or with the agency or instrumentality against which the proceeding was directed' were placed in square brackets to reflect continuing disagreement over them. In addition, however, it was proposed that the words 'It has been established that' be inserted at the beginning of draft article 18(*c*), in response to and in the exact words of a suggestion, endorsed by several delegations, 'to introduce an objective element into the text that would do away with the need to establish the intention of the State to use the property'.[41]

In 2002, the Ad Hoc Committee on Jurisdictional Immunities of States and Their Property, once again under the chairmanship of Gerhard Hafner, accepted the latter's proposal, in his last capacity, to split the former draft article 18 into a draft 'article XY', exclusively on pre-judgment measures of constraint, and a new draft article 18 dedicated to post-judgment measures.[42] The second provision reproduced verbatim the text proposed by Chairman Hafner in 2000, complete with square brackets around the 'connection' requirement, on which agreement remained elusive.

To general surprise, the issue of draft article 18(*c*) was resolved the following year, at the same time and by the same means as the resolution of the parallel controversy over State enterprises in the context draft article 10. It was agreed within the Ad Hoc Committee to drop from what had been renumbered draft article 19(*c*) the requirement of a connection between the property against which post-judgment measures of constraint were to be taken and the claim the object of the proceeding. Draft article 19(*c*) would retain stipulations only as to the actual or intended use of the property for other than government non-commercial purposes and the presence of the property in the territory of the forum State. But, to allay the fears of developing States, it would also contain the further proviso, salvaged from the 'connection' requirement in the ILC's draft article 18(1)(*c*), 'that post-judgment measures of constraint may only be taken against property that has a connection with the entity against which the proceeding was directed'.[43] By way of *quid pro quo*—along the lines of the deal that broke the deadlock in relation to draft article 10—for the inclusion of the 'connection' proviso in Article 19(*c*), a threefold 'understanding' with respect to draft article 19 was proposed,[44] to elaborate on issues relevant to State enterprises and, indeed, to other emanations of the State. The third limb of the understanding reproduced what was said in relation to draft article 10, namely that the provision '[did] not prejudge the question of "piercing the corporate veil", questions relating to a situation where a State entity ha[d] deliberately misrepresented its financial position or subsequently reduced its assets to avoid satisfying a claim, or other related issues'. The second limb explained that the expression 'property that has a connection with the entity' in draft article 19(*c*) was 'to be understood as broader than ownership or possession'.

In 2004, the various understandings were annexed to the draft convention,[45] and they were adopted as an integral part of it by the General Assembly later that year, along with the finalized Article 19.

[41] See 2000 report Chairman Sixth Committee Working Group, 22, para. 78.
[42] See 2002 report Ad Hoc Committee, annex, 10–11.
[43] 2003 report Ad Hoc Committee, annex I, 11.
[44] See 2003 report Ad Hoc Committee, annex II, 14.
[45] See 2004 report Ad Hoc Committee, annex I, 17–18.

3. Key Points

3.1 Article 19, chapeau: the general rule of immunity

The chapeau to Article 19 lays down a general rule, subject only to the exceptions subsequently enumerated in paragraphs (*a*) to (*c*), that '[n]o post-judgment measures of constraint, such as attachment, arrest or execution, against property of a State may be taken in connection with a proceeding before a court of another State'. This position is consonant with Article 23 ECSI, which, absent consent in writing to the contrary, prohibits 'measures of execution' against the property of a Contracting State in the territory of another Contracting State; accords with State practice, which, either absolutely or *prima facie*, posits the immunity of State property from foreign measures of constraint taken subsequent to judgment;[46] and was endorsed by the International Court of Justice in *Jurisdictional Immunities of the State*.[47] That said, Article 27(1) ECSI[48] and numerous States do not forbid the taking of such measures against the property of State agencies, instrumentalities, or other entities established by the State and enjoying municipal legal personality separate from it (known in some jurisdictions as 'separate entities'),[49] or at the very least they pose fewer legal obstacles to the taking of these measures against such entities.[50] But the difference in this regard with Article 19 may not be as great in practice as it may appear, given that in many instances separate entities will not qualify as a 'State' to begin with under Article 2(1)(*b*)(iii) of the Convention.[51]

The rule enunciated in the chapeau to Article 19 is straightforward, even if several elements of it are worthy of further consideration. The ILC commentary is not always helpful in this regard, since the draft article 18 to which it refers, which covered in a single provision both pre-judgment and post-judgment measures of constraint, was not the same as the eventual Article 19 of the Convention. At the same time, much of the commentary to draft article 18 retains whatever value it had to begin with.

A. 'property of a State'

Article 19's key term 'property of a State' is potentially ambiguous, and the ILC commentary sheds no real light on the point.[52] The preposition 'of' could, as a matter

[46] See eg s. 1609 FSIA (US); s. 13(2) SIA (UK); s. 12(1) chapeau SIA (Can); s. 14(2) SIO (Pak); s. 14(1) FStIA (SA); s. 30 FStIA (Aus); s. 15(2) SIA (Sing); s. 15(*a*) FSIL (Isr). The *prima facie* prohibition on post-judgment measures of constraint against State property is similarly found in the case-law of very many States.

[47] See *Jurisdictional Immunities of the State (Germany v Italy: Greece intervening), Judgment*, 3 February 2012, International Court of Justice, paras 113–120.

[48] Art. 27(1) ECSI provides: 'For the purposes of the present Convention, the expression "Contracting State" shall not include any legal entity of a Contracting State which is distinct therefrom and is capable of suing or being sued, even if that entity has been entrusted with public functions.'

[49] See eg s. 14(1) SIA (UK), declaring a separate entity not to be included within references to a 'State' (including for the purposes of the *prima facie* prohibition on post-judgment measures of constraint against State property). But see also s. 14(3) SIA (UK), prohibiting such measures against the property of a separate entity if it submits to the jurisdiction of the UK courts in a case where it would otherwise enjoy immunity by virtue of s. 14(2); and s. 14(4), second limb, preventing the taking of post-judgment measures of constraint against a State's central bank or other monetary authority in the event that it is a separate entity. See also s. 15(1), (3), and (4) SIO (Pak); ss. 1(2) and 15(2) and (3) FStIA (SA); ss. 3(3) and 35 FStIA (Aus); s. 16(1), (3), and (4) SIA (Sing); s. 18 FSIL (Isr). See too, without the provision in respect of waiver, s. 12(2) and (4) SIA (Can).

[50] See eg s. 1610(*b*) FSIA (US).

[51] See the commentaries to Art. 2(1)(*a*) and (*b*) and Part IV UNCSI.

[52] See ILC commentary, draft art. 18, para. 5.

of ordinary meaning,[53] be taken to mean 'belonging to'—that is, to denote ownership alone. But it could equally be taken to comprehend possession or control. Recourse to the *travaux préparatoires* to resolve the ambiguity[54] indicates plainly that the second reading is the correct one. The words 'property of a State', having been proposed as shorthand for the formulation 'its property or property in its possession or control' adopted on first reading, are to be construed as referring to any property that a State owns or that it possesses or controls.[55] On the other hand, any property in which a State has some lesser species of right or interest is excluded from the purview of Article 19, the bracketed words '[, or property in which it has a legally protected interest]' adopted on first reading having been deleted on second reading.[56]

It is important to note that nothing in Article 19 specifies that the State whose property benefits from the immunity from post-judgment measures of constraint laid down in the chapeau need be named as a party to the foreign proceeding in connection with which the measure or measures are to be taken. Article 19 stipulates simply that '[n]o post-judgment measures of constraint... against property of a State may be taken in connection with a proceeding before a court of another State'. Moreover, Article 6(2)(*b*) of the Convention indicates that a State enjoys immunity from jurisdiction in respect of itself and its property even when it is not named as a party to the proceeding, provided that 'the proceeding in effect seeks to affect the property... of that... State'; and it stands to reason the same goes for the immunity of the State's property from post-judgment measures of constraint in connection with such a proceeding.

B. *'post-judgment measures of constraint... against property of a State'*

The expression 'post-judgment measures of constraint' used in Article 19 is a generic term intended to embrace all measures of a judicial and related executive character capable of being taken against or in relation to property in connection with, and subsequent to the handing down of judgment in, court proceedings, with a view to executing that judgment.[57] The illustrative examples in Article 19 itself, namely attachment, arrest, and execution, give a useful and obviously non-exhaustive[58] indication of the sorts of measures to which the provision relates. The ILC commentary elaborates further, explaining that the measures of constraint referred to in the post-judgment context in draft article 18 covered not only attachment and arrest but also 'other forms of *saisie*, *saisie-arrêt* and *saisie-exécution* including enforcement of arbitral award[s] [and] sequestration'.[59]

The formulation 'post-judgment measures of constraint, such as attachment, arrest or execution, against property of a State' might be taken at first glance to exclude from the ambit of Article 19 those post-judgment measures of constraint directed not, like attachment, arrest, and execution, against a State's property as such but against the State itself in relation to its use or disposal of that property—that is, measures of

[53] See Art. 31(1) VCLT.
[54] See Art. 32(*a*) VCLT.
[55] Recall sections 2.1 and 2.2.
[56] Recall sections 2.1 and 2.2. See also, to this extent usefully, ILC commentary, draft art. 18, para. 5.
[57] See ILC commentary, introduction to draft Part IV, para. 2. Recall also the commentary to Part IV. As argued in section 3.1(C), the term as used in Art. 19 should be taken to extend to the same measures when taken in execution of an arbitral award—that is, to what might be called 'post-award' measures of constraint.
[58] See ILC commentary, draft art. 18, para. 4.
[59] ILC commentary, draft art. 18, para. 4.

constraint *in personam* such as an injunction or order for specific performance or for the recovery of land or other property. But such an exclusion would be unreasonable, first, in that the applicability of Article 19 would arbitrarily depend on the formal characterization of a measure under municipal law and, secondly, in that Article 19 would run counter to the State practice it seeks to codify, which expressly or by necessary implication prohibits (subject to exceptions) the giving of relief against a State by way of injunction or order.[60] In this light, interpretive recourse to the *travaux préparatoires* is permitted,[61] and these reveal clearly that the words 'post-judgment measures of constraint... against property of a State' are to be taken to encompass 'all... measures of judicial constraint under domestic law'.[62]

C. *'post-judgment measures... in connection with a proceeding before a court of another State'*

Article 19's reference to 'post-judgment' measures of constraint against State property in connection with 'a proceeding before a court of another State' would appear, on the face of it, to exclude the application of the provision to measures of constraint taken with a view to the execution of an award rendered in arbitral proceedings. At the same time, however, Article 19(*a*)(ii) provides that a State's consent to the taking of 'post-judgment' measures of constraint against its property can be expressed in an arbitration agreement.

Special Rapporteur Sucharitkul referred several times in his Seventh Report to the execution of arbitral awards;[63] cited in support of his proposed draft articles section 13(2)(*b*) SIA (UK) and section 14(2)(*b*) SIO (Pak), *inter alia*, which both provide that 'the property of a State shall not be subject to any process for the enforcement of a judgment or arbitration award';[64] and originally proposed texts of draft articles 22 and 23 which made no mention of proceedings before a court of another State. The execution of arbitral awards was also mentioned in the ensuing discussion in the ILC.[65] The words 'in connection with a proceeding before a court of another State' first appeared in the Special Rapporteur's revised version of his proposed draft article 22,[66] and there is no indication that the insertion or its endorsement the Drafting Committee[67] was motivated by an intention to exclude from the application of the proposed provisions measures of constraint in connection with pending or ongoing arbitration. It would seem, rather, to have been an instance of inattentive drafting, the potential implications of which were not divined at any point between 1985 and the adoption of the Convention in 2004. Paragraph 1(*a*)(ii) of draft article 18 referred, as Article 19(*a*)(ii) of the Convention refers, to a State's grant of express consent to measures of constraint 'by an arbitration

[60] See eg *S & S Machinery Co. v Masinexportimport*, 706 F2d 411, 418 (US (2nd Cir.) 1983), re s. 1609 FSIA (US); s. 13(2)(*a*) SIA (UK); s. 14(2)(*a*) SIO (Pak); s. 14(1)(*a*) FStIA (SA); s. 30 FStIA (Aus); s. 15(2)(*a*) SIA (Sing).

[61] See Art. 32(*b*) VCLT.

[62] Report ILC, thirty-seventh session, 55, para. 230.

[63] See Seventh report Sucharitkul, 34, paras 68 and 71, 35, para. 74, 36, para. 75, 39, para, 91, 41, para. 99, and 41, paras 99 and 100.

[64] See also, subsequently, s. 14(1)(*b*)(ii) FStIA (SA); s. 30 FStIA (Aus); s. 15(2)(*a*) SIA (Sing). The first two are cited in ILC commentary, draft art. 18, para. 7, fn. 171. S. 12(1) SIA (Can) refers simply to 'attachment and execution', without mention of either judgments or arbitral awards.

[65] See Report ILC, thirty-seventh session, 55–6, para. 235.

[66] See Report ILC, thirty-seventh session, 57, para. 247, fn. 206.

[67] See summary record 1968th ILC meeting (n. 11), 171, paras 82 and 83.

agreement'; and the ILC commentary to draft article 18 refers repeatedly to questions of immunity from measures of constraint taken in connection with arbitration.[68] The oversight was eventually compounded by the decision of the Ad Hoc Committee to refer, on the splitting of former draft article 18, to 'pre-judgment' and 'post-judgment' measures of constraint, thereby failing once more to take into account arbitral 'awards'.

It is certainly reasonable to argue—in light of the interpretative context provided by Article 19(*a*)(ii)'s reference to arbitration agreements, of the *travaux préparatoires*, and of the requirement of interpretation in good faith[69]—that what seems to have been the unwitting omission of any reference to arbitral awards or arbitral proceedings in the chapeau to Article 19 should not be taken to indicate *a contrario* that measures of constraint taken by a court against the property of a foreign State with a view to the execution of that award do not fall within the ambit of Article 19.[70] In this light, the expression 'post-judgment measures of constraint... taken in connection with a proceeding before a court of another State' should be construed as shorthand for 'post-judgment or post-award measures of constraint taken in connection with a proceeding before a court of another State or an arbitral tribunal'. It remains to be seen whether future States parties to the Convention enter interpretative declarations on this point. The absence of any such declarations to date may suggest that at least the current State parties see no real issue here.

Article 19's encompassing of post-award measures of constraint taken by a court against the property of a foreign State with a view to executing that award would, it might be added, accord with principle; with Article 23 ECSI, which provides unspecifically that '[n]o measures of execution... against the property of a Contracting State may be taken in the territory of another Contracting State'; and with certain national legislation, which either mentions arbitral awards alongside judgments or refers to neither.[71]

On a separate but related note, the ILC commentary to draft article 18 asserts that '[t]he word "State" in the expression "proceeding before a court of another State" refers to the State where the property is located, regardless of where the substantive proceeding takes place'.[72] The statement is manifestly unsound. The 'State' referred to in the words 'in connection with a proceeding before a court of another State' is clearly the State where the substantive proceeding takes place, wherever that may be. The ILC's comment appears to be a garbled version of the Chairman of the Drafting Committee's acknowledgment that the State in whose courts an application for measures of constraint against property of another State located in the territory is made may not be the State in whose courts the substantive proceeding takes place.[73]

[68] See ILC commentary, draft art. 18, paras 4, 7, including fn. 171, and 9.

[69] See Art. 31(1) and (2) and Art. 32 VCLT.

[70] Were, however, post-award measures of constraint taken by a court in execution of an arbitral award to be held not to be regulated by the Convention, their lawfulness as among States parties to the Convention would be governed instead by customary international law. As it happens, however, the present content of customary international law accords with Art. 19, although a question mark remains over the 'connection' proviso in Art. 19(*c*). See section 4.

[71] See s. 1610(*a*)(6) FSIA, inserted by way of Act to Implement the Inter-American Convention on International Commercial Arbitration, Pub L 100–669, 102 Stat 3969 (16 November 1988); s. 13(2)(*b*) SIA (UK); s. 12(1) SIA (Can); s. 14(2)(*b*) SIO (Pak); s. 14(1)(*b*)(ii) FStIA (SA); s. 30 FStIA (Aus); s. 15(2)(*a*) SIA (Sing).

[72] ILC commentary, draft art. 18, para. 6.

[73] See summary record 1968th ILC meeting (n. 11), 171, para. 83.

3.2 The exceptions to the general rule of immunity

*A. Article 19(*a*): express consent*

The first of the three exceptions in Article 19 to the general rule of the immunity of a State's property from post-judgment measures of constraint is, as provided for in Article 19(*a*), where and to the extent that the State whose property it is has expressly consented to such measures, whether by 'international agreement', by 'an arbitration agreement or in a written contract', or by 'a declaration before the court or by a written communication after a dispute between the parties has arisen'. The exception is based on State practice,[74] and has been acknowledged by the ICJ.[75] It is also in principle in line with Article 23 ECSI, which abrogates the immunity of State property from foreign 'measures of execution' only 'where and to the extent that the State has expressly consented thereto in writing'. But Article 19(*a*) UNCSI differs from Article 23 ECSI insofar as the latter goes on to require that express consent be given 'in any particular case', which could be taken to mean that consent can be given for the purposes of Article 23 ECSI only by means of a written communication after a dispute between the parties has arisen, to borrow the words of Article 19(*a*)(iii) UNCSI. In contrast, for the purposes of Article 19(*a*)(i) and (ii) UNCSI, an express grant of consent to post-judgment measures of constraint given in advance of the genesis of any dispute between the parties is to be considered effective.

The general considerations relevant to the express grant of consent to post-judgment measures of constraint in accordance with Article 19 are the same, *mutatis mutandis*, as those relevant to the express grant of consent to the exercise of jurisdiction in accordance with Article 7.[76] On the specific question of whether a State's express consent to the taking of post-judgment measures of constraint against its property can be revoked, it suffices for present purposes to say that there is reason to doubt the restrictiveness of the ILC's conclusions on this point,[77] for which there is no basis in the text of draft article 18(1)(*a*), let alone in Article 19(*a*) of the Convention.

A historically significant, albeit in practice unimportant example of States' consent by international agreement to post-judgment measures of constraint against their property is Article 26 ECSI, an optional provision potentially applicable as among only six States. It provides that, notwithstanding the prohibition on measures of execution against State property laid down in Article 23 ECSI, 'a judgment rendered against a Contracting State in proceedings relating to an industrial or commercial activity, in which the State is engaged in the same manner as a private person, may be enforced [*viz* executed] in the State of the forum against property of the State against which judgment has been given,

[74] See eg 1610(*a*)(1) FSIA (US); s. 13(3) SIA (UK); s. 14(3) SIO (Pak); s. 12(1)(*a*) SIA (Can); s. 14(2) FStIA (SA); s. 31 FStIA (Aus); s. 15(3) SIA (Sing); s. 17(*a*) and (*b*) FSIL (Isr). See also eg *Philippine Embassy Bank Account Case*, 65 ILR 146, 164 (FRG (FCC) 1977).

[75] See *Jurisdictional Immunities of the State* (n. 47), para. 118.

[76] For a full discussion, subject to the necessary modifications, see the commentary to Art. 7 UNCSI.

[77] See ILC commentary, draft art. 18, para. 9: 'Once consent has been given under paragraph . . . (*a*), any withdrawal of that consent may only be made under the terms of the international agreement (subparagraph (i)) or of the arbitration agreement or the contract (subparagraph (ii)). However, once a declaration of consent or a written communication to that effect (subparagraph (iii)) has been made before a court, it cannot be withdrawn. In general, once a proceeding before a court has begun, consent cannot be withdrawn.' For a full discussion of the general question of the revocability of a State's waiver of State immunity, see the commentary to Art. 7 UNCSI.

used exclusively in connection with such an activity', if three cumulative conditions are met. The conditions are that both the forum and judgment debtor States must have made special declarations under Article 24; the judgment debtor State must not have been entitled to immunity from the proceedings that resulted in the judgment; and the judgment, in the words of Article 20(1)(*b*) ECSI, 'cannot or can no longer be set aside if obtained by default, or if it is not or is no longer subject to appeal or any other form of ordinary review or to annulment'.

A classic contractual provision in accordance with which a State patently consented to the taking of, *inter alia*, post-judgment measures of constraint against its property was the dispute settlement provision in the fiscal agency agreement that was at issue before the UK Supreme Court in *NML Capital Ltd v Republic of Argentina*[78] (a case concerning immunity from jurisdiction, rather than from post-judgment measures of constraint). This provided in relevant part:

> To the extent that the Republic or any of its revenues, assets or properties shall be entitled, in any jurisdiction in which any specified court is located, in which any related proceeding may at any time be brought against it or any of its revenues, assets or properties, or in any jurisdiction in which any specified court or other court is located in which any suit, action or proceeding may at any time be brought solely for the purpose of enforcing or executing any related judgment, to any immunity . . . from attachment in aid of execution of judgment, from execution of a judgment or from any other legal or judicial . . . remedy, and to the extent that in any such jurisdiction there shall be attributed such an immunity, the Republic has hereby irrevocably agreed not to claim and has irrevocably waived such immunity to the fullest extent permitted by the laws of such jurisdiction . . . provided further that such agreement and waiver, in so far as it relates to any jurisdiction other than a jurisdiction in which a specified court is located, is given solely for the purpose of enabling the fiscal agent or a holder of securities of this series to enforce or execute a related judgment.[79]

Obviously the permissibility of post-judgment measures of constraint in such circumstances will depend on the terms of the contract or arbitration agreement, as the case may be. So, taking the example of the fiscal agency agreement in *NML Capital*, post-judgment measures of constraint against Argentine State property in 'any jurisdiction other than a jurisdiction in which a specified court is located' would not be permissible if the substantive proceedings were not 'for the purpose of enabling the fiscal agent or a holder of securities of [the relevant] series to enforce or execute a related judgment'.

*B. Article 19(*b*): the allocation or earmarking of property to satisfy the claim*

The second exception to the general rule of the immunity of a State's property from post-judgment measures of constraint is where and to the extent that 'the State has allocated or earmarked property for the satisfaction of the claim which is the object of that proceeding', in the words of Article 19(*b*). Such a situation clearly represents implied consent by the State to the taking of post-judgment measures of constraint against the property so allocated or earmarked.[80] The ILC commentary explains that the rule in what became Article 19(*b*) 'should have the effect of preventing extraneous or unprotected claimants from frustrating the intention of the State to satisfy specific claims or to make payment

[78] *NML Capital Ltd v Republic of Argentina*, 147 ILR 575 (UK (SC) 2011).
[79] *NML Capital Ltd v Republic of Argentina* (n. 78), 611–12.
[80] See eg Seventh report Sucharitkul, 38, para. 83(*c*).

for an admitted liability'.[81] It adds that 'the question whether particular property has or has not been allocated for the satisfaction of a claim may in some situations be ambiguous and should be resolved by the court'.[82]

No national State immunity legislation provides explicitly for an exception to the immunity of foreign State property from post-judgment measures of constraint in cases where the State has allocated or earmarked the property for the satisfaction of the claim the object of the proceeding. Both section 1610(*a*)(1) FSIA (US) and section 12(1)(*a*) SIA (Can) do, however, accept as effective a foreign State's waiver of immunity from such measures 'either explicitly or by implication', although the former applies only insofar as the property is used for a commercial activity in the US. In addition, a range of national courts have, one way or another, given effect to an exception more or less along the lines of Article 19(*b*) to the immunity of foreign State property from measures of execution. Some have permitted such measures where a State has earmarked or allocated the property for the satisfaction of commercial liabilities in general, rather than of a specific claim against it.[83] Others have deemed property of a State to be in use or intended for use for commercial purposes, and as a result statutorily unprotected by immunity from execution, where that property has been earmarked solely for the settlement of liabilities incurred in commercial transactions.[84] Either way, the ICJ has held that an exception exists to the immunity of foreign State property from post-judgment measures of constraint where the State 'has allocated the property in question for the satisfaction of a judicial claim'.[85]

C. *Article 19*(c)

(i) General

The most laboriously drafted paragraph of Article 19, namely paragraph (*c*), specifies an exception to the immunity of State property where and to the extent that 'it has been established that the property is specifically in use or intended for use by the State for other than government non-commercial purposes and is in the territory of the State of the forum', although the proviso is added that 'post-judgment measures of constraint may only be taken against property that has a connection with the entity against which the proceeding was directed'. The essence of the exception is based on a considerable degree of State practice.[86] In addition, although it has not said whether additional criteria must be met,[87] the ICJ has held that an exception exists to the immunity of foreign State

[81] ILC commentary, draft art. 18, para. 10.

[82] ILC commentary, draft art. 18, para. 10.

[83] See eg *Société Sonatrach v Migeon*, 77 ILR 525, 527 (Fra (CoC) 1985); *Société Creighton Ltd v Ministère des Finances et le Ministère des Affaires Municipales et de l'Agriculture du Gouvernement de l'Etat de Qatar* [2003] *Revue de l'Arbitrage* 417, 418 (Fra (Paris CA) 2001). See also A. Reinisch, 'European Court State Practice Concerning State Immunity from Enforcement Measures' (2006) 17 *EJIL* 803, 820.

[84] See *Alcom Ltd v Republic of Colombia*, 74 ILR 170, 187 (UK (HL) 1984), applying s. 13(4) SIA (UK).

[85] *Jurisdictional Immunities of the State* (n. 47), para. 118.

[86] See eg 1610(*a*)(2) FSIA (US); s. 13(4) SIA (UK); s. 14(2)(*b*) SIO (Pak); s. 12(1)(*b*) SIA (Can); s. 14(3) FStIA (SA); s. 32(1) and (3)(*a*) FStIA (Aus); s. 15(4) SIA (Sing); s. 16(1) FSIL (Isr). See also *Société Sonatrach v Migeon* (n. 83), 527; *Philippine Embassy Bank Account Case* (n. 74) and comparative case-law cited therein; *Kingdom of Spain v Company X SA*, 82 ILR 38, 41 (Swi (FT) 1986); *Abbott v Republic of South Africa*, 113 ILR 411, 419–24 (Spa (CC) 1992) and comparative case-law cited therein.

[87] See *Jurisdictional Immunities of the State* (n. 47), para. 117.

property from post-judgment measures of constraint where 'the property in question [is] in use for an activity not pursuing government non-commercial purposes'.[88]

It is paragraph (*c*) that, in terms of their respective requirements, distinguishes Article 19 from Article 18. The only exceptions to Article 18's prohibition on pre-judgment measures of constraint against State property are, in accordance with paragraphs (*a*) and (*b*), where the State consents, either expressly or, by allocating or earmarking the property for the satisfaction of the claim, implicitly to the taking of such measures. In contrast, Article 19(*c*) recognizes, not without controversy, an involuntary basis for the taking of post-judgment measures of constraint against property of a State.

Article 19(*c*) is linked closely to Article 21. The former provision lays down a general test for the non-consensual taking of post-judgment measures of constraint against State property. The latter specifies in turn certain categories of State property that, for the purposes of the exception to immunity from post-judgment measures of constraint laid down in Article 19(*c*), are deemed not to be in use or intended for use for other than government non-commercial purposes. In other words, Article 21 enumerates a range of State property against which, by definition, post-judgment measures of constraint may not be taken in the application of Article 19(*c*).[89] Such property may, however, be the subject of measures with a view to the execution of a judgment or arbitral award if and to the extent that the State has expressly consented by one of the means specified in Article 19(*a*) to the taking of such measures against the property or, as per Article 19(*b*), if and to the extent that the State has allocated or earmarked the property for the satisfaction of the claim that was the object of the judicial or arbitral proceeding on the merits.[90]

Article 19(*c*), unlike the draft article 18(1)(*c*) finally adopted by the ILC on second reading in 1991, does not require that the State property against which the post-judgment measure of constraint is taken have 'a connection with the claim which is the object of the proceeding'. It will be recalled[91] that the long struggle over this limb of draft article 18(1)(*c*) was finally resolved in 2003 by the decision of the Ad Hoc Committee to drop all reference to it. Inclusion of any such requirement would have represented a deviation from the practice of all bar one of the States whose State immunity legislation was influential in the inclusion in Article 19 of a 'commercial use' exception, although it is by no means unimportant that the odd one out is the US.[92] It would also have run counter to the judicial practice of many States, which 'look only at the purpose of the property concerned without requiring a specific connection or nexus'.[93]

The words 'it has been established' at the start of Article 19(*c*) were inserted, it will be recalled,[94] to lend an objective element to the question of the State's intended use of the

[88] *Jurisdictional Immunities of the State* (n. 47), para. 118.

[89] See Art. 21(1) UNCSI.

[90] See Art. 21(2) UNCSI.

[91] See section 2.2.

[92] See s. 1610(*a*)(2) FSIA (US) ('the property is or was used for the commercial activity upon which the claim is based').

[93] Reinisch (n. 83), 823. The French courts have seemingly been divided at times over whether a connection is required between the property and the object of the claim. Compare *Islamic Republic of Iran and Others v Société Eurodif and Others*, 77 ILR 513, 516 (Fra (CoC) 1984), where the court considered it relevant that there was a connection between the property and the object of the claim, and *Société Creighton Ltd v Ministère des Finances* (n. 83), where it is arguable that no connection was required. See Reinisch (n. 83), 822–3.

[94] Recall section 2.2, citing 2000 report Chairman Sixth Committee Working Group, 83, para. 78.

property, although whether they impart any more objectivity than is already inherent in the judicial determination of a subjective state is doubtful.

(ii) The 'commercial use' requirement

The central requirement of Article 19(*c*), that the property be specifically in use or intended for use by the State for other than government non-commercial purposes, is to be adjudged by reference to the time the proceeding for arrest, attachment, execution, or other post-judgment measure of constraint is instituted.[95] As for the adjectives 'government' and 'non-commercial', they are cumulative, although it is again difficult to discern the difference made by what is really no more than semantic redundancy. The import of the adverb 'specifically' is also elusive. The word was never the subject of recorded discussion, and is not explained in the ILC commentary. It may have been inserted as an oblique reference to the problem of so-called 'mixed' bank accounts—that is, where an embassy or other State organ or entity uses a single account for both sovereign and non-sovereign purposes. If so, it remains unclear what the qualifier is supposed to signal.

The 'commercial use' criterion goes to the purpose, rather than the nature, of the property's use. This stands in apparent contrast with the emphasis on the nature, rather than the purpose, of a transaction in the definition of a 'commercial transaction' specified in Article 2(1)(*c*) of the Convention, as elaborated on in Article 2(2) and applied in Article 10's 'commercial transaction' exception to immunity from jurisdiction. But any inconsistency is merely apparent, for the reason that a commercial transaction and commercial use are different, albeit closely related concepts, the latter being at one remove from the former. Interpreting Article 19(*c*) against the backdrop of Article 2(1)(*c*), which forms part of the former's context,[96] it is logical to construe the term 'non-commercial purposes' in Article 19(*c*) to mean 'purposes other than a "commercial transaction" as defined in Article 2(1)(*c*)'. In short, property of a State is used for 'other than ... non-commercial purposes' within the meaning of Article 19(*c*) when—stating it in the positive—it is used for the purpose of a commercial transaction as understood by the Convention. This would be in line with the national legislative practice that the Special Rapporteur sought to codify, which elsewhere defines the term 'commercial purposes' by reference to the 'commercial transaction' or 'commercial activity' exception to immunity also found in the legislation.[97]

(iii) The territorial requirement

Article 19(*c*) further requires that the property against which the post-judgment measure of constraint is sought be in the territory of 'the State of the forum'. At first glance the specification of the territory of the State of the forum might be taken to imply that measures may not be taken against State property in one State in execution of a judgment rendered by a court of another. Closer analysis, however, reveals this not to be so. Execution against property located in the territory of one State of a judgment rendered by a court of another State is, at least in widespread practice, preceded in the courts of the territory where the property is located by a proceeding for the recognition and enforcement of that judgment—that is, a proceeding to convert the foreign judgment into a

[95] See ILC commentary, draft art. 18, para. 11.

[96] See Art. 31(1) and (2) VCLT. See also R. Gardiner, *Treaty Interpretation* (Oxford: Oxford University Press, 2008), 185–6.

[97] See s. 17(1) SIA (UK); s. 7(1) SIA (Can); s. 1(1) FStIA (SA).

judgment of the local courts, in form or effect. When this occurs, it is the local proceeding for recognition and enforcement of the foreign judgment that will constitute, for the purposes of the chapeau to Article 19, the proceeding in connection with which the post-judgment measure of constraint is sought to be taken. In this light, it is the State where the property is located which is to be considered 'the State of the forum' for the purposes of Article 19(*c*). The same goes, *mutatis mutandis*, for the recognition and enforcement and the consequent execution of arbitral awards.

(iv) The proviso as to 'a connection with the entity against which the proceeding was directed'

Post-judgment measures of constraint may be taken against property of a State in accordance with Article 19(*c*) only if that property 'has a connection with the entity against which the proceeding was directed'. In this regard, the first limb of the 'understanding' with respect to Article 19 annexed to the Convention provides that the expression 'entity' in Article 19(*c*) 'means the State as an independent legal personality, a constituent unit of a federal State, a subdivision of a State, an agency or instrumentality of a State or other entity, which enjoys independent legal personality'.[98] It pays to recall too that, in accordance with Article 6(2), a proceeding is considered, for the purposes of the Convention, to be 'against' a State (in any of its various emanations) either if the State is named as a party to the proceeding[99] or if the proceeding 'in effect seeks to affect the property, rights, interests or activities of that other State'.[100]

What the 'connection' proviso in Article 19(*c*) means is that post-judgment measures of constraint may be taken against property of the State as such—that is, as a legal person separate as a matter of the municipal law of that State from any political subdivisions (such as constituent federal units, autonomous regions, counties, or cities) and from any agencies, instrumentalities, or other entities as may exist and enjoy independent legal personality under the law of that State—only if the proceeding on the merits was against the State as such. The proviso means equally that post-judgment measures of constraint may be taken against property of a constituent federal unit or of some other political subdivision of a State with independent legal personality under the law of that State only if the proceeding on the merits was against that constituent federal unit or other subdivision, as the case may be; and that the same measures may be taken against property of a State agency, instrumentality, or other entity enjoying independent legal personality under the law of that State only if the proceeding on the merits was against that agency, instrumentality, or other entity. In short, the final limb of Article 19(*c*) stipulates that, when it comes to post-judgment measures of constraint, the State of the forum must ensure that its courts respect the 'segregation' or division of foreign State property among the various, separate legal persons recognized by the municipal law of that foreign State.

No mention is made in the understanding to Article 19(*c*) of the other emanations of a State referred to in the definition of 'State' in Article 2(1)(*b*) of the Convention, namely the 'various organs of government' of a State, as cited in Article 2(1)(*b*)(i), among them the State's government as such or its various ministries and departments, and individual

[98] The final comma is extraneous. The closing words should read 'or other entity which enjoys independent legal personality'.

[99] See Art. 6(2)(*a*) UNCSI.

[100] See Art. 6(2)(*b*) UNCSI.

representatives of the State acting in that capacity, as cited in Article 2(1)(*b*)(iv). The reason for the omission of any mention of individual State representatives is obvious: property vesting in a State representative personally is by definition not State property, and on this account does not implicate Article 19(*c*). The reason for the understanding's silence as to the various organs of government of a State is less clear, and may come down to a plain desire to avoid cumbersome verbiage; but it is certainly reasonable to argue that reference to such organs is implicit in the understanding's reference to the State as an independent legal personality, alongside which 'its various organs of government' appear in Article 2(1)(*b*)(i).

In practice, what the 'connection' proviso in Article 19(*c*) seeks to obviate is the taking of post-judgment measures of constraint against property of a foreign State *eo nomine* where the judgment debtor is not the foreign State *eo nomine* but a State enterprise. The anxiety of what at the time was the socialist bloc, as well as of developing States, during the preparation of the ILC's draft articles and, in terms of the latter group, of the later Convention—an anxiety manifest as much in the controversy over what became Article 10(3)[101] as in the interminable debate over Article 19(*c*)—was that, in the absence of an absolute prohibition on the taking of non-consensual measures of constraint against property of a State, private claimants might seek to execute against property vesting in the State as such judgments obtained against the State's commercial enterprises, especially where the assets of the enterprise were insufficient to satisfy the judgment debt. The upshot was Article 19(*c*). But, as made clear by the Privy Council (on appeal from Jersey) in *Gécamines* and, indeed, by the facts of the case, a claimant may, conversely, seek 'to hold a state-owned corporation liable for the state's debts'.[102] Article 19(*c*) applies equally to this situation.

At the same time, the developed States expressed concern throughout the drafting process that a requirement to respect the independent legal personality of each municipal emanation of a foreign State might encourage States to frustrate the execution of judgments obtained against State enterprises by deliberating undercapitalizing such enterprises or dissipating their assets in anticipation of proceedings against them. The fruit, for what it is worth, of this second concern is the third limb of the understanding to Article 19 annexed to the Convention, which provides that 'Article 19 does not prejudge the question of "piercing the corporate veil", questions relating to a situation where a State entity has deliberately misrepresented its financial position or subsequently reduced its assets to avoid satisfying a claim, or other related issues'. It has to be said that it is not at all clear what this statement means. But the gist would appear to be that Article 19(*c*)'s 'connection' proviso—pertaining as it does solely to the question of the immunity from post-judgment measures of constraint of the property of the State as such or of any of its several emanations—is without prejudice to whether, as a matter of the substantive municipal law applied by the court, the State as such may be held liable in certain circumstances for the acts of a State enterprise. Putting it another way, as emphasized in the third limb of the understanding, Article 19(*c*) stipulates no more than that, if it was against the State as such that the claimant obtained her judgment, it is against the property of the State as such alone that she may levy execution; and that, as a

[101] See the commentary to Art. 10 UNCSI.

[102] *La Générale des Carrières et des Mines v F.G. Hemisphere Associates LLC* [2002] UKPC 27, para. 3 (UK (PC Jersey) 2012).

consequence, Article 19(*c*) has no bearing on the logically precedent and substantive question of municipal law of whether the State as such may be proceeded against in place of the State enterprise. And *vice versa*. It remains to be seen what practical effect this limb of the understanding has.

For its part, the second limb of the understanding to Article 19 provides that the words 'property that has a connection with the entity' in Article 19(*c*) 'are to be understood as broader than ownership or possession'. Even leaving aside the poor syntax, the statement is difficult to penetrate. For the purposes of Article 19 as a whole, the term 'property of a State' means property either owned or possessed or controlled by a State.[103] In this light, the second limb of the understanding may simply indicate that mere control of the property suffices for the purposes of Article 19(*c*)'s 'connection' proviso. But this ought to be taken as read by simple virtue of the application of Article 19(*c*) to 'property of a State'; and it is, moreover, telling in this regard that, as adopted on first reading, draft article 18(1) referred to 'its [*viz* the State's] property or property in its possession or control', the term 'control' being paired and treated as effectively synonymous with 'possession'.[104] What, then, the understanding to Article 19 must mean by a 'connection' between the property and the State 'broader than ownership or possession' is something akin to the mere 'legally protected interest' included in square brackets in the text of draft article 18(1) as adopted on first reading—that is, the same 'legally protected interest' rejected on second reading as insufficient to make property 'property of a State' within the meaning of Articles 18 and 19 of the eventual Convention.

Putting all this together and taking a State instrumentality by way of example, what the second limb of the understanding with respect to Article 19 would seem to indicate is that a judgment obtained in proceedings against a State instrumentality may, in full accordance with the 'connection' proviso in Article 19(*c*), be executed not only against property owned or possessed or controlled by that instrumentality but also against any property in which that instrumentality has a legally protected interest. The catch, however, is that where the legal or natural person that enjoys the greater rights (be they of ownership or of possession or control) in the property in which the State instrumentality has a mere legally protected interest is a private party, Article 19 does nothing to prohibit execution against the property in the first place, since the property, not being either owned or possessed or controlled by a State, is not 'property of a State' within the meaning of Article 19. The only situation, in other words, in which the second limb of the understanding to Article 19 has any purchase is where the party with the greater rights (whether of ownership or of possession or control) in the property is another emanation of the State, and in practice this is most likely to mean the State as such.

In the final analysis, then, the significance of the second limb of the understanding to Article 19 is to dilute to an extent the effect of the 'connection' proviso in Article 19(*c*). Although it remains contrary to the immunity of property of a State recognized in Article 19 to execute a judgment rendered against, for example, a State enterprise against property owned or possessed or controlled by the legal person of a foreign State as such and with which the State enterprise has no connection whatsoever, it would appear permissible—the requirements as to commercial use and presence in the forum State's

[103] See section 3.1(A).

[104] Report ILC, thirty-eighth session, 17.

territory being satisfied—to execute the same judgment against, for example, property owned by the foreign State as such but in which the State enterprise has a beneficial interest. Like the third limb of the understanding with respect to Article 19, the second is designed to meet in part the concerns of developed States as regards the execution of judgments obtained by private parties in proceedings, whether judicial or arbitral, against undercapitalized State enterprises. But, as with the third limb, it is worth reiterating that the second limb applies equally to the converse situation where a creditor seeks measures of execution against the property of a State enterprise to satisfy a debt of the State as such.

4. Evaluation

In *Jurisdictional Immunities of the State*, Germany relied on the provisions of Article 19, arguing that they 'codified, in relation to the issue of immunity from enforcement [*i.e.* execution], the existing rules under general international law'.[105] In response, the International Court of Justice stated:

> 117. When the United Nations Convention was being drafted, these provisions gave rise to long and difficult discussions. The Court considers that it is unnecessary for purposes of the present case to decide whether all aspects of Article 19 reflect current customary international law.
>
> 118. Indeed, it suffices for the Court to find that there is at least one condition that has to be satisfied before any measure of constraint may be taken against property belonging to a foreign State: that the property must be in use for an activity not pursuing government non-commercial purposes, or that the State which owns the property has expressly consented to the taking of a measure of constraint, or that that State has allocated the property in question for the satisfaction of a judicial claim.

In other words, the Court held that the essence of Article 19 reflects customary international law. What it did not say, and was not required to say, was whether the proviso to Article 19(*c*), 'that post-judgment measures of constraint may only be taken against property that has a connection with the entity against which the proceeding was directed', is also consonant with custom.

As for Article 19 itself, while the discontinuity between the chapeau's reference to 'post-judgments measures of constraint . . . taken in connection with proceedings before a court of another State' and paragraph (*a*)(ii)'s reference to arbitration agreements is a major drafting oversight, the interpretation of the chapeau in good faith and in context, as confirmed by recourse to the *travaux préparatoires*, ought to result in its embrace of measures of constraint taken by a court in execution of an arbitral award. As for Article 19(*c*) and its attendant understandings, their adoption represents a significant achievement, which carries with it the hope of what the preamble to the Convention refers to as 'the harmonization of practice in this area'.

[105] *Jurisdictional Immunities of the State* (n. 47), para. 115.

Article 20

Roger O'Keefe

Article 20

*Effect of consent to jurisdiction to [*sic*] measures of constraint*

Where consent to the measures of constraint is required under articles 18 and 19, consent to the exercise of jurisdiction under article 7 shall not imply consent to the taking of measures of constraint.

1. Introduction

Article 7 of the Convention provides that a State is not entitled to immunity from proceedings in a court of another State where it has expressly consented by one of several specified means to the exercise of jurisdiction over it.[1] Articles 18 and 19 lay down that no pre- or post-judgment measures of constraint may be taken against the property of a State in connection with proceedings in a court of another State unless, *inter alia*, the first State has expressly consented to the taking of such measures against its property.[2] For its part, Article 20 clarifies the relationship between consent for the purposes of Article 7 and consent for the purposes of Articles 18 and 19 by specifying that there is no relationship. A State's consent to foreign proceedings against it does not in any way establish its consent to the taking of measures of constraint against its property in connection with those proceedings. Insofar as Articles 18 and 19 require a State's express consent to measures of constraint against its property, such consent must be specifically to measures of constraint against its property. In short, Article 20 reiterates the fundamental distinction drawn in the Convention between the immunity of a State from proceedings (or, in the language of the Convention, from jurisdiction), as regulated by Parts II and III of the Convention, and the immunity of a State's property from arrest, conservatory attachment, attachment in aid of execution, execution itself, and all other pre- and post-judgment measures of constraint, as regulated by Part IV.

2. Drafting History

The drafting history of Article 20 is bound up closely with that of Articles 18 and 19. What ultimately became Article 20 of the Convention was introduced by the ILC's Drafting Committee as paragraph 2 of the then draft article 22,[3] as adopted by the Commission on first reading,[4] a provision which dealt with express consent to measures of constraint, whether pre- or post-judgment, and which varied considerably from what had been proposed by Special Rapporteur Sucharitkul in his Seventh Report as draft

[1] See Art. 7(1) UNCSI. [2] See Arts 18(*a*) and 19(*a*) UNCSI.

[3] See summary record 1968th ILC meeting, *YILC 1986*, vol. I, 165, 172–3, paras 97–104.

[4] See Report ILC, thirty-eighth session, 11–12 and 18.

article 23.[5] Although the Commission eventually combined in a single provision what had previously been two separate articles on measures of constraint against State property, the former draft article 22(2) remained substantively unchanged, and was finally adopted on second reading as draft article 18(2) of the ILC's 1991 draft articles. Draft article 18(2) stated that '[c]onsent to the exercise of jurisdiction under article 7 shall not imply consent to the taking of measures of constraint under paragraph 1 [of article 18], for which separate consent shall be necessary'.

In the event, the Ad Hoc Committee on Jurisdictional Immunities of States and Their Property divided draft article 18 into three separate draft articles, one each on pre- and post-judgment measures of constraint and a stand-alone article headed 'Effect of consent to jurisdiction to [*sic*] measures of constraint', applicable to both preceding provisions insofar as they demanded express consent to the taking of measures of constraint against State property.[6] The sole substantive difference between the ILC's draft article 18(2) and what was now provisionally numbered draft article 18 *bis* was the deletion of the former's final relative clause ('for which separate consent shall be necessary'), which was presumably deemed redundant.[7] Draft article 18 *bis* emerged substantively unaltered at the end of the drafting process as Article 20 of the Convention.

3. Key Points

3.1 Drafting

The English-language version of Article 20 is a sloppily drafted affair insofar as both its title and its text contain grammatical errors. The title 'Effect of consent to jurisdiction to measures of constraint' in fact makes no sense, the correct wording, as confirmed by comparison with the equally authentic Arabic, Chinese, French, Russian, and Spanish texts, being 'Effect of consent to jurisdiction *on* measures of constraint'.[8] While the mistake in the text of the provision—namely the insertion of an extraneous definite article in the opening clause ('Where consent to *the* measures of constraint is required under articles 18 and 19'[9])—is less egregious, it remains unbecoming of a major multilateral treaty.

3.2 Rationale

Article 20 is not strictly necessary, given the seemingly unambiguous insistence in the respective chapeaux to Articles 18(*a*) and 19(*a*) that consent by a State to the taking of measures of constraint against its property be express. All the same, there is no harm and

[5] See Seventh report Sucharitkul, 38, para. 84.

[6] See 2002 report Ad Hoc Committee, 10–11.

[7] See 2002 report Ad Hoc Committee, 11. The *travaux* offer no indication of the rationale for the deletion, but redundancy would stand to reason and is certainly the most likely explanation.

[8] The French version of the title of Art. 20 is 'Effet du consentement à l'exercice de la juridiction *sur* l'adoption de mesures de contrainte' (emphasis added), while the Spanish is 'Efecto del consentimiento a la jurisdicción *sobre* las medidas coercitivas' (emphasis added). The Arabic, Chinese, and Russian versions also use the equivalent of the English preposition 'on'.

[9] Emphasis added. Ironically, neither the French ('le consentement à l'adoption de mesures de contrainte') nor Spanish ('el consentimiento para la adopción de medidas coercitivas') version of Art. 20—from which an anglophone might, on the basis of linguistic stereotyping, have supposed the spare 'the' to have derived—uses the definite article at the same point in the text.

at least potential benefit in 'mak[ing] more explicit', *ex abundante cautela*, 'the requirement of separate consent for the taking of measures of constraint under part IV' of the Convention[10]—that is, in clarifying, if clarification be needed, that '[c]onsent under article 7 . . . is confined exclusively to immunity from the jurisdiction of a court of a State in a proceeding against another State'.[11]

3.3 Basis in customary international law

The proposition that a State's consent to the exercise by a foreign court of jurisdiction over it (whether in the form of submission to the jurisdiction or waiver of immunity from proceedings, insofar as the distinction is in any way domestically relevant) does not imply the consent of that State to the taking of pre- or post-judgment measures of constraint against its property finds ample support in State practice.[12] For example, section 13(3) SIA (UK)—which concerns written consent by a State to the enforcement of a judgment or arbitral award against its property or, in an action *in rem*, to the arrest, detention, or sale of such property—specifies that 'a provision merely submitting to the jurisdiction of the courts is not to be regarded as a consent for the purposes of this subsection'.[13] An analogous statement is to be found in each of section 31(1) FStIA (Aus), section 11(2) SIA (Can), section 17(*c*) FSIL (Isr), section 14(3) SIO (Pak), section 14(2) FStIA (SA), and section 15(3) SIA (Sing).[14] It has also been held in the French courts that a State's '[w]aiver of jurisdictional immunity does not in any way involve waiver of immunity from execution'.[15]

Since the adoption of Article 20 of the Convention, the International Court of Justice has declared unequivocally, in *Jurisdictional Immunities of the State*, that 'any waiver by a State of its jurisdictional immunity [ie immunity from jurisdiction] before a foreign court does not in itself mean that that State has waived its immunity from enforcement [ie execution] as regards property belonging to it situated in foreign territory'.[16]

3.4 Separate but simultaneous consent

Article 20 should not be taken to mean that a State may not expressly consent, by means of a single provision in an international agreement or written contract, a single oral declaration before the court, or a single written communication to the same, both to the exercise of foreign jurisdiction over itself and to the taking of pre- and/or post-judgment measures of constraint against its property in connection with the same proceedings. Provided that each expression of consent is—or, where relevant, provided that all three expressions of consent (*viz* to proceedings, to pre-judgment measures of constraint, and to

[10] ILC commentary, draft art. 18, para. 12.

[11] ILC commentary, draft art. 18, para. 12.

[12] The major exception in this regard is Switzerland. See the commentary to Part IV UNCSI.

[13] In this respect, the UK legislation does not merely follow Art. 23 ECSI, which, while permitting measures of execution and 'preventive measures' against State property only insofar as the State 'has expressly consented thereto in writing in any particular case', does not contain a clarificatory statement as per s. 13(3) SIA (UK).

[14] See also now, in implementation of Art. 20 of the Convention, Art. 17(3) ACJJFS (Jpn).

[15] *Socialist Federal Republic of Yugoslavia v Société Européenne d'Etudes et d'Entreprises*, 65 ILR 46, 49 (Fra (TGI Paris) 1970).

[16] See *Jurisdictional Immunities of the State (Germany v Italy: Greece intervening), Judgment*, International Court of Justice, 3 February 2012, para. 113.

post-judgment measures of constraint) are—explicit and specific, there is no reason why they may not be given together.[17] A clear-cut case of such an all-encompassing expression of consent was the waiver clause in the fiscal agency agreement at issue in the UK Supreme Court case of *NML Capital Ltd v Republic of Argentina*, which provided:

To the extent that the Republic or any of its revenues, assets or properties shall be entitled, in any jurisdiction in which any specified court is located, in which any related proceeding may at any time be brought against it or any of its revenues, assets or properties, or in any jurisdiction in which any specified court or other court is located in which any suit, action or proceeding may at any time be brought solely for the purpose of enforcing or executing any related judgment, to any immunity from suit, from the jurisdiction of any such court, from set-off, from attachment prior to judgment, from attachment in aid of execution of judgment, from execution of a judgment or from any other legal or judicial process or remedy, and to the extent that in any such jurisdiction there shall be attributed such an immunity, the Republic has hereby irrevocably agreed not to claim and has irrevocably waived such immunity to the fullest extent permitted by the laws of such jurisdiction ... provided further that such agreement and waiver, in so far as it relates to any jurisdiction other than a jurisdiction in which a specified court is located, is given solely for the purpose of enabling the fiscal agent or a holder of securities of this series to enforce or execute a related judgment.[18]

Lord Mance JSC appropriately referred to the clause as 'a comprehensive submission'.[19]

3.5 Separate consent to pre- and post-judgment measures of constraint?

What Article 20 does not clarify, as arguably it should have done, is whether a State's consent to the taking of post-judgment measures of constraint (such as execution and attachment in aid of execution) as per Article 19(*a*) suffices also for the express consent to the taking of pre-judgment measures of constraint (such as a *Mareva* injunction, or freezing order, in the common law or *une ordonnance de saisie conservatoire* under French law) demanded by Article 18(*a*), and, at least in principle, *vice versa*.[20] The insistence in Article 18(*a*) on a State's express consent to the taking of 'such measures', the term being unambiguously cross-referable to the 'pre-judgment measures of constraint, such as attachment or arrest, against property of a State' spoken of in the chapeau to Article 18, would seem to provide the answer, as would the analogous insistence, *mutatis mutandis*, in Article 19(*a*), obviously cross-referable to the 'post-judgment measures of constraint, such as attachment, arrest or execution, against property of a State' the subject of the chapeau to Article 19. In other words, just as consent to the exercise of jurisdiction in accordance with

[17] See also H. Fox, *The Law of State Immunity* (2nd end) (Oxford: Oxford University Press, 2008), 487, stating in relation to Art. 20 UNCSI that 'an express waiver of immunity may operate to constitute consent to remove immunity in respect of both the adjudication and execution stages of a proceeding'. See eg, under the SIA (UK), *A Company Ltd v Republic of X* 87 ILR 412 (UK (EWHC) 1989) and *Sabah Shipyard (Pakistan) Ltd v Islamic Republic of Pakistan* [2002] EWCA Civ 1643 (UK (EWCA) 2002). But whether the contractual clause at issue in the first case ought to have been taken as consent to both jurisdiction and measures of constraint, and whether in the second the clause should have been read to include pre-judgment measures of constraint, are another matter. Consider also in this light *Creighton Ltd v Minister of Finance of Qatar and Others*, 127 ILR 154 (Fra (CoC) 2000).

[18] *NML Capital Ltd v Republic of Argentina*, 147 ILR 575, 611–12 (UK (SC) 2011).

[19] *NML Capital Ltd v Republic of Argentina* (n. 18), 618, para. 98.

[20] In practice, it is far more likely that a State would consent by way of international agreement or contract to the taking of post-judgment measures of constraint (typically via a term like 'execution') without mentioning pre-judgment measures than that it would consent to the latter without mentioning the former.

Article 7 is not to be equated with consent to the taking of measures of constraint under either Article 18(*a*) or Article 19(*a*), so too consent to the taking of pre-judgment measures of constraint for the purposes of Article 18(*a*) is not to be treated as one and the same as consent to the taking of post-judgment measures of constraint in line with Article 19(*a*); and consent in line with Article 19(*a*) is not to be construed as consent for the purposes of Article 18(*a*).

This conclusion is supported by the ILC's commentary to the requirement of express consent to jurisdiction in what became Article 7, according to which there is 'no room for implying the consent of an unwilling State which has not expressed its consent in a clear . . . manner'.[21] Nor is the conclusion undermined by the commentary to draft article 18(1)(*a*) of the ILC's 1991 draft articles, which states that 'express consent can be given generally with regard to measures of constraint . . . or be given for particular measures'.[22] For a start, draft article 18 applied indiscriminately to all measures of constraint, whether pre- or post-judgment, whereas Articles 18 and 19 of the Convention reflect a deliberate decision on the part of the subsequent drafters of the Convention to treat measures of constraint prior to judgment and measures of constraint consequent on judgment, and with them the respective requirements of express consent to such measures in Articles 18(*a*) and 19(*a*), separately. But even taking the commentary to draft article 18(1)(*a*) on its own terms, it cannot be doubted that—just as a State can specify that it consents at one and the same time to both proceedings against itself and measures of constraint against its property—a State may indeed, provided it does so unambiguously, consent expressly via a single formula to all measures of constraint, both pre- and post-judgment, against its property. In contrast, what is impermissible under the terms of Article 18(*a*) of the Convention is for a court to imply a State's consent to the taking of 'preventive'[23] measures of constraint against its property from the mere fact that the State has consented to executory measures against the same, and *vice versa* under the terms of Article 19(*a*).[24]

The explanation for the omission from Article 20 (and, for that matter, from anywhere else in Part IV of the Convention) of any mention of the need for separate consent to pre- and post-judgment measures of constraint respectively can only be a matter of speculation. But it would seem that when the Ad Hoc Committee divided the ILC's draft article 18 into separate articles on pre- and post-judgment measures of constraint, with a third article corresponding to what is now Article 20, its attention was thereafter absorbed by the wording of what became Article 19(*c*)[25] at the understandable expense of considered reflection on Article 20, which essentially[26] remained as it had been as draft article 18(2), and on the relationship, or lack thereof, between Articles 18(*a*) and 19(*a*). Nor would knowledge of State legislative practice have turned the Committee's minds to the question, since the various national State immunity statutes do not explicitly delineate, as do Articles 18(*a*) and 19(*a*) of the Convention, between consent to pre-judgment measures and consent to post-judgment measures of constraint. In short, the drafters took no conscious decision to refrain from including in Article 20 or elsewhere in Part IV

[21] ILC commentary, draft art. 7, para. 8.

[22] ILC commentary, draft art. 18, para. 8.

[23] The language is that of Art. 23 ECSI.

[24] To this extent, Part IV of the Convention is at odds with the robust logic adopted in *Sabah Shipyard (Pakistan) Ltd v Islamic Republic of Pakistan* (n. 17), paras 22–23.

[25] See 2002, 2003 and 2004 reports Ad Hoc Committee.

[26] Recall from section 2 the immaterial deletion of the words 'for which separate consent shall be necessary'.

a clause that would do for Articles 18(*a*) and 19(*a*) respectively what Article 20 as adopted does for Article 7, on the one hand, and Articles 18(*a*) and 19(*a*) together, on the other. They appear never to have considered the issue.

4. Evaluation

Article 20, while strictly speaking redundant, is nonetheless a judicious inclusion for the avoidance of doubt. Just as a range of States have done, the drafters of the Convention have sensibly thought fit to seek to scotch artful pleading which might undermine the cardinal distinction the Convention draws between the immunity of a State from foreign proceedings against it and the immunity of that State's property from measures of constraint before or after judgment in those proceedings. The English-language version of the provision and its heading show signs of inattentive *toilettage*, but Article 20 is unambiguous in its affirmation of the need, for the purposes of Articles 18(*a*) and 19(*a*), for a State's express consent to measures of constraint against its property over and above any express consent to proceedings against itself given by the State in accordance with Article 7. While there is no reason why the two distinct expressions of consent cannot be given alongside each other, consent to the taking of measures of constraint against State property must relate explicitly and specifically to the taking of measures of constraint. It is only a pity that the drafters of Article 20 did not get around to emphasizing the same, *mutatis mutandis*, in relation to consent to measures of constraint after and before judgment respectively.

Article 21

CHESTER BROWN AND ROGER O'KEEFE*

Article 21

Specific categories of property

1. The following categories, in particular, of property of a State shall not be considered as property specifically in use or intended for use by the State for other than government non-commercial purposes under article 19, subparagraph (*c*):
   (*a*) property, including any bank account, which is used or intended for use in the performance of the functions of the diplomatic mission of the State or its consular posts, special missions, missions to international organizations or delegations to organs of international organizations or to international conferences;
   (*b*) property of a military character or used or intended for use in the performance of military functions;
   (*c*) property of the central bank or other monetary authority of the State;
   (*d*) property forming part of the cultural heritage of the State or part of its archives and not placed or intended to be placed on sale;
   (*e*) property forming part of an exhibition of objects of scientific, cultural or historical interest and not placed or intended to be placed on sale.
2. Paragraph 1 is without prejudice to article 18 and article 19, subparagraphs (*a*) and (*b*).

1. Introduction

Article 19(*c*) of the Convention provides that no post-judgment measures of constraint may be taken against property of a State in connection with a proceeding before a court of another State unless and to the extent that 'it has been established that the property is specifically in use or intended for use by the State for other than government non-commercial purposes'.[1] The purpose of Article 21 of the Convention is to deem certain categories of property of a State not to be 'specifically in use or intended for use by the State for other than government non-commercial purposes' within the meaning of Article 19(*c*). Putting it another way, the effect of Article 21 is to prohibit the taking of post-judgment measures of constraint against the categories of property listed in subparagraphs (*a*) to (*e*) of Article 21(1) unless and to the extent that the State has expressly consented to the taking of such measures in accordance with Article 19(*a*) or has allocated or earmarked the property for the satisfaction of the claim the object of the proceedings in accordance with Article 19(*b*).

* The authors would like to thank Ashique Rahman, LLM (Syd), for his valuable assistance in the preparation of this chapter.

[1] Art. 19(*c*), as elaborated on by the first limb of the 'understanding' with respect to Art. 19 annexed to the Convention, requires in addition that the property be in the territory of the State of the forum and that it have a connection with the particular emanation of the State against which the proceeding on the merits was directed. See the commentary to Art. 19 UNCSI.

The statement in Article 21(1) that the categories of State property specified in subparagraphs (*a*) to (*e*) 'shall not be considered as property specifically in use or intended for use by the State for other than government non-commercial purposes under article 19, subparagraph (*c*)' is without prejudice to the corresponding characterization of any category of State property not found on the list, as the words 'in particular' in the chapeau to the provision make plain. Moreover, as is obvious as a matter of both explicit wording and logic from the application of Article 21(1) to Article 19(*c*) alone, and as is additionally specified for the avoidance of doubt in Article 21(2), Article 21(1) has no bearing on whether a State is to be considered to have expressly consented to the taking of post-judgment measures of constraint against its property in accordance with Article 19(*a*) or to have allocated or earmarked the property for the satisfaction of the claim the object of the proceedings in accordance with Article 19(*b*).

It should also be apparent as a matter of wording and logic, and is again further specified in Article 21(2), that Article 21(1) has no bearing on the application of Article 18, which deals with pre-judgment measures of constraint. Article 18 embodies no 'commercial use' exception akin to that found, in relation to post-judgment measures, in Article 19(*c*). Instead, Article 18 makes clear that pre-judgment measures of constraint are prohibited against any and all State property unless and to the extent that the State has expressly consented to the taking of such measures in accordance with Article 18(*a*) or to has allocated or earmarked the property for the satisfaction of the claim the object of the proceedings in accordance with Article 18(*b*).[2]

2. Drafting History

2.1 The ILC's draft articles

When Special Rapporteur Sucharitkul first proposed to the ILC in his Seventh Report the texts of draft provisions on State immunity from foreign measures of constraint,[3] the relevant rules were initially presented in the form of a draft article 21 ('Scope of the present part'), a draft article 22 ('State immunity from attachment and execution'), a draft article 23 ('Modalities and effect of consent to attachment and execution'), and a draft article 24 ('Types of State property permanently immune from attachment and execution'). Article 21 of the Convention has its origins in draft article 24.

From the outset, as the title to his original draft article 24 indicates, Special Rapporteur Sucharitkul proposed that certain categories of State property be specified as permanently immune from attachment and execution. As initially put forward, draft article 24(1) provided:

1. Notwithstanding [the draft article on modalities of consent] and regardless of consent or waiver of immunity, the following property may not be attached, arrested or otherwise taken in forced execution of the final judgment by a court of another State:
   (*a*) property used or intended for use for diplomatic or consular purposes or for the purposes of special missions or representation of States in their relations with international organizations of universal character internationally protected by inviolability; or
   (*b*) property of a military character, or used or intended for use for military purposes, or owned or managed by the military authority or defence agency of the State; or

[2] See the commentary to Art. 18 UNCSI.

[3] See, generally, Seventh report Sucharitkul, 23–44, paras 4–117.

(*c*) property of a central bank held by it for central banking purposes and not allocated for any specified payments; or
(*d*) property of a State monetary authority held by it for monetary and non-commercial purposes and not specifically earmarked for payments of judgment or any other debts; or
(*e*) property forming part of the national archives of a State or of its distinct national cultural heritage.

2. Nothing in paragraph 1 shall prevent a State from undertaking to give effect to the judgment of a court of another State, or from consenting to the attachment, arrest or execution of property other than the types listed in paragraph 1.[4]

The principle embodied in the chapeau to paragraph 1 that a State's consent to the taking of measures of forced execution against property of the sort listed was to be considered ineffective was regarded by Special Rapporteur Sucharitkul as necessary to protect the interests of developing States. Such States 'might otherwise be lured into including in an agreement an expression of consent affecting certain types of property which should under no circumstances be seized or detained, owing to the vital nature of their predominantly public use (such as warships), or to their inviolability (such as diplomatic premises), or to their vulnerability (such as the funds of central banks)'.[5]

The Special Rapporteur's formulation was the subject of considerable debate within the Commission. Some members opposed restricting the effectiveness of a State's consent to measures of constraint against its property.[6] Not only, it was thought, did this impermissibly limit a State's sovereign discretion, but it was also possibly incompatible with existing 'codification conventions'.[7] Instead, '[s]ince article 24 listed the various types of State property that could not in any circumstances be regarded as being used for commercial purposes', the suggestion was made that 'it might be drafted in such a way as to present its provisions as an interpretation of what constituted property used for commercial purposes'.[8] As for some of the specific types of property mentioned, concern was expressed over the breadth of the term 'property of a military character'.[9] In consequence of members' comments, the Special Rapporteur revised his proposed text, which was referred, along with the rest of the provisions on immunity from measures of constraint, to the Drafting Committee,[10] which amended it further.[11]

The now renumbered draft article 23(1) specified categories of State property that were not to be considered in use or intended for use for 'commercial [non-governmental]' purposes, the phrase being the contentious one used at the time in what was the renumbered draft article 21(*a*), which embodied an exception to immunity from measures of constraint for property in or intended for such use.[12] The categories

[4] Seventh report Sucharitkul, 44, para. 117.
[5] Seventh report Sucharitkul, 42, para. 105.
[6] See Report ILC, thirty-seventh session, 56, para. 241.
[7] Report ILC, thirty-seventh session, 56, para. 241. The reference would seem to have been to Art. 23 ECSI.
[8] Report ILC, thirty-seventh session, 56, para. 241.
[9] See Report ILC, thirty-seventh session, 57, para. 244.
[10] See Report ILC, thirty-seventh session, 57, para. 247, text of revised provision at fn. 206.
[11] See summary record 1968th ILC meeting, *YILC 1986*, vol. I, Part 1, 165, 173, paras 105–110.
[12] The square brackets indicated text on which agreement had not been reached. See the commentary to Art. 19 UNCSI.

themselves were similar to those listed in the Special Rapporteur's original proposal, although the property of a central bank and the property of a State monetary authority were combined in a single subparagraph and a new category of 'property forming part of an exhibition of objects of scientific or historical interest which is in the territory of another State and not placed or intended to be placed on sale'[13] was added. The Commission then adopted draft article 23 on first reading.[14]

Several States submitted comments on draft article 23 as adopted on first reading. The UK, supported by Australia, Germany, and Switzerland, thought that subparagraph (*a*) of draft article 23(1) ought to clarify that the 'purposes of the diplomatic mission' referred only to 'the mission's purely diplomatic functions'.[15] Germany, supported by Australia, Qatar, and the five Nordic countries, voiced opposition to the proposition that all property of a central bank should be classified as not in use or intended for use for commercial purposes, proposing instead that only property serving monetary purposes should be deemed inherently uncommercial.[16] In response, the Special Rapporteur proposed the addition to draft article 23(1)(*c*) of the words 'and serves monetary purposes'.[17] But other members of the Commission opposed the proposal,[18] which was dropped 'for lack of general support'.[19]

What was eventually renumbered draft article 19 ('Specific categories of property') was finally adopted on second reading as follows:

1. The following categories, in particular, of property of a State shall not be considered as property specifically in use or intended for use by the State for other than government non-commercial purposes under paragraph 1(*c*) of article 18:
   (*a*) property, including any bank account, which is used or intended for use for the purposes of the diplomatic mission of the State or its consular posts, special missions, missions to international organizations, or delegations to organs of international organizations or to international conferences;
   (*b*) property of a military character or used or intended for use for military purposes;
   (*c*) property of the central bank or other monetary authority of the State;
   (*d*) property forming part of the cultural heritage of the State or part of its archives and not placed or intended to be placed on sale;
   (*e*) property forming part of an exhibition of objects of scientific, cultural or historical interest and not placed or intended to be placed on sale.
2. Paragraph 1 is without prejudice to paragraph 1(*a*) and (*b*) of article 18.

The scene now shifted to the Sixth Committee.

2.2 From draft article 19 to Article 21 of the Convention

When in 1992 the Working Group of the Sixth Committee discussed draft article 19, some States queried the need to spell out categories of government non-commercial property for the purposes of the 'commercial use' exception in draft article 18(1)(*c*) to the immunity of State property from measures of constraint.[20] Others considered draft

[13] Summary record 1968th ILC meeting (n. 11), 173, para. 105.
[14] See Report ILC, thirty-eighth session, 12.
[15] Preliminary report Ogiso, 119, para. 230.
[16] See Preliminary report Ogiso, 119, para. 233.
[17] Preliminary report Ogiso, 119, para. 239.
[18] See Report ILC, forty-second session, 42, para. 227.
[19] ILC commentary, draft art. 19, para. 5.
[20] See 1992 report Sixth Committee Working Group, 13.

article 19 essential.[21] As to specifics, differences arose again over whether all property of a central bank or only property used for monetary purposes should enjoy immunity *ipso facto* from measures of constraint; and the question was raised whether a blanket immunity should extend to 'mixed' bank accounts, where monies in or intended for use for government non-commercial purposes were mingled with monies held for commercial purposes.[22] Resolution of these issues proved impossible within the context of the Working Group over both 1992 and 1993,[23] and they were seemingly not alluded to during the informal consultations held in the Sixth Committee in 1994.[24]

The same questions were raised in 1999 in the context of the ILC Working Group,[25] while the Sixth Committee's reconvened Working Group barely discussed draft article 19 over the course of its sessions in 1999 and 2000.[26] In the event, the provision emerged from the 2002–2004 deliberations of the Ad Hoc Committee on Jurisdictional Immunities of State and Their Property in a form almost identical to that in which it was adopted by the ILC on second reading. The only changes were that the words 'for the purposes of the diplomatic mission' in paragraph 1(*a*) had become 'in the performance of the functions of the diplomatic mission' and that the words 'for military purposes' in paragraph 1(*b*) had become 'in the performance of military functions'.[27] Renumbered after the three-way division of the former draft article 18 into Articles 18, 19, and 20, it was in this form that Article 21 of the Convention was adopted.

3. Key Points

3.1 Article 21(1)

Article 21(1) of the Convention specifies that certain categories of State property are not to be considered 'specifically in use or intended for use by the State for other than government non-commercial purposes' within the meaning of the exception posited in Article 19(*c*) to the immunity of State property from post-judgment measures of constraint. In effect, it prohibits the taking of post-judgment measures of constraint against the categories of property listed in subparagraphs (*a*) to (*e*) unless and to the extent that the State has expressly consented to the taking of such measures in accordance with Article 19(*a*) or has allocated or earmarked the property for the satisfaction of the claim the object of the proceedings in accordance with Article 19(*b*). The ILC considered the rule 'necessary and timely in view of the trend in certain jurisdictions to attach or freeze assets of foreign States, especially bank accounts, assets of the central bank or other *instrumenta legati* and specific categories of property which equally deserve protection'.[28] Support for the a priori exclusion of certain types of property from the 'commercial use'

[21] See 1992 report Sixth Committee Working Group, 13.

[22] See 1992 report Sixth Committee Working Group, 13–14.

[23] As to the latter, see 1993 report Sixth Committee Working Group, 15, paras 81–82.

[24] See Report Sixth Committee informal consultations, 4–5, paras 11–13.

[25] See 1999 report ILC Working Group, 169, para. 115.

[26] See 1999 report Sixth Committee Working Group, 6–7, paras 35–45 and 9, para. 66; 2000 report Sixth Committee Working Group, 13–22, paras 53–83 and 27–29, para. 88.

[27] 2004 report Ad Hoc Committee, annex I, 13 (art. 21 Draft UNCSI).

[28] ILC commentary, draft art. 19, para. 2.

exception to the immunity of State property from post-judgment measures of constraint can be found in the legislative practice of a range of States.[29]

The words 'in particular' in Article 21(1) indicate that subparagraphs (*a*) to (*e*) are not to be taken as an exhaustive enumeration of the range of State property capable of being considered in use or intended for use for government non-commercial purposes and as thereby not falling within the exception to the immunity of State property from post-judgment measures of constraint provided for in Article 19(*c*). At the same time, to describe subparagraphs (*a*) to (*e*), as the ILC commentary does, as 'merely illustrative'[30] is to miss the point. The gist of Article 21(1) is not to provide examples of the sort of property of a State that might fall outside Article 19(*c*). It is to stipulate categories of State property that under no circumstances are to be considered as falling within that provision.

The term 'property of a State' in the chapeau to Article 21(1) has the same meaning as elsewhere in Part IV of the Convention.[31] That is, it encompasses not only property owned by a foreign State but also property possessed or, synonymously, controlled by it. It does not, however, extend to property in which the State has some lesser legally protected interest.

Neither Article 21(1) nor, for that matter, Article 19 makes provision for the certification by the foreign State of the government non-commercial purpose of the actual or intended use of any other of its property against which post-judgment measures of constraint may be sought. This is in contrast to the State immunity legislation of certain States. By way of example, section 13(5) SIA (UK) provides that a certificate from the head of a foreign State's diplomatic mission in the United Kingdom 'to the effect that any property is not in use or intended for use by or on behalf of the State for commercial purposes shall be accepted as sufficient evidence of that fact unless the contrary is proved'. The legislation of Australia, Pakistan, and Singapore makes respective provision to the same effect.[32] The lack of provision in either Article 21 or Article 19 for such certification also contrasts with the position under Article 16, on immunity from jurisdiction in relation to State-owned or -operated ships. Article 16(6) provides that, '[i]f in a proceeding there arises a question relating to the government and non-commercial character of a ship owned or operated by a State or cargo owned by a State, a certificate signed by a diplomatic representative or other competent authority of that State and communicated to the court shall serve as evidence of the character of that ship or cargo'.

In conceiving of how the various subparagraphs of Article 21(1) might apply in practice, it is essential to keep in mind that 'commercial use' is not the sole criterion of the exception to immunity from post-judgment measures of constraint posited in Article 19(*c*). In addition, the foreign State property in question must be present in the territory of the forum State (meaning the State to whose court the application for the post-judgment measure of constraint is made), and it must have a connection with the specific emanation of the foreign State against which the proceeding was directed.

[29] See eg s. 1611 FSIA (US); s. 14(4) SIA (UK); s. 12(3) and (4) SIA (Can); s. 15(4) SIO (Pak); s. 15(3) FStIA (SA); s. 32(3)(*a*) FStIA (Aus); s. 16(4) SIA (Sing); s. 18 FSIL (Isr). See also art. VIII(C) ILA Revised Draft Articles.

[30] See ILC commentary, draft art. 19, para. 1.

[31] For a fuller discussion, see the commentary to Arts 18 and 19 UNCSI.

[32] See s. 41 FStIA (Aus); s. 14(4) SIO (Pak); s. 15(5) SIA (Sing).

A. *Article 21(1)(a)*

Article 21(1)(*a*) provides that State property shall not be considered as property specifically in use or intended for use for other than government non-commercial purposes within the meaning of Article 19(*c*) if it is 'property, including any bank account, which is used or intended for use in the performance of the functions of the diplomatic mission of the State or its consular posts, special missions, missions to international organizations or delegations to organs of international organizations or to international conferences'.

When considering Article 21(1)(*a*), it pays first to recall Article 3(1)(*a*) of the Convention, which indicates that the Convention 'is without prejudice to the privileges and immunities enjoyed by a State under international law in relation to the exercise of the functions of... its diplomatic missions, consular posts, special missions, missions to international organizations or delegations to organs of international organizations or to international conferences'.[33] In turn, the customary and conventional rules of diplomatic and cognate international law provide that the premises of diplomatic missions, special missions, and missions to international organizations, along with their furnishings, any other property on such premises[34] or, in the case of special missions, used in the operation of such premises,[35] and the means of transport of such missions, are immune from attachment and execution in the receiving State. In short, Article 3(1)(*a*) deems the Convention to be without prejudice to the immunity of all these categories of State property from attachment and execution. In this light, neither Article 19(*c*) nor Article 21(1)(*a*) can apply in the first place to these specific categories of property.

Against this normative backdrop, the practical effect of Article 21(1)(*a*) is considerably less than it may appear. What Article 21(1)(*a*) in effect does is to render by definition immune from post-judgment measures of constraint any property of a State used or intended for use in the performance of the functions of the diplomatic mission etc of the State insofar as such property is not already covered by the special immunity regimes of diplomatic and cognate international law. Examples of such property include the premises or movable property of a consular post—which no rule of consular law serves to protect from attachment or execution[36]—to the extent that it is used or intended for use in the performance of the functions of the post. Another, highly significant example, and one explicitly mentioned in Article 21(1)(*a*), is any bank account of a diplomatic mission, consular post, special mission, mission to an international organization, or delegation to an organ of an international organization or to a diplomatic conference that is used or intended for use in the performance of the functions of the mission, post, or delegation.

While national State immunity legislation frequently excludes from its scope of application the immunities recognized under diplomatic and consular law,[37] only section 32(3)(*a*) FStIA (Aus) makes additional provision for 'diplomatic property' as such, defined in section

[33] See the commentary to Art. 3 UNCSI.

[34] See Art. 22(3) Vienna Convention on Diplomatic Relations, Vienna, 18 April 1961, 500 UNTS 95 (VCDR) and Art. 23(3) Vienna Convention on the Representation of States in their Relations with International Organizations of a Universal Character, Vienna, 14 March 1975, UN doc. A/CONF.67/16 (not in force) (VCRS), as regards diplomatic missions and missions to international organizations respectively.

[35] See Art. 25(3) Convention on Special Missions, New York, 8 December 1969, 1400 UNTS 231 (CSM), as regards special missions.

[36] A consular post may, however, operate from the premises of a diplomatic mission.

[37] See the commentary to Art. 3 UNCSI.

3(1) of the Act as 'property that, at the relevant time, is in use predominantly for the purpose of establishing or maintaining a diplomatic or consular mission, or a visiting mission, of a foreign State to Australia'. Section 32(3)(*a*) FStIA (Aus) has the effect of deeming diplomatic property not to be 'commercial property' within the meaning of section 32(1)'s 'commercial property' exception to the immunity of State property from measures of execution posited in section 30. But the jurisprudence of the courts of more than a few States is to similar effect, at least in relation to certain categories of diplomatic and analogous property, among them bank accounts in use or intended for use in the performance of the functions of the mission, post, or delegation.[38]

The expression 'the functions of the diplomatic mission [etc]' in Article 21(1)(*a*) of the Convention was settled on, it will be recalled, after the criticism levelled by several States at the expression 'the purposes of the diplomatic mission' adopted on first reading, which they considered too broad.[39] The words ultimately included in Article 21(1)(*a*) are intended to refer only to 'the mission's purely diplomatic functions'.[40] A useful, albeit non-exhaustive list of the functions of a diplomatic mission is to be found in Article 3(1) VCDR; an exhaustive and much longer list of consular functions is found in Article 5 VCCR;[41] a non-exhaustive list of the functions of a permanent mission to an international organization can be found in Article 6 VCRS;[42] and the functions of a permanent observer mission to an international organization are listed non-exhaustively in Article 7 VCRS. As for special missions, their functions are, in accordance with Article 3 CSM, to be determined by the mutual consent of the sending and receiving States.

Article 21(1)(*a*) does not do away with the difficult task of factual appreciation inherent in the judicial characterization of the relevant State property as in use or intended for use in the performance of the functions of the mission, post, or delegation. In the words of the ILC commentary, Article 21(1)(*a*) 'obviously excludes property, for example, bank accounts maintained by embassies for commercial purposes'.[43] But some purposes may be harder to delineate as either commercial or 'in the performance of the functions' of the mission, post, or delegation. Moreover, as in the case of mixed bank accounts, property in use or intended for use in the performance of the functions of the mission, post, or delegation may be hard to separate out from property in use or intended for use for commercial purposes.

In relation specifically to mixed accounts, the ILC commentary elaborates that '[t]he recent case law seems to suggest the trend' that they are to be accorded immunity, at least where one can speak of 'the non-commercial character of the account in general'.[44] But

[38] See eg *Philippine Embassy Bank Account Case*, 65 ILR 146 (FRG (FCC) 1977); *Alcom Ltd v Republic of Colombia*, 74 ILR 170 (UK (HL) 1984); *Republic of 'A' Embassy Bank Account Case*, 77 ILR 488 (Aut (SC) 1986); *MK v State Secretary for Justice*, 94 ILR 357 (Nth (CoS) 1986); *Banamar-Capizzi v Embassy of the Popular Democratic Republic of Algeria*, 87 ILR 56 (Ita (CoC) 1989); *Libyan Arab Socialist People's Jamahiriya v Actimon SA*, 82 ILR 30, 35 (Swi (FT) 1985) and *Z v Geneva Supervisory Authority for the Enforcement of Debts and Bankruptcy*, 102 ILR 205 (Swi (FT) 1990); *Abbott v Republic of South Africa*, 113 ILR 411 (Spa (CC) 1992); *Russian Federation v Noga Import/Export Company*, 127 ILR 156 (Fra (Paris CA) 2000); *Iraq v Vinci Constructions*, 127 ILR 101 (Bel (Brussels CA) 2002).

[39] See section 2.1.

[40] Preliminary report Ogiso, 119, para. 230.

[41] Vienna Convention on Consular Relations, Vienna, 24 April 1963, 596 UNTS 261 (VCCR).

[42] The VCRS is specifically mentioned in ILC commentary, draft art. 19, para. 3.

[43] ILC commentary, draft art. 19, para. 3.

[44] ILC commentary, draft art. 19, para. 3.

the statement, which as it is was made in 1991, is not intended prescriptively, and should not be taken as an indication of what Article 21(1)(*a*) itself dictates. In relation to mixed accounts, Article 21(1)(*a*) does not dictate anything.

B. *Article 21(1)(*b*)*

Article 21(1)(*b*) excludes from the application of Article 19(*c*)'s 'commercial use' exception 'property of a military character or used or intended for use in the performance of military functions'. The ILC commentary, stating the obvious somewhat, explains that the term 'military' encompasses the army, navy, and air force.[45] The words 'in the performance of military functions', it will be recalled, were substituted during the drafting of the provision for the previous words 'for military purposes', which were considered overly broad.[46]

The FStIA (Aus), SIA (Can), and FSIA (US) all make special provision for the immunity from post-judgment measures of constraint of at least certain sorts of foreign military property.[47] An equivalent rule is found in the jurisprudence of the courts of many States.

The specific, longstanding immunity from measures of constraint, whether post- or pre-judgment, of foreign warships present in the forum State's territorial sea is recognized in Article 32 United Nations Convention on the Law of the Sea (UNCLOS),[48] rights and obligations under which are unaffected as among States parties to both UNCSI and UNCLOS by virtue of Article 26 UNCSI. It may also be that any existing status of forces agreement (SOFA) or status of mission agreement (SOMA) between the foreign and forum States, rights and obligations under which will again be safeguarded from the effect of Article 19(*c*) of the Convention by Article 26, accords immunity *ipso facto* from post-judgment measures of constraint to the property of the foreign State's military forces stationed in the territory. In the case of property rendered immune by any subsequent, rather than existing, SOFA or SOMA, reliance will need to be placed not on Article 26 but instead on Article 21(1)(*b*).

C. *Article 21(1)(*c*)*

Article 21(1)(*c*) deems as not in use or intended for use for other than government non-commercial purposes 'property of the central bank or other monetary authority of the State'. Proposals during the drafting of the provision to limit the provision's scope to only such property of a central bank etc as was in use for monetary purposes were, it will be recalled, unsuccessful.[49] The resultant Article 21(1)(*c*) certifies as in use or intended for use for government non-commercial purposes any and all property of the central bank or other monetary authority of the State. The reference to 'other monetary authority of the State' is plainly to any authority of that State performing the functions of a central bank, whatever its title.[50]

[45] ILC commentary, draft art. 19, para. 4.

[46] Recall section 2.2.

[47] See s. 32(3)(*a*) FStIA (Aus), cross-referable to s. 32(1) and to the detailed definition of 'military property' in s. 3(1) FStIA (Aus); s. 12(3) SIA (Can); s. 1611(*b*)(2) FSIA (US). In addition, s. 17(*d*) FSIL (Isr) provides that waiver of immunity from execution may not apply to a 'military asset' as defined in s. 1 FSIL (Isr).

[48] Montego Bay, 10 December 1982, 1833 UNTS 3. For the suggestion that Art. 32 UNCLOS refers to the immunity from measures of constraint of warships in whatever waters they may be present, see *The 'ARA Libertad' Case (Argentina v Ghana), Request for the prescription of provisional measures, Order*, 15 December 2012, paras 63–67.

[49] Recall section 2. See also ILC commentary, draft art. 19, para. 5.

[50] See eg 1992 report Sixth Committee Working Group, 13 (Chairman Calero-Rodrigues).

The specification that the property of a foreign central bank or other foreign monetary authority is under no circumstances to be considered in use or intended for use for commercial purposes within the meaning of the 'commercial use' exception to immunity from post-judgment (and pre-judgment) measures of constraint is found in the SIA (UK), SIO (Pak), FStIA (SA), and SIA (Sing).[51] The wording of Article 21(1)(*c*) would also appear consistent with China's Law on Judicial Immunity from Measures of Constraint for the Property of Foreign Central Banks.[52] Less expansively, section 1611(*b*)(1) FSIA (US) extends a priori immunity from attachment and execution only to property of a foreign central bank or monetary authority 'held for its own account'. This is intended and taken to mean that the funds 'are used for central bank functions as these are normally understood', even if this means that they are 'used for commercial purposes'.[53] At the other end of the spectrum, the FStIA (Aus) and the FSIL (Isr) treat the property of a foreign central bank or monetary authority in the same way as they treat State property generally,[54] as does in effect section 12(4) SIA (Can), which provides that 'property of a foreign central bank or monetary authority that is held for its own account and is not used or intended for use for a commercial activity is immune from attachment and execution'.

Despite appearances, the effect of Article 21(1)(*c*) is not necessarily to render immune from foreign measures of constraint all property of a foreign central bank or other monetary authority. Insofar as a foreign central bank or other monetary authority may not be an organ of government within the meaning of Article 2(1)(*b*)(ii) of the Convention but rather a State agency, instrumentality, or other entity enjoying a municipal legal personality separate from the personality of the foreign State as such, it is to be considered a 'State' for the purposes of the Convention only to the extent, in accordance with Article 2(1)(*b*)(iii), that it is entitled to perform and is actually performing acts 'in the exercise of sovereign authority of the State'. In the case of a central bank etc that also engages in commercial conduct, Article 2(1)(*b*)(iii)'s proviso may make a crucial difference. While it can be assumed that, insofar as it is authorized to act as the State's monetary authority, the central bank etc is entitled to perform acts in the exercise of the State's sovereign authority, the question will be whether, when it engages in purely commercial conduct, it can be said actually to be performing such acts. If the answer is that it cannot be, it cannot be considered a 'State' in this context, and its property will not be 'property of a State' within the meaning of Article 19. As such, the property will not be protected in the first place by the immunity from foreign measures of constraint posited in that article. In short, Article 19(*c*), and therefore Article 21(1)(*c*), will not enter into it, because the property will not be 'property of a State'.

[51] See s. 12(4) SIA (UK); s. 15(4) SIO (Pak); s. 15(3) FStIA (SA); s. 16(4) SIA (Sing).

[52] See art. 1 Law on Judicial Immunity from Measures of Constraint for the Property of Foreign Central Banks 2005, quoted in L. Zhu, 'State Immunity from Measures of Constraints [*sic*] for the Property of Central Banks: The Chinese Perspective' (2007) 6 *Chinese JIL* 67, 75, para. 23.

[53] *Jurisdiction of United States Courts in Suits Against Foreign States*, H Rep No 94–1487, 94th Cong. (9 September 1976). See also the case-law of certain US District Courts cited in A. Dickinson, R. Lindsay, and J.P. Loonam, *State Immunity: Selected Materials and Commentary* (Oxford: Oxford University Press, 2004), 326, fn. 625.

[54] See s. 32(3)(*a*) FStIA (Aus), specifically in respect of those central banks or monetary authorities that are separate entities (all others being considered a 'State' within the meaning of the Act); s. 18 FSIL (Isr). Recall from section 2.1 that Australia was one of the States which queried the application of Art. 21(1)(*c*) to all property of a State's central bank or other monetary authority.

It is not clear whether—but unlikely that—this potential consequence of the interplay of the definition of 'State' in Article 2(1)(*b*)(iii) and the deeming provision in Article 21(1)(*c*) was intended. It is certainly the practice of some States to make special provision for the immunity from measures of constraint of the property of any central bank or other monetary authority which happens to constitute a separate entity within the meaning of the relevant legislation.[55] But only under the SIA (UK), SIO (Pak), FStIA (SA), and SIA (Sing) is such property deemed not to be in use or intended for use for commercial purposes.

It remains to be seen whether this apparent 'loophole' in Articles 19 and 21(1)(*c*) becomes a focus of litigation. Much will depend on how the courts give effect to the proviso in Article 2(1)(*b*)(iii)'s definition of 'State'.

*D. Article 21(1)(*d*)*

Article 21(1)(*d*) provides that 'property forming part of the cultural heritage of the State or part of its archives and not placed or intended to be placed on sale' shall not be considered property specifically in use or intended for use for other than government non-commercial purposes. The ILC commentary suggests that Article 21(1)(*d*) applies only insofar as the property in question belongs to the State.[56] But such a restrictive application would run counter to the meaning of the term 'property of a State' as used elsewhere in Part IV of the Convention, which, in addition to comprehending property owned by a State, extends to property merely possessed or controlled by it.[57] The distinction may be highly significant in the context of the cultural heritage of a State, given the common practice whereby many of the items in a State's national museums and galleries are technically not owned by the State but merely held by it on 'permanent loan' or the like from their private owners.

It can only be presumed that whether or not property forms part of the cultural heritage of a State or part of a State's archives is to be determined by reference to the relevant legislation of that State. In the case of a State's national cultural heritage, such legislation usually makes use of a system of 'listed' or 'scheduled' items, although whether an item's non-inclusion in such a list is to be treated as conclusive of the property's lack of requisite status will be an evidentiary question for the court.

It is worth bearing in mind that Article 21(1)(*d*) can apply only if Article 19(*c*) applies to the property and that Article 19(1)(*c*) applies only in relation to property of a foreign State present in the territory of the forum State. In other words, only rarely will immovable cultural property, such as historic buildings, be encompassed by Article 21(1)(*d*), and even then many such buildings are already likely to be immune per se from execution either by virtue of the interaction of Article 3 of the Convention and the rules of diplomatic or cognate international law or by virtue of Article 21(1)(*a*).[58] Article 21(1)(*d*) is likely to have greater practical import in relation to movable cultural property, insofar as

[55] See s. 12(4) SIA (UK); s. 15(4) SIO (Pak); s. 15(3) FStIA (SA); s. 32(3)(*a*) FStIA (Aus); s. 16(4) SIA (Sing).

[56] See ILC commentary, draft art. 19, para. 6.

[57] See section 3.1 and commentary to Arts 18 and 19 UNCSI.

[58] Many extraterritorial historic buildings belonging to or in the possession of a State form part of diplomatic premises or are otherwise property in use in the performance of the function of a diplomatic mission.

this may not already be covered by Article 21(1)(*e*), with which Article 21(1)(*d*) is likely in practice to overlap.

E. Article 21(1)(e)

Article 21(1)(*e*) prevents the 'commercial use' exception in Article 19(*c*) from applying to 'property forming part of an exhibition of objects of scientific, cultural or historical interest and not placed or intended to be placed on sale'. As with Article 21(1)(*d*), the ILC commentary suggests that Article 21(1)(*e*) applies only to State-owned property;[59] but, as with Article 21(1)(*d*), the suggestion is contrary to the meaning of 'property of a State' as used in Part IV of the Convention, which, as has been said, embraces also property possessed or controlled by a State. Again, the distinction may be significant in the context of artworks etc on loan from a State's national collections to a gallery or museum abroad, given the frequency with which objects in a State's national collections are not owned by the State but merely held by it on 'permanent loan' or the like from their private owners.

The ILC commentary further asserts that Article 21(1)(*e*) does not apply to 'exhibits for industrial or commercial purposes'.[60] Whether this is correct depends on what it means. If by 'exhibits for industrial or commercial purposes' the commentary has in mind property exhibited at a trade fair designed to promote sales, the comment makes sense, and is merely a gloss on the requirement in Article 21(1)(*e*) itself that the property not be placed or intended to be placed on sale. If, however, the suggestion is that Article 21(1)(*e*) does not apply to property forming part of an exhibition that the public pays to view, the commentary is on shakier ground. Nothing in the text of Article 21(1)(*d*) bars its application to such exhibits, provided they are 'not placed or intended to be placed on sale'.

It is regularly the case that States lend items from their national collections to museums or galleries in other States for inclusion in exhibitions, including in those for a fee-paying public. With a view to encouraging such loans, a range of States have in place legislation declaring, or permitting the declaration of, cultural exhibits on loan as immune per se from post- and pre-judgment measures of constraint.[61]

As previously stated,[62] Article 21(1)(*e*) is likely in practice to overlap with Article 21(1)(*d*).

3.2 Article 21(2)

Article 21(2) provides that Article 21(1) is 'without prejudice to article 18 and article 19, subparagraphs (*a*) and (*b*)'. This should already be apparent from the fact that Article 21(1) is stated to relate to Article 19(*c*), but it does not hurt to underline this. In short, pre- and

[59] See ILC commentary, draft art. 19, para. 7.

[60] ILC commentary, draft art. 19, para. 7.

[61] See eg 22 USC § 2459 ('Immunity from seizure under judicial process of cultural objects imported for temporary exhibition or display'); Part 6 ('Protection of Cultural Objects on Loan') Tribunals, Courts and Enforcement Act 2007 (UK). Austria, Belgium, France, and Germany have similar legislation. See N. van Woudenberg, 'Immunity from Seizure: A Legal Exploration', in S. Pettersson et al. (eds), *Encouraging Collections Mobility: A Way Forward for Museums in Europe* (2010), 184, 188 (http://www.lending-for-europe.eu/fileadmin/CM/public/handbook/Encouraging_Collections_Mobility_A4.pdf). See also, generally, N. van Woudenberg, *State Immunity and Cultural Objects on Loan* (The Hague: Martinus Nijhoff, 2011).

[62] See section 3.1(D).

post-judgment measures of constraint may still be taken against the categories of foreign State property listed in subparagraphs (*a*) to (*e*) of Article 21(1) if the State expressly consents to the taking of such measures against that property[63] or if the State has allocated or earmarked that property for the satisfaction of the claim the object of the proceeding.[64]

When it comes to express consent, the ILC commentary to the draft equivalent of Article 21(2) asserts that '[a] general waiver or a waiver in respect of all property in the territory of the State of the forum, without mention of any of the specific categories, would not be sufficient to allow measures of constraint against property in the categories listed in paragraph 1'.[65] But there is no compelling reason why this should be so. Nothing in Part IV of the Convention specifies that the conditions under which express consent to the taking of measures of constraint against State property is to be considered effective differ as between the categories of property mentioned in Article 21(1) and any other State property. As Article 21(1) itself makes plain and Article 21(2) reiterates, Article 21(1) relates solely to Article 19(*c*). Provided it is evident from the terms of the consent that the consent is applicable to the property in question, there is no reason to insist on specific mention of any particular category.

4. Evaluation

In *Jurisdictional Immunities of the State*, the International Court of Justice held that the gist of Article 19(1)(*c*)'s 'commercial use' exception to the immunity of foreign State property present in the forum State's territory from post-judgment measures of constraint represented a rule of customary international law.[66] The follow-up question is obviously whether Article 21(1) does as well. The cautious answer is that it probably does in part.

The rule in subparagraph (*a*) of Article 21(1), which as it is applies only insofar as the property is not already rendered immune from attachment and execution by diplomatic or analogous international law, has a solid body of State practice and *opinio juris* to support it;[67] and even though the application of the rule to mixed bank accounts has divided national courts, there is little reason to doubt the customary status of the rule itself. The same probably goes for the rule in subparagraph (*b*). The proposition in subparagraph (*c*) that all property of a State's central bank or other monetary authority, and not just such property as is in use or intended for use for monetary purposes, is entitled by definition to immunity from post-judgment measures of constraint is, in contrast, far more contentious. Even among those relatively few States that accord State immunity on a legislative basis, there is a marked divergence of practice, with some deeming all property of a foreign State's central bank or the equivalent immune, even when that bank or equivalent is a separate entity, and others treating such property like

63 See Arts 18(*a*) and 19(*a*) UNCSI.

64 See Arts 18(*b*) and 19(*b*) UNCSI.

65 ILC commentary, draft art. 19, para. 8.

66 See *Jurisdictional Immunities of the State (Germany v Italy: Greece intervening), Judgment*, 3 February 2012, International Court of Justice, para. 118. The Court declined to decide whether all the elements of Art. 19(*c*) of the Convention—by which it meant the proviso as to a connection between the property in question and the specific emanation of the foreign State against which the proceeding on the merits was directed—reflect customary international law.

67 Recall section 3.1(A).

any other State property.[68] A similar divide was reflected during the drafting process.[69] In this light, it is difficult to conclude that the blanket rule recognized in Article 21(1)(*c*) is currently reflective of customary international law. As for Article 21(1)(*d*), the rule embodied is a 'novel' one,[70] and there is as yet no indication that customary international law has evolved in its image. As for the potentially partially overlapping rule in Article 21(1)(*e*), it would be similarly hasty to assert its customary status, even if State practice in this regard is somewhat more developed.[71]

As for Article 21(1) itself, while it may impose, as among States parties to the Convention, a common set of rules in specific areas of the law on immunity from execution, it cannot, of itself, provide the answers to the nuanced questions of factual appreciation thrown up by key expressions like 'in the performance of the functions of the diplomatic mission', 'in the performance of military functions', or, indeed, 'intended for use'. It will probably remain the case, even in the application of Article 21(1), that one court's *actum jure imperii* is another's *actum jure gestionis.*

[68] Recall section 3.1(C). [69] See section 2.1.

[70] H. Fox, *The Law of State Immunity* (2nd edn) (Oxford: Oxford University Press, 2008), 647.

[71] Recall section 3.1(E).

PART V: MISCELLANEOUS PROVISIONS

Article 22

Tarcisio Gazzini

Article 22

Service of process

1. Service of process by writ or other document instituting a proceeding against a State shall be effected:
   (*a*) in accordance with any applicable international convention binding on the State of the forum and the State concerned; or
   (*b*) in accordance with any special arrangement for service between the claimant and the State concerned, if not precluded by the law of the State of the forum; or
   (*c*) in the absence of such a convention or special arrangement:
      (i) by transmission through diplomatic channels to the Ministry of Foreign Affairs of the State concerned; or
      (ii) by any other means accepted by the State concerned, if not precluded by the law of the State of the forum.
2. Service of process referred to in paragraph 1(*c*)(i) is deemed to have been effected by receipt of the documents by the Ministry of Foreign Affairs.
3. These documents shall be accompanied, if necessary, by a translation into the official language, or one of the official languages, of the State concerned.
4. Any State that enters an appearance on the merits in a proceeding instituted against it may not thereafter assert that service of process did not comply with the provisions of paragraphs 1 and 3.

1. Introduction

Article 22 ('Service of process') is the first of three articles comprising Part V ('Miscellaneous provisions') of the Convention. It does not itself deal with any issue of State immunity from proceedings or measures of constraint. Rather, it prescribes how the writ or other document instituting proceedings regulated by the Convention is to be served on the potential respondent State. What it prescribes, given the special character of the respondent, is a regime quite different from that applicable in national legal systems to service of process on a private respondent.

2. Drafting History

What became Article 22(1) of the Convention was first proposed in 1986 in Special Rapporteur Sucharitkul's eighth and final report as draft article 26(1).[1] The provision was stated in merely facultative terms and offered several equal alternatives for service of process, namely in accordance with any special arrangement or international convention

[1] See Eighth report Sucharitkul, 31–2.

binding on the forum State and the intended recipient State (referred to as 'the State concerned') or transmitted by registered mail requiring a signed receipt or through diplomatic channels addressed and dispatched to the head of the Ministry of Foreign Affairs of the latter State.

The Drafting Committee, however, favoured a mandatory formulation, replacing the words 'may be effected' with 'shall be effected'. As regards the methods of service of process, it preferred a more involved, hierarchical menu of options according to which service was to be effected in accordance with any special arrangement for service between the claimant and the State concerned; or, and only failing such an arrangement, in accordance with any international convention binding on the forum State and the State concerned; or, and only failing both prior avenues, by transmission through diplomatic channels to the Ministry of Foreign Affairs of the latter; or, and only failing all of the foregoing, and if permitted by the law of both the forum State and the State concerned, by registered mail, requiring a signed receipt, addressed to the head of the Ministry of Foreign Affairs of the latter, or by any other means. It was in this form that was what by then numbered draft article 24(1) was adopted by the ILC on first reading in 1986.[2]

Draft article 24(1) as adopted on first reading attracted few comments from governments. The Nordic countries, however, observed that special arrangements between the claimant and the State concerned for service of process could not be taken into account in many national legal systems without changing the rules of civil procedure, which was unlikely to happen.[3]

In the light of the foregoing concern, Special Rapporteur Ogiso proposed that the express reference to service of process in accordance with any special arrangement between the forum State and the State concerned be deleted.[4] What was finally adopted on second reading in 1991 as draft article 20(1) was a simplified version of Special Rapporteur Ogiso's text.[5] It confirmed the latter's preference for service in accordance with any applicable international convention binding on both forum and concerned States; but, in the absence[6] of such a convention, process could be served either through diplomatic channels to the Ministry of Foreign Affairs of the State concerned or by any other means accepted by the State concerned and not precluded by the law of the forum State.

The text of draft article 20(1) remained unchanged until 2004, when it was substantially amended by the Ad Hoc Committee on Jurisdictional Immunities of States and Their Property.[7] The Ad Hoc Committee re-introduced reference to any special arrangement between the claimant and the State concerned, to the extent that it was not precluded by the law of the forum State, and posited it as a preferred method of service alongside any applicable international convention. If and only if no international convention applied and no special arrangement had been made, service of process was to be effected by transmission through diplomatic channels to the Ministry of Foreign Affairs of the State concerned or by any other means accepted by the State concerned, if not precluded by the law of the forum State. It was in this form that what had by then

[2] See Report ILC, thirty-eighth session, 20.

[3] See 'Comments and observations received from Governments', UN doc. A/CN.4/410 and Add. 1–5, *YILC 1988*, vol. II(1), 45, 78, para. 13 (Nordic States).

[4] See Third report Ogiso, 20–1.

[5] Report ILC, forty-third session, 59.

[6] The expression 'in the absence of' was preferred to 'failing', as had appeared in previous texts.

[7] See 2004 report Ad Hoc Committee, annex, 13 (art. 22(1) Draft UNCSI).

become Article 22(1) passed into the Convention as adopted by the General Assembly later that same year.

Paragraph 2 of Article 22, dealing with receipt of documents, underwent amendment following its adoption by the ILC on first reading in 1986 only insofar as this was consequential on amendments to paragraph 1. Paragraphs 3 and 4 as eventually included in the Convention are identical to the drafts adopted on first reading.

3. Key Points

3.1 Article 22(1) and (2)

A. 'State'

Article 22(1) specifies how service of process is to be effected in a proceeding against a 'State', and a 'State' for these purposes refers not only to a State as such but also to any of the emanations of a State enumerated in the definition of 'State' in Article 2(1)(*b*) of the Convention. In other words, whenever any entity or individual qualifying as a foreign 'State' under Article 2(1)(*b*) is to be named as a respondent to proceedings governed by the Convention, service must be effected in accordance with Article 22(1). Unlike the FSIA (US),[8] the SIA (Can),[9] and the FSIL (Isr),[10] the Convention makes no separate provision for service of initiating process on an agency, instrumentality, or other entity of a State within the meaning of Article 2(1)(*b*)(iii).

B. 'shall be effected'

Article 22(1) embodies a mandatory rule. In order for proceedings regulated by the Convention to be instituted effectively, the writ or other relevant document 'shall' (that is, must) be served on the State concerned in accordance with the menu of options specified in the provision. Service by another means is to be treated by the State party of the forum as ineffective to institute proceedings under the Convention. The mandatory specification of the method or methods of service of process against a State is a common feature of international[11] and national[12] legal instruments on State immunity, although not all of the latter follow this pattern.[13]

The Convention is silent on where the burden of proof lies in any challenge to the effectiveness of service on the State concerned. But it stands to reason, as has been found to be the case *mutatis mutandis* under the FSIA (US),[14] that it is incumbent on the claimant to establish that service was in accordance with Article 22(1).

C. Type and form of initiating process

Article 22(1) speaks of service of process 'by writ or other document instituting a proceeding against a State'. The text was drafted in intentionally unprescriptive terms

[8] See s. 1608(*b*) FSIA (US). [9] See s. 9(3) and (4) SIA (Can).

[10] See s. 13(*d*) FSIL (Isr). [11] See Art. 16(1) and (2) ECSI.

[12] See s. 12(1) SIA (UK); s. 13(1) SIO (Pak); s. 13(1) FStIA (SA); s. 14(1) SIA (Sing); s.13(*a*) FSIL (Isr). Ss. 23–5 FStIA (Aus) provide claimants with the mandatory choice of one of two equal options. See also now, in implementation of Art. 22(1) UNCSI, s. 20(1) ACJJFS (Jpn).

[13] See s. 9(1) SIA (Can), the merely facultative character of which was stressed in *United States v Friedland*, 120 ILR 417, 451 (Can (Ontario CoJ) 1998).

[14] See eg *Seramur v Saudi Arabian Airlines*, 934 F.Supp. 48, 50 (US (EDNY) 1996).

to cater for the wide variety of documents by which court proceedings are initiated under the respective national laws of potential States parties. The type and form of document to be used is a question for the rules of civil procedure of the forum State.[15]

D. *Methods of service of process*

Article 22(1) offers two pairs of alternative methods of service, with a hierarchy as between these two pairs.[16] The ILC commentary explains that '[t]he variety of means available ensures the widest possible flexibility, while protecting the interests of the parties concerned'.[17] This variety stands in sharp contrast to the rigidity of the ECSI, Article 16(2) of which prescribes a single method of effecting service, namely through the diplomatic channel to the Ministry of Foreign Affairs of the State concerned, for onward transmission, where appropriate, to its competent authority.

Article 22(1) indicates that the methods of service cited in subparagraphs (*a*) and (*b*)—respectively, 'in accordance with any applicable international convention binding on the State of the forum and the State concerned' and 'in accordance with any special arrangement for service between the claimant and the State concerned, if not precluded by the law of the State of the forum'—enjoy priority over the two methods referred to in subparagraph (*c*), namely 'transmission through diplomatic channels to the Ministry of Foreign Affairs of the State concerned', as per sub-subparagraph (i), or 'any other means accepted by the State concerned, if not precluded by the law of the State of the forum', as per sub-subparagraph (ii). Subparagraph (*c*) is a default option to which recourse may be had only in the absence of a convention within the meaning of subparagraph (*a*) or a special arrangement within the meaning of subparagraph (*b*).

As between subparagraphs (*a*) and (*b*), in contrast, the choice is an unqualified one: both options are equally open to the claimant. The same goes as between the options provided for in sub-subparagraphs (i) and (ii) of subparagraph (*c*).

(i) Applicable international conventions

Pursuant to subparagraph (*a*) of Article 22(1), service of process may be effected 'in accordance with any applicable international convention binding on the State of the forum and the State concerned'. It is immaterial for the purposes of the provision when the convention was concluded or entered into force.

At present, the multilateral convention most relevant to Article 22(1)(*a*) is the Hague Convention on Service Abroad of Judicial and Extrajudicial Documents in Civil and Commercial Matters (Hague Convention),[18] which is widely,[19] although not unanimously,[20] considered to apply to service of process on foreign States. The main method of service of process under the Hague Convention is transmission of the writ or other

[15] See ILC commentary, draft art. 20, para. 1. See also Expl. Rep. ECSI, para. 60.

[16] Recall section 2.

[17] ILC commentary, draft art. 20, para. 1.

[18] The Hague, 15 November 1965, 658 UNTS 163.

[19] See Permanent Bureau of the Hague Conference on Private International Law, *Practical Handbook on the Operation of The Hague Service Convention* (3rd edn) (The Hague: HCCH Publications, 2006), 13, relying on *VS v Delsman*, NJ 1998, 887 (Nth (SC) 1997) and *Ohntrup v Kurumu*, 1992 US Dist. LEXIS 271 (US (ED Pa) 1992).

[20] See the position of Germany, cited in B.A. Ristau, *International Judicial Assistance: Civil and Commercial* (Washington: International Law Institute, 2000), vol. I, Part IV, 154–6.

document instituting proceedings through a designated 'Central Authority' of the foreign State.[21]

(ii) Special arrangements

Pursuant to subparagraph (*b*) of Article 22(1), service of process may be effected 'in accordance with any special arrangement for service between the claimant and the State concerned, if not precluded by the law of the State of the forum'. It is worth underlining in this regard between whom the special arrangement in question must have been agreed. Whereas any international convention as per subparagraph (*a*) must be between the State concerned and the forum State (and perhaps other States as well), a special arrangement as per subparagraph (*b*) must be agreed between the State concerned and the claimant. As a corollary, whereas an international convention within the meaning of subparagraph (*a*) will, perhaps needless to say, be an international legal instrument, an agreement on a special arrangement for service within the meaning of subparagraph (*b*) will be governed by national law, to which questions as to its effectiveness, in particular whether it need be in writing, and the construction of its terms must be directed. This national law does not need to be the national law of the forum State.

The only limitation placed by Article 22(1)(*b*) on the arrangements it envisages is that they not be precluded by the law of the forum State. That is, whatever national law may govern the agreement on a special arrangement for service of initiating process, the method of service specified in the arrangement must not, if it is to be effective for the purposes of the Convention, be inconsistent with the forum State's rules of civil procedure. Within these parameters, the terms of the arrangement are a matter for the claimant and the State concerned, and can obviously be diverse,[22] although in practice such arrangements tend to take the form of the appointment of an independent process agent. In this regard, a tribunal has pointed out that, '[w]hen a Party agrees to accept service [by way of an independent process agent], it takes upon itself the responsibility of maintaining sufficient link with the designated agent to ensure that process served upon the agent is brought to its attention'.[23]

In practice, States have proved reluctant to agree to special arrangements for service on them of initiating process.[24]

(iii) Default options

(a) Transmission through diplomatic channels to the Ministry of Foreign Affairs of State concerned

If neither of the two methods indicated in subparagraphs (*a*) and (*b*) of Article 22(1) is available, service of process may be effected, in accordance with Article 22(1)(*c*)(i), by transmission of the writ or other initiating document through diplomatic channels to the Ministry of Foreign Affairs of the State concerned. Process cannot be served, at least in accordance with Article 22(1)(*c*)(i), on that State's diplomatic or consular premises in the forum State. In accordance with Article 22(2), service of process by means of

[21] See Arts 2–6 Hague Convention.

[22] See J.W. Dellapenna, *Suing Foreign Governments and their Corporations* (2nd edn) (New York: Transnational Publishers, 2003), 277.

[23] *A.N. International Bank plc v Republic of Zambia and others*, 118 ILR 602, 609 (UK (EWHC) 1997).

[24] See A. Dickinson, R. Lindsay, and P. Loonam, *State Immunity: Selected Materials and Commentary* (Oxford: Oxford University Press, 2004), 386.

transmission through diplomatic channels is deemed to be effected by receipt of the initiating document by the Ministry of Foreign Affairs of the State concerned.

Aware of the need to respect the inviolability of diplomatic and consular premises that underpins the rules on service of process in the context of proceedings against a foreign State, national courts have generally applied domestic rules analogous to Article 22(1)(*c*)(i) strictly. In *Alberti v Empresa Nicaraguense de la Carne*, for instance, the US Court of Appeals for the Seventh Circuit relied on the legislative history of the FSIA (US) to hold as defective service of process on a foreign State's permanent diplomatic mission to the US.[25] Similarly, in *Kuwait Airways Corporation v Iraqi Airways Company and Republic of Iraq*, Evans J held that '[i]n no sense is a diplomatic mission in a foreign State the same as the Ministry of Foreign Affairs of the sending State'.[26] Strict compliance similarly means that, should it not be possible to transmit the writ or other document through the diplomatic channel, process has to be served through another method under Article 22(1)(*c*)(ii).[27] At the same time, in the event that the forum State and the State concerned do not have diplomatic relations, there is nothing in Article 22(1)(*c*)(i) to rule out the not-uncommon practice of recourse for the purposes of service of process to the good offices of the diplomatic representation of a third State.

Article 22(1)(*c*)(i) and (2), like Article 16 ECSI, do not stipulate that the State concerned is obliged to accept service of process, although it is certainly arguable that an undertaking to do so is implied by a State party's acceptance of the terms of Article 22 as manifest in its participation in the Convention.[28] Nor, however, do they stipulate that the writ or other initiating document must be 'accepted' by the Ministry of Foreign Affairs of the State concerned, as long as it is received there. The terminological distinction may well be significant, as in effect it was held to be in the English case of *Pocket Kings Ltd v Safenames Ltd and another*, where the refusal by the US Department of State to accept the initiating process served on it in Washington, DC by the Pro Consul at the UK's embassy there did not prevent the English Court of Chancery from ruling that the document had been 'received at the Ministry' for the purposes of section 12(1) SIA (UK).[29]

(b) Any other means accepted by State concerned and not precluded by law of forum State

The other default option offered in Article 22(1)(*c*) as an alternative to service through diplomatic channels is, in the words of sub-subparagraph (ii), 'by any other means accepted by the State concerned, if not precluded by the law of the State of the forum'. An example might be service by registered mail.

[25] 705 F.2d 250 (US (7th Cir) 1983).

[26] [1995] 3 All ER 694, 703–4.

[27] See eg *Westminster City Council v Islamic Republic of Iran*, 108 ILR 557 (UK (EWHC) 1986).

[28] Expl. Rep. ECSI, para. 60, elaborates: 'The Foreign Ministry is obliged to accept writs served on it even if it believes that the proceedings brought against the State are unjustified, that the court is not competent to entertain the proceedings, or that the defendant State may claim immunity. On the other hand, by accepting the documents, the defendant State in no way renounces its right to invoke its grounds of defence or to claim immunity.'

[29] *Pocket Kings Ltd v Safenames Ltd and another* [2010] Ch 438, 449–50, paras 25–26 (UK (EWHC) 2009). For its part, s. 24(3) FStIA (Aus) deems service to be effected when initiating process has been 'delivered to', rather than 'received by', the Ministry of Foreign Affairs of the State concerned. S. 9(5) SIA (Can) goes even further by deeming service to have been effected when the Canadian Deputy Minister of Foreign Affairs or someone designated by him or her 'certifies to the relevant court that the copy of the document has been transmitted to the foreign State'.

3.2 Article 22(3)

Article 22(3) requires that the writ or other document instituting a proceeding against a State under the Convention be accompanied, if necessary, by a translation into the official language or one of the official languages of the State concerned.[30] The text reproduces almost verbatim Article 16(2) ECSI.[31] The words 'if necessary', on which the obligation laid down in Article 22(3) hangs, were inserted by the Drafting Committee without recorded discussion, and no explanation of them is given in the ILC commentary. The most obvious and convincing meaning of 'if necessary' in this context is 'if the language used in the writ or other document instituting the proceeding against that State is not the official language or one of the official languages of the State concerned'. While there is scope to argue for a functional approach based on the actual familiarity of relevant persons linked to the State concerned with the language used in the document,[32] the argument is not convincing, not least because of the contingency—and therefore the unpredictability and resultant potential for endless squabbling over the effectiveness of service—involved.

Like Article 16(2) ECSI, Article 22(3) of the Convention does not require that the translation be certified or the like. The inclusion of such a certificate may make practical and tactical sense, but it is clearly not mandatory. The Explanatory Report to the ECSI states in this regard:

> The translation which must accompany the documents referred to in paragraph 2 is solely for purposes of information. The Convention does not require the translator to have any special qualifications or that the accuracy of the translation be confirmed by a duly authorised person.[33]

In contrast, section 24(*c*)(ii) FStIA (Aus) demands that the translation be accompanied by a certificate in the official language of the State concerned 'signed by the translator, setting out particulars of his or her qualifications as a translator and stating that the translation is an accurate translation of the initiating process'.

3.3 Article 22(4)

In accordance with Article 22(4), if the State concerned 'enters an appearance on the merits' in a proceeding instituted against it, it may not thereafter assert that service of process did not comply with the provisions of paragraphs 1 and 3 of Article 22. The corresponding provision of the ECSI, namely Article 16(6),[34] and of the FStIA

[30] When ratifying the Convention, Switzerland made the following 'Interpretative declaration concerning article 22, paragraph 3': 'If the State [i.e. the entity qualifying as the "State" for the purposes of the Convention under Article 2(1)(*b*)] concerned is a Swiss canton, Switzerland considers that "official language" should be understood as the official language or one of the official languages of the canton in which process is to be served.' See C.N.223.2010.TREATIES–2 (Switzerland: Ratification), 20 April 2010.

[31] Translation is also required by s. 1608(3) and (4) FSIA (US) and by s. 24(2)(*c*)(i) FStIA (Aus).

[32] See eg, in the context of the translation requirement in the FSIA (US), *Sherer v Construcciones Aeronauticas, S.A.*, 987 F.2d 1246 (US (6th Cir.) 1993) and *Straub v Green, Inc.*, 38 F.3d 448, 453 (US (9th Cir.) 1994).

[33] Expl. Rep. ECSI, para. 60.

[34] Art. 16(6) ECSI reads: 'A Contracting State which appears in the proceedings is deemed to have waived any objection to the method of service.' Expl. Rep. ECSI, para. 66, explains: 'Paragraph 6 refers only to the method of service of the document by which the proceedings are instituted. It does not prevent a State from appearing, in accordance with the procedure in force in the State of the forum, in order to claim that it had not been allowed the time for entering an appearance provided for in paragraphs 4 and 5.'

(Aus)[35] speak appropriately in terms of waiver of objection to service. The ILC commentary elaborates:

Paragraph 4 [of Article 22] provides that a State which has entered an appearance on the merits, that is to say without contesting any question of jurisdiction or procedure, cannot subsequently be heard to raise any objection based on non-compliance with the service of process provisions of paragraphs 1 and 3. The reason for the rule is self-evident. By entering an appearance on the merits, the defendant State effectively concedes that it has had timely notice of the proceeding instituted against it. The defendant State is, of course, entitled at the outset to enter a conditional appearance or to raise a plea as to jurisdiction.[36]

The qualification 'on the merits' was inserted by the ILC's Drafting Committee to clarify that, for the purposes of Article 22(4), 'appearance' does not include 'appearance for the sole purpose of challenging the jurisdiction of the court'.[37] This is in line with the understanding of the notion of 'the merits' in the context of Article 8(1)(*b*), which deals with the effect on a State's immunity from jurisdiction of its taking any step 'relating to the merits'.

At the same time, it is open to doubt whether the commentary is correct to exclude the entry of a plea as to jurisdiction from the concept of an appearance on the merits as used specifically in Article 22(4), at least if by 'a plea as to jurisdiction' and 'contesting... jurisdiction' the commentary is referring to the State concerned's submission that it is entitled to immunity from the proceeding. While this understanding of the notion of 'the merits' is clearly correct for the purposes of Article 8(1)(*b*), it might be thought for the purposes of Article 22(4) that by entering a plea as to jurisdiction—that is, by arguing before the court for its immunity from the proceeding—the State has implicitly accepted that the proceeding has been instituted, which in turn implies that the writ or other document instituting the proceeding was served effectively. In this light, it might be argued that, for the specific purposes of Article 22(4), 'the merits' include any question as to jurisdiction. It is telling in this connection that Article 16(6) ECSI refers to the State's appearance not 'on the merits' but simply 'in the proceedings'. The same is the case under the respective provisions of the SIA (UK), the SIO (Pak), the FStIA (SA), the FStIA (Aus), and the SIA (Sing).[38]

But a traditional canon of treaty interpretation militates in favour of the consistent construction of a term throughout the same treaty; and although a canon of construction is not a rule, and can be outweighed by more compelling considerations, the text of Article 22(4) of the Convention, read in the light of Article 8(1)(*b*), does appear to militate against any argument for an expanded understanding of the term 'the merits' for the purposes of challenges to the effectiveness of service of process under the Convention. In short, Article 22(4) does not seem to preclude the State concerned from challenging the effectiveness of service of process on it even after appearing before the court to assert its immunity.

[35] See s. 26 FStIA (Aus), entitled 'Waiver of objection to service'. The text, however, of the provision does not use this language.

[36] ILC commentary, draft art. 20, para. 4.

[37] Summary record 1969th ILC meeting, *YILC 1986*, vol. I, 173, 180, para. 68.

[38] See s. 12(3) SIA (UK); s. 13(3) SIO (Pak); s. 13(3) FStIA (SA); s. 26 FStIA (Aus) ('Where a foreign State enters an appearance in a proceeding without making an objection in relation to the service of the initiating process... '); s. 14(3) SIA (Sing).

4. Evaluation

Article 22 establishes a flexible, workable framework for service of process on a foreign State for the purpose of instituting proceedings under the Convention. The menu of options it specifies takes balanced account of the autonomy and interests of the three potential 'stakeholders', namely the claimant, the intended respondent State, and the intended forum State. While it remains to be seen, in relation to the default rule laid down in Article 22(1)(*c*)(i), how the courts of State parties construe 'receipt' of the documents by the Ministry of Foreign Affairs of the State concerned, Article 22 as a whole is for the most part clear, and should pose few problems of interpretation and application.

Article 23

TARCISIO GAZZINI

Article 23

Default judgment

1. A default judgment shall not be rendered against a State unless the court has found that:
   (*a*) the requirements laid down in article 22, paragraphs 1 and 3, have been complied with;
   (*b*) a period of not less than four months has expired from the date on which the service of the writ or other document instituting a proceeding has been effected or deemed to have been effected in accordance with article 22, paragraphs 1 and 2; and
   (*c*) the present Convention does not preclude it from exercising jurisdiction.
2. A copy of any default judgment rendered against a State, accompanied if necessary by a translation into the official language or one of the official languages of the State concerned, shall be transmitted to it through one of the means specified in article 22, paragraph 1, and in accordance with the provisions of that paragraph.
3. The time-limit for applying to have a default judgment set aside shall not be less than four months and shall begin to run from the date on which the copy of the judgment is received or is deemed to have been received by the State concerned.

1. Introduction

A claimant in a proceeding against a State under the Convention may have occasion to request the court to render judgment against that State in default of the latter's appearance before the court. This may occur where the State concerned has acknowledged or not objected to service on it of the writ or other document instituting the proceeding, but has subsequently failed to appear. It may also transpire where the State has failed to convince the court that service was defective[1] and has subsequently chosen either not to appear or to terminate its appearance before the court. The overarching concern of Article 23 of the Convention is to ensure that the immunity of a State provided for in the Convention is not undermined through judgments against it in default of appearance.

Article 23(1) stipulates the conditions under which a default judgment may be rendered against a State in proceedings under the Convention. It specifies three things: that the requirements of Article 22 in relation to service of initiating process on the State must have been satisfied; that four months must have elapsed between the effecting of service and judgment; and that the State must not enjoy immunity from the proceeding in accordance with Parts II and III of the Convention. Article 23(2) requires that a copy

[1] Whether and under what conditions a State may challenge the effectiveness of service of process depends on the *lex fori*.

of any default judgment be transmitted to the State concerned via one of the methods specified in Article 22 in relation to service of process.

Article 23(3) establishes a four-month minimum period within which a State may apply to have a default judgment against it set aside. Any other procedural questions relating to default judgments—such as whether the claimant must make out a *prima facie* case, whether a judgment debtor may apply to have a default judgment set aside, and, indeed, whether the courts of the forum State are empowered to render default judgments in the first place—are matters for the *lex fori* alone.

While prescribing conditions under which a default judgment may be rendered against a State in proceedings under the Convention, Article 23 does not regulate the legal effects of such a judgment. This, again, is a matter for the law of the forum state.

2. Drafting History

Article 23 underwent very few changes over the course of its drafting.[2] From the discussions within the ILC and the comments received from governments, it is clear that the provision enjoyed broad support, both in terms of its rationale and its formulation of the conditions under which a default judgment may be rendered. This should come as no surprise, as the provision draws in many respects on national legislation. Three changes nonetheless deserve mention.

The first concerns the opening sentence of paragraph 1. Until 1991, the relevant provision stated that a default judgment could not be rendered 'except on proof of compliance' with the required conditions for delivery of such a judgment.[3] In 1991, the Drafting Committee reformulated this to read that a default judgment could not be rendered 'unless the court has ascertained that' the required conditions for such a judgment have been satisfied.[4] As explained by the Chairman of the Committee, the change was intended 'to indicate clearly that it was incumbent on the court to ascertain that the required conditions were met and that it had to do so prior to rendering its judgment'.[5] In the final version of the 1991 draft articles, the verb 'to find' was preferred to the verb 'to ascertain',[6] possibly to emphasize further the proactive role to be played by the court.

The second change concerns the time-limits set in paragraphs (1)(*b*) and (3), the first specifying the lapse of time required from service of process to default judgment, the latter granting a 'grace period' for applying to have a default judgment set aside. Special Rapporteur Sucharitkul's initial draft provision set no firm time-limits. It merely required the lapse of a reasonable period between service of process and judgment on default, and indicated that any time for applying to have a judgment set aside began to run from the date on which the judgment was received by the State

[2] The provision goes back to Seventh report Sucharitkul, 45–6, paras 126–129, where the Special Rapporteur proposed a draft art. 26 addressing, in one provision, questions relating to service of process and default judgment. Following initial discussion, the two issues were separated out into two provisions (draft arts 24[25] and 25[26]) and regulated in more detail. For the revised draft provision and very brief debate, see summary record 1969th ILC meeting, *YILC 1986*, vol. I, 173, 182.

[3] See eg Report ILC, thirty-eighth session, 12, draft art. 25 and Report ILC, forty-third session, 60–1, draft art. 21.

[4] Summary record 2221th ILC meeting, *YILC 1991*, vol. I, 88, 92, para. 38.

[5] Summary record 2221th ILC meeting (n. 4), 92, para. 39.

[6] Report ILC, forty-third session, 60–1.

concerned.[7] But draft article 25 as provisionally adopted on first reading introduced a minimum of three months, as—in the words of the Special Rapporteur—'[i]t had been considered preferable to specify a time-limit, rather than rely on the subjective notion of a period of time subject to a reasonable extension' or on the applicable domestic law.[8] Since 'it might take over a month for the document instituting the proceeding to reach the authorities of the State concerned and as much time for those authorities' reaction to reach the forum State',[9] the Commission decided to extend the minimum period to four months.[10] No further modifications were proposed, and the four-month minimum period was kept in the final text of Article 23.

The third change relates to the conditions under which a default judgment may be rendered. The ILC's first-reading text mentioned only two conditions, namely compliance with the requirements on service of process and expiration of the mandatory time period (then three months).[11] In their comments on the first-reading text, both the Federal Republic of Germany and the German Democratic Republic had expressed concern that this might be construed to permit a default judgment merely by virtue of due service of process.[12] In response, the ILC decided to add what was to become paragraph (1)*(c)*, clarifying that, even where the State concerned did not appear, the court would have to ascertain that it would be permissible under the Convention to exercise jurisdiction.[13] In his brief explanation, the Chairman of the Drafting Committee noted that this addition 'had no bearing on the question of the competence of the court, which was a matter for each legal system to determine'.[14]

3. Key Points

3.1 'default judgment'

The term 'default judgment' is not defined in Article 23 of the Convention,[15] but it is clear that it is to be given an autonomous, 'international' meaning. That is, the meaning

[7] Seventh report Sucharitkul, 46, para. 129 (draft art. 26(3) and (4)).

[8] Summary record 1969th ILC meeting (n. 2), 182.

[9] Summary record 2221st ILC meeting (n. 4), 92, para. 39 (Chairman of the Drafting Committee).

[10] See Report ILC, forty-third session, 60–1.

[11] Report ILC, thirty-eighth session, 12. The suggestion came from Stephen McCaffrey, but no reasons were recorded. See summary record 2221st ILC meeting (n. 4), 92, para. 42.

[12] See 'Comments and observations received from Governments', UN doc. A/CN.4/410 and Add. 1–5, *YILC 1988*, vol. II(1), 45, 72, para. 33 (FRG) and 67, para. 29 (GDR). According to the Federal Republic of Germany, '[t]he defendant State would then have to claim immunity in court although it may not be brought before a court. This situation is intolerable and should be clarified by added the wording "if the court has jurisdiction"'. It is worth noting that, prior to the adoption of the Convention, the US Court of Appeals for the Eleventh Circuit was similarly concerned to see that the FSIA (US) 'provide foreign states protection from unfounded default judgment rendered solely upon a procedural default'. See *Compania Interamericana Export-Import, S.A. v Compania Dominicana de Aviacion*, 88 F.3d 948, 951 (US (11th Cir.) 1996).

[13] See eg Preliminary report Ogiso, 120, para. 254 (Special Rapporteur's recommendation); summary record 2221st ILC meeting (n. 4), 92, para. 40 (summary of changes by Chairman of the Drafting Committee); and Report ILC, forty-third session, 60–1 (text of provision on second reading).

[14] Summary record 2221st ILC meeting (n. 4), 92, para. 40.

[15] The same is the case with Art. 12(1) ECSI.

of the term is not to be limited to the meaning ascribed to it by any particular national legal system. Nor, for that matter, is Article 23 inapplicable simply because the law of the forum State does not use the term 'default judgment'. As employed in Article 23, the expression 'default judgment' refers generically to a judgment rendered on the failure or refusal of the respondent to appear in the proceeding.

3.2 'rendered against a State'

In contrast to Article 16(2) ECSI, which speaks of a default judgment 'against a State which was defendant in the proceedings', Article 23(1) and (2) of the Convention refer simply to a default judgment rendered 'against a State'. Moreover, Article 6(2) indicates that a proceeding under the Convention is considered to have been instituted 'against [a] State' if the State concerned is either named as a party to the proceeding, as per subparagraph (*a*), or, as per subparagraph (*b*), 'is not named as a party to the proceeding but the proceeding in effect seeks to affect the property, rights, interests or activities of that . . . State'. Nonetheless, the context of the expression 'rendered against a State' as used in Article 23(1) and (2)—in the form of, first, the cross-references in both provisions to Article 22's rules on service of process on a State and, secondly, of Article 23(3), the logic of which would be obscure were Article 22(1) and (2) to refer additionally to an indirectly impleaded State[16]—makes it clear that a default judgment 'rendered against a State' within the meaning of Article 23 does not include a default judgment that merely 'affect[s] the property, rights, interests or activities' of a State not named as respondent to the proceeding, but is limited to a judgment rendered against a respondent State. This construction is supported by the ILC commentary to the identically-worded draft article 21, which speaks of 'the defendant State'[17] and of the non-appearance of the State itself.[18]

3.3 Article 23(1)

Article 23(1) lays down three conditions that must be satisfied before a court of a State party may render a default judgment against another State party in a proceeding under the Convention. Any other, more general requirements for the rendering of a default judgment, such as the need for the claimant to make out a *prima facie* case, are matters for the law of the forum State.

The purpose of Article 23(1), as its negative formulation emphasizes, is to clarify that, if the domestic law of a State party permits default judgments, these can be rendered in accordance with the Convention only if the requirements of the three subparagraphs are complied with. While the competence of domestic courts to render default judgments is governed by the *lex fori*, Article 23(1) establishes conditions for the internationally-permissible exercise of such competence and imposes on States parties an obligation to ensure that their courts respect them.

[16] While Art. 23(3) does not dictate that the *lex fori* have any particular content, it nonetheless tends to be the case under national law that only the respondent to the proceeding that gave rise to a judgment in default is permitted to apply to set aside that judgment; and, where the State concerned is not that respondent, it makes little sense for the time-limit for an application by the person who *is* the respondent to run from the receipt of a copy of the judgment by the State.

[17] See ILC commentary, draft art. 23, paras 2 and 4.

[18] See ILC commentary, draft art. 23, para. 2.

The first, twofold condition, laid down in subparagraph (*a*) of Article 23(1), is that the document which initiates process must have been served on the State concerned in accordance with Article 22(1) and that the requirement in Article 22(3) as to translation into the official language or one of the official languages of the State concerned has, where necessary, been satisfied. Secondly, as per subparagraph (*b*), a period of at least four months[19] must have elapsed from the date on which service was effected or deemed to have been effected.[20] This is intended to grant the State enough time to prepare and file its defence. The period prescribed is a minimum, and nothing prevents domestic courts from extending it in accordance with the *lex fori*.

Thirdly, subparagraph (*c*) of Article 23(1) makes it clear that, should the *lex fori* permit the rendering of such judgments, a court of a State party may render a default judgment in a proceeding brought under the Convention against another State party only in the event that the Convention's rules on a State's immunity from the jurisdiction of the courts of another State do not oblige the forum State to refrain from exercising jurisdiction in the proceeding in question. In short, the Convention's rules on immunity from jurisdiction must be complied with. These rules include Article 6(1), which obliges the forum State to ensure—should it be necessary, as will often be the case in proceedings in default of the respondent State's appearance—that the court determines the question of immunity on its own initiative. All of this stands to reason, given that proceedings in default of appearance are no less proceedings, and, subject to the exceptions provided for in Parts II and III of the Convention, a State party enjoys immunity, as per Article 5 of the Convention, from proceedings in the courts of another State party.

3.4 Article 23(2)

Article 23(2) requires that a copy of any default judgment rendered in proceedings against a State under the Convention be transmitted to that State via one of the methods specified in Article 22 in relation to service of process and in accordance with the requirements laid down in the provision.[21] While subject to identical requirements under the Convention, service of process and transmission of a copy of a default judgment remain distinct procedural stages.

The object of Article 23(2) is to ensure that the State receives notice of the judgment rendered against it, to enable it to comply, should it wish and the *lex fori* allow, to have the judgment set aside and to defend, should it wish, any subsequent proceeding for the execution of the judgment against its property. Where the default judgment is reasoned, its provision to the State has the collateral benefit of enabling the latter to prepare better its submissions in support of any application it may make for the setting aside of the judgment.

3.5 Article 23(3)

Article 23(3) requires that any time-limit imposed on the making of an application to set aside a default judgment rendered against a State in a proceeding under the Convention

[19] *Cf* Art. 16(4) ECSI, specifying a minimum period of only two months.

[20] Art. 22(2) of the Convention provides that service is deemed to be effected by receipt of the documents by the Ministry of Foreign Affairs of the State concerned. See the commentary to Art. 22(2) UNCSI.

[21] For an outline and analysis of these methods, see the commentary to Art. 22(1) UNCSI.

be at least four months, calculated from the date on which the copy of the default judgment is received or deemed to have been received by the State. Once again, the four-month period specified is a minimum. A court may always, in accordance with the *lex fori*, require a longer period. As observed by the ILC, Article 23(3) aims at ensuring 'effective communication with the State concerned and to allow adequate opportunities to the defendant State to apply to have a default judgment set aside'.[22]

The obligation in Article 23(3) is premised on the provision in the first place by the law of the forum State of a procedure for applying to have a default judgment set aside. Should no such procedure exist under the *lex fori*, Article 23(3) does not, on its face, oblige the forum State to afford one.

3.6 Execution of a default judgment

Article 23 is silent on the question of the execution of default judgments. The question is governed, as far as the UNCSI is concerned, by Article 19, dealing with immunity from post-judgment measures of constraint, as supplemented by Article 21.

4. Evaluation

While it is undisputed that 'the interests of justice are best served by trials on the merits, not by default',[23] the domestic law of many States permits default judgments against foreign States. Under the Convention, the competence of a court to render judgment in default remains a matter for the *lex fori*. Article 23 applies only if such competence exists.

Article 23 successfully strikes a balance between the interest of the claimant in having the case adjudicated, even if the State concerned is reluctant to appear before the court, and the need to protect the rights and prerogatives of the State concerned. By imposing, as a matter of international law, a clear timeframe and basic conditions, which are uncontroversial and largely reflect those found in most national legal systems, Article 23 permits domestic courts to render default judgment in a manner respectful of the interests of all actors involved.

[22] Report ILC, forty-third session, 61.

[23] *Tohme v Sebaaly*, 2008 WL 878770, 2 (US (ED Mich) 2008).

Article 24

Tarcisio Gazzini

Article 24

Privileges and immunities during court proceedings

1. Any failure or refusal by a State to comply with an order of a court of another State enjoining it to perform or refrain from performing a specific act or to produce any document or disclose any other information for the purposes of a proceeding shall entail no consequences other than those which may result from such conduct in relation to the merits of the case. In particular, no fine or penalty shall be imposed on the State by reason of such failure or refusal.
2. A State shall not be required to provide any security, bond or deposit, however described, to guarantee the payment of judicial costs or expenses in any proceeding to which it is a respondent party before a court of another State.

1. Introduction

While judicial proceedings involving foreign States remain in principle governed by the *lex fori*, Article 24 grants foreign States certain privileges and immunities, which flow from their status as sovereign entities. It does so in two different ways.

Article 24(1) excludes sanctions for non-compliance with court orders. It leaves unaffected the competence of courts to issue, in accordance with domestic law, orders enjoining foreign States to perform a specific act or to produce any document or disclose any other information for the purposes of a proceeding. What it prohibits is the imposition of coercive measures if the foreign State fails, or refuses, to comply with such orders.

Article 24(2) singles out, and prohibits, one particular measure of coercion: it exempts foreign States appearing before the courts of another State from the obligation to provide any security, bond, or deposit, however described, to guarantee the payment of judicial costs or expenses.

2. Drafting History

Article 24 has maintained its essential content throughout its drafting history, although it has gone through a few changes.

2.1 Article 24(1)

What was to become Article 24(1) initially took the form of the first two paragraphs of draft article 27 proposed in Special Rapporteur Sucharitkul's Seventh Report, entitled 'Procedural Privileges'.[1] The two paragraphs provided, respectively, that a State was not

[1] Seventh report Sucharitkul, 46, paras 130–134. As the Commission had not been able to discuss it in 1985, the provision was resubmitted in Eighth report Sucharitkul, 32, para. 40.

required to comply with orders by a foreign court compelling it to perform a specific act or to refrain from specified action and that no fine or penalty could be imposed on a foreign State for failure or refusal to disclose or produce any document or other information for the purpose of the proceedings. When adopting the draft articles on first reading in 1986, the ILC separated out the two elements of the provision.[2] The first paragraph became draft article 26 of the 1986 text, entitled 'Immunity from measures of coercion', which read as follows:

> A State enjoys immunity, in connection with a proceeding before a court of another State, from any measure of coercion requiring it to perform or to refrain from performing a specific act on pain of suffering a monetary penalty.[3]

The second paragraph of Special Rapporteur Sucharitkul's draft article 27 became the first paragraph of draft article 27 of the 1986 text, entitled 'Procedural immunities'. It read:

> Any failure or refusal by a State to produce any document or disclose any other information for the purposes of a proceeding before a court of another State shall entail no consequences other than those which may result from such conduct in relation to the merits of the case. In particular, no fine or penalty shall be imposed on the State by reason of such failure or refusal.[4]

In 1991, the Commission reverted to the initial choice of a single provision, a decision that was apparently taken for reasons of convenience and left the substance of the provision unaffected.[5] The new provision was numbered draft article 22(1) in the 1991 text adopted on second reading and entitled 'Privileges and immunities during court proceedings'. No further changes were proposed after 1991, and draft article 22(1) of the 1991 text eventually became Article 24(1) of the Convention as adopted in 2004.

2.2 Article 24(2)

The drafting of Article 24(2) also proved largely unproblematic. The essence of the provision was agreed on at an early stage, and was subsequently the subject of only one clarification and one substantive change.[6] Like Article 24(1), Article 24(2) was first proposed in Special Rapporteur Sucharitkul's Eighth Report.[7] While the Special Rapporteur had specifically wished to exempt States from the duty to provide a 'security', the Commission clarified that the exemption would cover 'any security, bond or deposit, however described'.[8]

The substantive change concerns the range of States exempted from the duty to provide any security etc under Article 24(2). The exemption was initially intended to apply regardless of whether the foreign State was respondent or claimant. In their comments on the first-reading text, however, some States considered the application

[2] See the explanation provided by the Chairman of the Drafting Committee (Willem Riphagen) and the brief ensuing debate in summary record 1969th ILC meeting, *YILC 1986*, vol. I, 173, 182–3, paras 97–108.

[3] Report ILC, thirty-eighth session, 12.

[4] Report ILC, thirty-eighth session, 12.

[5] See summary record 2221st ILC meeting, *YILC* 1991, vol. I, 88, 93.

[6] See Report ILC, thirty-eighth session, 12 (draft art. 27(2)); Report ILC, forty-third session, 61 (draft art. 22(2)).

[7] Seventh report Sucharitkul, 46, paras 130–134, resubmitted in Eighth report Sucharitkul, 32, para. 40.

[8] See summary record 1969th ILC meeting (n. 2), 182, para. 97.

of the exemption to cases in which the foreign State was the claimant to be unwarranted.[9] The Federal Republic of Germany in particular took the view that

> [t]he non-requirement of security is not justified in cases where the State is acting as claimant... [T]he draft should therefore be restricted to cases in which a State is acting as defendant.[10]

Special Rapporteur Ogiso proposed to amend Article 22(2) accordingly.[11] The Commission, however, limited itself to recording reservations expressed by States in the commentary to draft article 22.[12] It was only during the debates of the Ad Hoc Committee that the change proposed by the Federal Republic of Germany was endorsed.[13]

3. Key Points

3.1 Article 24(1)

A. 'a State'

The application of Article 24(1) is not confined to cases in which the foreign State is respondent to the proceedings—as it is the case of Article 24(2) in its eventual form—or a party to the dispute. As the expression 'a State', without any further qualification, indicates, the provision applies to all State parties to the Convention, even when they are interveners in a dispute or simply a third party ordered to provide documentary or oral evidence. This interpretation, which is supported by the text and not contradicted by the *travaux préparatoires*, is at variance with the position under the ECSI, whose Article 18 is expressly limited to 'any Contracting State party to proceedings'. National legislation on the matter is not fully consistent. For instance, sections 34 and 39(1) FStIA (Aus)—addressing, respectively, orders in general and disclosure in particular—do not qualify the reference to a State for the purpose of privileges and immunities during proceedings.[14] Section 13(1) SIA (UK), in contrast, applies only to States that are parties to the proceedings.

B. 'an order of a court'

Nothing in Article 24(1), or the Convention more generally, prevents a domestic court from issuing, in accordance with the *lex fori*, the types of orders referred to in Article 24(1),

[9] See 'Comments and observations received from Governments', UN doc. A/CN.4/410 and Add. 1–5, *YILC 1988*, vol. II(1), 45, 72, para. 35 and 89–90, para. 37, respectively.

[10] 'Comments and observations' (n. 9), 72, para. 35.

[11] Preliminary report Ogiso, 121, para. 265.

[12] ILC commentary, draft art. 22, para. 5. The commentary was clear that '[t]he procedural immunities provided for in paragraph 2 apply to both plaintiff States and defendant' (ibid.).

[13] See 2004 report Ad Hoc Committee, 14.

[14] See also s. 13 SIA (Can).

either on an application from the private party or on its own initiative. In 1986 the Drafting Committee explained that 'it was not advisable or realistic to prohibit a court from exercising its usual power to order a party to perform or refrain from performing a specific act'.[15] In this light, Article 24(1) merely limits the court's options in response to non-compliance with an order.

As regards the types of orders covered, Article 24(1) adopts a comprehensive approach. It applies to orders enjoining States to perform a certain act, to produce documents, or to disclose other information, as well as to orders requiring States to refrain from certain conduct.[16] Because of the diversity of domestic systems, as regards both terminology and the conditions for the imposition of such orders, the provision uses generic language. The text covers a wide range of orders, among them orders for discovery and for specific performance, as well as what common law systems would refer to as interlocutory injunctions, preliminary injunctions, temporary restraining orders, and the like. Notwithstanding the rubric's use of the phrase 'during proceedings', Article 24(1) applies to both pre-judgment and post-judgment orders.

Article 24(1) is broader than its counterpart in the ECSI (Article 18), which refers only to the disclosure of any documents or other evidence. Domestic legislation, too, is often limited to disclosure, although there are important examples of a comprehensive approach along the lines of Article 22(1) UNCSI.[17]

Among the different orders covered, discovery deserves special mention. Its importance is demonstrated by the fact that it is expressly referred to in Article 24(1), in Article 18 ECSI, and in some national provisions, such as section 39 FStIA (Aus). Discovery orders can give rise to particular problems if issued to determine whether the respondent is immune from suit. On the one hand, a strict limitation on discovery may hinder the claimant's ability to pursue its action against a State. On the other hand, because it is often 'impossible to make a decision concerning subject matter jurisdiction without considering the merits' of the case, a permissive discovery rule may result in a significant encroachment on the State's sovereignty. Article 24(1) imposes no restrictions or conditions on the making of orders for discovery. The matter is for the *lex fori.* Some domestic courts have called for self-restraint in this regard. US courts, for instance, have held that, '[a]t the very least, discovery should be ordered circumspectly and only to verify allegations of specific facts crucial to an immunity determination'.[18]

[15] Statement by the Chairman of the Drafting Committee, summary record 1969th ILC meeting (n. 2), 182.

[16] See summary record 1942nd ILC meeting, *YILC 1986*, vol. I, 4, 8 (Sir Ian Sinclair) and summary record 1944th ILC meeting, *YILC 1986*, vol. I, 15, 16 (Stephen McCaffrey).

[17] See, in particular, ss. 34 and 39 FStIA (Aus).

[18] *Arriba Ltd v Petroleos Mexicanos*, 962 F.2d 528, 534 (US (5th Cir.) 1992). See also *EM Ltd v Republic of Argentina*, 473 F.3d 463, 486 (US (2nd Cir.) 2007); *Kelly v Syria Shell Petroleum Development B.V.*, 213 F.3d 841, 849 (US (5th Cir.) 2000).

C. *'shall entail no consequences'*

Article 24(1) categorically forbids coercive measures imposed on a foreign State in response to its failure to comply with a court order. If the State concerned refuses or fails to comply with such an order, the court must refrain from compelling compliance through the imposition of a fine or other penalty. Nor does Article 24(1) suggest that the State is required to justify its conduct.

In the text adopted on first reading in 1986, the ILC had included a separate provision expressly recognizing the immunity of States from any measure of 'coercion' imposed by a foreign court.[19] Chosen for its breadth, the word 'coercion' was intended to cover 'any court order for specific performance carrying with it the coercive measure of a pecuniary penalty for non-performance of the order'.[20] While the separate provision on measures of 'coercion' was not retained, its gist is embodied in Article 24(1).

D. *'no fine or penalty'*

Fines (that is, pecuniary sanctions) and penalties are obvious negative consequences of non-compliance with a court order and are specifically referred to in the second sentence of Article 24(1).[21] A fine being a species of penalty, the expression 'no fine or *other* penalty' would have been more accurate. Other sorts of penalty would include the committal of a State representative for contempt of court, as referred to in some national legislation ('committal'). The words '[i]n particular' and the broad notion of 'consequences' make clear that the reference to 'fines' and 'penalties' is merely illustrative.

Certain national legislation excludes the imposition of penalties by way of fine or committal in response to a foreign State's failure to comply with an order by a court.[22] In contrast, United States courts have not hesitated to exercise under the FSIA (US) an 'inherent contempt power' permitting them to impose pecuniary sanctions on States that have failed to comply with discovery orders.[23]

E. *'other than those which may result from such conduct in relation to the merits of the case'*

A State's failure to comply with a court order may have a negative impact on its case, insofar as the court may be deprived of information which would have either supported the State's submissions or undermined the claimant's. But this is no more than the natural and unavoidable consequence of the State's conduct and can in no way be equated with a

[19] See Report ILC, thirty-eighth session, 12 (draft art. 26).

[20] Report ILC, thirty-eighth session, 21.

[21] At times, the Commission seemed to draw a strict identity between coercive measures and pecuniary sanctions (sometimes also referred to, as in the French legal system, as *astreinte*). Towards the end of the first reading, the Chairman of the Drafting Committee explained that the coercive nature of the measures prohibited under Art. 24(1) derived from the imposition of a monetary penalty in the event of non-compliance. See summary record 1969th ILC meeting (n. 2), 182.

[22] See eg s. 34 FStIA (Aus).

[23] *FG Hemisphere Associates, LLC v Democratic Republic of Congo*, 637 F.3d 373 (US (DC Cir.) 2011). The US government took the opposite view.

sanction imposed for non-compliance.[24] In acknowledgment of this, Article 24(1) makes clear that the provision does not preclude any consequences for the State 'in relation to the merits of the case' which may result from its failure or refusal to comply with a relevant order of a court of another State. This aspect of Article 24(1) is drafted more precisely than the second sentence of Article 18 ECSI, which provides that 'the court may draw any conclusion it thinks fit from such failure or refusal'.

3.2 Article 24(2)

A. 'A State . . . in any proceeding to which it is a respondent party before a court of another State'

Article 24(2) exempts a State from the obligation to provide any security, bond, or deposit, 'however described', to guarantee the payment of judicial costs or expenses in any proceeding to which it is a respondent before a court of another State. In contrast to Article 24(1), Article 24(2) applies only where the State is a respondent to a proceeding and not where it is the claimant. It is worth noting that Article 24(2) contains no provision equivalent to the second sentence of Article 17 ECSI, pursuant to which '[a] State which is a claimant in the courts of another Contracting State shall pay any judicial costs or expenses for which it may become liable'.

B. 'shall not be required'

Article 24(2) differs in a second way from Article 24(1) in that it does not merely prohibit the imposition of coercive measures in response to the failure or refusal by a State to comply with an order. Instead, it prohibits the court from requiring any form of security from the State in the first place. This prohibition is unqualified. In contrast, under Article 17 ECSI, a court may require a foreign State to provide a security or similar if this could 'have been required in the State of the forum of a national of that State or a person domiciled or resident there'.

C. 'any security, bond or deposit, however described, to guarantee the payment of judicial costs or expenses'

The expression 'any security, bond or deposit, however described, to guarantee the payment of judicial costs or expenses' derives from Article 17 ECSI. It covers all forms of guarantee of the payment of judicial costs and expenses.

3.3 Relationship between Article 24 and other provisions

As Article 24 addresses certain types of coercive measures, its relationship to other provisions of the Convention permitting the use of coercion against a foreign State, notably Articles 18 and 19, needs to be addressed at least briefly. The difference and relationship between Article 24(1) and Articles 18 and 19 of the Convention call for brief elaboration. Which of the two regimes applies depends less on the object against which coercion is sought than on what is ordered.

[24] See ILC commentary, draft art. 22, paras 3 and 4.

Article 24(1) does not prohibit the making of any judicial order against a foreign State. All it does is to prohibit the imposition of any form of sanction on that State in the event that it fails or refuses to comply with any such order that may be made. In contrast, Articles 18 and 19 prohibit, except in specified circumstances, the making and taking of pre-judgment measures of judicial constraint (such as attachment or arrest) and post-judgment measures of judicial constraint (such as attachment, arrest, or execution) against the property of a foreign State or against the foreign State itself in respect of its property.[25] The judicial measures *prima facie* prohibited by Article 19 include orders for specific performance or for the recovery of land, while among the measures *prima facie* prohibited by Article 18 are orders such as a '*Mareva* injunction' (or 'freezing order'), compelling the enjoined party to refrain from dissipating its assets in anticipation of judgment, and an '*Anton Piller* order' (or 'search order'), by which the respondent is compelled to permit the applicant to search its premises or other property and to seize certain of its property as evidence.[26] In short, while Article 24(1) is without prejudice to the making of any such orders, Articles 19 and 18 together prohibit, subject to exception, certain 'order[s] of a court of another State enjoining [a State] to perform or refrain from performing a specific act', in the words of Article 24(1). Conversely, Article 24(1) prohibits the imposition of any form of sanction on a foreign State on account of its failure or refusal to comply with any court order, not just those regulated by Articles 18 and 19, 'enjoining it to perform or refrain from performing a specific act', as well as any court order, insofar as there may be a difference, to produce any document or disclose any other information for the purposes of a proceeding.

4. Evaluation

Article 24 strikes a delicate balance between the legitimate interests of private litigants and the prerogatives and rights of States. On the one hand, it leaves unaffected the competence of a domestic court to make an order against a foreign State for the purposes of a proceeding. On the other hand, it respects the sovereignty of that State by prohibiting the taking of coercive measures against it to compel compliance with any such order and by exempting it, insofar as it may be the respondent party, from the obligation to provide any form of guarantee of payment of judicial costs or expenses.

[25] See, generally, the respective commentaries to Part IV and Articles 18, 19, 20, and 21 UNCSI.

[26] See, respectively, *Mareva Compania Naviera SA v International Bulkcarriers SA* [1975] 2 Lloyd's Rep 509 (UK (EWCA) 1975) and *Anton Piller KG v Manufacturing Processes Limited* [1976] Ch 55 (UK (EWCA) 1975).

PART VI: FINAL CLAUSES

Article 25

Jean d'Aspremont

Article 25

Annex

The annex to the present Convention forms an integral part of the Convention.

1. Introduction

Article 25 constitutes the first of the final provisions of the Convention. It clarifies the status of the 'understandings' annexed to the Convention.[1]

2. Drafting History

Article 25 was added at a very late stage of the drafting process. It was included when the decision to agree on a binding Convention had been taken and it had become clear that, notwithstanding the work of the working groups and Ad Hoc Committee on Jurisdictional Immunities of States and Their Property, some of the provisions of the draft articles on jurisdictional immunities of States and their property remained controversial. Rather than prolonging the debate over the formulation of certain provisions, the Ad Hoc Committee decided in 2003 to elaborate on them in so-called 'understandings'.[2] During its final session the following year, the Committee agreed that these understandings should be annexed to, and should form an integral part of, the eventual Convention.[3] What was to become Article 25 passed unaltered into the Convention as adopted later the same year, having attracted only a single comment in the Sixth Committee.[4]

3. Key Points

Understandings such as those found in the annex to the Convention are intended by and large to clarify the meaning and wider import of potentially contentious provisions of the relevant treaty. Annexed understandings of this sort are not to be confused with unilateral interpretative declarations often made by States when expressing their consent to be bound by a treaty. In contrast to interpretative declarations, annexed understandings are formulated by the drafters of the treaty, are adopted or otherwise finally agreed on simultaneously with the treaty, and, as indicated in the chapeau to Article 31(2) VCLT,[5]

[1] The subsequent discussion deals solely with the formal legal status of the annex. The content of each understanding is examined in the commentary to the operative provision to which it refers.

[2] See 2003 report Ad Hoc Committee, Annex II.

[3] See art. 25 Draft UNCSI.

[4] See Sixth Committee, summary record 13th meeting, UN doc. A/C.6/59/SR.13, 8, para. 49 (PRC).

[5] The chapeau to Art. 31(2) VCLT provides: 'The context for the purpose of the interpretation of a treaty shall comprise, in addition to the text, including its preamble and annexes: . . . '

form part of the text of the treaty. The inclusion of Article 25 UNSCI, which was not strictly necessary, reflects the concern of the Ad Hoc Committee to dispel any doubts as to the status of the understandings annexed to the Convention.

When it comes to interpreting the Convention's operative provisions, Article 31(2) VCLT specifies that the annex—like the preamble and, indeed, the rest of the text—comprises part of the context of the terms for the purposes of Article 31(1) VCLT. In this light, and *pace* the view seemingly expressed by China in the Sixth Committee,[6] the respective understandings can be used as an aid to the interpretation not only of the provisions of the Convention to which they expressly refer but also of other articles.[7]

As an integral part of the treaty, the annex is itself subject to the rules on treaty interpretation codified in the VCLT.

4. Evaluation

Article 25 'anchors' the annexed understandings in the Convention and clarifies their formal legal status. While not strictly necessary, the provision usefully dispels any doubt as to the interplay between the understandings and the operative provisions.

[6] See Sixth Committee (n. 4), 8, para. 49 (PRC): 'Regarding the legal status of the understandings with respect to certain provisions of the Convention, it was true that, according to the draft Convention (article 25), the understandings formed an integral part of the Convention. However, as clearly stated in the chapeau of the understandings, the purpose of the annex was to set out understandings relating only to the provisions concerned. The understandings did not, therefore, share equal legal status with the provisions of the draft Convention.'

[7] While the various understandings are typically limited to matters arising under a specific provision, they could in principle assist in the interpretation of the treaty as a whole. It is not certain that this effect was envisaged by the drafters: see Sixth Committee (n. 4), 8, para. 49 (PRC).

Article 26

Jean d'Aspremont

Article 26

Other international agreements

Nothing in the present Convention shall affect the rights and obligations of States Parties under existing international agreements which relate to matters dealt with in the present Convention as between the parties to those agreements.

1. Introduction

Article 26 stipulates that, in the event of inconsistency between the provisions of the Convention and rights and obligations under any existing international agreement to which States parties to the Convention are parties, the latter are to prevail. In doing so, Article 26 aims not only to avoid placing the Convention's State parties in the invidious position of having to choose which of two or more conflicting treaty obligations to breach but also to safeguard any rights that States parties might enjoy under an existing agreement dealing with the same subject-matter as the Convention.

Savings clauses along the lines of Article 26 are commonly included in multilateral treaties with a view to obviating potential conflicts of norms between the treaty in question and any earlier or later treaties by which State parties may also be bound. A provision to this effect is found in Article 33 ECSI, which posits that nothing in the ECSI 'shall affect existing or future international agreements in special fields which relate to matters dealt with in the [ECSI]'. In contrast to Article 33 ECSI, however, Article 26 of the Convention applies only, on the one hand, to existing but also, on the other, to general agreements.

In preserving rights and obligations deriving from sources of international law extrinsic to the Convention, Article 26 is similar to the various 'without prejudice' clauses found in Article 3.[1] Unlike Article 3, however, it refers to extrinsic international rights and obligations only insofar as they derive from other treaties, not from customary international law as well, and only if those treaties can be characterized as 'existing'. Nonetheless, in terms of their effects, Articles 3 and 26 are analogous. Both provide that the Convention yields to another set of rules if the two prescribe incompatible results, while neither affects the validity of the Convention's provisions, both going instead only to their application.

2. Drafting History

Article 26 was included in the text of what became the Convention only in 2003, at the initiative of the Ad Hoc Committee on Jurisdictional Immunities of States and Their

[1] For details, see the commentary to Art. 3 UNCSI.

Property, which took the view that a general savings clause regulating the relationship between the eventual Convention and international agreements relating to the same subject-matter was necessary.[2] In 2004, the Committee's Chairman proposed specifying that the Convention did not affect 'existing or future international agreements in special fields or of a regional or sub-regional nature which relate to matters dealt with in the . . . convention'.[3] The Committee agreed with the idea of a general savings clause in respect of other treaties binding on the Convention's States parties but modified the Chairman's text significantly.[4] The reference to agreements 'in special fields or of a regional or sub-regional nature' was dropped and the provision restricted to 'existing' agreements. The Committee further specified that what was to be unaffected by the Convention were 'rights and obligations' under such agreements, as distinct from the agreements themselves. Amended in this way, the provision was included in the Convention as Article 12.

3. Key Points

3.1 'international agreements which relate to matters dealt with in the Convention'

Article 26 safeguards the rights and obligations of States parties under existing 'international agreements which relate to matters dealt with in UNCSI. Unlike the Chairman of the Ad Hoc Committee's proposal,[5] the provision does not require that such agreements pertain to a special field or be of a regional or sub-regional character.[6] As a result, Article 26 encompasses a diverse range of treaties touching on jurisdictional immunities of States and their property.

A. The ESCI

The ESCI undoubtedly constitutes an international agreement which relates to matters dealt with in the Convention, *viz* State immunity from jurisdiction and measures of constraint. As among States parties, then, to both the Convention and the ECSI, the ECSI will continue to govern their mutual relations to the extent of any inconsistency between the two treaty regimes.

In March 2006, however, the Committee of Legal Advisers on Public International Law of the Council of Europe (CAHDI) informally agreed that 'in due course' the UNCSI, once in force, should supersede the ESCI.[7] In CAHDI's view, this could be achieved either by way of denunciation of the ECSI in accordance with its Article 40 and Protocol or by way of an agreement in the sense of Article 41 VCLT that, on the entry into force of the UNCSI, the ECSI would cease to apply as among those of its parties that

[2] See 2003 report Ad Hoc Committee, 2, para. 12. See also Sixth Committee, fifty-eighth session, summary record 13th meeting, UN doc. A/C.6/58/SR.13, 3, para. 11 (Mex).

[3] Suggestions of the Chairman, 2, Art. B.

[4] See art. 15 Draft UNCSI.

[5] Recall section 2.

[6] The sole requirement is that an existing international agreement 'relate to matters dealt with in the . . . Convention'.

[7] See CAHDI, 'Interim report of the informal meeting of the parties to the European Convention on State Immunity', 23 March 2006, Council of Europe doc. CM(2006)59, 19 April 2006, Appendix 2.

were parties to the UNCSI.[8] A subsequent meeting of CAHDI in September 2006 concluded, however, that the most straightforward way to proceed was for each party to the ECSI to denounce that Convention once the UNCSI had entered into force.[9] It remains to be seen what transpires in this regard.[10]

B. Specialized agreements and provisions on immunity

While the application of Article 26 to general agreements on State immunity like the ESCI seems uncontroversial, the question arises whether other, more specialized international agreements which address aspects of the jurisdictional immunities of States and their property in particular contexts can also be considered to 'relate to matters dealt with in the... Convention'. The International Convention for the Unification of Certain Rules relating to the Immunity of State-owned Vessels (1926 Brussels Convention)[11] and its Additional Protocol[12] are a case in point.[13] While the *travaux préparatoires* provide no clear indication, the better view is that Article 26 covers specialized agreements as well. Nothing in Article 26 suggests that the provision covers only international agreements with an identical scope of application *ratione materiae* as the Convention. There is no textual reason why the 1926 Brussels Convention and its Protocol, for example, cannot be considered existing international agreements 'which relate to matters dealt with in the... Convention', in that they relate to the immunity of States, in respect of themselves and their ships, from foreign jurisdiction and measures of constraint, and the Convention deals with the immunity of States, in respect of themselves and, *inter alia*, their ships, from foreign jurisdiction and measures of constraint.

A further question, again not answered by the *travaux*, is whether Article 26 also covers specific provisions dealing with some aspect of the jurisdictional immunities of States and their property that may be found in existing international agreements of a more general scope. By way of example, one could think of Article 2(8) of the UNESCO Convention on the Protection of the Underwater Cultural Heritage and Articles 32, 95, 96, and 236 of the United Nations Convention on the Law of the Sea. Again, nothing in the text of Article 26 indicates otherwise. Moreover, the reference to 'rights and obligations... under' other international agreements, rather than to the agreements per se, might be thought to strengthen the conclusion that any such agreement need not be dedicated in its entirety to some aspect of the jurisdictional immunities of States and their property.'

The same reasoning applies to relevant provisions of status of forces agreements (SOFAs) and status of mission agreements (SOMAs). These bilateral or multilateral

[8] See CAHDI, 'Interim report' (n. 7).

[9] See CAHDI, 'Interim report of the second informal meeting of the parties to the European Convention on State Immunity,' 13 September 2006, Council of Europe in doc. CM(2006)171, 23 October 2006, Appendix 3.

[10] For details as to the Convention's entry into force, see the commentary to UNCSI Art. 30.

[11] Brussels, 10 April 1926, 176 LNTS 199.

[12] Brussels, 24 May 1934, 176 LNTS 215.

[13] Similar considerations would seem to apply to Convention on the Liability of Operators of Nuclear Ships, Brussels, 25 May 1962, IAEA Legal Series No. 4 (1966), (1963) 57 *AJIL* 268; Convention Relating to the Arrest Of Sea-Going Ships, Brussels, 10 May 1952, 439 UNTS 193; Convention on Third Party Liabilities in the Field of Nuclear Energy, Paris, 29 July 1960, 956 UNTS 251; Convention on Civil Liability for Nuclear Damage, Vienna, 21 May 1963, 1063 UNTS 265; Convention relating to Civil Liability in the field of Maritime Carriage of Nuclear Material, Brussels, 17 December 1971, 974 UNTS 255.

agreements typically specify the legal position of military forces and civilian personnel deployed by one or more States or by an international organization in the territory of another State with the latter's consent. In addition to dealing with issues like entry and departure of foreign personnel, the carrying of arms, taxation, the settlement of claims, SOFAs and SOMAs typically recognize the immunity of members of the visiting force or mission.[14] Leaving aside the question of the Convention's application in the first place to military activities,[15] there is no reason to exclude rights and obligations under SOFAs and SOMAs from the scope of Article 26. SOFAs and SOMAs require the receiving State to refrain from exercising jurisdiction, in the words of Article 6 of the Convention, over a foreign State, as defined in Article 2(1)(*b*) of the same. In short, they relate to matters dealt with in the Convention.

C. Agreements on the recognition and enforcement of judgments or awards

International agreements on the recognition and enforcement of foreign judgments and arbitral awards, such as the 1958 New York Convention or the 1971 Hague Convention,[16] raise specific issues in the context of Article 26, as do individual provisions on recognition and enforcement in other international agreements. Proceedings for the recognition (in effect, the conversion into a local judgment) and enforcement of a foreign judgment or arbitral award on an application for *exequatur* or the like constitute an exercise of jurisdiction by the local court. Where the respondent to such proceedings is a foreign State, the proceedings will implicate applicable international rules on the immunity of a State from the jurisdiction of the courts of another State.[17] To this extent, and depending always on the precise content of any rights and obligations arising for States parties to it (specifically, whether there arises any obligation to recognize and enforce a judgment or award rendered against a foreign State), a convention or provision for the recognition and enforcement of a foreign judgment or arbitral award could be said to 'relate to matters dealt with in the ... Convention', in the words of Article 26. The same may go, depending on the terms of any relevant convention or provision, as regards the execution of foreign judgments and arbitral awards.

But the question under Article 26 is whether the rights and obligations of States parties under existing international agreements which relate to matters dealt with in the

[14] Provisions in such instruments are classically formulated as follows: '[X] remain at all times under the jurisdiction of the sending state'. Such a formulation does not expressly specify that visiting forces or civilian personnel, and the sending State as such in respect of them, are entitled to immunity from proceedings in the courts of the receiving State, but this is usually what it is taken to indicate. Moreover, some SOFASs and SOMAs make explicit provision for jurisdictional immunities.

[15] On this question, see the commentary to the 'general understandings'.

[16] See Convention on the Recognition and Enforcement of Foreign Arbitral Awards, New York, 10 June 1958, 330 UNTS 38; Convention on the Recognition and Enforcement of Foreign Judgments in Civil and Commercial Matters, The Hague, 1 February 1971, 1144 UNTS 249, and Supplementary Protocol to the latter, The Hague, 1 February 1971, 1144 UNTS 271.

[17] The point has recently been addressed by the ICJ in *Jurisdictional Immunities of the State (Germany v Italy: Greece intervening), Judgment*, International Court of Justice, 3 February 2012, paras 124–133. At para. 128, the Court noted: 'The fact nonetheless remains that, in granting or refusing *exequatur*, the court exercises a jurisdictional power which results in the foreign judgment being given effects corresponding to those of a judgment rendered on the merits in the requested State.' It followed that 'the court seized of an application for *exequatur* of a foreign judgment rendered against a third State has to ask itself whether the respondent State enjoys immunity from jurisdiction—having regard to the nature of the case in which that judgment was given—before the courts of the State in which *exequatur* proceedings have been instituted' (*Jurisdictional Immunities of the State*, para. 130).

Convention conflict with the rights and obligations of States parties to the Convention. It may, depending on its true construction, be that the effect of a provision, like Article 54(1) ICSID Convention, which obliges States parties to recognize and enforce a foreign judgment or arbitral award is that a State party is taken to have consented to the exercise of jurisdiction over it by the courts of the other States parties to the relevant agreement, a consent which in turn would be effective for the purposes of Article 7(1)(a) UNCSI. Conversely, as regards measures of constraint, most relevant international agreements 'leav[e] the law on State immunity from execution intact'.[18] Indeed, Article 55 of the ICSID Convention—'the result of a conscious decision in the Convention's drafting'[19]—expressly preserves it.[20] In contrast, under the New York Convention, which contains no express provision on the matter, the immunity of foreign State property from execution can be treated as a legitimate 'public policy concern' in the sense of Article V(2)(*b*) or as a preliminary matter of procedural law in the sense of Article III;[21] either way, the New York Convention has not been considered to oblige the abrogation of the immunity of foreign State property.[22]

3.2 'existing'

Article 26 provides that only 'existing' international agreements relating to matters dealt with in the Convention displace the application of the latter. Unlike under Article 33 ECSI and the proposal by the Chairman of the Ad Hoc Committee,[23] 'future' agreements on the same subject-matter are not covered.

There is scope for argument over when an international agreement is to be treated as 'existing' for the purposes of Article 26. In contrast to more precisely worded safeguard clauses in other treaties,[24] Article 26 permits of different interpretations, and the *travaux préparatoires* are of limited assistance in ascertaining which is the correct one. The term 'existing' might refer solely to agreements in force on the date the Convention was adopted, namely 2 December 2004, or it might also encompass agreements merely concluded before that date, regardless of whether they had entered into force by then. Equally, the term could

[18] C. Schreuer et al., *The ICSID Convention: A Commentary* (2nd edn) (Cambridge: Cambridge University Press, 2009), 1154. See also A.K. Bjorklund, 'State Immunity and the Enforcement of Investor-State Arbitral Awards', in C. Binder et al. (eds), *International Investment Law for the 21st Century: Essays in Honour of Christoph Schreuer* (Oxford: Oxford University Press, 2009), 302.

[19] Schreuer et al. (n. 18), 1154.

[20] Art. 55 ICSID Convention provides: 'Nothing in Article 54 [dealing with the recognition and enforcement of awards] shall be construed as derogating from the law in force in any Contracting State relating to immunity of that State or of any foreign State from execution.' As Schreuer et al. (n. 18), 1155, observe, this 'must be read as a reference to the law on immunity from execution as it evolves over time.'

[21] See Bjorklund (n. 18), 308–9. Consider also Art. 31(1)(*c*) VCLT.

[22] Recall also, in this regard, Art. 20 UNCSI, according to which 'consent to the exercise of jurisdiction . . . shall not imply consent to the taking of measures of constraint.' For details, see the commentary to Art. 20.

[23] See section 2.

[24] See eg Art. 351 Treaty on the Functioning of the European Union, Rome, 25 March 1957, as amended, consolidated version, 2010 OJ C83/47: 'The rights and obligations arising from agreements concluded before 1 January 1958 or, for acceding States, before the date of their accession, between one or more Member States on the one hand, and one or more third countries on the other, shall not be affected by the provisions of this Treaty'.

be read as referring to agreements either in force or merely concluded by the date not of the Convention's adoption but of its entry into force. Likewise, the term might extend even to agreements either in force or concluded after the Convention's initial entry into force but prior to its entry into force between the States parties concerned. What is more, in the event that an 'existing' international agreement were to be limited to one whose entry into force predates either the adoption or entry into force of the Convention, it remains unclear whether the criterion would relate to the initial entry into force of that international agreement or to its entry into force between the States parties concerned.

It is not certain that the drafters of the Convention reflected on these manifold possibilities. Certainly the *travaux préparatoires* provide no indication that they did.[25] It remains to be seen what, if any, practical impact the uncertainty over the scope of the word 'existing' has.[26]

3.3 'rights and obligations under'

Article 26 has the effect of preserving 'rights and obligations under' existing international agreements. The reference to 'rights and obligations under', rather than to 'the provisions of', would seem to indicate that the focus is on the actual legal effect of the agreement for the States concerned. This means that the effect for those States of any reservations, of the severance of any invalid provisions, of the suspension of the agreement, and so on, is to be taken into account.[27] Whether what is involved is a 'right' or an 'obligation' is a matter of perspective. For example, pursuant to Article 15 ECSI, a foreign State's 'right' to immunity from proceedings corresponds to the 'obligation' of the forum State not to exercise jurisdiction. Conversely, where one of the exceptions set out in Articles 1–14 ECSI applies, the forum State's 'right' to exercise jurisdiction corresponds to the foreign State's 'obligation' to accept that exercise.

3.4 Article 26 and dispute settlement

The relationship between Article 26 and the dispute settlement regime of Article 27 (envisaging, if negotiations do not resolve a dispute over the interpretation or application of the Convention, the possibility of arbitration or adjudication) calls for brief mention. Where, pursuant to Article 26, the application of a provision of the Convention as between States parties is displaced by a rule in an existing international agreement to which those States are parties, the question arises whether a dispute over the interpretation or application of that rule is subject to any dispute settlement obligation to which the States concerned may have subscribed under Article 27 or whether any obligation or otherwise to settle the dispute is to be determined by reference to the other agreement. The answer is not self-evident and may depend on the precise facts.

[25] See section 2.

[26] The text has simply been said to be 'restrictive,' because it 'grants precedence to other conventions on this issue.' See G. Hafner, 'Accountability and Immunity: The United Convention on Jurisdictional Immunity of States and Their Property and the Accountability of States' (2005) 99 ASIL Procs 237, 241.

[27] Despite the differing formulation, the same would logically have to be the case in relation to the formulation 'nothing in the present convention,' which must mean 'no rights or obligations under the present convention'.

4. Evaluation

Article 26 is similar to savings clauses found in many treaties. But its interpretation and application are not without their problems. Its vague wording and the sketchiness of the *travaux préparatoires* make it difficult to ascertain the exact meaning of the provision. The Chairman's proposed text, which was closer to the savings clause in Article 33 ECSI, would have been clearer. Nonetheless, Article 26 permits a considerable number and range of existing agreements to trump the Convention to a greater or lesser extent. To this extent the Convention's regime is residual.

Article 27

CHRISTIAN J. TAMS

Article 27

Settlement of disputes

1. States Parties shall endeavour to settle disputes concerning the interpretation or application of the present Convention through negotiation.
2. Any dispute between two or more States Parties concerning the interpretation or application of the present Convention which cannot be settled through negotiation within six months shall, at the request of any of those States Parties, be submitted to arbitration. If, six months after the date of the request for arbitration, those States Parties are unable to agree on the organization of the arbitration, any of those States Parties may refer the dispute to the International Court of Justice by request in accordance with the Statute of the Court.
3. Each State Party may, at the time of signature, ratification, acceptance or approval or, of accession to, the present Convention, declare that it does not consider itself bound by paragraph 2. The other States Parties shall not be bound by paragraph 2 with respect to any State Party which has made such a declaration.
4. Any State Party that has made a declaration in accordance with paragraph 3 may at any time withdraw that declaration by notification to the Secretary-General of the United Nations.

1. Introduction

Article 27 is included among the final clauses of the Convention, but unlike some other final clauses it is of central importance. It deals with the settlement of disputes, and it does so by providing for a two-step process. First, paragraph 1 requires States parties to settle disputes relating to the Convention through negotiation. Secondly, and more significantly, in accordance with paragraph 2, any dispute not settled through negotiation may be brought by any of the parties to it before an arbitral tribunal or, failing agreement on arbitration, before the ICJ. Paragraph 3 provides, however, that States parties may opt out of this regime by making a declaration to the effect when signing or expressing their consent to be bound by the Convention. Such a declaration may be withdrawn later, as made clear in paragraph 4.

In setting out a procedure for the resolution of Convention-related disputes, Article 27 gives effect to the duty of States to settle their disputes peacefully.[1] It goes beyond this general duty, however, by specifying the available means of dispute resolution and in particular by recognizing, subject to the opt-out clause in paragraph 3, the principle of

[1] See Art. 2(3) UN Charter. For a discussion of this duty, see C. Tomuschat, 'Article 2(3)', in A. Zimmermann, C. Tomuschat, K. Oellers-Frahm, and C.J. Tams (eds), *The Statute of the International Court of Justice: A Commentary* (2nd edn) (Oxford: Oxford University Press, 2012), 75, 81–3. Possible means of dispute settlement are mentioned in Art. 33(1) UN Charter and spelled out in UNGA res. 37/10, 15 November 1982, Annex (Manila Declaration on the Peaceful Settlement of International Disputes).

binding settlement by an impartial institution in accordance with law. It stipulates in effect that States parties are required not only to settle disputes relating to the interpretation or application of the Convention peacefully but to do so by accepting the involvement of an arbitral tribunal or the ICJ.

Under the general law on the peaceful settlement of disputes, any form of binding dispute resolution depends on the consent of the parties.[2] One way this can be given is by including so-called compromissory clauses in international agreements.[3] Article 27(2) is one such compromissory clause. Indeed, given the breadth of issues covered by the Convention and the sensitive nature of disputes over jurisdictional immunities, it promises to be an important compromissory clause. Unsurprisingly, its proposed inclusion provoked concern among States unwilling to submit to binding dispute resolution on the basis of law. The result is a regime that in principle accepts the binding legal settlement of disputes but that allows States parties to opt out.

Provisions on dispute resolution are regularly included in treaties. The approaches adopted vary,[4] with some treaties setting up elaborate regimes involving external actors such as courts, tribunals, and/or other institutions, and others dealing with the matter in the leanest possible way by doing no more than essentially confirming the general (but unspecified) duty to settle disputes by some peaceful means. On the spectrum of dispute settlement provisions, Article 27 is situated somewhere in the middle, between straightforward compromissory clauses envisaging recourse to binding legal settlement without the possibility of opt-out[5] and the manifold versions of 'softer' provisions which either eschew binding legal settlement altogether or leave it to States parties to opt in. In mentioning both arbitration and adjudication by the ICJ, Article 27(2) leaves States parties a measure of discretion to choose their preferred means of legal settlement, while at the same time seeking to ensure through the inclusion of a time-limit that at least some form of binding settlement on the basis of law remains available. In attempting to balance flexibility and effectiveness in this way, Article 27(2) follows certain earlier compromissory clauses, among which Article 14(1) Convention for the Suppression of Unlawful Acts against the Safety of Civilian Aircraft has arguably become the best known.[6]

[2] See Tomuschat (n. 1), 81.

[3] For details, see C.J. Tams, 'The Continued Relevance of Compromissory Clauses as a Source of ICJ Jurisdiction', in T. Giegerich (ed.), *A Wiser Century? Judicial Dispute Settlement, Disarmament and the Laws of War 100 Years after the Second Hague Peace Conference* (Berlin: Duncker & Humblot, 2009), 461–92.

[4] For a concise overview, see *Final Clauses Handbook*, 90–4.

[5] Examples include the respective systems of compulsory binding legal settlement under Part XV United Nations Convention on the Law of the Sea, Montego Bay, 10 December 1982, 1833 UNTS 3 (UNCLOS) and the Understanding on Rules and Procedures Governing the Settlement of Disputes (DSU), Annex 2 to the Agreement Establishing the World Trade Organization, Marrakesh, 15 April 1994, 1869 UNTS 401. A further example is the recourse to international arbitration provided for in standard bilateral investment treaties. As far as dispute resolution by the ICJ is concerned, typical straightforward compromissory clauses can be found in Art. IX Convention on the Prevention and Punishment of the Crime of Genocide, Paris, 9 December 1948, 78 UNTS 277 (Genocide Convention), and in many 'friendship, commerce and navigation' treaties, eg Art. XXI(2) Treaty of Amity, Economic Relations and Consular Rights between the United States of America and Iran, Tehran, 15 August 1955, 284 UNTS 93.

[6] Convention for the Suppression of Unlawful Acts against the Safety of Civilian Aircraft, Montreal, 23 September 1971, 974 UNTS 177 (Montreal Convention). Art. 27 as a whole is very similar in substance to Art. 14 Montreal Convention, which reads as follows:

1. Any dispute between two or more Contracting States concerning the interpretation or application of this Convention which cannot be settled through negotiation, shall, at the request of one of them, be submitted to arbitration. If within six months from the date of the request for arbitration the Parties are unable to agree on the organization of the arbitration, any one of those Parties may refer the dispute to the International Court of Justice by request in conformity with the Statute of the Court.

The Convention is not the first treaty dealing with jurisdictional immunities to contain a dispute settlement provision. Such provisions can be found in or attached to the ECSI, the VCDR, and the VCCR. Just like Article 27 of the Convention, these earlier provisions lend specificity to the duty of States to settle their disputes peacefully. At the same time, each of these regimes adopts a somewhat different approach to binding dispute settlement. The VCDR and VCCR 'outsource' questions of dispute resolution to optional protocols, which provide for compulsory settlement by the ICJ or, in the agreed alternative, by an arbitral tribunal or non-binding conciliation procedure. Article 34(1) ECSI is less flexible: it stipulates compulsory settlement by the ICJ, but does not afford the possibility of opting out. Neither VCDR/VCCR nor ESCI require a prior attempt to arbitrate; but both allow the parties to agree on a different method of peaceful settlement. Compromissory clauses aside, immunity-related disputes can be submitted to binding settlement by way of special agreement or, in the case of the ICJ, optional clause declaration.[7]

While in many respects, the Convention codifies general international law, the regime of dispute settlement set out in Article 27 is treaty-specific. Of course, in light of what has been said in the previous paragraph, States are free to submit immunity-related disputes to binding settlement on the basis of some other jurisdictional title. However, by recognizing the principle of binding settlement of disputes about the Convention, Article 27 marks a considerable development. Unlike other provisions, it does not clarify, fine-tune, or confirm, the state of international law; but, once it takes effect, will establish dispute settlement options that are at present not available. In this respect as well, it is of central importance.

2. Drafting History

Unlike the issues addressed in the Convention's other final clauses, dispute settlement received more than token attention during the early stages of the ILC's work on the Convention. The real debates, however, on what was to become Article 27 took place during the final session of the Ad Hoc Committee on Jurisdictional Immunities of States and Their Property, whose deliberations were held *in camera*, making it difficult to draw conclusions from the *travaux*.

Dispute settlement was discussed in Special Rapporteur Sucharitkul's Eighth and final report, which considered the inclusion in the ILC's draft articles of a separate Part VI entitled 'Settlement of Disputes'.[8] The Special Rapporteur took no firm view on whether the Convention should include a section on dispute resolution. On the one hand, he

2. Each State may at the time of signature or ratification of this Convention or accession thereto, declare that it does not consider itself bound by the preceding paragraph. The other Contracting States shall not be bound by the preceding paragraph with respect to any Contracting State having made such as reservation.
3. Any Contracting State having made a reservation in accordance with the preceding paragraph may at any time withdraw this reservation by notification to the Depositary Governments.

The main difference is that Art. 14(1) Montreal Convention does not allot a specific period to negotiation.

[7] See Art. 36(1) and (2) ICJ Statute. A prime example of the settlement of a dispute over immunity by the ICJ on the basis of the parties' reciprocal optional clause declarations is *Arrest Warrant of 11 April 2000 (Democratic Republic of the Congo v Belgium), Judgment*, ICJ Rep 2002, 3.

[8] See Eighth report Sucharitkul, 32–4, paras 44–8.

suggested (rather surprisingly, in retrospect) that rules on dispute settlement might be unnecessary given the 'paucity of instances involving differences or disputes between states'.[9] On the other hand, his report proposed detailed draft articles covering negotiation, conciliation, arbitration, and judicial settlement.[10] With the slackening pace of the ILC's work on jurisdictional immunities, these provisions were never seriously discussed. Incoming Special Rapporteur Ogiso returned to the various options available in his Preliminary Report, and indicated that he would be willing to present his own views if the Commission so desired.[11] The Commission decided, however, to leave the matter for States to address during any eventual diplomatic conference. As a consequence, dispute settlement did not feature in the ILC's draft articles as finally adopted in 1991.

When work towards a binding text resumed in the late 1990s, dispute settlement could no longer be ignored. The Ad Hoc Committee eventually addressed the issue in 2004, when it 'proceeded with the formulation of a preamble and final clauses, on the basis of written and oral proposals submitted by delegations, as well as suggestions of the Chairman'.[12] The Chairman's suggested dispute settlement provision[13] was ultimately adopted unaltered as Article 27. Guatemala had submitted an alternative proposal, which included an arbitration annex laying down a procedure governing disputes relating to the interpretation and application of what would become the Convention.[14] There is no official record of the debates or any indication why the Chairman put forward the text he did, so it can only be assumed that, as with earlier dispute settlement clauses on which the Chairman's was modelled, the 'package' of binding legal dispute settlement accompanied by the possibility of opting out afforded a compromise acceptable to all.

3. Key Points

Article 27 seeks to facilitate the peaceful resolution of immunity-related disputes by encouraging negotiated settlement, while also providing—for those States that have not opted out—the surety of binding arbitration and, failing this, ICJ proceedings. This sequence of dispute settlement options is available in respect of disputes about the interpretation or application of the Convention.

3.1 'dispute[s] between two or more States Parties concerning the interpretation or application of the . . . Convention'

Article 27 envisages the diplomatic or legal resolution of a specific category of disputes, namely 'disputes . . . concerning the interpretation or application of the . . . Convention'. The language is typical of compromissory clauses, which are usually framed as ancillary provisions laying down procedures for the settlement of disputes related specifically to matters covered by the treaty in question. The formula clarifies the scope of Article 27 in three respects. First, there has to be a 'dispute'. This is generally understood in broad terms as a 'disagreement on a point of law or fact, a conflict of legal views or of

[9] Eighth report Sucharitkul,, 33, para. 47.

[10] See Eighth report Sucharitkul, n. 8, 33–4.

[11] See Preliminary report Ogiso, 122, para. 274.

[12] 2004 report Ad Hoc Committee, 3, para. 9.

[13] See Suggestions of the Chairman, 2, art. C.

[14] See Ad Hoc Committee on Jurisdictional Immunities of States and Their Property, 1–5 March 2004, Dispute Settlement Provisions: Proposal by Guatemala, UN doc. A/AC.262/2004/DP.3, 27 February 2004.

interests'.[15] Secondly, the dispute must be one between States parties to the Convention. This is an obvious restriction, which follows from the *pacta tertiis* principle.[16] It can also be read as affirming that Article 27 does not extend to disputes that materialized before the Convention's entry into force for the States concerned: in order to be 'States Parties' in the sense of Article 27, the two or more parties to the dispute must have been bound by the Convention when the dispute arose.[17] Thirdly, the parties' 'disagreement on a point of law or fact' must relate to the interpretation or application of the Convention. Article 27 is not intended to pave the way for dispute settlement, let alone legal claims before arbitral tribunals or the ICJ, concerning matters not covered by the Convention.[18] In legal proceedings, the formula 'disputes . . . concerning the interpretation or application of the . . . Convention' is understood to encompass disputes relating to remedies for breach of the Convention.[19]

Whether a particular dispute falls within the scope of a compromissory clause may become clear only during the dispute settlement process itself. Article 27 says nothing as to how this question is to be resolved. In arbitral or ICJ proceedings, it will be for the tribunal or Court to decide, in the exercise of its jurisdiction to rule on its jurisdiction ('*compétence de la compétence*' or '*Kompetenzkompetenz*').[20] Even then, it may be that the matter is put to rest only in any award or judgment on the merits. To filter out far-fetched claims, the ICJ, for its part, has adopted a '*prima facie*' approach. When faced with a jurisdictional objection, it has not 'limit[ed] itself to noting that one of the Parties maintains' that the dispute was covered by the terms of a compromissory clause,[21] but has gone on to ascertain whether the alleged breaches were 'capable of falling within'[22] the scope of the clause. The test typically requires an applicant State to make out at least a plausible case.

3.2 Negotiation

Paragraph 1 of Article 27 requires States parties to settle disputes with respect to the Convention by means of negotiation. This amounts to an obligation of conduct: States parties 'shall endeavour' to settle by means of negotiation disputes concerning the

[15] See *Mavrommatis Palestine Concessions*, PCIJ Ser. A No. 2 (1924), 11.

[16] See Art. 34 VCLT.

[17] The restriction is accepted in principle, but can be difficult to apply, as it requires precise identification of the dispute, which may have evolved over time. As noted by the ICJ in *Certain Property (Liechtenstein v Germany), Preliminary Objections*, ICJ Rep 2005, 6, 25, para. 46, the critical date is that of the 'source or real cause' of the parties' disagreement.

For details on the Convention's entry into force (and the distinction between its initial entry into force and its subsequent entry into force for a particular State) see the commentary on Art. 30.

[18] The point is frequently affirmed in international jurisprudence. See eg *Application of the Convention on the Prevention and Punishment of the Crime of Genocide (Bosnia and Herzegovina v Serbia and Montenegro), Merits*, ICJ Rep 2007, 43, 104, para. 147, noting in proceedings brought on the basis of Art. IX Genocide Convention that the Court had 'no power to rule on alleged breaches of other obligations under international law, not amounting to genocide'.

[19] Disputes as to the consequences of breach of the Convention are disputes as to the Convention's application, in the language of Art. 27.

[20] See C. Tomuschat, 'Article 36' in Zimmermann et al. (n. 1), 633, 694 *et seq.*

[21] *Oil Platforms (Islamic Republic of Iran v United States of America), Preliminary Objection*, ICJ Rep 1996, 803, 810, para. 16.

[22] *Legality of Use of Force (Yugoslavia v Belgium), Provisional Measures*, ICJ Rep 1999, 124, 137, para. 38. See also, similarly, ICJ Rep 1999, 124, 138, para. 41 ('capable of coming within').

interpretation or application of the Convention. Putting it a different way, States parties are obliged to negotiate with a view to settling Convention-related disputes, even if they are under no accompanying obligation of result to achieve a negotiated settlement. As the ICJ noted in a recent judgment, it is not unusual in compromissory clauses conferring jurisdiction on the Court and other international jurisdictions to refer to resort to negotiations. Such resort fulfils three distinct functions. In the first place, it gives notice to the respondent State that a dispute exists and delimits the scope of the dispute and its subject-matter. In the second place, it encourages the parties to attempt to settle their dispute by mutual agreement, thus avoiding recourse to binding third-party adjudication. In the third place, prior resort to negotiations or other methods of peaceful dispute settlement performs an important function in indicating the limit of consent given by States.[23]

That said, even though it serves (as the passage clarifies) to facilitate dispute resolution, negotiation is the archetypal example of the 'diplomatic', as distinct from 'legal', settlement of disputes. What this means is that the respective legal positions of the parties to the dispute need not be the sole determinant of the outcome. Indeed, they need not be a factor at all (although in the context of disputes concerning the interpretation of application of the Convention it stands to reason that they will be). In principle, what matters in diplomatic settlement is what is acceptable to both sides.

By the same token, a negotiated settlement must indeed be agreed to by both sides.[24] It cannot be imposed on an unwilling party. This does not, however, mean that an obligation to negotiate is worthless. Most international disputes—both as a matter of international law generally and in the specific area of jurisdictional immunities—are in fact settled by way of negotiation. Moreover, the range of potential negotiated outcomes is broad.[25] For example, in the present context, negotiation may lead to the waiver of immunity from proceedings by one party to the dispute, as per Article 7(1)(*c*) of the Convention, or to its waiver of immunity from execution, as per Article 19(*a*)(iii). Conversely, negotiation may result in the discontinuance of proceedings initiated against that party.

International law imposes few restrictions on the freedom of parties to any dispute to negotiate and to agree on a negotiated outcome. The approach is informed by pragmatism and by a respect for party autonomy and State sovereignty, and it is only in rare instances that public order considerations call for limitations.

In terms of the *negotiating process*, negotiation, while rightly viewed as a form of peaceful dispute settlement, need not be particularly pacific. Within the limits outlined below, it may involve pressure and threats as much as incentives—sticks as much as carrots. As to its organization, it may be strictly bilateral or part of a wider, perhaps more structured process. The main restriction imposed by international law on the conduct of

[23] *Application of the International Convention on the Elimination of All Forms of Racial Discrimination (Georgia v Russian Federation), Preliminary Objections,* ICJ, 1 April 2011, para. 131.

[24] For details, see eg UN Office of Legal Affairs (Codification Division), *Handbook on the Peaceful Settlement of Disputes between States* (United Nations: New York, 1992), UN doc. OLA/COD/2394, UN Sales No. E.92.V.7, 9–24, paras 21–73; J. Collier and V. Lowe, *The Settlement of Disputes in International Law* (Oxford: Oxford University Press, 1999), 20–4.

[25] See Collier and Lowe (n. 24), 20. In *North Sea Continental Shelf (Federal Republic of Germany/Denmark; Federal Republic of Germany/Netherlands),* ICJ Rep 1969, 3, 47, para. 86, the ICJ found 'no need to insist upon the fundamental character of this method of settlement'.

negotiation is the prohibition on the threat or use of inter-State force.[26] Treaties embodying negotiated settlements that were procured by the threat or use of force are void *ab initio*.[27] Similarly, a State's expression of consent may be void, or voidable, if it has been obtained through coercion or procured by corruption.[28] But these grounds are invoked rarely.

As regards the *outcome* of negotiations, as a general rule international law recognizes the result agreed upon by the disputants. Negotiation will typically produce a deal requiring both parties to agree to a compromise that falls short of their initial demands, and any such deal may well reflect the relative political clout of the respective States as much as the soundness of their legal arguments. It is only when a negotiated settlement conflicts with a peremptory norm (*jus cogens*) that international law interferes with party autonomy. Like treaties enshrining settlements procured by the threat or use of force, treaties embodying agreements in violation of *jus cogens* are invalid.[29] But the limitation is more of conceptual than practical relevance.

Although Article 27(1) mentions only negotiation, it should not be read to exclude other forms of dispute resolution. International lawyers are accustomed to distinguishing among various methods for the diplomatic settlement of disputes. Alongside negotiation, there exist mediation, conciliation, fact-finding, and good offices.[30] Like negotiation, these other diplomatic methods of dispute resolution presuppose the consent of both parties; they cannot be imposed on an unwilling State. Like negotiation, each of them may help to resolve a particular dispute.[31] Even though Article 27(1) refers only to negotiations, the parties remain free to agree to settle their dispute by other peaceful means such as conciliation, fact-finding, etc. However, these do not form part of the structured dispute settlement process envisaged by the provision. This means that recourse to any of these other diplomatic methods does not constitute a precondition to the binding legal settlement of Convention-related disputes provided for in Article 27 (2).

3.3 Binding Legal Settlement

A. From negotiation to legal settlement

If negotiation produces no result, paragraph 2 of Article 27 envisages a move from non-binding diplomatic means of dispute resolution to binding legal settlement, either by an arbitral tribunal or the ICJ. By 'legal' settlement is meant that the legal positions of the

[26] See Art. 2(4) UN Charter.

[27] See Art. 52 VCLT. For details, see A. Aust, *Modern Treaty Law and Practice* (2nd edn) (Cambridge: Cambridge University Press, 2007), 317–18.

[28] See Art. 49–51 VCLT.

[29] See Art. 53 VCLT. For a brief summary of the heated debates over the provision, see Aust (n. 27), 319–20.

[30] For details, see the Manila Declaration on the Peaceful Settlement of International Disputes, (n. 1); *Handbook on the Peaceful Settlement of Disputes between States* (n. 24), 24–55, paras 74–167.

It is worth recalling that, as noted above (section 2), Special Rapporteur Sucharitkul had at some point considered the establishment of a conciliation procedure: see Eighth report Sucharitkul, 33–4 (draft art. 30 and annex).

[31] To give an example, the involvement of a mediator may help put protracted negotiations back on track. For a useful discussion of examples of successfully mediated settlements, see F. Orrego Vicuña, 'Mediation', in R. Wolfrum (ed.), *Max Planck Encyclopedia of Public International Law* (Oxford: Oxford University Press, 2012), vol. VII, 45.

parties are the sole formal determinant of the outcome, an outcome which in turn is without formal regard to its acceptability to any or all of the parties. The move to binding legal settlement is discretionary—'at the request of any of th[e] States Parties' involved in the dispute, in the words of Article 27(2)—and the parties to the dispute may decide not to avail themselves of the option. The dispute may not, for example, be important enough to them to justify legal action, or the parties to it may harbour uncertainties as to the force of their respective legal arguments. The availability of the alternative is nonetheless significant, not least because the prospect of litigation may facilitate a negotiated settlement.

Article 27(2) stipulates that legal proceedings may be instituted only on the lapse of a six-month period (calculated from when the dispute over the interpretation or application of the Convention arose) during which the States parties must have sought to settle their disagreement by negotiation. The clause underlines the importance of negotiation within the scheme of Article 27 and is significant insofar as, in the absence of express provision to this effect, international law allows immediate recourse to arbitration or adjudication by the ICJ, without any prior attempt at diplomatic resolution of the dispute.[32] By contrast, Article 27 formulates a precondition that must be complied with before the dispute can be submitted to binding dispute legal settlement.[33]

The precise content of that precondition is difficult to identify and a matter 'for consideration in each case';[34] but the jurisprudence of the ICJ provides at least a starting point: 'Negotiations entail more than the plain opposition of legal views or interests between two parties, or the existence of a series of accusations and rebuttals, or even the exchange of claims and directly opposed counter-claims', the Court recently noted, but entailed '—at the very least—a genuine attempt by one of the disputing parties to engage in discussions with the other disputing party, with a view to resolving the dispute'.[35] These discussions need not necessarily have expressly referred to the treaty provision whose breach is alleged; however, 'the subject-matter of the negotiations must relate to the subject-matter of the dispute which, in turn, must concern the substantive obligations contained in the treaty in question'.[36]

All this is fairly unproblematic where the disputants maintain regular diplomatic relations, in the framework of which a specific immunity-related dispute can be addressed. Real questions arise if the relations between the states concerned are of such a nature as to make negotiated outcomes unlikely. In such instances, experience with similar (though not identical) compromissory clauses suggests that the requirement of prior negotiations can be interpreted flexibly. For example, in the *Lockerbie* case, the Court had been seised directly, even though the applicable compromissory clause made

[32] See *Land and Maritime Boundary between Cameroon and Nigeria (Cameroon v Nigeria), Preliminary Objections*, ICJ Rep 1998, 275, 303, para. 56.

[33] See *Application of the International Convention on the Elimination of All Forms of Racial Discrimination* (n. 23), para. 141, where the ICJ made the following observation with respect to the applicable compromissory clause: 'the terms of Article 22 of CERD, namely "[a]ny dispute . . . which is not settled by negotiation or by the procedures expressly provided for in this Convention", establish preconditions to be fulfilled before the seisin.'

[34] *Mavrommatis Palestine Concessions* (n. 15), 13.

[35] *Application of the International Convention on the Elimination of All Forms of Racial Discrimination* (n. 23), para. 157.

[36] *Application of the International Convention on the Elimination of All Forms of Racial Discrimination* (n. 23), para. 161.

ICJ proceedings dependent on the failure to reach a negotiated settlement ('cannot be settled through negotiation') and fruitless attempts to pursue arbitration ('If within six months of the date of the request for arbitration the Parties are unable to agree on the organization of the arbitration'). The Court held that the requirement of prior, unsuccessful negotiations could not be used to delay proceedings if one party refused to negotiate or if the further pursuit of negotiation was patently pointless.[37] This no doubt makes sense where the compromissory clause—like Article 14 of the Montreal Convention—simply requires negotiations to have failed. However, it is worth noting that the underlying (purposive) reasoning is more difficult to apply to a provision that—like Article 27 UNCSI—allots a specific time-period to negotiation.[38] In this case, it remains to be seen how the balance between flexibility and strict adherence to the text is to be struck.

B. From arbitration to judicial settlement by the ICJ

Article 27(2) does not stop at providing that any of the States parties involved in a dispute over the interpretation or application of the Convention may initiate recourse to binding legal settlement six months after the dispute has arisen. It also regulates the method of legal dispute resolution open to the requesting party by stipulating that arbitration is to be attempted first, with recourse to judicial settlement before the ICJ becoming an alternative if, 'six months after the date of the request for arbitration, th[e] States Parties are unable to agree on the organization of the arbitration'. This further mandatory sequence of dispute resolution options would appear to reflect a perceived preference on the part of States for arbitration over judicial settlement, the former presenting a more flexible form of binding legal dispute resolution which allows the parties to retain a greater degree of control over the conduct of proceedings. In the scheme of Article 27(2), recourse to the ICJ is envisaged as a fall-back, to prevent a party to a dispute from frustrating binding legal settlement altogether by stymieing arbitral proceedings.[39]

Whether this hierarchy is respected in practice remains to be seen. As noted above with respect to the six-month period allotted to negotiations preceding binding dispute settlement, insistence on the lapse of time may appear formalistic where the parties manifestly are not going to agree on arbitration.[40] As has also been observed, the express reference to a specific time-period argues against too much flexibility. Still, when faced with similar dispute settlement clauses, the ICJ has not been averse to considerations of flexibility. On the one hand, it has made clear that 'the lack of agreement between the

[37] See eg *Questions of Interpretation and Application of the 1971 Montreal Convention arising from the Aerial Incident at Lockerbie (Libyan Arab Jamahiriya v United States of America), Preliminary Objections,* ICJ Rep 1998, 115, 122, para. 20.

[38] The Court has correctly observed that 'though similar in character, compromissory clauses containing a reference to negotiation (and sometimes additional methods of dispute settlement) are not always uniform' (*Application of the International Convention on the Elimination of All Forms of Racial Discrimination* (n. 23), para. 136).

But note that in the *Lockerbie* case (n. 37), the ICJ seemed willing to adopt a flexible interpretation of the requirement that six months lapse between the request for arbitration and the institution of ICJ proceedings. See further section 3.3.B.

[39] It should be noted that nothing precludes parties to a Convention-related dispute from continuing to pursue arbitration after the end of the six-month period.

[40] See section 3.3.A.

parties as to the organization of an arbitration cannot be presumed'.[41] An applicant State would therefore be expected to provide evidence of its attempts to initiate arbitral proceedings. On the other hand, it is implicit in the Court's statement that where the parties' failure to agree on the arbitration is manifest, the six-month period need not be observed. In this event, the 'refusal of the Respondent to enter into arbitration . . . absolve[s] [the applicant State] from any obligation . . . to observe a six-month period starting from the request for arbitration, before seising the Court'.[42]

Beyond these controversial instances pitting flexibility versus textual strictness, nothing precludes the parties from directly submitting their dispute, by common agreement, to the ICJ, instead of pursuing arbitration first. In such a case, the parties would be taken to have waived the exhaustion of the six-month period by mutual consent.

C. The framework of binding legal settlement

(i) Common elements

Article 27(2) is silent on the conduct and the formal outcome and effect of any arbitral or ICJ proceedings which may arise in respect of disputes concerning the interpretation or application of the Convention. These questions are to be answered by reference to the constitutive instrument and rules of procedure of the arbitral tribunal in question or of the ICJ, as the case may be, as elaborated on by any relevant international jurisprudence. On the basis of the corpus of such instruments and jurisprudence, however, it is possible to speak, at a necessary level of generality, of the principles common to arbitration and ICJ adjudication. This 'normative framework' for the binding legal settlement of international disputes, within which Article 27(2) is situated, is in many respects the same whether the dispute is brought before an arbitral tribunal or the ICJ.[43]

In procedural terms, both arbitration and judicial settlement by the ICJ can be requested unilaterally, by the disputant wanting to move to binding legal settlement, or by joint submission of the parties. Provision is generally made for a preliminary phase, prior to and separate from consideration of the merits, during which the respondent State may object to the jurisdiction of the tribunal or the Court or to the admissibility of the claim.[44] When it comes to the admissibility of a claim, the applicant State must establish a legal interest in the subject-matter of the dispute, usually in the form of injury as a result of the respondent State's alleged international wrong,[45] and it must show that

[41] *Armed Activities on the Territory of the Congo (New Application: 2002) (Democratic Republic of the Congo v Rwanda), Jurisdiction and Admissibility*, ICJ Rep 2006, 6, 41, para. 92.

[42] *Lockerbie* (n. 37), 122, para. 20. It is important to note that this particular statement was made in relation to a compromissory clause that—just like Art. 27—made recourse to the ICJ dependent upon the lapse of a six-month period during which arbitration was to be pursued.

[43] Recent years have witnessed a flurry of studies seeking to determine the content of a 'common law of international adjudication'. See, notably, C. Brown, *A Common Law of International Adjudication* (Oxford: Oxford University Press, 2007); and M. Benzing, *Das Beweisrecht vor internationalen Gerichten und Schiedsgerichten in zwischenstaatlichen Streitigkeiten* (Berlin: Springer, 2010); as well as the earlier study by V.S. Mani, *International Adjudication: Procedural Aspects* (The Hague: Martinus Nijhoff, 1980). For a clear summary of the general principles of international proceedings, see Collier and Lowe (n. 24), 189–273.

[44] See Collier and Lowe (n. 24), 227–9. It is at this preliminary stage that the respondent State will have the opportunity to challenge the tribunal or the Court's jurisdiction, eg by contesting the existence of a dispute between the parties and/or whether any such dispute as may be found to exist concerns the interpretation or application of the Convention.

[45] This requirement is referred to in a multiplicity of ways which are not always clearly distinguished. Terms include *locus standi*, *jus standi*, legal interest, interest to sue, *intérêt pour agir*, capacity or special capacity,

the dispute is not merely hypothetical.[46] In the context of the Convention, legally actionable injury can be expected generally to consist in either the denial to the applicant State by the courts of the respondent State of a jurisdictional immunity to which the Convention entitles the former or, conversely, in the grant of immunity by the respondent State's courts to a third State, in proceedings brought by a national of the applicant State, in circumstances where the Convention denies such immunity. Both the preliminary objections phase and the merits phase of proceedings will typically comprise in turn both a written and a later oral phase of pleadings.

As for their formal outcome and effect, proceedings before an arbitral tribunal and before the ICJ result (unless the dispute is settled diplomatically in the meantime) in a decision, termed an 'award' and a 'judgment' respectively, which, in accordance with the constitutive instrument of the relevant body,[47] will be binding. If there is a need for the tribunal or the Court to pronounce on objections raised at the preliminary stage, this will be done in a separate decision rendered before written pleadings on the merits are submitted. Awards and judgments are final, and are subject subsequently, and in practice rarely, only to proceedings for their revision or interpretation. The content of what is decided naturally depends on the nature of the parties' submissions and the merits of their claims. Claims that are without legal merit will be rejected. If the tribunal or Court upholds the applicant's claim for breach of the Convention, it will declare that the respondent State has violated its international obligations. As the Convention does not address consequences of breaches expressly, remedies will be determined on the basis of general international law. Of particular relevance in this respect are the ILC's Articles on State Responsibility, which are widely seen as a codification of the existing law, and which require states responsible for wrongful acts to cease wrongful conduct (if ongoing)[48] and to make reparation, aimed at 'wip[ing] out all the consequences of the illegal act'.[49] Reparation in turn may consist of restitution (designed to re-establish the situation which existed before the wrongful act was committed), compensation (for financially assessable damages), or satisfaction (for non-material damage).[50] The precise content of reparation of course depends on the nature of the breach in question; in disputes brought under Article 27(2), a judgment or award might, for example, require a State to stop domestic

and right or cause of action. For details, see C.A. Günther, *Die Klagebefugnis der Staaten in internationalen Streitbeilegungsverfahren* (Cologne: C. Heymanns, 1999), 20–8; C.J. Tams, *Enforcing Obligations* Erga Omnes *in International Law* (Cambridge: Cambridge University Press, 2005), 25–47. Controversial decisions typically relate to issues of 'public interest enforcement'. See eg *South West Africa (Ethiopia v South Africa; Liberia v South Africa), Second Phase*, ICJ Rep 1966, 6 (in which the ICJ controversially denied the applicant States' legal interest to challenge the South African mandate over South West Africa/Namibia) and the subsequent 'correction' of this decision in *Barcelona Traction, Light and Power Company, Limited (Belgium v Spain), Second Phase*, ICJ Rep 1970, 3 (recognizing the concept of obligations *erga omnes* such as to permit a limited form of public interest litigation).

[46] See *Northern Cameroons (Cameroon v United Kingdom), Preliminary Objections*, sep. op. Fitzmaurice, ICJ Rep 1963, 15, 97 *et seq*; *Nuclear Tests (Australia v France)*, ICJ Rep 1974, 253, 270–2, paras 55–59; *Nuclear Tests (New Zealand v France)*, ICJ Rep 1974, 457, 476–7, paras 58–62.

[47] See eg Art. 84 Convention for the Pacific Settlement of International Disputes, The Hague, 18 October 1907, 205 CTS 233; Art. 59 ICJ Statute.

[48] Art. 30 Articles on Responsibility of States for Internationally Wrongful Acts.

[49] Art. 31 Articles on Responsibility of States for Internationally Wrongful Acts and commentary thereto, para. 2, citing *Factory at Chorzów, Merits*, PCIJ Ser. A No. 17 (1928), 47.

[50] Arts 34–37 Articles on Responsibility of States for Internationally Wrongful Acts.

legal proceedings disregarding existing claims to immunity or to compensate for material losses.

It appears from the foregoing that arbitration and ICJ proceedings in many respects are subject to a 'common law' of international dispute settlement. However, the claim that under contemporary international law, 'the modalities of arbitration are essentially the same as adjudication'[51] is an overstatement, neglecting as it does important differences of which the following sections provide a brief summary.[52]

(ii) Arbitration

Although leading, like ICJ adjudication, to a binding outcome on the basis of law, arbitral proceedings take place not before a pre-existing, permanently constituted court but before an ad hoc tribunal constituted by way of agreement between the parties for the resolution of the particular dispute and operating within a procedural framework established or otherwise identified by those parties. Indeed, arbitration is often defined in contradistinction to adjudication by a standing court, for example as 'the determination of a difference... through a legal decision of... a tribunal other than the International Court of Justice or another permanent tribunal'.[53] As a consequence of this basic distinction, arbitration generally affords a greater degree of party autonomy by granting the disputants more control over the organization and conduct of proceedings than they would enjoy before the ICJ. Parties to arbitration benefit from a wide measure of discretion in defining the parameters of the arbitral process. They may specify the size and seat of the tribunal, its composition, its procedural powers, its applicable law, and the role before it, if any, of third parties.[54]

Since to provide *de novo* for an arbitral procedure is potentially burdensome, various standard rules have been developed to serve as models for parties to international disputes. Among these, the relevant provisions of the Hague Conventions of 1899 and 1907 respectively, regulating proceedings before the Permanent Court of Arbitration, are of historical importance,[55] while later inter-State arbitral frameworks include the Model Rules on Arbitral Procedure developed by the ILC and adopted by the United Nations General Assembly in 1958;[56] the PCA Optional Rules for Arbitrating Disputes between Two States, in effect since 1992;[57] and the arbitral mechanism set up the same year under

[51] I. Brownlie, 'The Peaceful Settlement of International Disputes' (2009) 8 *Chinese JIL* 267, 273.

[52] For further details, see R. Jennings, 'The Difference between Conducting a Case in the ICJ and in an *Ad Hoc* Arbitration Tribunal', in N. Ando et al (eds), *Liber Amicorum Judge Shigeru Oda* (The Hague: Kluwer, 2002), 893.

[53] Collier and Lowe (n. 24), 31.

[54] See *Handbook on the Peaceful Settlement of Disputes between States* (n. 24), 58, para. 176. Unlike with a standing court, the parties will also have to pay for the establishment and running of the arbitral tribunal and for the services of the arbitrators, which can make arbitration more costly than litigation before the ICJ.

[55] For the 1907 Hague Convention, revising the original version of 1899, see n. 47. For the 1899 version, see International Convention for the Pacific Settlement of International Disputes, The Hague, 29 July 1899, 187 CTS 410. The PCA has not functioned as an arbitral tribunal in its own right since rendering its award in 1956 in the protracted *Affaire relative à la Concession des Phares de l'Empire Ottoman*, 12 RIAA 155 (*compromis* concluded in 1931). But the facilities and administrative resources of the PCA have frequently been used since then for ad hoc arbitration not governed by the rules in the 1899 and 1907 Hague Conventions. For details, see N. Ando, 'Permanent Court of Arbitration (PCA)', in R. Wolfrum (ed.), *Max Planck Encyclopedia of Public International Law* (Oxford: Oxford University Press, 2012), vol. VIII, 251, paras 25–28.

[56] See Report ILC, tenth session, 83–6, para. 22 and UNGA res. 1262 (XIII), 14 November 1958.

[57] See 32 ILM 572 (1993).

the auspices of what is now the OSCE.[58] Typically, States submitting to inter-State arbitration choose to conduct proceedings on the basis of one of the existing sets of procedural rules, perhaps as 'customized' by the parties themselves. The same approach is likely to be followed should States parties decide to institute arbitral proceedings pursuant to Article 27(2). But the provision does not itself specify which set of rules is to apply. Nor—unlike some other multilateral treaties[59] and the scheme proposed by Guatemala to the Ad Hoc Committee[60]—does it prescribe Convention-specific rules for the arbitration of disputes concerning the treaty's interpretation or application. The matter is for the parties to decide.

Beyond that it is at times argued that, as ad hoc bodies set up to address specific disputes, arbitral tribunals approach their task differently from the ICJ.[61] Being established for a specific dispute, they are said to be less willing to follow previous decisions than the ICJ; and more inclined to focus on settling the dispute to hand (at the expense of developing the law). These allegations are plausible, but difficult to establish conclusively. There is no shortage of arbitral awards which adopt past decisions or which develop the law,[62] just as there are ICJ judgments which place little emphasis on consistency or which focus on settling the dispute before the Court regardless of the wider legal implications.[63] That said, even if it is not borne out by the facts, the perceived difference between the ICJ and arbitral tribunals may of course influence the approach of States parties to the binding legal settlement of disputes under the Convention.

(iii) Judicial settlement by the ICJ

Judicial settlement by the ICJ, while bearing similarities to arbitration, displays a number of features that set it apart. Notably, the parties have less control over the conduct of proceedings. By the same token, since the Court already exists, it does not have to be set up and paid for[64] simply to hear the one case, although the parties may be entitled to nominate judges ad hoc to supplement the bench.[65] Nor is there any need to agree on procedure, which is addressed in detail in the ICJ Statute and Rules of Court.[66] What is more, as has just been noted,[67] the fact that the Court is a permanent judicial institution with a long tradition of adjudication may perhaps influence the dispute settlement

[58] See Convention on Conciliation and Arbitration within the Conference on Security and Co-operation in Europe, Stockholm, 15 December 1992, 1842 UNTS 150. See also Rules of the Court of Conciliation and Arbitration within the OSCE, 1 February 1997, http://www.osce.org/files/documents/f/f/40108.pdf.

[59] See eg Annexes VII and VIII UNCLOS, laying down rules for arbitration pursuant to Part XV UNCLOS.

[60] See n. 14.

[61] See eg C. Gray and B. Kingsbury, 'Developments in Dispute Settlement: Inter-State Arbitration Since 1945' (1992) 63 *BYIL* 97, especially at 109–19. See also Jennings (n. 52), for a balanced assessment.

[62] See Gray and Kingsbury (n. 61), 119–33.

[63] For an illustration see F.L. Bordin, 'Continuation of Membership in the United Nations Revisited: Lessons from Fifteen Years of Inconsistency in the Jurisprudence of the ICJ' (2011) 10 *The Law and Practice of International Courts and Tribunals* 315.

[64] See Art. 3 ICJ Statute, stating that the expenses of the Court are to be borne by the UN. See also *Final Clauses Handbook* (n. 4), 89.

[65] See Art. 31 ICJ Statute.

[66] To be sure, the ICJ Statute and Rules are designed to accommodate the special interests of the parties. For example, in accordance with Art. 26 ICJ Statute, the parties may decide to hold proceedings before a Chamber of the Court; subject to Art. 39, they may decide on the language of proceedings; and subject to Arts 43 and 48, they can influence the length of proceedings. Where the parties fail to agree, however, the Court will apply its general procedural rules.

[67] See section 3.3.C (ii).

process. All these factors will no doubt inform the parties' approach to litigation, and may lead them to favour one of the two methods of binding legal dispute settlement envisaged in Article 27(2) over the other.

3.4 Opting Out

Arbitration and adjudication by the ICJ are intrusive forms of international dispute settlement that not all States consider desirable.[68] For a range of reasons, from principled objections to binding legal dispute resolution to bad experiences with international litigation, the sensitive character of immunity-related disputes, and so on, some States during the drafting of the Convention opposed the idea of making binding legal settlement compulsory. Others were keen to enshrine binding legal settlement as the principle, and to allow States that initially refuse to accept the principle to change their minds subsequently. Paragraphs 3 and 4 of Article 27 embody a compromise between these approaches. In accordance with Article 27(3), States parties may opt out of Article 27(2)'s regime of binding legal dispute resolution by means of a declaration made when signing or expressing their consent to be bound by the Convention. In accordance with Article 27(4), however, they may at any time withdraw such declaration.

The fact that Article 27(3) renders optional the binding settlement according to law of Convention-related disputes between States parties is no doubt of concern to certain States. But the provision does no more than reflect the ambivalent attitude of many other States to the binding legal settlement of international disputes, and is by no means an exception among modern dispute resolution clauses. Quite the contrary, multilateral treaties concluded in recent decades typically approach dispute settlement in a cautious fashion. Some treaties make no mention of binding legal settlement at all.[69] Others leave it to States parties to opt in, rather than requiring them, should they wish, to opt out.[70] Moreover, even the straightforward compromissory clauses found in some multilateral treaties are typically subject to reservations.[71] Against this background, the inclusion of

[68] See eg Sir Gerald Fitzmaurice, in Institut de Droit international, *Livre du Centenaire, 1873–1973: évolution et perspectives du droit international* (Basel: S. Karger, 1973), 279: '[G]overnments prefer to deal with disputes by political means rather than by submission to adjudication, and fight shy of the commitment involved by going to law: they dislike the loss of control that is entailed over the future of the case, the outcome of which they can no longer influence politically once it is before a court of law, since this will then depend upon legal considerations with which they do not find themselves at home.'

[69] See eg Arts 8 and 10 Convention on the Prohibition of the Use, Stockpiling, Production and Transfer of Anti-Personnel Mines and on their Destruction, Oslo, 18 September 1997, 2056 UNTS 211, establishing a deliberately non-judicial compliance mechanism and relying for the resolution of Convention-related disputes on consultation and cooperation between the parties, with, if desired by those parties, the involvement of the Meeting of the States Parties.

[70] See eg Art. 15(2) Convention on Environmental Impact Assessment in a Transboundary Context, Espoo, 25 February 1991, 1989 UNTS 309, which provides: 'When signing, ratifying, accepting, approving or acceding to this Convention, or at any time thereafter, a Party may declare in writing to the Depositary that for a dispute not resolved in accordance with paragraph 1 of this Article [ie through negotiation or any other mutually accepted means], it accepts one or both of the following means of dispute settlement as compulsory in relation to any Party accepting the same obligation: (*a*) Submission of the dispute to the International Court of Justice; (*b*) Arbitration in accordance with the procedure set out in Appendix VII.' The provision's 'opt-in' approach is typical of many modern multilateral standard-setting treaties in the fields of international environmental law and arms reduction.

[71] See Arts 19–23 VCLT. Whether reservations to dispute settlement provisions are compatible with the object and purpose of a treaty is much discussed, but international practice provides plentiful examples of such reservations, and the ICJ upheld a reservation to Art. IX Genocide Convention in *Armed Activities in the*

paragraph 3 in Article 27 should come as no great surprise, and could even be seen in a positive light insofar as the Convention's drafters managed to salvage the principle of binding legal settlement and require recalcitrant States to declare their recalcitrance openly.

As Article 27(3) specifies, the declaration by which a State party may opt out of Article 27(2)'s regime of binding legal settlement must be made 'at the time of signature, ratification, acceptance or approval of, or accession to, the . . . Convention'. In other words, if a State party has signed or expressed its consent to be bound by the Convention without making such a declaration, it may not subsequently opt out of Article 27(2). But the converse is not true. As Article 27(4) affirms, a State party which has made such a declaration at the time of its signature or expression of consent to be bound may later withdraw the declaration, thereby accepting the regime of binding legal dispute settlement provided for in Article 27(2). The situation is analogous to that relating to reservations.[72] The omnibus reference in Article 27(3) to 'signature, ratification, acceptance or approval of, or accession' is less than elegant, but is intended not only to indicate that a declaration may be made under the provision at either signature or expression of consent to be bound but also to reflect, as regards the latter, the diverse formal means recognized in Article 29 by which States may express their consent to be bound by the Convention.[73]

Article 27(3) makes no mention of procedural requirements. But declarations of this sort in respect of multilateral treaties are always made in writing,[74] and, as is implied by Articles 27(4) and 32(2)(*c*) of the Convention, are to be notified to the depositary of the treaty,[75] which in this case is the UN Secretary-General.[76] In accordance with Article 32(2)(*c*) of the Convention, the Secretary-General must then inform all States (and not just States parties and signatories) of the declaration.

A valid declaration under Article 27(3), the effect of which is that the declarant state is not bound by Article 27(2), has two consequences: first, the declarant State cannot be required to submit disputes about the interpretation or application of the Convention to arbitration or adjudication by the ICJ; and second, as is made clear in the insistence on reciprocity in the second sentence of Article 27(3), the declarant State may not take advantage of the Convention's regime of binding legal settlement (ie cannot institute proceedings).

Of the 13 States to have become parties to the Convention to date,[77] two (Iran and Saudi Arabia) have made a declaration under Article 27(3).[78] While the figure may seem

Territory of the Congo (n. 41), 32, para. 67. For a fuller discussion in the context of Art. IX Genocide Convention, see *Armed Activities in the Territory of the Congo* (n. 41), joint sep. op. Higgins, Kooijmans, Elaraby, Owada, and Simma, 65 *et seq.*

72 See Arts 2(1)(*d*) and 19 VCLT. On the handling of late reservations, see Aust (n. 27), 158–9.

73 For details see the commentary to Art. 29.

74 See eg, by implication, Art. 77(1)(*c*) and (*d*) VCLT. In its *Treaty Handbook*, 17, para. 3.6.4, the UN Office of Legal Affairs (Treaty Division) states: 'Optional and mandatory declarations [under a treaty] impose legal obligations on the declarant and therefore must be signed by the Head of State, Head of Government or Minister for Foreign Affairs or by a person having full powers for that purpose issued by one of the above authorities.' The same would seem to apply where, by means of a declaration, a State 'opts out' of a legal framework, as is the case with Art. 27(3). See also *Final Clauses Handbook* (n. 4), 55.

75 See also Art. 78(*a*) VCLT.

76 See Art. 32 UNSCI.

77 As of July 2012.

78 See Status of Multilateral Treaties deposited with the Secretary-General, chap. III, no. 13 (United Nations Convention on Jurisdictional Immunities of States and Their Property, New York, 2 December 2004), http://treaties.un.org/Pages/ParticipationStatus.aspx.

low, experience with other multilateral treaty regimes which allow States parties to opt out of binding legal dispute resolution suggests that the number of declarations is likely to grow as the number of States parties increases. To give just one example, 21 of the 151 States parties to the Convention against Torture have opted out of the inter-State dispute settlement mechanism provided for by Article 30 of that convention.[79] This suggests that the number of States which 'dislike the loss of control that is entailed'[80] in recourse to binding legal dispute resolution is by no means negligible.

4. Evaluation

Article 27 is of considerable importance in the scheme of the Convention, and it is only because of the peculiar history of the Convention's text and States' long experience with dispute settlement clauses that this is not fully reflected in the *travaux*. The provision may be expected to have a significant impact on the settlement of immunity-related disputes between States. While its emphasis on negotiated settlement is relevant, Article 27 is noteworthy mainly because it increases the chance of inter-State litigation, whether in the form of arbitration or adjudication by the ICJ, in relation to the broad range of matters covered by the Convention. As the scale of this effect is proportionate to the number of States parties to the Convention,[81] it will take some time to discern. But paragraph 2 of Article 27 clearly has the potential to emerge as an important compromissory clause.

As for the dispute settlement process it embodies, Article 27 seeks to strike a balance between the interest in a legalized framework and the desire for flexibility—a flexibility which extends, in accordance with paragraphs 3 and 4, to whether a State is bound by paragraph 2's regime of binding legal settlement. In distinguishing not only between negotiations and binding legal settlement but also between arbitration and ICJ proceedings, Article 27 is perhaps overly prescriptive. It remains to be seen too whether the provision's preference for arbitration over the ICJ will be borne out in practice.

Irrespective of its role in the resolution of disputes between States parties, Article 27 is significant in paving the way for international pronouncements on the law of State immunity. While formally binding only between the parties to the dispute in question, it might be expected that arbitral awards and ICJ judgments pursuant to Article 27(2) will help to clarify the Convention's provisions and perhaps whether they comport with customary international law. Experience with other treaties envisaging recourse to arbitration or the ICJ, among them the Genocide Convention and the VCDR and VCCR, suggests that this ancillary benefit cannot be underestimated.

Naturally, at this stage, neither Iran nor Saudi Arabia has withdrawn its declaration in accordance with Art. 27(4). Experience with other multilateral treaties suggests that reliance by a State on Art. 27(4) is not out of the question, the most prominent example of the withdrawal of reservations to compromissory clauses being action taken by former socialist States in the late 1980s and early 1990s.

[79] As of July 2012: see Status of Multilateral Treaties deposited with the Secretary-General, chap. IV, no. 9 (Convention against Torture and Other Cruel, Inhuman or Degrading Treatment or Punishment, New York, 10 December 1984), http://treaties.un.org/Pages/ParticipationStatus.aspx.

[80] Fitzmaurice, in Institut de Droit international (n. 68), 279.

[81] It also depends on the number of States parties opting out of binding legal settlement via a declaration under Art. 27(3).

Article 28

James Devaney

Article 28

Signature

The present Convention shall be open for signature by all States until 17 January 2007, at United Nations Headquarters, New York.

1. Introduction

It is usual for modern multilateral treaties to include a provision like Article 28 of the Convention indicating when and where the treaty may be signed.[1] Article 28 fixes a discrete period during which the Convention is, or rather was, open for signature. On expiry of this period, accession[2] becomes, and has now become, the only means by which a State that has not signed the Convention may become party to it. In contrast, those States which availed themselves of the opportunity to sign the Convention may become party to it by means of ratification, acceptance, or approval.[3] Article 28 indicates that the Convention was open for signature by all States, not just by UN member States. Twenty-eight States became signatories to the Convention.[4]

2. Drafting History

A provision on signature was floated, alongside other final provisions, in Special Rapporteur Sucharitkul's Eighth Report,[5] but the ILC opted not to include final provisions in its 1991 draft articles. It was not until the last session, in 2004, of the Ad Hoc Committee on Jurisdictional Immunities of States and Their Property that such provisions were adopted. The wording of Article 28 was suggested by the Chairman of the Ad Hoc Committee.[6]

3. Key Points

3.1 When and where

Some multilateral treaties, for example the various UN conventions on human rights, remain open for signature indefinitely.[7] But it is far more common for treaties elaborated

[1] See *Final Clauses Handbook*, 33; *Treaty Handbook*, 5, para. 3.1.1.

[2] See Art. 29(2) UNCSI.

[3] See Art. 29(1) UNCSI.

[4] See Status of Multilateral Treaties deposited with the Secretary-General, chap. III, no. 13 (United Nations Convention on Jurisdictional Immunities of States and Their Property, New York, 2 December 2004), http://treaties.un.org/pages/ViewDetails.aspx?src=TREATY&mtdsg_no=III-13&chapter=3&lang=en.

[5] See Eighth report Sucharitkul, 35.

[6] See Suggestions of the Chairman, 2, art. D.

[7] See *Summary of Practice of the Secretary-General as Depositary*, 34, para. 116; *Final Clauses Handbook*, 30; *Treaty Handbook*, 5, para. 3.1.2.

and adopted under the aegis of the UN to remain open for signature only for a specified period.[8] The Convention followed the latter pattern. It was opened for signature on 17 January 2005[9] and closed for signature, as indicated in Article 28, on 17 January 2007. That the Convention was made available for signature at UN headquarters in New York is further consistent with contemporary UN practice.[10]

3.2 'all States'

The decision to open the Convention for signature by 'all States', in accordance with what is known as the 'all-States formula',[11] afforded States not members of the UN the opportunity to become party to the treaty. The formula is a not-infrequent feature of multilateral treaties that aspire to universal participation.[12] The UN's near-universal contemporary membership reduces considerably the formula's practical significance. But it does nothing to lessen its potential for diplomatic controversy. Whereas opening a multilateral treaty for signature by all UN member States is unproblematic insofar as it is self-evident when a State is and is not a member of the UN, the 'all States' formula is liable to place the Secretary-General—in his capacity as the Convention's depositary, one of whose tasks it is to ascertain whether an aspiring signatory may indeed sign the Convention[13]—in the invidious position of having to reach a conclusion as to whether a territorial-political entity from which he may receive a request to sign the Convention but whose claim to statehood is contested is indeed a State and, as such, eligible to sign the Convention.[14] In the event, however, the Secretary-General was spared the embarrassment. Only UN member States approached him for signature.[15]

3.3 Effect

Article 28 provides for what is referred to as 'simple' signature.[16] That is, signature of the Convention, as is usual with multilateral treaties elaborated and adopted within the framework of the UN, represents merely the expression of the signatory State's intention to take steps to become party to the treaty in the future[17] by means of the further act of ratification, acceptance, or approval, as provided for in Article 29(1) of the Convention. Simple signature, as distinct from so-called 'definitive' signature,[18] does not constitute consent to be bound by the Convention. Only ratification, acceptance, or approval, in the case of a signatory, or accession, in the case of a non-signatory and as provided for in Article 29(2) of the Convention, does. Signature does, however, commit the signatory State to refrain from any act which would defeat the object and purpose of the

[8] See *Final Clauses Handbook*, 30.

[9] See 'In witness whereof' clause UNCSI.

[10] See *Summary of Practice of the Secretary-General as Depositary*, 33–4, para. 116; *Final Clauses Handbook*, 30.

[11] See *Summary of Practice of the Secretary-General as Depositary*, 22, para. 81; *Final Clauses Handbook*, 12–15.

[12] See *Final Clauses Handbook*, 12.

[13] See *Summary of Practice of the Secretary-General as Depositary*, 21, para. 73 and 32, para. 108.

[14] See *Final Clauses Handbook*, 14.

[15] For how the Secretary-General is to proceed if approached by an entity whose statehood is contested, see the commentary to Art. 29(2) UNCSI.

[16] See *Final Clauses Handbook*, 32 and 124; *Treaty Handbook*, 5–6, para. 3.1.3.

[17] See *Final Clauses Handbook*, 32; *Treaty Handbook*, 5, para. 3.1.3.

[18] See *Final Clauses Handbook*, 34 and 124; *Treaty Handbook*, 6, para. 3.1.4. See also Arts 11 and 12 VCLT.

Convention, unless and until it makes clear its intention not to become party to the treaty.[19] Examples of such acts might be the adoption of legislation providing for the absolute immunity of foreign States from the civil jurisdiction of the signatory State's courts or, conversely, for the unavailability to foreign States in civil proceedings before those courts of any jurisdictional immunity whatsoever. Another example is provided by the recent practice of the People's Republic of China, a signatory to the Convention. On 8 June 2011, in *Democratic Republic of the Congo v FG Hemisphere Associates LLC*, a majority of the Court of Final Appeal of the Hong Kong Special Administrative Region, ruling that it was not open to the Court as a matter of constitutional law to apply a doctrine of State immunity different from the policy practised by the Central People's Government of the People's Republic of China, held that '[t]he doctrine of state immunity which presently applies in the HKSAR is the doctrine of absolute immunity'.[20] This technically provisional judgment was effectively affirmed on 26 August 2011 by a constitutionally-required 'interpretation' of the Basic Law of the HKSAR issued by the Standing Committee of the National People's Congress (SCNPC) of the PRC, on receipt of which the Court of Final Appeal, finding the majority's provisional judgment consistent with the SCNPC's interpretation, declared the judgment final.[21]

4. Evaluation

Provision for a procedure of simple signature followed by ratification, acceptance, or approval does no harm, and from the systemic point of view of the Convention it affords the bonus of creating a class of States which, though not parties, are obliged to refrain from acts which would defeat the object and purpose of the instrument. From the perspective of those States signatories, however, none of the supposed practical benefits of the two-stage procedure appears compelling in the context of a multilateral treaty elaborated over decades, merely rubber-stamped by the General Assembly, open for signature for a period of two years, and deposited with the Secretary-General.

The chief advantage to a signatory of the two-stage procedure over definitive signature—namely that the State is not bound by the provisions of a freshly-minted agreement signed in the heat of the moment by a plenipotentiary but, rather, has pause for thought before committing itself to participation—arises only in the context of conclusion and on-the-spot signature of a treaty at the close of a diplomatic conference or some

[19] See Art. 18(*a*) VCLT, as consonant with customary international law.

[20] *Democratic Republic of the Congo v FG Hemisphere Associates LLC*, FACV Nos 5, 6 & 7 of 2010, 8 June 2011, para. 226 (Chan and Ribeiro PJJ and Mason NPJ) (PRC (CFA HKSAR) 2011).

[21] See *Democratic Republic of the Congo v FG Hemisphere Associates LLC*, FACV Nos 5, 6 & 7 of 2010, 8 September 2011 (PRC (CFA HKSAR) 2011). The SCNPC's interpretation is found at annex 2 to this later judgment. In an explanation of the then-draft interpretation presented to the SCNPC on 24 August 2011 by the Deputy Director of the Legislative Affairs Commission of the SCNPC, the relationship between the PRC's continuing adherence to an absolute doctrine of State immunity and China's signature of UNCSI was explained as follows: 'On 14 September 2005, China signed the United Nations Convention on Jurisdictional Immunities of States and Their Property. The Convention confers on foreign states and their properties immunity from court jurisdiction and execution and provides, at the same time, for certain exceptions to state immunity by excluding commercial activities of states and their properties used for the purpose of commercial activities from the scope of state immunity. However, the Convention has not yet entered into force. The Standing Committee of the National People's Congress has not yet ratified the Convention. At present, China still implements the rules and policies on state immunity to which it has consistently and firmly adhered.' The explanation is found at annex 1 to the later judgment of the Court of Final Appeal.

other intensive period of negotiation. A State which, sometime between 17 January 2005 and 17 January 2007, signs a text over twenty-five years in the making and finalized by the Sixth Committee three weeks in advance of its adoption by the General Assembly in plenary[22] has had ample time for reflection. The same goes, *mutatis mutandis*, for the argument[23] that the two-stage procedure grants a signatory State the opportunity to arrange, where necessary, for legislative approval of its entry into the treaty and/or to get its legislative house in order before being bound by a treaty with implications for its domestic law. Both of these arguments are even weaker when the comparison drawn is not between simple and definitive signature within a limited period but between simple signature within a limited period and accession at the acceding State's leisure.

Nor, in the depositary practice of the Secretary-General, is it the case that signatories are notified of signatures, expressions of consent to be bound, and similar communications by other States while non-signatories are not. Quite apart from the fact that such information is readily available both online and in hard copy,[24] the Secretary-General sends depositary notifications to all States,[25] a practice rendered obligatory under the Convention by Article 32(2). The Secretary-General also sends to all States notification of any error in, and proposed correction of, an authentic text or certified true copy of a multilateral treaty deposited with him.[26] That said, 'it is to be understood', in the words of the Treaty Section of the UN Office of Legal Affairs, 'that only the States parties and signatories may object to the proposed correction'.[27]

[22] See 2004 Report Sixth Committee, 2, para. 8, indicating that the Sixth Committee adopted on 9 November 2004 the draft text of what would be UNGA res. 59/38, 2 December 2004.

[23] See eg *Final Clauses Handbook*, 36; *Treaty Handbook*, 8–9, para. 3.3.2.

[24] See Multilateral Treaties Deposited with the Secretary-General (MTDSG), available online and updated daily at <http://treaties.un.org/pages/ParticipationStatus.aspx>. The most recent print version, also available online (<http://treaties.un.org/Pages/Publications.aspx?pathpub=Publication/MTDSG/Page1_en.xml>), is current only to 1 April 2009.

[25] See *Final Clauses Handbook*, 33, note 37.

[26] See *Summary of Practice of the Secretary-General as Depositary*, 14–15, paras 51–52.

[27] *Summary of Practice of the Secretary-General as Depositary*, 15, para. 52.

Article 29

James Devaney

Article 29

Ratification, acceptance, approval or accession

1. The present Convention shall be subject to ratification, acceptance or approval.
2. The present Convention shall remain open for accession by any State.
3. The instruments of ratification, acceptance, approval or accession shall be deposited with the Secretary-General of the United Nations.

1. Introduction

Article 29 addresses the formal means by which a State may express its consent to be bound by the Convention and the procedure by which it must do so. Paragraph 1 concerns by implication only States signatories to the Convention, which in line with standard practice may, and which alone may, become party to the treaty by means of ratification, acceptance, or approval. Paragraph 2 concerns by implication all other States—that is, States which did not sign the Convention during the period from 17 January 2005 to 17 January 2007 specified for its signature.[1] In accordance again with established practice, these non-signatory States may, and should they wish to become party must, accede to the Convention. Paragraph 3 of Article 29 specifies that a State's expression of consent to be bound by the Convention under paragraph 1 or 2 is to be effected by the deposit with the UN Secretary-General (the Convention's depositary[2]) of the State's instrument of ratification, acceptance, approval, or accession, as the case may be. Deposit of the relevant instrument does not, however, bring the Convention into immediate force for the depositing State, the question of entry into force, both initial and subsequently for individual States parties, being dealt with in Article 30.

At time of going to press,[3] eight States had ratified the Convention, one had accepted it, one had approved it, and three had acceded to it.[4]

2. Drafting History

Separate provisions on ratification (no mention being made of acceptance or approval) and accession were floated, alongside other final provisions, in Special Rapporteur Sucharitkul's Eighth Report,[5] but the ILC opted not to include final provisions in its

[1] See Art. 28 and 'In witness whereof' clause UNCSI.

[2] See Art. 32(2) UNCSI.

[3] 28 September 2012.

[4] See Status of Multilateral Treaties deposited with the Secretary-General, chap. III, no. 13 (United Nations Convention on Jurisdictional Immunities of States and Their Property, New York, 2 December 2004), <http://treaties.un.org/pages/ViewDetails.aspx?src=TREATY&mtdsg_no=III-13&chapter=3&lang=en>.

[5] See Eighth report Sucharitkul, 35.

1991 draft articles. It was not until the last session, in 2004, of the Ad Hoc Committee on Jurisdictional Immunities of States and Their Property that such provisions were adopted. The Chairman of the Ad Hoc Committee suggested a simple article on consent to be bound which stated, without recourse to separate paragraphs, that the Convention was 'subject to ratification, acceptance, approval or accession', specifying in a second sentence that the relevant instruments were to be deposited with the Secretary-General.[6] But unlike the other final provisions suggested by the Chairman, the text underwent substantial modification at the hands of the Committee, which divided it into three paragraphs and decided to use in paragraph 2 the formula 'shall remain open for accession by any State'. The provision eventually adopted by the Committee[7] emerged unaltered as Article 29 of the Convention.

3. Key Points

3.1 Different formal means, identical legal effects

Although it is not indicated in Article 29(1), established treaty practice dictates that only those States which have signed the Convention may express their consent to be bound by it via ratification, acceptance, or approval. For any other State wishing to become party to the Convention, accession in accordance with Article 29(2) is the only option. But whatever the formal means open to a State for the expression of its consent to be bound by the Convention, the legal effect is the same.[8] Deposit by a State with the Secretary-General of its instrument of, variously, ratification, acceptance, approval, or accession establishes the State's consent to be bound by the treaty.

3.2 Ratification, acceptance, and approval

A. Equivalent for the purposes of international law

As Article 29(1) suggests, the terms 'ratification', 'acceptance', and 'approval' are, when used together in this way, functionally synonymous as a matter of international law. At first blush, Article 14(2) VCLT—which provides that '[t]he consent of a State to be bound by a treaty is expressed by acceptance or approval under conditions similar to those which apply to ratification'—might, in its use of the phrase 'similar to', be thought equivocal in this regard; but it is sufficiently clear from the article as a whole and from the ILC commentary to its draft forerunner[9] that 'similar to' should be taken in this context to mean 'substantively the same as'. Moreover, State practice leaves no room for doubt but that, as international acts, ratification, acceptance, and approval are to be treated as perfectly congruent when ranged alongside each other. The Treaty Section of the UN Office of Legal Affairs, for example, states:

> Acceptance or approval of a treaty following signature has the same legal effect as ratification, and the same rules apply, unless the treaty provides otherwise.[10]

A treaty may provide *contra* that acceptance and approval may be effected without prior signature, in which case they are treated as equivalent to accession, and the rules on

[6] Suggestions of the Chairman, 2, art. E.
[7] See art. 29 Draft UNCSI.
[8] See Arts 2(1)(*b*) and 11 VCLT; *Final Clauses Handbook*, 37 and 121; *Treaty Handbook*, 10, para. 3.3.4.
[9] See ILC commentary DALT, draft art. 11, para. 9.
[10] *Final Clauses Handbook*, 36.

accession are taken to apply.[11] As a general rule, however, '[r]atification, acceptance and approval all refer to the act undertaken on the international plane whereby a [signatory] State establishes its consent to be bound by a treaty'.[12]

The differences between ratification, acceptance, and approval lie solely at the level of national (*viz* constitutional) law, and are immaterial for present purposes. By making identical international provision for all three constitutional acts, Article 29(1) seeks to accommodate the varying demands of States' domestic legal orders, thereby facilitating participation in the Convention.[13]

B. 'Ratification'

'Ratification' within the meaning of the international law of treaties differs from 'ratification' as the term is often used in the domestic legal context,[14] particularly in relation to those domestic legal orders in which treaties are incapable of self-execution. 'Ratification' in the domestic sense usually refers to a legislative act by which some or all of the rules enunciated in a treaty are given effect within the law of the State in question. Such an act has no bearing on whether the State can be said to have ratified the Convention within the meaning of Article 29(1). Legislative enactment of this sort may predate or postdate the State's ratification, in the international legal sense, of the Convention. Either way, it is a different legal phenomenon entirely.

3.3 Accession

A. A one-step process

Accession, as provided for in Article 29(2) of the Convention, is the usual means by which States not signatories to a treaty may become party to it.[15] Whereas signature followed by ratification, acceptance, or approval is obviously a two-step process, a State's entry into the Convention by means of ratification requires only a single act,[16] namely deposit by that State with the Secretary-General of its instrument of accession, as provided for in Article 29(3).

B. 'any State'

Just as Article 28 specifies that the Convention was open for signature by 'all States',[17] Article 29(2) provides that the Convention is open for accession by 'any State'. No substantive difference exists between the 'all States' and 'any State' formulas.[18] The widespread use in multilateral treaties elaborated under the auspices of the UN of the former in relation to signature and the latter in relation to accession is perhaps intended

[11] See ILC commentary DALT, draft art. 11, paras 9, 10, and 12; *Treaty Handbook*, 9, para. 3.3.3.

[12] *Final Clauses Handbook*, 124.

[13] See ILC commentary DALT, draft art. 11, paras 11–12.

[14] See eg ILC commentary DALT, draft art. 11, para. 1; *Treaty Handbook*, 9, para. 3.2.2.

[15] See eg ILC commentary DALT, draft art. 12, para. 1.

[16] See, in relation to the law of treaties generally, *Final Clauses Handbook*, 37–8 and 121; *Treaty Handbook*, 10, para. 3.3.4.

[17] Note that, since ratification, acceptance, and approval are all premised on a State's prior signature of the Convention, it was unnecessary for the drafters to specify in Art. 29(1) UNCSI the range of States to which these three forms of expression of consent are open. Art. 28 UNCSI specifies that the Convention is open for signature by all States, and only those States which signed the Convention may ratify, accept, or approve it.

[18] See eg *Summary of Practice of the Secretary-General as Depositary*, 23, para. 81; *Final Clauses Handbook*, 12–14.

to connote (and, if so, is unsuccessful in connoting) that the facility of accession is not available to States which have signed the treaty.

Opening the Convention for accession by any State affords States not members of the UN the opportunity to become party to the treaty. The formula is a not-infrequent feature of multilateral treaties that aspire to universal participation.[19] But while the Organization's near-universal contemporary membership reduces the provision's practical significance, it does nothing to lessen its potential for diplomatic controversy. Whereas opening a multilateral treaty for accession by any UN member State is unproblematic insofar as it is self-evident when a State is and is not a member of the UN, the 'any State' formula is liable to place the Secretary-General—in his capacity as the Convention's depositary, one of whose tasks it is to ascertain whether an aspiring State party may indeed become party to the Convention[20]—in the invidious position of having to reach a conclusion as to whether a territorial-political entity from which he may receive an instrument of accession but whose claim to statehood is contested is indeed a State and, as such, eligible to accede to the Convention.[21]

Some cases are likely to prove less problematic than others. Significantly, it would appear that, in accordance with the canon of logic that the greater includes the lesser, the 'all States'/'any State' formula is taken to subsume the alternative 'Vienna formula', which embraces—in addition to UN members and parties to the Statute of the ICJ, both of which must be States[22]—those entities admitted as a member State to one or more of the UN specialized agencies.[23] As explained by the *Summary of Practice of the Secretary-General as Depositary* prepared by the Treaty Section of the UN Office of Legal Affairs, such entities are 'in essence recognized as States by the international community'.[24] On the basis of this past practice, Palestine, for example, as a member State of UNESCO, would be eligible to accede to the Convention.

But not every entity claiming to be a State is a member of one of the UN specialized agencies. The *Summary of Practice of the Secretary-General as Depositary* explains what happened in the past in relation to such entities:

> In reply to questions raised in connection with the interpretation to be given to the all States formula, the Secretary-General has on a number of occasions stated that there are certain areas in the world whose status is not clear. If he were to receive an instrument of accession from any such area, he would be in a position of considerable difficulty unless the [General] Assembly gave him explicit directives on the areas coming within the 'any State' or 'all States' formula. He would not

[19] See *Final Clauses Handbook*, 12.

[20] See *Summary of Practice of the Secretary-General as Depositary*, 21, para. 73 and 36, para. 120.

[21] See *Final Clauses Handbook*, 14.

[22] See Art. 4 UN Charter and Art. 35 ICJ Statute, respectively.

[23] See *Summary of Practice of the Secretary-General as Depositary*, 22–3, paras 79–81 and 83 (with erratum to para. 79 indicated at iii); *United Nations Juridical Yearbook 1974*, 158, para. 4. See also *Summary of Practice of the Secretary-General as Depositary*, 24, para. 86: '[O]n the basis of the Cook Islands' membership in the World Health Organization, and of its subsequent admittance to other specialized agencies (Food and Agriculture Organization of the United Nations, United Nations Educational, Scientific and Cultural Organization and International Civil Aviation Organization) as a full member without any specifications or limitations, the Secretary-General considered that the Cook Islands could henceforth be included in the "all States" formula, were it to wish to participate in treaties deposited with the Secretary-General.' The crucial distinction between the procedure, on the one hand, for admission to the UN and (in the case of non-member States) participation in the Statute of the ICJ and, on the other, for admission to one of the UN specialized agencies is that the latter is not subject to the veto of the five permanent members of the Security Council.

[24] *Summary of Practice of the Secretary-General as Depositary*, 22, para. 79 (with erratum indicated at iii).

wish to determine, on his own initiative, the highly political and controversial question of whether or not the areas whose status was unclear were States. Such a determination, he believed, would fall outside his competence. He therefore stated that when the 'any State' or 'all States' formula was adopted, he would be able to implement it only if the General Assembly provided him with the complete list of the States coming within the formula, other than those falling within the 'Vienna formula', i.e. States that are Members of the United Nations or members of the specialized agencies, or Parties to the Statute of the International Court of Justice.[25]

In the event, the General Assembly gave the Secretary-General no such list. Rather, on 14 December 1973, the Assembly adopted the following statement:

It is the understanding of the General Assembly that the Secretary-General, in discharging his functions as depositary of a convention with an 'all States' clause, will follow the practice of the Assembly in implementing such a clause and, whenever advisable, will request the opinion of the Assembly before receiving a signature or an instrument of ratification or accession.[26]

The *Summary of Practice of the Secretary-General as Depositary* elaborates on what is meant in this regard by 'the practice of the Assembly':

The 'practice of the General Assembly' referred to in the above-mentioned understanding is to be found in unequivocal indications from the Assembly that it considers a particular entity to be a State even though it does not fall within the 'Vienna formula'. Such indications are to be found in General Assembly resolutions . . .[27]

One type of General Assembly resolution taken in the past by the Secretary-General as an unambiguous indication of the statehood of a non-member State was the common resolution which noted with satisfaction the accession to independence of a former non-self-governing territory.[28] In contrast, on the basis of General Assembly resolution 2758 (XXVI), in which the Assembly recognized the representatives of the government of the People's Republic of China as the only legitimate representatives of China to the UN,[29] 'instruments received from the Taiwan Province of China will not be accepted by the Secretary-General in his capacity as depositary'.[30]

3.4 An open-ended opportunity

Unlike signature of the Convention, for the performance of which Article 28 afforded States a fixed period of two years, there is no time-limit on the availability to a signatory State of ratification, approval, or acceptance of the Convention in accordance with Article 29(1) or on the availability to any other State of accession in accordance with Article 29(2). As is usual for multilateral standard-setting treaties,[31] the opportunity to become party to the Convention is temporally open-ended.

[25] *Summary of Practice of the Secretary-General as Depositary*, 23, para. 81. See also *Final Clauses Handbook*, 14.

[26] *United Nations Juridical Yearbook 1973*, 79, note 9. See also *United Nations Juridical Yearbook 1974*, 158, para. 2; *Summary of Practice of the Secretary-General as Depositary*, 23, para. 82; *Final Clauses Handbook*, 14.

[27] *Summary of Practice of the Secretary-General as Depositary*, 23, para. 83.

[28] See *Summary of Practice of the Secretary-General as Depositary*, 24, para. 84.

[29] UNGA res. 2758 (XXVI), 25 October 1971.

[30] *Final Clauses Handbook*, 15.

[31] See *Treaty Handbook*, 9, para. 3.3.2. See also *Final Clauses Handbook*, 38, in specific relation to accession.

Where a signatory State shows no signs of moving towards ratification, acceptance, or approval, its obligation to refrain from acts which would defeat the object and purpose of the Convention will remain on foot unless and until it makes clear its intention not to become party to the treaty.[32]

3.5 Deposit of the instrument of ratification, acceptance, approval, or accession

The obligation on a State wishing to express its consent to be bound by the Convention to deposit its instrument of ratification, acceptance, approval, or accession with the Secretary-General is more than merely administrative. Although Article 29(3) does not spell this out, a State's expression of consent to be bound is effected as a matter of law by its deposit with the Secretary-General[33] and, as a corollary, is effective from the date of such deposit.

3.6 Consent to be bound and entry into force

Deposit by a State of its instrument of ratification, acceptance, approval, or accession does not render the Convention in force for the depositing State.[34] The Convention's entry into force, both initial and for individual States parties thereafter, is dealt with in Article 30.[35] The twofold upshot of this latter provision is that, for the first thirty States to deposit their respective instruments of consent, the Convention will enter into force only on the thirtieth day following the date of deposit of the thirtieth such instrument;[36] and that, for each State depositing its instrument of consent after the deposit of the thirtieth such instrument, the Convention will enter into force only on the thirtieth day after the deposit by that State of its own instrument.[37]

Once it has expressed its consent to be bound, a State is obliged to refrain from acts which would defeat the Convention's object and purpose 'pending the entry into force of the [Convention] and provided that such entry into force is not unduly delayed'.[38] This obligation applies as much in respect of the Convention's entry into force for a specific State after its initial entry into force as in respect of that initial entry into force, even if the proviso as to undue delay makes sense only in the second context. In other words, just as (subject to the foregoing proviso) any and all of the first thirty States to express their consent to be bound under Article 29 must refrain from acts contrary to the Convention's object and purpose while they await the Convention's initial entry into force, so too must a State which expresses its consent to be bound under Article 29 sometime after the thirtieth such expression of consent refrain from like acts during the thirty-day interim between the deposit of its instrument of consent to be bound and the Convention's entry into force for it.

[32] See Art. 18(*a*) VCLT. See also *Summary of Practice of the Secretary-General as Depositary*, 41, para. 139; *Treaty Handbook*, 10–11, para. 3.3.5.

[33] See Art. 16(*b*) VCLT.

[34] See eg *Summary of Practice of the Secretary-General as Depositary*, 42, para. 142; *Treaty Handbook*, 8, para. 3.1.1.

[35] See commentary to Art. 30 UNCSI. See also, more generally, Art. 24(1) VCLT.

[36] See Art. 30(1) UNCSI.

[37] See Art. 30(2) UNCSI.

[38] Art. 18(*b*) VCLT.

4. Evaluation

Article 29 is a straightforward provision affording flexibility as to the formal means by which a State may express its consent to be bound by the Convention. Its use of the 'any State' formula in relation to accession may raise sensitive questions for the Secretary-General as depositary, but a procedure is in place for answering these questions.

Article 30

Antonios Tzanakopoulos

Article 30

Entry into force

1. The present Convention shall enter into force on the thirtieth day following the date of deposit of the thirtieth instrument of ratification, acceptance, approval or accession with the Secretary-General of the United Nations.
2. For each State ratifying, accepting, approving or acceding to the present Convention after the deposit of the thirtieth instrument of ratification, acceptance, approval or accession, the Convention shall enter into force on the thirtieth day after the deposit by such State of its instrument of ratification, acceptance, approval or accession.

1. Introduction

The common-sense customary rule codified in the first limb of Article 24(1) VCLT states that a treaty enters into force 'in such manner and upon such date as it may provide'. For the purposes of the Convention, it is Article 30 which provides for this manner and date. Article 30 belongs to that set of final provisions which are considered to apply, in accordance with Article 24(4) VCLT, from the moment of the adoption of the text, dealing as they do with 'matters arising necessarily before the entry into force of the treaty'[1]—that is, in the terminology of the Treaty Section of the UN's Office of Legal Affairs, before the treaty's 'initial'[2] (or definitive'[3]) entry into force. As is the usual practice for multilateral standard-setting treaties concluded under the auspices of the UN,[4] Article 30 makes provision for two dates of entry into force,[5] namely a date of initial entry into force, when the Convention becomes effective in its entirety for the first time, albeit only for those States within the quorum required to trigger this occurrence, and a date of 'subsequent entry into force for additional parties'[6] (or 'entry into force for a State'[7]), when the Convention becomes applicable to any State becoming party to it subsequent to the achievement of the quorum for its initial entry into force.

[1] Art. 24(4) VCLT.

[2] See *Summary of Practice of the Secretary-General as Depositary*, 66, heading A.

[3] See *Final Clauses Handbook*, 58, heading 1; *Treaty Handbook*, 20, para. 4.2.1.

[4] See *Final Clauses Handbook*, 57–66.

[5] On the various dates of a multilateral treaty's entry into force, see G.E. do Nascimento e Silva, 'Le facteur temps et les traités' (1977) 154 *RdC* 215, 225; E. Roucounas, 'Uncertainties Regarding the Entry into Force of Some Multilateral Treaties', in K. Wellens (ed.), *International Law: Theory and Practice—Essays in Honour of Eric Suy* (The Hague: Martinus Nijhoff, 1998), 179, 179.

[6] See *Summary of Practice of the Secretary-General as Depositary*, 72, heading B.

[7] See *Treaty Handbook*, 21, para. 4.2.2, and 59. See, similarly, *Final Clauses Handbook*, 65, referring to the date of '[e]ntry into force for a State after the treaty has entered into force'.

2. Drafting History

A provision on entry into force appeared among other final provisions floated in 1986 in Special Rapporteur Sucharitkul's Eighth Report;[8] but, true to the spirit if not the letter of the latter's observation that consideration of the issue 'could be postponed . . . until the plenipotentiary conference [was] convened',[9] the ILC decided against incorporating final provisions in its 1991 draft articles. The matter was taken up again only in the final session, in 2004, of the Ad Hoc Committee on Jurisdictional Immunities of State and Their Property, shortly before the eventual adoption of the Convention. The wording of Article 30 was put forward by the Chairman of the Ad Hoc Committee,[10] who further suggested an additional sentence in each paragraph specifying that the Convention was to apply only to proceedings introduced after its initial entry into force (paragraph 1) or its entry into force for the particular State in question (paragraph 2). The non-inclusion of the respective sentences almost certainly[11] reflects their superfluity, given Article 4 of the Convention.[12] There is no indication as to how or why the Chairman settled on the respective figures of thirty ratifications and thirty days as the trigger for the Convention's entry into force or whether these figures were the subject of debate.

3. Key Points

A wide range of formulae are available for the specification of a treaty's initial entry into force. Figures aside, the formula employed in Article 30(1), namely a minimum number of expressions of consent to be bound followed by the lapse of a set period, is the most common among modern multilateral treaties.[13] The threshold of thirty instruments of consent is a mid-range one for a universal multilateral treaty. By way of comparison, the United Nations Convention on the Law of the Sea and the Rome Statute of the International Criminal Court each required sixty,[14] whereas the Geneva Conventions of 1949 required only two.[15] In the words of the Treaty Section of the UN Office of Legal Affairs, '[a] significant number of instruments of consent to be bound are specified to ensure broad acceptance of the treaty before its entry into force'.[16] It makes sense,

[8] See Eighth report Sucharitkul, 35.

[9] Eighth report Sucharitkul, 35, para. 50.

[10] See Suggestions of the Chairman, 3, art. F.

[11] The Committee's debates were conducted *in camera*, the only account of them being the extremely terse announcements of their respective outcomes in the Committee's sessional reports.

[12] Art. 4 UNCSI provides in relevant part that the Convention 'shall not apply to any question of jurisdictional immunities of States or their property arising in a proceeding instituted against a State before a court of another State prior to the entry into force of the present Convention for the States concerned'. For more, see commentary to Art. 4 UNCSI.

[13] See *Final Clauses Handbook*, 58–9; *cf* A. Aust, 'Article 24—Convention of 1969', in O. Corten and P. Klein (eds), *The Vienna Conventions on the Law of Treaties: A Commentary* (Oxford: Oxford University Press, 2011), vol. I, 628, 634, para. 11; C. Denis, 'Article 84—Convention of 1969', in Corten and Klein (n. 13), vol. II, 1825, 1825, para. 1.

[14] See Art. 308(1) United Nations Convention on the Law of the Sea, Montego Bay, 10 December 1982, 1833 UNTS 3; Art. 126(1) Rome Statute of the International Criminal Court, Rome, 17 July 1998, 2187 UNTS 3.

[15] See Art. 58 Convention for the Amelioration of the Condition of the Wounded and Sick in Armed Forces in the Field, Geneva, 12 August 1949, 75 UNTS 32; Art. 57 Convention for the Amelioration of the Condition of the Wounded, Sick and Shipwrecked Members of the Armed Forces at Sea, Geneva, 12 August 1949, 75 UNTS 86; Art. 138 Convention relative to the Treatment of Prisoners of War, Geneva, 12 August 1949, 75 UNTS 136; Art. 153 Convention relative to the Protection of Civilian Persons in Time of War, 12 August 1949, 75 UNTS 288.

[16] *Final Clauses Handbook*, 58.

however, not to set the bar prohibitively high. In these twin lights, the figure of thirty strikes a judicious balance. As for the figure of thirty days between deposit of the thirtieth instrument of consent to be bound and the Convention's initial entry into force, this is at the low end of the spectrum of UN practice, which ranges from thirty days to twelve months.[17] The Treaty Section of the Office of Legal Affairs explains the lapse-of-time requirement as follows:

> The time so provided may give contracting States time to enact domestic legislation or to bring into effect implementing legislation previously enacted. It also gives the depositary time to notify contracting States of the forthcoming entry into force.[18]

In this light, thirty days is a surprisingly short period, especially given the constitutional or practical requirement in many States for the passage of legislation to give effect to the Convention. States would be well advised to enact and bring into effect any necessary legislation in anticipation of deposit of their instrument of consent.

It is worth emphasizing that Article 30(2) relates not (as is often said by way of shorthand of this type of provision[19]) to any State which deposits its instrument of consent to be bound after the Convention's initial entry into force but rather to any State which deposits its instrument of consent anytime after the deposit of the minimum number of instruments of consent required for the Convention's initial entry into force—that is, in the case of the Convention, anytime after the deposit of the thirtieth instrument of consent. This means, for example, that if the thirtieth instrument of ratification, acceptance, approval, or accession is deposited on 26 April and the thirty-first on 27 April, the Convention will enter into force for the thirty-first State party on 27 May, only one day after its initial entry into force. This explains why the specified interim period between an additional State's expression of consent to be bound and the treaty's entry into force for it tends to be the same as the specified interim period between the achievement of the necessary quorum of expressions of consent and the treaty's initial entry into force.[20] If the former were shorter than the latter, the treaty might be scheduled to enter into force for an additional State party before it had entered into force in the first place.

4. Evaluation

The text of Article 30 does not give rise to problems of interpretation. The most important questions posed by the provision are whether and when the Convention will enter into force. Most multilateral treaties deposited with the Secretary-General enter into force within three to five years of their adoption.[21] The Convention has already passed that mark. As well as being significant in its own right, uncertainty over the Convention's entry into force has implications for the obligation on those States already parties to it to refrain, pending its entry into force, from any act which would defeat its object and purpose, an obligation which is subject to the proviso that 'such entry into force is not unduly delayed'.[22]

[17] *Final Clauses Handbook*, 59.
[18] *Final Clauses Handbook*, 59.
[19] See eg *Final Clauses Handbook*, 65; *Treaty Handbook*, 21, para. 4.2.2.
[20] See *Final Clauses Handbook*, 65.
[21] Roucounas (n. 5), 184–5.
[22] See Art. 18(b) VCLT, as consonant with custom.

That said, it might be asked whether any real benefit is to be had by the Convention's entry into force. It is arguable that most of the instrument's substantive provisions simply codify existing customary rules and that those which may not are shaping customary international law in their image. An analogy might be drawn with the VCLT and the ILC's Articles on Responsibility of States for Internationally Wrongful Acts, the practical value of each of which lies in its codification or crystallization of custom. The Convention or individual provisions of it have already been relied on as statements of customary international law by the ECtHR and a range of national courts.[23] Moreover, the questions of State immunity in relation to which custom remains—or, until 3 February 2012, remained[24]—in flux, and thus in relation to which the Convention might usefully have served to harmonize practice,[25] are precisely the questions understood not to be covered by the instrument or on which it is silent, chief among them being the respective questions of criminal proceedings; of civil proceedings in respect of violations of international human rights law, international humanitarian law or other international rules for the protection of the human person; and of civil proceedings in respect of the acts of foreign military forces in the forum State's territory.

In the final analysis, however, the Convention's entry into force would doubtless be a good thing. Just as with the VCLT, the application *inter partes* of the Convention in its quality as treaty law would be without prejudice to any value it may have as a statement of custom, and would usefully serve to harmonize practice among the parties' courts on those crucial questions to which the Convention relates.

[23] See commentary to Preamble UNCSI.

[24] As regards the second question and aspects of the third, see now *Jurisdictional Immunities of the State (Germany v Italy: Greece intervening), Judgment*, International Court of Justice, 3 February 2012, <http://www.icj-cij.org/docket/files/143/16883.pdf>.

[25] See Preamble (third recital) UNCSI.

Article 31

ANTONIOS TZANAKOPOULOS

Article 31

Denunciation

1. Any State Party may denounce the present Convention by written notification to the Secretary-General of the United Nations.
2. Denunciation shall take effect one year following the date on which notification is received by the Secretary-General of the United Nations. The present Convention shall, however, continue to apply to any question of jurisdictional immunities of States or their property arising in a proceeding instituted against a State before a court of another State prior to the date on which the denunciation takes effect for any of the States concerned.
3. The denunciation shall not in any way affect the duty of any State Party to fulfil any obligation embodied in the present Convention to which it would be subject under international law independently of the present Convention.

1. Introduction

Article 31 makes provision for the denunciation of the Convention by any State party, a possibility foreshadowed by the customary rule[1] codified in Article 54(*a*) VCLT.[2] The term 'denunciation', which is functionally synonymous with 'withdrawal',[3] 'denotes a unilateral act by which a party terminates its participation in a treaty'.[4] As a general rule, the consequence of a State party's denunciation of a multilateral treaty, such as the Convention, is that from the date the denunciation takes effect the denouncing State, on the one side, and each of the remaining States parties, on the other, are reciprocally released from any obligation further to perform the treaty the one towards the other.[5] The multilateral treaty itself remains on foot as among the other States parties to it.[6] A savings clause in Article 31(2) of the Convention, however, lays down that, in proceedings instituted before the date on which any denunciation takes effect for any of the States concerned, the Convention shall continue to dictate the scope of the

[1] See V. Chapaux, 'Article 54—Convention of 1969', in O. Corten and P. Klein (eds), *The Vienna Conventions on the Law of Treaties: A Commentary* (Oxford: Oxford University Press, 2011), vol. II, 1236, 1238, para. 4.

[2] Art. 54(*a*) VCLT provides in relevant part that 'the withdrawal of a party [to a treaty] may take place . . . in conformity with the provisions of the treaty'.

[3] See eg Art. 56 VCLT. See also *Final Clauses Handbook*, 109; *Treaty Handbook*, 25, para. 4.5. In the specific context of a multilateral treaty, Aust considers 'withdrawal' to be the 'better term'. See A. Aust, *Modern Treaty Law and Practice* (2nd edn) (Cambridge: Cambridge University Press, 2007), 277.

[4] Aust (n. 3), 277. See, similarly, *Final Clauses Handbook*, 109: 'Denunciation (or withdrawal) is a procedure initiated unilaterally by a State to terminate its legal engagements under a treaty.'

[5] See Art. 70(2) VCLT, cross-referable to Art. 70(1)(*a*) VCLT. Article 70(2) VCLT reflects customary international law. See H. Ascensio, 'Article 70—Convention of 1969', in Corten and Klein (n. 1), vol. II, 1585, 1590–1, paras 8–10.

[6] See *Final Clauses Handbook*, 109; Aust (n. 3), 277.

jurisdictional immunities of the denouncing State and its property before the courts of the remaining States parties, and *vice versa*. Article 31(2) specifies that denunciation of the Convention pursuant to Article 31(1) takes effect one year after the date on which written notification is received by the UN Secretary-General, the Convention's depositary.

2. Drafting History

The final provisions of the Convention were discussed and adopted only during the final session, in early 2004, of the Ad Hoc Committee on Jurisdictional Immunities of States and Their Property, not long before the final adoption of the Convention itself by the General Assembly later that year.[7] No final provisions are to be found in the ILC's draft articles, and although Special Rapporteur Sucharitkul did tentatively suggest some in his eighth and final report in 1986,[8] he included no provision on denunciation.

Paragraph 3 of Article 31 did not appear in the Chairman's suggestions on final clauses to the Ad Hoc Committee,[9] perhaps because it states the obvious, and must have been inserted *ex abundante cautela* during discussion within the Committee.[10] As for paragraph 2, the second sentence suggested by the Chairman, which mirrored Article 40(2) ECSI, read:

> The present Convention shall, however, continue to apply to proceedings introduced before the date on which the denunciation takes effect, and to judgments given in such proceedings.[11]

Article 31(2) of the eventual Convention, however, makes no mention of judgments. No reason for the deletion is recorded, although it almost certainly relates to the fact that the ECSI, unlike the Convention, obliges Contracting States to give effect to judgments rendered against them in the courts of other Contracting States.[12]

3. Key Points

3.1 Right of denunciation unconditional

Article 31(1) of the Convention, as is common for multilateral treaties concluded under the auspices of the UN,[13] allows for the Convention's unconditional denunciation by a State party, by which is meant that the State party need establish no objective[14] or even subjective[15] justification for its decision. Indeed, as is also common under UN

[7] See 2004 Report Ad Hoc Committee, 3, paras 9–10 and Part VI Draft UNCSI.

[8] See Eighth report Sucharitkul, 35.

[9] See Suggestions of the Chairman, 3, Art. G.

[10] The Committee's debates were conducted *in camera*, the only account of them being the extremely terse announcements of their respective outcomes in the Committee's sessional reports.

[11] See Suggestions of the Chairman, 3, Art. G(2).

[12] See Art. 20 ECSI.

[13] See eg Art. 21 International Convention on the Elimination of All Forms of Racial Discrimination, New York, 7 March 1966, 660 UNTS 195; Art. 9 Protocol relating to the Status of Refugees, New York, 31 January 1967, 606 UNTS 267; Art. 52 Convention on the Rights of the Child, New York, 20 November 1989, 1577 UNTS 3; Art. 15 Optional Protocol to the Convention on the Rights of the Child on the Sale of Children, Child Prostitution and Child Pornography, New York, 25 May 2000, 2171 UNTS 227; Art. 11 Optional Protocol to the Convention on the Rights of the Child on the Involvement of Children in Armed Conflict, New York, 25 May 2000, 2173 UNTS 222. See also Aust (n. 3), 279.

[14] See eg Arts 56(1)(*b*), 61, and 62 VCLT.

[15] See eg Art. X(1) Treaty on the Non-Proliferation of Nuclear Weapons, Washington Moscow London, 1 July 1968, 729 UNTS 161 (NPT); Art. XVI(2) Convention on the Prohibition of the Development,

conventions, the denouncing State party need not even give reasons for its decision.[16] Nor is there any requirement that the Convention be in force for a specified period before it can be denounced.[17]

3.2 Procedure

As the ILC noted in its commentary to what was to become Article 54 VCLT, when a treaty provides for its own denunciation, 'how and when this is to happen is essentially a question of interpreting and applying the treaty'.[18] Article 31(1) of the Convention specifies that a State party may denounce the Convention simply by addressing a written notification to the effect to the UN Secretary-General, who acts as the Convention's depositary in accordance with Article 32(1). The procedure is significantly more straightforward than the default procedure for withdrawal in Articles 65, 66, and 67(1) VCLT. This makes sense, given that the VCLT's procedure is aimed at establishing whether one of the objective conditions for withdrawal enumerated in the VCLT has been satisfied.[19]

Article 67(2) VCLT, applicable as much to denunciation pursuant to a provision in the treaty (here, the Convention) as to denunciation in accordance with the default procedure laid down in the VCLT, stipulates that any act of withdrawing from a treaty 'shall be carried out through an instrument communicated to the parties'. Under the Convention, the task of communicating a State party's notification of denunciation falls to the UN Secretary-General as depositary, in accordance with Article 32(2)(*a*). Unlike under the VCLT's default procedure, there is no scope under the Convention for objections to a notification of denunciation, since a State party is free to denounce the Convention for whatever reason it thinks fit.

The first sentence of Article 31(2) specifies that denunciation of the Convention becomes effective one year after receipt by the Secretary-General of the denouncing State's written notification.

3.3 Effects

A. Article 31(2)'s savings clause

Once its denunciation becomes effective, the denouncing State is no longer a party to the treaty. As a general rule, it owes no further treaty obligations towards the remaining

Production, Stockpiling and Use of Chemical Weapons and on their Destruction, Geneva, 3 September 1992, 1974 UNTS 45 (Chemical Weapons Convention).

[16] A requirement to provide reasons is common in arms control treaties: see eg Art. X(1) NPT; Art. XVI(2) Chemical Weapons Convention; Art. 20(2) Convention on the Prohibition of the Use, Stockpiling, Production and Transfer of Anti-Personnel Mines and on their Destruction, Oslo, 18 September 1997, 2056 UNTS 211 (Ottawa Convention). The validity of denunciation despite the absence of any required statement of reasons can be assumed in all cases where no objective conditions precedent to denunciation are posited. See S. Maslen, *Commentaries on Arms Control Treaties. Volume 1: The Convention on the Prohibition of the Use, Stockpiling, Production, and Transfer of Anti-Personnel Mines and on their Destruction* (Oxford: Oxford University Press, 2004), 308, para. 20.7.

[17] By way of contrast, see Art. XIV Convention on the Prevention and Punishment of the Crime of Genocide, Paris, 9 December 1948, 78 UNTS 277 (ten years); Art. 19(1) Vienna Convention for the Protection of the Ozone Layer, Vienna, 22 March 1985, 1513 UNTS 293 (four years); Art. 28(1) Stockholm Convention on Persistent Organic Pollutants, Stockholm, 22 May 2001, 2256 UNTS 119 (three years).

[18] ILC commentary DALT, draft art. 51, para. 1.

[19] See M Prost, 'Article 65—Convention of 1969', in Corten and Klein (n. 1), 1483, 1484–5, paras 2–3.

States parties, and they owe none to it.[20] But in a minor deviation from this general rule, the second sentence of Article 31(2) of the Convention inserts a savings clause according to which the Convention will continue to apply, despite the denunciation, to any question of jurisdictional immunities of States or their property which may arise in proceedings against the denouncing State before the courts of one of the remaining State parties, and *vice versa,* if the proceedings were instituted before the denunciation took effect for either of these States. Effectively, then, the second sentence of Article 31(2) turns the one-year notification period specified by the first sentence of the same article into a 'grace period' during which a prospective claimant (before the denouncing State's courts against another State party or before another State party's courts against the denouncing State), having been put on notice of the denunciation, is given the opportunity to institute proceedings to which the Convention will apply. An analogous situation prevails under Article 40(2) ECSI. The words 'for any of the States concerned' in the final phrase of Article 31(2) of the Convention ('the date on which the denunciation takes effect for any of the States concerned') are not insignificant. A State which becomes a party to the Convention only after a former State party's denunciation has become effective is not bound by, and may not benefit from, the special obligation imposed by the savings clause in Article 31(2).

The savings clause in Article 31(2) might perhaps be characterized as an application of the customary rule reflected in Article 70(1)(*b*) VCLT (applicable to denunciation of a multilateral treaty via Article 70(2) VCLT), whereby denunciation does not affect any 'legal situation of the parties created through the execution of the treaty' prior to the date when the denunciation takes effect.[21] A proceeding before a domestic court might plausibly be qualified as a 'legal situation' within the meaning of Article 70(1)(*b*) VCLT. The savings clause in Article 31(2) might equally be thought of as an analogical application to the domestic level of the principle that international jurisdiction by way of a compromissory clause in a treaty may not be frustrated by the treaty's denunciation if the relevant proceedings were initiated before the denunciation took effect.[22]

B. Article 31(3)'s savings clause

Article 31(3) contains a further savings clause which provides that denunciation of the Convention shall not affect obligations binding independently of the Convention on either the denouncing State or any of the remaining States parties. The provision corresponds in substance to Article 43 VCLT,[23] and serves, out of an abundance of caution,[24] merely to affirm the juridical truism that obligations owed by or towards the

[20] See n. 5.

[21] See also eg Art. 317(2) United Nations Convention on the Law of the Sea, Montego Bay, 10 December 1982, 1833 UNTS 3 (UNCLOS).

[22] See *Northern Cameroons (Cameroon v United Kingdom), Preliminary Objections,* ICJ Rep 1963, 15, 35. See also, to equivalent effect, Art. 12(2) Optional Protocol to the International Covenant on Civil and Political Rights, New York, 16 December 1966, 999 UNTS 171; Art. 31(2) second sentence United Nations Convention against Torture and Other Cruel, Inhuman or Degrading Treatment or Punishment, New York, 10 December 1984, 1465 UNTS 85.

[23] Article 43 VCLT reads in relevant part: 'The ... denunciation of a treaty ... as a result ... of the provisions of the treaty, shall not in any way impair the duty of any State to fulfil any obligation embodied in the treaty to which it would be subject under international law independently of the treaty.' See also eg Art 318(3) UNCLOS; Art. 16(3) Chemical Weapons Convention; Art. 20(4) Ottawa Convention.

[24] See M. Villiger, *Customary International Law and Treaties: A Manual on the Theory and Practice of the Interrelation of Sources* (2nd edn) (The Hague: Kluwer, 1997), 270, para. 428, referring to Art. 43 VCLT.

denouncing State under either customary international law[25] or another treaty touching on the same subject-matter as the Convention continue in force regardless of the Convention's denunciation.

4. Evaluation

Article 31's allowance for denunciation of the Convention subject to its two savings clauses is uncontroversial treaty practice in the UN context, and does not give rise to significant problems of interpretation or application. But it might be asked whether the inclusion of a denunciation clause casts doubt on any codificatory character to which the Convention or at least some of its provisions may lay claim. On the one hand, it might be argued that, if all or part of the Convention were truly thought consonant with customary international law, its drafters would not have provided for denunciation from it, since denunciation would be to no substantive avail: the States concerned would remain bound in relation to each other by the non-procedural obligations embodied in the instrument, albeit on the basis of parallel, identical rules of custom. On the other hand, one could argue that, if the drafters believed the Convention to reflect custom in whole or in part, they would, it stands to reason, have seen no problem in allowing for denunciation, precisely because the States concerned would remain bound vis-à-vis each other by the substantive customary rules codified in the instrument. Moreover, the drafters would no doubt have appreciated that provision for denunciation does remain of considerable practical advantage, and therefore attractiveness, to prospective States parties insofar as it permits States parties to disencumber themselves of any subsequently unwanted procedural or other ancillary obligations laid down in the Convention (notably the dispute settlement obligation in Article 27, with its compromissory clause in paragraph 2) to which they did not enter a reservation (or, in the case of Article 27, a declaration under paragraph 3) when expressing their consent to be bound. It also pays to keep in mind that many domestic legal orders make different constitutional allowance for customary international law and treaty law. In this light, the inclusion in the Convention of provision for denunciation has no necessary implications for the putative correspondence with custom of any or all of the instrument's substantive provisions.

[25] See *Military and Paramilitary Activities in and Against Nicaragua (Nicaragua v United States of America), Jurisdiction and Admissibility*, ICJ Rep 1984, 392, 424, para. 73; *Military and Paramilitary Activities in and Against Nicaragua (Nicaragua v United States of America), Merits*, ICJ Rep 1986, 14, 93–7, paras 174–182.

Article 32

Tobias Thienel

Article 32

Depositary and notifications

1. The Secretary-General of the United Nations is designated the depositary of the present Convention.
2. As depositary of the present Convention, the Secretary-General of the United Nations shall inform all States of the following:
   (*a*) signatures of the present Convention and the deposit of instruments of ratification, acceptance, approval or accession or notifications of denunciation, in accordance with articles 29 and 31;
   (*b*) the date on which the present Convention will enter into force, in accordance with article 30;
   (*c*) any acts, notifications or communications relating to the present Convention.

1. Introduction

The UN Secretary-General is usually the depositary of conventions elaborated under the auspices of the UN.[1] But even when this is the case, he or she is not always explicitly designated as such.[2] It has often been thought sufficient simply to indicate in the final provisions of a convention that instruments of ratification, accession, approval, or acceptance, as well as the original text, are to be deposited with the Secretary-General; that States parties may denounce the Convention by written notification to the Secretary-General; and that the Secretary-General has duties relating to the transmission of certified copies of the Convention and, as provided for in Article 32(2) of the Convention, to notification of treaty actions and of the date of the Convention's entry into force. That said, a specific provision in the terms of Article 32(1) of the Convention is not uncommon,[3] and arguably represents best practice.

[1] See *Treaty Handbook*, 3, para. 2.3. The Secretary-General's policy in relation to acceptance of designation as depositary is spelled out in *Summary of Practice of the Secretary-General as Depositary*, 7–8, paras 28–30; in part III of the Secretary-General's bulletin entitled *Procedures to be followed by the departments, offices and regional commissions of the United Nations with regard to treaties and international agreements*, UN doc. ST/SGB/2001/7, 28 August 2001; in *Final Clauses Handbook*, 6–7; and in *Treaty Handbook*, 3–4, para. 2.3.

[2] See, generally, *Final Clauses Handbook*, 3–5.

[3] See eg Art. 25(2) Convention on the Elimination of All Forms of Discrimination against Women, New York, 18 December 1979, 1249 UNTS 13; Art. 319(1) United Nations Convention on the Law of the Sea, Montego Bay, 10 December 1982, 1833 UNTS 3; Art. 53 Convention on the Rights of the Child, New York, 20 November 1989, 1577 UNTS 3; Art. 41(1) United Nations Convention against Transnational Organized Crime, New York, 15 November 2000, 2225 UNTS 209; Art. 71(1) United Nations Convention against Corruption, New York, 31 October 2003, 2349 UNTS 41; Art. 41 Convention on the Rights of Persons with Disabilities, New York, 13 December 2006, 2515 UNTS 3.

In designating the Secretary-General as depositary of a treaty, States are in reality designating the Treaty Section of the Office of Legal Affairs of the UN Secretariat,[4] to which the Secretary-General has assigned all his depositary functions 'because of the extreme importance that those functions be performed in a legally correct and absolutely consistent manner and that all information on United Nations treaties be available in and published by one office'.[5]

2. Drafting History

When eventually, on receipt in late 2003 of the penultimate report of the Ad Hoc Committee on Jurisdictional Immunities of States and Their Property, the General Assembly reconvened the Committee for what would be its final session, it mandated the latter to formulate final clauses 'with a view to completing a convention on jurisdictional immunities of States and their property'.[6] What became Article 33 was suggested by the Chairman of the Ad Hoc Committee in 2004.[7] The Committee adopted the provision, which passed into the Convention on its adoption later the same year.

3. Key Points

Neither the obligation on UN member States under Article 102(1) UN Charter[8] to register treaties with the UN Secretariat nor the similar obligation under Article 80(1) VCLT[9] entails an obligation to designate the Secretary-General as depositary. Article 32(1) of the Convention is no more than a practical consequence of the fact that the Convention was adopted under the UN's aegis. The designation of the Secretary-General as depositary does, however, in accordance with Article 80(2) VCLT, constitute authorization for him or her to register the Convention with the Secretariat, which, as it is, is one of the inherent functions of a treaty depositary specified in Article 77(1) VCLT.[10]

The exercise by the Secretary-General of his depositary functions under Article 32 is informed by his longstanding practice as depositary of what are now over 500 multilateral treaties.[11] This established practice, 'though differing somewhat from that described in the [VCLT]', 'take[s] into account the most relevant provisions of the Vienna Convention as regards the usual function of a depositary'.[12]

Article 76(2) VCLT is one provision relevant to the discharge by the Secretary-General of the functions of depositary of the Convention, whether they be the functions expressly assigned by the Convention or those, adumbrated in Article 77(1) VCLT, inherent in designation as depositary. Article 76(2) states that '[t]he functions of the

[4] *Summary of Practice of the Secretary-General as Depositary*, 7, para. 27; *Treaty Handbook*, 1 and 3, para. 2.2.

[5] *Summary of Practice of the Secretary-General as Depositary*, 7, para. 27.

[6] UNGA res. 58/74, 9 December 2003, para. 2.

[7] See Suggestions of the Chairman, 3, Art. H.

[8] Art. 102(1) UN Charter provides: 'Every treaty and every international agreement entered into by any Member of the United Nations after the present Charter comes into force shall as soon as possible be registered with the Secretariat and published by it.'

[9] Art. 80(1) VCLT reads: 'Treaties shall, after their entry into force, be transmitted to the Secretariat of the United Nations for registration or filing and recording, as the case may be, and for publication.'

[10] See Art. 77(1)(*g*) VCLT.

[11] *Treaty Handbook*, 1 and 3, para. 2.1.

[12] *Summary of Practice of the Secretary-General as Depositary*, 4, para. 13.

depositary of a treaty are international in character' and that 'the depositary is under an obligation to act impartially in their performance'. The provision adds that 'the fact that a treaty has not entered into force between certain of the parties or that a difference has appeared between a State and a depositary with regard to the performance of the latter's functions shall not affect that obligation'. Additionally relevant is Article 77(2) VCLT, which provides that, '[i]n the event of any difference appearing between a State and the depositary as to the performance of the latter's functions, the depositary shall bring the question to the attention of the signatory States and the contracting States'.

The tasks of notification incumbent on the Secretary-General under Article 32(2) of the Convention correspond in substance to those specified in Article 77(1)(*e*) and (*f*) VCLT. But Article 32(2) of the Convention teases apart the duty, on the one hand, to inform States of what Article 77(1)(*e*) VCLT and Article 32(2)(*c*) of the Convention refer to generically as 'any acts, notifications or communications relating to' the Convention and the duty, on the other, to inform States specifically of expressions of consent to be bound by the Convention and of withdrawals from it, *viz* of 'signatures of the... Convention and the deposit of instruments of ratification, acceptance, approval or accession or notifications of denunciation', as referred to in Article 32(2)(*a*). The reason for hiving off the lesser from the greater is not apparent. The practice of the Secretary-General to date under Article 32(2) of the Convention confirms, consistently with his general practice as treaty depositary,[13] that notification pursuant to Article 32(2)(*a*) extends to notification of any unilateral statement—whether it be labelled a reservation, an interpretative declaration, a declaration *simpliciter*, something else, or nothing—which may accompany a State's expression of consent to be bound,[14] including any declaration made pursuant to Article 27(3) of the Convention.[15] The residual category of 'acts, notifications or communications relating to the Convention' within the meaning of Article 32(2)(*c*) includes declarations of succession,[16] objections to reservations, withdrawals of reservations, and withdrawals in accordance with Article 27(4) of declarations made under Article 27(3). As for Article 32(2)(*b*), the obligation therein to inform States of the date on which the Convention will enter into force is no different in substance from the function of a depositary specified in Article 77(1)(*f*) VCLT.[17]

Article 32(2) obliges the Secretary-General to inform 'all States,' and not just the States parties to the Convention, of the treaty actions and facts specified in subparagraphs (*a*) to (*c*). This is in accordance with the Secretary-General's established practice.[18] It also reflects the gist of subparagraphs (*e*) and (*f*) of Article 77(1) VCLT, which require a

[13] See *Summary of Practice of the Secretary-General as Depositary*, 92, para. 311.

[14] See UNCSI depositary notifications C.N.280.2006.TREATIES–2 (Norway: Ratification), 6 April 2006; C.N.744.2008.TREATIES-3 (Iran: Ratification), 8 October 2008; C.N.912.2009.TREATIES–1 (Sweden: Ratification), 24 December 2009; C.N.223.2010.TREATIES-2 (Switzerland: Ratification), 20 April 2010; C.N.675.2010.TREATIES-4 (Saudi Arabia: Accession), 3 November 2010.

[15] See UNCSI depositary notifications C.N.744.2008.TREATIES-3 (Iran: Ratification), 8 October 2008; C.N.675.2010.TREATIES-4 (Saudi Arabia: Accession), 3 November 2010.

[16] See F. Ouguergouz, S. Villalpando, and J. Morgan-Foster, 'Article 77—Convention of 1969,' in O. Corten and P. Klein (eds), *The Vienna Conventions on the Law of Treaties: A Commentary* (Oxford: Oxford University Press, 2011), vol. II, 1715, 1733, para. 38.

[17] Art. 77(1)(*f*) VCLT imposes on a depositary the duty of 'informing the States entitled to become parties to the treaty when the number of signatures or of instruments of ratification, acceptance, approval or accession required for the entry into force of the treaty has been received or deposited'.

[18] See *Final Clauses Handbook*, 33, fn. 37.

depositary to inform, respectively, 'the parties and the States entitled to become parties to the treaty' and 'the States entitled to become parties to the treaty' of, respectively, treaty actions and the treaty's imminent entry into force, although the expression 'States entitled to become parties to the treaty' in Article 77(1)(*e*) and (*f*) is taken to refer solely to signatory States and not to all States to which the treaty is open.[19]

As indicated in Article 77(1)(*d*) VCLT, one of the functions of a treaty depositary is that of examining whether any signature to the treaty or any instrument, notification, or communication relating to the treaty is 'in due and proper form' and, if necessary, of 'bringing the matter to the attention of the State in question'. The depositary's authority in this regard extends solely to formal validity. In this light, the Secretary-General, as the Convention's depositary, may scrutinize whether, for example, any purported treaty action in relation to the Convention by a person purporting to represent a State is backed by *bona fide* full powers.[20] In contrast, the Secretary-General may not engage in an assessment of whether, for example, any unilateral statement made by a State when expressing its consent to be bound by the Convention (which is silent on the question of reservations) constitutes an impermissible reservation.[21] Indeed, in the wake of the ICJ's words to this effect in *Reservations to the Genocide Convention*,[22] the General Assembly, in resolution 598 (VI) of 12 January 1952, requested the Secretary-General, '[i]n respect of future conventions concluded under the auspices of the United Nations of which he is the depositary',

(i) To continue to act as depositary in connection with the deposit of documents containing reservations or objections, without passing upon the legal effect of such documents; and
(ii) To communicate the text of such documents relating to reservations or objections to all States concerned, leaving it to each State to draw legal consequences from such communications.[23]

By way of resolution 1452 B (XIV) of 7 December 1959, the General Assembly extended its injunction to treaties concluded under UN auspices before 12 January 1952.[24] Perhaps needless to say, the Secretary-General has followed this practice under the Convention.[25]

[19] See *Final Clauses Handbook*, 33, fn. 37, where the practice of sending notifications to all States is described only as a matter of practical convenience. The Secretary-General's practice in identifying the States to which a treaty is open, on the other hand, appears to relate only to Art. 77(1)(*b*) VCLT and to the formal validity of treaty actions. See *Summary of Practice of the Secretary-General as Depositary*, 20–30, paras 70–100. See also, generally, H. Tichy and P. Bittner, 'Article 77,' in O. Dörr and K. Schmalenbach (eds), *Vienna Convention on the Law of Treaties: A Commentary* (Heidelberg: Springer, 2012), 1309, 1322–3, paras 37–38; M.E. Villiger, *Commentary on the 1969 Vienna Convention on the Law of Treaties* (Leiden: Martinus Nijhoff, 2009), 934, 940, criticizing the breadth of the notion of 'States entitled to become parties to the treaty'.

[20] See Ouguergouz, Villalpando, and Morgan-Foster (n. 16), 1734–44, paras 40–53. See also s. 7 ('Full powers') *Procedures to be followed with regard to treaties and international agreements* (n. 1): 'All instruments of full powers received by any department, office or regional commission authorizing representatives to sign treaties and international agreements deposited with the Secretary-General shall be forwarded to the Treaty Section for verification prior to signature of such treaties and international agreements. Any exceptions to this rule shall be arranged in advance with the Treaty Section.'

[21] See Ouguergouz, Villalpando, and Morgan-Foster (n. 16), 1734–44, paras 40–53; A. Behnsen, *Das Vorbehaltsrecht völkerrechtlicher Verträge* (Berlin: Duncker & Humblot, 2007), 244–8.

[22] See *Reservations to the Convention on the Prevention and Punishment of the Crime of Genocide, Advisory Opinion*, ICJ Rep 1951, 15, 26–7.

[23] UNGA res. 598 (VI), 12 January 1952, para. 3(*b*).

[24] See UNGA res. 1452 B (XIV), 7 December 1959, para. 1. For the Secretary-General's practice in this general regard, see *Summary of Practice of the Secretary-General as Depositary*, 52–4, paras 173–181.

[25] See eg the depositary notifications cited (n. 14). No objections have been entered to date to any of the unilateral statements made so far on expression of consent to be bound by the Convention.

The established practice of the Secretary-General makes it clear that he will not permit to sign a multilateral treaty of which he is depositary, nor formally accept an instrument of consent to be bound from, any entity (whether State, international organization, or other) that is not permitted to sign or become party to the treaty in accordance with its terms.[26] As regards a treaty, such as the Convention, which employs the 'all States' formula in specifying its permissible signatories and parties,[27] this may place the Secretary-General in the position of having to ascertain whether a given territorial-political entity is a State, a task on which the longstanding policy is to seek guidance from the General Assembly.[28]

Where, as with the Convention, the treaty designates a depositary, any notification or communication made by any State in relation to the treaty must, in accordance with Article 78(*a*) VCLT, be transmitted to the depositary, rather than, where relevant, to the State or States for which it was intended. As provided for in Article 78(*b*) VCLT, any such notification or communication is considered as having been made only when it is received by the depositary; and, as per Article 78(*c*) VCLT, if a notification or communication is intended for another State, it is considered as having been received by that State only when the latter has received notification from the depositary.[29]

The Secretary-General, as depositary, has duties under Article 79 VCLT in relation to any necessary correction of errors in any of the authentic texts or certified true copies of the Convention, although his practice in this regard differs slightly from that laid down in Article 79 VCLT in that, in line with his general practice in relation to treaty notification, he brings the error and proposed correction to the attention of all States, not just the States parties and signatories.[30] He has twice to date had to fulfil these duties, with respect to the original Chinese and Arabic versions respectively of the text and of the certified true copies of them. On 28 February 2005, he notified States of apparent errors in the Chinese version of the text, and, '[i]n accordance with the established depositary practice', proposed to effect the proposed corrections, subject to objection by any State.[31] He later duly notified States of the corrections effected.[32] The Secretary-General subsequently observed the same procedure in relation to the Arabic version.[33]

[26] See *Summary of Practice of the Secretary-General as Depositary*, 21, para. 73, 32, para. 108 and 36, para. 120.

[27] See the commentaries to Arts 28 and 29 UNCSI.

[28] See *Summary of Practice of the Secretary-General as Depositary*, 23, paras 81–83; *United Nations Juridical Yearbook 1973*, 79, fn. 9; *United Nations Juridical Yearbook 1974*, 158, para. 2. See also the commentaries to Arts 28 and 29 UNCSI.

[29] Note that Art. 78(*c*) VCLT does not purport to govern the entry into force of a treaty, which, absent specific provision in the treaty in question, is regulated by Arts 16 and 24 VCLT. See *Land and Maritime Boundary between Cameroon and Nigeria (Cameroon v Nigeria), Preliminary Objections, Judgment*, ICJ Rep 1998, 275, 293–4, paras 29–31. As specifically regards the Convention, the question of entry into force is governed by Art. 30 UNCSI.

[30] See *Summary of Practice of the Secretary-General as Depositary*, 14–15, paras 51–52. As explained, however, *Summary of Practice of the Secretary-General as Depositary*, 15, para. 52, it is to be understood that only the States parties and signatories may object to the proposed correction.

[31] UNCSI depositary notification C.N.141.2005.TREATIES-4 (Proposal of Corrections to Original Text of Convention (Chinese Version) and to the Certified True Copies), 28 February 2005. See, in this regard, Art. 79(2), (3), and (6) VCLT.

[32] See UNCSI depositary notification C.N.419.2005.TREATIES-6 (Corrections to Original Text of Convention (Chinese Version) and to the Certified True Copies), 31 May 2005.

[33] See UNCSI depositary notification C.N.359.2008.TREATIES-1 (Proposal of Corrections to Original Text of Convention (Arabic Version) and to the Certified True Copies), 6 May 2008; C.N.556.2008. TREATIES-2 (Corrections to Original Text of Convention (Arabic Version) and to the Certified True Copies), 21 August 2008.

4. Evaluation

The choice of the Secretary-General as the Convention's depositary was the logical one, and he—in reality, the Treaty Section of the Office of Legal Affairs of the UN Secretariat—is already, and wholly unsurprisingly, acquitting the depositary's various duties in accordance with Article 32(2) and with his sensible and efficient past practice.

Article 33

TOBIAS THIENEL

Article 33

Authentic texts

The Arabic, Chinese, English, French, Russian and Spanish texts of the present Convention are equally authentic.

1. Introduction

As is normal practice for treaties elaborated under the auspices of the UN,[1] Article 33 declares the text of the Convention to be equally authentic in each of the official languages of the Organization.[2] What this means is that the Arabic, Chinese, English, French, Russian, and Spanish texts may each be relied on as authoritative when determining the meaning of the Convention's provisions.[3] Article 33 corresponds in essence to one of the standard final clauses found in UN conventions, although the clause is often[4] accompanied by the stipulation that the convention is to be deposited in the UN archives[5] or with the Secretary-General.[6]

2. Drafting History

A final clause embracing the twin questions of authentic texts and deposit with the Secretary-General was proposed in the Eighth and final report of Special Rapporteur

[1] See *Summary of Practice of the Secretary-General as Depositary*, 11, para. 40; *Final Clauses Handbook*, 77.

[2] Chinese, English, French, Russian, and Spanish were designated at the outset as the official languages of the various UN organs, while Arabic was added in 1973. See now eg Rule 51 Rules of Procedure of the General Assembly (as amended), UN doc. A/520/Rev.17; Rule 41 Provisional Rules of Procedure of the Security Council (as amended), UN doc. S/96/Rev.7. The ICJ constitutes the sole exception in this regard. Art. 39 of the ICJ Statute provides that the Court's only official languages are English and French.

[3] See *Final Clauses Handbook*, 121. See also ILC commentary DALT, draft art. 29, paras 1–2.

[4] But *cf* the subsequent Art. 50 Convention on the Rights of Persons with Disabilities, New York, 13 December 2006, 2515 UNTS 3.

[5] See eg Art. 25(1) International Convention on the Elimination of All Forms of Racial Discrimination, New York, 7 March 1966, 660 UNTS 195; Art. 31(1) International Covenant on Economic, Social and Cultural Rights, New York, 16 December 1966, 993 UNTS 3; Art. 53(1) International Covenant on Civil and Political Rights, New York, 16 December 1966, 999 UNTS 171; Art. XXIX(1) International Convention on the Suppression and Punishment of the Crime of Apartheid, New York, 30 November 1973, 1015 UNTS 243; Art. 33(1) United Nations Convention against Torture and Other Cruel, Inhuman or Degrading Treatment or Punishment, New York, 10 December 1984, 1465 UNTS 85.

[6] See eg Art. 30 Convention on the Elimination of All Forms of Discrimination against Women, New York, 18 December 1979, 1249 UNTS 13; Art. 320 United Nations Convention on the Law of the Sea, Montego Bay, 10 December 1982, 1833 UNTS 3; Art. 54 Convention on the Rights of the Child, New York, 20 November 1989, 1577 UNTS 3; Art. 41(2) United Nations Convention against Transnational Organized Crime, New York, 15 November 2000, 2225 UNTS 209; Art. 45(1) International Convention for the Protection of All Persons from Enforced Disappearance, New York, 20 December 2006.

Sucharitkul,[7] who at the same time remarked that 'consideration of the question of final provisions or final clauses could be postponed until the [ILC's] second reading or until the plenipotentiary conference [was] convened'.[8] In the event, the ILC chose not to adopt final clauses on either first or second reading of the draft articles, presumably because such provisions were required only in the context of a finalized convention. When eventually, on receipt in late 2003 of the penultimate report of the Ad Hoc Committee on Jurisdictional Immunities of States and Their Property, the General Assembly reconvened the Committee for what would be its final session, it mandated the latter to formulate final clauses 'with a view to completing a convention on jurisdictional immunities of States and their property'.[9] Article 33 in its present form was suggested by the Chairman of the Ad Hoc Committee in 2004.[10] The Committee adopted the provision,[11] which passed unaltered into the Convention on the latter's adoption later the same year.

3. Key Points

In accordance with Article 33(3) VCLT, the terms of a treaty are presumed to have the same meaning in each authentic text. But the reality is that divergence among languages is difficult to eliminate,[12] with the consequence that provision for six authentic texts risks giving rise to competing interpretations. The formal solution to any such problem is to be found in Article 33(4) VCLT, which provides in relevant part:

> [W]hen a comparison of the authentic texts discloses a difference of meaning which the application of articles 31 and 32 [VCLT] does not remove, the meaning which best reconciles the texts, having regard to the object and purpose of the treaty, shall be adopted.[13]

In this light, failing resolution of the issue via Articles 31 and 32 VCLT, the existence of six authentic texts can be as much a help as a hindrance, in that the likelihood of a particular term bearing a different meaning in each of the six languages—indeed, in more than two of them—is exceedingly slim. A side-by-side comparison of the six versions can be expected to expose the oddity or oddities, tending to make reconciliation of the texts for the purposes of Article 33(4) VCLT in practice, albeit not formally,[14] a majority verdict.

As it is, with six authentic languages, it tends to be readily apparent that any divergence in one or perhaps more of the texts is as a result of some sort of error, which can be corrected by recourse to the procedure laid down in Article 79 VCLT or, in the case of

[7] See Eighth report Sucharitkul, 35.

[8] Eighth report Sucharitkul, 35, para. 50.

[9] UNGA res. 58/74, 9 December 2003, para. 2.

[10] See Suggestions of the Chairman, 3, art. I.

[11] See 2004 Report Ad Hoc Committee, 3, para. 10 and art. 33 Draft UNCSI.

[12] See also M. Hilf, 'Article 111', in B. Simma et al. (eds), *The Charter of the United Nations: A Commentary* (2nd edn) (Oxford: Oxford University Press, 2002), 1379, para. 1.

[13] The rule codifies customary international law. See *LaGrand (Germany v US), Judgment*, ICJ Rep 2001, 466, 502, para. 101; *Sunday Times v United Kingdom*, ECHR Series A No. 30, (1979–1980) 2 EHRR 245, 270, para. 48.

[14] The minority version or versions, while compatible with the others, may state the point more precisely or may better accord with the object and purpose of the treaty. As a matter of law, Art. 33(4) VCLT can never be a question of a simple head count. See I. Schübel-Pfister, *Sprache und Gemeinschaftsrecht* (Berlin: Duncker & Humblot, 2004), 140. See also Case C-257/00, *R v Commissioner of Customs and Excise, ex parte EMU Tabac SARL* [1998] ECR I-1605, 1644–5, para. 36.

the Secretary-General, to his almost-identical procedure.[15] The latter has been invoked twice so far with respect to the Convention. The Chinese-language version of the original text and certified copies was corrected in 2005, although in relation only to 'the outline style (numbering and lettering denoting the various levels of organization within the text)'.[16] The Arabic version of the original text and certified copies was corrected in 2008 by the removal of an extraneous preambular recital.[17]

4. Evaluation

The current practice is for the texts of multilateral treaties concluded under the UN's aegis to be authentic in the six official languages of the Organization.[18] The potential for dispute is always present in a polyglot arrangement of this sort. But so too are the tools for its resolution.

[15] See the slight difference noted in *Summary of Practice of the Secretary-General as Depositary*, 14–15, paras 51–52, in that the Secretary-General brings the error and the proposed correction to the attention of all States, not simply the States parties and signatories.

[16] UNCSI depositary notification C.N.141.2005.TREATIES-4 (Proposal of Corrections to Original Text of Convention (Chinese Version) and to the Certified True Copies), 28 February 2005. For the notification of the eventual effecting of the corrections, see UNCSI depositary notification C.N.419.2005.TREATIES-6 (Corrections to Original Text of Convention (Chinese Version) and to the Certified True Copies), 31 May 2005.

[17] See UNCSI depositary notification C.N.359.2008.TREATIES-1 (Proposal of Corrections to Original Text of Convention (Arabic Version) and to the Certified True Copies), 6 May 2008. See also UNCSI depositary notification C.N.556.2008.TREATIES-2 (Corrections to Original Text of Convention (Arabic Version) and to the Certified True Copies), 21 August 2008.

[18] See *Final Clauses Handbook*, 77.

APPENDIX

1. United Nations Convention on Jurisdictional Immunities of States and Their Property

The States Parties to the present Convention,

Considering that the jurisdictional immunities of States and their property are generally accepted as a principle of customary international law,

Having in mind the principles of international law embodied in the Charter of the United Nations,

Believing that an international convention on the jurisdictional immunities of States and their property would enhance the rule of law and legal certainty, particularly in dealings of States with natural or juridical persons, and would contribute to the codification and development of international law and the harmonization of practice in this area,

Taking into account developments in State practice with regard to the jurisdictional immunities of States and their property,

Affirming that the rules of customary international law continue to govern matters not regulated by the provisions of the present Convention,

Have agreed as follows:

PART I
INTRODUCTION

Article 1 Scope of the present Convention

The present Convention applies to the immunity of a State and its property from the jurisdiction of the courts of another State.

Article 2 Use of terms

1. For the purposes of the present Convention:
   (*a*) 'court' means any organ of a State, however named, entitled to exercise judicial functions;
   (*b*) 'State' means:
      (i) the State and its various organs of government;
      (ii) constituent units of a federal State or political subdivisions of the State, which are entitled to perform acts in the exercise of sovereign authority, and are acting in that capacity;
      (iii) agencies or instrumentalities of the State or other entities, to the extent that they are entitled to perform and are actually performing acts in the exercise of sovereign authority of the State;
      (iv) representatives of the State acting in that capacity;
   (*c*) 'commercial transaction' means:
      (i) any commercial contract or transaction for the sale of goods or supply of services;
      (ii) any contract for a loan or other transaction of a financial nature, including any obligation of guarantee or of indemnity in respect of any such loan or transaction;
      (iii) any other contract or transaction of a commercial, industrial, trading or professional nature, but not including a contract of employment of persons.

2. In determining whether a contract or transaction is a 'commercial transaction' under paragraph 1(*c*), reference should be made primarily to the nature of the contract or transaction, but its purpose should also be taken into account if the parties to the contract or transaction have so agreed, or if, in the practice of the State of the forum, that purpose is relevant to determining the non-commercial character of the contract or transaction.
3. The provisions of paragraphs 1 and 2 regarding the use of terms in the present Convention are without prejudice to the use of those terms or to the meanings which may be given to them in other international instruments or in the internal law of any State.

Article 3 Privileges and immunities not affected by the present Convention

1. The present Convention is without prejudice to the privileges and immunities enjoyed by a State under international law in relation to the exercise of the functions of:
   (*a*) its diplomatic missions, consular posts, special missions, missions to international organizations or delegations to organs of international organizations or to international conferences; and
   (*b*) persons connected with them.
2. The present Convention is without prejudice to privileges and immunities accorded under international law to heads of State *ratione personae.*
3. The present Convention is without prejudice to the immunities enjoyed by a State under international law with respect to aircraft or space objects owned or operated by a State.

Article 4 Non-retroactivity of the present Convention

Without prejudice to the application of any rules set forth in the present Convention to which jurisdictional immunities of States and their property are subject under international law independently of the present Convention, the present Convention shall not apply to any question of jurisdictional immunities of States or their property arising in a proceeding instituted against a State before a court of another State prior to the entry into force of the present Convention for the States concerned.

Part II

General principles

Article 5 State immunity

A State enjoys immunity, in respect of itself and its property, from the jurisdiction of the courts of another State subject to the provisions of the present Convention.

Article 6 Modalities for giving effect to State immunity

1. A State shall give effect to State immunity under article 5 by refraining from exercising jurisdiction in a proceeding before its courts against another State and to that end shall ensure that its courts determine on their own initiative that the immunity of that other State under article 5 is respected.
2. A proceeding before a court of a State shall be considered to have been instituted against another State if that other State:
   (*a*) is named as a party to that proceeding; or
   (*b*) is not named as a party to the proceeding but the proceeding in effect seeks to affect the property, rights, interests or activities of that other State.

Article 7 Express consent to exercise of jurisdiction

1. A State cannot invoke immunity from jurisdiction in a proceeding before a court of another State with regard to a matter or case if it has expressly consented to the exercise of jurisdiction by the court with regard to the matter or case:
   (*a*) by international agreement;

(*b*) in a written contract; or
(*c*) by a declaration before the court or by a written communication in a specific proceeding.

2. Agreement by a State for the application of the law of another State shall not be interpreted as consent to the exercise of jurisdiction by the courts of that other State.

Article 8 Effect of participation in a proceeding before a court

1. A State cannot invoke immunity from jurisdiction in a proceeding before a court of another State if it has:
(*a*) itself instituted the proceeding; or
(*b*) intervened in the proceeding or taken any other step relating to the merits. However, if the State satisfies the court that it could not have acquired knowledge of facts on which a claim to immunity can be based until after it took such a step, it can claim immunity based on those facts, provided it does so at the earliest possible moment.
2. A State shall not be considered to have consented to the exercise of jurisdiction by a court of another State if it intervenes in a proceeding or takes any other step for the sole purpose of:
(*a*) invoking immunity; or
(*b*) asserting a right or interest in property at issue in the proceeding.
3. The appearance of a representative of a State before a court of another State as a witness shall not be interpreted as consent by the former State to the exercise of jurisdiction by the court.
4. Failure on the part of a State to enter an appearance in a proceeding before a court of another State shall not be interpreted as consent by the former State to the exercise of jurisdiction by the court.

Article 9 Counterclaims

1. A State instituting a proceeding before a court of another State cannot invoke immunity from the jurisdiction of the court in respect of any counterclaim arising out of the same legal relationship or facts as the principal claim.
2. A State intervening to present a claim in a proceeding before a court of another State cannot invoke immunity from the jurisdiction of the court in respect of any counterclaim arising out of the same legal relationship or facts as the claim presented by the State.
3. A State making a counterclaim in a proceeding instituted against it before a court of another State cannot invoke immunity from the jurisdiction of the court in respect of the principal claim.

PART III

PROCEEDINGS IN WHICH STATE IMMUNITY CANNOT BE INVOKED

Article 10 Commercial transactions

1. If a State engages in a commercial transaction with a foreign natural or juridical person and, by virtue of the applicable rules of private international law, differences relating to the commercial transaction fall within the jurisdiction of a court of another State, the State cannot invoke immunity from that jurisdiction in a proceeding arising out of that commercial transaction.
2. Paragraph 1 does not apply:
(*a*) in the case of a commercial transaction between States; or
(*b*) if the parties to the commercial transaction have expressly agreed otherwise.
3. Where a State enterprise or other entity established by a State which has an independent legal personality and is capable of:
(*a*) suing or being sued; and
(*b*) acquiring, owning or possessing and disposing of property, including property which that State has authorized it to operate or manage, is involved in a proceeding which relates to a commercial transaction in which that entity is engaged, the immunity from jurisdiction enjoyed by that State shall not be affected.

Article 11 Contracts of employment

1. Unless otherwise agreed between the States concerned, a State cannot invoke immunity from jurisdiction before a court of another State which is otherwise competent in a proceeding which relates to a contract of employment between the State and an individual for work performed or to be performed, in whole or in part, in the territory of that other State.
2. Paragraph 1 does not apply if:
   (*a*) the employee has been recruited to perform particular functions in the exercise of governmental authority;
   (*b*) the employee is:
      (i) a diplomatic agent, as defined in the Vienna Convention on Diplomatic Relations of 1961;
      (ii) a consular officer, as defined in the Vienna Convention on Consular Relations of 1963;
      (iii) a member of the diplomatic staff of a permanent mission to an international organization or of a special mission, or is recruited to represent a State at an international conference; or
      (iv) any other person enjoying diplomatic immunity;
   (*c*) the subject-matter of the proceeding is the recruitment, renewal of employment or reinstatement of an individual;
   (*d*) the subject-matter of the proceeding is the dismissal or termination of employment of an individual and, as determined by the head of State, the head of Government or the Minister for Foreign Affairs of the employer State, such a proceeding would interfere with the security interests of that State;
   (*e*) the employee is a national of the employer State at the time when the proceeding is instituted, unless this person has the permanent residence in the State of the forum; or
   (*f*) the employer State and the employee have otherwise agreed in writing, subject to any considerations of public policy conferring on the courts of the State of the forum exclusive jurisdiction by reason of the subject-matter of the proceeding.

Article 12 Personal injuries and damage to property

Unless otherwise agreed between the States concerned, a State cannot invoke immunity from jurisdiction before a court of another State which is otherwise competent in a proceeding which relates to pecuniary compensation for death or injury to the person, or damage to or loss of tangible property, caused by an act or omission which is alleged to be attributable to the State, if the act or omission occurred in whole or in part in the territory of that other State and if the author of the act or omission was present in that territory at the time of the act or omission.

Article 13 Ownership, possession and use of property

Unless otherwise agreed between the States concerned, a State cannot invoke immunity from jurisdiction before a court of another State which is otherwise competent in a proceeding which relates to the determination of:

(*a*) any right or interest of the State in, or its possession or use of, or any obligation of the State arising out of its interest in, or its possession or use of, immovable property situated in the State of the forum;

(*b*) any right or interest of the State in movable or immovable property arising by way of succession, gift or *bona vacantia*; or

(*c*) any right or interest of the State in the administration of property, such as trust property, the estate of a bankrupt or the property of a company in the event of its winding up.

Article 14 Intellectual and industrial property

Unless otherwise agreed between the States concerned, a State cannot invoke immunity from jurisdiction before a court of another State which is otherwise competent in a proceeding which relates to:

(*a*) the determination of any right of the State in a patent, industrial design, trade name or business name, trademark, copyright or any other form of intellectual or industrial property which enjoys a measure of legal protection, even if provisional, in the State of the forum; or

(*b*) an alleged infringement by the State, in the territory of the State of the forum, of a right of the nature mentioned in subparagraph (*a*) which belongs to a third person and is protected in the State of the forum.

Article 15 Participation in companies or other collective bodies

1. A State cannot invoke immunity from jurisdiction before a court of another State which is otherwise competent in a proceeding which relates to its participation in a company or other collective body, whether incorporated or unincorporated, being a proceeding concerning the relationship between the State and the body or the other participants therein, provided that the body:
   (*a*) has participants other than States or international organizations; and
   (*b*) is incorporated or constituted under the law of the State of the forum or has its seat or principal place of business in that State.
2. A State can, however, invoke immunity from jurisdiction in such a proceeding if the States concerned have so agreed or if the parties to the dispute have so provided by an agreement in writing or if the instrument establishing or regulating the body in question contains provisions to that effect.

Article 16 Ships owned or operated by a State

1. Unless otherwise agreed between the States concerned, a State which owns or operates a ship cannot invoke immunity from jurisdiction before a court of another State which is otherwise competent in a proceeding which relates to the operation of that ship if, at the time the cause of action arose, the ship was used for other than government non-commercial purposes.
2. Paragraph 1 does not apply to warships, or naval auxiliaries, nor does it apply to other vessels owned or operated by a State and used, for the time being, only on government non-commercial service.
3. Unless otherwise agreed between the States concerned, a State cannot invoke immunity from jurisdiction before a court of another State which is otherwise competent in a proceeding which relates to the carriage of cargo on board a ship owned or operated by that State if, at the time the cause of action arose, the ship was used for other than government non-commercial purposes.
4. Paragraph 3 does not apply to any cargo carried on board the ships referred to in paragraph 2, nor does it apply to any cargo owned by a State and used or intended for use exclusively for government non-commercial purposes.
5. States may plead all measures of defence, prescription and limitation of liability which are available to private ships and cargoes and their owners.
6. If in a proceeding there arises a question relating to the government and non-commercial character of a ship owned or operated by a State or cargo owned by a State, a certificate signed by a diplomatic representative or other competent authority of that State and communicated to the court shall serve as evidence of the character of that ship or cargo.

Article 17 Effect of an arbitration agreement

If a State enters into an agreement in writing with a foreign natural or juridical person to submit to arbitration differences relating to a commercial transaction, that State cannot invoke immunity from jurisdiction before a court of another State which is otherwise competent in a proceeding which relates to:

(*a*) the validity, interpretation or application of the arbitration agreement;

(*b*) the arbitration procedure; or

(*c*) the confirmation or the setting aside of the award, unless the arbitration agreement otherwise provides.

Part IV

State immunity from measures of constraint in connection with proceedings before a court

Article 18 State immunity from pre-judgment measures of constraint

No pre-judgment measures of constraint, such as attachment or arrest, against property of a State may be taken in connection with a proceeding before a court of another State unless and except to the extent that:

(*a*) the State has expressly consented to the taking of such measures as indicated:
  (i) by international agreement;
  (ii) by an arbitration agreement or in a written contract; or
  (iii) by a declaration before the court or by a written communication after a dispute between the parties has arisen; or

(*b*) the State has allocated or earmarked property for the satisfaction of the claim which is the object of that proceeding.

Article 19 State immunity from post-judgment measures of constraint

No post-judgment measures of constraint, such as attachment, arrest or execution, against property of a State may be taken in connection with a proceeding before a court of another State unless and except to the extent that:

(*a*) the State has expressly consented to the taking of such measures as indicated:
  (i) by international agreement;
  (ii) by an arbitration agreement or in a written contract; or
  (iii) by a declaration before the court or by a written communication after a dispute between the parties has arisen; or

(*b*) the State has allocated or earmarked property for the satisfaction of the claim which is the object of that proceeding; or

(*c*) it has been established that the property is specifically in use or intended for use by the State for other than government non-commercial purposes and is in the territory of the State of the forum, provided that post-judgment measures of constraint may only be taken against property that has a connection with the entity against which the proceeding was directed.

Article 20 Effect of consent to jurisdiction to measures of constraint

Where consent to the measures of constraint is required under articles 18 and 19, consent to the exercise of jurisdiction under article 7 shall not imply consent to the taking of measures of constraint.

Article 21 Specific categories of property

1. The following categories, in particular, of property of a State shall not be considered as property specifically in use or intended for use by the State for other than government non-commercial purposes under article 19, subparagraph (*c*):
   (*a*) property, including any bank account, which is used or intended for use in the performance of the functions of the diplomatic mission of the State or its consular posts, special

missions, missions to international organizations or delegations to organs of international organizations or to international conferences;

(*b*) property of a military character or used or intended for use in the performance of military functions;

(*c*) property of the central bank or other monetary authority of the State;

(*d*) property forming part of the cultural heritage of the State or part of its archives and not placed or intended to be placed on sale;

(*e*) property forming part of an exhibition of objects of scientific, cultural or historical interest and not placed or intended to be placed on sale.

2. Paragraph 1 is without prejudice to article 18 and article 19, subparagraphs (*a*) and (*b*).

Part V

Miscellaneous provisions

Article 22 Service of process

1. Service of process by writ or other document instituting a proceeding against a State shall be effected:

   (*a*) in accordance with any applicable international convention binding on the State of the forum and the State concerned; or

   (*b*) in accordance with any special arrangement for service between the claimant and the State concerned, if not precluded by the law of the State of the forum; or

   (*c*) in the absence of such a convention or special arrangement:

      (i) by transmission through diplomatic channels to the Ministry of Foreign Affairs of the State concerned; or

      (ii) by any other means accepted by the State concerned, if not precluded by the law of the State of the forum.

2. Service of process referred to in paragraph 1 (*c*) (i) is deemed to have been effected by receipt of the documents by the Ministry of Foreign Affairs.

3. These documents shall be accompanied, if necessary, by a translation into the official language, or one of the official languages, of the State concerned.

4. Any State that enters an appearance on the merits in a proceeding instituted against it may not thereafter assert that service of process did not comply with the provisions of paragraphs 1 and 3.

Article 23 Default judgment

1. A default judgment shall not be rendered against a State unless the court has found that:

   (*a*) the requirements laid down in article 22, paragraphs 1 and 3, have been complied with;

   (*b*) a period of not less than four months has expired from the date on which the service of the writ or other document instituting a proceeding has been effected or deemed to have been effected in accordance with article 22, paragraphs 1 and 2; and

   (*c*) the present Convention does not preclude it from exercising jurisdiction.

2. A copy of any default judgment rendered against a State, accompanied if necessary by a translation into the official language or one of the official languages of the State concerned, shall be transmitted to it through one of the means specified in article 22, paragraph 1, and in accordance with the provisions of that paragraph.

3. The time-limit for applying to have a default judgment set aside shall not be less than four months and shall begin to run from the date on which the copy of the judgment is received or is deemed to have been received by the State concerned.

Article 24 Privileges and immunities during court proceedings

1. Any failure or refusal by a State to comply with an order of a court of another State enjoining it to perform or refrain from performing a specific act or to produce any document or disclose any

other information for the purposes of a proceeding shall entail no consequences other than those which may result from such conduct in relation to the merits of the case. In particular, no fine or penalty shall be imposed on the State by reason of such failure or refusal.

2. A State shall not be required to provide any security, bond or deposit, however described, to guarantee the payment of judicial costs or expenses in any proceeding to which it is a respondent party before a court of another State.

Part VI
Final clauses

Article 25 Annex

The annex to the present Convention forms an integral part of the Convention.

Article 26 Other international agreements

Nothing in the present Convention shall affect the rights and obligations of States Parties under existing international agreements which relate to matters dealt with in the present Convention as between the parties to those agreements.

Article 27 Settlement of disputes

1. States Parties shall endeavour to settle disputes concerning the interpretation or application of the present Convention through negotiation.
2. Any dispute between two or more States Parties concerning the interpretation or application of the present Convention which cannot be settled through negotiation within six months shall, at the request of any of those States Parties, be submitted to arbitration. If, six months after the date of the request for arbitration, those States Parties are unable to agree on the organization of the arbitration, any of those States Parties may refer the dispute to the International Court of Justice by request in accordance with the Statute of the Court.
3. Each State Party may, at the time of signature, ratification, acceptance or approval of, or accession to, the present Convention, declare that it does not consider itself bound by paragraph 2. The other States Parties shall not be bound by paragraph 2 with respect to any State Party which has made such a declaration.
4. Any State Party that has made a declaration in accordance with paragraph 3 may at any time withdraw that declaration by notification to the Secretary-General of the United Nations.

Article 28 Signature

The present Convention shall be open for signature by all States until 17 January 2007, at United Nations Headquarters, New York.

Article 29 Ratification, acceptance, approval or accession

1. The present Convention shall be subject to ratification, acceptance or approval.
2. The present Convention shall remain open for accession by any State.
3. The instruments of ratification, acceptance, approval or accession shall be deposited with the Secretary-General of the United Nations.

Article 30 Entry into force

1. The present Convention shall enter into force on the thirtieth day following the date of deposit of the thirtieth instrument of ratification, acceptance, approval or accession with the Secretary-General of the United Nations.
2. For each State ratifying, accepting, approving or acceding to the present Convention after the deposit of the thirtieth instrument of ratification, acceptance, approval or accession, the Convention shall enter into force on the thirtieth day after the deposit by such State of its instrument of ratification, acceptance, approval or accession.

Article 31 Denunciation

1. Any State Party may denounce the present Convention by written notification to the Secretary-General of the United Nations.
2. Denunciation shall take effect one year following the date on which notification is received by the Secretary-General of the United Nations. The present Convention shall, however, continue to apply to any question of jurisdictional immunities of States or their property arising in a proceeding instituted against a State before a court of another State prior to the date on which the denunciation takes effect for any of the States concerned.
3. The denunciation shall not in any way affect the duty of any State Party to fulfil any obligation embodied in the present Convention to which it would be subject under international law independently of the present Convention.

Article 32 Depositary and notifications

1. The Secretary-General of the United Nations is designated the depositary of the present Convention.
2. As depositary of the present Convention, the Secretary-General of the United Nations shall inform all States of the following:
   (*a*) signatures of the present Convention and the deposit of instruments of ratification, acceptance, approval or accession or notifications of denunciation, in accordance with articles 29 and 31;
   (*b*) the date on which the present Convention will enter into force, in accordance with article 30;
   (*c*) any acts, notifications or communications relating to the present Convention.

Article 33 Authentic texts

The Arabic, Chinese, English, French, Russian and Spanish texts of the present Convention are equally authentic.

IN WITNESS WHEREOF, the undersigned, being duly authorized thereto by their respective Governments, have signed this Convention opened for signature at United Nations Headquarters in New York on 17 January 2005.

Annex to the Convention

Understandings with respect to certain provisions of the Convention

The present annex is for the purpose of setting out understandings relating to the provisions concerned.

With respect to article 10

The term 'immunity' in article 10 is to be understood in the context of the present Convention as a whole.

Article 10, paragraph 3, does not prejudge the question of 'piercing the corporate veil', questions relating to a situation where a State entity has deliberately misrepresented its financial position or subsequently reduced its assets to avoid satisfying a claim, or other related issues.

With respect to article 11

The reference in article 11, paragraph 2 (*d*), to the 'security interests' of the employer State is intended primarily to address matters of national security and the security of diplomatic missions and consular posts.

Under article 41 of the 1961 Vienna Convention on Diplomatic Relations and article 55 of the 1963 Vienna Convention on Consular Relations, all persons referred to in those articles have the duty to respect the laws and regulations, including labour laws, of the host country. At the same time, under article 38 of the 1961 Vienna Convention on Diplomatic Relations and article 71 of the 1963 Vienna Convention on Consular Relations, the receiving State has a duty to exercise its jurisdiction in such a manner as not to interfere unduly with the performance of the functions of the mission or the consular post.

With respect to articles 13 and 14

The expression 'determination' is used to refer not only to the ascertainment or verification of the existence of the rights protected, but also to the evaluation or assessment of the substance, including content, scope and extent, of such rights.

With respect to article 17

The expression 'commercial transaction' includes investment matters.

With respect to article 19

The expression 'entity' in subparagraph (*c*) means the State as an independent legal personality, a constituent unit of a federal State, a subdivision of a State, an agency or instrumentality of a State or other entity, which enjoys independent legal personality.

The words 'property that has a connection with the entity' in subparagraph (*c*) are to be understood as broader than ownership or possession.

Article 19 does not prejudge the question of 'piercing the corporate veil', questions relating to a situation where a State entity has deliberately misrepresented its financial position or subsequently reduced its assets to avoid satisfying a claim, or other related issues.

2. List of States Parties and Signatories

Status as at 05-10-2012: Signatories: 28. Parties: 13

Participant	**Signature**	**Ratification, Acceptance (A), Approval (AA), Accession (a)**
Austria	17 January 2005	14 September 2006
Belgium	22 April 2005	
China	14 September 2005	
Czech Republic	13 October 2006	
Denmark	19 September 2006	
Estonia	30 March 2006	
Finland	14 September 2005	
France	17 January 2007	12 August 2011 AA
Iceland	16 September 2005	
India	12 January 2007	29 September 2008
Iran (Islamic Republic of)	17 January 2007	
Japan	11 January 2007	11 May 2010 A
Kazakhstan		17 February 2010 a
Lebanon	11 November 2005	21 November 2008
Madagascar	15 September 2005	
Mexico	25 September 2006	

Continued

Continued

Participant	Signature	Ratification, Acceptance (A), Approval (AA), Accession (a)
Morocco	17 January 2005	
Norway	8 July 2005	27 March 2006
Paraguay	16 September 2005	
Portugal	25 February 2005	14 September 2006
Romania	14 September 2005	15 February 2007
Russian Federation	1 December 2006	
Saudi Arabia		1 September 2010 a
Senegal	21 September 2005	
Sierra Leone	21 September 2006	
Slovakia	15 September 2005	
Spain		21 September 2011 a
Sweden	14 September 2005	23 December 2009
Switzerland	19 September 2006	16 April 2010
Timor-Leste	16 September 2005	
United Kingdom of Great Britain and Northern Ireland	30 September 2005	

3. List of Reservations and Declarations

(Unless otherwise indicated, the declarations and reservations were made upon ratification, acceptance, approval, or accession.)

Iran (Islamic Republic of)

Reservation:

'Pursuant to Article 27, paragraph 3 of the United Nations Convention on Jurisdictional Immunities of States and Their Property, the Government of the Islamic Republic of Iran does not consider itself bound by the provisions of Article 27, paragraph 2 of the Convention. The Government of the Islamic Republic of Iran affirms that the consent of all parties to such a dispute is necessary, in each individual case, for the submission of the dispute to the International Court of Justice. The Government of the Islamic Republic of Iran can, if it deems appropriate, for the settlement of such a dispute, agree with the submission of the dispute to arbitration in accordance with its related domestic law.'

Norway

Declaration:

'Recalling inter alia resolution 59/38 adopted by the General Assembly of the United Nations on 2 December 2004, in which the General Assembly took into account, when adopting the Convention, the statement of 25 October 2004 of the Chairman of the Ad Hoc Committee on Jurisdictional Immunities of States and Their Property introducing the Committee's report, Norway hereby states its understanding that the Convention does not apply to military activities, including the activities of armed forces during an armed conflict, as those terms are understood under international humanitarian law, and activities undertaken by military forces of a State in the exercise of their official duties. Such activities remain subject to other rules of international law. Similarly, as also noted in the said statement, the Convention does not apply where there is a special immunity regime, including immunities ratione personae. Thus, the express mention of heads of State in Article 3 should not be read as suggesting that the immunity ratione personae of other State officials is affected by the Convention.

Furthermore, in cases where it has been established that property of a State is specifically in use or intended for use by the State for other than government non-commercial purposes and is in the territory of the State of the forum, it is the understanding of Norway that Article 18 does not prevent pre-judgement measures of constraint from being taken against property that has a connection with the entity against which the proceeding was directed.

Finally, Norway understands that the Convention is without prejudice to any future international development in the protection of human rights.'

Saudi Arabia

Reservation:

'. . . the Kingdom of Saudi Arabia does accede to and accept the United Nations Convention on Jurisdictional Immunities of States and Their Property, with the following reservation to article 27, paragraph 2, of the Convention regarding referral of disputes to the International Court of Justice:

The Kingdom does not consider itself bound by the provision that disputes concerning the interpretation or application of the Convention may be referred to the International Court of Justice. Disputes should not be referred to the International Court of Justice without the agreement of all parties involved.'

Sweden

Declarations:

'Recalling inter alia resolution 59/38, adopted by the General Assembly on 16 December 2004, taking into account inter alia the statement of the Chairman of the Ad Hoc Committee introducing the report of the Ad Hoc Committee to the General Assembly, as well as the report of the Ad Hoc Committee, Sweden hereby declares its understanding that the Convention does not apply to military activities, including the activities of armed forces during an armed conflict, as those terms are understood under international humanitarian law, and activities undertaken by military forces of a State in the exercise of their official functions.

Sweden also declares its understanding that the express mention of heads of State in article 3 should not be read as suggesting that the immunity ratione personae which other State officials might enjoy under international law is affected by the Convention.

Sweden furthermore declares its understanding that the Convention is without prejudice to any future international legal development concerning the protection of human rights.'

Switzerland

Interpretative declarations

'General interpretative declaration:

In accordance with General Assembly resolution 59/38, adopted on 2 December 2004, Switzerland hereby understands that the Convention does not cover criminal proceedings;

Interpretative declaration concerning article 12:

Switzerland considers that article 12 does not govern the question of pecuniary compensation for serious human rights violations which are alleged to be attributable to a State and are committed outside the State of the forum. Consequently, this Convention is without prejudice to developments in international law in this regard;

Interpretative declaration concerning article 22, paragraph 3:

If the State concerned is a Swiss canton, Switzerland considers that "official language" should be understood as the official language or one of the official languages of the canton in which process is to be served.'

4. General Assembly resolution 59/38

Resolution adopted by the General Assembly

[*on the report of the Sixth Committee (A/59/508)*]

59/38. United Nations Convention on Jurisdictional Immunities of States and Their Property

The General Assembly,

Bearing in mind Article 13, paragraph 1 (a), of the Charter of the United Nations,

Recalling its resolution 32/151 of 19 December 1977, in which it recommended that the International Law Commission take up the study of the law of jurisdictional immunities of States and their property with a view to its progressive development and codification, and its subsequent resolutions 46/55 of 9 December 1991, 49/61 of 9 December 1994, 52/151 of 15 December 1997, 54/101 of 9 December 1999, 55/150 of 12 December 2000, 56/78 of 12 December 2001, 57/16 of 19 November 2002 and 58/74 of 9 December 2003,

Recalling also that the International Law Commission submitted a final set of draft articles, with commentaries, on the law of jurisdictional immunities of States and their property in chapter II of its report on the work of its forty-third session,

Recalling further the reports of the open-ended Working Group of the Sixth Committee, as well as the report of the Working Group on Jurisdictional Immunities of States and Their Property of the International Law Commission, submitted in accordance with General Assembly resolution 53/98 of 8 December 1998,

Recalling that in its resolution 55/150 it decided to establish the Ad Hoc Committee on Jurisdictional Immunities of States and Their Property, open also to participation by States members of the specialized agencies, to further the work done, consolidate areas of agreement and resolve outstanding issues with a view to elaborating a generally acceptable instrument based on the draft articles on jurisdictional immunities of States and their property adopted by the International Law Commission and also on the discussions of the open-ended Working Group of the Sixth Committee,

Having considered the report of the Ad Hoc Committee on Jurisdictional Immunities of States and Their Property,

Stressing the importance of uniformity and clarity in the law of jurisdictional immunities of States and their property, and emphasizing the role of a convention in this regard,

Noting the broad support for the conclusion of a convention on jurisdictional immunities of States and their property,

Taking into account the statement of the Chairman of the Ad Hoc Committee introducing the report of the Ad Hoc Committee,

1. *Expresses its deep appreciation* to the International Law Commission and the Ad Hoc Committee on Jurisdictional Immunities of States and Their Property for their valuable work on the law of jurisdictional immunities of States and their property;
2. *Agrees* with the general understanding reached in the Ad Hoc Committee that the United Nations Convention on Jurisdictional Immunities of States and Their Property does not cover criminal proceedings;
3. *Adopts* the United Nations Convention on Jurisdictional Immunities of States and Their Property, which is contained in the annex to the present resolution, and requests the Secretary-General as depositary to open it for signature;
4. *Invites* States to become parties to the Convention.

65th plenary meeting
2 December 2004

5. Statement of the Chairman of the Ad Hoc Committee on Jurisdictional Immunities of States and Their Property

General Assembly, Fifty-ninth session
Sixth Committee
Summary record of the 13th meeting [*excerpt*]

Held at Headquarters, New York, on Monday, 25 October 2004, at 10 a.m.

Agenda item 142: Convention on jurisdictional immunities of States and their property (A/59/22)

29. Mr. Hafner, (Chairman of the Ad Hoc Committee on Jurisdictional Immunities of States and Their Property), introducing the report of the Ad Hoc Committee on Jurisdictional Immunities of States and Their Property (A/59/22), recalled that the Ad Hoc Committee had been established by General Assembly resolution 55/150 of 12 December 2000. Pursuant to paragraph 2 of Assembly resolution 58/74, of 9 December 2003, the Ad Hoc Committee had been reconvened at Headquarters from 1 to 5 March 2004 and given the mandate to formulate a preamble and final clauses, with a view to completing a convention on jurisdictional immunities of States and their property, which would contain the results already adopted at its previous sessions.

30. The Ad Hoc Committee, having made great progress at its third session, had concluded its work on the text of the draft United Nations Convention on Jurisdictional Immunities of States and Their Property. It had based its work on the draft articles on jurisdictional immunities of States adopted by the International Law Commission at its forty-third session (A/46/10, para. 28), and on the discussions of an openended working group of the Sixth Committee. The text of the draft Convention, contained in annex I of the report of the Ad Hoc Committee, was therefore the culmination of 27 years of sometimes difficult work by the Commission, the Sixth Committee and the Ad Hoc Committee. The drafting of the text had been possible only because several States belonging to different legal systems and regions had made considerable concessions and shown great flexibility. Such flexibility was not easy to offer when domestic legislation was already in force, and for that reason, the flexibility and the concessions had to be mentioned particularly.

31. The report was composed of three chapters and two annexes. The first two chapters contained, respectively, the usual introductory information and a summary of the proceedings; chapter III contained the Ad Hoc Committee's recommendations. Annex I A/C.6/59/SR.13 contained the text of the draft Convention. Annex II contained the texts of two written proposals submitted in the course of the 2004 session.

32. He drew attention to the Ad Hoc Committee's recommendations in paragraphs 13 and 14 of the report. The first was that the General Assembly should adopt the draft Convention; the second was that the General Assembly should include in its resolution adopting the draft Convention, the general understanding that it did not cover criminal proceedings.

33. With the adoption of the text of the United Nations Convention on Jurisdictional Immunities of States and Their Property, the work of many years would come to a successful conclusion. As always, of course, some minor drafting corrections were still to be made in order to harmonize the text and avoid subsequent difficulties of interpretation. Such corrections, which would be done by the Secretariat, would not in any case change the substance of the draft text and should be no problem.

34. He listed the corrections that were needed in the English text. In article 2, paragraph 1 (b) (ii), the word 'the' should be deleted before the words 'sovereign authority'. In article 11, paragraph 2 (b) (iii) should read: 'A member of the diplomatic staff of permanent missions to an international organization, of a special mission, or is recruited to represent a State at an international conference'. In paragraph 2, subparagraphs (c) and (d), of article 11, the word 'subject-matter' should replace the word 'subject', and in subparagraph (f) a hyphen should be inserted between the words 'subject' and 'matter'. In article 27, paragraphs 3 and 4, the words 'of this article' should be deleted.

In article 33, the usual final clause beginning with the phrase 'In witness thereof...'needed to be added. In article 28, the date until which signature of the Convention would be possible still had to be inserted.

35. Generally, it must be borne in mind that the Convention would have to be read in conjunction with the commentary prepared by the International Law Commission, at least insofar as the text submitted by the Commission had remained unchanged. The Commission's commentary, the reports of the Ad Hoc Committee and the General Assembly resolution adopting the Convention would form an important part of the *travaux préparatoires* of the Convention. That common reading of the text of the Convention and the commentary would certainly clarify the text if certain questions of interpretation remained.

36. One of the issues that had been raised was whether military activities were covered by the Convention. The general understanding had always prevailed that they were not. In any case, reference should be made to the Commission's commentary on article 12, stating that 'neither did the article affect the question of diplomatic immunities, as provided in article 3, nor did it apply to situations involving armed conflicts' (A/46/10, p. 114). It had to be borne in mind that the preamble stated that the rules of customary international law continued to govern matters not regulated by the provisions of the Convention.

37. That was an example of the general approach of the Convention: it did not apply where there was a special immunity regime, including immunities *ratione personae* (*lex specialis*). Sometimes that was expressly stated in the text, sometimes not. Thus, for example, the express mention of heads of State in article 3 should not be read as suggesting that the immunity *ratione personae* of other state officials was affected by the Convention.

38. He expressed his gratitude to all delegations for their valuable contributions to the work of the Ad Hoc Committee. Given the strong interest elicited by that increasingly important and ever-developing area of the law, it should be seen as a significant accomplishment to have reached agreement on an instrument which, if adopted, promised to harmonize the practice of States and facilitate commercial relations between States and private actors. In that regard, the flexibility and creativity demonstrated by delegations during the negotiations was noteworthy. He also thanked the members of the Bureau of the Ad Hoc Committee, Mr. Medrek (Morocco), Mr. Ogonoswki (Poland), Mr. Gandhi (India) and the Rapporteur, Ms. Plazas (Colombia), for their hard work and wise counsel, without overlooking the tireless efforts made over a number of years by the coordinators of the informal consultations, Mr. Yamada (Japan) and Mr. Bliss (Australia).

39. The Chairman commended the Ad Hoc Committee for its success in fulfilling its mandate of formulating the preamble and the final clauses of the draft Convention and expressed appreciation for Mr. Hafner's contributions in that.

6. ILC Draft Articles on Jurisdictional Immunities of States and Their Property

Part I
Introduction

Article 1 Scope of the present articles

The present articles apply to the immunity of a State and its property from the jurisdiction of the courts of another State.

Article 2 Use of terms

1. For the purposes of the present articles:
   (*a*) 'court' means any organ of a State, however named, entitled to exercise judicial functions;
   (*b*) 'State' means:
      (i) the State and its various organs of government;
      (ii) constituent units of a federal State;
      (iii) political subdivisions of the State which are entitled to perform acts in the exercise of the sovereign authority of the State;
      (iv) agencies or instrumentalities of the State and other entities, to the extent that they are entitled to perform acts in the exercise of the sovereign authority of the State;
      (v) representatives of the State acting in that capacity;
   (*c*) 'commercial transaction' means:
      (i) any commercial contract or transaction for the sale of goods or supply of services;
      (ii) any contract for a loan or other transaction of a financial nature, including any obligation of guarantee or of indemnity in respect of any such loan or transaction;
      (iii) any other contract or transaction of a commercial, industrial, trading or professional nature, but not including a contract of employment of persons.
2. In determining whether a contract or transaction is a 'commercial transaction' under paragraph 1(*c*), reference should be made primarily to the nature of the contract or transaction, but its purpose should also be taken into account if, in the practice of the State which is a party to it, that purpose is relevant to determining the non-commercial character of the contract or transaction.
3. The provisions of paragraphs 1 and 2 regarding the use of terms in the present articles are without prejudice to the use of those terms or to the meanings which may be given to them in other international instruments or in the internal law of any State.

Article 3 Privileges and immunities not affected by the present articles

1. The present articles are without prejudice to the privileges and immunities enjoyed by a State under international law in relation to the exercise of the functions of:
   (*a*) its diplomatic missions, consular posts, special missions, missions to international organizations, or delegations to organs of international organizations or to international conferences; and
   (*b*) persons connected with them.
2. The present articles are likewise without prejudice to privileges and immunities accorded under international law to Heads of State *ratione personae.*

Article 4 Non-retroactivity of the present articles

Without prejudice to the application of any rules set forth in the present articles to which jurisdictional immunities of States and their property are subject under international law independently of the present articles, the articles shall not apply to any question of jurisdictional immunities of States or their property arising in a proceeding instituted against a State before a court of another State prior to the entry into force of the present articles for the States concerned.

Part II

General principles

Article 5 State immunity

A State enjoys immunity, in respect of itself and its property, from the jurisdiction of the courts of another State subject to the provisions of the present articles.

Article 6 Modalities for giving effect to State immunity

1. A State shall give effect to State immunity under article 5 by refraining from exercising jurisdiction in a proceeding before its courts against another State and to that end shall ensure that its courts determine on their own initiative that the immunity of that other State under article 5 is respected.
2. A proceeding before a court of a State shall be considered to have been instituted against another State if that other State:
   (*a*) is named as a party to that proceeding; or
   (*b*) is not named as a party to the proceeding but the proceeding in effect seeks to affect the property, rights, interests or activities of that other State.

Article 7 Express consent to exercise of jurisdiction

1. A State cannot invoke immunity from jurisdiction in a proceeding before a court of another State with regard to a matter or case if it has expressly consented to the exercise of jurisdiction by the court with regard to the matter or case:
   (*a*) by international agreement;
   (*b*) in a written contract; or
   (*c*) by a declaration before the court or by a written communication in a specific proceeding.
2. Agreement by a State for the application of the law of another State shall not be interpreted as consent to the exercise of jurisdiction by the courts of that other State.

Article 8 Effect of participation in a proceeding before a court

1. A State cannot invoke immunity from jurisdiction in a proceeding before a court of another State if it has:
   (*a*) itself instituted the proceeding; or
   (*b*) intervened in the proceeding or taken any other step relating to the merits. However, if the State satisfies the court that it could not have acquired knowledge of facts on which a claim to immunity can be based until after it took such a step, it can claim immunity based on those facts, provided it does so at the earliest possible moment.
2. A State shall not be considered to have consented to the exercise of jurisdiction by a court of another State if it intervenes in a proceeding or takes any other step for the sole purpose of:
   (*a*) invoking immunity; or
   (*b*) asserting a right or interest in property at issue in the proceeding.
3. The appearance of a representative of a State before a court of another State as a witness shall not be interpreted as consent by the former State to the exercise of jurisdiction by the court.
4. Failure on the part of a State to enter an appearance in a proceeding before a court of another State shall not be interpreted as consent by the former State to the exercise of jurisdiction by the court.

Article 9 Counterclaims

1. A State instituting a proceeding before a court of another State cannot invoke immunity from the jurisdiction of the court in respect of any counterclaim arising out of the same legal relationship or facts as the principal claim.
2. A State intervening to present a claim in a proceeding before a court of another State cannot invoke immunity from the jurisdiction of the court in respect of any counterclaim arising out of the same legal relationship or facts as the claim presented by the State.
3. A State making a counterclaim in a proceeding instituted against it before a court of another State cannot invoke immunity from the jurisdiction of the court in respect of the principal claim.

Part III

Proceedings in which State immunity cannot be invoked

Article 10 Commercial transactions

1. If a State engages in a commercial transaction with a foreign natural or juridical person and, by virtue of the applicable rules of private international law, differences relating to the commercial transaction fall within the jurisdiction of a court of another State, the State cannot invoke immunity from that jurisdiction in a proceeding arising out of that commercial transaction.
2. Paragraph 1 does not apply:
   (*a*) in the case of a commercial transaction between States; or
   (*b*) if the parties to the commercial transaction have expressly agreed otherwise.
3. The immunity from jurisdiction enjoyed by a State shall not be affected with regard to a proceeding which relates to a commercial transaction engaged in by a State enterprise or other entity established by the State which has an independent legal personality and is capable of:
   (*a*) suing or being sued; and
   (*b*) acquiring, owning or possessing and disposing of property, including property which the State has authorized it to operate or manage.

Article 11 Contracts of employment

1. Unless otherwise agreed between the States concerned, a State cannot invoke immunity from jurisdiction before a court of another State which is otherwise competent in a proceeding which relates to a contract of employment between the State and an individual for work performed or to be performed, in whole or in part, in the territory of that other State.
2. Paragraph 1 does not apply if:
   (*a*) the employee has been recruited to perform functions closely related to the exercise of governmental authority;
   (*b*) the subject of the proceeding is the recruitment, renewal of employment or reinstatement of an individual;
   (*c*) the employee was neither a national nor a habitual resident of the State of the forum at the time when the contract of employment was concluded;
   (*d*) the employee is a national of the employer State at the time when the proceeding is instituted; or
   (*e*) the employer State and the employee have otherwise agreed in writing, subject to any considerations of public policy conferring on the courts of the State of the forum exclusive jurisdiction by reason of the subject-matter of the proceeding.

Article 12 Personal injuries and damage to property

Unless otherwise agreed between the States concerned, a State cannot invoke immunity from jurisdiction before a court of another State which is otherwise competent in a proceeding which relates to pecuniary compensation for death or injury to the person, or damage to or loss of tangible property, caused by an act or omission which is alleged to be attributable to the State, if the act or omission occurred in whole or in part in the territory of that other State and if the author of the act or omission was present in that territory at the time of the act or omission.

Article 13 Ownership, possession and use of property

Unless otherwise agreed between the States concerned, a State cannot invoke immunity from jurisdiction before a court of another State which is otherwise competent in a proceeding which relates to the determination of:

(*a*) any right or interest of the State in, or its possession or use of, or any obligation of the State arising out of its interest in, or its possession or use of, immovable property situated in the State of the forum;

(*b*) any right or interest of the State in movable or immovable property arising by way of succession, gift or *bona vacantia*; or

(*c*) any right or interest of the State in the administration of property, such as trust property, the estate of a bankrupt or the property of a company in the event of its winding-up.

Article 14 Intellectual and industrial property

Unless otherwise agreed between the States concerned, a State cannot invoke immunity from jurisdiction before a court of another State which is otherwise competent in a proceeding which relates to:

(*a*) the determination of any right of the State in a patent, industrial design, trade name or business name, trade mark, copyright or any other form of intellectual or industrial property, which enjoys a measure of legal protection, even if provisional, in the State of the forum; or

(*b*) an alleged infringement by the State, in the territory of the State of the forum, of a right of the nature mentioned in subparagraph (*a*) which belongs to a third person and is protected in the State of the forum.

Article 15 Participation in companies or other collective bodies

1. A State cannot invoke immunity from jurisdiction before a court of another State which is otherwise competent in a proceeding which relates to its participation in a company or other collective body, whether incorporated or unincorporated, being a proceeding concerning the relationship between the State and the body or the other participants therein, provided that the body:
   (*a*) has participants other than States or international organizations; and
   (*b*) is incorporated or constituted under the law of the State of the forum or has its seat or principal place of business in that State.
2. A State can, however, invoke immunity from jurisdiction in such a proceeding if the States concerned have so agreed or if the parties to the dispute have so provided by an agreement in writing or if the instrument establishing or regulating the body in question contains provisions to that effect.

Article 16 Ships owned or operated by a State

1. Unless otherwise agreed between the States concerned, a State which owns or operates a ship cannot invoke immunity from jurisdiction before a court of another State which is otherwise competent in a proceeding which relates to the operation of that ship, if at the time the cause of action arose, the ship was used for other than government non-commercial purposes.
2. Paragraph 1 does not apply to warships and naval auxiliaries nor does it apply to other ships owned or operated by a State and used exclusively on government non-commercial service.
3. For the purposes of this article, 'proceeding which relates to the operation of that ship' means, inter alia, any proceeding involving the determination of a claim in respect of:
   (*a*) collision or other accidents of navigation;
   (*b*) assistance, salvage and general average;
   (*c*) repairs, supplies or other contracts relating to the ship;
   (*d*) consequences of pollution of the marine environment.
4. Unless otherwise agreed between the States concerned, a State cannot invoke immunity from jurisdiction before a court of another State which is otherwise competent in a proceeding which relates to the carriage of cargo on board a ship owned or operated by that State if, at the time the cause of action arose, the ship was used for other than government non-commercial purposes.
5. Paragraph 4 does not apply to any cargo carried on board the ships referred to in paragraph 2 nor does it apply to any cargo owned by a State and used or intended for use exclusively for government non-commercial purposes.
6. States may plead all measures of defence, prescription and limitation of liability which are available to private ships and cargoes and their owners.

7. If in a proceeding there arises a question relating to the government and non-commercial character of a ship owned or operated by a State or cargo owned by a State, a certificate signed by a diplomatic representative or other competent authority of that State and communicated to the court shall serve as evidence of the character of that ship or cargo.

Article 17 Effect of an arbitration agreement

If a State enters into an agreement in writing with a foreign natural or juridical person to submit to arbitration differences relating to a commercial transaction, that State cannot invoke immunity from jurisdiction before a court of another State which is otherwise competent in a proceeding which relates to:
(*a*) the validity or interpretation of the arbitration agreement;
(*b*) the arbitration procedure; or
(*c*) the setting aside of the award; unless the arbitration agreement otherwise provides.

Part IV

State immunity from measures of constraint in connection with proceedings before a court

Article 18 State immunity from measures of constraint

1. No measures of constraint, such as attachment, arrest and execution, against property of a State may be taken in connection with a proceeding before a court of another State unless and except to the extent that:
   (*a*) the State has expressly consented to the taking of such measures as indicated:
      (i) by international agreement;
      (ii) by an arbitration agreement or in a written contract; or
      (iii) by a declaration before the court or by a written communication after a dispute between the parties has arisen;
   (*b*) the State has allocated or earmarked property for the satisfaction of the claim which is the object of that proceeding; or
   (*c*) the property is specifically in use or intended for use by the State for other than government non-commercial purposes and is in the territory of the State of the forum and has a connection with the claim which is the object of the proceeding or with the agency or instrumentality against which the proceeding was directed.
2. Consent to the exercise of jurisdiction under article 7 shall not imply consent to the taking of measures of constraint under paragraph 1, for which separate consent shall be necessary.

Article 19 Specific categories of property

1. The following categories, in particular, of property of a State shall not be considered as property specifically in use or intended for use by the State for other than government non-commercial purposes under paragraph 1(*c*) of article 18:
   (*a*) property, including any bank account, which is used or intended for use for the purposes of the diplomatic mission of the State or its consular posts, special missions, missions to international organizations, or delegations to organs of international organizations or to international conferences;
   (*b*) property of a military character or used or intended for use for military purposes;
   (*c*) property of the central bank or other monetary authority of the State;
   (*d*) property forming part of the cultural heritage of the State or part of its archives and not placed or intended to be placed on sale;
   (*e*) property forming part of an exhibition of objects of scientific, cultural or historical interest and not placed or intended to be placed on sale.
2. Paragraph 1 is without prejudice to paragraph 1(*a*) and (*b*) of article 18.

Part V
Miscellaneous provisions

Article 20 Service of process

1. Service of process by writ or other document instituting a proceeding against a State shall be effected:
   (*a*) in accordance with any applicable international convention binding on the State of the forum and the State concerned; or
   (*b*) in the absence of such a convention:
      (i) by transmission through diplomatic channels to the Ministry of Foreign Affairs of the State concerned; or
      (ii) by any other means accepted by the State concerned, if not precluded by the law of the State of the forum.
2. Service of process referred to in paragraph 1(*b*)(i) is deemed to have been effected by receipt of the documents by the Ministry of Foreign Affairs.
3. These documents shall be accompanied, if necessary, by a translation into the official language, or one of the official languages, of the State concerned.
4. Any State that enters an appearance on the merits in a proceeding instituted against it may not thereafter assert that service of process did not comply with the provisions of paragraphs 1 and 3.

Article 21 Default judgement

1. A default judgement shall not be rendered against a State unless the court has found that:
   (*a*) the requirements laid down in paragraphs 1 and 3 of article 20 have been complied with;
   (*b*) a period of not less than four months has expired from the date on which the service of the writ or other document instituting a proceeding has been effected or deemed to have been effected in accordance with paragraphs 1 and 2 of article 20; and
   (*c*) the present articles do not preclude it from exercising jurisdiction.
2. A copy of any default judgement rendered against a State, accompanied if necessary by a translation into the official language or one of the official languages of the State concerned, shall be transmitted to it through one of the means specified in paragraph 1 of article 20 and in accordance with the provisions of that paragraph.
3. The time-limit for applying to have a default judgement set aside shall not be less than four months and shall begin to run from the date on which the copy of the judgement is received or is deemed to have been received by the State concerned.

Article 22 Privileges and immunities during court proceedings

1. Any failure or refusal by a State to comply with an order of a court of another State enjoining it to perform or refrain from performing a specific act or to produce any document or disclose any other information for the purposes of a proceeding shall entail no consequences other than those which may result from such conduct in relation to the merits of the case. In particular, no fine or penalty shall be imposed on the State by reason of such failure or refusal.
2. A State shall not be required to provide any security, bond or deposit, however described, to guarantee the payment of judicial costs or expenses in any proceeding to which it is a party before a court of another State.

Select Bibliography

Andrews, S., 'US Courts Rule on Absolute Immunity and Inviolability of Foreign Heads of State: The Cases against Robert Mugabe and Jiang Zemin', *ASIL Insight*, vol. 8, issue 27, November 2004

Atteritano, A. (ed.), *Le immunità giurisdizionali degli stati e degli altri enti internazionali: con raccolta di giurisprudenza italiana* (Padua: CEDAM, 2008)

——'Immunity of States and Their Organs: The Contribution of Italian Jurisprudence over the Past Ten Years' (2009) 19 *Italian Yearbook of International Law* 33

Babu, R., 'Foreign State Immunity in Contracts of Employment with Particular Reference to Indian State Practice' (2007) 49 *Journal of the Indian Law Institute* 129

Bankas, E., *The State Immunity Controversy in International Law: Private Suits Against Sovereign States in Domestic Courts* (Berlin: Springer, 2005)

Barton, G.P., 'Foreign Armed Forces: Qualified Jurisdictional Immunity' (1934) 15 *British Year Book of International Law* 341

Bederman, D.J., 'The "Common-Law Regime" of Foreign Sovereign Immunity: The Actual Possession Rule in Admiralty' (2010) 44 *Vanderbilt Journal of Transnational Law* 837

Bellinger, J.D., 'The Dog that Caught the Car: Observations on the Past, Present and Future Approaches of the Office of the Legal Adviser to Official Act Immunities' (2011) 44 *Vanderbilt Journal of Transnational Law* 819

Bianchi, A., 'Denying State Immunity to Violators of Human Rights' (1994) 46 *Austrian Journal of Public and International Law* 195

——'Immunity versus Human Rights: the *Pinochet* case' (1996) 10 *European Journal of International Law* 266

——'Serious Violations of Human Rights and Foreign States', in Vorah, L.C. et al. (eds), *Man's Inhumanity to Man: Essays in honour of Antonio Cassese* (The Hague: Kluwer Law International, 2003), 149

——'L'immunité des Etats et les violations graves des droits de l'homme: la fonction de l'interprète dans la détermination du droit international' (2004) 108 *Revue générale de droit international public* 63

——'Ferrini c. Repubblica Federale di Germania (Italian Court of Cassation, Judgment of 11 March 2004): a Comment' (2005) 99 *American Journal of International Law* 242

——'The Act of State, the State of the Act: Judicial Interpretation and Human Rights Enforcement', in Kohen, M. (ed.), *Promoting Justice, Human Rights and Conflict Resolution through International Law* (Leiden: Brill, 2007), 151

Bjorklund, A., 'State Immunity and the Enforcement of Investor-State Arbitration Awards', in Binder, C. et al. (eds), *International Investment Law for the 21st Century: Essays in Honour of Christoph Schreuer* (New York: Oxford University Press, 2009), 302

Blair, W., 'The Legal Status of Central Bank Investments under English Law' (1998) 57 *Cambridge Law Journal* 149

Bolla Arocena, M.D., 'Soberanía, justicia universal e inmunidad de jurisdicción en los asuntos: República del Congo c. Bélgica y Republica del Congo c. Francia' (2004) 56 *Revista española de derecho internacional* 91 [summary available in English]

Bordoni, M., '"Default" nel debito pubblico ed immunità dello Stato destero dalla giurisdizione civile' (2006) 89 *Rivista di diritto internazionale* 1031

——'L'ordine pubblico internazionale nella sentenza della Cassazione sulla esecuzione della decisione greca relativa al caso Distomo' (2009) 92 *Rivista di diritto internazionale* 496

Bornkamm, P.B., 'State Immunity Against Claims Arising from War Crimes: The Judgment of the International Court of Justice in *Jurisdictional Immunities of the State*' (2012) 13 *German Law Journal* 773

Bouchez, N., 'The Nature and Scope of State Immunity from Jurisdiction and Execution' (1979) 10 *Netherlands Yearbook of International Law* 3

Bröhmer, J., *State Immunity and the Violation of Human Rights* (The Hague: Kluwer Law International, 1997)

Buzzini, G.P., 'Lights and Shadows of Immunities and Inviolability of State Officials in International Law: Some Comments on the Djibouti v. France Case' (2009) 22 *Leiden Journal of International Law* 455

Caflisch, L., 'Immunité de juridiction et respect des drois de l'homme', in Boisson de Chazournes, L. and Gowlland-Debbas, V. (eds.), *The International Legal System in Quest of Equity and Universality/L'ordre juridique international: un système en quête d'équité et universalité* (The Hague: Kluwer Law International, 2001)

Caplan, L.M., 'State Immunity, Human Rights and *Jus Cogens*: A Critique of the Normative Hierarchy Theory' (2003) 97 *American Journal of International Law* 741

Carnerero Castilla, R., 'La imunidad de jurisdicción de los jefes de Estado y de gobierno extranjeros en la jurisprudencia de la Audiencia Nacional española' (2003) 16 *Anuario hispano-luso-americano de derecho internacional* 289

Carrera Hernández, F.J., 'La inmunidad de ejecución de los Estados en la Convención de Naciones Unidas sobre las inmunidades jurisdiccionales de los Estados y sus bienes' (2007) 58 *Revista española de derecho internacional* 711

Crawford, J., 'Execution of Judgments and Foreign Sovereign Immunity' (1981) 75 *American Journal of International Law* 820

——'International Law and Foreign Sovereigns: Distinguishing Immune Transactions' (1983) 54 *British Year Book of International Law* 75

Dabu, A.B.C., 'Sovereign Immunity vis-à-vis the Municipal Legal Remedy of Specific Performance' (2007) 51 *Ateneo Law Journal* 878

Damrosch, L.F., 'Changing the International Law of Sovereign Immunity through National Decisions' (2011) 44 *Vanderbilt Journal of Transnational Law* 1185

Delaume, G.R., 'Economic Development and Sovereign Immunity' (1985) 79 *American Journal of International Law* 318

Dellapenna, J., *Suing Foreign Governments and Their Corporations* (2nd edn) (Ardsley, New York: Transnational, 2003)

Denza, E., *Diplomatic Law. A Commentary on the Vienna Convention on Diplomatic Relations* (3rd edn) (Oxford: Oxford University Press, 2008).

——'The 2005 [*sic*] UN Convention on State Immunity in Perspective' (2006) 55 *International Comparative Law Quarterly* 395

DeSena, P., 'Immunità degli Stati dalla giurisdizione e violazioni di diritti dell'uomo: la sentenza della Cassazione italiana nel caso Ferrini' (2005) 157 *Giurisprudenza italiana* 255

De Vittor, F., 'Recenti sviluppi in tema di immunità degli Stati dalla giurisdizione: la Convenzione di New York del 2 dicembre 2004' (2007) 23 *Comunicazioni e studi* 47

De Wet, E., 'The Prohibition on Torture as an International Norm of *Jus Cogens* and its Implications for National and Customary Law' (2004) 15 *European Journal of International Law* 97

Dickinson, A., 'Status of Forces under the UN Convention on State Immunity' (2006) 55 *International Comparative Law Quarterly* 427

Dickinson, A., Lindsay, R., and Loonam, J., *State Immunity: Selected Materials and Commentary* (Oxford: Oxford University Press, 2004)

Dinstein, Y., 'Diplomatic Immunity from Jurisdiction *Rationae Materiae*' 1966 15 *International Comparative Law Quarterly* 76

Distefano M., 'Immunità degli Stati e art. 6 della Convenzione europea dei diritti dell'uomo: coeranza sistemica e garanzie di non impunità' (2007) 23 *Comunicazioni e studi* 205

Douglas, Z., 'State Immunity for the Acts of State Officials' (2011) 82 *British Year Book of International Law* [forthcoming]

Eboe-Osuji, C., 'State Immunity, State Atrocities and Civil Justice in the Modern Era of International Law' (2007) 45 *Canadian Yearbook of International Law* 223

El Boudouhi, S., 'La motivation de la jurisprudence recente de la Corte Suprema di Cassazione Italienne sur les immunités jurisdictionnelles de l'État' (2010) 114 *Revue générale de droit international public* 747

Espósito Massicci, C., *Inmunidad del estado y derechos humanos* (Cizur Menor: Thomson Civitas, 2007)

——'Sobre la emergencia de una excepción de los estados en la práctica jurisprudencial española' (2006) 22 *Anuario español de derecho internacional* 63

Fenet, A., 'La responsabilité pénale international du Chef d'État' (2002) 32 *Revue générale de droit* 585 [summary available in English]

Ferrer Lloret, J., 'La inmunidad de ejecución en la Convención de 2004: un análisis desde la práctica de España' (2006) 22 *Anuario español de derecho internacional* 3

——'La inmunidad de jurisdicción del Estado ante violaciones graves de los derechos humanos' (2008) 59 *Revista española de derecho internacional* 29

Finke, J., 'Sovereign Immunity: Rule, Comity or Something Else?' (2010) 21 *European Journal of International Law* 853

Foakes, J. and Wilmshurst, E., *State Immunity: The UN Convention and its Effects*, Chatham House Briefing Paper, ILP BP 05/01, May 2005

Focarelli, C., 'Diniego dell'immunità giurisdizionale degli Stati stranieri per crimini, "jus cogens" e dinamica del diritto internazionale' (2008) 91 *Rivista di diritto internazionale* 748

——'Denying Foreign State Immunity for Commission of International Crimes: The *Ferrini* Decision' (2005) 54 *International Comparative Law Quarterly* 951

——'Immunité des Etats et *jus cogens*. La dynamique du droit international et la fonction du *jus cogens* dans le processus de changement de la règle sur l'immunité juridictionnelle des Etats étrangers' (2008) 112 *Revue générale de droit international public* 761

Forcese, C., 'De-immunizing Torture: Reconciling Human Rights and State Immunity' (2007) 52 *McGill Law Journal* 127

Fox, H., 'In Defence of State Immunity: Why the UN Convention on State Immunity is Important' (2006) 55 *International Comparative Law Quarterly* 399

——'State Immunity and the International Crime of Torture' (2006) 11 *European Human Rights Law Review* 142

——'State Immunity and Other Norms of International Law: Possible Methods of Accommodation', in Erauw, J.A. (ed.), *Liber memorialis Petar Šarčević* (Munich: Sellier European Law Publishers, 2006)

—— *The Law of State Immunity* (2nd edn) (Oxford: Oxford University Press, 2008)

——'The Merits and Defects of the 2004 UN Convention on State Immunity: Gerhard Hafner's Contribution to its Adoption by the United Nations', in Buffard, I. et al. (eds), *International Law Between Universalism and Fragmentation: Festschrift in Honour of Gerhard Hafner* (The Hague: Martinus Nijhoff, 2008), 413

——'International Law and Restraints on the Exercise of Jurisdiction by National Courts of States', in Evans, M. (ed.), *International Law* (3rd edn) (Oxford: Oxford University Press, 2010), 340

Frulli, M., *Immunità e crimini internazionali: l'esercizio della giurisdizione penale e civile nei confronti degli organi statali sospettati di gravi crimini intrernazionali* (Turin: Giappichelli, 2007)

——'Some Reflections on the Functional Immunity of State Officials' (2010) 19 *Italian Yearbook of International Law* 91

Gaillard, E., 'Effectivité des sentences arbitrales: immunité des Etats et autonomie des personnes morales dépendant d'eux', in Pingel-Lanuzza, I. (ed.), *Droit des immunités et exigencies du procès equitable* (Paris: Pedone, 2004), 120

Gardiner, R., 'UN Convention on State Immunity: Form and Function' (2006) 55 *International Comparative Law Quarterly* 407

Garnett, R., 'Should Foreign State Immunity be Abolished?' (1999) 20 *Australian Yearbook of International Law* 175

——'State Immunity Triumphs in the European Court of Human Rights' (2002) 118 *Law Quarterly Review* 367

Gattini, A., 'War Crimes and State Immunity in the *Ferrini* Decision' (2005) 3 *Journal of International Criminal Justice* 224

Gavouneli, M., *State Immunity and the Rule of Law* (Athens: Sakkoulas, 2001)

Giegerich, T., 'Do Damages arising from *Jus Cogens* Violations Override State Immunity from the Jurisdiction of Foreign Courts?', in Tomuschat, C. and Thouvenin, J.-M. (eds), *The Fundamental Rules of the Legal Order: Jus Cogens and Erga Omnes* (The Hague: Martinus Nijhoff, 2006), 203

Goldmann, M., 'Arrest Warrant Case (Democratic Republic of Congo v Belgium)', in Wolfrum, R. (ed.), *Max Planck Encyclopedia of International Law* (Oxford: Oxford University Press, 2012), vol. I, 653

Goren, J., 'State-to-State Debts: Sovereign Immunity and the "Vulture" Hunt' (2010) 41 *George Washington International Law Review* 83

Gouttes, R., 'L'actualité de l'immunité de juridiction des États étrangers' (2006) 182 *Recueil Dalloz* 606

Hafner, G., 'Accountability and Immunity: The United Nations Convention on Jurisdictional Immunity of States and Their Property and the Accountability of States' (2005) 99 *Proceedings of the American Society of International Law* 237

——'United Nations Convention on Jurisdictional Immunities of States and Their Property (2004)', in Wolfrum, R. (ed.), *Max Planck Encyclopedia of International Law* (Oxford: Oxford University Press, 2012), vol. X, 319

Hafner, G. and Köhler, U., 'The United Nations Convention on Jurisdictional Immunities of States and Their Property' (2004) 35 *Netherlands Yearbook of International Law* 3

Hafner, G. et al. (eds), *State Practice Regarding State Immunities* (Leiden: Martinus Nijhoff/Council of Europe, 2006)

Hall, C.K., 'UN Convention on State Immunity: The Need for a Human Rights Protocol' (2006) 55 *International Comparative Law Quarterly* 411

Heß, B., 'The International Law Commission's Draft Convention on the Jurisdictional Immunities of States and Their Property' (1993) 4 *European Journal of International Law* 269

Hirobe, K., 'Immunity of State Property: Japanese Practice' (1979) 10 *Netherlands Yearbook of International Law* 233

Hope, D. (Lord Hope of Craighead), 'The Rule of Law Legacy of the House of Lords' Pinochet Judgments' (2009) 43 *International Lawyer* 45

Howard, D., 'Achieving a Level Playing Field in Space-related Public-private Partnerships: Can Sovereign Immunity Upset the Balance?' (2008) 73 *Journal of Air Law and Commerce* 723

Huang Jin and Ma Jingsheng, 'The Immunities of States and Their Property: The Practice of the People's Republic of China' (1988) 1 *Hague Yearbook of International Law* 163

Humes-Schulz, S., 'Limiting Sovereign Immunity in the Age of Human Rights' (2008) 21 *Harvard Human Rights Journal* 105

Iwasawa, Y., 'Japan's Interactions with International Law: The Case of State Immunity' in Ando, N. (ed.), *Japan and International Law. Past, Present and Future* (The Hague: Kluwer Law International, 1999), 123

Jennings, R.Y., *The Place of Jurisdictional Immunity of States in International and Municipal Law* (Saarbrücken: Europa-Institut der Universität des Saarlandes, 1987)

Jiménez, A.S., *La excepción por actividades comerciales a las inmunidades estatales* (Madrid: Gráficas Arias Montano, 1995)

Kalb, N., 'Immunities, Special Missions', in Wolfrum, R. (ed.), *Max Planck Encyclopedia of International Law* (Oxford: Oxford University Press, 2012), vol. V, 94

Keitner, C.I., 'Foreign Official Immunity After *Samantar*' (2010) 44 *Vanderbilt Journal of Transnational Law* 837

——, 'Germany v. Italy: The International Court of Justice Affirms Principles of State Immunity', *ASIL Insights*, vol. 16, issue 5, 14 February 2012

Knoeplfer, F., 'L'immunité d'exécution contre les États' (2003) 3 *Revue de l'arbitrage* 1017 [summary available in English]

Köhler, U., 'Contracts of Employment under the UN Convention on Jurisdictional Immunities of States and Their Property' (2006) 9 *Austrian Review of International and European Law* 191

Lange, L., 'La convention des Nations Unies sur les immunités juridictionnelles des États et de leurs biens' (2004) 50 *Annuaire français de droit international* 45

Lalive, P., 'Swiss Law and Practice in Relation to Measures of Execution Against the Property of a Foreign State' (1979) 10 *Netherlands Yearbook of International Law* 153

Lauterpacht, E., *Aspects of Administration of International Justice* (Cambridge: Cambridge University Press, 1991)

Lauterpacht, H., 'The Problem of Jurisdictional Immunities of Foreign States' (1951) 28 *British Year Book of International Law* 220

Lloyd Jones, D., 'Article 6 ECHR and Immunities Arising in Public International Law' (2003) 52 *International Comparative Law Quarterly* 463

Lopez, 'Is the Head of State above International Law? The Applicability of Head of State Immunity to the Commission of International Core Crimes' (2007) 51 *Ateneo Law Journal* 1079

Luzzatto, R., 'La giurisdizione sugli stati stranieri tra convenzione di New York, norme internazionali generali e diritto interno' (2007) 23 *Comunicazioni e studi* 1

McGregor, L., 'State Imunity and *Jus Cogens*' (2006) 55 *International Comparative Law Quarterly* 437

——'Torture and State Immunity: Deflecting Impunity, Distorting Sovereignty' (2008) 18 *European Journal of International Law* 903

Mizushima, T., 'The Individual as Beneficiary of State Immunity: Problems of the Attribution of *ultra vires* Conduct' (2001) 29 *Denver Journal of International Law and Policy* 261

——'Foreign State Immunity in Japanese Courts at the Beginning of the Twenty-first Century' (2007) 18 *Japanese Annual of International Law* 903

——'Denying Foreign State Immunity on the Grounds of the Unavailability of Alternative Means' (2008) 71 *Modern Law Review* 734

O'Keefe, R., 'European Convention on State Immunity (1972)', in Wolfrum, R. (ed.), *Max Planck Encyclopedia of International Law* (Oxford: Oxford University Press, 2012), vol. III, 889

—— 'State Immunity and Human Rights: Heads and Walls, Hearts and Minds' (2010) 44 *Vanderbilt Journal of Transnational Law* 99

Orakhelashvili, A., 'State Immunity and International Public Order Revisited' (2006) 49 *German Yearbook of International Law* 327

——'State Immunity and Hierarchy of Norms: Why the House of Lords Got It Wrong' (2008) 18 *European Journal of International Law* 955

—— *The Interpretation of Acts and Rules in Public International Law* (Oxford: Oxford University Press, 2008)

Ostrander, J., 'The Last Bastion of Sovereign Immunity: a Comparative Look at Immunity from Execution of Judgements' (2004) 22 *Berkeley Journal of International Law* 541

Panken, H., Ryngaert C., and Van Eeckhoutte, D., 'Het arrest Sharon van het Hof van Cassatie: bouwstenen voor de verdere rol van universele jurisdictie, internationale immuniteiten en de doorwerking van het internationaal gewoonterecht' (2004) 211 *Revue belge de droit international* 240–52

Parlett, K., 'Immunity in Civil Proceedings for Torture: the Emerging Exception' (2006) 11 *European Human Rights Law Review* 49

Pavoni, R., 'La jurisprudence italienne sur l'immunité des États dans différends en matière de travail: tendances récentes à la lumière de la Conventions des Nations Unies' (2007) 53 *Annuaire français de droit international* 211

——'A Decade of Italian Case Law on the Immunity of Foreign State Officials in the Light of Recent Judgements of Italian Courts' (2010) 19 *Italian Yearbook of International Law* 666

Pierini, P., 'The Jurisprudence of the European Court of Human Rights in Respect of Conduct of a Foreign State or an International Organization in the Territory of a Contracting State and the Extraterritorial Effect of Foreign Acts' (2006) 45 *Revue de droit militaire et de droit de la guerre* 389

Pingel, I., 'Observations sur la Convention du 17 Janvier 2005 sur les immunités jurisdictionelles des États et de leurs biens' (2005) 132 *Journal du droit international* 1045

Qi, D., 'State Immunity, China and its Shifting Position' (2008) 7 *Chinese Journal of International Law* 307

Reinisch, A., 'European Court State Practice Concerning State Immunity from Enforcement Measures' (2006) 17 *European Journal of International Law* 803

Riblett, P., 'A Legal Regime for State-owned Companies in the Modern Era' (2008) 18 *Journal of Transnational Law & Policy* 1

Robinson, D., 'The Impact of the Human Rights Accountability Movement on the International Law of Immunities' (2002) 40 *Canadian Yearbook of International Law* 151

Schlemmer, E.C., 'The Immunity of State-owned Ships' (2002) 27 *South African Yearbook of International Law* 248

Schreuer, C., *State Immunity: Some Recent Developments* (Cambridge: Cambridge University Press, 1988)

Sciso, E., 'Italian Judges' Point of View on Foreign States' Immunity' (2010) 44 *Vanderbilt Journal of Transnational Law* 1201

Sornarjah, M., 'Problems in Applying the Restrictive Theory of State Immunity' (1982) 31 *International Comparative Law Quarterly* 668

Steinhardt, R.G., 'United States Foreign Sovereign Immunities Act (1976)', in Wolfrum, R. (ed.), *Max Planck Encyclopedia of International Law* (Oxford: Oxford University Press, 2012), vol. X, 550

Stephan, P.B., 'The Political Economy of *Jus Cogens*' (2010) 44 *Vanderbilt Journal of Transnational Law* 1073

Stephens, B., 'Abusing the Authority of the State: Denying Foreign Official Immunity for Egregious Human Rights Abuses' (2011) 44 *Vanderbilt Journal of Transnational Law* 163

Stern, B., 'Immunités et doctrine de l'Act of State: Différences théoriques et similitudes pratiques de deux modes de protection des chefs d'État devant les juridictions étrangères' (2006) 133 *Journal du droit international* 63

Stewart, D.P., 'The UN Convention on Jurisdictional Immunities of States and Their Property' (2005) 99 *American Journal of International Law* 194

——'The Immunity of State Officials Under the UN Convention on Jurisdictional Immunities of States and Their Property' (2010) 44 *Vanderbilt Journal of Transnational Law* 1047

Stoll, P.-T., 'State Immunity', in Wolfrum, R. (ed.), *Max Planck Encyclopedia of International Law* (Oxford: Oxford University Press, 2012), vol. IX, 498

Sucharitkul, S., *State Immunities and Trading Activities in International Law* (New York: Praeger, 1960)

Sucharitkul, S., 'Jurisdictional Immunities in Contemporary International Law from Asian Perspectives' (2005) 4 *Chinese Journal of International Law* 1

Sun, J., 'The Linkage Requirement in Enforcement Immunity' (2010) 9 *Chinese Journal of International Law* 699

Talmon, S.A.G., '*Jus Cogens* after Germany v. Italy: Substantive and Procedural Rules Distinguished' (2012) 25 *Leiden Journal of International Law* 979

Tams, C.J., 'Well Protected Enemies of Mankind' (2002) 61 *Cambridge Law Journal* 246

——*Enforcing Obligations Erga Omnes in International Law* (Cambridge: Cambridge University Press, 2005)

Tanzi, A., 'Immunità ed evoluzione della società internazionale' (2007) 23 *Comunicazioni e studi* 23

Tomuschat, C., 'L'immunité des États en cas de violations graves des droits de l'homme' (2005) 109 *Revue générale de droit international public* 51 [summary available in English]

——'The International Law of State Immunity and Its Development by National Institutions' (2010) 44 *Vanderbilt Journal of Transnational Law* 1105

Totten, C.D., 'Head-of-state and Foreign Official Immunity in the United States after *Samantar*: a Suggested Approach' (2011) 34 *Fordham International Law Journal* 332

Trapp, K.N. and Mills, A., 'Smooth Runs the Water Where the Brook Is Deep: The Obscured Complexities of *Germany v Italy*' (2012) 1 *Cambridge Journal of International and Comparative Law* 153

Turck, N.B., 'French and US Courts Define Limits of Sovereign Immunity in Execution and Enforcement of Arbitral Awards' (2001) 17 *Arbitration International* 327

Ubertazzi, B., 'Immunità statale dalla giurisdizione e priopriettà intellettuale nella Convenzione di New York del 2004' (2007) 23 *Comunicazioni e studi* 87

Uriondo de Martinoli, A., 'Jurisprudencia argentina y la inmunidad de ejecución de los estados extranjeros' (2003) 16 *Anuario hispano-luso-americano de derecho internacional* 525

Van Alebeek, R., *The Immunity of States and Their Officials in International Criminal Law and International Human Rights Law* (Oxford: Oxford University Press, 2008)

Van Woudenberg, N., *State Immunity and Cultural Objects on Loan* (The Hague: Matinus Nijhoff, 2011)

——'Immunity, Diplomatic Missions', in Wolfrum, R. (ed.), *Max Planck Encyclopedia of International Law* (Oxford: Oxford University Press, 2012), vol. V, 98

Villagrán Kramer, F., 'Immunidad absoluta e inmunidad relativa: Excepciones a la regla *par in parem non habet imperium*' (2003) 16 *Anuario hispano-luso-americano de derecho internacional* 553

Watts, A. and Foakes, J., 'Heads of Governments and Other Senior Officials', in Wolfrum, R. (ed.), *Max Planck Encyclopedia of International Law* (Oxford: Oxford University Press, 2012), vol. IV, 754

Watts, A. and Foakes, J., 'Heads of State', in Wolfrum, R. (ed.), *Max Planck Encyclopedia of International Law* (Oxford: Oxford University Press, 2012), vol. IV, 758

Wen, A.H., 'Suing the Sovereign's Servant: the Implications of Privatization for the Scope of Foreign Sovereign Immunities' (2003) 103 *Columbia Law Review* 1538

Wittich, S., 'The Definition of Commercial Acts' in Hafner, G. et al. (eds), *State Practice Regarding State Immunities* (Leiden: Martinus Nijhoff/Council of Europe, 2006), 21

——'Recent Austrian Cases on Questions of Jurisdictional Immunities' (2003) 8 *Austrian Review of International and European Law* 309

——'Immunity from Seizure: A Legal Exploration', in Pettersson, S. et al. (eds), *Encouraging Collections Mobility: A Way Forward for Museums in Europe* (Helsinki: Finnish National Gallery, 2010), 184

Wuerth, I., 'Foreign Sovereign Immunity at Home and Abroad' (2010) 44 *Vanderbilt Journal of Transnational Law* 1233

Yang, Z., 'State immunity in the European Court of Human Rights: Reaffirmations and Misconceptions' (2003) 74 *British Year Book of International Law* 333

——*State Immunity in International Law* (Cambridge: Cambridge University Press, 2012)

Yarkov, V.V., 'The Evolution of the Jurisdictional Immunity Doctrine', in Trunk, A. (ed.), *Russland in Kontext der internationalen Entwicklung: Internationales Privatrecht, Kulturgüterschutz, geistiges Eigentum, Rechtsvereinheitlichung* (Berlin: Berliner Wissenschafts-Verlag, 2004), 231

Yee, S., 'Foreign Sovereign Immunities, *acta jure imperii* and *acta jure gestionis*: a recent Exposition from the Canadian Supreme Court' (2003) 2 *Chinese Journal of International Law* 649

Yokomizo D., 'State Immunity from Civil Jurisdiction' (2009) 51 *Japanese Yearbook of International Law* 485

Zarbiev, F., 'Quelques observations sur le traitement de l'exception d'immunité juridictionnelle de l'État étranger par la Cour européene des droits de l'homme' (2004) 15 *Revue trimestrielle des droits de l'homme* 621

Zhu L., 'State Immunity from Measures of Constraints for the Property of Central Banks: The Chinese Perspective' (2007) 6 *Chinese Journal of International Law* 67

Index

Introductory Note

References such as '138–9' indicate discussion of a topic across a range of pages. Wherever possible in the case of topics with many references, the topics have been divided into sub-topics or only the most significant discussions of the topic have been listed. Because the entire volume is about 'jurisdictional immunities', the use of this term as an entry point has been restricted. This is also the case with certain other very common terms. Information will be found under the corresponding detailed topics.

The manufacturer's authorised representative in the EU for product safety is Oxford University Press España S.A. of El Parque Empresarial San Fernando de Henares, Avenida de Castilla, 2 - 28830 Madrid (www.oup.es/en or product.safety@oup.com). OUP España S.A. also acts as importer into Spain of products made by the manufacturer.
Printed and bound by CPI Group (UK) Ltd, Croydon, CR0 4YY
14/09/2026
02216288-0011